Sunset

California
——TRAVEL GUIDE——

By the Editors of Sunset Books
and Sunset Magazine

SCOTT ATKINSON

Spring view of Daffodil Hill, 3 miles northwest of the tiny gold-rush town of Volcano.

Sunset Publishing Corporation ■ Menlo Park, California

CHUCK PLACE

Cruises from Fisherman's Village at Marina del Rey explore the West Coast's largest man-made marina.

Discover the Californias

To offer visitors a complete look at this vast vacationland, we combine guides to the state's northern and southern regions into one comprehensive volume. This book tours all of California, from its scenic redwood coast to its sun-splashed desert oases.

We are grateful to the many state, county, and city tourist organizations who took time to verify our material. Our special thanks to Joan Beth Erickson for her assistance in preparing this book and to Lois Lovejoy for her illustration of California's state flower, the poppy.

Research and Text
Barbara J. Braasch

Book Editor
Phyllis Elving

Coordinating Editor
Suzanne Normand Mathison

Design
Cynthia Hanson
Kathy Avanzino Barone

Maps
Eureka Cartography

Editor, Sunset Books
Elizabeth L. Hogan

First Printing May 1991

Copyright © 1991, 1986, Sunset Publishing Corporation, Menlo Park, CA 94025. Second Edition. World rights reserved. No part of this publication may be reproduced by any mechanical, photographic, or electronic process, or in the form of a phonographic recording, nor may it be stored in a retrieval system, transmitted, or otherwise copied for public or private use without prior written permission from the publisher. Library of Congress Catalog Card Number: 90-71533. ISBN 0-376-06127-8. Lithographed in the United States.

Marilyn Monroe's star shines on Hollywood's Walk of Fame, a 3½-mile stretch of sidewalk commemorating some 2,500 celebrities.

Cover: On the picturesque Mendocino coast, red-hot pokers (*Kniphofia uvaria*) stand sentinel over Cuffy Cove near the little town of Elk. Design by Susan Bryant. Photography by Carr Clifton.

Contents

Introducing the Golden State

Northern California

Southern California

Introducing the Golden State

From snowy mountains to sunny beaches, from redwoods to Hollywood, California encompasses scenic and man-made attractions in amazing variety. This great diversity is one of the state's prime lures for visitors and residents alike.

Not surprisingly, the country's most populous state (almost 30 million people) is also its primary tourist destination. Drawn by its year-round mild climate, variety of topography, last-frontier setting, and Hollywood-portrayed lifestyle, millions of tourists arrive each year. And smog, fog, traffic congestion, and the occasional earthquake aside, the Golden State satisfies their expectations.

Its casual lifestyle belies the state's position as a trendsetter in fashion, cuisine, arts, entertainment, business, and environmental concerns. Thanks to the temperate climate, Californians spend more time outdoors than residents in the rest of the country. But most of these weekend surfers, skiers, cyclers, hikers, and campers are hard-working business people during the rest of the week.

Land of dreams

California was founded on dreams. Juan Rodriguez Cabrillo, a Portuguese navigator, was searching for treasure in 1542 when he landed at what is now San Diego. Sir Francis Drake, an English privateer, was preying on Spanish gold ships when he paused for repairs around Point Reyes in 1579.

In 1768, it was dreams of colonization (and the hope of finding fabled cities of gold) that prompted Spain to send Gaspar de Portola and his Franciscan cohort, Father Junipero Serra, north from Mexico. They established forts and a chain of missions from San Diego to Sonoma, beginning the state's settlement in a process that decimated much of its Native American population.

But it was the discovery of a few flakes of yellow metal in John Sutter's millrace on the South Fork of the American River in 1848 that prompted the biggest dreams of all—fortunes in gold and manifest destiny for a nation pulled inexorably to the continent's western shore.

After Spanish and Mexican rule, and a brief period as a republic (1846), California became a United States territory in 1848—just before gold was struck to make a reality of all these early dreams. Statehood arrived in 1850 at the height of the gold rush.

Some of the miners who raced here from around the world remained after the gold panned out. They were soon joined by other immigrants seeking their own dreams, creating an eclectic blend of cultures and races matched nowhere else in the country.

Land of travel

California stretches north and south along the coast for more than 1,300 miles and expands inland for almost 300 miles at its widest point. It boasts some 30,000 miles of rivers and streams

MARK E. GIBSON

Mariachi band performs at one of the many colorful festivals held on the plaza at El Pueblo de Los Angeles, the city's historic heart.

and more than 5,000 lakes. About 25 million acres of this diverse topography is protected in national and state parks and national forests.

If superlatives are the measure of a destination, the Golden State has more than its share. For starters, it contains the top visitor attraction in the entire world (Disneyland), the country's favorite national monument (Cabrillo's landing site in San Diego outdraws even the Statue of Liberty) and best-loved national park (Yosemite), and North America's largest alpine lake (Tahoe). Here, too, are the world's tallest trees (coast redwoods), its most massive (giant sequoias), and its oldest (ancient bristlecone pines).

California also boasts the highest point in the contiguous United States, lofty Mount Whitney (14,494 feet), only 85 miles from the lowest point, Badwater in Death Valley (282 feet below sea level). Death Valley also has the dubious honor of having recorded the continent's highest temperature (134° in July, 1913).

Using the book

As a convenience for travelers, this edition combines Sunset's *Northern California Travel Guide* and *Southern California Travel Guide* into a single volume. Our division of the state—defined by personality as well as geography—is shown by the map on this page.

This comprehensive guide is not an abridgement; everything in the two separate regional books is included in this *California Travel Guide,* except for the book covers shown below. The Northern and Southern California sections are self-contained, so that each has its own table of contents, general introductory information, index, and page numbers. Halfway through this volume, page number-ing starts over again for Southern California.

Color is used to help readers find their way through this guide—green for Northern California, sepia for Southern California. Maps, special features, back-of-the-book activity guides, indexes, and color spots next to page numbers are printed in these hues.

Since there are separate color-coded indexes for Northern California and Southern California, be sure to check both if you don't know exactly where a particular attraction is located, or if you're looking for a category of destinations, such as missions or wineries. Note that a few "borderline" places (for example Hearst Castle) are covered in both halves of this book.

Each chapter includes regional maps, and there are a number of detailed city maps. Special sections at the end of both Northern California and Southern California describe popular active pursuits within the regions; the combined activity guides serve as a quick statewide reference to everything from camping to whale watching.

Getting acquainted

This guide to the state's attractions calls out state and local visitor and convention bureaus and chambers of commerce that can supply current information on transportation, accommodations, dining options, and special events. Take advantage of these regional resources to make the most of your California travels.

The California Office of Tourism can be particularly helpful (address on page 4 of both Northern California and Southern California); it publishes several useful lists, such as a roster of bed-and-breakfast inns. The introductions to the two books give additional details for seniors and disabled travelers.

American Automobile Association members can obtain free maps and comprehensive guides to the state's hotels and campgrounds. The California Travel Parks Association publishes a directory ($2) showing the location and facilities of RV parks and private camp-

State map (above) indicates area boundaries and chapter breakdowns for the Northern California and Southern California travel guides. Individual book covers are shown at right.

SCOTT ATKINSON

Resembling a floral patchwork quilt, these commercial flower fields lie east of Gilroy. Travelers on State 152 across Pacheco Pass enjoy the colorful view in spring and autumn.

grounds; write to P.O. Box 5648, Auburn, CA 95604, or phone (916) 885-1624.

We make every effort to include up-to-date admission fees and hours of operation for all attractions described. They change constantly, however, so check locally to make certain.

When to visit

The state's biggest asset might be its weather. Lots of sun, little rain, low humidity, and moderate extremes of temperature make it possible to enjoy outdoor activities the year around.

For the most part, California's climate is determined more by rainfall than by the calendar. There are two seasons, wet and dry, with most of the rain (snow in high elevations) coming in winter, though deserts get occasional brief summer thunderstorms. (So little precipitation has fallen in recent years that you may have to ask for a glass of water in a restaurant.)

Surprisingly, fog can shroud the coast in summer and shut down road travel in the Central Valley from time to time in winter. (If San Francisco is on your itinerary as a summer stop, forget shorts and pack a warm jacket.)

Coastal temperatures are generally mild year-round. Inland seasons are somewhat more distinct, with temperatures varying with elevation; high-mountain regions have the most dramatic weather and definite seasons. A typical summer day in California can range from 80° at a beach around Los Angeles to 65° in San Francisco, 99° or more in Palm Springs or Redding, and 70° at Lake Tahoe.

Getting around

The state's major international air terminals are at Los Angeles, San Francisco, San Diego, and San Jose; the first three cities are cruise ports as well. Greyhound buses travel to and around the state.

By train, Amtrak serves California from the east and north; call (800) USA-RAIL for information. Oakland (San Francisco) and Los Angeles are primary terminals.

The *Coast Starlight* runs between Seattle and Los Angeles via Portland, Sacramento, Oakland, San Jose, and Santa Barbara. The *California Zephyr* streaks from Chicago to Oakland (San Francisco connection) via Sacramento. In Southern California, Amtrak's *San Diegan* makes 8 daily trips each way between Los Angeles and San Diego.

Though public transportation reaches many sites, you'll need a car to thoroughly explore the state's far-flung diversions. All major and many local car rental firms are located in big cities. The principal highways connecting Northern and Southern California are Interstate 5 and State 99 through the Central Valley and, to the west, U.S. 101 and coastal State 1. Los Angeles and San Francisco are some 400 miles apart by the most direct route.

Regional transportation is discussed within the individual chapters of this guide.

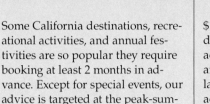

Tips for Booking Ahead

Some California destinations, recreational activities, and annual festivities are so popular they require booking at least 2 months in advance. Except for special events, our advice is targeted at the peak-summer travel season.

If you can't arrange your time to avoid crowds, don't give up; cancellations do occur. Prices given are for summer months (off-season rates can be more favorable).

Death Valley National Monument. For the desert's high season (November through March), book rooms 4 months ahead at the elegant Furnace Creek Inn ($218 to $300) or rustic Furnace Creek Ranch a mile away ($94). Call (619) 786-2345.

Lassen Volcanic National Park. Ask to be put on a reservations list a year in advance for summer bookings at Drakesbad, the only dude ranch in the national park (rooms and cabins $70, bungalows and annex $80). On February 1, call to confirm or learn of cancellations. Arrangements are through California Guest Services, (916) 529-1512.

Yosemite National Park. Book rooms a year ahead at the stately Ahwahnee ($188), Tuolumne Meadows Lodge ($32), White Wolf Lodge ($30, $49 for cabins), Wawona Hotel ($55 to $75), or Curry Village cabins ($32).

Book tent cabins ($28) two months ahead. In early November, request applications (they *must* be received by the first Monday in December) for summer stays in High Sierra camps ($66, including tent cabin, breakfast and dinner).

The first week in November a year ahead, request a lottery application for the famous multicourse Bracebridge holiday dinner at the Ahwahnee Hotel ($128 for adults,

$107 for children) and New Year's Eve dinner dance ($120). Applications are accepted *only* between December 15 and January 15. Losers are notified by late March, winners later in the year; acceptance assures a room (additional cost).

For all Yosemite reservations, call (209) 252-4848 or write to Yosemite Reservations Office, 5410 E. Home Avenue, Fresno, CA 93727.

Camping. For tent sites in Yosemite Valley or high country ($10 to $12 a night), be on the phone at 10 A.M. sharp 8 weeks in advance. Valley sites sell out in 5 minutes. Also plan 8 weeks ahead for Sequoia National Park and Whiskeytown Lake. Call Ticketron at (800) 452-1111 (reservations) or (213) 642-4242 (information).

For campsite reservations at state parks ($12 to $18 a night plus $3.95 service charge), call MISTIX at (800) 444-7275 at 8 A.M. sharp 8 weeks ahead to the day for popular beach parks: Seacliff, Carpinteria, Doheny, Morro Bay, New Brighton, Refugio.

Malakoff Diggins State Historic Park. To book the 3 cabins ($20) in this forested old gold-mining area near Nevada City, call (916) 265-2740 at least 2 months ahead.

Mount Tamalpais. Two months ahead to the day, call MISTIX, (800) 444-7275, to book one of 10 cabins ($30) overlooking the Pacific at Steep Ravine in Marin County.

Santa Catalina Island. Six months ahead, book rooms ($150 to $490) at the Georgian-style Inn on Mount Ada (formerly the Wrigley Mansion). Call (213) 510-2030.

Houseboating. For Lake Shasta, reserve 2 months ahead for a week on a 6- to 16-person boat ($1,060 to $2,495). Call (916) 225-4433 for a list of operators.

In the Sacramento–San Joaquin Delta, plan 4 months ahead for a week of midsummer cruising aboard boats ranging from basic to luxury ($740 to $1,680). For a list of operators, call (209) 477-1840.

Mount Whitney. The 22-mile climb to the 14,995-foot summit is limited to 50 overnight hikers. The Forest Service is presently changing its reservation systems; call (619) 876-5542 for information.

Special events. It's hard to get last-minute tickets to many annual performances. To be sure you can attend, here are some guidelines.

Carmel Bach Festival tickets ($35) must be booked at least 3 months ahead for the three July weekend concerts at 200-year-old Carmel Mission basilica; weekday tickets cost $15 to $35.

Tickets to the *Pageant of the Masters* in Laguna Beach ($9 to $38) should be reserved by May. The July and August pageant features live models portraying famous paintings or sculptures. Call (714) 494-1145 for details.

You can get tickets for reserved seating at Pasadena's January 1 *Tournament of Roses Parade* until the day before ($35), but you need to reserve 9 months ahead for choice TV-camera vantage near the parade's start on Orange Grove Avenue at Colorado Boulevard. Call (818) 795-4171.

Order tickets in November for the *Glory of Easter* play March 15 to 31 at Garden Grove's Crystal Cathedral ($14 to $25). The event features a cast of 200 as well as live animals; call (714) 544-5679.

To attend the *Christmas folk productions* at historic San Juan Bautista Mission, order your tickets ($12) 3 months ahead. Call (408) 623-2444.

MARK E. GIBSON

San Francisco's distinctive skyline appears miniaturized in this bird's-eye view of the bay from above the Golden Gate Bridge.

Northern
California
——— TRAVEL GUIDE ———

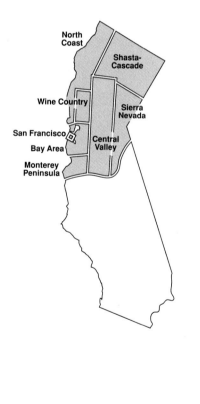

By the Editors of Sunset Books
and Sunset Magazine

Sunset Publishing Corporation
Menlo Park, California

Research and Text
Barbara J. Braasch

Book Editor
Phyllis Elving

Coordinating Editor
Suzanne Normand Mathison

Design
Cynthia Hanson
Kathy Avanzino Barone

Maps
Eureka Cartography

Cover: Warm sunset glow enriches the vibrant hue of San Francisco's Golden Gate Bridge. View is looking north from the city's Baker Beach toward the Marin Headlands. Cover design by Susan Bryant. Photography by Jeff Gnass Photography.

Our thanks...

to the many people and organizations who assisted in the preparation of this travel guide. Special appreciation goes to city and county visitor bureaus, chambers of commerce, and other visitor service agencies throughout Northern California.

We would also like to thank Joan Beth Erickson and Pamela Evans for their editorial contributions to this manuscript and Lois Lovejoy for her illustration of the California poppy.

Photographers

R. Valentine Atkinson: 2, 114; **Larry Brazil:** 34; **Carr Clifton:** 47, 78, 106; **Betty Crowell:** 127; **Mark Gibson:** 18, 26, 31, 39, 42, 55, 70, 119; **Jeff Gnass Photography:** 86, 91; **Dave G. Houser:** 58; **Rolland A. Meyers:** 10, 67; **Chuck Place Photography:** 111; **Mickey Pfleger/Photo 20-20:** 122; **Galen Rowell:** 50; **David Ryan/Photo 20-20:** 23; **Larry Ulrich Photography:** 15, 63, 75, 83, 94, 98, 103.

Editor, Sunset Books
Elizabeth L. Hogan

First Printing May 1991

Copyright © 1991, 1980, 1975, 1970, 1964, 1959, Sunset Publishing Corporation, Menlo Park, CA 94025. Sixth Edition. World rights reserved. No part of this publication may be reproduced by any mechanical, photographic, or electronic process, or in the form of a phonographic recording, nor may it be stored in a retrieval system, transmitted, or otherwise copied for public or private use without prior written permission from the publisher. Library of Congress Catalog Card Number: 90-71701. ISBN 0-376-06559-1. Lithographed in the United States.

Prairie Creek Redwoods State Park, carpeted and canopied in greenery, contains some of the last remaining old-growth redwoods along the northern coast.

Contents

Discovering Northern California

"**K**aleidoscopic"—that's the word to describe Northern California. From waterfall-laced mountains to grape-filled valleys, giant redwood forests to sandy coastal stretches, and slumbering ghost towns to one of the world's most cosmopolitan cities, this region really does offer something for everyone, any time of the year.

This is an area devoted to outdoor recreation, and your choices are almost unlimited. You can hike, camp, fish, boat, cycle, beachcomb, run river rapids, and climb mountains. Swimmers and windsurfers take to the lakes and rivers in summer, and winter finds skiers heading for slopes at dozens of high-country resorts. Tennis players and golfers pursue their games year-round, thanks to the mild climate.

San Francisco—famous for its bay, bridges, hills, waterfront, and fine food—draws a majority of Northern

California's tourists with its big-city attractions. Together with the surrounding Bay Area cities (as far south as San Jose), it's the region's largest cultural, business, and industrial center.

Scenic riches

The best of Northern California's diversions were created by nature— Yosemite Valley and Lake Tahoe in the mighty Sierra Nevada range, Mount Shasta, the Big Sur coast, Redwood National Park, and more. These scenic splendors, and the wealth of outdoor recreation such areas make possible, lure visitors and residents alike. But if you're looking for solitude, you can head for the mountain wilderness north of Redding.

Northern California boasts the state's most dramatic coastline and the majority of its mountains, forests, natural lakes, and rivers. The region encompasses the continent's highest waterfall (Yosemite Falls) and the world's tallest trees.

That's not to say you won't find man-made attractions. Popular destinations beyond San Francisco include Sonoma, with its Spanish landmarks; the Napa Valley wine district; Monterey's historic buildings and waterfront; Carmel's quaint shops; and Mendocino, with its dramatic coastal setting and artsy atmosphere.

Sacramento, the main city in the agriculturally important Central Valley, is often overlooked by tourists. Its river setting, historic waterfront, and world-famous railroad museum, however, make it well worth visiting. East of the valley in the foothills of the Sierra are remnants from the days when gold created California.

The northern half of the state also has its share of theme parks (Marine World/Africa USA and Great America, for example), zoos, museums, galleries, shopping centers, and an array

of wineries to tour. And it offers such unique diversions as the Skunk train that chugs through the redwoods up north, the island prison of Alcatraz offshore from San Francisco, a Russian fort on the Sonoma coast, and the Santa Cruz Boardwalk, one of the coast's few fun zones remaining from another age.

A golden frontier

Mountain men, Russian fur traders, Spanish explorers, and Franciscan monks—all had a hand in creating Northern California. But it took the shouts of "Gold!" in 1848 to turn the world's attention to San Francisco and the Sierra foothills.

Sir Francis Drake had set anchor along the coast in 1579, claiming the region for England. Yet it was Spanish explorers and accompanying Franciscan monks who began settlement, nearly two centuries later. They built forts in San Francisco and Monterey and extended a chain of missions as far north as Sonoma.

Monterey became Alta California territorial capital for both Spain and Mexico (after its declared independence in 1822). Still, the Spanish-Mexican reign had less of an influence in Northern California than it did in the south. The U. S. flag had already been raised at Monterey and San Francisco two years before Mexico finally surrendered its territory to the United States in 1848.

And then gold was discovered. The fabled wealth of the Mother Lode helped achieve statehood for California by 1850. It catapulted San Francisco into prominence as the financial center for those who made their fortunes in the mines. And gold fever called global attention to the area,

Contacts

Agencies listed on the first page of each chapter in this book can provide information about accommodations and attractions in their locales. Contact the following offices for general information about traveling in California.

California Office of Tourism
801 K St., Suite 1600
Sacramento, CA 95814
(800) 862-2543 *(for maps and brochures)*
(916) 322-1397 *(for specific travel questions)*

Redwood Empire Association
785 Market St., 15th Floor
San Francisco, CA 94103
(415) 543-8334 *(for North Coast and Wine Country)*

Rodeo competitions, Dixieland jazz, ethnic and historic celebrations, art fairs, and festivities celebrating everything from jumping frogs and racing crabs to wine, pumpkins, and garlic—lively events throughout the year showcase Northern California's diversity. Below are 15 of the region's most colorful celebrations. For a calendar of events throughout the state, contact the California Office of Tourism (address on page 4).

AT&T Pebble Beach National Pro-Am, late January–early February at Pebble Beach. Legendary golf tournament shows off the Monterey Peninsula's renowned golf courses. Sightseers have a field day as celebrities and high-profile sports figures team with top golfers for several rounds. Contact: (408) 372-4711 outside California or (800) 541-9091 within the state.

Chinese New Year, February in San Francisco. North America's largest Chinese community salutes the lunar new year with the Golden Dragon parade, Miss Chinatown USA pageant, martial arts demonstrations, and cultural events. Contact: (415) 391-2000.

World Championship Crab Races, mid-February (Saturday of Presidents' Day weekend) in Crescent City. Dungeness crabs claw their way down a short race course; the winner is returned ceremoniously to the sea. The celebration climaxes with a huge crab feed. Contact: (707) 464-3174.

Mendocino Whale Festival, mid-March in Mendocino. Bring your binoculars to scan the sea for migrating whales, then join in wine tasting, boutique and gallery browsing, and other activities. Contact: (707) 964-3153.

Cherry Blossom Festival, mid- to late-April in San Francisco. This street party in Japantown celebrates spring with entertainment by kimono-clad performers, martial arts experts, and masters in origami (paper folding), ikebana (flower arranging), and bonsai (tree pruning). You can take in a tako drum concert, attend a Japanese film festival, and sample teriyaki, yakitori, sushi, and other treats in the food bazaar. Contact: (415) 922-6776.

Jumping Frog Jubilee, third weekend in May in Angels Camp. Mark Twain publicized the first frog jump in this gold country community; now hundreds of colorfully named frogs jump in various divisions. Contact: (209) 736-2561.

Dixieland Jazz Jubilee, Memorial Day weekend in Sacramento. Jazz takes over California's capital city for a 4-day jam session with lively performances by more than 100 bands from around the world. Contact: (916) 372-5277.

Carmel Bach Festival, last three weeks in July in Carmel. Outstanding baroque music draws classical music enthusiasts to this coastal town each summer for performances of instrumental and choral works, young people's concerts, recitals, and lectures. Book 3 months ahead for weekends. Contact: (408) 624-1521.

California Rodeo, mid-July in Salinas. Top cowboys compete during one of North America's biggest rodeos. Other events include horse races, horse show, chili cookoff, barbecue, and square dancing. Contact: (408) 757-2951.

Gilroy Garlic Festival, last full weekend in July in Gilroy. Garlic-lovers by the thousands feast on garlic-seasoned recipes from appetizers to desserts in Gourmet Alley. Though food

is its main attraction, the festival also features lively entertainment, cooking demonstrations by celebrity chefs, and an arts and crafts show. Contact: (408) 842-1625.

California State Fair, mid-August through Labor Day in Sacramento. The state's largest agricultural fair (held at the Cal Expo grounds) includes a carnival, exhibits, and top-name entertainment. Contact: (916) 924-2000 or (916) 924-2032.

Monterey Jazz Festival, third weekend in September in Monterey. Venerable 3-day event draws many top jazz performers. Contact: (408) 373-3366.

Valley of the Moon Vintage Festival, late September in Sonoma. This oldest of California's wine festivals celebrates the harvest with the "blessing of the grapes," an old-fashioned grape stomp, and re-enactments of events from Sonoma history. Wine tasting and food sampling take place in and around Sonoma's historic town square. Contact: (707) 996-2109.

Half Moon Bay Art & Pumpkin Festival, mid-October in Half Moon Bay. You can pick out your Halloween pumpkin, then enjoy a giant street fair featuring regional artists and craftspeople, food booths, and varied entertainment. Contact: (415) 726-9652.

Gold Country Christmas, Thanksgiving weekend to mid-December in various towns: *Placerville*, Festival of Trees, (916) 621-5885; *Columbia*, Christmas Lamplight Tour and Miners' Christmas Celebration, (209) 532-4301; *Auburn*, Old Town Auburn Village Christmas, (916) 885-5616; *Coloma*, Christmas in Coloma, (916) 622-3470.

bringing an influx of people from around the world who were looking for something more permanent than gold. Many of these immigrants played important parts in Northern California's development.

Over the years, San Francisco's unique blend of races, cultures, and lifestyles has transformed it from a sleepy pueblo into a Pacific Basin gateway. Central Valley agriculture, too, owes much to the early farmers who came here from other parts of the world.

About this book

Based on the state's regional differences, we've chosen a boundary line for Northern California that extends from the coast at San Simeon (site of Hearst Castle) east across the Coast Range into the Central Valley as far south as Fresno.

Then this imaginary border turns northward along the Sierra Nevada range just south of Yosemite National Park.

The area below this boundary is described in Sunset's companion *Southern California Travel Guide*.

This book begins with one of the world's most visited cities, San Francisco, starting point for most Northern California visits. Subsequent chapters cover the surrounding Bay Area, the Monterey Peninsula, Napa and Sonoma wine valleys, the northern coast, the mountainous reaches north of Redding, the Sierra Nevada region, and the Central Valley.

The map on page 7 shows how we've divided the state, chapter by chapter. Regional maps within each chapter, and detailed downtown maps of San Francisco, Monterey, and Sacramento, are included as further aids in planning driving or walking tours.

A special guide at the back of the book breaks down Northern California by activity. Look here for specifics on camping in national and state parks, plus directories of golf courses, ski resorts, boat cruises, whale-watching excursions, river runs, underground explorations, and train trips.

Some destinations may be covered in special features or in the activity guide as well as in the chapter describing that region; use the index at the back of the book to make sure you locate each entry.

A note on prices and hours: we've made every effort to be up to date. Admission fees and hours are constantly changing, however, so check locally to be sure.

When to visit

Thanks to its equable climate, Northern California is a year-round destination, though there are "best" seasons for various areas.

Coastal temperatures are mild the year around, with extremes a rarity. Spring and autumn are especially good times to tour the coast—you'll find clearer and warmer weather than in summer, when fog frequently blankets the region, especially in the morning and evening. Winter brings the year's

Global Dining

No matter what cuisine you choose, you'll probably find it among San Francisco's 3,300 restaurants. Along with trendy California cuisine eateries and more traditional European and American favorites, this city abounds in restaurants spotlighting Pacific Rim and other lesser-known fares.

The ethnic dining spots listed here are but a small sampling of what's available. The tab at such places is usually low to moderate; we've noted any exceptions. Unless mentioned, you won't need reservations weekdays, though you may have to wait for an empty table in small establishments. Most are open for both lunch and dinner.

Afghanistani. *The Helmand*, 430 Broadway, (415) 362-0641. Locally acclaimed exotic fare, closed Sunday; you might call ahead.

Brazilian. *Bahia*, 41 Franklin Street, (415) 626-3306. Open weekdays for spicy seafood, music; reservations advisable for both lunch and dinner.

Cambodian. *Angkor Wat*, 4217 Geary Boulevard, (415) 221-7887. Longtime favorite, closed Monday.

Chinese. Of hundreds of possibilities, try *China Moon Cafe*, 639 Post Street, (415) 775-4789, for Chinese-California blend; popular with theater crowd, expensive. *Hunan Restaurant* at three locations (924

Sansome Street, 853 Kearny Street, 5723 Geary Boulevard) has bare-bones atmosphere but fine spicy fare.

Ethiopian. *Rasselas*, 2801 California Street, (415) 567-5010. Spicy food, good jazz bar.

Greek. *Stoyanof's*, 1240 9th Avenue, (415) 664-3664. Turkish and eastern Mediterranean specialties, closed Monday.

Indian. *North India Restaurant*, 3131 Webster Street, (415) 931-1556. Well-prepared curries and tandoori.

Japanese. *Tachibana*, 301 Mission Street, (415) 957-0757. Traditional favorites and American versions of Asian appetizers; popular for lunch, closed weekends.

Korean. *Korea House*, 1640 Post Street, (415) 563-1388. Well presented fiery food.

Spanish. *Alejandro's*, 1840 Clement Street, (415) 668-1184. Good tapas bar, not open for lunch.

Thai. *Khan Toke Thai House*, 5937 Geary Boulevard, (415) 668-6654. Pleasantly prepared seafood, poultry, and meats; Sunday dancing.

Vietnamese. *Golden Turtle*, 2211 Van Ness Avenue, (415) 441-4419. Long list of delicacies, closed Monday.

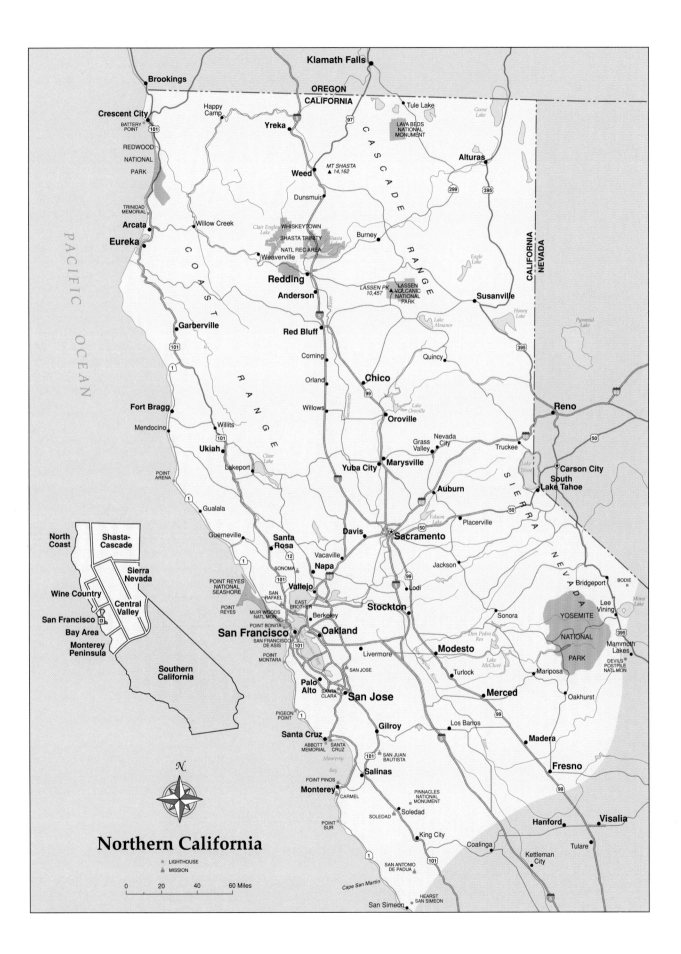

Northern California

LIGHTHOUSE
MISSION

0   20   40   60 Miles

supply of rain, decreasing as you head south. Crescent City and Eureka in the north receive twice as much precipitation as do Santa Cruz and Monterey on down the coast.

As you move inland, the seasons become more pronounced. Summers get hotter (with relatively little humidity), winters colder (with occasional snow). Spring and autumn are the best times to visit Sacramento and the Central Valley, and also the gold-rush ghost towns nestled in the Sierra foothills. These destinations sizzle in mid-summer, and the valley is subject to low-lying fogs in winter.

The Sierra Nevada has the most dramatic seasonal changes. Summer days are warm, ideal for outdoor activity, the nights cool. Autumn brings a crispness to the air and creates dramatic splashes of red and gold foliage, and winter's usually heavy snowfalls make the mountains a mecca for skiers. Some Sierra highways do close for the winter at the first snowfall, and others require chains over high mountain passes.

The mountains to the north are best visited from spring to early autumn. Many small-town attractions and accommodations in this part of the state are closed in winter.

How to get around

San Francisco and the Greater Bay Area serve as Northern California's main gateway—with three international airports (San Francisco, San Jose, Oakland), two railway terminals (Oakland and San Jose), Greyhound bus terminals, port cities, and a network of teeming freeways.

Sacramento, at the intersection of major east-west and north-south routes, is served by many major airlines, Amtrak, and Greyhound.

Freeways. Northern California's major north-south corridor is Interstate 5, a fast albeit not too scenic route which streaks north through the Central Valley en route to the Oregon border. Other principal north-south highways include U.S. 101, State 99, and State 1, the latter a slow but dramatic route up the coast.

The main east-west artery, Interstate 80, crosses the Sierra into California west of Reno, Nevada. U.S. 50 enters the state from the east at Lake Tahoe, then joins Interstate 80 at Sacramento.

The only freeway congestion you're likely to find in Northern California lies around the Greater Bay Area and, to a lesser degree, the Sacramento metropolitan area. While freeways into San Francisco damaged by the 1989 earthquake are being repaired, traffic on other routes is heavier than usual. To save time, avoid normal commute hours.

Public transportation. Ways to get around specific areas within Northern California are discussed in each chapter. Besides San Francisco's picturesque cable cars and ferries, the Bay Area is served by the modern Bay Area Rapid Transit System (BART) plus municipal bus lines and trains. In other large cities, buses reach most attractions; the capital city shuttles visitors to and from its Old Sacramento attractions.

Tours. Don't overlook sightseeing tours as a means of getting around. They give good background information and spotlight the high points of an area. For details, check with your travel agent, hotel desk, or area visitor center.

Where to stay

Northern California accommodations range from sophisticated city hotels and elegant coastside resorts to guest ranches, small bed-and-breakfast inns, motels, and RV parks. In heavily traveled areas, advance reservations are almost always advisable in summer and on weekends year-round.

This guide takes a look at some San Francisco "boutique" hotels, North Coast bed-and-breakfast inns, and a variety of guest ranches. Other notable accommodations are mentioned throughout the book. For more comprehensive suggestions in any given area, write or call the contacts listed on the first page of each chapter.

Many of Northern California's national and state parklands offer camping facilities; for some choices see pages 120–122. For a listing of national forest campgrounds, contact the Office of Information, U.S. Forest Service, 630 Sansome Street, Room 529A, San Francisco, CA 94111; (415) 705-2874.

The U.S. Bureau of Land Management (2800 Cottage Way, Sacramento, CA 95825) can also provide camping information.

Information sources

Advance planning will help you make the most of your Northern California trip. For up-to-the-minute information on transportation, accommodations, dining options, and special events, contact the local visitor and convention bureaus and chambers of commerce listed in each chapter.

For general information about the state, contact the California Office of Tourism (address on page 4). Another good source of information is the Redwood Empire Association (also listed on page 4); this organization publishes a booklet (small fee) about coastal and Wine Country counties from San Francisco north to the Oregon border.

Every May the Department of Fish & Game (1416 9th Street, Sacramento, CA 95814) publishes a free pamphlet outlining current hunting and freshwater and saltwater fishing regulations for the coming year.

Handicapped travelers. In the last few years California has made great progress in assisting disabled travelers. Special license plates and permits, available from the state's Department of Motor Vehicles, allow the physically impaired to park in convenient slots close to entryways. California also honors permits and plates issued by other states. For additional information, contact the Department of Motor Vehicles, P.O. Box 942869, Sacramento, CA 94269-0001; (916) 732-7243.

Many attractions provide free or rental wheelchairs. And most new and recently refurbished hotels have a few rooms equipped especially for the handicapped. For referrals, contact the California Travel Industry Association, 2500 Wilshire Boulevard, Suite 603, Los Angeles, CA 90057; (213) 384-3178.

Senior citizens. Older travelers will receive hotel and transportation discounts, special dining rates, and reduced entrance fees at many places. The age of eligibility varies widely, so ask about special fares in advance.

Cuisine in California

Northern California has been influencing what America eats and drinks for more than a century. From food staples to regional recipes, the area has a rich history of culinary innovation.

The state's fertile farmlands, vast pasturelands, and hundreds of miles of coastal waters have created a bountiful harvest of fresh ingredients to inspire Northern California chefs. And because of the region's diverse ethnic makeup, varied international tastes have become basic fare here.

The following is a sampling of historic Northern California culinary specialties, including some that date back to gold-rush days.

Coffee. From the earliest days of the gold rush, the smell of roasting coffee has infused the air in San Francisco. By 1890, the city boasted 27 coffee and spice mills, 24 importers, and more than 100 coffee houses.

Three of the country's java giants started here: Folger's, MJB, and Hills Bros. You can sample the dark-roasted blends introduced more than 50 years ago at such places as Caffe Malvina, Caffe Trieste, and Cafe Italia in North Beach.

Stan Delaplane, the late San Francisco newspaper columnist, is credited with introducing Irish coffee in the 1950s. He showed Buena Vista Cafe bartenders how to mix this coffee, whiskey, and cream concoction. The stomach-warming drink can still be sipped at the BV (2765 Hyde Street).

Sourdough bread. Whether the "starter" for this distinctive bread came from the French and Basque settlers who arrived in 1840, the Alaska prospectors—called "sourdoughs"— who rushed here in 1849, or some unknown quality in San Francisco's atmosphere is still debated. But the Boudin brand of sourdough, made by San Francisco's first bakery, is still a favorite.

Chocolate. Domingo Ghirardelli arrived in San Francisco in 1849 via Italy and South America and quickly set up shop as a purveyor of spices, liqueurs, and chocolate. Less than 20 years later, he produced his famous ground chocolate. Take a look at the original equipment at the Chocolate Manufactory in Ghirardelli Square, his old factory.

Another Bay Area chocolate company, Guittard, has been around since 1868. Most of its production is used for cooking and to coat candies.

Jack cheese. This mild, semisoft cheese is another Northern California native. Two of the best-known brands, Sonoma and Vella, are made in the city of Sonoma. You can tour the plants on a visit to the city.

Dungeness crab. Some 140 years ago, Italian fishermen searching the waters around San Francisco for salmon, mackerel, herring, and smelt discovered a crustacean called Dungeness crab. During crab season (November to mid-June), you can sample it at Fisherman's Wharf as a walk-away cocktail in a paper cup.

Fortune cookies. No one is sure who made the first fortune cooky, but some credit Makoto Hagiwara, the developer of the Japanese Tea Garden in San Francisco's Golden Gate Park, with its creation in 1909. You can taste an up-to-date version at the teahouse or watch cookies being made in Chinatown's Golden Gate Fortune Cookies Company (56 Ross Alley).

Green Goddess Salad. One of the most popular items on the Garden Court menu at San Francisco's Sheraton Palace Hotel, this salad was created in the 1920s at the request of actor George Arliss, who was performing in a production called *Green Goddess*. The original dressing recipe calls for anchovy fillets, green onion, minced parsley, tarragon, mayonnaise, tarragon vinegar, and chives.

Joe's Special. This dish was born at New Joe's restaurant in San Francisco in 1932. When the chef informed a late-night customer that there was nothing left to eat but spinach, onions, mushrooms, ground beef, and eggs, he was told to "mix 'em together." It's still a favorite entrée.

Hangtown Fry. Restaurants from San Francisco to the Sierra serve the gold-rush favorite first prepared in Placerville, then called Hangtown. The dish of scrambled eggs, oysters, and bacon was reportedly a condemned prisoner's last request.

Steam beer. San Francisco's Anchor Brewing Co., founded in 1896, was the only steam beer survivor of Prohibition. Though devotees of this Potrero Hill brew admire its classic flavor, no one is certain what "steam beer" means.

Bottled water. From the Martinez area comes Alhambra Water, a company that benefited by being able to supply potable water after the 1906 earthquake. You can watch the operations of two Napa Valley bottled water plants, Calistoga and Crystal Geyser, both in Calistoga.

Wine. Long-lived wineries attest to the region's close ties between wine and food. Tours and tastings take place at such Napa Valley survivors as Beaulieu, Beringer, Inglenook, and Charles Krug; Buena Vista and Simi in Sonoma Valley; and Mirassou, Wente, and Concannon in the Greater Bay Area.

San Francisco

*P*olls consistently rank San Francisco in the top 10 of the world's favorite cities. The beautiful setting certainly has a lot to do with its allure. Pacific Ocean and San Francisco Bay waters enclose the city on three sides. And San Francisco's naturally air-conditioned climate, carefully preserved Victorian architecture, 19th-century cable cars, and cosmopolitan attitude all contribute to its popularity.

Then, too, this is a *manageable* city for visitors. Its compact size concentrates its considerable charms within a small area, making them easily accessible even without a car.

This is a city built on hills. Someone once said that if you get tired of climbing them, you can always lean against them. But it's from these peaks that you get the well-touted views—fog rolling in over the Golden Gate Bridge, cargo ships heading into the harbor, and sailboats tacking past islands in the channel.

Connecting links

Whether you drive across San Francisco's bay-spanning bridges or merely glimpse them from one of many observation spots, you'll notice their importance to the city.

Most glamorous of the bridges is the Golden Gate, one of the longest single-span suspension bridges ever built (6,450 feet). It's a bridge you can walk and bike across, enjoying a gull's-eye look 220 feet down. The turnout at its

View from the top of Twin Peaks stretches east across the city and the Bay Bridge all the way to Oakland in the East Bay.

north end offers exceptional city views. Motorists pay tolls only when entering San Francisco from the north.

The San Francisco–Oakland Bay Bridge is the city's main connection to the east. A hardworking double-decker, part suspension span and part cantilevered, it tunnels through Yerba Buena Island on its 8¼-mile route across the bay. Tolls are collected westbound only.

Tales of a city

San Francisco became a city quite out of proportion to its actual size from the first cry of "Gold!" in 1848. With a population of less than 725,000 in an area of less than 47 square miles, it's still a big city without being big.

It has qualities common to all of the world's great cities: rich historical background, great diversity of activity, cultural depth, and pervasive charm. And its problems are those of a large city, often magnified because they occur in such a compact area: traffic congestion, environmental concerns, and an ever-growing number of homeless.

Costanoan Indians had lived in the Bay Area for thousands of years before the Spaniards, in 1776, established a military post at what is now the Presidio and founded Mission San Francisco de Asis. But the pueblo drowsed until the mid-1800s, when the gold rush and the subsequent silver bonanza made it a magnet for those who hoped to get rich—and sometimes did. The city was changed forever.

By the start of the 20th century, the city, which had already been rebuilt seven times after devastating fires, boasted a population of 342,000. Then came the 1906 earthquake and fire, which destroyed 28,000 buildings and killed 500 people. San Franciscans rebuilt once more, showing off their new

look at the Panama-Pacific International Exposition in 1915.

Those early tourists wouldn't recognize today's city: ultramodern skyscrapers jostle venerable Victorians, old factories have become shopping areas, and part of the once-raucous Barbary Coast provides sedate quarters for antique dealers, attorneys, and architects.

Another serious earthquake occurred in 1989, and though San Francisco suffered less damage than other parts of the Bay Area, some freeways are still being repaired and realigned.

A cultural mosaic

Its early settlers, a unique blend of races and cultures, set the pattern for San Francisco's tolerant attitude. Over the years the city has been enriched by the colorful traditions of Chinese, Japa-

---

Contacts

These agencies offer information on attractions and accommodations. See additional contacts throughout this chapter.

San Francisco Convention & Visitors Bureau
201 3rd St., Suite 900
San Francisco, CA 94103-3185
(415) 974-6900

Visitor Information Center
Hallidie Plaza, Lower Level
Powell and Market Streets
(P.O. Box 6977)
San Francisco, CA 94101-6977
(415) 391-2000

---

nese, Southeast Asian, Italian, Hispanic, and other ethnic groups. Some 50 foreign language publications are currently sold around town.

A more recent addition to the city's cultural heritage is its gay community, now estimated to comprise about 15 percent of the total population.

Planning a trip

Part of the pleasure of visiting San Francisco is the ease with which a visitor can move from attraction to attraction. A car is not a necessity—you can get around on foot or aboard public transportation.

The city is noted as being eternally springlike, which means that it's seldom hot (and often foggy and cold in summer, when tourists least expect it). September and October are usually the warmest months, January the coldest (average 55°).

The San Francisco Visitor Information Center at Hallidie Plaza (address on page 11) can provide additional travel details. For an around-the-clock rundown of events, call (415) 391-2001.

Accommodations. A sampling of city hotels is shown on page 16; contact the visitors bureau (page 11) for a complete guide. You can call hotels directly or book through a travel agency or reservation service such as San Francisco Reservations, (800) 333-8996, and San Francisco Lodging, (800) 356-7567.

Getting there. Major north-south highways into San Francisco are U.S. 101 and State 1. Interstate 280 also reaches the city from San Jose. Interstate 80 is the most direct east-west corridor.

Some 35 domestic and foreign carriers serve San Francisco International Airport, 14 miles south of the city via U.S. 101. Oakland and San Jose have alternative international airports. An information board in the baggage claim areas of each of the three SFO terminals lists ground transportation, including door-to-door shuttles and limousines. Most major car rental agencies have desks here. A free shuttle connects airport terminals.

SFO Airporter shuttles ($7 one-way, $11 round-trip) run every 20 minutes from 5 A.M. to midnight between the airport and Union Square area hotels. Cab fare into the city is about $25.

Amtrak train and Greyhound bus passengers arrive at the Transbay Terminal, 1st and Mission streets. (Train passengers are transported across the bay by bus from Oakland.)

From the Transbay Terminal, regional bus lines also connect the city with destinations around the Bay Area. AC Transit buses, (415) 839-2882, serve the East Bay; Golden Gate Transit, (415) 332-6600, reaches the North Bay; and SamTrans, (415) 761-7000, heads south to the airport and peninsula cities. CalTrain commuter train service extends south to San Jose; for information, call (415) 557-8661.

Getting around by car. It's wise to avoid driving in the heart of the city. Streets are crowded, parking limited and expensive.

After the 1989 earthquake put the Embarcadero Freeway out of business, the city posted color-coded directional signs to help visitors find their way to Fisherman's Wharf, Chinatown, and North Beach. Drivers from the East Bay should leave Interstate 80 at the Embarcadero exit; from the South Bay, exit U.S. 101 at Civic Center. Then follow the green boot of Italy, the red Chinese lantern, or the orange crab to your destination.

San Francisco Municipal Railway. The city operates one of the country's most convenient and efficient fleet of buses, light-rail vehicles, and cable cars. Route information is published in the Yellow Pages, or you can call 673-MUNI for specific help. A comprehensive route map is sold at stores throughout the city.

You'll need exact change—currently about $1 ($2 on cable cars), reduced rates for seniors and disabled. Free transfers can be used on any Muni vehicle. Passports valid for one day ($6) or three days ($10) are sold at the visitor information center (address on page 11) and STBS outlets (see page 14).

Cable cars. Riding San Francisco's "municipal roller coaster" is not only fun, but an excellent means of transportation on congested streets.

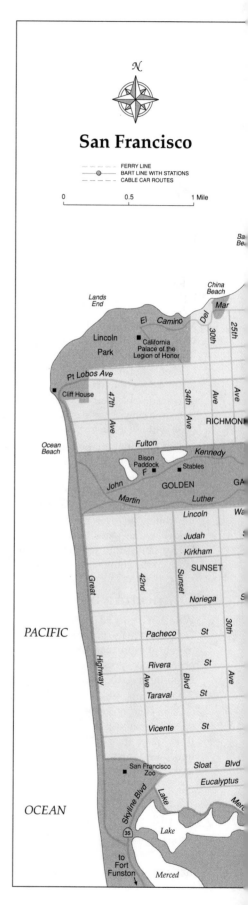

San Francisco Bay

to Marin County

Golden Gate Bridge
Fort Point

Golden Gate National Rec Area

Marina Green

Crissy Field

Ferry to Angel Island, Tiburon, Vallejo

Ferry to Alcatraz Island

Ferry to Sausalito

Ferry to Tiburon

Ferry to Vallejo

Fisherman's Wharf
Pier 45
Pier 43½
Pier 41
Pier 39
Pier 35

Hyde St Pier
Aquatic Park
Cannery
Anchorage

Beach
Bay

Ghirardelli Square

Fort Mason

Palace of Fine Arts/ Exploratorium

Marina Blvd
Doyle Dr
Lincoln Blvd

Lincoln Blvd

Presidio Army Museum & Pershing Square

MARINA
Lombard St
Union St
Broadway
Washington

PRESIDIO

Julius Kahn Playground

West Pacific
Washington St

Mtn Lake Park

California St
Clement

Park Presidio Blvd

Balboa

7th Ave

Geary

Arguello Blvd

Masonic Ave

Blvd

Stanyan

PACIFIC HEIGHTS
Sacramento

Steiner St
Fillmore St
Webster St
Laguna St
Gough St

Divisadero St
Lyon St
Presidio Ave

Polk St
Leavenworth
Taylor St

RUSSIAN HILL

Columbus Ave
Powell
Grant
Montgomery
Battery St

Coit Tower

TELEGRAPH HILL

NORTH BEACH

Pier 7
The Embarcadero
Drumm

BART Transbay Tube to Oakland

Ferry to East Bay

Bay Bridge

Main St

Transbay Bus Terminal

NOB HILL

CHINA TOWN

Portsmouth Square

FINANCIAL DISTRICT

Washington
California
Sutter
Geary
O'Farrell

Van Ness Ave
Larkin St

Union Square

Howard
Folsom
Harrison

1st St
2nd St
3rd St

Japan Center
JAPANTOWN
St Mary's Cathedral

Turk

CIVIC CENTER
City Hall
Opera House

Fulton St

Alamo Square

Fell St

Oak St

Univ of San Francisco

De Young/ Asian Art Museum
Conservatory of Flowers
McLaren Lodge

Calif Academy of Sciences
Playground

Japanese Tea Garden
Stow Lake

PARK

Strybing Arboretum
Frederick

HAIGHT
Haight
Clayton St
Ashbury St

Buena Vista Park

J. Randall Museum

Market St

Mission St
8th
9th
10th
11th
7th

Freeway Closed

MOSCONE Center
Moscone Center

SOUTH OF MARKET

4th
5th
6th

Bryant
Brannan

6th St
3rd St

Duboce Ave

15th

16th St

Mission Dolores

MISSION

Potrero

De Haro

Arkansas St

Pennsylvania

3rd

19th Ave

7th Ave

10th Ave

Univ of Calif SF

Clarendon
Twin Peaks
Market St
Douglass St
Castro St

17th St
19th St
20th
22nd
24th

Mission Dolores Park

South Van Ness Ave
Folsom
Harrison
Bryant
Potrero Ave

20th
23rd

POTRERO

14th Ave

19th Ave

TWIN PEAKS

CASTRO

NOE VALLEY

27th

30th St

Guerrero
Valencia
Dolores

Army

Evans

Jerrold Ave

Closed For Repairs

Industrial St

Oakdale
Quint

Cargo Way

Dewey Blvd
Portola Dr

O'Shaughnessy Blvd

Yerba Buena Ave

MT DAVIDSON

Bosworth St

San Jose St

Courtland Ave

Freeway

BAYVIEW

Ave

Mendell

Sigmund Stern Grove
Dr

Junipero Serra Blvd

Monterey Blvd

Silver Ave

Mission

University

McLaren Park

Keith St
Thomas Ave
3rd St

HUNTERS POINT

Ocean

Holloway Ave

San Francisco State Univ

City College of SF

to Daly City, San Jose

San Jose Ave
Alemany Blvd

to SF Intl Airport, San Jose

San Francisco ■ 13

The two lines that leave from the turntable at Powell and Market streets (Hallidie Plaza) reach the waterfront. Cars marked "Bay and Taylor" clang through the edge of Chinatown and along a section of North Beach en route to Fisherman's Wharf. "Hyde and Beach" cars bypass most of Chinatown and North Beach but provide grand bay views and hang-on-tight rides to Aquatic Park.

The California Street line runs from the foot of Market Street, through the financial district and Chinatown, up steep Nob Hill, and west to Van Ness Avenue.

It's best to buy tickets ($2) before boarding; be prepared for long lines. Look for self-service ticket machines at terminals and major stops. All-day passes are also available there.

Bay Area Rapid Transit. This modern, direct, and comfortable subway system links San Francisco with Daly City to the south and with the East Bay (the latter via a tube under the bay). BART trains run to midnight daily (weekdays from 4 A.M., Saturday from 6 A.M., Sunday from 8 A.M.). Discounted senior and children's tickets are also available; call (415) 464-7133. Downtown San Francisco has four stations (see map on page 19). Phone (415) 788-BART for other details.

Ferries. Several ferry companies provide daily transport as well as sightseeing. Golden Gate Ferries serve Sausalito and Larkspur in Marin County from the Ferry Building at the foot of Market Street; call (415) 332-6600 for fares and schedules. The Red & White Fleet, (415) 546-BOAT, makes daily runs to Sausalito, Tiburon, and Vallejo (shuttle to Marine World). Oakland/Alameda service is operated by the Blue & Gold Fleet; for information, call (415) 522-3300.

Tours. Gray Line offers several popular guided sightseeing tours, including a 3-hour look at the city and a trip to Chinatown at night. Other companies offer limousine and minivan tours; check with your hotel desk, the visitors bureau (page 11), or the Yellow Pages.

You can join the knowledgeable City Guides, (415) 558-3981, for a free walking tour. The Foundation for San Francisco's Architectural Heritage, (415) 441-3004, is another good choice (small fee). For other specialized walks, check with the visitors bureau.

Harbor tours operate from piers at Fisherman's Wharf (see page 124).

Dining. The city's 3,300 restaurants offer every kind of dining, from haute cuisine to family-style meals. Service comes at cloud level at posh aeries on Nob Hill and downtown. For a list of restaurants offering fare from Afghanistani to Vietnamese, stop by the visitor center (page 11); also see page 6.

For inexpensive choices, try "walk-away" seafood cocktails at Fisherman's Wharf, dim sum in Chinatown, sushi in Japantown, tacos in the Mission District, and pasta in North Beach.

Entertainment. San Francisco has always had a zest for performing arts. At least 15 legitimate theaters flourished here in 1850 amid the saloons of the Barbary Coast, and ebullient audiences threw gold nuggets at the feet of the performers. The pace has not slackened.

City entertainment includes everything from trendy nightclubs South of Market to quiet piano bars and lively discos in downtown and Nob Hill hotels. The Civic Center is home to renowned opera, symphony, and ballet companies. For plays and musical shows, theaters are concentrated downtown on Geary, Mason, and Market streets and on the waterfront at Fort Mason. Check the visitors bureau or the weekend entertainment sections of the local newspapers for current events.

Club Fugazi (678 Green Street in North Beach) is the venue for the city's longest-running musical revue, the zany *Beach Blanket Babylon,* presented cabaret-style Wednesday through Sunday nights plus Sunday matinees. For reservations, call (415) 421-4222.

Stop by San Francisco Ticket Box Office Service outlets (STBS) on the Stockton Street side of Union Square or at One Embarcadero Center (street level) for half-price day-of-performance tickets or full-price tickets for future events. The Union Square office is open noon to 7:30 P.M. Tuesday through Saturday; Embarcadero is open 10 A.M. to 6 P.M. daily except Sunday. For recorded information, call (415) 433-STBS.

Spectator sports. San Francisco hosts professional baseball (Giants) and football (49ers); both teams currently share the stadium at Candlestick Park, 8 miles south of the city off U.S. 101. Across the bay, the Oakland A's baseball team and the Golden State Warriors basketball team perform in the Oakland Coliseum. San Jose has pro hockey (Sharks).

The Cow Palace sports arena on Geneva Avenue in Daly City is the site of the Grand National livestock exposition, horse show, and rodeo every October.

A Bay Model

For a graphic illustration of the immensity of the West's largest estuary, cross the Golden Gate Bridge to visit Sausalito's impressive hydraulic model of San Francisco Bay and Delta region. Though only a thousandth of the bay's actual size, the scale model takes up 1½ acres in a warehouselike stucture.

A tape tour describes tidal movement, flow and current of water, and other forces affecting the sea.

Anecdotes about Humphrey the humpback whale and the area's humming toadfishes enliven the tour.

Operated by the U.S. Army Corps of Engineers, the visitor center is open 9 A.M. to 4 P.M. Tuesday through Saturday. Admission and tape tour are free. From U.S. 101, take the Marin City/Sausalito exit east and head south on Bridgeway; turn left on Marinship Way, and follow the signs.

Called the city's municipal roller coasters, cable cars provide thrills and views. This line terminates downhill at the Hyde Street Pier, where you can climb aboard several vintage ships at San Francisco's Maritime National Historical Park.

At one time the names of San Francisco's grand hotels could roll right off your tongue: Clift, Fairmont, Mark Hopkins, Palace, St. Francis, and Sir Francis Drake. These are still top-notch contenders (the Sheraton Palace reopened in 1991 after an 18-month renovation), but they've been joined by other well-known names.

In addition to the oldtimers, the downtown roster of major hotels now includes Grand Hyatt, Hilton, Holiday Inn, Huntington, Hyatt Regency, Mandarin, Marriott, Meridien, Nikko, Pan Pacific, Parc Fifty Five, Park Hyatt, Ritz-Carlton, and Stanford Court.

Motels (mostly along Van Ness Avenue and Lombard Street) and bed-and-breakfast inns are scattered throughout the city. Twenty chain hotels, from Best Western to Westin, are located south of the city at the airport.

"Boutique" hotels are another popular lodging option. These small hotels (under 150 rooms), often recently renovated and conveniently located, usually offer such complimentary services as breakfast, tea, or limo transfers. Our sampling focuses on what's available around Union Square.

Rates begin around $100 at some, climb well upward at others. For a complete list of San Francisco hotels, contact the visitors bureau (address on page 11).

Campton Place Hotel, 340 Stockton Street; (415) 781-5555. Small, elegant, top-of-the-line hotel with traditional European ambience; 126 rooms and a restaurant rated one of the city's finest. Complimentary limo.

Cartwright Hotel, 524 Sutter Street; (415) 421-2865. Built in 1915 and renovated in 1990, with 114 antique-furnished rooms; coffee shop for breakfast only. Complimentary afternoon tea.

Hotel Diva, 440 Geary Street; (415) 885-0200. Ultramodern hostelry in a transformed 1912 building; 107 rooms with down comforters, safes, minirefrigerators, and VCRs (video library in lobby). Complimentary continental breakfast and morning limo.

Donatello, 501 Post Street; (415) 441-7100. Intimate, grande-luxe hotel; 95 rooms furnished with many 18th- and 19th-century antiques; top-rated Ristorante Donatello.

Inn at Union Square, 440 Post Street; (415) 397-3510. Charming English country atmosphere with European-style service; 30 antique-decorated rooms, some with garden views. Complimentary breakfast, afternoon tea with goodies, and evening wine and hors d'oeuvres on each floor.

Hotel Juliana, 590 Bush Street; (415) 392-2540. Rotating art collection from local galleries hangs in the 107 guest rooms. Complimentary limo to Financial District, evening wine, coffee and tea all day.

Kensington Park Hotel, 450 Post Street; (415) 788-6400. Intimate lobby, 84 Queen Anne–styled rooms, just off Union Square. Complimentary continental breakfast, afternoon high tea and sherry.

Monticello Inn, 127 Ellis Street; (415) 392-8800. Ninety-one rooms in renovated 1906 building; popular Corona Bar & Grill. Complimentary breakfast, evening wine, and limo service.

Orchard Hotel, 562 Sutter Street; (415) 433-4434. Renovated 1907 building with 96 rooms; large lobby offering cocktails beneath crystal chandeliers; Sutter Garden Restaurant. Complimentary coffee, limo.

Petite Auberge, 863 Bush Street; (415) 928-6000. Twenty-six country French–furnished rooms, 18 with fireplaces. Complimentary breakfast buffet, afternoon tea, wine and hors d'oeuvres, morning paper, home-baked cookies, and terry robes.

Prescott Hotel, 545 Post Street; (415) 563-0303. Opened in 1989 with 109 traditional-styled rooms; Postrio Restaurant featuring Wolfgang Puck's cuisine.

Regis Hotel, 490 Geary Street; (415) 928-7900. Luxury hotel with Louis XVI styling, French and English antiques in its 86 rooms; Regina's restaurant. Complimentary morning limo.

Hotel Union Square, 114 Powell Street; (415) 397-3000. The 131 rooms have honor bars, hair dryers, comforters, and remote-control TV; Mermaid Seafood Bar & Bar is off the lobby. Complimentary continental breakfast and limo.

Vintage Court Hotel, 650 Bush Street; (415) 392-4666. European-style decor with 106 rooms; outstanding French cuisine in Masa's—rated by some as the city's best restaurant. Complimentary morning coffee and tea, limo, afternoon wine.

White Swan Inn, 845 Bush Street; (415) 775-1755. London-style inn with 26 antique-decorated rooms featuring sitting areas and fireplaces, wet bars and refrigerators. Complimentary breakfast; afternoon tea, wine, and sherry; home-baked cookies; newspaper; shoeshine.

York Hotel, 940 Sutter Street; (415) 885-6800. Ninety-six room hotel with high-ceilinged, Victorian-style lobby; Plush Room cabaret and bar; wet bars, coffeemakers, and vanities in guest rooms; and 24-hour executive gym. Complimentary continental breakfast, limo.

Unlocking the City

One way to grasp the city on your own is to follow the 49-Mile Drive past important scenic and historic points. Later you can return to explore areas that interest you most.

Marked by blue, white, and orange seagull signs, the drive takes you along some congested downtown streets. For that reason, it's best enjoyed on Sunday. Pick up a free map at the visitor center (address on page 11), and start anywhere along the route.

City hills

For a good overview, climb the city's hills. The following are the most accessible and interesting.

Nob Hill. This posh crest is easily reached by any of the city's three cable car lines. Disembark at California and Powell for a spectacular look down California to the bay. The lofty plateau has long been synonomous with the city's elite. Before the 1906 earthquake, it was the site of grand mansions; the imposing brownstone at California and Mason (now the Pacific Union Club) is the single complete survivor.

Several of the city's most luxurious hotels (Fairmont, Mark Hopkins Inter-Continental, Huntington, Stanford Court, and Ritz-Carlton) rise atop or around the hill. Other cachets include the California Masonic Memorial Temple at California and Taylor, a spacious auditorium for performing arts, and Gothic-style Grace Cathedral across the street, begun in 1910 and consecrated in 1964. The east entry doors at the Episcopalian church are gilded bronze replicas of the Ghiberti doors at the Florence Baptistry.

Telegraph Hill. At the northeast corner of the city, Telegraph was named for the semaphores once used to signal ships. Coit Tower at its summit was built as a memorial to volunteer firemen from funds left by Lillie Hitchcock Coit, a great fire buff. Even the 210-foot tower's shape roughly resembles a hose nozzle. Inside, 25 murals of "Life in California, 1934" were painted by WPA artists. An elevator to an observation platform operates daily (small charge). To get there, take Lombard Street from the west.

Russian Hill. West of Telegraph, bounded roughly by Polk, Taylor, Broadway, and Bay streets, Russian Hill is an area of small green parks and quaint cottages squeezed amidst apartment buildings. Filbert between Hyde and Leavenworth is one of the city's steepest streets; brick-paved Lombard between Hyde and Leavenworth is its most crooked.

Twin Peaks. Situated in the center of the city, the Twin Peaks are noted for some of the best views of the Bay Area. Now a 65-acre park, the crests are particularly popular lookouts at night. To get there, take upper Market Street west to Twin Peaks Boulevard.

City streets

Knowing these famous and not-so-famous streets will help you get around.

Market Street. The city's best-known thoroughfare slices diagonally across town from Twin Peaks to the Ferry Building. Heart of the gay community lies around Market and Castro; the strip south of Union Square is a continuation of the downtown shopping center.

Across from the Ferry Building at the foot of Market lies Justin Herman Plaza; its monumental Vaillancourt Fountain is a walk-through arrangement of 101 concrete boxes.

High-rises accent the street's lower end. The 20-story building at Market and Bush rises above a pleasant park (popular at lunch). At 555 Market you can stroll through gardens outside the 43-story building or see a free Chevron petroleum exhibit inside (9 A.M. to 4 P.M. weekdays).

At Market and New Montgomery streets stands the refurbished Sheraton Palace Hotel, built by silver king William Ralston in 1875. Its glass-roofed Garden Court—a historical landmark—is a popular dining spot.

Geary Street. The city's oldest street, Geary extends west from Market all the way to Sutro Heights Park near the ocean. En route it passes some of the city's smartest shops, Union Square, the theater district, stunning St. Mary's Cathedral on Gough Street, and Japantown (page 24).

Mission Street. Paralleling Market Street to the south, Mission cuts through the South of Market (SoMa) district, home to trendy restaurants, clubs, and galleries—see page 21. Upscale hotels edge close to the Moscone Convention Center, a block south of Mission between 3rd and 4th streets. Mission Street takes an abrupt turn south after it crosses Van Ness Avenue, heading into the heart of the Hispanic Mission District (see page 24).

California Street. Taking off from Market at Justin Herman Plaza, California extends all the way west to Lincoln Park, site of the California Palace of the Legion of Honor museum. En route, it climbs from the canyons of the financial district through colorful Chinatown to the heights of Nob Hill.

Union Street. Passing North Beach and upper Grant Avenue, Union becomes a shopping and dining compound after crossing Van Ness. In pre–gold rush days, the district became known as Cow Hollow, the city's dairyland.

The Octagon House at Gough Street, built in 1861, is open for tours (donations) from noon to 3 P.M. the second and fourth Thursday and second Sunday of every month except January. Another vintage charmer a few blocks south, the Haas-Lilienthal House at Franklin and Jackson, welcomes visitors from noon to 4 P.M. Wednesday, 11 A.M. to 4:30 P.M. Sunday; there's a nominal admission.

Polk Street. The 10-block length of Polk between Union and Pine streets—one of the city's main gay areas—sandwiches antique stores, galleries, and restaurants between odds-and-ends emporiums.

At the heart of downtown shopping, Union Square serves as an outdoor setting for colorful city festivals; underneath is a large parking garage. On its west side stands the elegant Westin St. Francis Hotel, a 1906 earthquake survivor.

18

Downtown

Unlike many big cities, San Francisco still has its government, financial, and major retail centers centrally located downtown. Stretching roughly from Van Ness Avenue to the waterfront, this downtown area encompasses the Civic Center, Union Square, the Financial District, Embarcadero Center, historic Jackson Square, and the revitalized South of Market district.

Chinatown and North Beach, two colorful sections in the heart of the city, are discussed on pages 22 and 24. For shopping highlights, see page 20.

Civic Center

A monumental group of federal, state, and city structures, Civic Center extends east from Franklin Street to the United Nations Plaza (scene of lively produce markets on Wednesday and Sunday) at Market and 7th streets. The buildings that make up the performing arts center lie along Van Ness Avenue, and around them spreads a fresh crop of restaurants, inns, galleries, bookstores, and antique shops.

Public buildings. Ornate City Hall, a model of French Renaissance grandeur crowned by a lofty dome higher than the nation's capitol, presides over Civic Center Plaza. Underneath, Brooks Hall adds exhibit space to the Civic Auditorium complex. The History Room at the Main Public Library (east of the plaza) holds maps, photographs, and exhibits salvaged from the 1906 earthquake; call (415) 558-3949 for hours.

Performing Arts Center. West of City Hall along Van Ness Avenue is one of the country's largest performing arts centers. The War Memorial Opera House (home to fine opera and ballet companies) is bracketed by the gleaming modern Louise M. Davies Symphony Hall on the south and the War Memorial Veterans Building on the north. Center tours are offered every half-hour Monday (except holidays) from 10 A.M. to 2:30 P.M.; you can also tour Davies on Wednesday and Saturday afternoons (moderate admission). Phone (415) 552-8338 for details.

The Veterans Building (Van Ness and McAllister) was the site of the signing of the United Nations Charter in 1945. It houses the intimate Herbst Theatre and the Museum of Modern Art, acclaimed for its abstract expressionist works. The museum is open 10 A.M. to 5 P.M. Tuesday through Friday (to 9 P.M. Thursday), 11 A.M. to 5 P.M. weekends. Admission is $4 adults, $2 seniors and

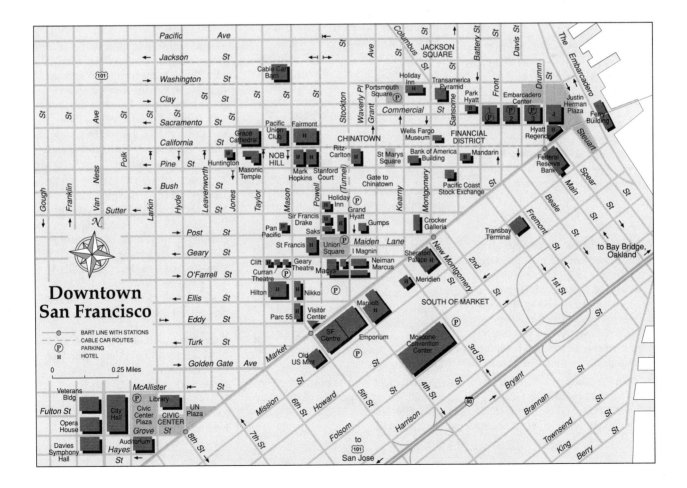

San Francisco is a world marketplace with everything from tourist trifles to antique treasures for sale. Most shops are open 7 days a week, with extended evening hours on certain weekdays.

The d.a.s. Bus (Dining and Shopping) offers loop service to Pier 39, Fisherman's Wharf, Union Square, North Beach, Union Street, Chinatown, South of Market, and Civic Center. For fares and schedules, call (415) 775-SHOW.

Don't overlook museum and gallery stores. Check out the San Francisco Zoo (Sloat Boulevard at Skyline), San Francisco Opera Shop (199 Grove Street), Museum of Modern Art (401 Van Ness Avenue), and Craft & Folk Art Museum at Fort Mason (Building A) for T-shirts, books, posters, and many one-of-a-kind items.

To buy souvenirs and support a cause at the same time, shop at the Greenpeace Store (890 North Point) for handcrafted and recycled items or the UNICEF Store (3419 Sacramento Street) for international gifts.

Downtown, Union Square's wealth of stores, convenient parking, good restaurants, and nearby attractions make it hard to bypass. Only a few blocks away lie other unique malls, and farther afield you'll find discount outlets, crafts galleries, and trendy boutiques.

Union Square. This is San Francisco's answer to Rodeo Drive in Beverly Hills. Elegant department stores and richly appointed specialty shops cater to an upscale crowd, but their decor makes them fun to browse. When you tire, a variety of restaurants and hotel dining rooms offer a change of pace.

Serious shoppers concentrate on the blocks bounded by Geary, Powell, Post, and Stockton streets. Besides the large stores like Neiman Marcus, Saks Fifth Avenue, I. Magnin, and Macy's, take a look at Gump's (250 Post Street), famous for its Orientalia, and FAO Schwarz (48 Stockton), a playland for children. Sutter Street has art galleries and exclusive clothing stores.

San Francisco Shopping Centre. Spiral escalators reach 9 floors of shops and restaurants in this vertical mall at Market and Powell streets. Nordstrom department store occupies the top 5 stories; more than 90 boutiques and 9 restaurants fill the rest of the space.

The large Emporium department store just up Market Street, connected by walk-throughs to the Centre, is one of the city's oldest retailers.

Crocker Galleria. This three-level center on the block bounded by Post, Kearny, Sutter, and Montgomery streets encompasses more than 50 boutiques, restaurants, and services under a spectacular glass dome. Modeled after Milan's vast Galleria Vittorio Emmanuelle, it's the place to look at the wares of American and European designers. Two rooftop gardens offer picnic possibilities.

Embarcadero Center. On the site of San Francisco's other-era produce market, this high-rise complex of offices, stores, restaurants, and hotels near the waterfront north of Market Street resembles a city of the future. You can park in the garage and spend the day wandering around. Information boards at the base of the escalators will help orient you.

South of Market. You don't really need a map to shop the discount and factory outlets South of Market—just follow the crowds. Discount shopping in the city is so popular that several guidebooks have been published on the subject, and special bus tours are available; check with the visitor center (page 11).

Stores usually open around 10 A.M. and close about 5 P.M.; most are closed Sunday. Go early; merchandise can become a mad tangle by mid-day.

Six-Sixty Center (660 3rd Street) has 20 outlets offering savings on brand-name shoes, clothing, and accessories. Happy Times, across the street, discounts jewelry, watches, and sunglasses.

Yerba Buena Square (Howard and 5th streets, open daily) offers outlets for toys, coats, dance and exercise wear, and more.

Among San Francisco designer outlets worth visiting are Esprit (Illinois and 16th streets, open daily, sportswear); Eileen West (39 Bluxome Street, women's clothing); and Gunne Sax (35 Stanford Alley between 2nd and 3rd streets, open daily, period-look prom dresses and other women's clothing).

Waterfront. While most of the stores at Fisherman's Wharf and Pier 39 sell souvenir-type merchandise, street vendors often display good handicrafts. But your best bet for crafts and unique gifts will be the Anchorage, Cannery, or Ghirardelli Square malls (see pages 27–28 for information).

Union Street. Trendy upscale shops west of Van Ness Avenue in the 1500 to 2200 blocks mingle happily with bakeries, cafes, and lively bars. Victorians have been transformed into shopping malls, and passages between buildings lead to small courtyards and antique-filled backyard barns.

Sacramento Street. A browsable 5-block area south of the Presidio between Lyon and Spruce streets is reminiscent of early Union Street. Interspersed with vintage homes are galleries, boutiques, and coffee houses.

...Downtown

students, free 12 and under (free for all the first Tuesday of the month). The museum will move to South of Market in 1993 (see below right).

Around Union Square

The 20-odd blocks around Union Square are a magnet for shoppers, diners, and theatergoers. You can park in the cavernous garage beneath the square to stroll around this walkable area. (Two other convenient garages are Mason-O'Farrell and Sutter-Stockton.)

The square. The landscaped square (bounded by Geary, Powell, Post, and Stockton streets) got its name from a series of 1860 pro-Union demonstrations. Its 97-foot monument to victory in the Spanish-American war and the Westin St. Francis hotel across Powell Street are 1906 earthquake survivors.

Today, its benches are lined with a motley assortment of street artists, panhandlers, and people feeding the pigeons. But it's also the site of fashion shows, rallies, concerts, and colorful events like the annual Cable Car Bell Ringing Contest in June.

Around the square. Framing the square and fanning out around it are such noted stores as Neiman Marcus, I. Magnin, Saks Fifth Avenue, Macy's, Gump's, and FAO Schwarz (see page 20 for more shopping details). West on Geary lie the Curran and Geary theaters and the venerable Clift Hotel (its Redwood Room bar is a favorite pre-theater stop).

Sutter Street, a block north of Union Square, showcases an array of haute couture, art, and antique stores in the 300 to 500 blocks. Two blocks east is the glass-canopied Crocker Galleria shopping center.

The fountain in the plaza of the Grand Hyatt north of the square on Stockton near Sutter gives a whimsical picture of city history. It was created by sculptor Ruth Asawa, who also designed fountains at Ghirardelli Square and Japantown's Buchanan Mall.

On the east side of Union Square across Stockton lies Maiden Lane, a pedestrianway that began life as the Barbary Coast's most lurid red light district. Architecturally, the lane's chief claim to fame is the yellow brick gallery at 140, designed by Frank Lloyd Wright in 1948 as a prototype for New York City's Guggenheim Museum.

Financial district

North of Market Street, impressive office buildings shade the narrow slot that is Montgomery Street, San Francisco's business center. Heart of the district is the Pacific Coast Stock Exchange (Pine and Sansome streets), where business begins around 6 A.M. to coincide with New York trading. At lunchtime, well-clad crowds hurry through the doors of such dining temples as Doro's, Ernie's, Jack's, Sam's Grill, Tadich Grill, and Tommy Toy's.

It's hard to realize that this dapper domain of bankers and brokers was a muddy morass deemed "impassable, not even jackassable" in gold-rush days when A. P. Giannini founded his Bank of America at the corner of Montgomery and California.

Two high-rises offer bird's-eye views: the Bank of America's 52nd-floor Carnelian Room restaurant and bar (see page 30) and the 27th floor of the 853-foot-high Transamerica Pyramid at 600 Montgomery Street.

Three banks have free museums open during banking hours. The Wells Fargo History Museum, 420 Montgomery Street, brims with memorabilia from the 1800s to 1915. The Bank of California's one-of-a-kind gold collection, 400 California Street, includes privately minted coins and Western currency. The Bank of Canton's Pacific Heritage Museum, Commercial and Montgomery streets, looks at contributions made to the state by Pacific Rim immigrants.

Embarcadero Center

Laced on three levels by landscaped plazas and malls, this 10½-acre complex near the waterfront combines offices, shops, restaurants, and hotels in five soaring towers. Its showplace is the Hyatt Regency at the foot of California. Another hotel, the Park Hyatt, faces Battery Street.

In the neighboring Federal Reserve Bank (101 Market Street), a surprisingly interesting World of Economics display describes banking with cartoons, electronic devices, and computer games. Stop by at noon for a 20-minute movie. You can see the free exhibits weekdays from 9 A.M. to 4:30 P.M.

Jackson Square

Built on the wharves and ships of those hungry for gold, this historic district is roughly bounded by Washington, Columbus, Pacific, and Sansome streets. It's now a quiet enclave of tiny alleys and tree-lined streets, a far cry from its rowdy Barbary Coast beginnings.

Converted into a showplace for designers in the 1950s, it became home to attorneys, architects, and ad agencies when the decorators fled south to design complexes around Potrero Hill. Some of the elegant buildings house antique shops and restaurants.

Landmarks of interest on Jackson Street include the original iron-shuttered A. P. Hotaling Co. liquor distillery (451), the factory used by Domingo Ghirardelli for his chocolate works (415–31), and an early 1850s survivor supported by ship masts (472), used as the French Consulate from 1865 to 1876.

South of Market

Explore the industrial neighborhood south from Market Street to find some of the city's trendiest nightclubs, eateries, discount shops, gay clubs, and avant garde galleries, museums, and theaters. This is a funky community with warehouse-size buildings, later-day apartments, wino bars, and train tracks. Parking is tight weekdays.

SoMa's gentrification started with the 1981 opening of Moscone Convention Center (Howard between 3rd and 4th streets), now the focal point for upscale hotels such as the Meridien and Marriott, discount outlets (see page 20), and restaurants. Part of the Yerba Buena Center construction across the street is the new Museum of Modern Art, scheduled to move here in 1993.

Most art galleries are sprinkled along Folsom Street, and several popular restaurants and clubs cluster around 11th and Folsom.

Neighborhoods

Most of San Francisco's immigrants settled in tightly knit communities—a happy circumstance for anyone who has ever prowled Chinatown's back alleys, enjoyed a *caffelatte* in North Beach, joined a spring festival in Japantown, or eaten nachos in the Mission District.

San Francisco's districts are often called cities within a city, and they grow and change just as the city itself does. For example, the funky Haight-Ashbury residential district at the east end of Golden Gate Park, home to flower children in the 1960s, is as likely to attract young professionals these days. And the predominantly gay Castro area south of Market has become increasingly gentrified, its Victorians spruced up and its streets lined with boutiques and pubs.

Chinatown

Benevolent dragons and stone lions guard the green-tiled gateway to Chinatown at Grant Avenue and Bush Street. The center for the largest Asian community in North America, Chinatown covers an area of about 24 square blocks between Kearny, Mason, Bush, and Broadway.

The 8-block stretch of Grant Avenue attracts most tourists. But more local flavor is found along the cross streets and side alleys paralleling Grant. You'll find typical Chinese markets and food stores along the northern reaches of Stockton Street and around Broadway. Plan to explore the avenue on foot, as the streets are narrow and very heavily congested.

A neighborhood stroll. Busy, crowded Grant Avenue bulges with shops, restaurants (venerable favorites with Westerners include Empress of China, Kan's, and Imperial Palace), bars, bakeries, teahouses, theaters, and Asian markets. Fine wares from China, Taiwan, and Hong Kong mingle with curios made in Korea, Japan, and the U.S. One local axiom: the best stock is never found in the front of the shop.

Old St. Mary's Church, a landmark since 1854, stands at Grant and California. This Gothic structure was built largely by Chinese laborers with granite from China and brick brought around Cape Horn from New England.

Diagonally across the street is St. Mary's Square, a quiet little park with sculptor Beniamino Bufano's imposing marble and stainless steel statue of Sun Yat-sen, founder of the Chinese Republic and onetime Chinatown resident. Underneath the park lies a parking garage (entrances on Kearny, Pine, and California).

The Bank of Canton branch at 743 Washington (east of Grant) is another landmark. From 1909 to 1949 the building held the Chinese Telephone Exchange; operators memorized as many as 2,400 names and numbers of Chinatown subscribers.

Waverly Place, a 2-block stretch paralleling Grant Avenue west between Washington and Sacramento streets, reveals some of Chinatown's colorful old buildings and few remaining temples. Of special interest is the Tien Hou Temple (top floor of 125 Waverly), which dates back to gold-rush days. Tourists might take note: the main shrine is dedicated to the protectress of travelers.

Down the street on Waverly is the Chinese Culture and Art Center, where instructors teach calligraphy, *tai chi chuan*, Chinese violin, and butterfly harp during weekend classes.

Continue west to Stockton Street; the lively food stalls and markets in the 1000–1200 blocks sell everything from squawking chickens and ducks to crocks of pickled vegetables and packages of rare herbs and fragrant teas. Buyers gather not only to shop, but also to socialize.

Portsmouth Square. Just east of Grant Avenue, between Washington and Clay, is the place where Captain John B. Montgomery raised the American flag in 1846 to proclaim the Mexican village a possession of the United States. Named for Montgomery's ship, the

square today is a landscaped park atop a parking garage.

Portsmouth Square may not have a Chinese name, but it is the area's village plaza. In the early morning, students practice *tai chi chuan* exercises; by afternoon elders gather for chess and conversation while youngsters romp in the nearby playground.

Museums. Two museums help unlock the history and culture of this famous section of town. The Chinese Culture Center (750 Kearny Street), on the third floor of the Holiday Inn on Portsmouth Square, offers a collection of contemporary and historical art. The free gallery is open Tuesday through Saturday from 10 A.M. to 4 P.M.

The free Chinese Historical Society Museum, 650 Commercial Street, is a small downstairs gallery with a treasurehouse of Chinese-American artifacts, among them unusual tools from early herb shops and a small, flat-bottomed boat dating back to the bay's first shrimping industry. You can visit Wednesday through Sunday from noon to 4 P.M.

Walking tours. Guided tours can uncover Chinatown's hidden heart. Docents from the Chinese Culture Center lead a 1- to 2-hour Chinese Heritage Walk with stops at an herb shop, fortune cooky factory, Buddhist temple, and other architectural and historical gems ($9 adults, $2 children under 18). A culinary tour also is offered ($18 adults, $9 children under 12). For details and reservations, call (415) 986-1822.

Several other walking tours of the area are conducted by knowledgeable locals; for a complete list of options, check with the visitors bureau (address on page 11).

North Beach

Not really a beach at all, this district between Chinatown and Fisherman's Wharf acquired its name in the 1850s when a finger of bay extended inland

Stone lions guard the ornate gateway to Chinatown at Grant Avenue and Bush Street. Most tourist shops and restaurants lie along Grant, but side-street prowls reveal temples, museums, and workshops.

to the sunny shore cradled between Telegraph and Russian hills. The bohemian era of the 1950s and a later influx of Chinese newcomers erased some of the original Italian imprint, but North Beach is still a distinctive neighborhood.

An enticing mosaic of cappuccino houses, cafes, bakeries, and Italian specialty stores is found on and around aptly named Columbus Avenue north of Broadway's titillating nightspots. Remnants of the 1950s Beat Generation live on in the City Lights Bookstore at 216 Columbus (onetime gathering spot for Beat poets) and neighboring Vesuvio cafe and bar.

Beach Blanket Babylon packs Club Fugazi at 678 Green in an area of moderately priced, family-run Italian restaurants. And photos and relics of old days are on display in the North Beach Museum, located above Eureka Federal Savings at 1435 Stockton Street. The free museum is open during regular bank hours.

Heart of this Little Italy is Washington Square (Columbus Avenue and Union Street), actually a pentagon adorned with a statue of Benjamin Franklin. Just as early immigrants gathered here to socialize with neighbors, oldtimers today sit on benches conversing with friends in Italian.

The annual blessing of the local fishing fleet in October begins with a procession from the twin-spired Church of Saints Peter and Paul, across Filbert Street from the square. Spiritual home of city Italians, the church now also offers masses in English and Cantonese.

The upper floors of the building at the southwest corner of Union and Stockton serve as a retirement home for elderly Italians, while the ground floor is occupied by Fior d'Italia, the city's oldest Italian restaurant.

Japantown

More than 12,000 people of Japanese descent live in San Francisco. Though the first Japanese arrived in the 1860s, it wasn't until after the 1906 earthquake that many chose to rebuild homes in this area west of downtown, bounded by Post, Geary, Laguna, and Fillmore streets.

For visitors the focal point is the Japan Center at Post and Buchanan, a 5-acre, pagoda-crowned complex of hotels, shops, theaters, restaurants, and sushi bars. Street signs are in both Japanese and English.

Colorful ceremonies take place in the central plaza, including the week-long Spring Cherry Blossom Festival in April.

A little over a mile from Union Square, Japantown is easy to reach on public transportation; take a bus west along Geary and get off at Buchanan or Laguna. Motorists can park in the center's underground garage.

Mission District

The Latino section of the city is unfamiliar to many tourists, but in this colorful area south of Market Street you'll find vibrant outdoor murals, lively street markets, galleries of traditional and contemporary art, and some outstanding food.

You can also see the city's oldest building. The Mission District's heart is Mission San Francisco de Asis (called Mission Dolores), founded in 1776 by Father Junipero Serra. The 1791 mission church at 16th and Dolores streets survived the 1906 earthquake to claim senior status among San Francisco structures. Note the Indian art on the ceilings and the ornate altar. A small museum displays artifacts, and the cemetery is a final resting place for San Francisco pioneers. The mission is open from 9 A.M. to 4 P.M. daily (small admission fee).

District streets are crowded and parking is at a minimum, so it's easiest to take BART from downtown. From the station at 24th and Mission, wander east on 24th Street for 10 blocks to York Street, with a small detour into Balmy Alley, to see more than 30 murals. The Precita Eyes Mural Center conducts tours the first and third Saturday of the month; for information and reservations, call (415) 285-2287.

The free Galeria de la Raza, 2851 24th Street (open Tuesday through Saturday, noon to 6 P.M.), is a setting for traditional and contemporary art. The adjacent shop sells folk art.

For south-of-the-border taste treats, the 5-block stretch of 24th between Harrison and Hampshire streets has bakeries, candy stores, markets, and inexpensive eateries like tiny Roosevelt Tamale Parlor at 2817 24th Street.

Clement Street

In the Richmond District, some 3½ miles west of downtown, Clement Street (north of Geary Boulevard) is multicultural. In this section of town, bagel shops and Asian food markets jostle Russian bakeries and Greek delis.

With an estimated third of the city's Chinese population living nearby, it's not surprising that eateries lean heavily toward dim sum and roast duck. But a stroll along the friendly street (best from 1st to 12th or 19th to 26th avenues) also reveals a peppering of Irish bars and French bistros plus lots of Indonesian and Vietnamese restaurants. And Bill's Place (2315 Clement) is regarded as one of the best in the city for a hamburger.

Alamo Square

The classic view of a prim line of Victorian houses backdropped by downtown skyscrapers is taken from Hayes and Steiner streets in the Alamo Square Historic District. This picture-pretty setting also embraces the Imperial Russian consulate of czarist days (1198 Fulton Street) and a 1904 chateau (1000 Fulton) that was once home to the city's Roman Catholic archbishops, and then an inn.

Pacific Heights

Some of the city's finest homes lie around Fillmore Street north of California. Interspersed among the mansions are consulates, private schools, and posh condominiums. House browsing is best along Broadway between Webster and Lyon streets. Where Broderick crosses Broadway, the sidewalk is so steep it's a stairway. Climb up to the top; the views down to the bay are superb.

Small collections of treasures and historical tidbits form surprising additions to San Francisco's rich museum scene. Everyone in the family should find something of interest in this eclectic sampling. Many are free, others charge only nominal fees, and all close on major holidays.

African-American Historical and Cultural Society, Building C, Fort Mason; (415) 441-0640. This museum, art gallery, and history center devoted to African-Americans and black Californians is open noon to 5 P.M. Wednesday through Sunday. Admission: Donations.

Cable Car Museum, Powerhouse, and Car Barn, 1201 Mason Street; (415) 474-1887. Tours of the cable car control center are offered daily from 10 A.M. to 6 P.M. It's a treasure house of photos, scale models, and original cars designed by Andrew S. Hallidie in 1873. A 16-minute film shows continously. Admission: Free.

Cartoon Art Museum, 665 3rd Street, 5th Floor; (415) 546-9481. Exhibits highlight the history of cartoon art with illustrations and animation (Wednesday through Friday from 11 A.M. to 5 P.M., Saturday from 10 A.M. to 5 P.M.). Admission: $3 adults, $2 seniors and students, $1 children 12 and under. On the same floor is the free Explore Print! museum, with motorized models to explain printing processes (8:30 A.M. to 5 P.M. weekdays).

Craft and Folk Art Museum, Building A, Fort Mason; (415) 775-0990. Witty exhibits showcase contemporary crafts, American folk art, and traditional ethnic art from around the world (daily except Monday from 11 A.M. to 5 P.M., from 10 A.M. on Saturday). Admission: $1; free Saturday morning.

Fire Department Pioneer Memorial Museum, 655 Presidio Avenue; (415) 861-8000. Horse-drawn engines and other equipment that fought fires after the 1906 earthquake are featured in this tribute to early volunteer fire units, open 1 to 4 P.M. Thursday through Sunday. Admission: Free.

Friends of Photography, Ansel Adams Center, 250 4th Street; (415) 495-7000. Five galleries of creative photography showcase works by Ansel Adams and other photographers (11 A.M. to 6 P.M. Tuesday through Sunday). Admission: $3 adults, $2 seniors and students 12 to 17.

Jewish Community Museum, 121 Steuart Street; (415) 543-8880. A lively collection of art and artifacts explores Jewish culture past and present. You can visit Tuesday through Friday from 10 A.M. to 4 P.M. Admission: Free.

Levi Strauss, 250 Valencia Street; (415) 565-9153. To see the small museum chronicling the history of this San Francisco jeans giant, make a reservation for a 45-minute factory tour, offered at 10:30 A.M. Wednesday. Admission: Free.

Mexican Museum, Building D, Fort Mason; (415) 441-0404. Fine art collections focus on pre-Hispanic, colonial, folk, Mexican, and Mexican-American works. The museum is open Wednesday through Sunday from noon to 5 P.M. Admission: $2 adults, $1 seniors and children above 10.

Musée Mécanique, Cliff House, 1090 Point Lobos Avenue; (415) 386-1170. Rescued from former fun zones, 140 ancient amusement devices accept your quarters for games and music. A few modern video games beep at the back of this arcade, open from 11 A.M. to 7 P.M. weekdays, from 10 A.M. weekends. Admission: Free, but you pay to play.

Museo Italo American, Building C, Fort Mason; (415) 673-2200. This collection of Italian-American and Italian art, culture, and history focuses on contemporary artists. It's open Wednesday through Sunday, noon to 5 P.M. Admission: Free.

Museum of Ophthalmology, 655 Bush Street, Suite 300; (415) 561-8500. This engaging but serious shrine to mankind's attempts to improve vision displays 6,000 artifacts from as far afield as Sri Lanka and China. Hours are 8:30 A.M. to 5 P.M. weekdays. Admission: Free.

Old Mint, 5th and Mission streets, (415) 744-6830. Opened in 1874, this building contains restored rooms, western art, pioneer gold coins, and a pyramid of gold bars valued at $5 million. The mint is open Tuesday through Saturday from 9 A.M. to 1 P.M. with tours offered Saturday at 10 and 11:30 A.M. Admission: Free.

Society of California Pioneers, 456 McAllister Street; (415) 861-5278. A Children's Gallery featuring the state's history, gold-rush artifacts, and costumes is open weekdays from 10 A.M. to 4 P.M. (closed in August). Admission: Free.

Telephone Pioneers Communications Museum, 140 New Montgomery Street, Suite 111; (415) 542-0182. This display of telephone communication from the days of antique switchboards to the technology of the future is open weekdays from 10 A.M. to 2 P.M. Admission: Free.

Treasure Island Museum, Building l, Treasure Island; (415) 395-5067. Halfway across the Bay Bridge, this museum chronicles the history of military service in the Pacific, the 1939 World's Fair, and the China Clipper. It is open daily from 10 A.M. to 3:30 P.M. Admission: Free.

A chocoholic haven, the Chocolate Manufactory at Ghirardelli Square sells gigantic sundaes and splits; some of Domingo Ghirardelli's original candy-making equipment is still operating on the premises.

Along the Waterfront

San Francisco's waterfront is its chief drawing card. Attractions around Fisherman's Wharf and Pier 39 draw the most visitors, but you can also take a sightseeing tour around the bay, boat across to the former island prison of Alcatraz or to Angel Island (see page 37), board a flotilla of venerable ships, visit some noted museums, and explore a Spanish fort. Many of the sites are part of the Golden Gate National Recreation Area (page 29).

Piers are numbered from the Ferry Building at the foot of Market Street; even-numbered piers lie to the south, odd-numbered piers to the north. From the 1896 Ferry Building (site of the World Trade Center) along the Embarcadero southeast to the base of the Bay Bridge, a waterfront promenade provides a place to stroll.

Northwest at the foot of Broadway, 840-foot-long Pier 7 has been fitted with ornate lamps and a brass railing and opened to strollers and fishers (no license required). Pier 35 is the major dock for passenger liners.

Getting around. Parking lots around Fisherman's Wharf and garages across from Pier 39 and under Ghirardelli Square provide space for all but the busiest weekends. Traffic to the wharf is always congested, but it's particularly bad since the elevated Embarcadero Freeway was closed by earthquake damage in 1989 (and then demolished). Avoid driving by catching a cable car from downtown (even though lines can be long and waits exasperating), or taking a taxi.

You can also ride through the area by horse-drawn carriage (Carriage Charter at Pier 41), pedicab, or motorized cable car (Cable Car Charters at Piers 39 and 41), or see it from along the water's edge in a 17-foot inflatable boat (Bay Adventure, Pier 41).

Boat tours. The most striking views of San Francisco come from the water. Sightseeing boats leave from Piers 41 and 43½ near Fisherman's Wharf and from Pier 39's west marina. The *City of San Francisco*, a re-created bay steamer, offers dinner cruises from Pier 33 at the foot of Bay Street. For all cruise details, see page 124.

Fisherman's Wharf

Visitors far outnumber fishermen in the wharf district which stretches east from the Hyde Street Pier to Pier 39. Most of the activity is centered in the 22-square-block district around the pier at Jones and Jefferson streets, where you'll find what is left of San Francisco's fishing fleet.

This world-famous destination is a combination of tourist-oriented shops and galleries, offbeat museums, sidewalk stalls, and seafood restaurants. Along the dock, a vast open-air fish market offers oceans of steaming crabs, piles of prawns, and heaps of San Francisco sourdough bread.

The 312-foot submarine *U.S.S. Pampanito* tied up at Pier 45 saw action in the Pacific during World War II. It's now open for touring daily (from 9 A.M. to 9 P.M. in summer, closing at 6 P.M. weekdays the rest of the year). Admission is $4 adults, $2 students 12 to 17, and $1 ages 5 to 11, seniors, and military.

Dining. To many who come to the city, a visit calls for a meal at Fisherman's Wharf. The view is the big reason. Bayside tables let you see bobbing fishing boats and cavorting sea lions below you, while the towers of the bridges loom in the distance.

Specialties at seafood restaurants such as Scoma's (Pier 47) include fresh crab (season runs from November to July), cracked and served cold with lemon and mayonnaise; crab Louis, the classic wharf salad, served with sourdough bread; and cioppino, the heroic shellfish stew you dip into with your fingers.

Shopping. Waterfront district stores sell souvenirs ranging from seashell jewelry and T-shirts to bronze turnbuckles and model ships. The biggest retailer, Cost Plus Imports at 2252 Taylor Street, is a rambling bazaar of housewares, antiques, foods, jewelry, and home garden supplies.

At the west end of the district sprawl warehouses converted into stores and restaurants. Most famous is Ghirardelli Square (page 28); others include the Cannery and the Anchorage.

The Cannery (bounded by Beach, Leavenworth, and Jefferson streets) was constructed in 1894 by the Del Monte Company. Today, the restored brick building holds three levels of lively shops and restaurants and a comedy club. Jugglers, mimes, magicians, and musicians perform in the flower-filled courtyard.

The Anchorage occupies the block bounded by Jones, Leavenworth, Beach, and Jefferson. Its contemporary design is bedecked with nautical flags and banners, and a two-story anchor sculpture rises in the central plaza. When shopping palls, you can have a snack and watch street performers.

Pier 39

Once an abandoned cargo shipping pier, Pier 39 was transformed into a waterfront marketplace in the late 1970s. Just east of Fisherman's Wharf, the long pier (length of three football fields) embraces two levels of restaurants, tourist-oriented specialty shops, and entertainment areas.

One of its nicest features is the 5-acre waterfront park that stretches along the southwestern edge of Pier 39 as far as Pier 35. In the marinas flanking the pier, fishing boats and pleasure craft bob and sea lions bark. The Blue & Gold Fleet runs sightseeing excursions from here (see page 124).

There's no lack of free entertainment on the pier's stages, and children enjoy the double-deck Venetian carousel and the amusement arcade. The San Francisco Experience, a multimedia presentation of the city's colorful history, is offered daily every half hour from 10 A.M. to 10 P.M. ($6 adults, $5 seniors and military, $3 children ages 6 to 16).

A pedestrian bridge over Beach Street leads from a large parking garage to the pier's second level.

Alcatraz Island

Noted chiefly as a prison, Alcatraz was also the site of the first lighthouse and permanently fortified military outpost on the West Coast. Old Fort Alcatraz started housing military criminals in 1861, but it wasn't until after Prohibition in the 1930s that the island acquired the name "the rock" and its reputation as a secure site for America's most hardened criminals. Its roster of inmates included Al Capone and "Birdman" Robert Stroud.

The federal prison was abandoned in 1963, occupied in a protest movement by Native Americans from 1969 to 1971, and opened to the public in 1973 as a part of the Golden Gate National Recreation Area. Tours include a self-guiding trail, a slide show, and an audio tour of the cellblock featuring the voices of former guards.

Ferries depart Pier 41 daily every 30 minutes from 9:45 A.M. to 2:45 P.M. ($7.50 adults and children ages 12 to 18, $4 children ages 5 to 11). Get a ticket at least a day in advance during the busy summer season, from the ticket booth at Pier 41 or through Ticketron.

Visitors can stay on the island as long as they wish; the last boat back leaves at 4:35 P.M. Dress warmly, and wear comfortable shoes. For tour information, call (415) 546-BOAT or (800) 229-2784 within California.

Aquatic Park

Once part of the Golden Gate National Recreation Area (facing page), the bayside park east of Fort Mason is now the San Francisco Maritime National Historical Park. In addition to an acclaimed maritime museum and a flotilla of historic ships at Hyde Street Pier, the park contains a curving pier popular with anglers, bocce ball courts, grassy lawns alive with vendors, and one of the city's few sandy beaches.

Best way to reach the park is on the Powell and Hyde Street cable car; the turntable lies just east of the ship-shaped museum at Beach and Polk.

Investigate San Francisco's seagoing past at the *streamline moderne* Maritime Museum, which houses an extensive collection of meticulously crafted ship models, figureheads, nautical relics, photographs, and paintings. The free museum is open daily from 10 A.M. to 5 P.M.

Queen of the fleet at the Hyde Street Pier is the *Balclutha*, a regal three-masted sailing ship. Refurbished and restored, she looks like what she was: a Scottish-built square-rigger that plied the seas between the 1880s and the 1920s and logged 17 Cape Horn doublings.

Other ships include the schooner *C.A. Thayer*, river tug *Eppleton Hall*, ferryboat *Eureka*, scow schooner *Alma*, and steam tug *Hercules*. Admission to the pier is a modest $3 (free for seniors and children under 12). It's open from 10 A.M. to 6 P.M. daily.

Ghirardelli Square

Just south and west of the Hyde Street Pier, this shopping and dining complex covers the square block bounded by Beach, Larkin, North Point, and Polk streets. Though it was first a woolen works (Civil War uniforms were made here), Ghirardelli Square is better known for its years as a chocolate factory.

In 1964, the red-brick compound was renovated to contain an enticing miscellany of shops, galleries, restaurants, and a theater, all situated around an inviting plaza with an innovative fountain. Part of the square's charm lies in the outdoor cafes and the variety of food outlets available here. You can still see some of the machines used to make the rich chocolate at the Ghirardelli Chocolate Manufactory, noted for its ice cream concoctions.

Marina district

This lovely residential area with its Mediterranean flavor made headlines when it suffered extensive damage in the 1989 earthquake. But the damage has been repaired, and this stretch of waterfront still offers the best bayside viewing in San Francisco.

Fort Mason. Once Army land, Fort Mason is now the headquarters and visitor center for the Golden Gate National Recreation Area (facing page). Its old wharves and warehouses burst with museums (page 25), craft studios, theaters, bookstores, a vast maritime library (open to the public), workshops, and classrooms.

Greens, a top-rated vegetarian restaurant, serves up great views with lunch and dinner. Lawns and gardens offer picnic sites, and piers afford prime views along with fishing (California fishing license required).

Star of the show at the fort's Pier 3 is the *S.S. Jeremiah O'Brien*, an unaltered World War II Liberty Ship. A taped self-guided tour lets you clamber about the great welded-steel decks on your own. The ship is open 9 A.M. to 3 P.M. daily except holidays (small admission charge). The third weekend of each month (except May and December), the steam engine is fired up. An annual bay cruise on the third weekend of May includes a buffet luncheon; for information, call (415) 441-3101.

Fort Mason's main entrance is at Franklin and Bay streets. Best entrance for visitor attractions is Marina Boulevard at Buchanan Street.

Get maps and additional details from the information center in Building A, open 8:30 A.M. to 5 P.M. weekdays. For further information, call (415) 441-5705. To find out about guided walks, call (415) 441-5706.

Golden Gate Promenade. The 3½-mile shoreline walk between Aquatic Park and Fort Point leads to the Marina Green, a favorite place for flying kites, sunbathing, and jogging. Crissy Field, beyond, is a quiet stretch of shoreline that skirts the water's edge for about a mile; it's a favorite windsurfing spot. The orange-roofed building at the water's edge is the St. Francis Yacht Club.

At the end of the breakwater, a 20-pipe organ engineered by the Exploratorium (facing page) creates music through wave action.

To reach the end of the promenade, head west past a U.S. Coast Guard station to Long Avenue, which leads to Fort Point (page 30) and the Golden Gate Bridge. The hardy can climb the hill to the Golden Gate Bridge toll plaza and catch an inbound Golden Gate Transit bus back to the downtown area.

Palace of Fine Arts. The Greco-Romanesque rotunda at Marina Boulevard and Baker Street was built as a showcase for fine art exhibits for the 1915 Panama-Pacific International Exposition. The original building on the natural lagoon was plaster, but it was recast in concrete in 1967 to keep it from deteriorating. The palace now houses the Exploratorium museum and a 1,000-seat theater.

Exploratorium. This internationally acclaimed museum of science, art, and human perception delights both children and adults. There are some 700 exhibits to be manipulated, tinkered with, or activated by a push of a button. A visit to the Tactile Gallery, a pitch-black sensory chamber, requires reservations; call (415) 561-0362.

The museum, in the Palace of Fine Arts, is open Wednesday through Sunday from 10 A.M. to 5 P.M. (until 9:30 P.M. Wednesday) in summer. Hours the rest of the year are 1 to 9:30 P.M. Wednesday, 1 to 5 P.M. Thursday and Friday, and 10 A.M. to 5 P.M. weekends. Admission (valid for 6 months) is $6 adults, $3 seniors, $2 ages 6 to 17 (free the first Wednesday of the month and every Wednesday after 6 P.M.).

The Presidio

Location led to the Presidio's original founding by Spanish explorer Juan Bautista de Anza in 1776, and proximity to San Francisco kept it going. The U.S. Army needed the fort to protect the Pacific gateway. But in recent years, global action has passed it by.

An Urban National Park

Within a short distance of San Francisco's skyscrapers lies the country's largest urban national park. The Golden Gate National Recreation Area (GGNRA) sprawls over 74,000 acres, all the way from San Mateo County in the south to Tomales Bay in Marin County, offering diverse historic and scenic attractions.

On the north side of the Golden Gate, the park includes Marin's dramatic headlands, Muir Woods and Mount Tamalpais (see page 37), and Muir and Stinson beaches (page 68). South of the Golden Gate, the park extends out in the bay to Angel Island (page 37), wraps around San Francisco's northern and western waterfronts, and extends south into San Mateo County.

San Francisco's MUNI system provides transportation to most park attractions. For route information, call (415) 673-MUNI. For more information on GGNRA parklands, visit the headquarters in Fort Mason (open weekdays, 7:30 A.M. to 5 P.M.) or call (415) 556-0560. A detailed guidebook to all area attractions, published by the Golden Gate National Park Association, is available at many park locations and area bookstores.

The following is a brief rundown on waterfront attractions in the San Francisco part of the GGNRA. For detailed information, turn to the page reference given for each site.

Fort Mason. On the waterfront north of Fisherman's Wharf, this former Army post served as the embarkation point for Pacific-bound soldiers and supplies during World War II. Today, the recycled military warehouses brim with museums, theaters, galleries, classrooms, and a vegetarian restaurant. The last unaltered operational Liberty Ship, the *S.S. Jeremiah O'Brien*, is tied up at Fort Mason's Pier 3. (See page 28.)

Alcatraz Island. Guided tours tracing this 22-acre island's history from fort to federal prison leave from Pier 41 at Fisherman's Wharf. (See page 28.)

Golden Gate Promenade. This scenic bayshore walk with its magnificent waterfront views stretches 3½ miles from Hyde Street Pier to Fort Point and the Golden Gate Bridge. (See page 28.)

Fort Point. This brick and granite coastal fortification underneath the Golden Gate Bridge is open daily for tours. (See page 30.)

Presidio. The 1,440-acre military post at the city's northern tip (see above) will become part of the GGNRA after its scheduled closure in 1995. Rangers lead free weekend tours of the facility.

Baker Beach. On the northwest shore of the Presidio, Baker Beach is a good place to hike and fish (swimming is unsafe). Behind the beach is Battery Chamberlin, with a 95,000-pound cannon. Rangers lead tours on weekends; call (415) 556-8371 for details.

Cliff House. This San Francisco landmark, now a restaurant and museum, offers sweeping views of the Pacific Ocean and Marin coast. (See page 33.)

Ocean Beach. The 4-mile stretch of windswept sandy beach south of Cliff House is a dramatic place to hike, though unsafe for swimming.

Fort Funston. At the city's southwest corner (off Skyline Boulevard opposite Lake Merced), this fort was a military reservation from 1898 to 1972. Now its seaward bluffs are a popular launching spot for hang gliders. A loop trail offers grand views.

...Waterfront

This 215-year-old, 1,440-acre Army base overlooking the Golden Gate is scheduled for closure in 1995. Thanks to its rich history and grand scenery, the Presidio will become a national park administered by the Golden Gate National Recreation Area.

Until then, it's still a working Army post, through which you can walk, bicycle, and drive—a city within a city with more than 1,100 housing units, hospital, supermarket, churches, bowling alley, theaters, and 18-hole golf course.

On the wilder ocean and bay sides, the wind sculpts trees and hikers' hairdos. To the south, joggers and dog-walkers invade its woods and creek-lands. The eastern part is the main post and hospital.

You can go anywhere in the Presidio unless it is marked otherwise. Pick up a free map showing points of interest at the Presidio Army Museum (see right), or join a ranger-led weekend tour; call (415) 556-0865 for reservations. Parking is easy, except on the lot near the Golden Gate Bridge toll plaza (try the free unpaved lot off Lincoln between the road to Fort Point and the bridge turnoff).

Presidio Army Museum. This free museum (open 10 A.M. to 4 P.M. Tuesday through Sunday) stands near the corner of Lincoln Boulevard and Funston Avenue on the east side of the Presidio.

Built in 1864, the building was the original post hospital. Displays on two floors document the fort's history from the Spanish period through the Vietnam era, with detours into Black military history and military propaganda. Models and dioramas of the 1906 earthquake and the 1915 Panama-Pacific Exposition are particularly interesting.

The two small shacks behind the museum, built as temporary housing after the 1906 earthquake, now contain exhibits.

Pershing Square. On the grassy square around which the museum lies, an old cannon is still fired daily when the flag is raised and lowered. The square was named for John J. Pershing, General of the Armies of World War I, whose home once stood here. In 1915, while Pershing was chasing Pancho Villa in Mexico, his house burned down. His wife and daughters perished; only a son escaped.

Fort Point National Historic Site. The most popular Presidio attraction is Fort Point, huddled directly under the south end of the Golden Gate Bridge. Completed in 1861, it was once the West Coast's principal defense bastion; its 126 cannons guarded the entrance to the bay from 1861 until the fort was abandoned in 1886—though it never saw actual battle.

The fort is open from 10 A.M. to 5 P.M. daily. Guides in period uniforms lead free tours that visit the restored powder magazine and cannon display; you're on your own in the bookstore.

Room to roam. Off West Pacific Avenue along the Presidio's southern boundary lie two places to pause: Mountain Lake Park (fitness course, playground, tennis courts) and, over the hill to the east, Julius Kahn Playground (picnic tables, tennis courts, baseball diamond, gated play area).

Sky-high Retreats

Restaurants and lounges scattered across the city welcome those looking for high—literally—society. These lofty vantage points range in age from the Top of the Mark, a 1939 landmark, to the View Lounge, Marriott's new vista site. You can go sky-high even if you only want to look.

Carnelian Room, 52nd Floor, Bank of America Building, 555 California Street; (415) 433-7500. Opens 3 P.M. weekdays, 4 P.M. Saturday, 10 A.M. Sunday; cocktails, dinner, Sunday brunch.

Cityscape, 46th Floor, San Francisco Hilton, O'Farrell Street between Taylor and Mason; (415) 776-0215. Cocktails daily from 5 P.M., dinner, Sunday brunch, nightly entertainment.

Club 36, 36th Floor, Grand Hyatt, 345 Stockton Street; (415) 398-1234. Cocktails daily from 2 P.M., live entertainment from 4 P.M.

Crown Room, 24th Floor, Fairmont Hotel, 950 Mason Street; (415) 772-5131. Buffet lunch and dinner Monday through Saturday, Sunday brunch, cocktails daily from 11 A.M.

Equinox, 18th Floor, Hyatt Regency, 5 Embarcadero Center (foot of California Street); (415) 788-1234. Revolving restaurant, daily lunch and dinner, cocktails from 11 A.M.

Oz, 32nd Floor, Westin St. Francis, 335 Powell Street; (415) 397-7000. Cocktails from 4:30 P.M., music for dancing (cover charge) nightly from 9:30 P.M.

S. Holmes, Esq., 30th Floor, Holiday Inn-Union Square, 480 Sutter Street; (415) 398-8900. Cocktails daily from 4 P.M. (from 8 P.M. Saturday), live entertainment Tuesday through Friday from 5 P.M.

Starlite Roof, 21st Floor, Sir Francis Drake Hotel, 450 Powell Street; (415) 392-7755. Cocktails daily from 4:30 P.M., dancing until 1 A.M.

Top of the Mark, 19th Floor, Mark Hopkins Inter-Continental, California and Mason; (415) 392-3434. Cocktails daily from 4 P.M., Sunday buffet brunch.

Victor's, 32nd Floor, Westin St. Francis, 335 Powell Street; (415) 956-7777. Cocktails daily from 5 P.M., dinner, Sunday champagne brunch.

View Lounge, 39th Floor, San Francisco Marriott Hotel, 727 Market Street; (415) 896-1600. Cocktails daily from noon, piano music.

Swans and ducks share the lagoon fronting the Palace of Fine Arts in the Marina District. The neo-classic structure (home to the Exploratorium museum) is the sole survivor of the 1915 Panama-Pacific International Exposition complex.

The West Side

San Francisco owes a great debt of gratitude to William Hammond Hall and John McLaren, two pioneer park designers whose vision and perseverance turned 1,017 acres of rolling sand dunes into one of the world's best-loved parks. Golden Gate Park stretches all the way across the western half of the city.

The city's western edge, defined by the Pacific Ocean, was part of an 1854 coastal fortification plan that established a natural greenbelt south as far as Fort Funston. The region is now part of the Golden Gate National Recreation Area (see page 29).

Golden Gate Park

San Francisco's premier park is a place for people to walk, play, and picnic in grassy meadows. Hiking and riding trails and bicycle paths wind through the urban oasis close to three museums, gardens, lakes, waterfalls, sports fields, polo grounds, tennis and horseshoe courts, lawn bowling greens, flycasting pools, and an archery range.

A children's playground at the eastern end of the park has a handsomely restored 1912 carousel. Toward the western end of the park, a small herd of bison grazes in a paddock not far from a 9-hole golf course. Trail rides are available from the nearby stables; call (415) 666-7201 for reservations.

Two main drives—John F. Kennedy and Martin Luther King, Jr.—run the 3-mile length of the park. Some roads in the east end close to auto traffic on Sunday.

Stop by McLaren Lodge at the east end (Stanyan and Fell streets) weekdays for maps and brochures. Friends of Recreation and Parks offers free walking tours on weekends from May through October; call (415) 221-1311.

Three of the city's finest museums flank the Music Concourse (free outdoor concerts Sunday at 1 P.M.) in the eastern half of the park. Museum admission is free on the first Wednesday of the month.

A trio of distinctive gardens offers abundant floral displays. Note also the rhododendron dell near McLaren Lodge and the rose gardens near Stow Lake (center of park).

California Academy of Sciences. The West's oldest scientific museum (founded in 1853) includes a natural history center, an aquarium, and a planetarium. Crowd-pleasing exhibits include a simulated earthquake ride, California wildlife dioramas, "Life through Time" evolutionary evidence, and a gem and mineral display.

Among the most popular aquarium residents are penguins (feedings at 11:30 A.M. and 4 P.M. daily), dolphins and seals (fed every 2 hours beginning at 10:30 A.M.), turtles, octopi, and alligators.

The Fish Roundabout lets you stand in the center of a tank while a dazzling array of sharks, tuna, and other fish flash past around you. A re-created tidepool introduces children to starfish and hermit crabs.

Daily shows at the Morrison Planetarium revolve around a specially built star projector. One-hour performances (modest admission) take place at 2 P.M. weekdays, on the hour from 1 to 4 P.M. weekends and holidays. Laserium shows are offered some evenings; call (415) 750-7138 for information.

The museum is open 10 A.M. to 5 P.M. daily. Admission is $6 adults, $3 seniors and children 12 to 17, and $1 children 6 to 11.

M. H. de Young Memorial Museum. Refurbished and reorganized, this venerable art museum (started in 1894) concentrates on American art from colonial times to the 20th century. Heart of the show is the acclaimed John D. Rockefeller III collection of paintings, sculpture, furniture, and decorative arts. The country's great artists from Paul Revere to Richard Diebenkorn are represented.

The museum (good cafeteria, gift store) is open 10 A.M. to 4:45 P.M. Wednesday through Sunday. Admission of $4 adults, $2 seniors and children ages 12 to 17, includes the Asian Art Museum (see below) and a same-day visit to the California Palace of the Legion of Honor (see facing page).

Asian Art Museum. Though it's in the same building as the de Young Museum and costs no more to visit, this impressive museum is a separate institution, the largest of its kind outside of Asia. Heart of the collection is the Avery Brundage collection of more than 12,000 works spanning 6,000 years. Note especially the Chinese jades and ancient bronzes.

Japanese Tea Garden. Just west of the M. H. de Young Museum, this lavish display of Oriental landscaping boasts a moon bridge, hand-carved gates, pagodas, a large bronze Buddha, and a teahouse (tea and cookies served from 10:30 A.M. to 4:30 P.M. daily). Spring cherry blossoms peak around April 1, turning the 5 acres into a fairyland. The modest admission is waived on the first Wednesday of the month. The garden is open from 9 A.M. to 5 P.M. daily.

Strybing Arboretum. This self-contained 70-acre world of plants includes 6,000 species from all over the world. Highlights include a fragrance garden for the visually impaired, home demonstration gardens, and a stunning display of California redwoods.

The free gardens, located at 9th Avenue and Lincoln Way, are open weekdays from 8 A.M. to 4:30 P.M., weekends from 10 A.M. to 5 P.M. Guided tours take place at 1:30 P.M. weekdays, 10:30 A.M. and 1:30 P.M. weekends.

Conservatory of Flowers. The atmosphere in this jungle setting (open daily 9 A.M. to 5 P.M.; small admission) is warm and humid. Lush tropical plants include bright crotons, large-flowered hibiscus, rare cycads, graceful ferns, and a variety of orchids. Pathways are lined with tall palms and huge old philodendrons.

The wooden greenhouse, a replica of the conservatory at London's Kew

Gardens, was transported from England around the Horn on a sailing ship and erected here in 1878. The conservatory is off John F. Kennedy Drive in the park's northeast corner.

The western edge

A tumultous meeting of sand and surf, the 4-mile stretch of Ocean Beach alongside the Great Highway is a favorite lookout for tourists and sunset watchers. Like most of the city's beaches, it's not safe for swimming. (Swimmers should head for secluded and often sunny China Beach to the north at 28th and Sea Cliff avenues.)

Overlooking the Pacific at the city's northwest corner, Adolph Sutro opened the elaborate gingerbread Cliff House resort in 1896. It was destroyed by fire in 1907, and the current incarnation, built in 1909, is the third to occupy the site. It houses a restaurant, lounge, and the Musée Mécanique amusement arcade (see page 25).

In those early days people frolicked happily at Sutro Baths, the largest indoor swimming pools in the world, just north of Cliff House. Closed in 1952, the concrete ruins can still be discerned, though the elaborate stained glass, fountains, and gardens are long gone. Offshore, at the foot of Point Lobos Avenue, Seal Rocks are alive with shore birds and stellar sea lions. Bring binoculars for a closeup. On a clear day, you can see the Farallon Islands some 30 miles away.

Other western attractions include Lincoln Park's renowned art museum, the San Francisco Zoo, and an open-air amphitheater for summer music performances.

California Palace of the Legion of Honor. This fine-arts museum commands a heady view from its hilltop site in Lincoln Park near 34th Avenue and Clement Street. Modeled after the Palais de la Legion d'Honneur in Paris, the elegant museum was given to the city in 1924 by the Spreckels family.

A sister museum to the M. H. de Young (see page 32), it was once devoted exclusively to French art but now houses an eclectic collection of European works from medieval days to the 20th century. Auguste Rodin's *The Thinker* graces the entry.

Admission to the museum (open Wednesday through Sunday from 10 A.M. to 5 P.M.) is $4 adults, $2 seniors and children 12 to 17 (free the first Wednesday of the month). Admission entitles you to a same-day visit to the M. H. de Young and Asian Art museums in Golden Gate Park.

San Francisco Zoo. This top-ranking zoo at the edge of Ocean Beach includes snow leopards, koalas, a rare white tiger, and pygmy hippos among its resident species. (Turn inland from the Great Highway at either Sloat Boulevard or Park Road; the entrance is near 45th Avenue.)

Of special interest are the Penguin Island, one-horned rhinos (a gift from the King of Nepal), and the Primate Discovery Center and Gorilla World. A Children's Zoo within the zoo (small separate entrance fee) corrals petting animals and an unusual collection of insects. Kids will also be attracted by the zoo's carousel and trackless train (20-minute guided circuits, small charge).

The zoo is open daily from 10 A.M. to 5 P.M. To hear the lions roar, get there for the 2 P.M. feeding. Zoo admission is $6 adults, $3 ages 12 through 15, free under 12 accompanied by an adult (free for all the first Wednesday of every month).

Sigmund Stern Grove. A wooded open-air amphitheater just east of the zoo at 19th Avenue and Sloat Boulevard is the setting for an annual Midsummer Music Festival. Free musical entertainment, from classical offerings to pops concerts, takes place Sunday around 2 P.M.; come early to reserve a patch of lawn, spread out a blanket, and enjoy a picnic.

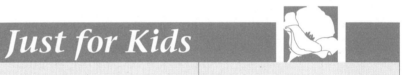

Just for Kids

Children love San Francisco at first glance, for the toylike cable cars that swoop down the hills, the bridges, and the array of boats along the waterfront. And the city bulges with other tot-sized delights, from forts to fortune cookies.

Many places described in this chapter appeal to youngsters, especially the Zoo, the children's playground and other attractions in Golden Gate Park, the Exploratorium at the Palace of Fine Arts, Fort Point under the Golden Gate Bridge (cannon is fired at 1:30 and 2:30 P.M.), Hyde Street Pier (sea chantey singalongs on the first Saturday afternoon of the month), and Pier 39's fun zone.

The Josephine D. Randall Junior Museum (199 Museum Way off Roosevelt Way) is an informal place for tykes to experience nature first hand. Among the attractions are a petting corral, a working seismograph, and mineral and fossil displays. The free museum is open 10 A.M. to 5 P.M. Tuesday through Saturday.

For a hands-on approach to art, youngsters can take part in free Saturday programs at the M.H. de Young Museum in Golden Gate Park. For 7- to 13-year-olds, "Doing & Viewing Art" includes a docent-led tour and an art activity. "Big Kids, Little Kids" is geared to ages 3½ to 6 (an adult must accompany). Both programs run from 10:30 A.M. to noon (no reservations needed). Call (415) 750-3658 for details.

If cookies intrigue, head for Chinatown's Golden Gate Fortune Cookies Company, at 56 Ross Alley (1 block west of Grant Avenue, north of Washington Street). You'll see workers deftly placing the fortunes inside.

And at bedtime, youngsters may dial (415) 626-6516 for a story, courtesy of the San Francisco Public Library.

The Bay Area

The San Francisco Bay covers some 900 square miles from its mouth at the Golden Gate. Around its perimeter lie towns that hide a wealth of attractions, some of the state's finest parks, and several top entertainment complexes.

North of the Golden Gate Bridge are upscale Marin County's bayside villages and bucolic parks. East of the Bay Bridge, communities like the port of Oakland and university-oriented Berkeley parallel the shoreline, while new development turns once-sleepy inland towns into burgeoning cities.

The peninsula south of San Francisco is divided into distinctly different regions by its forested mountain ridge. The bay side is lined with cities, while the ocean side from San Francisco to Santa Cruz sports unspoiled beaches and peaceful farmland.

At the south end of the bay, the Santa Clara Valley was known for its orchards before high-tech industries dubbed the area Silicon Valley. San Jose, its largest city, was founded in 1777.

Planning a trip

Weather is no factor when planning a Bay Area trip; the climate is mild, and most locations are at least several degrees warmer than San Francisco. Summers are dry, and spring and autumn days can sparkle.

Getting there. Three international airports serve the Bay Area: San Francisco (14 miles south of the city), Oakland (6 miles south of downtown off Interstate 880), and San Jose (northwest of down-

One of the stars at Marine World/Africa USA, 30 miles northeast of San Francisco at Vallejo, gives a gracious "hand" to an appreciative audience.

town off U.S. 101). Greyhound buses connect area towns, and Amtrak trains stop at Oakland and San Jose.

Major north-south highways are U.S. 101 in Marin and the South Bay, Interstates 880 and 680 in the East Bay, Interstate 280 in the South Bay, and State 1 on the coast. From the east, Interstates 80 and 580 reach the region.

A series of toll bridges links bay communities—Golden Gate and Bay bridges from San Francisco to Marin and Oakland, Richmond–San Rafael from Marin to the East Bay, and San Mateo and Dumbarton bridges from the East Bay to the peninsula.

Several ferry lines serve the North Bay (page 36). Blue and Gold Fleet operates from San Francisco to Oakland/Alameda; call (415) 522-3300. Red and White Fleet, (415) 546-BOAT, serves Vallejo. Bay Area Rapid Transit (BART) covers the East Bay and dips under the bay to San Francisco (see page 14). Various bus lines provide transbay and regional service, and commuter trains run down the peninsula (see page 12).

Where to stay. Most chain hotels cluster around airports or in main cities such as San Rafael, Sausalito, Oakland, Berkeley, San Mateo, Palo Alto, and San Jose. Small inns and motels are scattered along the coast.

Activities. You can watch professional baseball (Oakland Athletics) and basketball (Golden State Warriors) at the Oakland–Alameda County Coliseum 5 miles south of downtown Oakland on Interstate 880. The South Bay is headquarters for the San Francisco 49ers football team and home of the San Jose Sharks hockey team. Bay Meadows Racecourse in San Mateo and Golden Gate Raceway across the bay in Albany draw crowds for horse racing.

The East Bay has the touted Oakland Ballet and Berkeley Repertory Theater, plus symphony, opera, jazz clubs, and more theater. Call (415) 835-ARTS for Oakland events, (415) 642-9988 for University of California performances. Varied events are staged at Marin County's Veteran's Memorial Auditorium-Theater (San Rafael), Walnut Creek's Regional Center for the Arts, the Mountain View Center for the Performing Arts, and San Jose's Center for Performing Arts. The Concord Pavilion and Mountain View's Shoreline Amphitheatre host summer outdoor concerts.

Contacts

These agencies offer information on attractions and accommodations. See additional contacts throughout this chapter.

NOTE: The telephone area code in East Bay counties will change from (415) to (510) as of October 1991.

Marin County Convention and Visitors Bureau
30 N. San Pedro Rd., Suite 150
San Rafael, CA 94903
(415) 472-7470

Oakland Convention and Visitors Bureau
1000 Broadway, Suite 200
Oakland, CA 94607-4020
(415) 839-9000

San Jose Convention and Visitors Bureau
333 W. San Carlos St., Suite 1000
San Jose, CA 95110
(408) 283-8833 *(information)*
(408) 295-2265 *(activities)*

North Bay

Visitors to the San Francisco Bay Area often find Marin County the surprise treat of their visit. Its bay side is one of the most photogenic shorelines in California. Captivating waterside towns, impressive Mount Tamalpais, and several ancient redwood groves are part of its rich mosaic.

The county's scenic Pacific coast is discussed on page 68.

Arriving by water. Many Marin residents prefer to commute to San Francisco by boat—also a good way for tourists to see the area without a car. Golden Gate Ferries make 10 daily round trips on weekdays and six daily on weekends and holidays from the San Francisco Ferry Building to Sausalito, Tiburon, and Larkspur Landing (north end of the bay near Point San Quentin). For details, call (415) 332-6600.

The Red & White Fleet also has ferry service to Sausalito, Tiburon, and Angel Island from Piers 41 and 43½ at Fisherman's Wharf. For information, call (415) 546-BOAT.

The Tiburon–Angel Island Ferry runs daily in summer, on weekends and holidays the rest of the year. For details, call (415) 435-2131.

Roaming through Marin

Alongside the bay, picturesque Sausalito clings to a hill, while Tiburon includes 10 square miles of salt water in its city limits. Other towns are grouped northward along U.S. 101 or lodged in canyons west of the highway.

En route to these communities, at the northern foot of the Golden Gate Bridge, the former Army garrison of Fort Baker is home for the Bay Area Discovery Museum, a hands-on facility for children 2 to 12 (modest fee).

Sausalito. With a setting reminiscent of a southern European seacoast village, Sausalito has harbors full of small vessels in all sizes and shapes. Shops and restaurants line its waterfront and crawl up the narrow, winding side streets. The most scenic approach by car is Alexander Avenue off U.S. 101 just north of the Golden Gate Bridge.

Sausalito's town center is tidy little Plaza Viña del Mar on Bridgeway. Ferries arrive here, drivers park in nearby lots, and shops and galleries line the blocks on either side. Village Fair at 777 Bridgeway (a multilevel mall with 40 shops and restaurants) has been an opium and gambling den, a gangster hideout, and a Prohibition distillery.

Two historic hotels (Casa Madrona above Bridgeway and Alta Mira on Bulkley Avenue) afford sweeping views. The Alta Mira dining deck is a favorite in nice weather. Waterside restaurants include Horizons, Scoma's, and the Spinnaker.

Sausalito is also home to a working model of San Francisco Bay (see page 14). Visitors are welcome.

Tiburon. On the shore of Richardson Bay at the tip of a peninsula opposite Sausalito (signed exit east from U.S. 101), Tiburon epitomizes the good life. Tourists join locals for alfresco dining at dockside restaurants, shopping on block-long Main Street, or wine tasting at Windsor Vineyards/Tiburon Vintners at 72 Main (10 A.M. to 7 P.M. daily).

On a hill overlooking town, splendid Old St. Hilary's Church is open 1 to 4 P.M. Wednesday and Sunday from April through October. Take Beach Road/Esperanza Street northwest from Tiburon Boulevard.

To the southwest, Beach Road takes you over Belvedere Lagoon past the expensive homes and yacht club of Belvedere. The 1866 China Cabin, formerly the social saloon of a clipper ship, is a free museum (open Sunday and Wednesday from 1 to 4 P.M.).

Trails at the Richardson Bay Audubon Center at the north end of the bay (376 Greenwood Beach Road) meander down to 900 acres of tidelands where birdlife abounds. The center is open Wednesday through Sunday from 9 A.M. to 5 P.M; you can tour its 1876 Lyford House (fee) from 1 to 4 P.M. Sunday, October through April.

Mill Valley. This town got its name from a sawmill that provided lumber for early San Francisco homes. A reconstruction stands in Old Mill Park, just down the street from the town plaza at Throckmorton and Miller. From here, you can see the steeply gabled roofs of homes tucked into the hills.

Sir Francis Drake Boulevard. Marin's most traveled east-west corridor starts at the junction of U.S. 101 and Interstate 580 just west of the Richmond–San Rafael Bridge and threads its way west to the Point Reyes Peninsula. It passes through the towns of Ross (stately homes and an Art and Garden Center at an old estate) and San Anselmo (a center for antique stores).

San Rafael. At 1102 5th Avenue in Marin's largest city, you'll find a replica of Mission San Rafael Arcangel, founded in 1817 (11 A.M. to 4 P.M. daily). A lavish Victorian in Boyd Park (1125 B Street) houses the Marin County Historical Society Museum; call (415) 454-8538 for hours. And the Guide Dogs for the Blind facility at 350 Los Ranchitos welcomes visitors to its kennels and campus; call (415) 499-4000 to arrange a free tour.

Take North San Pedro Road east of U.S. 101 to the bayside China Camp State Park (picnicking, fishing, sailing, camping), which contains the remnants of an 1800s Chinese fishing village. A turn-of-the-century store is now a museum (10 A.M. to 5 P.M. daily).

Nestled in the hills along the highway just to the north is the blue-domed Marin County Civic Center, designed by Frank Lloyd Wright. For a free tour, call (415) 499-7407.

Novato. In the rolling hills of northern Marin County, Novato gives no hint of its Spanish founding, but the town does acknowledge its original settlers with a free Museum of the American Indian (2200 Novato Boulevard, open Tuesday through Saturday from 10 A.M. to 4 P.M., Sunday from noon to 4 P.M.).

Marin parks

From an island in the bay to one of the Bay Area's highest peaks, Marin's parks are a varied lot. The county's climate also varies sharply between east and west, principally because Mount Tamalpais and the high ridges leading up to it form a barrier against fog.

Angel Island State Park. Once called the Ellis Island of the West, this 740-acre wilderness in San Francisco Bay has served as military base, war-prisoner detention center, and immigration camp.

Ferries from Tiburon and San Francisco dock at Ayala Cove on the northwest side of the island. You can sun at the beach, picnic, ride your bicycle around the island on a 5-mile unpaved road, or climb the interior slopes. Free guided tours of Civil War–era military buildings take place in summer.

Mount Tamalpais State Park. Draped across the upper slopes of 2,586-foot "Mount Tam" and reaching down to the sea at Muir Beach, the state park offers a labyrinth of hiking and riding trails. Picnic grounds lie near park headquarters on winding Panoramic Highway; take the State 1/Stinson Beach exit from U.S. 101 and follow the signs. From here you can drive nearly to the summit, 4 miles beyond. There are campsites near headquarters and at East Peak. Stage plays are presented in a hillside amphitheater in May and June; for details, call (415) 388-2070.

Muir Woods National Monument. Cool and green, this 502-acre park named for naturalist John Muir preserves a stand of virgin coast redwoods. The central part of the park and most of the 27 miles of trails are on a relatively level stretch of forest floor, making it accessible by wheelchair. There's also a marked trail for the blind.

To get a map of the park, which is surrounded by Mount Tamalpais State Park, stop by the handsome stone-and-cedar interpretive center. No camping or picnicking are allowed, but there is a coffee shop.

The park is 3½ miles west of Mill Valley, via Panoramic Highway/State 1. The road in is narrow and winding.

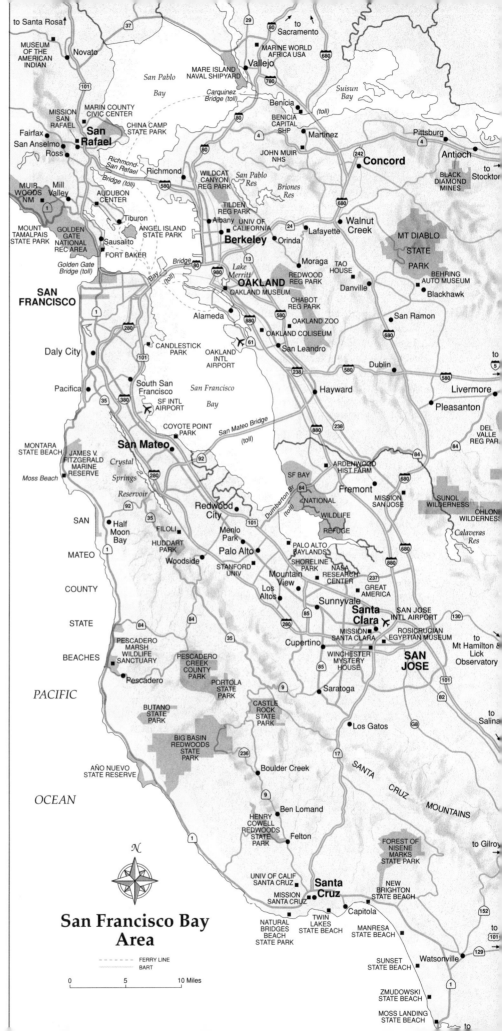

San Francisco Bay Area

```
FERRY LINE
BART
```

0   5   10 Miles

East Bay

A long ridge of low hills parallels San Francisco Bay on its eastern side, forming the backdrop for a continuous string of bayside cities. A second tier of communities is a rapidly growing counterpart on the other side of the hills.

This is a region rich in family-oriented attractions and outdoor recreation areas. It also has its share of fine museums and intriguing historic sites.

Regional parklands. In the hills that rise behind the East Bay cities, more than 50,000 acres of countryside have been set aside for recreational use under the aegis of the East Bay Regional Park District. Some parks are small, some large; some are wilderness areas, others highly developed.

You can camp at Chabot (above Oakland/San Leandro), Del Valle (near Livermore), and Sunol Wilderness (near Fremont). For a guide to all the parks, contact the East Bay Regional Park District, 11500 Skyline Boulevard, Oakland, CA 94619; (415) 531-9300.

Dining and shopping. The East Bay is where "California cuisine" was launched in the 1970s, at Alice Waters' Chez Panisse Restaurant in Berkeley (1517 Shattuck Avenue). Subsequently the nearby area, with its upscale food shops and restaurants, has come to be known as "Gourmet Gulch." But the whole East Bay offers a wealth of top-rated dining places.

Among pleasant dining and shopping streets are College Avenue through Berkeley and Oakland (Oliveto Cafe & Restaurant), Oakland's Piedmont Avenue (Bay Wolf Restaurant), Berkeley's 4th Street north of University (Fourth Street Grill), and Solano Avenue through Berkeley and Albany. Berkeley's Telegraph Avenue near the campus has fine bookstores and plenty of local color.

Oakland

Stretched out between the bay and a greenbelt of hilltop parks, the city of Oakland is one of the country's largest container shipping ports. Several attractive redevelopment efforts in recent years have focused on the downtown and waterfront areas, and visitors can take a look during free walking tours at 10 A.M. Wednesday and Saturday from May through October. Call (415) 273-3234 for details.

Oakland Museum. Oakland's acclaimed and handsome museum at 10th and Oak streets presents a different aspect of California in each of its three levels. In the Cowell Hall of California History, vivid displays suggest historical periods. The natural sciences gallery simulates a walk through the state's eight biotic zones, and the Gallery of California Art exhibits more than 550 works. The roof of each level is a garden terrace for the level above.

The museum is at the south end of Lake Merritt, a block east of the Lake Merritt BART Station. It's open Wednesday through Saturday from 10 A.M. to 5 P.M., Sunday from noon to 7 P.M. (closed major holidays). Admission is free, except for some special exhibits.

Around the lake. A 155-acre saltwater tidal basin just east of downtown, Lake Merritt is encircled by a 3¼-mile "necklace of lights" at night and by joggers and strollers during the day.

The country's oldest waterfowl refuge, established in 1870, is at the north end of the lake. Children's Fairyland offers fairytale-based scenes, puppet shows, tot-scaled rides and climbing structures (10 A.M. to 4:30 P.M. daily in summer, Friday through Sunday the rest of the year; modest admission).

Nearby, you can rent boats (daily in summer, weekends the rest of the year) or board the paddle-wheeler *Merritt Queen* for a cruise around the lake (weekend afternoons; modest charge).

At the south end, a rare three-panel Tiffany glass mosaic at Lake Merritt United Methodist Church (1330 Lakeshore Avenue) can be viewed from 2 to 4 P.M. Wednesday (free). Across the lake at 1418 Lakeside Drive, you can tour the elegant 1876 Camron-Stanford House from 11 A.M. to 4 P.M. Wednesday and 1 to 5 P.M. Sunday (small charge).

Downtown. Broadway is Oakland's "main street," cutting through a mixture of ornate early-1900s brick and tile buildings (some seriously damaged in the 1989 earthquake) and modern office towers. At 21st and Broadway is the city's Paramount Theater, a glittery 1931 art deco movie palace that hosts performing arts events. Tours are conducted the first and third Saturday of the month at 10 A.M. (small fee).

The modern-day focal point downtown is the tiered plaza stretching west from Broadway at 13th Street. A sculptural swirl of color called *There* is the city's answer to Gertrude Stein's comment about her Oakland home town, "There is no there there."

The Oakland Museum Sculpture Court at the 1111 Broadway office building is open free from 7 A.M. to 7 P.M. Down the street is downtown's only high-rise hotel, the Parc Oakland, with adjoining convention center.

Two square blocks of restored 1870s commercial buildings west of Broadway between 8th and 10th streets constitute the Old Oakland shopping and office complex. A couple of lunchtime favorites are Pacific Coast Brewing Company brew pub at 906 Washington Street and Ratto's grocery and deli at 821 Washington Street.

Across Broadway to the east, Oakland's Chinatown is concentrated between Franklin and Harrison, 10th and 7th streets. An influx of new Asian residents in recent years has added vitality to this district of food markets, shops, and many fine restaurants.

Waterfront. At the foot of Broadway, the Jack London Square area has restaurants, shops, and a hotel. The First and Last Chance Saloon (50 Webster Street) was once a hangout of author London. You can also peek into a rustic cabin in which London supposedly spent a Yukon winter, reconstructed here.

You can board a ferry to San Francisco from Jack London Square—call

Oakland's Jack London Square provides opportunities for watching waterfront activities. Giant container-loading cranes loom like harbor mascots; the busy seaport has the West Coast's largest container facility.

(415) 522-3300 for details—or take a free 1½-hour harbor cruise (every Thursday, May through August); call (415) 272-1188 to reserve. At the foot of Clay Street, take a look at Franklin Roosevelt's former yacht *Potomac*.

Along the hills. Attractions perched above the city would be worth a look if only for the views their hilltop sites afford. Castlelike Claremont Resort Hotel & Spa, built in 1915, straddles the Oakland-Berkeley city line off Claremont Avenue just north of State 13. Equally eye-catching is the Mormon Temple at Lincoln Avenue and State 13 (Warren Freeway). Free tours of its exterior and geneological library are offered daily, 9 A.M. to 9 P.M.

A string of wooded parks borders Skyline Boulevard: Joaquin Miller, Redwood, Roberts, and Chabot.

In the foothills just off Interstate 580, the Oakland Zoo has increased in stature in recent years with the addition of such naturalistic animal enclosures as a 1-acre elephant compound. Eighty species are housed at the zoo, open daily from 10 A.M. to 4 P.M. (moderate admission). Take Golf Links Road east from Interstate 580.

Berkeley

Immediately to the north of Oakland, Berkeley is known both for student activism and culinary preoccupations (see page 38). The University of California at Berkeley provides a lively mix of ideas and slate of events.

University of California. The 720-acre campus is home to more than 30,000 students. Stop at the visitor center in University Hall, University Avenue and Oxford Street, to pick up a map or to join a 1½-hour free walking tour (weekdays at 1 P.M., also Monday, Wednesday, and Friday at 10 A.M.). Take the 50-cent elevator ride up 300-foot Sather Tower for an overview.

Another sweeping view is from the Lawrence Hall of Science, on Centennial Drive above the football field. Inside are all sorts of hands-on science exhibits (10 A.M. to 4:30 P.M. weekdays,

to 5 P.M. weekends; moderate admission). The center's Holt Planetarium has weekend shows at 1, 2:15, and 3:30 P.M. (no children under 6 years).

The free 33-acre Botanical Garden is off Centennial Drive on the way up to Lawrence Hall (9 A.M. to 4:45 P.M. daily).

Also notable are the Lowie Museum of Anthropology (10 A.M. to 4:30 P.M. Tuesday through Friday, noon to 4:30 P.M. weekends; small admission); the free Paleontology Museum (8 A.M. to 5 P.M. weekdays, 1 to 5 P.M. Saturday); and the University Art Museum (11 A.M. to 5 P.M. Wednesday through Sunday, moderate admission).

Tilden Regional Park. One of the East Bay's favorite family playgrounds, this 2,000-acre area in the hills above Berkeley has an antique merry-go-round, pony rides, and a miniature steam train (daily in summer, weekends the rest of the year; small fees). At the free Little Farm, youngsters can pet farm animals, while the adjacent nature center has exhibits about wild ones. There are picnic areas, trails, a swimming lake, a botanic garden, and a golf course.

From Interstate 80, take University Avenue, turn left at Oxford, right at Cedar, and left at Spruce, then continue uphill to cross Grizzly Peak Boulevard and take the first left (Cañon Drive).

Heading south

A trip south to Fremont offers a look at earlier eras, plus a chance to glimpse bayside birdlife.

Ardenwood Historic Farm. Some 20 miles south of Oakland, you can ride a horse-drawn train or wagon, tour a Victorian home, and see demonstrations of turn-of-the-century farm skills.

Ardenwood Farm is open April through mid-November, from 10 A.M. to 4 P.M. Thursday through Sunday; admission is $5 adults, $3 seniors, $2.50 ages 4 through 17. Leave Interstate 880 at State 84 , drive west a mile, and turn right at Ardenwood Boulevard.

San Francisco Bay National Wildlife Refuge. Some 150 different species of birds call at this bayside refuge near the

eastern end of the Dumbarton Bridge. To reach the headquarters, open 10 A.M. to 5 P.M. daily, take State 84 west from Interstate 880 for 2 miles, then turn left onto Thornton Avenue. For a schedule of slide shows, walks, and bird-watching programs, call (415) 792-0222.

Mission San Jose. This 1797 Spanish mission was completely reconstructed in the 1980s. The imposing white structure and the adjacent museum are open daily between 10 A.M. and 5 P.M. (small donation suggested); a 20-minute slide show is presented on the hour. Mission San Jose is at 43000 Mission Boulevard, just south of Interstate 680 (Mission Boulevard exit) or 4 miles east of Interstate 880 (Warren/Mission Boulevard exit).

Carquinez Strait

Fresh and salt water come together in the Carquinez Strait, some 20 miles north of Oakland between Interstate 80 and Interstate 680. Near the western end, Vallejo is home to Marine World/Africa USA (see page 41) and Mare Island Naval Shipyard. For a look at the city's maritime history, stop at the Vallejo Naval and Historical Museum at 734 Marin Street (10 A.M. to 4:30 P.M. Tuesday through Friday, to 4 P.M. weekends; admission by donation).

Benicia. At the eastern end of the strait, the onetime state capital and port of Benicia is now a thriving artists' community. Stop at the Benicia Chamber of Commerce office at 601 1st Street for a walking tour guide.

Founded in 1847, Benicia became California's capital in 1854, a distinction that lasted only 13 months. The restored brick capitol building at 1st and West G streets is operated as a state historic park, generally open Thursday through Monday from 10 A.M. to 5 P.M. (small fee); call (707) 745-3385.

Browse along 1st Street from the waterfront as far as K Street to see a concentration of historic structures, antique stores, and the restored 1882 Union Hotel at 1st and West D streets (notable restaurant). On East H Street, the Yuba Arts Center (600 block) and nearby buildings house the studios of glass blowers and other artisans.

Among the more intriguing structures at the 1851 Benicia Arsenal at the east end of town are sandstone warehouses that once served as camel barns, the aftermath of an Army experiment in using the animals in the Southwest. Now they house a free city museum (weekends from 1 to 4 P.M.).

John Muir Historic Site. South of the strait in the town of Martinez is the elegant Victorian farmhouse where the West's premier conservationist lived from 1890 to 1914. You can take a self-guided tour of the house, orchard, and 1849 Martinez Adobe any day between 10 A.M. and 4:30 P.M. (small admission). John Muir National Historic Site is on Alhambra Avenue just north of State 4.

Over the hills

Across the hills, business parks and suburban housing developments are overtaking pastureland near such burgeoning communities as Concord, Walnut Creek, Livermore, and Pleasanton. Interstate 680 connects towns along this East Bay "sun belt."

Mount Diablo State Park. For an unparalleled view of the Bay Area, head up to the summit of 3,849-foot Mount Diablo. The 15,000-acre state park on the mountain's slopes offers more than 100 miles of trails, a summit visitor center, and a quartet of campgrounds that can sometimes be reserved through MISTIX; call (800) 444-7275.

To get to the park, exit Interstate 680 at Danville (Diablo Road exit) or Walnut Creek (Ygnacio Valley Road to Walnut Avenue).

Black Diamond Mines. A preserve operated by the East Bay Regional Park District offers a glimpse at area mining history and a 1930s underground sand mine. Call (415) 757-2620 to make reservations for the mine tour (expected to reopen in 1992 after repairs; small fee) and to find out about free weekend programs. Take Somersville Road south from State 4 below Antioch.

Danville. This suburban community at the foot of Mount Diablo has a purposefully quaint and countrified downtown and several cultural attractions.

Playwright Eugene O'Neill wrote some of his best-known works while living here from 1937 to 1944. You can tour his Tao House residence, operated as a national historic site, Wednesday through Sunday at 10 A.M. and 12:30 P.M. Call (415) 838-0249 for reservations for the free tour; you'll be picked up in downtown Danville.

In Danville's posh Blackhawk real estate development, the Behring Auto Museum at 3750 Blackhawk Plaza Circle displays more than 60 vintage luxury cars (10 A.M. to 5 P.M. daily except Monday, to 9 P.M. Wednesday and Friday). Admission is $8 adults, $6 seniors, $5 students. Next door , the Museum of Art, Science, and Culture exhibits University of California art and artifacts.

To get to Blackhawk, exit Interstate 680 at Crow Canyon Road and head east 4 miles to Camino Tassajara, then turn right. At the plaza, take a look at FJ's Blackhawk Market, which provides live piano music and cellular phones for the brass-trimmed shopping carts.

Livermore Valley. Interstate 580 cuts through the hills to the Livermore Valley, where nine wineries offer a leisurely approach to wine touring.

Wente Brothers Estate Winery (5565 Tesla Road in Livermore) and Concannon Vineyard (4590 Tesla Road), both founded in 1883, offer tours and tasting. Take Vasco Road south from Interstate 580 to Tesla. Southwest at 5050 Arroyo Road, Wente Bros. Sparkling Wine Cellars has tours, tastings, and the elegant Restaurant, open Wednesday through Sunday.

Pick up a touring map from any winery or from the Livermore Chamber of Commerce at 2157 1st Street.

Livermore is also the home of Lawrence Livermore National Laboratory, known for its nuclear research. A visitor center 3 miles south of Interstate 580 via Greenville Road has scientific exhibits (9 A.M. to 4:30 P.M. weekdays, noon to 5 P.M. weekends); call (415) 422-9797 to visit and to get directions to the lab's computer museum.

Drive east a few miles on Interstate 580 to see a strange landscape of thousands of wind turbines set amidst grazing lands in the Altamont Hills—the world's largest wind-fueled power plant.

Marine World

Where else can you have a tug of war with an elephant and get splashed by a whale on the same day? Marine World/Africa USA, 25 miles north of Oakland at Vallejo, is part zoo, part animal theater, and part elaborate playground.

Highlights of a visit to this 165-acre park are seven shows—killer whales and dolphins, sea lions, tigers, chimpanzees, birds, a wildlife conservation theater, and waterskiing.

The park's Elephant Encounter lets you see elephants in a variety of situations. You can also walk through the steamy tropical Butterfly World, see tidepool activity in an aquarium, observe handlers caring for giraffes, rhinos, and tigers, and glimpse park babies in a glass-walled nursery.

At the Showcase Theater various entertainment is scheduled. And a children's play area offers climbing and scrambling opportunities.

Admission, including all entertainment except elephant rides, is $19.95 adults, $14.95 ages 4 through 12, and $16.95 seniors. Marine World is open daily from 9:30 A.M. to 6 P.M. in summer, Wednesday through Sunday from 9:30 A.M. to 5 P.M. September through May.

From Interstate 80, go west on State 37, then south on Fairgrounds Drive. Or take a Red and White Fleet ferry from San Francisco to Vallejo; a combination ticket includes shuttle to the park.

A favorite family getaway, Santa Cruz lures visitors with wide, sandy beaches and a venerable boardwalk. The wooden Giant Dipper roller coaster, a national landmark, has been thrilling riders since 1924.

Peninsula & South Bay

Geographically, Palo Alto marks the end of the San Francisco Peninsula. But the cities of Mountain View, Los Altos, Sunnyvale, Cupertino, Santa Clara, and San Jose are still considered part of the South Bay.

Separating bayside communities from the pastoral coast are the Santa Cruz Mountains, a spur of the Coast Range, rising 2,000 to 3,000 feet. A string of public parks straddling their spine protects venerable redwood groves.

You can drive from San Francisco to San Jose (some 50 miles) on U.S. 101 (Bayshore Freeway) or Interstate 280 (Junipero Serra Freeway). Skyline Boulevard (State 35) winds along the ridge of the mountains, and State 1 skirts the coast.

Daily commuter trains run between San Francisco and San Jose; call CalTrain, (415) 495-4546, for information. San Mateo County Transit, (415) 761-7000, has bus service as far south as Palo Alto, and Santa Clara County Transit, (408) 287-4210, blankets the southern end of the bay.

Along the Bayshore

U.S. 101 provides the most convenient access to cities, harbors, and parks along the bay. Several major routes connect this highway with Interstate 280, a few miles inland. The two routes join in San Jose.

Bayside parks. Displays and hands-on exhibits at the nature center in Coyote Point Park (Coyote Point Drive exit in San Mateo) provide family fun. Besides the indoor Coyote Point Museum, the indoor-outdoor Wildlife Habitats let you take a look at live animals native to the Bay Area. The center is open Tuesday through Saturday from 10 A.M. to 5 P.M. and Sundays noon to 5 P.M. There's a modest admission along with a $4 per-car park entry fee. Picnic tables around the park offer grand views.

Birding and biking are popular on miles of trails along the levees in Palo Alto Baylands (Embarcadero Road east from U.S. 101). A free nature center is open 1 to 5 P.M. weekends. A 4-mile pathway extends south from here to Shoreline Park in Mountain View, a free 654-acre recreation and wildlife area (Shoreline Park exit from U.S. 101).

Around Palo Alto. This college town is noted for its tree-shaded streets of grand old houses, plus a good range of restaurants and entertainment. Don't overlook the beautifully renovated Stanford Theatre, downtown at 221 University Avenue (1920s Wurlitzer organ, pre-1950s films).

Sunset Publishing Corporation, Middlefield and Willow roads in adjacent Menlo Park, offers free weekday tours of its test kitchens and gardens; call (415) 321-3600 for times. At Arbor Road and Creek Drive in Menlo Park, Allied Arts Guild's shops and dining room inhabit part of an old Spanish rancho. For lunch and tea reservations (closed Sunday), call (415) 324-2588.

Stanford University. In 1891, Leland Stanford opened this private university on his horse farm. You can tour the campus, see the largest collection of Rodin sculptures outside of Paris (on the grounds of Stanford Museum of Art), and ride to the top of the Hoover Tower (small fee) for the view. Hour-long student-led walks start at the stone information booth at the south end of the Oval (end of Palm Drive) at 11 A.M. and 3:15 P.M. daily, except school holidays; call (415) 725-3335. University Avenue leads southwest from downtown Palo Alto into the campus.

NASA Research Center. At Moffett Field naval air station, south in Mountain View, the Ames Research Center offers weekday tours (2½ hours, 2-mile walk) of its wind tunnels and hangars. For reservations, call (415) 694-6497.

Off Interstate 280

En route south from San Francisco, the Junipero Serra Freeway—Interstate 280—passes Crystal Springs Reservoir, which holds San Francisco's water supply. The classic Greek-style Pulgas Water Temple at its southern tip marks the end of the Hetch Hetchy aqueduct, a 162-mile pipeline that begins in Yosemite National Park.

Filoli. This 654-acre estate in Woodside (Edgewood Road exit west to Cañada Road) is reason enough for a drive 25 miles south of San Francisco. The 43-room mansion—featured on TV's *Dynasty*—was built in 1916 by William Bowers Bourn II, who pulled millions in gold out of his Empire Mine in Grass Valley. Its name is a contraction of Bourn's code—Fight, Love, Live.

First-time visitors should join a docent-led tour ($8) of the house (no children under 12) and vast formal gardens (Tuesday through Saturday from mid-February to mid-November). A 3-mile nature hike ($4 adults, $1 children) is offered Monday through Saturday morning. Call (415) 364-2880 for tour reservations.

Stanford Linear Accelerator. Heart of this research center operated by Stanford University for the U.S. Department of Energy (Sand Hill Road exit) is a 2-mile-long accelerator generating high-energy electron and positron beams. Allow about 2 hours for the free guided bus tour. For reservations, phone (415) 926-3300, ext. 2204.

Around San Jose

If you haven't been in downtown San Jose recently, you'll be surprised at the changes. Thanks to major urban renewal, this oldest and biggest of Bay Area cities (population 740,000—the nation's 11th largest) has blossomed into a pleasant melange of old and new.

Downtown. A light-rail system runs along city streets and northeast to Santa Clara's Great America (see page 45). New and renovated hotels (Fairmont, upcoming Hilton, DeAnza, Holiday Inn), restaurants, and shops give visitors a reason to stay downtown.

Hub of the renaissance is the Convention Center (west of San Carlos Street between Almaden and Market) and its attendant cultural complex: Center for Performing Arts (opera, symphony, and ballet companies), Civic Auditorium, and Montgomery Theater (San Jose Repertory).

The new engenders a growing respect for the old. A self-guided history tour (check with the visitors bureau, address on page 35) leads past some of the city's architectural treasures: the Peralta Adobe (San Jose's oldest building), reconstructed St. Joseph's Cathedral, nearby San Jose State College, and the University of Santa Clara (reconstruction and remnants of the Santa Clara Mission, founded in 1777).

Museums of note. The Garage, a high-tech museum named for the scene of several startup Silicon Valley computer companies, will delight both children and adults. Among its displays: a larger-than-life microchip, robots, and the latest computers. The museum, located at 145 W. San Carlos Street, is open 10 A.M. to 5 P.M. (closed Monday). Admission is $6 adults, $4 children over 6 and seniors.

The purple exterior of the Children's Discovery Museum at Guadalupe River Park is your first clue that this lively world of hands-on fun is for kids 2 to 6 or so. Of parental interest: a changing room and a cafe geared to small appetites. The West's largest children's museum, it's open 10 A.M. to 5 P.M. Tuesday through Saturday, from noon Sunday; arrive early to avoid a crowd. Enter on Auzerais Street off Almaden Boulevard; admission is $6 adults, $3 children over 4 and seniors.

To catch a glimpse of turn-of-the-century life, visit 21 original and restored buildings that make up the San Jose Historical Museum in Kelley Park (Story Road exit south off U.S. 101). The museum is open weekdays from 10 A.M. to 4:30 P.M., weekends from noon (separate park entry and admission fees). Elsewhere in the park: a small playground and zoo and a picturesque Japanese garden.

The free San Jose Museum of Art (110 S. Market Street) is best known for its exhibits of post-war modernist and contemporary paintings. Hours are 10 A.M. to 4:30 P.M. Tuesday through Saturday, noon to 4 P.M. Sunday.

The renowned Rosicrucian Egyptian Museum at 1342 Naglee Avenue displays mummies, scarabs, and other artifacts from Egypt, Babylon, and Assyria. Admission fees to the museum (open 9 A.M. to 5 P.M. Tuesday through Saturday, 9 to 11 A.M. Sunday) and the adjacent planetarium are separate. Planetarium shows take place at 11 A.M. and 2 and 3:30 P.M. on weekends.

Across from Santa Clara's City Hall at 1505 Warburton, the stunning Triton Museum showcases turn-of-the-century American paintings, many depicting the Santa Clara Valley. The free museum is open 10 A.M. to 5 P.M. weekdays, noon to 5 P.M. weekends.

Winchester Mystery House. Sarah Winchester, heir to her father-in-law's gun fortune, believed that if she stopped adding rooms onto her house she would die. The 160-room result (Winchester Boulevard and Interstate 280) is a memorial to her obsession. The mansion, gardens, and large gift shop are open daily except Christmas for tours ($10.95 adults, $8.95 seniors, and $5.95 children 6 to 12). Hours vary with the season; call (408) 247-2101.

Lick Observatory. Twenty miles east of San Jose, the narrow and winding Mount Hamilton Road (State 130) climbs up to one of the world's largest telescopes. Visitors get a free look from 10 A.M. to 5 P.M. daily except holidays. The road isn't recommended in bad weather.

Los Gatos and Saratoga. Nestled in the foothills west of San Jose, the neighboring towns of Los Gatos and Saratoga have a well-heeled country village charm. Both are distinguished by an array of boutiques and restaurants. To get there from San Jose, take State 17 west to the Los Gatos exit; Saratoga is 4 miles to the north via State 9.

Tucked into the hills behind Saratoga (follow Big Basin Way west about a mile) are the 15½-acre Hakone Gardens, formerly a private estate, now a city park. The hillside gardens (open 10 A.M. to 5 P.M. weekdays, 11 A.M. to 5 P.M. weekends) feature Japanese plantings, teahouses, and koi ponds.

Through the mountains

South of San Francisco, Skyline Boulevard leads to woodsy communities and some of the area's busiest day-use and overnight parks: Huddart, Sam McDonald, San Mateo County Memo-'rial, and Portola State Park.

From Skyline Boulevard, campers, hikers and sightseers can head south on State 9 to redwood-shaded state parks—Castle Rock, Big Basin, and Henry Cowell—and the charming San Lorenzo Valley towns of Boulder Creek (golf course), Ben Lomond, and Felton.

Roaring Camp & Big Trees Railroad. At Roaring Camp, a simulated 1880s logging town half a mile south of Felton, a narrow-gauge steam train carries passengers on a 6-mile, 75-minute loop through thick redwood groves. For information on this trip and a second route to the Santa Cruz Boardwalk, see page 126.

Along the coast

Though not as spectacular a scenic stretch as the Big Sur coast, the San Mateo County shoreline along State 1 between San Francisco and Santa Cruz reveals many beaches and a few small towns to explore.

Beaches. Your best look at tidepools is from the rocky reef at James V. Fitzgerald Marine Reserve at Moss Beach. A free museum gives you information (collecting is prohibited).

The San Mateo Coast State Beaches, nine narrow strands scattered along 50 miles of the coast (headquarters in Half Moon Bay), are popular for strolling, picnicking, sunbathing, wading, and surf and rock fishing (license required), though the water's not safe or warm enough for swimming.

Año Nuevo State Reserve, a winter breeding ground for elephant seals, is open for docent-led guided tours from December through March. For reservations, call MISTIX, (800) 444-7275.

Towns. An agricultural and fishing center, Half Moon Bay is crowded in mid-October for its annual Pumpkin Festival. The rest of the year it's a good choice for a lazy weekend of fishing, golfing, hiking, or taking in a Sunday afternoon jazz session at the funky Bach Dancing and Dynamite Society. Among lodging choices: San Benito House (noted for its food), Mill Rose Inn, Half Moon Bay Lodge.

Ranches, flower fields, and artichoke farms surround Pescadero, 15 miles south, but most visitors head for nearby beaches, Pescadero Marsh (533-acre wildlife sanctuary), or Butano State Park (hiking, camping), 7 miles inland. Duarte's Tavern, an 1894 landmark, is the place to eat.

Santa Cruz

This seaside town was severely damaged by the 1989 earthquake (the epicenter was in nearby Forest of Nisene Marks State Park). But its visitor attractions, numerous accommodations, and restaurants were almost untouched.

For area details, contact the visitor center at 701 Front Street; phone (408) 425-1234. An information booth on Ocean Street between Water and Soquel is open during summer months.

Attractions. At the long municipal wharf (Center and Beach streets), you can fish, buy souvenirs, and dine at such seafood restaurants as Sea Cloud. Wide white beaches stretch to either side, and the vintage boardwalk (see below) lies at the pier's foot.

Art galleries, museums, wineries, golf courses, and the gravity-defying Mystery Spot (1953 Branciforte Drive, admission fee) are among other choices. You can visit a replica of the 1791 Santa Cruz Mission (126 High Street) or head into the hills to the wooded campus of the University of California at Santa Cruz (take High Street west from State 1).

Along the beach. To watch surfers at Steamer Lane and visit a free surfing museum, follow cove-hugging West Cliff Drive southwest from the pier. The Lighthouse Point museum is open daily except Tuesday from 1 to 4 P.M. in summer, also closed Wednesday the rest of the year.

To the west lies Natural Bridges Beach State Park (migrating butterflies in winter, guided tidepool tours). Nearby Long Marine Laboratory & Aquarium (foot of Delaware Avenue) is open to the public from 1 to 4 P.M. Tuesday through Sunday (free).

Twin Lakes, a day-use beach east of the wharf, is a favorite with local picnickers. One of the park's lagoons is a wildfowl refuge; a second is a yacht harbor.

Southeast of Santa Cruz. South of town are many excellent beach parks popular with swimmers, surfers, and anglers. Water is warmer here than farther north, and the surf is usually gentle.

Campsites are available at Manresa, New Brighton, and Sunset state beaches (see page 121); Seacliff offers trailer hookups, and you can fish from an unusual pier—a 45-foot cement ship. Zmudowski, Moss Landing, and Salinas River are day-use beaches.

Capitola, next door to Santa Cruz, was one of California's first beach resorts, dating back to the late 1880s. Today it sparkles with shops, galleries, eating spots, and begonias—at the Capitola National Begonia Festival in September and at Antonelli Begonia Gardens (2545 Capitola Road). Peak blossom season at the commercial gardens is August and September.

Moss Landing, a former whaling village halfway between Santa Cruz and Monterey, has a hardworking harbor, a bird sanctuary (visitor center and hiking trails inland from the highway), seafood restaurants, and some 25 antique shops.

South Bay Fun Zones

Thrill rides, arcades, and live shows draw crowds to Santa Clara's Great America and the Santa Cruz Beach Boardwalk. Both have acclaimed roller coasters and carousels, but one is a self-contained theme park and the other the last of the West's great beach boardwalks.

Great America. The plaza of this 100-acre park opens onto five Americana theme areas, each with wild and mild rides, shows, shops, and restaurants. There's even a special zone for tiny tots, with kiddie-sized attractions.

An amphitheater hosts summer concerts, spirited musical revues appear in theaters, and films flicker on the world's largest motion picture screen—7 stories tall, 96 feet wide.

In addition to the Bay Area's largest wooden roller coaster, rides include the West's only stand-up roller coaster, corkscrews, loop rollers, and white-water rafts.

The park is open daily for Easter vacation and from Memorial Day through Labor Day, weekends only in spring and autumn (closed in winter); call (408) 988-1800 for seasonal hours. Admission is $17.95 adults and children over 6, $10.95 seniors, and $8.95 children 3 to 6. Take Great America Parkway exit north from U.S. 101 at Santa Clara.

Santa Cruz Beach Boardwalk. Since it opened in 1924, this mile-long beach fun zone's most popular rides have been the Giant Dipper wooden roller coaster and the 1911 hand-carved Looff carousel, where you can still reach for the brass (now steel) ring. Both are national historic landmarks.

Other attractions include rides, games, restaurants and snack stands, and an indoor miniature golf course. Rides operate daily in summer, on weekends the rest of the year; seasonal hours vary. Boardwalk admission is free; unlimited ride tickets cost $15.95 (individual tickets available).

Monterey Peninsula

*P*ristine beaches, surf crashing against craggy rocks, and wave-warped cypresses—along with miles of golf courses—have made the Monterey Peninsula famous around the world. Formed by Monterey and Carmel bays, the peninsula juts into the Pacific Ocean 120 miles south of San Francisco. Here you can explore carefully preserved historic adobes in Monterey; browse through art galleries in carefully quaint Carmel; and drive among grand estates in the dense woods of Del Monte Forest. To the south, Big Sur is one of the state's most spectacular stretches of coast.

Inland lie the caves and peaks of Pinnacles National Monument, picturesque mission towns, a cluster of wineries, and the agricultural center of Salinas, birthplace of author John Steinbeck and site of a top rodeo.

Contacts

These agencies offer information on attractions and accommodations. See additional contacts throughout this chapter.

Monterey Peninsula Chamber of Commerce and Visitors & Convention Bureau
380 Alvarado St. (P.O. Box 1770)
Monterey, CA 93942
(408) 649-1770

Salinas Area Chamber of Commerce
119 E. Alisal St. (P.O. Box 1170)
Salinas, CA 93901
(408) 424-7611

Mexico's last bastion

The peninsula was settled thousands of years ago by the Esselen and later the Ohlone Indians. The first European to sight Monterey Bay was Juan Rodriguez Cabrillo, a Portuguese explorer sailing for Spain, who couldn't land in 1542 because of high seas. Sebastian Vizcaino named the bay on a 1602 visit, but it wasn't until 1770 that the area was settled.

Then Gaspar de Portola and Father Junipero Serra established the first of Spain's four California presidios and the second of the Franciscans' 21 California missions on the south shore of the bay.

Until the middle of the 19th century, Monterey was California's most important settlement. Beginning the century as the Spanish capital of Alta California, it became the Mexican capital in 1822 and the American capital in 1846. After the discovery of gold in 1848 moved the focus north to San Francisco, Monterey turned to whaling, then to fishing and finally tourism.

Planning a visit

The ocean setting conditions the peninsula's weather. Summer months along the coast are likely to be overcast, with early morning and late afternoon fog. Spring and autumn months can be sparkling—warm days, crystal skies. Rain is frequent from December to March, but even January, the wettest month, has occasional crisp, sunny days.

Getting there. Monterey Peninsula Airport, 3 miles east of Monterey on State 68, has daily scheduled flights on some half dozen domestic carriers. Hotel shuttles, local buses, and taxis provide transfers, and rental cars are available.

Salinas is a stop on Amtrak's coastal rail route, and Greyhound has bus terminals in Salinas, Fort Ord, and Monterey. Monterey-Salinas Transit, (408) 899-2555, connects towns within the area (as far south as Big Sur in summer).

If you drive, the most scenic north-south route is coastal State 1. Connecting roads between U.S. 101 (fastest route to inland attractions) and State 1 include State 152 across Hecker Pass from Gilroy, State 156 through the artichoke capital of Castroville, and State 68 between Salinas and Monterey.

Where to stay. The greatest selection of resorts, hotels, motels, and inns is found between Monterey and Carmel; Pacific Grove boasts several beachside Victorian inns. For a list of choices, contact area visitor bureaus. Among the biggest and best-known lodgings in the Monterey-Carmel area are Doubletree, Highlands Inn, Hotel Pacific, Hyatt Regency, Monterey Bay Inn, Monterey Hotel, Monterey Plaza, Monterey Sheraton, Old Carmel Mission Inn, Spindrift Inn, and Tickle Pink Motor Inn.

There are several scenic public campgrounds along the Big Sur coast (see page 54), plus a number of private facilities for RV and tent campers. Other state parks inland from Salinas welcome campers (page 57). For additional details on area camping, turn to page 121.

Fog creeps across the rugged Santa Lucia Mountains along the Big Sur coast. State 1, blasted out of the high bluffs, hugs the shore for some 90 miles between Carmel and San Simeon, site of Hearst Castle.

Monterey Area

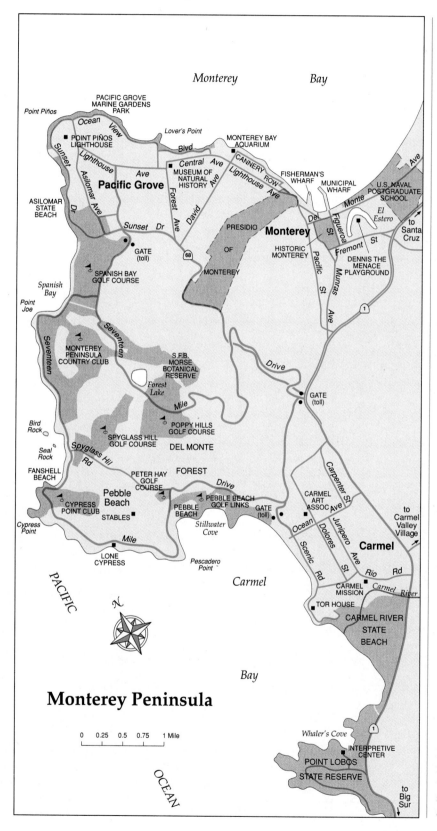

Monterey Bay

PACIFIC GROVE
MARINE GARDENS
PARK

Point Piños

Lover's Point

Ocean View

Point Piños
Lighthouse

MONTEREY BAY
AQUARIUM

MONTEREY
BAY
AQUARIUM

Lighthouse

Central Ave

Blvd

CANNERY ROW

FISHERMAN'S
WHARF

MUNICIPAL
WHARF

Ave

MUSEUM OF
NATURAL
HISTORY

Lighthouse Ave

U.S. NAVAL
POSTGRADUATE
SCHOOL

Monte

to
Santa
Cruz

Pacific Grove

ASILOMAR
STATE
BEACH

Forest Ave

David Ave

Ave

PRESIDIO

Del

Monterey

Figueroa St

El
Estero

Fremont St

Sunset Dr

OF

HISTORIC
MONTEREY

Pacific St

Munras Ave

DENNIS THE
MENACE
PLAYGROUND

GATE
(toll)

68

MONTEREY

1

SPANISH BAY
GOLF COURSE

Spanish
Bay

Seventeen

Point
Joe

MONTEREY
PENINSULA
COUNTRY CLUB

S.F.B.
MORSE
BOTANICAL
RESERVE

Drive

GATE
(toll)

Forest
Lake

Mile

Bird
Rock

POPPY HILLS
GOLF COURSE

Seal
Rock

SPYGLASS HILL
GOLF COURSE

DEL MONTE

Spyglass Hill Rd

FANSHELL
BEACH

PETER HAY
GOLF
COURSE

FOREST

Carpenter St

CYPRESS
POINT CLUB

**Pebble
Beach**

Drive

STABLES

PEBBLE BEACH
GOLF LINKS

GATE
(toll)

CARMEL
ART
ASSOC

Ave

to
Carmel
Valley
Village

Cypress
Point

PEBBLE
BEACH

Ocean

Juniper Ave

Dolores St

Carmel

LONE
CYPRESS

Mile

Stillwater
Cove

Scenic Rd

Pescadero
Point

Carmel

Rio Rd

CARMEL
MISSION

Carmel River

PACIFIC

N

TOR HOUSE

CARMEL RIVER
STATE
BEACH

Carmel

Bay

Monterey Peninsula

0   0.25   0.5   0.75   1 Mile

Whaler's Cove

INTERPRETIVE
CENTER

POINT LOBOS

OCEAN

STATE RESERVE

1

to
Big
Sur

Much of the old Spanish and Mexican village of yesteryear Monterey still stands in the midst of today's modern city of 31,500. Many buildings erected before 1850 are in good repair; about a dozen are preserved in downtown Monterey State Historic Park (see facing page). Stop first at the Custom House Plaza just inland from Fisherman's Wharf for a tour map.

An Adobe Tour each April features other buildings open to the public only for this event. Other events on the peninsula's crowded calendar include the famed Monterey Jazz Festival in September, plus a Bach Festival in July and a Dixieland celebration in March. Golf tournaments are also major events—the area is Northern California's golf capital (see page 123).

Monterey has a compact downtown area, easy to navigate on foot if you have a good map. Pedestrian walkways provide access to its most scenic areas. Parking in 2- and 4-hour metered public lots near Fisherman's Wharf is convenient, albeit crowded on summer weekends.

For the younger set, the free Dennis the Menace Playground downtown on Pearl Street at El Estero Lake makes a nice break from sightseeing. Cartoonist Hank Ketcham, creator of the comic strip character, designed the unusual playground.

A waterfront stroll. A popular Recreation Trail for strollers and cyclists follows the waterfront east for 5 miles from Lover's Point in Pacific Grove (Ocean View Boulevard and 17th Street), through Monterey's Cannery Row and Shoreline Park, past Fisherman's Wharf and Custom House Plaza, and along the Window on the Bay waterfront park and Del Monte Beach. Eventually the linear park will stretch to Castroville, 18 miles away.

Municipal Wharf. Monterey's Municipal Wharf extends into the bay from the foot of Figueroa Street. Here you'll see commercial fishing boats unload anchovies, cod, halibut, salmon, shark,

Scattered around downtown Monterey are good examples of a distinctive architecture still called "Monterey style." Some of these balcony-fronted two-story adobes are preserved and maintained as the Monterey State Historic Park. Others, operated independently, are included on a walking tour map of the city.

Start at the Custom House Plaza near Fisherman's Wharf. At the visitor center, you pay a single admission ($3.50 adults, $2 children 6 through 17) to visit all the following buildings except for Colton Hall, a free museum operated by the city. Most buildings are open 10 A.M. to 5 P.M. daily in summer, to 4 P.M. in winter.

Custom House. At 1 Custom House Plaza stands the Pacific Coast's oldest government office; one section dates back to 1827. Here the U.S. flag was officially raised for the first time in 1846. A collection center for revenue from foreign shipping until 1867, the restored building (free admission) displays 1840s goods.

Pacific House. This two-story structure on the Plaza dates back to 1847. First used for military offices and storage and later as a tavern, it now contains historical exhibits and Indian artifacts.

Boston Store. This building at Scott and Olivier streets, named Casa del Oro because it was supposedly a gold depository at one time, is again operated as a store (closed Monday, Tuesday, and Sunday morning).

Old Whaling Station. The garden of this former boarding house near the corner of Pacific and Scott streets is open for touring.

First Brick House. Next door stands the area's first brick structure, home to a pioneer family.

First Theater. At Scott and Pacific streets, the building that housed the state's first theater was originally a tavern and lodging house for sailors. Plays are still presented on weekends; call (408) 375-4916 for reservations.

Casa Soberanes. This well-preserved house at 336 Pacific was built in 1830. Period antiques decorate its interior.

Colton Hall. On Pacific Street facing Friendly Plaza, this impressive building (free admission) was where the state's first constitution was written in 1849. A second-floor museum displays early government documents. An old jail adjoins.

Larkin House. The two-story adobe at Jefferson Street and Calle Principal was built by Thomas Larkin, American Consul from 1843 to 1846. You see original furnishings on the guided tour (daily except Tuesday).

Cooper-Molera Adobe. The restored Victorian home at the corner of Polk and Munras (closed Wednesday) belonged to Captain John Cooper, a trader and entrepreneur, who married General Mariano Vallejo's sister.

Stevenson House. Named for Robert Louis Stevenson, who lived here in 1879, the restored and well-furnished house at 530 Houston Street is open for tours daily except Wednesday.

Royal Presidio Chapel. Founded by Father Junipero Serra in 1770 and rebuilt in 1794, San Carlos Cathedral (Church Street at Figueroa) has been in use ever since.

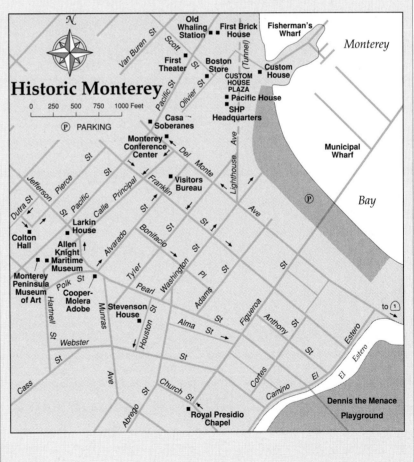

Historic Monterey

On a tour of the Monterey Bay Aquarium, visitors pause at fish-eye level in front of kelp forest exhibit. The world-famous undersea museum on Cannery Row in Monterey houses more than 6,500 sea creatures.

sole, squid, swordfish, and tuna at processing plants. If you don't mind getting your feet damp, you can watch from doorways as workers clean and pack fish. This is also the best place for pier fishing (licenses are sold at Joe's Boat Hoist on the pier).

Fisherman's Wharf. Built in 1846 as a pier for trading vessels bringing goods around Cape Horn, this wharf (4 blocks west of Municipal Wharf) was home to whaling vessels and sardine boats before its metamorphosis into a pier filled with fish markets, shops, and restaurants (Domenico's is a favorite).

Sportfishing, sightseeing, and whale-watching boats line the wood-planked pier, offering first-hand enjoyment of the bay (see page 125). Seals, sea lions, and otters provide daily entertainment along the length of the wharf.

Near the wharf's expansive plaza sprawls the city's convention center, a handsome three-level complex at One Portola Plaza. It's flanked by two large hotels and a shopping plaza. Other hotels and restaurants lie nearby.

Cannery Row. The row of canneries and warehouses John Steinbeck described as "a poem, a stink, a grating noise" still stands to the north of Fisherman's Wharf, a monument to the sardines that vanished abruptly from the bay in 1948. But the street is very different from the one portrayed in Steinbeck's novel *Cannery Row.*

The old buildings now house restaurants, antique stores, art galleries, shops, hotels, and the area's showcase, the innovative Monterey Bay Aquarium. There are several wine-tasting rooms: Bargetto, Monterey Peninsula, Roudon-Smith, and the striking glass-fronted Paul Masson facility at 700 Cannery Row (small museum, free film). Downstairs from Paul Masson, Steinbeck's Spirit of Monterey Wax Museum covers 400 years of area history (9 A.M. to 10 P.M. daily; admission). Across the street, a turn-of-the-century carousel delights children.

A few reminders of Steinbeck's novel do remain. A private club inhabits Doc Rickett's Western Biological Laboratory

at 800 Cannery Row; Lee Chong's Heavenly Flower Grocery across the street is now a shop (free museum at back); and La Ida's Cafe (one of the novel's houses of ill repute) serves food.

At 125 Ocean View Boulevard, around the corner from the row, rises the American Tin Cannery. Once a factory, the refurbished building is now home to 45 discount outlets.

Several parking lots, including a big garage on Foam Street between Hoffman and Prescott, are within easy walking distance of attractions.

Military touches. Founded by Portola in 1770, Monterey's Presidio is a subpost for the U.S. Army's 22,000-acre Fort Ord nearby, a language institute, and a training center. A free museum (open Thursday through Monday from 9 A.M. to 4 P.M.) exhibits military items from Spanish days to the present. The main gate is at Pacific and Artillery streets, near Vizcaino's original 1602 landing site.

Just east of downtown Monterey along State 1 lies the Del Monte Hotel, an early-day seaside resort and now the Naval Postgraduate School. Visitors may stroll around its lushly landscaped acres daily from 9 A.M. to 4 P.M. From State 1, exit onto Aguajito Road and

turn right on 3rd Street to reach the main entrance.

Other downtown museums. The Allen Knight Maritime Museum (550 Calle Principal) boasts a large nautical collection, including scale models of ships and the Point Sur light. In summer, the free museum is open Tuesday through Sunday from 10 A.M. to 4 P.M.

The Monterey Peninsula Museum of Art (559 Pacific Street) exhibits paintings, photography, graphics, and ethnic art. The museum welcomes viewers Tuesday through Saturday from 10 A.M. to 4 P.M. and Sunday from 1 to 4 P.M. (donation suggested). The museum also operates tours of the 22-room La Mirada Adobe (720 Via Mirada) on Wednesday and Saturday at 1, 2, and 3 P.M. A $5 donation is suggested.

Pacific Grove

Each October thousands of orange and black monarchs (*Danaus plexippus*) congregate in the pretty town of Pacific Grove just northwest of Monterey, earning it the title of "Butterfly City, USA." Most of these winter visitors prefer the 6-acre grove of trees at the end of Lighthouse Avenue; signs mark the route.

Bay Aquarium

At the edge of Monterey Bay sprawls one of the world's largest and finest aquariums. Some 6,500 marine creatures are dramatically housed in the rambling Monterey Bay Aquarium complex at the west end of Cannery Row.

With its multilevel roofs, boiler stacks, and corrugated walls, the aquarium manages to retain the waterfront feeling that inspired novelist John Steinbeck.

Sea life is displayed here in more than 100 display tanks—including an above-and-below-water sea otter world and a 3-story mature kelp forest.

A 90-foot-long tank, complete with deep reefs, a sandy ocean floor, and old wharf pilings, replicates life in the bay. Several species of large sharks cruise here among other bay denizens.

One end of the building is devoted to touchable displays—bat rays to pet and feed, for example, and tidepools to explore. A stunning walk-through aviary is home to marsh and shore birds.

Admission to the aquarium (open daily except Christmas from 10 A.M. to 6 P.M.) is $8 adults, $5.75 teens and seniors, and $3.50 children. Ticketron sells advance tickets.

...Monterey Area

It was Methodists, not butterflies, who founded Pacific Grove in 1875 when they held the first of many seashore camp meetings here. Incorporated in 1889, the town was corseted with ordinances regulating dancing, drinking, and public bathing.

Nowadays the city at the northern gate of the 17-Mile Drive is better known for its ornate Victorian houses and inns and its 3-mile stretch of rocky coast. Three annual events draw crowds: the Victorian Home Tour in April, the Feast of Lanterns festival in July, and the Butterfly Parade in October. For information on these and other activities and attractions, stop by the Pacific Grove Chamber of Commerce offices in the little blue Victorian at Forest and Central avenues, or call (408) 373-3304.

Museum of Natural History. Across the street from the chamber of commerce at 165 Forest, this little museum is a gem. Of particular interest are its "touchable" collections of native plants and animals. On an area relief map, you get an idea of the great chasm of Monterey Bay, some 8,400 feet deeper than the Grand Canyon. The free museum (donations welcomed) is open daily except Monday from 10 A.M. to 4 P.M.

Pacific Grove Marine Gardens Park. A walking and cycling path runs the length of Ocean View Boulevard, providing plenty of places to stop and enjoy the view. A white sand "pocket" beach offers good tidepooling (don't disturb the creatures), and Lover's Point (Ocean View at 17th) is a good place for picnicking, birding, and watching scuba divers.

Point Piños Lighthouse. The lighthouse just north of the intersection of Lighthouse and Asilomar avenues has stood at the entrance to the harbor since 1855. The West Coast's oldest continuously operating lighthouse, the Cape Cod–style structure is now a museum (see page 77).

Asilomar State Beach. A boardwalk lets you explore the rolling sand dunes between Point Piños and Asilomar State Beach without harming the plants. Asilomar Conference Center, inland from Sunset Drive, welcomes individuals as well as large groups; for information, call (408) 372-8016.

17-Mile Drive

One of the state's most beautiful roads, the 17-Mile Drive winds through the Del Monte Forest between Pacific Grove and Carmel. It takes less than an hour to tour the area, but you'll want to linger longer to savor the views of dramatic coastline and impressive homes, enjoy a beachside picnic lunch, overnight in a famed resort, or play a round on one of the golf courses overlooking the ocean.

The privately-owned road (part of Ben Hogan Properties) can be entered through several gates. There's one at Pacific Grove (off Sunset Drive), a marked exit off State 1 midway between Monterey and Carmel, and another in Carmel (west end of Ocean Avenue).

Entrance fee of $5.75 per car includes a map of the area. The gate charge is waived for golfers with tee times, hotel guests, and restaurant patrons with advance reservations. Cyclists enter free but must sign a liability release; biking is permitted daily except when special events are scheduled.

Seaside sights. From the Pacific Grove Gate, skirt the Inn and Links at Spanish Bay (resort and golf course), veering west along the shore at the road's fork. After passing Spanish Bay, you reach Point Joe, site of many early-day shipwrecks. The fury of colliding offshore currents can be seen even on calm days.

Sea lions and birds bask within viewing distance on Bird and Seal rocks. Neighboring Fanshell Beach boasts a nearly perfect crescent of white sand. For best views of the Pacific coastline and Point Sur Lighthouse (20 miles south), stop at the Cypress Point Lookout.

All along the rocky shore, weathered Monterey cypresses cling to the bluffs, their branches and foliage dramatically distorted by the wind. Lone Cypress, the most famous, stands by itself on a rocky outcropping above the surf. You'll see the eerie bleached white form of the Ghost Tree near Pescadero Point.

Activities. Overnight camping isn't allowed, but you can picnic at Spanish Bay and Seal Rock and fish from Fanshell Beach north. Access to Stillwater Cove (popular with divers) is through the Beach & Tennis Club parking lot; to reserve one of the limited number of parking spaces, phone (408) 625-8507.

The Pebble Beach Equestrian Center on Sombria Lane offers assorted rides on 36 miles of bridle trails through Del Monte Forest; for information, call (408) 624-2756. The adjacent Collins Polo Field hosts major West Coast equestrian events.

The area's golf courses are famous. For information on 18-hole public courses, see page 123. Scenic Cypress Point and Monterey Peninsula Country Club courses are not open to the public.

Resorts. Lingering for a fine meal or perhaps an overnight stay at one of the two deluxe resort hotels allows time to enjoy the area's beauty. The Lodge at Pebble Beach first opened its doors to guests in 1919. The Inn at Spanish Bay was added in 1989. Both have an array of shops.

Carmel Area

Celebrated by poets, writers, and photographers, Carmel has been home to such diverse personalities as poet Robinson Jeffers, photographer Ansel Adams, actress Kim Novak, and actor and former mayor Clint Eastwood.

Carmel prides itself on remaining a simple village by the ocean. Houses have no street numbers and no mail delivery; its 5,000 residents meet at the post office. Downtown there are no billboards, no neon signs, no stoplights, and almost no street lights. Side streets have no curbs and no sidewalks.

This very lack of commercialism, however, acts as a drawing card, attracting far too many tourists in summer. The sidewalks are crowded and the main street, Ocean Avenue, is jammed with cars almost every weekend. For maximum enjoyment, time your visit for a weekday out of season.

Plenty of motels, inns, and cottages line Carmel's streets, but there are only two hotels downtown—Pine Inn and La Playa. Restaurants—dozens of them—are small and run the gamut from tea shops to elegant establishments serving haute cuisine.

Shopping. Carmel is a village of shops, more than 150 of them, mostly small. Dozens of galleries displaying artists' works are scattered around town; the largest concentration is near the Carmel Art Association gallery on Dolores Street between 5th and 6th.

Along the shore. Carmel's classically beautiful beach at the foot of Ocean Avenue is ideal for strollers and, in good weather, sunbathers. It's unsafe for swimming, but most bathers find the water too cold anyway.

Scenic Road offers fine views along the shoreline. Robinson Jeffers' stone home, Tor House, faces Scenic Road at Carmel Point; you can tour the house Friday and Saturday from 10 A.M. to 3 P.M. Call (408) 624-1813 for advance reservations; on tour days, call (408) 624-1840. Admission is $5 for adults, $1.50 high school students (no younger children admitted).

South of the village limits, at the end of Scenic Road, is Carmel River State Beach, a gentle and usually sunny stretch of coast. It's a good place to picnic.

Carmel Mission. South of town, the second California mission founded by Franciscan Father Junipero Serra provides one of the most authentic and picturesque links to early California history. Father Serra is buried inside the Basilica San Carlos Borromeo del Rio Carmelo, established here in 1771 after being founded the previous year along Monterey Bay.

The mission is fully restored, and you could spend several hours wandering through the chapel, museum (donations encouraged), gardens, and cemetery (final resting place for some 3,000 Indians). You can visit from 9:30 A.M. to 4:30 P.M. Monday through Saturday and from 10:30 A.M. to 4:30 P.M. Sunday. To get there, turn west from State 1 at Rio Road; or follow Junipero Avenue south from downtown Carmel.

Point Lobos State Reserve. "Strange, introverted, and storm-twisted beauty"—so poet Robinson Jeffers described Point Lobos, the promontory jutting into the Pacific 4 miles south of Carmel. For many visitors, the reserve's 6-mile-long coastline represents nature at its most magnificent.

The 1,500-acre park (per-car entrance fee) offers a place to hike, picnic, look at rich tidepools, sun on the beach, scuba dive, watch birdlife, and fish. Pick up a map (small fee) at the entrance or at the information station at the Sea Lion Point parking lot. The interpretive center at Whaler's Cove on the north shore is a restored Chinese frame cabin built in 1851. Inside, artifacts trace cabin—and area—history from whaling days to movie fame.

Reserve hours are 9 A.M. to 5 P.M. daily. In summer, parking lots fill up quickly, so plan to arrive before 11 A.M. on weekends. Dogs are not permitted.

Scuba divers can reserve one of the 15 diving permits issued daily by calling MISTIX at (800) 444-7275 up to 28 days in advance. Unreserved slots are distributed by lottery at the entrance station each morning at 8:30 A.M. Divers must show proof of certification.

Carmel Valley

Just south of Carmel, Carmel Valley Road (County G16) heads inland from State 1 along the Carmel River. You turn onto the road at Carmel Rancho shopping center, which fronts the beautifully landscaped Barnyard shopping mall, location of the acclaimed Thunderbird Bookshop (also a restaurant).

Driving through the valley, you pass artichoke fields, fruit orchards, nurseries, strawberry fields, small shopping centers, and elegant resorts with golf courses. The Begonia Gardens, about 6 miles into the valley, are at their peak bloom in July and August. Chateau Julien (8940 Carmel Valley Road) offers wine tasting and touring daily from 10:30 A.M. to 2:30 P.M. Laid-back Carmel Valley Village lies about 12 miles southeast of State 1 on the Carmel Valley Road.

Recreational playground. When fog hangs over the rest of the Monterey Peninsula, the Carmel Valley is usually sunny, making it an ideal setting for some of the area's premier resorts and recreational sites. John Gardiner's first tennis ranch is here, as are three championship golf courses. The Carmel River holds an abundance of trout, and steelhead fishing is excellent in season.

Just beyond Carmel Valley Ranch Resort (about 8 miles inland from State 1), the 540-acre Garland Ranch Regional Park has hiking and equestrian trails, and a visitor center where you can pick up maps and brochures. You can camp at Riverside Park and Saddle Mountain Recreation Park.

Valley lodging. Carmel Valley's resorts and small lodges all offer interesting activities. For a list of accommodations, write to the Carmel Valley Chamber of Commerce, P.O. Box 288, Carmel Valley, CA 93921; or call (408) 659-4000.

Big Sur Coast

The 90-mile drive along the Big Sur coast on State 1 from Carmel to San Simeon, site of Hearst Castle, takes several hours. The two-lane road (built in the 1930s) dips and rises, clinging precariously to the seaward face of the Santa Lucia Mountains as it follows the rugged coastline.

One dramatic vantage point is just a few miles southwest of Carmel at Bixby Creek Bridge, 260 feet above the creek bed. Park your car and walk out to an observation alcove for a view of the surf, beach, and headlands. In winter, you'll often see California gray whales on their annual migration south to Baja California.

Along the route you'll pass other lookouts, too: cliff-perched eating places like Rocky Point, Nepenthe (where Henry Miller lived and wrote and Rita Hayworth and Orson Welles honeymooned), and Ventana Inn (an exclusive hideaway resort).

The village of Big Sur has several rustic resorts, grocery stores, restaurants, and shops. The Coast Gallery (center for local artisans) maintains two showrooms.

For additional information on area attractions, hotels, and activities, contact Big Sur Chamber of Commerce, Box 87, Big Sur, CA 93920; (408) 667-2156.

Parks along the way

Some of the finest meetings of land and water occur in four state parks along this coast. Two offer camping, but you have to walk in to one of them. For state park campsite reservations, call MISTIX, (800) 444-7275. For information on wilderness area camping sites in Los Padres National Forest, call (408) 385-5434.

Point Sur State Historic Park. Point Sur Lighthouse, rising on a headland of rock high above the surf, was completed in 1889. Guided tours (small fee) take place on Saturday and Sunday, weather permitting. For tour details, call (408) 625-4419. Parking at the lighthouse is limited; only 15 cars are admitted at a time.

Tours take 2 to 3 hours and include a half-mile hike with a 300-foot climb; for additional information, see page 77.

Andrew Molera State Park. You have to park your car along the road and hike into this 2,088-acre park along the lower section of the Big Sur River. Somewhat primitive campsites (chemical toilets, no showers) are available on a first-come, first-served basis (small fee). Fire-control roads make it easy to get around this preserve of redwoods, rocky bluff, meadowland, and sandy beach.

Pfeiffer Big Sur State Park. Though it isn't large (821 acres of river flats and canyons in the middle of Big Sur), this is one of the state's most popular nonbeach parks. In summer, you'll need advance reservations for its 218 riverside campsites (no hookups). For additional details, see page 121.

The most scenic public ocean beach in the Big Sur area is 2-mile-long Pfeiffer Beach (not part of the park), accessible from Sycamore Canyon Road just to the south.

Julia Pfeiffer Burns State Park. Among the attractions of this day-use park are a dramatic waterfall, redwood groves, and vantage points for viewing gray whales during their winter migration. You'll also find 2 miles of scenic coastline and upcountry canyons laced with trickling creeks.

Nearly 2 miles north of the park, a small parking area marks the entrance to Partington Cove. On your walk down the hill you cross a footbridge and pass through a 50-foot solid-rock tunnel. Scuba diving is popular at the cove, but you need a permit; check with the ranger at Pfeiffer Big Sur State Park (above).

Hearst Castle

The flamboyant former estate of newspaper tycoon William Randolph Hearst brings more than a million visitors annually to the coast 96 miles south of Monterey. The palatial residence, completed in 1947 after decades of work, is now operated as a state historic monument.

Hearst Castle crowns a hillside above the town of San Simeon on State 1. Four guided tours award glimpses of a lifestyle that once rivaled those of the media mogul's celebrity guests.

Tour 1, best introduction to the 123-acre estate, covers the gardens, guest house, pools, and main floor of Hearst's residence.

Tour 2 covers the main building's upper floors, including Hearst's private quarters and libraries, guest rooms, and kitchen.

Tour 3 takes in the guest wing, a guest house, gardens, pools, and home movie theater. From April through October, another tour visits the wine cellar, pools, underground vaults, and bowling alley.

The castle is open daily except New Year's, Thanksgiving, and Christmas. Each tour costs $12 ($6 children), lasts about 2 hours, and requires considerable walking and climbing.

Some tickets are available on a first-come, first-served basis, but advance reservations are recommended. Call or visit any MISTIX outlet; in California, the toll-free number is (800) 444-7275; from out of state, phone (619) 452-1950.

Perched on a cliff overlooking the Big Sur coast, Nepenthe restaurant is a favorite watering hole for locals and tourists. It was built in 1944 as a honeymoon cottage for Orson Welles and Rita Hayworth.

In & Around Salinas

Salinas, the heart of the valley dubbed the "salad bowl of the world," is also the birthplace of Nobel and Pulitzer prize–winning novelist John Steinbeck (1902–1968). The city and surrounding valley provided local color for Steinbeck novels such as *East of Eden*.

Visit the John Steinbeck Library, 110 W. San Luis Street, to learn about the writer's life and works. The library is open 10 A.M. to 9 P.M. Monday through Thursday, from 10 A.M. to 6 P.M. Friday and Saturday. Steinbeck's home, a gracious two-story Victorian at 132 Central Avenue, has been restored and opened as a luncheon restaurant and gift shop; for reservations, call (408) 424-2735.

Historical museums. Two of the city's oldest buildings contain county artifacts and photographs. The Boronda Adobe (open weekdays from 9 A.M. to noon and weekends from 1 to 4 P.M.) stands at the intersection of Boronda Road and Calle del Adobe in northwest Salinas; take Laurel Drive exit from U.S. 101. Admission is free.

The Harvey-Baker House (home of the city's first mayor) at 238 E. Romie can be toured from 1 to 4 P.M. the first Sunday of each month. For more information, call the Monterey County Historical Society, (408) 757-8085.

Rodeo. The wild West is alive and well in Salinas when the California Rodeo comes to town the third weekend in July. More than 700 competitors participate in the state's largest rodeo, culmination of a week-long celebration with thoroughbred racing, parades, barbecues, and hoedowns. For tickets and schedule information, contact the California Rodeo Office, P.O. Box 1648, Salinas, CA 93902; (408) 757-2951.

Three missions

Three of California's original Spanish missions are short detours off U.S. 101 in the Salinas Valley. Popular Mission San Juan Bautista is north of Salinas; Soledad and San Antonio de Padua lie to the south.

San Juan Bautista. About 21 miles north of Salinas, 3½ miles east of U.S. 101, is the town of San Juan Bautista, where Father Fermin Lasuen founded a mission in 1797. Its success was due largely to the energy and zeal of two other friars. Father Felipe del Arroyo, a linguistic whiz, preached to the Indians in seven dialects and even taught them the writings of Plato and Cicero. Father Estevan Tapis was an ebullient musician; by depicting different musical parts in brightly colored notes, he formed Indian choirs that continued his legacy for 40 years.

Restored mission buildings still overlook the valley, but the frame structures that stand shoulder-to-shoulder along 3rd Street in the old town—a state historic park since 1933—now house shops, galleries, and other attractions. To add to the ambience of the mid-1860s, power lines have been laid underground and vintage lighting installed. On the first Saturday of every month, state park personnel don period attire.

Among the historic sites open for touring are the 1840 Castro-Breen adobe, the Plaza Hotel (built in 1858), the two-story Plaza Hall (formerly a combination residence and dance hall), the Plaza Stable (blacksmith's shop, carriages, and wagons on display), the jail, and an early settler's cabin. Several of the buildings charge admission.

Soledad. Some 25 miles south of Salinas stands Mission Nuestra Señora de la Soledad, California's 13th mission, founded by Father Fermin Lasuen in 1791.

This mission reached its peak in 1820, but life was hard in this remote area, and by the 1830s the mission personified its name, "loneliness." When Father Vicente Francisco de Sarria died in 1835, the mission was officially closed. Winds and rain later reduced the adobe structure to crumbling ruins, but the chapel and the wing where the friars resided have been rebuilt.

The mission is west of U.S. 101 near the junction of Mission and Fort Romie roads. You can visit between 10 A.M. and 4 P.M. daily except Tuesday.

San Antonio de Padua. Father Serra founded this mission near King City in 1771. Though somewhat isolated in the middle of a military reservation, it's a rewarding place to visit. Some of the original tiles still top the roof of the restored mission. Besides the chapel, you'll see a water-powered grist mill, a tannery, an original wine vat, and early artwork.

To get to the mission, turn south from U.S. 101 at the Jolon Road (County G14) exit; it's about 18 miles farther.

Winery trails

Stretching along U.S. 101 from Morgan Hill to Greenfield and west along State 152 between Gilroy and Watsonville across the Hecker Pass, wineries cluster like so many grapes on the vine. Not all are open for tours, but most offer daily tasting.

Monterey Vineyard at Gonzales has good tours of its sprawling facilities. But what makes it an interesting stop is the gallery housing Ansel Adams' *Story of a Winery*, photographs shot in Monterey and Santa Clara counties between 1960 and 1963.

The winery is open from 10 A.M. to 5 P.M. daily, with tours on the hour from 11 A.M. to 4 P.M. Exit U.S. 101 on Gloria Road and go west to Alta; turn north to the winery.

State 152 from Gilroy (not recommended for trailers and RVs) is a gateway to scenic sites and picnic grounds. Just after passing A. Conrotto Winery, you'll come to Goldsmith Seed Company's test fields, a brilliant sight from late spring through summer. Due west the D'Arigo Cactus Pear Farm comes into view (no tours).

Wineries along State 152 include Fortino (excellent Italian deli), Hecker Pass, Thomas Kruse, Kirigin, Live Oak, and Sarah's Vineyard. All have pleasant tasting rooms and picnic grounds. At the top of the pass, Mount Madonna County Park (day-use fee) is another option; from Mount Madonna Inn you can see to the ocean.

Two state parks

Among nearby camping spots is Fremont Peak State Park, a rich historic and botanical area 11 miles south of San Juan Bautista on the San Juan Canyon Road (day-use and overnight fees). A winding road leads up to an observatory, open to the public on selected Saturdays for viewing through a 30-inch telescope; call (408) 623-4255.

Henry W. Coe State Park, 14 miles east of Morgan Hill on East Dunne Avenue, is little known and usually uncrowded (fee). The park headquarters occupy old ranch buildings perched at 2,600 feet. When wildflowers bloom, scores of would-be Monets flock to the park's rolling, grassy hills, their paints and canvases in hand. You'll find picnic tables and a few campsites.

Pinnacles National Monument

Laced with a surprising variety of trails, Pinnacles National Monument's spectacular spires and crags rise to 1,200 feet above the canyon floors, presenting a sharp contrast to the surrounding countryside. Below the ground lies a chain of caves.

This rugged territory, a remnant of ancient volcanic action, is a magnet for mountain climbers, hikers, and spelunkers (carry your own flashlight or buy one at the visitor center). A brochure showing the trail network (15 cents) is a good investment.

There are two entrances to the park, but no through roads. The best way to get there is from the east on State 25 through Hollister, then turn west on State 146 to the privately owned Pinnacles Campground; call (408) 389-4462 for reservations. The park's east entrance and visitor center lie just beyond.

To reach the west entrance, visitor center, and more primitive park-operated Chaparral Campground, exit U.S. 101 at Soledad and drive east on State 146 (too narrow for RVs). For information on campsites, turn to page 120.

Summer at the monument is *hot.*

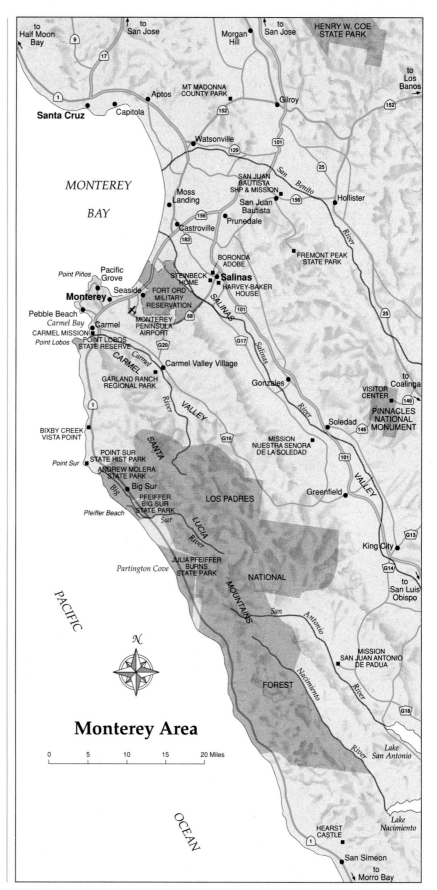

Monterey Area

Wine Country

North of San Francisco lie the valleys and hills synonymous with California wine. Some 3 million people visit the bucolic Napa and Sonoma valleys each year, primarily to watch the winemaking process and sample the results. This venerable wine district contains most of the state's best-known cellars and attractions, although Sonoma County's Alexander Valley and Russian River areas and the emerging Mendocino and Lake county districts are challengers.

The whole area abounds with other activities, too, from mud baths and swimming pools to quiet fishing lakes and flat viney byways ideal for cycling. You can ride in a hot-air balloon, tour by train, and browse through a multitude of intriguing galleries and shops.

Geography and climate combine in the Napa and Sonoma regions to create ideal grape-growing conditions. Wine was produced in the area as early as 1780 by Franciscan monks who planted cuttings from European grape stock. But it is Hungarian winemaker Agoston Haraszthy, who in 1857 introduced a number of European varietals at his Buena Vista Winery in Sonoma, who is widely credited as being the father of the state's wine industry.

Planning a trip

You *could* visit 20 cellars a day. But you would miss the details—and details are what make wine. Experienced travelers limit themselves to three, or at most four stops a day.

This chapter mentions major wineries and others with outstanding archi-

You have to get up early for this bird's-eye view of Napa Valley vineyards. Hot-air balloons lift off shortly after dawn.

tecture, gardens, or another particular reason to visit. For a complete list of visitable wineries, check with the tourist bureaus listed at right. The Sunset book *Wine Country California*, a guide to all the state's wineries, makes a valuable companion.

Getting there. Napa and Sonoma lie only some 15 miles apart, about 1½ hours from San Francisco. Napa County sandwiches neatly between U.S. 101 to the west and Interstate 80 to the southeast. State Highways 12, 29, 37, 121, and 128 connect the valley in various ways to the two freeways.

U.S. 101 also serves as entrée to Sonoma wineries. Sonoma and Napa valleys combine easily via State 12/121, through the Carneros Valley, and State 128, through Alexander and Knights valleys.

There's Greyhound bus service to both Napa and Sonoma valleys, and to towns along U.S. 101.

Dining and lodging. The wine country lends itself to lazy lunches; bring along a picnic basket or stop at bakeries, delis, and cheese shops along the way. Many wineries offer picnic sites; several have dining rooms. Virtually all have wine for sale. A wealth of intimate inns and romantic—and highly acclaimed—dining spots make it possible to extend wine forays.

When to go. A wine country visit can be rewarding at any time of the year. Spring is the most picturesque season, autumn (the time of the crush) the most dramatic. In winter, vintners may have more time to explain the steps from vine to wine. And, though summer temperatures can soar, that's when you'll find the most visitor activities.

Most wineries are open daily year-round. To avoid crowds, schedule a midweek visit and include cellars off the main highways.

Touring & tasting

Wineries vary in size from tiny family-run cellars requiring advance appointments to large operations with formal tours, tasting rooms, and gift shops. Old-line cellars with developed tours make good targets for newcomers to wine touring. Some wineries discourage visits due to size and staff limitations or remote location.

Touring and tasting used to be almost synonymous. Now, with many wineries often swamped with visitors, tasting is no sure bet. Where it is offered, visitors sample only two or three vintages, and there's often a fee to sip at Napa Valley cellars.

Contacts

These agencies offer information on attractions and accommodations. See additional contacts throughout this chapter.

Napa Valley Conference & Visitors Bureau
1556 1st St.
Napa, CA 94559
(707) 226-7459

Sonoma Valley Visitors Bureau
453 1st St. East
Sonoma, CA 95476
(707) 996-1090

Sonoma County Convention & Visitors Bureau
10 4th St., Suite 100
Santa Rosa, CA 95401
(800) 326-7666; (707) 575-1191

Napa Valley

Cradled between the redwood-forested Mayacamas Mountains to the west and the oak- and pine-studded Vaca Range on the east, the Napa Valley is only 30 miles long and 3 miles across at its widest point. Yet the little valley boasts some 220 wineries, many open for touring or tasting. A 24-hour hotline gives up-to-date information on wines and events; call (707) 963-1112.

The greatest concentration of wineries flanks State 29 north from Napa to Calistoga. To avoid the traffic that fills this main thoroughfare, knowledgeable travelers use the Silverado Trail, a scenic, winery-lined parallel road along the eastern edge of the valley. Crossroads among the vineyards connect the two arteries.

Though the city of Napa is by far the largest (53,000), each of the valley towns has its charms. In Calistoga you find spas and geysers; St. Helena claims many of the region's best dining and lodging choices as well as a wine library and the Silverado Museum; and Yountville offers dozens of shops, eating spots, and galleries, many tucked into a great brick winery.

Outside of these towns lie more wineries, markets, inns, quiet picnic spots, and historic parklands.

Plotting your route. Most visitors start a winery tour from the south end of the valley; you might consider reversing the order. Beginning in Calistoga gives you an opportunity to visit cellars such as Sterling, Chateau Montelena, and Clos Pegase that you might miss if you're here for only a day.

An alternative tour option, though you only clickety-clack past wineries, is the Napa Valley Wine Train, beautifully refurbished albeit controversial (residents resent its intrusion). See page 126 for details.

For yet another view, go aloft in one of the colorful hot-air balloons that brighten the sky above the valley vineyards. Balloon companies operate out of several valley towns; check with the Napa Valley Conference & Visitors Bureau (address on page 59).

Napa & Carneros region

The city of Napa is skirted by major highways and often passed unnoticed by motorists. A century ago, when the Napa River served as a main transportation route to the valley, it was a bustling port. The Napa Riverboat Co. lets you see the area as the oldtimers did—from the water (see page 125).

A walk down Napa's Main Street gives you a look at the refurbished historic downtown. Near the riverside park at 2nd Street, you can sip gourmet coffee or enjoy an alfresco lunch. For self-guided walking tours or to arrange a guided walk (small fee), stop at Napa County Landmarks (1144 Main Street), open Monday, Wednesday, and Friday from 8 A.M. to 5 P.M. To learn about valley history, go by the free historical society museum at 1219 1st Street, open noon to 4 P.M. Tuesday and Thursday.

Wineries. Just west of Napa, the Carneros district on the northern shores of San Pablo Bay is the first wine-growing region you pass if you're coming from San Francisco on State 12/121. The showplace of the region, Domaine Carneros (1240 Duhig Road), was built by the Taittinger sparkling wine people. You tour and taste (fee) in a replica of a Loire Valley chateau. Handicapped access avoids the steps from the parking lot.

The Hess Collection Winery (4411 Redwood Road) lies in the mountains 8 miles northwest of Napa. It's worth the trip to take a self-guided tour of this handsome winery, a former Christian Brothers novitiate, and multilevel modern art gallery. An excellent 20-minute wine film is shown in a small theater. Tasting is extra.

Yountville area

Named for George Yount, Napa Valley's first white settler, Yountville is chockful of quaint shops, lodging choices (Napa Valley Lodge and Vintage Inn are the largest), and historic sites. Vintage 1870, housed in on old brick winery, has be-

come a rural Ghirardelli Square shopping complex (shops, restaurants, bakery, tasting room). Two other specialty shopping areas lie just off the highway nearby, as do such trend-setting restaurants as Domaine Chandon (within the winery of the same name), French Laundry, Mustards Grill, Piatti, and the Diner.

Historic sites. Yount's final resting place is in the Pioneer Cemetery off Jackson Street, hard by the land in which he planted the valley's first vines in the 1850s. A free museum in the century-old Veterans Home west of the freeway is open noon to 2 P.M. Wednesday through Sunday.

Wineries. Architecture is one reason to visit historic Trefethen Vineyards (reached via Oak Knoll Avenue south of town) and Monticello Cellars (just east on Big Ranch Road). Trefethen's redwood winery was built a century ago, while Monticello, a replica of Thomas Jefferson's home, is a relative newcomer. Both wineries are open daily from 10 A.M. to 4:30 P.M.

French-owned Domaine Chandon (1 California Drive, just west of State 29) offers hourly tours explaining the manufacture of sparkling wine. Also at the sophisticated facility are a tasting center (fee), a restaurant (reservations usually required), and a small museum.

On the Silverado Trail east of Yountville, stop by S. Anderson (at Yountville Cross Road) to tour wine-aging caves carved from volcanic rock. Across the street, a huge red metal sculpture marks the entrance to Robert Sinskey Vineyards.

Oakville & Rutherford

Grand wine estates in this wide, flat part of the valley make the landscape around these two crossroads particularly impressive. You get a good look at the valley floor from Auberge du Soleil, an elegant inn and restaurant at 180 Rutherford Hill Road east of the

Silverado Trail. The Oakville Grocery (on State 29) offers the area's best one-stop shopping for picnic supplies.

Wineries. One of the best overviews of the wine-making process is given at Robert Mondavi Winery (west of State 29 at Oakville). Avoid this popular stop on weekends, when you need an advance reservation to tour. The winery's handsome artwork includes a Beniamino Bufano sculpture.

Other worthwhile winery stops along State 29 include historic Inglenook, venerable Beaulieu, and Franciscan's tasting center. East of the highway between Oakville and Rutherford, St. Supéry boasts both a state-of-the-art winery and a restored Queen Anne Victorian containing a wealth of Napa Valley history.

Guided tours of Mumm's extremely pleasant Napa Valley facility (8445 Silverado Trail) give a good look at sparkling wine production. Tasting takes place on an enclosed porch overlooking the vineyards.

St. Helena

The 1890s look of St. Helena's Main Street is proudly maintained by the city's 5,000 residents, and so is the town's century-old emphasis on wine. A small hotel, Meadowood resort (off Silverado Trail), and many inns offer lodging. Bay Area travelers often come just to dine in such eateries as Terra, Trilogy, and Tra Vigne. You can buy picnic fixings at the Model Bakery on Main Street, the Olive Oil Company (835 McCorkle Avenue), and V. Sattui Winery's deli (1111 White Lane). The latter also offers underground caves to tour and shady picnic sites.

Attractions. A major collection of wine literature, assembled by the Napa Valley Wine Library Association, takes up part of the town library 2 blocks west of Main on Adams Street. A separate wing of the library contains the free Silverado Museum, a large display of Robert Louis Stevenson memorabilia (noon to 4 P.M. daily except Monday).

The peripatetic author honeymooned in an abandoned bunkhouse of the defunct Silverado Mine on Mount St.

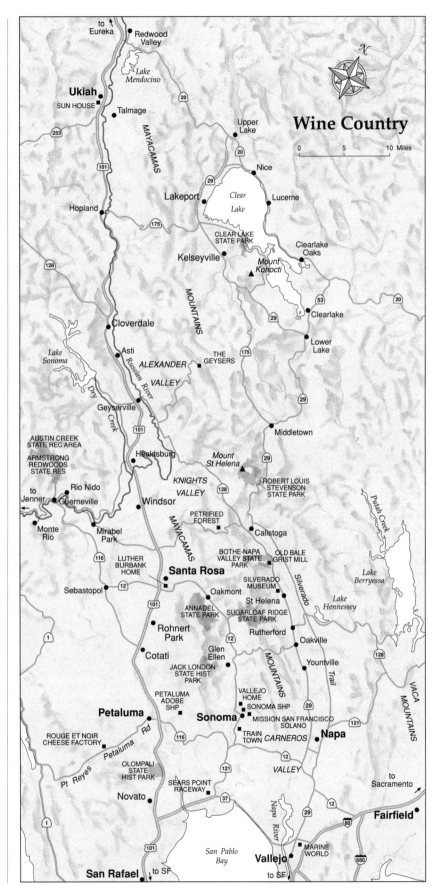

...Napa Valley

Helena in 1880–81. He recounted that experience in *Silverado Squatters*.

Wineries. Beringer, Christian Brothers, and Charles Krug, three romantic old wineries on State 29 north of town, offer complimentary tours and tastings. Even if you're only marginally interested in wine, you'll enjoy the historic structures. South of St. Helena on State 29 lie Louis M. Martini (tours and tasting) and Heitz (tasting only). Spring Mountain Vineyards (2805 Spring Mountain Road west of town) is the winery of *Falcon Crest* television fame.

Calistoga

The town situated at the foot of looming Mount St. Helena has long been famous as a center for health and relaxation. Thousands of tourists slither into mud baths and slide into mineral pools here every year. They've been arriving ever since millionaire entrepreneur Samuel Brannan built the first local spa in 1859. The unique Sharpsteen Museum at 1311 Washington Street gives you a free look at those early days. It's open 10 A.M. to 4 P.M. in summer, noon to 4 P.M. the rest of the year.

Lodging choices include bed-and-breakfast inns and the refurbished Mount View Hotel. A glider port, one-of-a-kind shops, and dozens of restaurants invite lingering. Calistoga Mineral Water and Crystal Geyser bottling plants downtown welcome visitors during working hours. For information on other attractions, contact the Calistoga Chamber of Commerce, 1458 Lincoln Avenue, (707) 942-6333.

Diversions. The Old Bale Grist Mill, off State 29 just south of Calistoga, takes visitors back to 1846, a time when wheat, not grapes, was the basis of the local economy. The 1-acre historic park (admission fee) is open daily from 10 A.M. to 5 P.M.; the immense overshot waterwheel actually grinds corn weekends at 1 and 4 P.M.

California's "Old Faithful" geyser spews steam and vapor skyward at about 40-minute intervals. The geothermal field on Tubbs Road about 1½ miles north of town (turn east from State 128) is open daily (small charge).

Wineries. Sterling Vineyards (1111 Dunaweal Lane east of State 29) provides an aerial tram ($5) to get up to its hilltop winery. Self-guided tours show winery works; the tasting room overlooks the upper Napa Valley.

Down the road, striking Clos Pegase winery's entrance leads you through an atrium; self-guided tours include a gallery and aging caves. Drop in for tours and tasting at longtime favorite Hanns Kornell Champagne Cellars (1091 Larkmead Lane east of State 29), and explore Vintners Village (west side of the highway), a collection of premium winery tasting rooms, shops, restaurants, and picnic grounds.

Hiking & camping

Hiking and cycling are good ways to get around the valley floor; heading up into the encircling hills provides plenty of exercise.

Bothe–Napa Valley State Park. About 4 miles north of St. Helena, this vast parkland with more than 1,000 acres of broad-leafed trees and second-growth redwoods extends west into the hills from State 29. Facilities include hiking trails and a swimming pool. For campsite reservations (April to October), phone MISTIX, (800) 444-7275.

Robert Louis Stevenson State Park. Eight winding miles north of Calistoga, this 3,000-acre undeveloped site sprawls along the eastern slopes of Mount St. Helena. A fire trail leads to the remnants of the author's cabin and the old Silverado Mine, continuing 4 miles to the 4,334-foot summit.

A Trio of Lakes

Three of the wine country's largest bodies of water attract anglers, water-skiers, and boaters.

Clear Lake. Anglers looking for trophy-sized bass head for Clear Lake in the spring, but a summer water temperature of 76° brings flocks of water-skiers and boaters to the 110 miles of shoreline at the state's largest lake (Tahoe is larger but is shared with Nevada). You can rent boats at resorts.

Clear Lake State Park on Soda Bay Road northeast of Kelseyville makes a good first stop. The center has geology exhibits, slide shows, and an aquarium. Kelsey Slough, a lush inlet snaking through the park, offers secluded bank-fishing sites and a remarkable array of birds. Four campgrounds accommodate tents and recreational vehicles; see page 121. The most direct route from the Bay Area (about 120 miles) is State 29 through Napa Valley.

Lake Berryessa. A popular year-round fishing hole in the dry hills separating the Napa and Sacramento valleys, Berryessa is best explored by boat. Launches are spaced at close intervals from Markley Canyon near the dam up to Putah Creek. In summer, anglers give way to skiers and motorboats.

All of the modest development, ranging from campsites to motels, lies along 12 miles of the west shore. Call (707) 966-2111 for information. Easiest access with a boat or camper is from Interstate 80.

Lake Sonoma. About 11 miles northwest of Healdsburg, massive Warm Springs Dam created the Lake Sonoma Recreation Area. A visitor center (open daily in summer, Thursday through Monday the rest of the year) gives a good overview of this fishing, boating, and swimming haven. Tent and RV camps and boat-in sites are on a first-come, first-served basis. A private marina offers boat rentals.

The most direct route from U.S. 101 is Canyon Road from Geyserville.

Picturesque Hop Kiln Winery in the Russian River area near Healdsburg recalls an era when Sonoma County was known more for growing hops than grapes. The 1905 stone kiln is a state historic landmark (tasting daily, tours by appointment).

Valley of the Moon

Historically, Sonoma is one of the state's most interesting towns. Site of Mission San Francisco Solano, last and northernmost of the 21 missions founded by the Franciscans in California, the Sonoma pueblo was also headquarters for General Mariano Vallejo, the Mexican administrator at the time of the Bear Flag Revolt in 1846.

Sonoma is also where Agoston Haraszthy laid the groundwork for some premium California wines at his Buena Vista winery. And it was the last home of author Jack London, who gave the valley its romantic "Valley of the Moon" name.

Sonoma Valley lies 45 miles north of San Francisco. From U.S. 101, take State 37 east to an intersection with State 121, which heads north toward the town of Sonoma. One more turn onto State 12, clearly marked, leads you right to the town plaza.

The main approach from the north is State 12, cutting inland from U.S. 101 at Santa Rosa. Coming from the east on Interstate 80, you turn west onto State 12 and follow the signs.

Sonoma Valley wineries

Two separate clusters of wineries are open to visitors. One begins in Sonoma town and stretches a mile or two east. The other lies north toward the head of the valley. In or near Sonoma: Sebastiani (sizable, with tours and tasting), Buena Vista (tours and tasting), Gundlach-Bundschu (tasting), and Haywood and Hacienda (tasting, picnic areas). Gloria Ferrar's champagne center (tours and tasting) lies southeast of town off State 121.

To the north, from Glen Ellen to Kenwood: Valley of the Moon (old-line family cellar), Glen Ellen (self-guided tour), Smothers Brothers, St. Francis, and Grand Cru. The Wine Gallery in Kenwood offers tastings of Caswell and Las Montanas vintages. Chateau St. Jean (self-guided tour, tasting, picnic sites) has a free "Wineline" reporting on valley grape crops and specific releases; call (800) 332-WINE.

In & around Sonoma

Historic sites, hotels, restaurants, and craft and food shops surround the town's central plaza. Of several annual events staged on the plaza, the Vintage Festival in September and the Ox Roast in June are the most famous.

Pick up a walking tour map from the Sonoma Valley Visitors Bureau office on the plaza. Parking is behind the Sonoma Barracks; turn in from 1st Street East just beyond Spain Street.

Dining and lodging. Two restored city hotels, El Dorado and Sonoma, face the plaza. Nearby are bed-and-breakfasts, motels, and the upscale Sonoma Mission Inn & Spa (north on State 12 in Boyes Hot Springs).

Dining choices in town include popular La Casa (across from the mission) and the two hotel restaurants. Out of town, head to the spa for an elegant meal or to the historic Grist Mill Inn, off State 12 in Glen Ellen.

Stroll around the plaza to assemble picnic fixings from the French Bakery, Sonoma Sausage Co., Sonoma Cheese Factory (or Vella Cheese Factory on 2nd Street East), and Wine Exchange.

History and trains. Across from the plaza's northeast corner stands the Sonoma Mission, founded July 4, 1823. Now part of Sonoma State Historic Park, it contains an outstanding museum collection (10 A.M. to 5 P.M. daily).

Several other park buildings can be toured for the single admission fee: the Sonoma Barracks, the servants' wing of Casa Grande (Vallejo's first home, mostly destroyed by fire in 1867), and General Mariano Vallejo's home (2 blocks west and north of the plaza on 3rd Street West). The adjacent warehouse (now a museum) was built in 1852 from timber and bricks shipped around Cape Horn.

Other historic buildings on the plaza include Blue Wing Inn (a gambling hall in the gold rush era), the Toscano Hotel, Swiss Hotel (now a restaurant), and the home of Salvador Vallejo.

Train Town, on State 12 about a mile south of the plaza, provides a change of pace. A 20-minute ride on a scale model railroad carries you through 10 acres of landscaped grounds with a stop at a replica of an old mining town. The park (admission charge) is open daily from 10:30 A.M. to 5:30 P.M. in summer, weekends from Labor Day to mid-June.

Into the hills

In the upper end of the valley, several state parks invite visitors to picnic, hike, and ride. Sugarloaf welcomes campers. In April and May these open spaces are carpeted with wildflowers.

Jack London State Historic Park. In the hills west of Glen Ellen, the House of Happy Walls, built by London's wife Charmian after his death in 1916, is a museum of the author's life (10 A.M. to 5 P.M. daily). At the end of a ¾-mile trail from the museum loom the rock walls of Wolf House, which burned before the couple could move into it. Nearby are London's grave, the ruins of his winery, his cottage, and several barns.

To reach the 803-acre park, open dawn to dusk daily, follow State 12 north about 6½ miles to Glen Ellen, then follow signs. There's a per-car admission.

Sugarloaf Ridge State Park. North of Kenwood, follow Adobe Canyon Road northeast from State 12 for 2 miles to a mountainous 2,500-acre park that was once a cattle ranch. Some 25 miles of trails crisscross the park, which has 50 campsites; reserve through MISTIX (800) 444-7275. There's a day-use fee.

Annadel State Park. First Pomo Indian land, then part of a Spanish rancho, this free 5,000-acre retreat boasts 35 miles of trails. The 3-mile hike to Lake Ilsanjo (no swimming or boating) is the most popular.

To reach the park, follow State 12 toward Santa Rosa; turn south on Los Alamos Road. At Channel Drive turn left and follow the signs.

Other Wine Valleys

Some of the most visitor-friendly wine districts stretch north from Santa Rosa to Ukiah alongside U.S. 101. Here, too, are the recreation-rich Russian River Valley, redwood groves, and charming towns. Backroads are good sources of fresh farm produce, Christmas trees, and handicrafts. For a free guide, write to Sonoma County Farm Trails, P.O. Box 6675, Santa Rosa, CA 95406.

Stops along U.S. 101

Santa Rosa and Healdsburg are gateways to the Russian River, Dry Creek, and Alexander Valley wine regions. Petaluma, to the south, is a quintessential small town, its setting used in such movies as *Peggy Sue Got Married* and *American Graffiti*.

Petaluma. Though it's now known for farms, Petaluma was once one of the country's foremost carriage-building centers. Prosperous times left an architecturally wealthy downtown; pick up a walking tour guide from the chamber of commerce (215 Howard Street). An old waterfront mill (6 Petaluma Boulevard) is now a warren of shops.

Four miles east of town at Adobe Road and Casa Grande Avenue lies Petaluma Adobe State Historic Park (open 10 A.M. to 5 P.M. daily; small admission), the restored headquarters of General Vallejo's old ranch. Nine miles southwest of town stands the venerable Rouge et Noir Cheese Factory (take C Street, which becomes the Pt. Reyes Petaluma Road). You can tour (10 A.M. to 4 P.M.), buy snacks, and picnic.

Santa Rosa. Sonoma County's largest city and county seat has an array of accommodations and good dining choices, such as John Ash & Co. next to the Vintners Inn amid the vineyards at the north end of town. Railroad Square, the restored and antique-filled historic district just west of the freeway, is worth a detour; browse along 4th and 5th streets west to the restored 1907 La Rose Hotel and the landmark 1870s-era stone train station.

Other highlights include the home and gardens of horticulturalist Luther Burbank. Guided tours of his furnished home (corner of Santa Rosa and Sonoma avenues) take place from 10 A.M. to 3:30 P.M. Wednesday through Sunday from April through mid-October (small fee). The free gardens are open daily from 8 A.M. to 5 P.M.

One block west, at 492 Sonoma Avenue, a chapel built from a single redwood appropriately houses the "believe it or not" Robert Ripley Museum of oddities (11 A.M. to 4 P.M. Wednesday through Sunday, small fee).

Healdsburg. Wineries, bed-and-breakfast inns, and a downtown plaza that almost rivals Sonoma's mark the town of Healdsburg, 14 miles north of Santa Rosa. Shops, restaurants, the Downtown bakery (don't miss the sticky buns), and small hostelries attract tourists and locals. You get a good idea of the town's past at a free museum at 221 Matheson Street, open noon to 5 P.M. except Sunday and Monday.

Russian River region. Northern Californian vacationers have long swarmed to the 12-mile stretch of river from Mirabel Park to Monte Rio to canoe, raft, splash, and sun. Today they also tour wineries.

The region (a popular gay vacation retreat) extends west to Jenner at the river's Pacific mouth. It has no one center, but Guerneville is its traditional hub, with most of the lodging and dining choices. You can make a leisurely loop trip on Eastside and Westside roads, which run on either side of the river from Healdsburg to Guerneville. The quickest approach to the river is to pick up River Road 4 miles north of Santa Rosa.

Canoeing. With a durable canoe or kayak, you can float between Asti/Healdsburg (canoe rentals) and Guerneville. The season runs from about April to October. Trips can last from 4 hours to 2 days. Take along food, water, and sun protection.

Parks. Two miles north of Guerneville sprawl the side-by-side Armstrong Redwoods State Reserve (a forest of ancient giants) and Austin Creek State Recreation Area (a 4,000-acre meadowland with springs and a fishing lake). Picnic sites nestle among the trees at Armstrong. Austin Creek has primitive campsites and an equestrian camp; for information on pack trips, call (707) 887-2939.

Wine touring

Several Russian River wineries offer tours, including Piper Sonoma (daily picnic lunches), Korbel, Mark West, and Rodney Strong. Others welcome tasters and provide picnic sites. Foppiano (near Healdsburg) is the area's oldest.

From Healdsburg north to Cloverdale, the tour roster includes William Wheeler, White Oak, Simi, and Chateau Souverain (noted restaurant). Trentadue and Geyser Peak (tasting only) have nice picnic facilities. West of U.S. 101 near Healdsburg lie Dry Creek, Robert Stemmler, and Lambert Bridge. Northwest of Cloverdale, Anderson Valley offers more wineries (page 76).

For another scenic setting, head southeast from Healdsburg on State 128 to the Alexander Valley, noted for its cabernet wines. Alexander Valley Fruit & Trading Co. (picnic baskets), Johnson's Alexander Valley, Alexander Valley Vineyards (gardens), and Field Stone (unusual architecture) are some taste choices.

Ukiah Valley boasts several easily visited wineries, among them Parducci (patriarch of Mendocino County cellars), Cresta Blanca, and Weibel. South at Hopland, don't miss Fetzer Vineyards' winery, gardens, and respected Sundial Grill.

A walker's guide to Ukiah's old homes is available at the Sun House, 431 S. Main Street. Once the home of painter Grace Carpenter Hudson, the building now contains her paintings and Indian artifacts (10 A.M. to 4 P.M. Wednesday through Saturday, noon to 4:30 P.M. Sunday; donations requested).

North Coast

Stretching almost 400 miles from San Francisco Bay to the southern border of Oregon, the virtually unspoiled North Coast delights sightseers. Sheer cliffs, pounding waves, rocky headlands, and photogenic offshore rocks characterize much of its shoreline. A national seashore, pocket beaches, and secluded coastal inlets invite visitors.

State 1, often termed the state's most beautiful highway, passes by Fort Ross (a former Russian fur-trading outpost), old fishing and logging ports, and weathered farmsteads and fences. Mendocino, an artists' mecca, is physi-cally reminiscent of New England, while Eureka, a Victorian lumber town on U.S. 101, provides entrée to sheltered Humboldt Bay. And just to the north lies the soaring stillness of magnificent Redwood National Park.

A wealth of activities

It's near-impossible to list all the attractions of this stretch of Northern California. Anglers tussle with fighting steelhead where mighty rivers empty into the sea; campers choose between parks in sandy dunes or dense forest; and crowds of urbanites flock to unique rural festivals.

The charms of Mendocino and its bustling fishing and lumbering neighbor, Fort Bragg, rank high. To the north, trails through groves of mighty coast redwoods tempt hikers and backpackers, who pass fern-choked waterfalls, tranquil lagoons, and herds of Roosevelt elk munching in grassy meadows.

Planning a trip

To thoroughly explore the North Coast, you need a car. Only Eureka and Crescent City have regularly scheduled air service, and bus travel is similarly limited. It's easiest (and usually less expensive) to pick up a car in San Francisco; other areas may have no rental agencies.

Greyhound bus service is available to cities along U.S. 101, and from Cloverdale to Fort Bragg via State 128. Golden Gate Transit offers scheduled bus service from San Francisco to Point Reyes National Seashore.

Getting there. Heading north across the Golden Gate Bridge from San Francisco, you follow U.S. 101 (an inland route until it meets the ocean at Humboldt Bay) or take the slower, coast-hugging State 1. Backcountry roads connect these two parallel highways before they join at Leggett, just south of the redwood-lined Avenue of the Giants.

When to visit. Oddly enough, weather is usually foggy and cold along the coast during the summer, but winter often brings clear, warm days. The most sparkling days can occur in spring and autumn. Weekends are crowded almost year-round. For the most elbow room, time your visit for weekdays.

Where to stay. Historic hotels and charming bed-and-breakfast inns (many in Victorian residences) dot the coastline and are sprinkled around many interior towns (see page 72). Most motels congregate along U.S. 101, but you'll also find a number along State 1 near Point Reyes National Seashore, Tomales Bay, Bodega Bay, and from Mendocino to Fort Bragg.

For complete listings of lodging, contact the visitor bureaus listed at left. The California Office of Tourism also publishes a free guide to bed-and-breakfast inns; its address is on page 4. The American Automobile Association also puts out a guide to California inns for members.

Campers find a variety of sites throughout the region; for additional details, see pages 120 and 122. Advance reservations are required almost everywhere in summer and are recommended at any time of year.

Contacts

These agencies offer information on attractions and accommodations. See additional contacts throughout this chapter.

Marin County Visitors Bureau
30 N. San Pedro Rd., Suite 150
San Rafael, CA 94903
(415) 472-7470

Mendocino County Convention and Visitors Bureau
P.O. Box 244
Ukiah, CA 95482
(707) 462-3091

Redwood Empire Association
785 Market St., 15th Floor
San Francisco, CA 94103
(415) 543-8334

Sonoma County Convention and Visitors Bureau
10 4th St., Suite 100
Santa Rosa, CA 95401
(707) 575-1191

You'll descend three ramps and 307 steps (and then climb back up) to visit the squat iron tower of Point Reyes Lighthouse, in winter a popular whale-watching site.

Marin Beaches

As far as mariners are concerned, the Marin County shore from Point Reyes to the Golden Gate has little to recommend it. For them it's a treacherous obstacle to reaching San Francisco, composed of sea fogs, howling winds, reefs, and shoals.

But for shorebound creatures, it means something else: good rock-fishing, wave-watching, rockhounding, and clamming. In its shallow bays, the hardy even enjoy swimming. Only one remote beach is more than an hour from San Francisco, and some of the shore is barely 15 minutes away.

In spite of its proximity to the city, Marin's coast has not been subjected to any permanent overcrowding, because the terrain rises sharply skyward in many places. Development has also been discouraged by the creation of parks along all but a handful of miles of shoreline.

Marin's shores from the north end of the Golden Gate Bridge are practically all open to the public as part of the Golden Gate National Recreation Area, which extends as far north as Olema. The land is a mixture of former army forts, ruggedly undeveloped open areas, and once-private ranch lands.

Marin Headlands

Just minutes north of San Francisco, the Marin Headlands are now part of the Golden Gate National Recreation Area. Plummeting from bare-crested hills to deep water all along their length, the headlands stretch west from the Golden Gate Bridge to Point Bonita. The region offers protected coastal valleys, windswept beaches, former army forts, abandoned artillery bunkers, and magnificent views of San Francisco, the Golden Gate Bridge, and the Pacific Ocean.

For solitude, take a hike. The Miwok, Coast, and Tennessee Valley trails begin in the headlands and traverse the coastal hills. Kirby Cove (a pocket beach in the shadow of the bridge) and Rodeo Beach (a broad beach near the California Marine Mammal Rescue Center, opposite Bird Island) offer fine spots for a picnic. These beaches afford sweeping ocean views, but their waters are not safe for swimming.

To reach the headlands from San Francisco, take the Alexander Avenue exit off U.S. 101 and turn left, following the GGNRA signs toward Forts Baker, Barry, and Cronkhite. From the north, take the last exit before reaching the Golden Gate Bridge and follow the signs.

You loop through the area by following Conzelman Road along the bluffs beyond Point Bonita to Bunker Road. (A left turn on Bunker Road leads to the ranger station, for maps and information.) Bunker Road heads back from Rodeo Valley through a tunnel to U.S. 101.

A hostel at Fort Barry offers overnight facilities for a slight fee; call (415) 331-2777 for information.

Point Bonita light station. The old lighthouse perched on the eroding tip of the headlands is now open for weekend tours; for information, see page 77.

A prime weather station and warning point for the bay, it's a reliable gauge of the comings and goings of the summer fog bank. The islands in the distance are the Farallons, now protected as a national wildlife refuge.

The first sounding device installed at Point Bonita in 1856 to help befogged mariners was an army sergeant charged with firing a muzzle-loading cannon at half-hour intervals whenever the weather demanded. At the end of two months he was exhausted, and had to petition for relief.

Fort Cronkhite. This outermost of three sentinel forts on the north side of San Francisco Bay welcomes visitors. Reasons for making the trip are many: rockhounds roam the gravelled shore in search of jadeite and jasper (especially good pickings in winter); the summer crowd comes to bask in the lee of bluffs that offer some protection from the prevailing westerlies; and people who like to watch seabirds have a superior arena.

Along the coast

State 1 leads to Marin County's west coast. Earthquake damage in 1989 closed a section of the highway south of Stinson Beach, rerouting traffic via the Panoramic Highway on the shoulder of Mount Tamalpais (see page 37).

If you're going to Point Reyes and Tomales Bay, State 1 is best reached from U.S. 101 via Sir Francis Drake Boulevard (exit west at Greenbrae). Or you can take Lucas Valley Road from U.S. 101 north of San Rafael west past Nicasio, then west 6 miles farther on the Point Reyes–Petaluma Road.

Stinson Beach. This is the name not only of a small town but also of a day-use park that's now part of the Golden Gate National Recreation Area. Anglers do well fishing for ling cod, cabezone, and blenny at several rocky points toward the park's southern boundary.

Just opposite the town's entrance is a 4,500-foot-long swimming beach, its waters warmed by the shoal of Bolinas Bay. Swimming is permitted from late May to mid-September, when lifeguards are on duty and the weather is most temperate.

Audubon Canyon Ranch. About 3 miles north of Stinson Beach on State 1 lies a 1,000-acre bird sanctuary. On weekends and holidays from March through July 4, rookery outlooks (open 10 A.M. to 4 P.M.) afford close-up views of flocks of great blue herons and egrets. The birds nest in trees overlooking the Bolinas Lagoon.

Bolinas. Sitting just across from Stinson Beach on the mouth of a small lagoon, the artists' haven of Bolinas tries hard not to attract visitors (residents tear down direction signs)—but it gets them anyway. To get there, turn left at the foot of the lagoon, then left again immediately. Follow the road to the other side of the lagoon and make another left.

Duxbury Reef, a principal cause of the town's popularity, creates ideal conditions for surfing, tidepooling, clamming, and rock-fishing. Each end of the town's east-west main street dips down to a beach access. The one nearest Stinson Beach serves bass anglers and surfers; the westerly end is closest to the foot of Duxbury Reef.

Tomales Bay

Headquarters for the Point Reyes National Seashore (see right) is Bear Valley Visitor Center, about a half-mile west of Olema. Tomales Bay, north of the park, is a tranquil alternative.

En route to the 13-mile-long bay, State 1 passes through the small town of Point Reyes Station (an arts and crafts center). Just south of town, it crosses Sir Francis Drake Boulevard, which leads to Inverness (marina, restaurants, inns) on the west side of the bay.

About 1½ miles north on State 1, a parking lot marks one entrance to the bay's eastern edge. Walk west about a mile to the shore for good picnicking spots (no facilities) and views of the bird life in the marshland sanctuary below.

Tomales Bay State Park. Pierce Point Road leads into the park (small fee) and to protected Heart's Desire Beach, where you can spread a picnic blanket or take a half-mile marked nature trail to learn how native Miwok Indians used plants and dug for oysters around the bay. In addition to its shoreside charms, the park is a preserve for Bishop pines.

A county boat launch lies just south of the point where State 1 bends inland toward the town of Tomales. Beach areas all along the bay are accessible for cockling or fishing during the winter run of herring. You can buy oysters from one of the commercial growers in the tiny town of Marshall or enjoy a casual lunch at a cafe perched over the bay.

Dillon Beach. This raffishly charming summer village at the mouth of the bay is almost due west of Tomales on a spur road. Clamming for gapers on a low-tide island, fishing, and swimming (for the hardy only) are popular sports.

Point Reyes

Like a wild land apart, the windswept, triangular-shaped Point Reyes Peninsula juts into the Pacific Ocean 50 miles northwest of San Francisco. Its pine-forested hills, rolling pasturelands, and rocky, wave-battered beaches are all part of the 66,000-acre Point Reyes National Seashore.

Geologically speaking, Point Reyes is really an island of land (on the Pacific plate) divided from the mainland (on the American plate) by the San Andreas Fault that runs through the Olema Valley. Olema was the epicenter of the 1906 San Francisco earthquake, during which the Point Reyes Peninsula moved 20 feet northwestward.

Point Reyes is easily reached from U.S. 101 via Sir Francis Drake Boulevard or from State 1. It's about a 1½-hour drive from San Francisco.

U.S. Weather Bureau statistics cite Point Reyes as the foggiest and windiest spot, bar none, between Canada and Mexico. That goes for summer, too—so bring warm clothing. Ideal months for active outings are August, September, and October. From February through July, colorful wildflowers carpet the land.

Exploring the park. Begin your exploration at the Bear Valley Visitor Center (open 9 A.M. to 5 P.M. daily) off State 1 on Bear Valley Road, a short drive west of Olema; phone (415) 663-1092. Here you can get maps, trail guides, nature books, and schedules of nature programs.

You'll also find dioramas depicting the area's natural and cultural history. Nearby points of interest include two short hikes, the Earthquake Trail along the San Andreas Fault and the Woodpecker Nature Trail; a replica of a coastal Miwok Indian village; and a Morgan horse–breeding ranch.

Several paved roads lead to other sites within the park. Bear Valley is

the gateway to more than 100 miles of trails, providing access to the park's remote beauty for hikers, bicyclists, and horseback riders. Horses can be rented at Five Brooks Stables, 4 miles south of Olema on Highway 1, and at Stewart's Horse Camp, on State 1 a quarter-mile north of the Five Brooks Trailhead.

No fees or permits are required for day use, but there are a few rules: don't bring dogs or other pets on trails, carry your own water, and stay back from the cliffs.

Wave-watching. This park's grandeur owes much to its varied seashore, popular for picnicking, strolling, beachcombing, and whale watching. Before beginning a beach walk, check the tide tables at the visitor center. Be alert for unexpectedly large waves and falling rocks from the steep cliffs.

A number of beaches dot the protected, curving crescent of Drakes Bay, considered by many historians the site of the first landing on this continent by an English explorer. Some claim that Sir Francis Drake arrived here in 1579 aboard his ship, the *Golden Hinde*.

Two Drakes Bay beaches of note are Limantour and Drakes, where you'll find the Kenneth C. Patrick Visitor Center, Drakes Bay Cafe, and sheltered picnic tables.

On Point Reyes Promontory, at the end of Sir Francis Drake Boulevard, stands Point Reyes Lighthouse and the Lighthouse Visitor Center (see page 77).

Bird-watching. Point Reyes Bird Observatory is the only full-time ornithological field research station on the continent. Here you'll see land birds, shorebirds, and waterfowl the year around. Located on the south end of the peninsula, the station is reached by Mesa Road from Bolinas.

Visitors tour the sturdy stockade at Fort Ross, a 19th-century North American outpost for Russian fur traders on the Sonoma Coast.

Sonoma Coast

Shorter and less developed than the Mendocino coast, its more famous neighbor to the north, the Sonoma coastline begins at Bodega Bay and runs north to the mouth of the Gualala River. Its principal attractions are a series of beach parks, awesome scenery, and Fort Ross, the last surviving sign of the 19th-century Russian settlements in California.

The Sonoma coast divides into three distinct parts: two lengths of coastal shelf divided by a file of steep hills marching into the sea. The shelves extend from Bodega Bay to Jenner on the south and from Fort Ross to Gualala on the north.

Getting there. State 1 continues north from Marin County through Mendocino County. More direct routes to the Sonoma coast from U.S. 101 are State 116, which winds along the Russian River from Guerneville through the recreated town of Duncans Mills to Jenner, or State 12, through the apple country around Sebastopol to the coast below Bodega Bay.

Lodging. Overnight accommodations are becoming more numerous along this scenic coastal stretch, though most still cluster around Bodega Bay and Jenner. It's wise to make reservations in advance. For a list of facilities, contact the Sonoma County Convention and Visitors Bureau (address on page 66).

Around Bodega Bay

The Bodega Bay-to-Jenner segment is the most developed and easiest to view. A gently sloping shelf permits State 1 to skirt a series of sandy beaches only 1½ hours from San Francisco.

Bodega Bay. Discovered by Spanish explorers in 1775, this harbor provides the only protected small-boat anchorage of any size between San Francisco and Noyo in Mendocino County. Both charter and commercial boats operate out of Bodega, chasing salmon from May to October and bottom fishing when salmon are scarce. If you're there in the early afternoon, watch a party fishing boat unload the day's catch at Spud Point Marina.

Perch feed in the lagoon shoals, especially along the western shore. Some gaper clams lurk along the shore, but most are clustered offshore on a low-tide island.

Outside the lagoon, surfers ride toward the spit, starting at a point 400 yards east of the breakwater. Rock fishers work the jetties and the exposed side of Bodega Head, a high, treeless knob at the northern end of the bay that's now part of the Sonoma Coast State Beach park. It's a good place to sight migrating gray whales from mid-December to mid-April.

Active children can romp endlessly in the rolling dunes that run all the way from the head north to Salmon Creek. A state campground at Bodega Dunes has more than 100 sites.

For information on shops, galleries, parks, restaurants, golf links, sport-fishing vessels, and lodging, contact the Bodega Bay Chamber of Commerce, 555 Coast Highway, Box 146, Bodega Bay, CA 94923, or call (707) 875-3422.

Sonoma Coast State Beach

Small coves, rocky headlands, and massive offshore rock stacks characterize Sonoma Coast State Beach. This collection of beaches and bays extends along State 1 from Bodega Bay to the mouth of the Russian River—over 14 miles of uninterrupted shore.

Beachcombers and anglers find this stretch fascinating. For a park brochure, stop at the entrance to Bodega Dunes or at park headquarters at Salmon Creek Beach.

Salmon Creek. About 1½ miles north of the town of Bodega, Salmon Creek forms an inviting summer wading pond. After autumn rains break down the sand bar, it becomes a spawning stream for salmon and steelhead. Local surfers, night smelters, and surf fishers use the outer beach. Sand dunes roll away to the south, crisscrossed by foot and bridle paths.

Duncan's Landing. A sign on this dangerous section of coast warns that a number of people have been swept to their deaths in a pounding sea by unexpectedly high waves. Yet there's plenty of safe rock fishing in other spots en route.

On sandy beaches, surf fishing and dip-netting for smelt are good. Duncan's Cove, just in the lee of the point, is one of the most productive day smelt beaches in the region.

Wrights Beach. North of Duncan's Landing, this beach is another camping unit for the state beach. It's also a favorite with picnickers, as much for its broad, sandy strand as for its facilities.

Goat Rock Beach. This site combines a protected cove with a long, sandy beach (which reaches out to form the mouth of the Russian River) and a sandy length of riverbank. Its northern end is a popular daytime beach with good smelt fishing in summer and steelheading in winter. The beach road forks off of State 1 near a long upgrade crest and descends across nearly a mile of meadows to sea level.

A Russian fort

Fort Ross is about 13 miles north of Jenner, where State 1 finally winds down from elevations that are either awe inspiring or terrifying, depending on the density of the sea fog and how you feel about steep dropoffs. You see the stout wooden buildings set high on the headlands before you reach them. The parking lot turnoff is just beyond the park.

The fort was originally the North American outpost for 19th-century Russian fur traders. Later, loggers and ranchers used the site. The Russians and Aleuts arrived in 1812 and stayed 30 years. During their sojourn these

Mellow old inns along the coast offer a warm welcome to travelers. From south to north, our sampling focuses on bed-and-breakfasts housed in vintage facilities from former farmhouses to a hospital. Rates vary (from $50 to more than $150 for two), depending on location and season. Prices include breakfast and other extras.

Book well in advance in summer and weekends year-round; most inns require 2-night stays on weekends. For a complete list of B & Bs, check with the county visitor bureaus and the California Office of Tourism (address on page 4). The American Automobile Association also publishes a free guide to B & Bs for members.

Bear Valley Inn, 88 Bear Valley Rd., Olema, CA 94950; (415) 663-1777. Two-story Victorian ranch house close to Point Reyes; full breakfast; 3 rooms (2 share bath).

Ten Inverness Way, Inverness, CA 94937; (415) 669-1648. Turn-of-the-century inn near national seashore; hot tub; 4 rooms.

Heart's Desire Inn, 3657 Church St., Occidental, CA 95465; (707) 874-1311. Mid-Victorian country residence; complimentary sherry; wheelchair accessible; 6 rooms, 1 suite with fireplace.

Murphy's Jenner Inn, 10400 State 1, Jenner, CA 95450; (707) 865-2377. Early Sonoma coast inn; ocean views; hot tub; complimentary aperitifs; 9 rooms, 3 suites, and 1 cabin, some with deck and fireplace.

Old Milano Hotel, 38300 State 1, Gualala, CA 95445; (707) 884-3256. Historic hotel opened in 1905; restaurant; hot tub; ocean views; 9 rooms (some share bath).

Coast Guard House, 695 Arena Cove, Point Arena, CA 95468; (707) 882-2442. Cape Cod–style house (1901) overlooking lighthouse; ocean or canyon views; continental breakfast; 6 rooms, (some share bath).

Elk Cove Inn, 6300 S. State 1, Elk, CA 95432; (707) 877-3321. Bluffside Victorian home and 4 ocean-view cottages with private beach access; 6 rooms, 2 with fireplace.

Harbor House, 5600 S. State 1, Elk, CA 95432; (707) 877-3203. Oceanside inn with private beach; full breakfast; 9 rooms, each with fireplace.

Fensalden Inn, 33810 Navarro Ridge Rd., (P.O. Box 99), Albion, CA 95410; (707) 937-4042. Restored 1860s stagecoach station 7 miles south of Mendocino; free hors d'oeuvres; 8 rooms, 6 with fireplace.

Glendeven, 8221 N. State 1, Little River, CA 95456; (707) 937-0083. New England–style farmhouse and converted barn; art gallery; 10 rooms and suites (2 share bath), 6 with fireplace.

Victorian Farmhouse, 7001 N. State 1, Little River, CA 95456; (707) 937-0697. Early Victorian near Mendocino and state parks; complimentary sherry; continental breakfast in room; 10 rooms, 6 with fireplace.

Agate Cove Inn, 11201 N. Lansing St., Mendocino, CA 95460; (707) 937-0551. Nineteenth-century farmhouse and cottages with sea views; complimentary sherry; 10 cottages, 9 with fireplace.

Brewery Gulch Inn, 9350 State 1, Mendocino, CA 95460; (707) 937-4752. Farmhouse (more than 130 years old) on 10 acres near town; full breakfast; 5 rooms (most share baths), 2 with fireplace.

John Dougherty House, 571 Ukiah St., Mendocino, CA 95460; (707) 937-5266. Cape Cod–style home in midst of the village; complimentary wine and chocolates; 6 rooms, 2 suites (2 with fireplace).

Joshua Grindle Inn, 44800 Little Lake Rd., Mendocino, CA 95460; (707) 937-4143. Two acres surrounding 1879 Victorian; full breakfast; 10 rooms, 6 with fireplace.

Gray Whale Inn, 615 N. Main St., Fort Bragg, CA 95437; (707) 964-0640. Large 1915 redwood building in heart of town near Skunk train depot; lounge; TV and game rooms; 14 rooms, 2 with fireplace, 4 overlooking ocean, 1 with jacuzzi and sun deck.

Bowen's Pelican Inn, 38921 N. State 1, (P.O. Box 35), Westport, CA 95488; (707) 964-5588. Turn-of-the-century hotel; restaurant and bar; 8 rooms (3 share bath).

Gingerbread Mansion, 400 Berding St., (P.O. Box AA40), Ferndale, CA 95536; (707) 786-4000. Well-photographed Queen Anne Victorian; English garden; afternoon tea; bicycles; 9 rooms, 3 with fireplace.

Shaw House Inn, 703 Main St., Ferndale, CA 95536; (707) 786-9958. Large yard surrounds 1854 gabled Gothic-style house; complimentary tea; 5 rooms (3 share bath).

Old Town Bed and Breakfast Inn, 1521 3rd St., Eureka, CA 95501; (707) 445-3951. Antique-furnished 1871 home in historic area; evening social hours; 5 rooms (2 share bath).

The Plough and The Stars, 1800 27th St., Arcata, CA 95521; (707) 822-8236. Midwestern-style 1860 farmhouse in suitable setting; croquet and horseshoes; 5 rooms (2 share bath), 1 with fireplace.

...Sonoma Coast

hunters, helped by their American and British rivals, wiped out the sea otter herds to the point of extinction.

Painstakingly restored and reconstructed after the 1906 earthquake and several later fires, the fort, which includes a tiny chapel, looks much as it must have originally. A modern visitor center's artifacts and displays illustrate the fort's colorful history, and the gift shop sells authentic Pomo basketry.

Free audio wands in the Rotchev house, the only Russian-built structure still standing in the compound, let visitors tune into the period simply by pointing at numbered listening posts.

The fort is open from 10 A.M. to 4:30 P.M. daily except Thanksgiving, Christmas, and New Year's; a small day-use fee is charged. Two holidays— Living History Day, July 22, and Ranch Day, on the last Sunday in September—attract many visitors. For more information, contact Fort Ross State Historic Park, 19005 Coast Highway 1, Jenner, CA 95450; phone (707) 847-3286.

A paved loop walk takes you to the bluff. From here, you can view rock fishers and rockhounds. The well-situated campground (see page 122) has redwoods and splendid views.

North to Gualala

From Fort Ross to Mendocino, the coastal shelf is narrow but gently sloping, sometimes wooded but mostly covered by meadow grass. Take along a picnic basket; restaurants are scarce. Immediately north of Fort Ross is the Timber Cove development. Walk around the seaward side of the hotel to look at sculptor Beniamino Bufano's last finished work, *Peace*.

Stillwater Cove County Park. Some 3½ miles north of Fort Ross is a day-use park much favored by scuba divers. Features include picnic tables, a canyon trail, and the old Fort Ross schoolhouse.

Salt Point State Park. Midway between Jenner and Stewarts Point, this park's rich environment makes it worth a stop. The strange offshore formations are sandstone columns eroded by waves. The park has open and secluded campsites (see page 122), miles of hiking trails, an underwater park for scuba divers, small stands of pygmy pines and redwoods, and deer and other wildlife. For picnicking, head for Fisk Mill Cove.

Kruse Rhododendron State Reserve. This large preserve on Plantation Road 22½ miles north of Jenner is at its best from April to June, the peak blossom period. Sorry, no picnic tables.

Sea Ranch. The architectural contrast between the weathered buildings of tiny Stewarts Point (general store and schoolhouse) and this private development just up the road is striking. Built in 1868, Stewarts Point's general store is one of the oldest buildings along this stretch of coast; it has picnic food, tackle sales and rentals, bait, and eclectic oddities.

At modern Sea Ranch, award-winning houses, designed to blend into the landscape, are scattered around more than 5,000 acres of grassy beachlands and forested slopes. Sea Ranch Lodge has 20 rooms with fireplaces or ocean views, plus a restaurant. Many of the trend-setting residences also can be rented.

Six marked trails (Black Point is the most dramatic; Walk-On is wheelchair accessible) lead the public to the beaches. Note that the trails are open for day use only (small fee), and that parking lots are tiny (holding four to six cars and no RVs). No parking is allowed along State 1 or on Sea Ranch streets.

Gualala Point Regional Park. This 75-acre park just beyond the northern boundary of Sea Ranch occupies the headland and spit that form the south side of the Gualala River and mark the northern boundary of Sonoma County. You can camp beside the river in which Jack London liked to cast for steelhead, visit a small nature center (open weekends from Memorial Day to Labor Day), and scramble out along the often-windy point for ocean views.

St. Orres, a renowned restaurant and inn a few miles north of Gualala, is vaguely reminiscent of Fort Ross in its Russian-inspired architecture.

North Coast

Mendocino Coast

Summer fog doesn't daunt the thousands of annual visitors who come to enjoy the 19th-century charm and scenic beauty of Mendocino's splendid coast. Urbanization doesn't threaten yet either, thanks to environmental activism and the narrow, crooked roads. Towns are still small and spaced well apart.

Blue sea and white surf contrast with the area's deep green forests and weathered gray barns. In the 100 miles from Gualala to Rockport, the mood changes around every headland, making this stretch a photographer's paradise: even the gap-toothed fences are appealing.

For most visitors the heart of this rugged coast is the short distance between the art colony of Mendocino and Fort Bragg, terminus for the strangely named Skunk trains. At either end of this 11-mile stretch, you'll find less deep-sea fishing, Victoriana, and tourism, but more expansive beaches for strollers, driftwood hunters, and surf fishers.

Logging opened up the coast between Point Arena and Fort Bragg in the 1850s, and mill towns and ports sprang up along the ragged coastline. In the 1940s nearly 50 sawmills worked this stretch of coast; now sheep graze the once-forested beachlands.

Getting there. Most visitors feel they need at least 3 days to linger in comfortable old inns, browse among shops and galleries, and picnic on pebbly beaches.

The county's southern boundary is only 125 miles north of San Francisco, its northern one 250. And yet following sinuous State 1 from San Francisco to Fort Bragg takes about 6 hours.

If perusing Mendocino's art and charm is your goal, there's a delightful alternative route. Head north on U.S. 101 as far as Cloverdale, then take State 128 through the Anderson Valley, a 57-mile sequence of rolling hills parting around a tunnel of towering redwoods. It's about a 3½-hour drive from the Bay Area.

To the north, State 20 also offers coastal access, heading west from Willits. It parallels the route of the Skunk trains through 34 miles of fine stands of redwood and Douglas fir, and joins State 1 just south of Fort Bragg.

Accommodations. Most lodging is around Mendocino and Fort Bragg, though you'll find historic hotels or upscale inns at Gualala, Point Arena, Elk, Albion, Little River, Noyo, and Westport. Some choices are listed on page 72.

Reservations are essential in summer and are advisable all year. For a complete list of facilities, contact the Mendocino County Convention and Visitors Bureau (see page 66) or the Fort Bragg–Mendocino Coast Chamber of Commerce, P.O. Box 1141, Fort Bragg, CA 95437; phone (707) 964-3153.

Beach parks

Public beaches are scattered along the coast from Gualala to Fort Bragg. Ranging from flat, sandy coves to tunneled headlands, most offer fine camping or picnicking facilities and abundant scenery. For park information, write to Department of Parks and Recreation, Mendocino Area State Parks, P.O. Box 440, Mendocino, CA 95460. Reservations are made through MISTIX, (800) 444-7275. For more camping details, see page 122.

Schooner Gulch State Park. Newest and southernmost of the county's state beaches, Schooner Gulch is a little more than 11 miles north of the Gualala River. Picnickers can descend a trail to the driftwood-littered sands or climb to the top of the bluffs for a fine view.

Manchester State Beach. The last generous sand stretch south of Fort Bragg, this park's 7 miles of wide shore span most of the distance between Garcia River and Alder Creek. Middling good for sand castles, the beach is far roomier than the minimally developed campground, which is sheltered behind sand dunes from frequent

winds. To the south lies Point Arena Lighthouse (see page 77).

Van Damme State Park. The beach side of this park on scenic Little River makes a pleasant wayside stop, but the main section (with campsites) is on the inland side of the highway. Activities include reasonably safe (but cold) swimming, skin diving, and cycling and hiking trails. One trail leads to an ancient forest of stunted conifers in the southeast quarter of the park (wheelchair access via Little River Airport Road).

Mendocino Headlands State Park. Beginning as a sandy beach at the mouth of Big River, this splendid park becomes a wall of rock looping west beneath the bluffs and then broadens to cover the flat fields of the headlands as well as their wave-swept edge. Heeser Drive, a loop road west of town, circles along the bluff's edge and extends down to the beach. Public fishing access is from the road's northern end.

This highly sculpted shore abounds with wave tunnels, arched rocks, narrow channels, and even a few lagoons. Skin divers fare well; tidepoolers should take a look-but-don't-touch attitude. For details, stop by the Ford House visitor center on Main Street.

Russian Gulch State Park. This parkland, which looks back at Mendocino across a broad bay from the next headland to the north, is a compacted replay of the sheltered beach at Van Damme and Mendocino's exposed headlands. A creek cutting out of the gulch pauses in a low, sandy spot, seemingly so that children can splash around in safety, and then slips into the sea in the lee of a craggy, lofty headland. A blowhole just north of the main overlook performs during storms.

From this dramatic boundary, the park runs deeply inland; protected campsites nestle in the mouth of a canyon. It's an easy hike upstream to a lacy waterfall set amidst a forest underlaid with beds of ferns.

Dining on the Noyo River at the southern end of Fort Bragg guarantees your "catch of the day" to be right off the boat.

...*Mendocino*

MacKerricher State Park. North of Fort Bragg, where Pudding Creek empties into the sea, this versatile park (three campgrounds) includes headlands, beaches, heavily forested uplands, and a small lake for fishing and boating.

A road wanders down to the shore between a rocky beach to the south and a sandy one to the north. The chief reasons for heading out along the dunes are smelt fishing or driftwood hunting. You can get to the Ten Mile River end of the beach from an old logging road off State 1.

Mendocino

Startlingly in contrast to its time and place, this small cluster of wooden towers and carpenter's Gothic houses contains a contemporary society of artists and artisans. When you amble through the town's galleries, you'll see how they've translated the stunning setting into artworks.

Mendocino's top galleries may be the sprawling Mendocino Art Center (45200 Little Lake Street) and its offshoot, the Mendocino Art Center Showcase (560 Main Street). Both combine studios with rotating exhibits by local and international artists. Another good choice is Gallery Glendeven (next to the Glendeven Inn on State 1 about 1½ miles south of town).

Settled as a mill town in 1852 by timber baron Henry Meiggs, Mendocino may look like a Cape Cod relic (and indeed is a stand-in for Cabot Cove on the TV series *Murder, She Wrote*), but its weathered buildings are bursting with life: cleverly named shops, studios, restaurants, and inns.

You can drive around it in 10 minutes, but it's best to park your car and walk, picking up the free map available at most stores. The terrain is also easily covered by bike. But perhaps the best way to learn about town history is to stop by the Kelley House Museum, 45007 Albion Street. Besides being a repository of memorabilia, it serves as an unofficial tourist center.

A number of area restaurants soothe hunger pangs. Town dining ranges from the homey Sea Gull Restaurant

(10481 Albion Street) to the highly respected MacCallum House (45020 Albion Street) and the acclaimed Cafe Beaujolais (961 Ukiah Street). Other favorites (Ledford House and Little River Restaurant) are a few miles south.

Anderson Valley

State 128 through the Anderson Valley is a scenic drive popular with travelers heading to and from the Bay Area. At the beginning of its route from the coast, the highway parallels the Navarro River, with big redwoods rising between road and river.

Paul M. Dimmick Wayside Camp, a 12-acre park, makes a handy base for trailer and tent campers. Nearby Hendy Woods State Park has two camping areas, a stream for summer swimming and fishing, and fine redwood stands.

About 30 miles from the coast, amid vineyards, orchards, and quiet ranchland, lies Boonville, settled in the 1850s. For many years, its claim to fame was "Boontling," a tongue-in-cheek dialect.

Now it's a good place to overnight (at Anderson Creek Inn and The Toll House, or Philo Pottery Inn in nearby Philo), eat (New Boonville Restaurant and Boont Berry Farm are two choices), or assemble a picnic. Between Philo and Boonville, fruit and juice stands thrive in season. Wineries (tasting rooms) cluster around Philo, and the Anderson Valley Brewing Company in Boonville produces several beers.

North to Fort Bragg

The beaches at two state parks (Caspar Headlands and Jug Handle) are good picnic spots en route to Fort Bragg. At Jug Handle, an "ecological staircase" (a series of terraces formed by wave action and varying sea levels) gives you a cram course on a half million years of natural history. Pick up a map from the vending machine (small charge) at the top of the stairs.

Mendocino Coast Botanical Gardens. A lavish display of flowers covers 47 acres of bluffs 2 miles south of Fort Bragg. It's at its best in spring, when the rhododendrons bloom. The reserve is open daily year-round; there's a small charge to visit.

Fort Bragg. As you enter Fort Bragg, you cross a bridge high over the Noyo River. The harbor east of the highway is home port to a big commercial fishing fleet. Visitors charter fishing boats or enjoy seafood restaurants.

Fort Bragg, the largest town on the coast (about 6,000 people), was settled as an army post in 1857, then resettled as a lumber town when the first sawmill was built in 1885. Paul Bunyan Days (Labor Day weekend) bring big crowds to watch loggers compete.

Visitors can pick up a walking tour map at the chamber of commerce office, 332 North Main Street (closed Wednesday and Sunday), visit the Guest House Museum (a former lumber company house filled with displays illustrating logging and shipping history), hop aboard the Skunk train for a trip through the redwood groves to Willits on U.S. 101 (see page 126 for details), or go beachcombing at Glass Beach, just north of town.

To the Lost Coast

Beyond Fort Bragg the coastal shelf narrows to next to nothing. Highway 1 suddenly veers inland above Rockport, unable to engineer its way along the formidable coastal terrain. Its failure results in a ruggedly unspoiled stretch known as the Lost Coast.

Westport. Weathered Westport's New England–style houses have changed little since the heyday of lumbering. The tiny town has only a couple of inns (one of them the rustic Cobweb Palace Inn) and restaurants.

Shore fishing is productive at Westport–Union Landing State Beach and at South Kibesillah Gulch Coast Angling Access Area, where a pair of parking lots provide access to several hundred yards of vertical shoreline.

Sinkyone Wilderness State Park. Access to the southern part of this skinny, 7,400-acre coastal preserve is only mildly difficult, at least in dry weather. A 6-mile dirt road (no RVs or trailers) departs State 1 about 13 miles north of Westport. The northern entrance is off U.S. 101 near Garberville. For details, call (707) 446-2311 or (707) 986-7711.

Not-so-lonely Lighthouses

Romanticized and treasured, the West Coast's surviving lighthouses have become as popular as they once were lonely. Some of these shoreline landmarks have been preserved and opened to the public as museums, hostels, and even a bed-and-breakfast inn.

Many of the beacons are on coastal promontories of stunning scenic beauty; others stand in or near parks or wildlife refuges. So your visit may also include beachcombing and driftwood collecting (check area regulations), tidepooling, camping, and wildlife watching (especially for gray whales).

We list, from north to south, 10 you can visit along the Northern California coast. Another, south of Mendocino at Point Cabrillo, is now part of the Coastal Conservancy and scheduled to open soon. For a free list of all state lighthouses, send a self-addressed stamped envelope to the U.S. Lighthouse Society, 244 Kearny Street, San Francisco, CA 94108.

Battery Point (1856). Topping a wave-washed rock nearly engulfed at high tide, this tiny Cape Cod–style stone lighthouse at Crescent City was among the first along the coast. You reach it at low tide via a 200-yard spit; the hike is an adventure. Visit a fine museum, climb into the 45-foot tower, picnic, and whale-watch. From April to October, the light is open Wednesday through Sunday from 10 A.M. to 4 P.M. Admission: $2 adults, 50 cents children under 12. For access times and directions, call (707) 464-3089.

Point Arena (1870). The 1906 quake toppled the first lighthouse on this long peninsula, 65 miles north of Point Reyes. You'll find a museum here and three bungalows to rent ($80 to $110 a night). Steps wind up into the 115-foot tower. The light is

open 11 A.M. to 2:30 P.M. daily, except December, and 10 A.M. to 3:30 P.M. summer weekends. Admission: $2 adults, 50 cents children under 12. For information, call (707) 882-2777.

Point Reyes (1870). A squat, 16-sided iron tower sits three ramps and 307 steps below the bluff. Foggy, barren, beset by storms, it was one of the West's least desirable locations; many keepers quit or went mad. Open Thursday through Monday 10 A.M. to 4:30 P.M., the light station is now part of a national park. Whale-watchers crowd it on winter weekends; go early in the day. The second and last Saturday evening of the month you can watch the lens being relighted; call (415) 669-1534 for reservations. Admission: free (park entry fee).

Point Bonita (1877). Clinging to a basalt outcrop northwest of the Golden Gate Bridge, the low iron tower (part of the Golden Gate National Recreation Area) is reached by trail, tunnel, and 180-foot steel suspension bridge; children under 12 are not permitted. The light is open 12:30 to 4 P.M. weekends, with guided tours at 1 P.M. For directions and to reserve monthly moonlight tours, call (415) 331-1540. Admission: free.

East Brother Light Station (1873). On a 1-acre island off Point Richmond in San Francisco Bay, a bed-and-breakfast inn ($295 a couple including dinner, breakfast, and transportation; book 6 months ahead) occupies the restored Victorian buildings. For overnight reservations or day visits ($10, minimum 4 people), call (415) 233-2385.

Point Montara (1875). After two cargo steamers piled up on a shallow ledge offshore, a fog signal was built at this spot, 20 miles south of San Francisco. The light tower, atop 70-foot cliffs, was added later. Restored buildings house a hostel ($10 a night).

Lodging is bunk-bed style, and you help with chores. For information, call (415) 728-7177 from 7:30 to 9:30 A.M. and 4:30 to 9:30 P.M.

Pigeon Point (1872). This station 30 miles north of Santa Cruz is named for a ship that broke up on nearby rocks in 1853. Weekend tours are hourly from 11 A.M. to 2 P.M. by reservation and 3 to 4 P.M. without. Admission: $2 adults, $1 children. There's also a dormitory-style hostel ($10 a night). For information, call (415) 879-0633.

Santa Cruz (1967). A snug brick structure on W. Cliff Drive, Mark Abbott Memorial Lighthouse was built on the site of an 1860s light by parents of a surfer who drowned nearby. The museum (historical surfing artifacts) is open daily except Tuesday from 1 to 4 P.M. in summer, also closed Wednesday the rest of the year. Admission: free.

Point Piños (1855). The oldest continuously operating lighthouse on the West Coast, this New England-style Pacific Grove structure operated for more than 40 years by women, is now a museum. Its tower rises over a cozy red-roofed house filled with period furniture and marine artifacts. The museum, on Asilomar Avenue at Pacific Grove, is open weekends from 1 to 4 P.M. Admission: free (donations accepted).

Point Sur (1889). This lighthouse 20 miles south of Carmel was recently acquired by the state parks department, which offers 2½-hour tours of keepers' homes, storehouses, and the lighthouse (includes a steep ½-mile hike). Tours take place on weekends, weather permitting. For information and parking directions, call (408) 625-4419. Admission: $2; no small children allowed because of hazardous site conditions.

Rhododendrons brighten this sequoia grove in Redwood National Park. These giant redwoods grow naturally nowhere else in the country except this coastal region.

Redwood Country

Before the gold rush brought a surge of new population to Northern California, a vast forest of the world's tallest trees—the coast redwood or *Sequoia sempervirens*—blanketed an area up to 30 miles wide and 450 miles long. Magnificent redwood groves extended from the Santa Lucia Mountains south of Monterey northward into a corner of Oregon. The oldest known coast redwood had reached the age of 2,200 years before being cut in the 1930s.

Civilization's demands have left only small parts of the forest primeval. The majority of the remaining redwoods are located along U.S. 101 from Leggett (where it merges with State 1) north to Crescent City.

Getting there. Via U.S. 101, it takes between 4 and 5 hours to drive from San Francisco to the southern edge of redwood country. Garberville, the northern entrance to the Sinkyone Wilderness State Park on the Lost Coast, is a favorite overnight stop. Most of the air service is to the Eureka/Arcata area, though some flights reach Crescent City. Rental cars are limited at airports. Greyhound also connects the region. Year-round 2- and 3-day sightseeing trips are also offered by several companies.

Accommodations. The supply of rooms in this region is often exceeded by the demand, especially in summer. A cluster of motels around Garberville and Miranda is your best bet in the south. Stop for a meal or just to take a look at the Tudor-style Benbow Inn, even if you're not planning to stay.

Farther north, Eureka and Arcata have the largest number of motels and inns. It pays to make reservations. Without them, you'll have better luck finding a place in Orick, Klamath, or Crescent City.

Weather. Climate in redwood country is changeable. The finest season is autumn, when crowds thin out, the air turns brisk, and a seasonal show of color brightens the countryside. Wild-flower season extends from March into August, but peaks from April to June. You may encounter rain even in summer; redwoods flourish in moist climates.

Avenue of the Giants. North of Garberville a 33-mile alternative scenic route (State 254) roughly parallels U.S. 101. Winding leisurely through a cathedral-like aisle of 300-foot-high trees, it offers a closer view of these "ambassadors from another age." Staying on U.S. 101 saves half an hour, but you'll miss grand groves, public campgrounds, picnicking and swimming spots, and an interesting mill town.

The avenue's entrance is at Sylvandale; it ends about 5 miles north of Pepperwood, which is 30 miles south of Eureka. Numerous turnouts and parking areas allow for neck-craning; trails lead through tranquil glens and along the Eel River.

Scotia. Pacific Lumber Company operates the world's largest redwood mill; mill tour permits and brochures are available at its office on Main Street. (In summer, get tickets at the company museum across the street; the mill is closed the first week in July.) Hours are 7:30 to 10:30 A.M. and 12:30 to 2:30 P.M. weekdays.

For a bit of luxury, stay at the Scotia Inn (11 antique-furnished rooms); call (707) 764-5683 to reserve. The dining room is open Wednesday through Sunday evenings. For information on other area lodging and dining choices, call the Rio Del–Scotia Chamber of Commerce at (707) 764-3436.

Pick a park

Some of the best remaining coast redwoods are preserved in Redwood National Park and several state parks along U.S. 101. Parks are busy throughout the summer, offering informative naturalist programs, nature hikes, and evening campfires.

South of Eureka, scenic attractions and the highway play tag with the South Fork of the Eel River. Sprawling Humboldt Redwoods State Park is the main attraction, but there are other good spots for campers.

Standish-Hickey State Recreation Area, just north of Leggett, has plenty of camping but only one mature redwood among its dense forest. Picnicking is popular at Smithe Redwoods State Reserve, a little farther north. You can hike to a waterfall or take a footpath down to the Eel River. The Benbow Lake State Recreation Area, south of Garberville, features picnic and limited camping facilities.

For details on these parks, write to California Department of Parks and Recreation, District 1 headquarters, 3431 Fort Avenue, Eureka, CA 95501. For camping details, see page 122.

Richardson Grove State Park. You can't miss this relatively small park: the highway runs right through its 800 acres. Swimming holes, highly developed campgrounds, and 10 miles of trails make it a popular choice. Though it can be wet and chilly in winter, it's open year-round. In winter, silver and king salmon and steelhead trout attract many anglers.

Humboldt Redwoods State Park. Scattered along most of the length of the Avenue of the Giants, this park was acquired piece by piece and now consists of more than 70 memorial groves. It begins unobtrusively at the Whittemore Grove across the river from the highway; take Briceland Road at Redway.

At Burlington, in a dark copse of second-growth trees, an all-year campground adjoins the park headquarters and museum. Rangers have information on camping and picnic facilities in other parts of the park; in autumn they'll tell you where to see the best color.

Park highlights include the Founders Tree, for many years considered the world's tallest (364 feet before a broken top brought the figure down to 347); the solemn depths of the Rockefeller

...Redwood Country

Forest; the wide pebble beach of the Eel, where you can stand back and look at redwoods from top to bottom instead of being encircled and overwhelmed; and Bull Creek flats, site of the present tallest tree.

Grizzly Creek Redwoods State Park. This small, secluded area along the Van Duzen River (18 miles east of U.S. 101 on State 36) is highly prized by picnickers and campers for its climate, which is often warmer and less foggy than parks right along the coast. Its 234 acres include a virgin redwood grove, more than a mile of river front, hiking trails, and improved campsites—but no grizzlies. Summer trout fishing is fair to good; steelheading is good from mid-February to mid-April.

In & around Eureka

Lumbering and fishing made Eureka, and they're still its main industries. Located midway between San Francisco and Portland, this city of some 25,000 is the North Coast's largest, and a perfect place to break up your drive. Sniff the air: the odors come from docks along Humboldt Bay or pulp mills south of town.

A cache of historic homes, hotels, and saloons, many dating from the late 1800s, and a fine harbor are hidden behind the blur of motels, gas stations, and coffee shops that line U.S. 101.

For an accommodations guide (Carter House, Hotel Carter, and the imposing Eureka Inn are among your choices) and brochures on attractions, stop by the Eureka Chamber of Commerce (2112 Broadway; open 8:30 A.M. to 5 P.M. weekdays).

In summer, the chamber offers a 5-hour narrated bus tour of the area, including lunch and a bay cruise. The price is around $15, and reservations are a must. For more information, call (707) 442-3738.

Old Town. It was once a collection of raucous bars and bordellos along the harbor. Now Old Town (1st and 2nd streets, just off U.S. 101) is a renovated shopping center with restored buildings that house shops, restaurants, and vintage museums. Stop by the Clarke Memorial Museum at 240 E Street (open noon to 4 P.M. Tuesday through Saturday; donations) to see Indian artifacts. The free Humboldt Bay Maritime Museum at 1410 2nd Street (open daily 11 A.M. to 4 P.M.) exhibits historical marine paraphernalia.

Victorian-sighting. A brick-lined promenade with old-fashioned street lamps leads up 2nd Street to the flamboyant and much-photographed Carson Mansion, called the "queen of Victorians." Now a private men's club, the mansion looks much as it did when completed by lumber baron William Carson in 1886. The smaller house across the street was also built by Carson, as a wedding gift for his son.

Fort Humboldt State Historic Park. Constructed in the 1850s and abandoned as a military post in 1865, the partly restored fort (open daily 9 A.M. to 5 P.M.) is a half-mile off U.S. 101 on the southern edge of town; follow signs on Highland Avenue, east of U.S. 101.

A small museum gives a brief history, including the time Ulysses S. Grant spent there prior to his resignation from the army. But most of the fort is now devoted to documenting logging life. Peek into a logger's cabin, see steam engines used to haul logs, and ride on a steam train (third Saturday of the month). Donations are welcome.

Sequoia Park. A woodland oasis at Glatt and W streets in the heart of Eureka contains one of the region's best forests. Here you can walk leafy trails past ferns and streams, stop at a zoo and children's playground, or feed ducks the remains of your picnic lunch.

Humboldt Bay. Just beyond the waterfront section of downtown Eureka and almost concealed from the highway is Humboldt Bay, the largest deepwater port between Portland and San Francisco. You can explore the harbor on an old ferry (see page 124), study birdlife, and go boating, fishing, or beachcombing along great stretches of land guarding the harbor.

Samoa. Following State 255 northwest across the Samoa Bridge takes you over Woodley and Indian islands. Marshy Indian Island, part of the Humboldt Bay National Wildlife Refuge, is the northernmost egret and heron rookery on the Pacific Coast. Roosting birds look like a feathery white cloud.

A sign marks the turnoff to the Samoa Cookhouse (open 6 A.M. to 9 P.M. daily), where you dine family-style in a barnlike structure that served loggers from a nearby lumber mill from 1890 until the 1950s. A hearty breakfast or lunch costs about $5; dinner is around $10. A museum displays antique cookware that matched lumberjacks' appetites.

Arcata. From Samoa you can continue along the North Spit across Mad River Slough to Arcata, where a self-guided architectural tour takes you back to the time of Bret Harte and the heyday of gold mining. Jacoby's Storehouse, an original one-story stone building on the plaza (791 8th Street), has been enlarged to include shops and restaurants. At Humboldt State University's Natural History Museum (1315 G Street), some of the plant and animal artifacts date back 500 million years.

Azalea reserve. A few miles north of Arcata on State 200 (accessible from U.S. 101 and State 299), the 30-acre Azalea State Reserve bursts into bloom around Memorial Day. Trails lead you through masses of colorful overhanging blossoms.

Trinidad. Settled in 1850, this small fishing village 22 miles north of Eureka is one of the North Coast's oldest towns. As you enter its Main Street from U.S. 101, turn left onto Trinity Street and park by Memorial Lighthouse. The harbor, dotted with colorful boats, lies straight ahead.

At Edwards and Ewing streets, Humboldt State's marine lab aquarium (free tours; open 8 A.M. to 4 P.M. weekdays and 1 to 5 P.M. Saturdays) contains pettable local critters. Below the lab, Edwards Street leads to Trinidad State Beach, a good place for picnics or beachcombing. To your left is Trinidad Head. A pleasant 1½-mile trail leads around the dramatic promontory.

Patrick's Point State Park. A forest- and meadow-covered headland, this 625-acre park lies 6 miles north of Trinidad. Its surprisingly varied area contains a beachful of agates, trees that stand on octopuslike arms, sea stacks, and even a tiny museum. The 2-mile Rim Trail leads through the forest and along the jagged shoreline.

A valley loop. A 73-mile road loops through pastoral Mattole Valley to the sea and back into the redwoods. You can begin at the refurbished town of Ferndale, about 15 miles south of Eureka. Here you'll find some of the coast's best-preserved Victorians, from small white cottages to intricate gingerbread mansions (several are now quaint bed-and-breakfast inns; see page 72).

Stop at the Ferndale Museum (3rd and Shaw streets; small admission) to look at the memorabilia and pick up a self-guided walking tour. Two houses, known locally as "butterfat palaces" because they were built by wealthy dairy farmers, also invite touring.

For information on 28-room Fern Cottage on Centerville Road, call (707) 786-4835. Linden Hall, a 15-room mansion at Bush Street and Port Kenyan Road, is surrounded by lovely grounds; call (707) 786-4908 for details.

From Ferndale, the Mattole Road heads south over Bear Ridge to the ocean and then sneaks inland past the little hamlets of Petrolia, site of California's first oil wells, and Honeydew, one of the state's smallest towns. The latter consists of a general store, gas station, and post office—all under one roof.

Redwood National Park

A representative segment of old-growth redwoods and some outstanding coastal scenery have been protected in a 106,000-acre park 330 miles north of San Francisco. Eight miles of shoreline roads and more than 150 miles of trails afford close-ups of magnificent trees and the abundant plant and animal life they nurture.

Included within its boundaries are three long-established state parks (Prairie Creek, Del Norte Coast, and Jedediah Smith), sites for most camp-

ing; for details, see page 120. Motels are found in Orick and Crescent City, to the north. Klamath, at the mouth of the Klamath River, is known for fine salmon and steelhead fishing, and for white-water rafting (see page 125) and jet boat tours. Paul Bunyan greets visitors at the Trees of Mystery (admission fee) just beyond town.

Visitor information. A visitor information center on the highway south of Orick provides park information and handles tickets for summer shuttles to the Tall Trees Grove (the loftiest giant is 367.8 feet high). The center is open daily from 9 A.M. to 5 P.M. (to 6 P.M. in summer) except Thanksgiving, Christmas, and New Year's. For more information, call (707) 488-3461.

The main park headquarters is located in Crescent City at 1111 2nd Street; phone (707) 464-6101. Information on area attractions is also available across the street from the chamber of commerce; phone (707) 464-3174.

Prairie Creek Redwoods State Park. A favorite of many campers, Prairie Creek has more than its share of special wonders: a handsome creek, a herd of native Roosevelt elk, the wide expanse of sand at Gold Bluffs Beach (tent campsites), and scenic Fern Canyon. Hiking its more than 100 miles of trails (including one for the blind) is the best way to explore. Lady Bird Johnson Grove, reached by a short trail off Bald Hill Road, has a cluster of giant trees.

Del Norte Coast Redwoods State Park. A drive through the park lets you enjoy both rugged inland forest and fine Pacific Ocean vistas. The Damnation Creek Trail leads through dense forest to the sea, where giant redwoods grow almost to the shore. From April to July, you'll see outstanding displays of rhododendrons and azaleas.

Jedediah Smith Redwoods State Park. At the northern end of the national park (9 miles northeast of Crescent City), Jed Smith presents views of skyline ridges still tightly furred with giant redwoods. The highway runs through two of the 18 memorial groves and then out to a flat, where the most imposing trees soar.

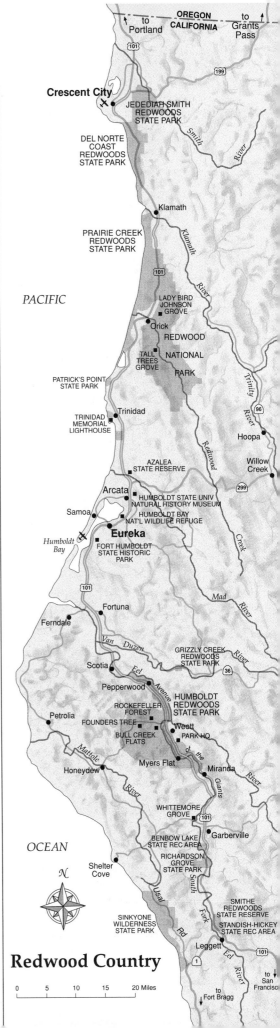

Redwood Country

Shasta-Cascade Region

Splashing streams, towering snow-covered peaks, snug valleys encircled by forested slopes, miles of deep blue waters, and some of nature's most unusual attractions make up the Shasta-Cascade region, an area stretching from the Coast Range east to Nevada and from the upper Sacramento Valley to the Oregon border.

In this vast land (about the size of Ohio) lie six national forests, eight national and state parks, the Trinity Alps, and the California Cascade range, which includes two gigantic glaciated volcanoes: the dormant 14,162-foot Mount Shasta and the still-active 10,457-foot Mount Lassen.

Though the gold rush here was never as well chronicled as the one in the Sierra Nevada, millions in ore were extracted by miners who thronged north in the 1850s.

A bonanza of recreation

This scenic northern wonderland offers plenty of open space in which to unwind and unlimited outdoor recreation to pursue, from leisurely sightseeing to adventurous mountain climbing. You can fish and raft along the Klamath River, waterski on Whiskeytown Lake, steer a houseboat around Lake Shasta and Trinity Lake, ride horseback through magnificent wilderness, sail across Eagle Lake, and camp among piney forests beside clear mountain streams.

Mountain lakes and streams offer good catches all year, making the region an angler's paradise. It's also salmon and steelhead country, boasting chinook of up to 55 pounds. Before you wet your line, check the regulations and restrictions on limits, size of hooks, types of lures, and stream closures.

Lava Beds National Monument and Lassen Volcanic National Park showcase unusual geologic formations, while Lake Shasta Caverns provide an underground look at equally impressive landscapes. Several hundred miles of the Pacific Crest National Scenic Trail (a route extending 2,600 miles from Canada to Mexico) traverse the region.

Planning your trip

This chapter covers only the most popular wilderness retreats. To reach them or other, more secluded areas in this far-flung empire, you'll need a car. Interstate 5 is the main north-south route through the northern mountains, State 299 the main east-west highway. U.S. 395 runs along the northeastern corner.

Rental cars are available at Redding, a destination of several intrastate airlines. Amtrak train stations are located at Redding and Dunsmuir (near Mount Shasta). Greyhound buses reach the largest towns.

When to visit. A popular summer vacation site, Shasta-Cascade is most active from May to October. Though Redding and Red Bluff can be sweltering in midsummer, the region's plentiful lakes provide cooling retreats. And in the nearby high country, you'll sleep under a blanket.

An autumn drive through the mountains offers a spectacular display of color. This season is also a good time to greet the wintering clan of bald eagles arriving at Tule Lake.

Many visitor attractions close in winter and heavy snowfall limits backroad driving, but Shasta and Lassen parks host skiers, snowshoers, and dogsled racers.

Where to stay. Redding, the area's largest city (population 65,000), offers the widest choice of lodging. The biggest motor lodges line Interstate 5. Other accommodations can be found in town along major highways.

A wealth of public and private campgrounds welcomes tourists throughout the region. Particularly popular is the Whiskeytown-Shasta-Trinity National Recreation Area, a 243,000-acre vacationland northwest of Redding.

Majestic Mount Shasta (14,162 feet) dominates the surrounding landscape for more than 100 miles. This view is from Grass Lake, off U.S. 97 to the north.

Contacts

These agencies offer information on attractions and accommodations. See additional contacts throughout this chapter.

Shasta-Cascade Wonderland Association
1250 Parkview Ave.
Redding, CA 96001
(916) 243-2643 *(for entire region)*

Redding Convention & Visitor Bureau
777 Auditorium Dr.
Redding, CA 96001
(800) 874-7562

Lassen Volcanic National Park
Box 100
Mineral, CA 96063
(916) 595-4444

Redding Area

Located at the junction of Interstate 5 and State 299, 4 hours from San Francisco and 3 hours from Sacramento, Redding makes a good base from which to explore the surrounding region. Majestic Mount Shasta looms to the north, and many other natural and man-made attractions lie within a 70-mile radius.

River walk. Taking full advantage of its picturesque setting on the Sacramento River, the city has developed a 5-mile nature walk along its banks. The starting point is from the Diestlehorst Bridge at Benton Drive.

Town museums. Caldwell Park along the river contains two museums. The Carter House Science Museum (small fee), open 10 A.M. to 4 P.M. Tuesday through Sunday, has natural history displays and a small collection of live animals.

A free city museum exhibits artwork, historical mementos, and Native American artifacts. From June through August, it's open Tuesday through Sunday, 10 A.M. to 5 P.M. The rest of the year, it's open Tuesday through Sunday afternoons and all day Saturday (closed major holidays).

Red Bluff

Named for the area's colored sand-and-gravel cliffs, this small city (population 13,000) 30 miles south of Redding is noted for its Victorians—and for the adobe ranchhouse of California's only president.

William B. Ide Adobe. Ide, a carpenter from Massachusetts, led a small band of settlers against the Mexican authorities in the so-called Bear Flag Revolt of 1846. He was elected president of the short-lived California Republic.

His restored ranch house and outbuildings are now part of a 4-acre state park on Adobe Road, east of Interstate 5. Picnic facilities and natural valley oaks make this park on the west bank of the Sacramento River a shady oasis. It's open daily from 8 A.M. to 5 P.M.

Kelly-Griggs House Museum. To see a classic resentative of the city's fine collection of Victorians, tour the two-story Kelly-Griggs house (311 Washington Street). Though there's no charge to visit the well-furnished mansion, donations are encouraged. Hours are 2 to 4 P.M. Thursday through Sunday (to 5 P.M. in summer).

Salmon viewing. At Diversion Dam south of State 36, underwater cameras record the action of salmon climbing fish ladders on their way upstream to spawn. The best viewing takes place between September and April. The area (open daily from 8 A.M. to 8 P.M.) offers picnicking, camping (fee), and boat-launching facilities.

Shasta Lake

Nine miles north of Redding soars Shasta Dam, an enormous structure holding back the bright blue waters of Shasta Lake, the state's largest man-made lake and part of a vast three-lake national recreation area. With a spillway three times the height of Niagara Falls, the 602-foot-high dam is a popular visitor attraction. Open daily, the visitor center offers historical and geological exhibits and a film on the dam workings. There are no tours of the dam itself.

Activities. Long popular for its houseboating, waterskiing, swimming, and fishing, the four-pronged lake is big enough (30,000 surface acres, with 365 miles of shoreline) to offer plenty of secluded anchorage for its houseboat armada. The Shasta-Cascade Wonderland Association (address on page 82) has boat rental and resort information.

The calmer waters of the Pit River arm and Jones Valley area are best for skiing. A waterskiing show takes place on summer evenings near Bridge Bay.

Of the 22 species of fish found here, bass, catfish, and crappie are the most prevalent in summer. Trout go deep when the water warms, but you can try for them in front of the dam or in the cold waters farther up the McCloud

River. Bass fishing is at its best on the Pit River.

Accommodations. Motels line Interstate 5 at Bridge Bay (south side of the lake) and Lakehead (north end). You can camp anywhere on shore with a fire permit, or in one of 1,200 Forest Service campsites, the most private and scenic of which are accessible only by boat. Your best chance of a quiet camp is on the McCloud, Pit, or Squaw arms.

Lake Shasta Caverns. The deep, complex limestone caves overlooking the McCloud River arm of Shasta Lake are fun to explore; just getting there is an adventure. You travel by boat and then transfer to a bus for the spectacular 800-foot ascent to the cavern entrance, a deceptively normal-looking door into the mountainside.

The 2-hour tour (including boat and bus ride) takes you through well-lighted tunnels and up and down stairs to see geologic formations possibly a million years old. Bring a sweater, as temperatures average 58°.

The caverns are open daily except Thanksgiving and Christmas. From April through October tours take place on the hour from 9 A.M. to 4 P.M.; service is reduced to three daily trips (10 A.M., noon, and 2 P.M.) the rest of the year.

To reach the caves, take the O'Brien–Lake Shasta Caverns exit off Interstate 5 about 15 miles north of Redding. Follow the signs for about 2 miles to the visitor center. If you're boating, you can dock at the landing on the east side of the McCloud arm. Admission is $12 adults, $6 ages 4 to 12; call (916) 238-2341 for specifics.

Whiskeytown Lake area

The other units that make up the Whiskeytown-Shasta-Trinity National Recreation Area lie off State 299 west of Redding. For detailed information on this recreation area, write to the Shasta-Cascade Wonderland Association or the Redding Convention & Visitors Bureau (addresses on page 82).

Shasta State Historic Park. Shasta, 6 miles west of Redding on State 299, is a mere ghost of its former lusty self. On a self-guided tour (modest park admission), you'll see the courthouse and jail (now a museum) and a refurbished general store. The museum is open daily March through October (except major holidays), closed Tuesday and Wednesday the rest of the year.

Whiskeytown Lake. Some of Northern California's most beautiful scenery surrounds this reservoir 8 miles west of Redding. A number of hiking and riding trails climb high enough to afford sweeping views of the lake's wooded islands. The National Park Service visitor center is on the east side of the lake adjacent to State 299.

The 36-mile-long cove-indented shoreline has plenty of room for waterskiing, scuba diving, swimming, and boating—it offers some of the region's top sailing waters. Fishing is good for trout, kokanee, bass, and bluegill, especially in autumn and early spring.

Two marinas—Oak Bottom and Brandy Creek—provide services; boats launch from the Whiskey Creek picnic area north of the highway. Other picnic and camping areas (some close to the beach) are marked; for more information, see page 120. No fires are allowed on the beach.

Trinity Lake. Though Clair Engle Lake is its official name, Trinity County residents still call this 16,500-surface-acre impoundage Trinity. Anglers come for good trout and smallmouth bass trophy fishing. An irregular shoreline creates many secluded hideaways for small boats and houseboats.

You can launch your own boat from five ramps or rent fishing boats or houseboats from four marinas. Motels and campgrounds (some with sandy swimming beaches) stretch along the Stuart Fork Arm.

Shasta-Cascade Region

Rainbows often form in the mist at the foot of Burney Falls, once described by Theodore Roosevelt as "the eighth wonder of the world." Downstream lies Lake Britton, a popular water sports site.

Into the Wilderness

The Shasta-Cascade Region contains many of the state's wilderness areas. These uniquely scenic and undeveloped spots are roadless, open only to hikers, horseback riders, packers, and campers. Fishing and hunting are permitted in many locations. We sample only a few. For specific area maps ($2 each), contact the Office of Information, U.S. Forest Service, 630 Sansome Street, Room 529A, San Francisco, CA 94111; phone (415) 705-2874. Several areas require a free entry permit; campers need a free fire permit.

Few roads lead into the heart of the northern mountains where three large ranges—Klamath-Scott (including the Trinity, Salmon, and Marble mountains), Cascades, and Warner—contain beckoning wilderness areas. Here, trails rise steeply to high peaks; the timberline is low (7,000 feet), so you quickly reach alpine terrain.

It's easy to sample the fringes by car and even to take day hikes into some regions. Isolated towns on the perimeter provide overnight lodging, and some remote mountain resorts offer lodging, meals, and pack trips.

Trinity Alps

Rugged and sawtoothed, the Trinity Alps are camouflaged by lower mountains. You scarcely notice them from Interstate 5, and even their easy approach from State 299 has never brought them heavy traffic.

You need a wilderness permit even for day hikes. Call the Forest Service in Redding, (916) 246-5222, for maps and permits. Before heading out, ask about trail conditions at ranger stations in Weaverville, Big Bar, or Coffee Creek.

Three roads form a circle around the Trinity Alps, linking old gold towns. The main road, State 299, parallels the Trinity Trail, famous as an Indian path, pioneer trail, and gold rush road; State 3, from Weaverville to Callahan and Yreka, was part of the old California-Oregon Wagon Road; and the third links Salmon River settlements on the mountains' west and north slopes.

Weaverville. Gateway to the Trinity Alps and Trinity County seat, this former boomtown at the junction of State 3 and State 299 came to life in the 1850s, when gold brought a flood of miners—including some 2,500 Chinese immigrants.

Brick facades and exterior spiral stairways remain almost unchanged on Main Street. The Weaverville Drug Store (founded in 1854) displays early remedies and potions, and the free J. J. "Jake" Memorial Museum (closed from December to April) contains mementos of the town's gold roots, including a stamp mill.

At Joss House State Historic Park (Oregon and Main streets) the Chinese left a lovely legacy in the form of an 1874 temple. Tours are offered from 10 A.M. to 5 P.M. The temple is closed Tuesday and Wednesday.

Into Scott Valley. From Weaverville, State 3 roams along the edge of Trinity Lake, over a mountain pass into peaceful Scott Valley, and north to meet Interstate 5. Several bed-and-breakfast inns open sporadically in the valley, but your best lodging bets are at Weaverville and Yreka.

The Scott Museum (open most of the year) at Trinity Center gives you an idea of how it was to live in the early mining days. And block-long Callahan, a former trading center for miners and ranchers, still has century-old buildings lining its boardwalks.

Tiny Etna, 13 miles to the north, appears almost a metropolis by contrast. The Native Daughters of the Golden West Museum is usually open summer afternoons, and you shouldn't miss the drugstore (sodas, antiques, and gifts).

Noted for its fine museum of Indian crafts (open Memorial Day to October 1), Fort Jones, 12 miles up the road, was the site of an old army outpost.

Wild West lawlessness, Chinese tong wars, and an 1871 fire were not enough to destroy Yreka. Though the area is booming, some fine old restored 1850-era survivors can be found along Miner Street. The Siskiyou County Court-house exhibits nugget and placer gold, and a free history museum (910 S. Main Street) contains other exhibits.

Marble Mountains

A loop road (State 96 on the west and north and good, partly gravel roads to the east and south) encircles the 280,000-acre Marble Mountains. The best way to approach them from Interstate 5 is to turn west onto State 96 some 10 miles north of Yreka. From Hamburg (35 miles to the west) a winding road follows the Scott River to Fort Jones and Etna and continues down the North Fork of the Salmon River to the tiny towns of Sawyers Bar, Forks of Salmon, and Somes Bar, all wilderness entry points.

The Marble Mountains are easier to get around in than the Trinity Alps to the south. The Sky High Lakes are almost in the center of the wilderness. From here, trails radiate in all directions.

Cascades

Extending all the way from British Columbia through Washington and Oregon, the Cascade Range ends at Lassen Volcanic National Park. Two wilderness areas around Lassen are popular with backpackers and anglers.

Thousand Lakes Wilderness. About 12 miles north of Lassen Park, four major trails lead into the heart of the wilderness. All are demanding, but the scenery and number of lakes in the valley compensate for the rigors of the hike. Cyprus Camp Trail, the easiest route, leads to large Lake Eiler. You can drive to the area on several unimproved roads from State 89; check with the ranger at Hat Creek. Bunchgrass Campground lies to the south.

Caribou Peak Wilderness. A series of lakes with good trout fishing and easy access from Silver Lake in Lassen County make Caribou popular. To reach the lake, take County A21 eastward 11 miles from State 44. Several campgrounds lie nearby.

Whether it's for a get-away-from-it-all vacation or a family reunion, consider a guest ranch for a relaxing change of pace in a friendly western setting. You can even select your favorite area of Northern California, as ranches are sprinkled throughout the northern mountains, the Sierra Nevada, the coastal valleys, and the high northeastern desert.

While most ranches cater specifically to guests, a few are working ranches with guest activities. We also include two upscale resorts with stables.

Typically, ranches include lodging, all meals, and activities in the daily price; horses may be extra. Accommodations vary from rustic tent cabins to deluxe suites, and daily rates range accordingly: from $300 a week to $300 a day.

Canyon Ranch Resort, P.O. Box 6, Sierraville, CA 96126; (916) 944-3340. Fishing (both creek and lake), hunting, and hiking are the lures of this year-round resort in Sierra Valley. It also boasts a swimming pool, hot tub, and stocked trout pond. Riding is available nearby. Meals are extra.

Coffee Creek Guest Ranch, Star HC 2, Box 4940, Trinity Center, CA 96091; (916) 266-3343. Located in the Trinity Alps northwest of Redding, this rustic and friendly resort offers horseback riding (extra charge), fishing, canoeing, riflery and trap shooting, square dancing, and special children's programs.

Drakesbad Guest Ranch, Warner Valley, Chester, CA 96020 (June through September) or California Guest Services, 2150 N. Main St., Suite 7, Red Bluff, CA 96080 (off-season); (916) 529-1512. The only lodging in Lassen Volcanic National Park, this comfortable (and all-too-popular) resort boasts a spring-heated pool, nearby fishing, and plenty of hiking and riding (extra fee).

Flying "AA" Ranch, Ruth Star Rte., Box 700, Bridgeville, CA 95526; (707) 574-6227. Guests at this site east of Fortuna stay in motel rooms, tent cabins, or mobile homes. On hand are a swimming pool, tennis, volleyball, horseshoe courts, and a tots' playground. Meals and horses are additional.

Greenhorn Creek Guest Ranch, P.O. Box 7010, Spring Garden, CA 95971; (916) 283-0930, (800) 33-HOWDY. Daily maid service in the cabins and a two-story lodge pamper guests on this 840-acre ranch east of Quincy. Among the activities are horseback riding, fishing, and evening singalongs.

JH Guest Ranch, 8525 Homestead Ln., Etna, CA 96027; (916) 467-3468. At this Christian retreat in Scott Valley, take your choice of white-water rafting (extra), mountain climbing, backpacking trips, horseback riding (extra), swimming, or fishing. A western rodeo tops your week.

Josephine Creek Lodge, Star Rte. 2, Box 5703, Trinity Center, CA 96091; (408) 353-1663. This adult hideaway lies deep in the Trinity Alps, 30 miles north of Coffee Creek. Guests are tucked away in cabins; meals are provided in the main lodge. Activities include fishing and hiking.

Spanish Springs Guest Ranch, P.O. Box 70, Ravendale, CA 96123 or Information Center, 1102 2nd St., San Rafael, CA 94901; (800) 272-8282 (in California), (800) 228-0279 (out of state). This 70,000-acre working cattle ranch in Lassen County is open year-round. Guests are housed at the main ranch or in other refurbished historic homesteads and participate in cattle drives, brandings, wild horse tours, pack rides, and trail rides. Winter fun includes sleigh rides, sledding, cross-country skiing, and ice skating. The ranch is not set up for children.

Stonepine, 150 E. Carmel Valley Rd., Carmel Valley, CA 93924; (408) 659-2245. Built as a getaway by the Crocker family, this small, elegant resort bears little resemblance to a ranch, but its stables are one of its main attractions. Others are a swimming pool and tennis courts. You'll feel like you're visiting a private mansion.

Timberhill Ranch, 35755 Hauser Bridge Rd., Cazadero, CA 95421; (707) 847-3458. Though the exterior of this inn and working ranch may look rustic, the interiors are beautifully decorated and the meals are gourmet, not pork and beans. Tennis, swimming, horseback riding, and picnic lunches at the beach are just some of its features. Leave the children at home for this stay.

Trinity Alps Resort, Star Rte., Box 490, Lewiston, CA 96052; (916) 286-2205. This large, family-oriented resort (restaurant and lounge) on Trinity Lake, with more than 40 cabins along the Stuart Fork River, is open summers through September. The facility offers swimming, fishing, horseback riding (extra), and tennis, volleyball, and badminton courts.

Trinity Mountain Meadow Ranch, Star Rte. 2, Box 5700, Trinity Center, CA 96091; call (408) 353-1663 for information. Despite its wild setting 28 miles north of Trinity Lake, this well-appointed, comfortable ranch has a heated pool and volleyball and badminton courts. Hiking trails lead into the Trinity Alps for fishing; adults can rent mountain bikes (no horses).

Shasta Country

The most massive cone volcano in the Cascade chain, Mount Shasta juts up abruptly from the landscape just north of Redding, dominating the region 100 miles around it. Eight glaciers mantle the 14,162-foot peak and Shastina, the 12,330-foot cone that rises from its western flank.

Here climbers tackle mountain slopes, wilderness hikers and campers head for the 37,000-acre wild area around the peak or the 7,300-acre Castle Crags Wilderness (abutting the state park) to the south, and anglers have a choice of good rivers and lakes. In winter, Mount Shasta Ski Park (at the 5,500-foot level) hosts downhill skiers (see page 124). The Forest Service also offers Nordic skiing and snowmobiling at areas around Mount Shasta.

The big mountain is off Interstate 5 about 5 hours from San Francisco. From the freeway, you can head east to more parks, fishing streams, and small towns. The area is sparsely populated—its towns slow paced and its high lakes and streams uncrowded—even in midsummer.

Hiking. Each year 7,000 hikers attempt Shasta's summit. If you're determined to try, contact the Forest Service in Mt. Shasta at 204 West Alma Street—(916) 926-4511—for information.

Day hikes on Shasta's shoulders are an easier option. Carry plenty of liquids and dress in layers (cold winds can pick up). A 2-mile trail from Bunny Flat, on the southwest slope at a cool 6,800 feet, to Avalanche Gulch rewards hikers with fine valley views. The trailhead is 11 miles east of the city of Mt. Shasta, on the Everitt Memorial Highway.

Lodging. Bustling Mt. Shasta is a good base for exploring the mountain and nearby Castle Crags State Park. It has over a dozen hotels and inns and twice that many restaurants. Because the mountain is considered sacred by many people, a dozen or more religious sects flourish around town.

Historic Dunsmuir, a few miles south, faded when railroad jobs dwindled, but a number of motels and a half-dozen restaurants make it a convenient stop. Railroad Park Resort, just off the freeway, is a train buff's dream. You can lodge in a caboose, dine in a railroad car, and admire the 1927 Willamette Shay engine and other rolling stock. Camping and RV facilities are nearby.

Castle Crags

A landmark off Interstate 5 near Dunsmuir, the gray granite outcroppings of Castle Crags are carved into snaggle teeth. Easy access makes this state park a popular place to camp (no hookups) from about the first of April to the end of October.

Fishing, swimming, inner tubing, and picnicking take place along the Sacramento River, a 2-mile stretch of which meanders through the park. If you're in shape, try the short (2½ miles), steep Crags Trail up to the rocks. The 8,544-foot formations perch in the wilderness area beyond.

Lake Siskiyou

This 430-acre lake on the Sacramento River was constructed solely for recreation. Facilities include 50 picnic areas, 299 campsites (with hookups), and a broad, sandy beach. Besides swimming, wind surfing, and boating (from a launch ramp and marina), the lake offers year-round fishing for brown and rainbow trout and bass. From Interstate 5, the lake is 4 miles southwest of Mt. Shasta town, off Barr Road.

Around McCloud

Queen of the lumber mill days, gaslit McCloud (10 miles east of Interstate 5 on State 89) was a company town founded in 1827. The mill workers were paid in scrip, spent it at the company store, and lived in houses made of the pine they had milled. Today, the 1890s Mercantile Building on Main Street contains a hardware store and a cafe with great milkshakes.

The Dance Country Restaurant, at 424 Main, serves up lumberjack meals. Up the hill, the beautifully restored 1907 McCloud Guest House is now a small bed-and-breakfast inn and restaurant.

South of town lies the Nature Conservancy–protected McCloud River Preserve, a 6-mile corridor of prime wild trout stream. Take Squaw Valley Road 9 miles to Lake McCloud, follow signs on a dirt road 9 miles to Ah-Di-Na camp, and then go 1 mile to the road's end. From there, it's a half-mile hike to the preserve cabin. (Check on road conditions first with the Forest Service at (916) 964-2184.)

McArthur-Burney Falls

One of the state's most scenic waterfalls is the chief attraction of this park near the junction of State 299 and State 89. A short nature trail brings you to the base of the misty 129-foot falls.

The 565-acre state park (open year-round) includes 6 miles of hiking trails and a portion of Lake Britton, a popular 9-mile-long reservoir. A grocery store and snack bar are open from mid-April to mid-October. The town of Burney offers a few motels and restaurants, groceries, and fly-fishing shops.

Two top streams

Several streams on Shasta's east side are renowned for their trout. Angling is at its best in September—cooler weather and fewer mosquitoes. Double-check fish and game regulations; they can vary on the same stream.

The icy, spring-fed waters of Hat Creek and Fall River, two meadow streams full of wily rainbow and brown trout, present a challenge even to experienced anglers. One good access point on Hat Creek is a PG&E day-use area off State 299, some 9 miles northeast of Burney. You can only get to Fall River from Cal Trout's Island Bridge, off Glenburn Road north of Fall River Mills (canoes or cartop boats only; no gas engines), and Fall River/Glenburn access (limited to cartop boats).

Lassen Country

Until May 30, 1914, Mount Lassen was simply a landmark for early emigrant parties on their way across the mountains into the Sacramento Valley. Then began the year-long eruptions of smoke, stones, steam, gases, and ashes that culminated in the spectacular events of May 19, 1915.

On that day a red, glowing bulge of lava spilled over the sides of the crater, melting the snow on the mountain's northeastern flank and sending 20-ton boulders and devastating floods of warm mud 18 miles down into the valleys of Lost and Hat creeks.

Three days later, Lassen literally blew its top, blasting hot gases and ash that scythed down forests and sent up a mushroom cloud darkening skies as far east as central Nevada. Though the mountain is quiet today, visitors to Lassen Volcanic National Park see striking reminders of its volcanic activity, such as bubbling mud pots and hissing fumaroles. Even place names ring with geologic drama: Devils Kitchen, the Devastated Area, Bumpass Hell. You'll find six lakes to fish (non–power boats are allowed on the largest) and 150 miles of backcountry trails to hike, including a 17-mile segment of the Pacific Crest National Scenic Trail.

As the state's national parks go, 106,000-acre Lassen is not overcrowded, seeing about 500,000 annual visitors (compared to Yosemite's nearly 3½ million). Even on a summer weekend you should be able to find a campsite, and if you visit in autumn you may get downright lonesome.

Getting to the park. Lassen is about 180 miles north of Sacramento. Most people approach it from Redding via State 44, or from Red Bluff on State 36. The park headquarters is in Mineral, 40 miles east of Red Bluff; its hours are 8 A.M. to 4:30 P.M. daily in summer, weekdays the rest of the year. You can get information there or at the park's entrances on State 89.

Camping. Seven campgrounds dot the park (see page 120); only Juniper Lake is free. All are filled on a first-come basis, and those at Summit and Manzanita lakes are the most popular. You'll need a wilderness permit (free at any ranger station) for backcountry camping.

Accommodations. The sole lodging in Lassen Park is rustic, comfortable, hard-to-get-into Drakesbad Guest Ranch in Warner Valley (see page 88). Outside the park, you'll find a number of unpretentious resorts along State 36 between Mineral and Chester and a smaller number along State 89 to the north. For a listing of all area accommodations, request a copy of the Lassen Park Guide from the park (address on page 82).

A park drive

A good introduction to Lassen, State 89 ribbons for 30 miles among many of the park's most interesting features. It crosses a shoulder of the volcano at 8,512 feet. Pick up a Road Guide (small charge) at one of the entrance stations. After the first snowstorm, the road is closed until late spring, except for the section leading to the park's ski area (see page 124).

Bumpass Hell. Biggest and showiest of the thermal areas, Bumpass Hell is 6 miles north of the southern entrance. From the parking lot, a 1½-mile trail leads to the rotten-egg wonderland of boiling sulfur springs, hot mud pools, and other mineralized landscape phenomena.

Lassen Peak Trail. Almost 8 miles from the entrance you'll find the trailhead to the top of the mountain. The hike is not difficult; it takes about 2 hours to ascend the 2,000 feet from the highway. A hat, sunscreen, and a windbreaker might come in handy.

If your summit arrival coincides with a ranger talk, you'll get an introduction to volcanoes; check information stations for talk schedules. Otherwise, your reward is a good view of Mount Shasta, the Coast Range north to the Trinity Alps, and the distant Sierra Nevada.

Devastated Area. About 3 miles northwest of Summit Lake, you'll see evidence of the swath of destruction carved by Lassen's eruptions.

Chaos Crags. The splintered rocks off to the west beyond the Devastated Area are plug volcanoes, similar to Lassen but only 1,000 to 1,200 years old. The massive boulder field in front was probably the result of an avalanche of rock that sped across the slope at speeds of up to 100 miles per hour.

Lassen's eastern side

Spectacular as State 89 is, it reveals only a small portion of the park. If you have the time, good scenery is also to be found elsewhere.

Butte Lake. The largest of Lassen's cinder cones rises near Butte Lake (stocked with rainbow trout) in the park's northeastern corner. To get there from the park, follow State 44 east 24 miles to Forest Road 32N21; then follow signs 6½ miles to Butte Lake Campground.

A trail ascends the 700-foot cone, which last erupted in 1851. The trek is arduous; you sink back one step for every two you take. But the summit view is eerily beautiful.

Warner Valley. Well known for its Drakesbad Guest Ranch, this glacier-scalloped valley is also a lovely place to camp. A 2⅓-mile trail to Boiling Springs Lake starts at the campground below, crosses Hot Springs Creek, and runs through white firs and lodgepole pines to the lake. A 2-mile trail leads to the bubbling mud pots at Devils Kitchen.

To get there from Chester, on State 36, take Feather River Drive north and follow the signs for 17 miles.

Juniper Lake. Largest and deepest of Lassen's lakes, Juniper is tucked into the park's southeastern corner. A good 2-mile trail takes you up to 8,048-foot Mount Harkness, a shield volcano with views of Lassen and Chaos Crags. From Chester, take Feather River Drive about 13 miles north to the campground.

A wooden trail snaking through Bumpass Hell, largest and showiest of Lassen Volcanic National Park's thermal areas, gives visitors a good look at boiling springs and gurgling pools.

Lassen's backcountry. Fully three-quarters of the park is wilderness, inviting day hikers and backpackers. One favorite midsummer hike starts at Summit Lake Campground (on State 89, midway through the park) and pokes almost 2 miles east to Echo Lake, then an additional 2 miles to Upper and Lower Twin Lakes.

Around the park

Two large lakes and a collection of smaller waters lie within close range of Lassen. Popular with swimmers, water-skiers, boaters, and anglers, Almanor and Eagle are just a few miles from the park; Lakes Basin Recreational Area is almost on the border of Plumas and Sierra counties. Hikers enjoy the Bizz Johnson Trail, a 30-mile entrée to the country between Westwood and Susanville; access is from State 36.

Lake Almanor. In Plumas County, 80 miles east of Red Bluff on State 36, 52 square miles of azure water mirror snow-capped Mount Lassen. The forest-rimmed lake, created by a dam on the Feather River, is also easily reached from U.S. 395 and State 70. Small resorts along the shore offer boat rentals, docking, and launching areas.

Fishing is excellent for trophy rainbow and brown trout, kokanee salmon, bass, catfish, and perch. Gould Swamp is the "hot spot" in spring; summer night fishing near the shore is productive. Other recreational choices include a nine-hole golf course, sailboat races, hunting, and rock collecting. Several cross-country ski areas operate in winter.

Eagle Lake. This Lassen County lake, one of the state's largest, is also one of its cleanest and least crowded. Here are plenty of spacious, tree-sheltered campgrounds and 27,000 acres of clear blue water for excellent sailing. At its southern end, Gallatin Beach has a store, marina, boat rentals, ramp, sandy beach, and shady picnic area.

The lake serves as a feeding ground for a rare breeding colony of osprey. Fishing is good for the large Eagle trophy trout, a natural hybrid that is the only game fish adapted to the unusually alkaline water. The limit is three, and 7-pound catches are possible.

To get to the lake from Lassen, head east on either State 44 or State 36; the highways join west of Susanville, the closest town. County A1 reaches Gallatin Beach and the campgrounds; State 139 runs along the eastern shore.

Lakes Basin Recreational Area. About halfway between Lassen Park and Lake Tahoe, a collection of small lakes is located conveniently close to State 89. Grassy Lake (closest to the highway) is often overfished; nearby Big Bear and Little Bear lakes hold rainbow trout, and Cub and Silver lakes harbor brook trout. At Long Lake, the largest of the group, you can rent boats.

Distances between lakes are short; you can hike, fish, and return to your car the same day. There's trailside camping at Silver Lake, an easy walk to less fished lakes. To get to the lakes from State 89, turn off at Graeagle (a golfer's getaway) and follow Gold Lake Road south.

Wildlife Watching

Some of the largest concentrations of wildlife in North America are in Northern California, several just a day trip from a major urban area. Animals tend to be most active early and late in the day. Bring warm clothes and binoculars. Sometimes it's best to stay in your vehicle; it may act as a blind.

Bald eagles. Up to 800 bald eagles come to the Klamath Basin refuges near the Oregon border each year. The visitor center at Tule Lake National Wildlife Refuge (see facing page) issues self-guided tour maps and information.

Elephant seals. The only mainland rookery of these huge, lumbering pinnipeds (bulls weigh up to 7,700 pounds) is at Año Nuevo State Reserve off State 1, 55 miles south of San Francisco. Reservations are required to join 2½-hour, 3-mile guided walks over the dunes daily from December through March; call MISTIX at (800) 444-7275. There's a small fee to visit.

Pronghorn antelopes. Pronghorns are second only to cheetahs in speed, having been clocked at 61 miles per hour. Fortunately for onlookers, they're curious, so don't bother trying to hide. For best viewing, follow U.S. 395 south from Susanville to Honey Lake or north to Alturas.

Sandhill cranes. The Merced National Wildlife Refuge in the Central Valley hosts some 12,000 of these stately, shy, and skittish creatures each winter. Drive 8 miles south of Merced on State 59 and 6 miles west on Sandy Mush Road.

Snow geese. You'll probably hear these vociferous white waterfowl before you see them. The Sacramento National Wildlife Refuge gets up to 300,000 (peak population in January). From Interstate 5, take the Norman Road exit (south of Willows) and follow the signs.

Tule elk. A good herd of these small elk is found in the San Luis Wildlife Refuge. Leave Interstate 5 at Los Banos and head north on State 165. In August and September, bulls round up a harem and defy challengers.

The Northeastern Corner

Centuries ago, flaming volcanoes in northeastern California spread rivers of liquid rock over the land below. On cooling, they formed one of the state's most fascinating landscapes—a rugged terrain of yawning chasms, cinder cones, and craters. Its official name is Lava Beds National Monument.

Adjoining the monument to the north are Tule Lake and Lower Klamath national wildlife refuges, havens for millions of migratory birds. Some 200 species have been sighted there, among them the largest collection of bald eagles in the continental United States. They're usually in residence between November and March.

If the Warner Mountains were near a large city, they would be famed for their scenery and aswarm with visitors. But because they are in the state's lightly traveled northeastern corner, they still promise adventures and discoveries.

Wildlife refuges

The Tule Lake and Lower Klamath wildlife refuges along the California-Oregon border make this area a stop-off for the largest concentration of waterfowl on the North American continent. Some 2 million birds drop by the Tule Lake wetlands each year.

Bird-watching and photography are two reasons for a visit; seasonal hunting is also permitted in some areas. Best viewing is in spring and autumn; peak numbers of waterfowl arrive in early November.

For a map, stop by the visitor center on Hill Road, west of Tulelake. The best route to the refuges from Interstate 5 is via State 97 north from Weed to 161 (State Line Road), along the top of the Lower Klamath Lake.

Lava Beds

"Nobody will ever want these rocks. Give me a home here," requested Modoc Indian Chief Captain Jack. Though he was wrong (the area was given monument status in the 1800s), he and his renegade band successfully defended their stronghold against federal and volunteer troops for 5 months in 1872 and 1873. Plaques document major battlegrounds and hideouts of the Modoc War.

Just off State 139, almost at the Oregon border, the 72 square mile national monument contains 1,500-year-old lava flows, high cinder buttes, pictographs and petroglyphs, and what may be the world's most outstanding exhibit of lava tubes. The largest group is on Cave Loop Road near park headquarters in the southeastern section. Mushpot Cave, an extension of the visitor center, is the only lighted lava tube. Check at the center about others; rangers lead walks and lend flashlights for exploration. Rattlesnakes are active in warm weather.

A 40-unit campground (no hookups) adjoins the southeastern entrance. Water is available in summer; check with the visitor center the rest of the year. Closest rooms, food, and gasoline are in Tulelake, the horseradish capital, 30 miles to the east.

The most direct route is to take State 299 east toward Canby and go north 26 miles on State 139. Coming from the Tule Lake National Wildlife Refuge, go south on State 139 for 4 miles to Great Northern Road and follow the signs to the entrance near Tulelake.

Medicine Lake

Medicine Lake is an easy detour from Lava Beds National Monument. You follow a paved road around Glass Mountain, a 7,622-foot pile of black obsidian, the rock once prized by Indians for tools and weapon points. For directions and road conditions, call the monument at (916) 667-2282.

To get to the lake from Tulelake, head south on State 139 and follow the signs west on County 97. This remote lake is big (600 acres), high (6,700 feet), starkly beautiful, and so clear that you can usually see 30 feet down.

You're likely to have the beach on the southeastern shore practically to yourself, your pick of campsites at the three Forest Service campgrounds, and plenty of elbow room when swimming or angling for trout.

Warner Mountains

The topography of the Warner Mountains may bring to mind parts of the Rockies, with their abrupt rocky summit ridges and long western slopes covered in a patchwork of pine, aspen, fir, juniper, sage, and grasses. You won't find resorts or lodges in this high country, but you can take day trips or arrange for packers from Alturas, the closest town, at the junction of State 299 and U.S. 395.

Along the town's Main Street you'll find a free Modoc County Museum (Indian and pioneer relics; open daily May to November) and the refurbished, last-century Niles Hotel and Saloon. The Brass Rail on U.S. 395 is a good bet for inexpensive family-style Basque dinners.

Getting there. State 299, the only paved road across the Warners, descends into Surprise Valley, a ranching area north of Cedarville. A gravel road across Fandango Pass to the north lets you make a loop trip back to U.S. 395.

Cedarville's most historic building is the Bonner Trading Post, built in 1865 for immigrants and settlers. Fort Bidwell, at the valley's northern tip (bed-and-breakfast inn, little theater), was an army outpost from 1866 to 1892 and a school for Paiute Indians until 1930.

South Warner Wilderness. The highest part of the mountains is a 70,000-acre wild area where the only signs of civilization are grazing sheep and cattle. For information, contact the Forest Service in Alturas (441 North Main Street) or phone (916) 233-5811.

The 24-mile Summit Trail hugs the top of the range and skirts the three highest peaks: Squaw, Warner, and Eagle, all climbworthy. Side trails lead to fine trout fishing in Pine, Mill, and East creeks and South Emerson and Patterson lakes.

Sierra Nevada

*T*he great naturalist John Muir described it as a "range of light": the Sierra Nevada, largest single mountain range in the country. Rising gradually from the floor of California's Central Valley, these snowcapped mountains ascend to jagged crests more than 14,000 feet high before plunging almost vertically to the east. They stretch along nearly two-thirds of the state's eastern border, encompassing mile after mile of alpine lakes, thundering waterfalls, and towering forests.

It's the wealth of outdoor recreation found in these lofty elevations that most attracts visitors. Hiking trails climb mountain slopes, cross lush meadows, and drop into river-carved canyons. Anglers try their luck in crystalline lakes and streams, and stunningly blue Lake Tahoe provides miles of boating and waterskiing opportunities. In winter, skiers flock to the Sierra's famous slopes.

Dramatic Yosemite Valley, sculpted by glaciers, attracts visitors with awe-inspiring scenery year-round, but the national park is at its most dramatic in spring. Then waterfalls cascade over the valley walls to splash on rocks more than 1,000 feet below, creating some of the Sierra's most spectacular vistas.

A golden era

Snuggled into the Sierra foothills between Tahoe and Yosemite lie remnants of gold rush days—historic towns and rushing streams where visitors still pan for "color." Some of the old mines have

"Grandest of all the special temples of nature" was John Muir's accolade to Yosemite National Park. From El Capitan's dome in the background, Yosemite Valley's Merced River would resemble a silver thread.

been reopened, but most of the region's wealth today comes from the antique stores, gift shops, restaurants, and inns that crowd old towns along State 49.

Hamlets off this main highway are also worth a visit. Many are covered by a facade of modernity; others verge on ghost town status. A few have been preserved as state historic parks.

Planning your trip

The fastest and most direct way to approach the northern Sierra from the San Francisco area is via Interstate 80, which cuts east through the foothills and Tahoe National Forest to cross the mountains at Donner Pass, named for an ill-fated pioneer party.

Other all-year highways reach Lake Tahoe at its southern rim: U.S. 50 links Sacramento and Carson City, Nevada, and State 88 joins State 89 after crossing 8,573-foot Kit Carson Pass.

To the south, State 4, State 108, and State 120 (through Yosemite National Park) are closed in winter due to snow. All-year routes to Yosemite are State 140 and State 41. State 49 is a year-round gold country highway.

When to go. All roads in and around the Sierra Nevada are open from late spring to early autumn. Summer daytime temperatures in the higher elevations usually range upward from the 70s, with nights cooling to the 50s and 60s. Summer rain is unusual.

In winter, expect crisp days and cold nights. Though snowfalls have been much below normal in recent years, a storm can quickly drop several feet of snow and force temporary highway closures. Always carry chains on winter drives.

The Sierra foothills are at their most colorful in spring and autumn. Summer temperatures can climb to 100°, and winter rains make sightseeing a chilly business.

Where to stay. An array of lodging from luxurious alpine resorts to modest cottages and roadside motels awaits Sierra travelers. Gold rush communities abound with quaint bed-and-breakfast inns and century-old hotels. Campers will find plenty of tent sites in state and national parks, but prime locations like Lake Tahoe and Yosemite Valley require reservations well in advance for summer (see pages 120–122).

Contacts

These agencies offer information on attractions and accommodations. See additional contacts throughout this chapter.

Lake Tahoe Visitors Authority
1156 Ski Run Blvd.
(P.O. Box 16299)
South Lake Tahoe, CA 95706
(800) 288-2463 (*trip planning, lodging*)
(900) 776-5050 (*road, ski, weather conditions; $1 per minute*)

Tahoe North Visitors & Convention Bureau
950 N. Lake Blvd., Suite 3
(P.O. Box 5578)
Tahoe City, CA 95730
(800) 824-6348

Yosemite National Park
Yosemite, CA 95389
(209) 372-0265 (*information weekdays*)
(209) 372-0264 (*24-hour recorded information*)

The Northern Sierra

Thousands of acres of forested land north of Lake Tahoe offer secluded spots for trout fishing, swimming, camping, hiking, and horseback riding. Much of Plumas National Forest is in Feather River country; Tahoe National Forest extends south and east to the Nevada border.

For a map of roads, trails, campsites, and lakes, contact Plumas National Forest, P.O. Box 1500, Quincy, CA 95971, or Tahoe National Forest, Highway 49, Nevada City, CA 95959 ($2 charge).

Feather River country

Rich in scenery and history, the Feather River region presents a varied topography—rocky canyons, fern-filled ravines, high mountains, leaf-covered foothills, chaparral-swathed slopes, and second-growth forests of pine and fir. Through all this flows the river named in 1820 by Spanish explorer Don Luis Arguello, who happened to reach its lower end when band-tailed pigeons were migrating and scattering feathers on the water.

State 70 follows the North Fork of the Feather, affording fine views of the canyon. Cabins and campgrounds line much of the highway. Stub roads lead to old mining settlements, pocket valleys cultivated since 1850, and trout-filled lakes. Trails take off where roads end. You'll find a backpack handy for spur-of-the-moment hikes.

The Middle Fork (the most rugged) provides some of the state's finest trout fishing. Site of early placer mining, the South Fork has swimming holes and streamside trails. Along its stretches lie seven reservoirs; the highest (5,000 feet) is 500-acre Little Grass Valley Lake.

Oroville. Gateway to the Feather River country, Oroville (population 10,000) lies 70 miles north of Sacramento on State 70. It began life as Ophir City, a boisterous tent town of gold rush days. In the 1870s its Chinatown was California's largest.

One visible reminder of that era is the Chinese Temple at Elma and Broderick streets. Built in 1863, it's now a museum of Oriental artifacts. A self-guiding tour (small fee) reveals chapels, a garden, and collections of puppets, costumes, and tapestries. Hours and days vary, but the museum is open from mid-January through November.

Another landmark is the Judge C. F. Lott Memorial Home in Sank Park (Montgomery Street between 3rd and 4th avenues). Completed in 1856, the white frame dwelling is furnished with period pieces. It's open Friday through Tuesday from 11 A.M. to 4:30 P.M. year-round, Wednesday and Thursday afternoons in summer (small fee).

Cherokee. Ten miles north of Oroville on Cherokee Road you'll see the shells and foundations of buildings that once made up the tiny gold-mining town of Cherokee. The first diamonds discovered in the United States were picked out of a sluice box here in 1866, but no extensive diamond mining was ever done.

Lake Oroville. With a surface area of about 15,800 acres and about 167 miles of shoreline, this lake 5 miles northeast of Oroville was created by the towering Oroville Dam built on the Feather River in 1968. The adjoining powerhouse can generate enough electricity to supply a city of a million people. Films on the project are shown at the visitor center.

Now a state recreation area, the lake is popular with sailors, boaters (houseboat and power boat rentals), water-skiers, swimmers, and anglers. Both drive-in and boat-in campsites can be reserved through MISTIX.

Feather Falls. North and east of Lake Oroville is Feather Falls Scenic Area, a 14,890-acre preserve of forested canyons, soaring granite domes, and plunging waterfalls. The region got its name from the 640-foot, plumelike cascade of the Feather River.

In the spring and early summer you get a good view of the falls by boating to the end of the Middle Fork arm of Lake Oroville and then climbing a hazardous ½-mile trail. For an eagle's-eye overlook, follow a 3½-mile trail from a road turning off at the village of Feather Falls, south of the falls on Lumpkin Road.

Though the Milsap Bar Road crosses the Middle Fork at the upper end of Bald Rock Canyon, not even a foot trail descends to its inner depths. To reach the Milsap Bar Bridge from Lake Oroville, follow the Oroville-Quincy Highway (County 162) north to the Brush Creek Ranger Station (about 18 miles from the Forbestown Road junction at the south end of the lake). Then head east on Milsap Bar Road about 7 miles.

Bucks Lake. At an altitude of 5,000 feet, this 20,000-acre lake near the old gold-mining town of Quincy glitters peacefully amid forested valleys and rocky mountaintops. Boating, swimming, waterskiing, and fishing are its prime attractions. Trails lead to other lakes; the Pacific Crest National Scenic Trail crosses Bucks Lake Road about 3 miles east.

Two south shore resorts (open May through October) offer cabins, restaurants, stores, gas pumps, launch ramps, and boat rentals. Sites at five U.S. Forest Service campgrounds are available on a first-come basis. Pick up campground maps (small charge) at Plumas National Forest offices, 159 Lawrence Street, Quincy (open weekdays).

To reach the lake from Oroville, follow State 70 for 80 scenic but winding miles to Quincy and then head west on County 162 for 17 miles. The Oroville-Quincy Highway (County 162) is scenic and shorter (50 miles), but the last 17 miles are unpaved.

A scenic trio

On to the east, three parcels of Sierra scenery offer more recreational opportunities and some glimpses of California history.

Plumas-Eureka State Park. On the slopes of Eureka Peak in Plumas

County, the nearly 5,000-acre Plumas-Eureka State Park surrounds the old mining town of Johnsville, 6 miles west of the intersection of State 70 and State 89. Hiking trails lead around Eureka Peak and south to the Sierra Buttes and more than 30 lakes in the Lakes Basin Recreation Area. The area is known for brook and rainbow trout fishing.

Summer campers will find 67 sites along Jamison Creek (reserve through MISTIX). The area's gold-mining past can be explored at a mining museum (open daily in summer); the nearby stamp mill is being restored. Though the campground closes in October, the park is open year-round. Heavy snowfall attracts cross-country and downhill skiers to Eureka Bowl.

Donner Lake. Along Interstate 80 about 2 miles west of Truckee lies Donner Lake, a favorite trout fishing and sailing spot. The state park museum tells the story of the Donner Party, trapped here for the winter of 1846–47. Almost half of the 89 pioneers perished; a monument to them rests on a stone base 22 feet high, the depth of the snow that fateful winter. There's a small fee to visit the museum, open year-round.

Desolation Wilderness. Southwest of Lake Tahoe, Desolation Wilderness is a favorite of Sierra high country devotees. "Desolation" describes some of the area's wild and lonely terrain, its huge boulders and glacier-polished slopes nearly devoid of trees. Peaks ranging from 6,500 to 10,000 feet cradle more than 70 named lakes.

Within these 63,469 acres, you can hike about 100 miles of trails from 11 major trailheads. The much-used Pacific Crest trail connects many lakes, tranquil oases for fishing. Pack trips are extremely popular.

Despite its name, Desolation is the most crowded wilderness in the United States. It's so popular that wilderness permits are required year-round, and a quota system is in effect from mid-June to Labor Day. Free wilderness permits, required for both day and overnight use, are available in person or by mail from the U.S. Forest Service, 870 Emerald Bay Road, Suite 1, South Lake Tahoe, CA 96150. For reservations, call (916) 573-2600.

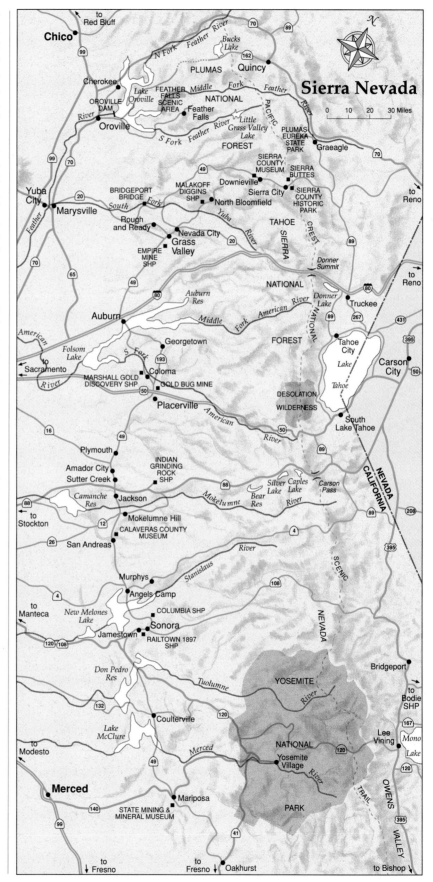

Sierra Nevada

Lake Tahoe's alpine setting and array of entertainment ensure year-round visitors. The view is across the lake from Nevada's Sand Harbor to the snow-tipped mountains on the California side.

Lake Tahoe

Between the two main emigrant routes of California's early settlers—now Interstate 80 and U.S. 50—lies large and lovely Lake Tahoe. Rimmed by snow-capped Sierra Nevada peaks, this clear and unbelievably blue lake is shared by California and Nevada.

North America's largest alpine lake, Tahoe is 22 miles long, 8 to 12 miles wide, and 1,645 feet at its deepest point. It contains enough water to cover the entire state of California to a depth of 14 inches.

The lake basin was a gathering spot for the native Washoe Indians; later its heavily timbered slopes became a prime source of lumber. Tahoe blossomed as a resort area as early as the 1870s. Fifty years later skiing was introduced, and roads to the lake were kept open all winter. But it wasn't until the late 1950s that the building boom began. Then, ski lodges and gambling casinos (Nevada side) sprang up, turning Tahoe into an all-year attraction.

Planning a visit

Tahoe boasts an average 247 sunny days a year and an annual snowfall of 25 to 40 feet. Snow can fall anytime from October to June. You can expect summer days to be warm, but Tahoe's 6,227-foot elevation makes for cool nights.

Getting there. Planes, trains, buses, and major highways make it easy to reach Lake Tahoe. Two major airports serve the area: Cannon International in Reno (about 1 hour away) and the smaller Lake Tahoe Airport at the southern end of the lake. Both provide shuttles, taxis, limos, and rental cars. Tahoe-Truckee Airport north of the lake welcomes small planes.

Amtrak trains between the San Francisco area and Chicago stop north of the lake at quaint Truckee, a former lumber and railroad town turned gentrified ski center; it's about a 6-hour rail trip from the Bay Area. Greyhound buses reach both ends of the lake.

By car, it takes about 5 hours in good traffic from the Bay Area via Interstate 80 to reach the north shore, slightly longer to get to the south shore on U.S. 50. (On either route, traffic is at its worst on summer weekends and on ski weekends, when weather conditions may add to the congestion.) If you're not in a hurry, a combination of State 88 and State 89 offers a scenic alternative. From Southern California, the fastest route north to Tahoe is U.S. 395 to U.S. 50.

Lodging. Cozy cabins, condos, country-style inns, budget motels, modern lodges, and glamorous resorts—Tahoe has them all. Once you've decided on a north or south shore base, a single toll-free call to the appropriate visitor center (see page 95) lets you make reservations at many lake properties.

Camping. More than 20 public and private campgrounds around Tahoe offer a choice of sites. With a few exceptions (including Mount Rose, Zephyr Cove, and Nevada Beach), most are in California. For information on state campgrounds, see page 122; for U.S. Forest Service campgrounds, call (916) 573-2600.

The Tahoe Douglas Chamber of Commerce (Highway 50 at Round Hill Shopping Center a couple of miles north of the state border), has information on Nevada campsites; call (702) 588-4591.

Activities at the lake

The snowy slopes around the lake are the focus of winter fun—the Tahoe Basin is one of the most compactly developed ski regions in the world. Summer pastimes revolve around the lake itself, but they aren't limited to boating, swimming, and waterskiing. You can cruise across the lake on a stern-wheeler, or get a bird's-eye view from an aerial tram or even a hot-air balloon (check the Yellow Pages). Golfers head for one of the area's dozen resort courses (see page 123). And casinos just across the Nevada border, south and north, offer year-round, around-the-clock gambling as well as big-name entertainment, splashy revues, and a variety of lounge acts.

Boating. Lake Tahoe is a mecca for boaters and water-skiers. There's plenty of room for everyone, and the coves and harbors along the lakeshore are appealing. If you bring your own boat, you'll find plenty of launching ramps, but during the busy summer season, you may have trouble securing a mooring. If a storm appears imminent, don't venture far from shore; the water can become very rough.

Several companies offer raft trips on the Truckee River north of Tahoe City. Check the Yellow Pages for listings.

Cruising. Two stern-wheelers offer sightseeing cruises on the lake. The 500-passenger *Tahoe Queen* operates Emerald Bay and dinner cruises year-round from South Lake Tahoe. The 360-passenger *M.S. Dixie,* based at Zephyr Cove (Nevada), operates Emerald Bay, Glenbrook Bay, brunch, and cocktail cruises April through October. North Tahoe Cruises also offers boat tours out of Tahoe City. (See page 124.)

Swimming. Polar bears would love this lake; the icy waters only get up to 68° in midsummer. The hardy will find plenty of public beaches around the lake. At the south end, the U.S. Forest Service oversees three stretches of sand off State 89: Pope, Kiva, and Baldwin. You can also swim at Emerald Bay, D. L. Bliss, and Sugar Pine Point state parks just to the north off State 89, and at South Lake Tahoe Recreation Area off U.S. 50.

The north shore offers public beaches at Tahoe City and Kings Beach. On the Nevada side, try Sand Harbor Beach State Recreation Area (north shore) and Nevada Beach Campground (east shore). Boat harbors such as Zephyr Cove (east shore) also have beaches.

Fishing. Lake Tahoe never freezes, so you can fish all year. Kokanee salmon and rainbow and brown trout abound in the lake and nearby streams. A li-

...Lake Tahoe

cense from either California or Nevada is valid all over the lake; sporting goods stores offer 1-day licenses.

You can fish from one hour before sunrise to two hours after sunset. Chumming is illegal, and there's a five-fish limit (no more than two mackinaw). Half-day fishing charters are available at both the south and north ends of the lake; check the Yellow Pages under "Fishing Parties."

Cycling. Bikers may choose from more than 12 miles of safe, paved biking trails with great lake views. The longest runs more than 5 miles from Tahoe City south to Homewood on the west shore. Near Camp Richardson at the southern end, a delightful 3½-mile trail meanders through forest and along streams close to the beaches. Ask for maps at bicycle rental shops.

Hiking and riding. More than 90 miles of a planned 150-mile circle of hiking and equestrian trails have been com-

pleted. Present access points are Tahoe City, State 50 at Spooner Summit (Nevada side), and State 89 at Luther Pass (south of the lake). A maximum 10 percent grade makes the trails good for beginners as well as advanced walkers. For information on camping (allowed along the trail), call the U.S. Forest Service at (916) 573-2600.

In summer, horses can be rented for trail rides from Cascade, Camp Richardson, Stateline, Sunset Corral, and Zephyr Cove stables on the south shore. North shore stables include Alpine Meadows, Cold Stream, Hilltop, Northstar, Ponderosa Ranch, Squaw Valley, and Tahoe Donner.

Skiing Tahoe. Downhill enthusiasts enjoy a variety of terrain in a cluster of fine ski areas, from the country's largest (Heavenly Valley) to the site of the 1960 Olympics (Squaw Valley). For the Nordic buff, the area boasts more than 30 ski-touring centers, some of which are located at the major downhill areas. Most offer rentals, instruction, and group tours.

For maps and general information, contact Lake Tahoe Visitors Authority or Tahoe North Visitors & Convention Bureau (see page 95). For information on specific resorts, see pages 123–124.

Aerial trams. For the best area view from the south shore, ride the Heavenly Valley Aerial Tram at South Lake Tahoe. It climbs to a restaurant about 2,000 feet above the lake. Take Ski Run Boulevard southeast from U.S. 50 to get to the tram, open 10 A.M. to 10 P.M. daily in summer, 9 A.M. to 5 P.M. at other times ($9.50 adults).

Across the lake, the Squaw Valley Cable Car operates from 9 A.M. to 10 P.M. in winter, 9 A.M. to 5 P.M. the rest of the year ($10 adults, $5 ages 12 and under). The tram takes you to the ski area's High Camp at 8,200 feet (restaurants, ice rink). Squaw Valley is off State 89 north of Tahoe City.

Circling the lake

A 72-mile road encircles the lake close to shore, offering beautiful views on all sides. Occasional winter snows may close a section of State 89 on the west shore around Emerald Bay.

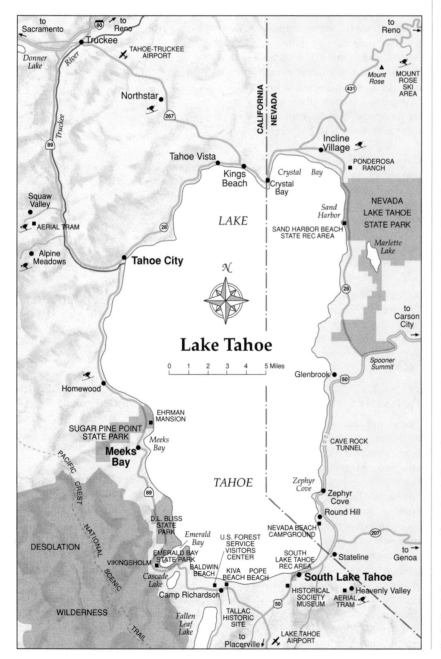

South shore. Lake Tahoe's lively south shore is the most heavily populated part of the lake. Resorts, motels, condominiums, restaurants, and shopping centers line U.S. 50 from the sprawling city of South Lake Tahoe past the border. Nevada's Stateline area is the gaming center, with such high-rise casino hotels as Caesar's, Harrah's, Harvey's (first on the lake), and Horizon.

A stop at the free Historical Society Museum (open 10 A.M. to 5 P.M. daily in summer), 3058 State 50 in South Lake Tahoe, provides a good introduction to the area's colorful past. You can also pick up a map to a self-guided auto tour of 20 historical landmarks.

From its split with U.S. 50 at the "Y" (location of discount outlets such as Mikasa and London Fog), State 89 winds north into national forest lands and provides access to two smaller lakes, Fallen Leaf and Cascade.

You can stroll around former summer estates and enjoy art shows and museums (summer only) at Tallac Historic Site, a 74-acre area on State 89 between Camp Richardson and Kiva Beach. The area is open spring through autumn. For information on hours and fees, call (916) 542-4166.

Just to the west, the U.S. Forest Service Visitor Center on Taylor Creek (open 8 A.M. to 6 P.M. daily in summer) has a nature trail and a stream profile chamber where you can observe the run of kokanee salmon in October.

West shore. Emerald Bay, at the southwest tip of the lake, is Tahoe's jewel. Completely surrounded by state parklands, the deep bay boasts the lake's only island, Fannette. The stone teahouse that you can see atop the island was built by the woman who erected Vikingsholm, a 38-room mansion at the head of the bay.

Tours of this onetime summer residence, patterned after an 800 A.D. Norse fortress, take place 10 A.M. to 4 P.M. June through September (small admission fee). From the lookout where you park your car, it's a 1-mile hike to the house; the return is uphill.

From the same parking area, you can take a short trail up to Eagle Falls, a good spot for photos. Picnic facilities lie nearby.

Northward on State 89, Meeks Bay has a beautiful beach and campground, and Sugar Pine Point State Park affords excellent views of the lake. In summer, tours of Sugar Pine's Ehrman Mansion are offered for a fee from 11 A.M. to 4 P.M. Parts of *Godfather II* were filmed here.

North shore. Tahoe City, at the junction of State highways 89 and 28, is the center for north shore skiing. Squaw Valley (aerial tram, new hotel) and Alpine Meadows ski areas are worth a detour in summer, as well, for the great scenery.

Gigantic trout can be viewed from Fanny Bridge (you'll see why it got its name), at Tahoe City. And you can bone up on early Tahoe history at the free Gatekeeper's Log Cabin Museum at 139 W. Lake Boulevard, open daily 11 A.M. to 5 P.M. from mid-May to mid-October.

Crystal Bay, on State 28 just into Nevada, is the hub of the north shore gaming. Several of the old casinos have been refurbished, including the Cal-Neva Club (once owned by Frank Sinatra).

The upscale Incline Village complex, 3 miles east, has a nearby ski area (Mount Rose), two 18-hole golf courses, tennis courts, riding trails, and the Hyatt resort and casino. A bit farther east on State 28, location scenes for TV's *Bonanza* series were filmed at the Ponderosa Ranch, open 9:30 A.M. to 5 P.M. May through October (ranchhouse tour, pony rides, gold panning). Admission is $7.50 adults, $5.50 ages 5 through 11.

East shore. South of Incline Village, State 28 passes one of the lake's most beautiful beaches, Sand Harbor at Nevada Lake Tahoe State Park (a day-use facility). Midway down the shore it intersects with State 50, which enters the Tahoe basin near historic Glenbrook Lodge, one of the first on the lake.

South at Cave Rock, the road goes through 25 yards of solid stone. The Washoe Indians regarded this rocky outcropping as holy; they placed their dead to rest in the waters below.

Zephyr Cove, a few miles farther, has another old-time lodge, cabins, a campground, a stable, and a beach. Before you reach the California state line, you'll pass the Round Hill shopping area; Nevada Beach Campground lies along the shore here.

Foothill Wineries

Forget the crowds in the Napa and Sonoma valleys. The serene Sierra foothills are home to several dozen small wineries eager for visitors. Most lie on back roads east of State 49 between Placerville and Murphys. Amador County's Shenandoah Valley, for example, boasts a cluster of 12 wineries ideally set up for an 18-mile, figure-eight tour.

Winemaking was a major industry here beginning around the time of the gold rush. But mine closings, a population exodus, Prohibition, and phylloxera did in all but a few cellars. Today the area is experiencing a renaissance, particularly in robust Zinfandels, as well as Sauvignon Blanc, Muscat, and Barbera.

You can explore the valley by car or bicycle; traffic is light. Weekends are the best time to assure open doors. Start your tour at the general store on State 49 in Plymouth (20 miles south of Placerville, or 32 miles east of Sacramento) and follow the signs. The wineries line Shenandoah Road and Shenandoah School, Bell, and Steiner side roads.

Sobon Estates (formerly the venerable D'Agostino Winery) is the best place to glean local wine history; it's 8 miles northeast of Plymouth on Shenandoah Road. Several wineries have picnic areas. For details on nearby food and lodging, call the Amador Chamber of Commerce at (209) 223-0350.

Gold Country

James Marshall changed the course of California history in January 1848 when he discovered gold in the millrace of Sutter's sawmill in Coloma. Within a year, California was known worldwide, and fortune seekers started the migration that would open the West.

Remnants of those times still exist in the gold rush country of the Sierra foothills. State 49 twists and turns for almost 300 miles through these rolling grass- and fir-clad hills, its elevation around 2,000 feet except where it dips into deep river canyons or climbs the mountains above Downieville.

Though the road could be driven in a day or two, a week is not too long for leisurely browsing. Many charming inns offer choices of lodging. Camping in summer can be uncomfortably hot except in higher, northern reaches.

Northern mines

Deep quartz mining was first developed in the region between Grass Valley and Sierra City. The area is also the birthplace of hydraulic mining, a highly destructive process in which entire mountain ridges were washed away.

Unlike the rest of the gold country, this region is best in summer. Your richest wanderings will be on side roads, often impassable with winter snows and spring runoff. Grass Valley and Nevada City make good bases for exploring. Make sure you have enough fuel and supplies for your outings; services are sparse.

Around Grass Valley. A disastrous 1855 fire destroyed the early community of Grass Valley, leaving little to recall the town's mining camp days except its narrow streets, scattered headframes, and the Empire Mine (see page 105), once the state's largest and richest gold mine.

Even the most sophisticated traveler is impressed by the vast display of mining equipment at the free Northstar Powerhouse Mining Museum (foot of S. Mill Street west of State 49). It's open 10 A.M. to 5 P.M. daily May through mid-

October; call (916) 273-4255 for other seasonal hours.

Several blocks up the street is a replica of the house occupied for some years by exotic dancer Lola Montez and her pet bear. Furnished with many of her belongings, the house is now occupied by the Grass Valley–Nevada County Chamber of Commerce: 248 Mill Street, phone (916) 273-4667.

Among the displays at the Grass Valley Museum in the century-old Mount St. Mary's Convent and Orphanage building (Church and Chapel streets) are a period schoolroom and an early-day doctor's office. The free museum is open noon to 3 P.M. Wednesday and weekends from June through October.

West of town. Detour 4 miles to see tiny Rough and Ready, which seceded from the Union in 1850 and did not legally return until 1948. (From Grass Valley, take West Main Street, which becomes Rough and Ready Highway). The I.O.O.F. Hall and the Fippin Blacksmith Shop, where Lotta Crabtree sang and danced, are among the town's oldest survivors. The Old Toll House now extracts revenues from the sale of antiques.

Several miles northwest is the longest remaining single-span covered bridge in the West. The 1862 Bridgeport Bridge (now closed to traffic) stretches 230 feet across the South Fork of the Yuba River and will soon be part of a new state park.

Nevada City. This appealing town has a well-deserved reputation for beautiful homes, intriguing shops, and carefully preserved antiquity. From here, you can head north 16 miles to the old mining town of North Bloomfield and Malakoff Diggins State Historic Park, an impressive example of hydraulic mining.

Prim Victorian houses with old-fashioned gardens (a few are inns) perch atop Nevada City's hills, sugar maples blaze with fall color, and a neat brick downtown is crammed with in-

triguing shops and museums. Pick up a walking tour map from the chamber of commerce, 132 Main Street.

Downieville and beyond. The mountain settlement of Downieville is still one of the most entrancing of the remaining gold towns. Its old stone, brick, and frame buildings, many built in the 1860s or earlier, face onto quiet, crooked streets and cling to mountainsides above the Yuba River. The Sierra County Museum (open daily in summer) is housed in an old Chinese store and gambling place along the highway.

The jagged Sierra Buttes overshadow the half-ghost town of Sierra City, 13 miles east. Between 1850 and 1852, miners tunneled through these dramatic granite peaks searching for gold. Sierra County Historical Park, an indoor-outdoor museum about a mile to the east, contains the Kentucky Mine's stamp mill, mining equipment, and Indian relics. You can take a guided tour (fee) Wednesday through Sunday from Memorial Day through September, weekends only in October.

Central Mother Lode

Much of California's gold country was called the Mother Lode, but the section between Auburn and Sonora contained the primary gold vein that gave the area its name. Thanks to tourism, this region retains many relatively intact mining towns, a concentration of inns, restaurants, and shops, and plenty of places to pan for gold, fish, boat, swim, or ski.

Auburn. The bustling town at the junction of State 49 and Interstate 80 has long since outgrown its historic heart, now marked "Old Town." For a look at some of its original brick and stone structures, walk along Lincoln Way and Court and Commercial streets just southwest of the highway junction. The gigantic gold-panner statue visible from the freeway honors Claude Chana's first strike.

The Gold Country Museum (1273 High Street in the fairgrounds south of

Quaint Nevada City's downtown streets are lined with vintage structures from 49er days; many house museums of the past.

103

...Gold Country

Old Town) focuses on mining history. Exhibits include a walk-through shaft, working stamp mill model, gold dredge, and assay office. The museum is open 10 A.M. to 4 P.M. Tuesday through Sunday. The small admission charge includes nearby Bernhard Museum, built in 1851 as a hotel and later the home of a pioneer vintner.

Coloma. One of the most important historical stops in the Mother Lode, Coloma today is barely an echo of the boom town that flourished here in the early 1850s. Only a handful of original buildings still stand, most as part of a 265-acre state park (per-car fee).

Stop at the park's visitor center for a walking guide and a look at a small museum (good film). But most of the best exhibits and demonstrations (mostly in summer) are outdoors.

James Marshall discovered gold at Sutter's Mill, where a replica stands. You can try your luck with a pan across the river. On the hill behind town stands a statue of Marshall—who died a penniless recluse. On the way back, peer into his cabin and the nearby restored 1858 Catholic church.

Georgetown detour. A 13-mile detour leads east on State 193 to Georgetown, its 19th-century buildings still intact because a wide main street protected them against fires. Among them are the Balzar House (a former hotel and dance hall), the American Hotel (now the American River Inn), the Georgetown Hotel, and the Wells Fargo Building.

Placerville. Though it was one of the great camps of the Gold Country, Placerville retains only a few mementos of its lusty past. The city center on Main Street is squeezed into a long, narrow strip at the bottom of a ravine south of U.S. 50. Founded in 1848 as Dry Diggins, the town picked up the name of Hangtown next year after some grisly lynchings. The Old City Hall (built in 1857) and its next-door neighbor still serve as city offices.

The free county museum in the fairgrounds north of U.S. 50 includes replicas of an early-day store and country kitchen. It's open 10 A.M. to 4 P.M. Wednesday through Saturday, 1 to 4 P.M. Sunday in summer. In Bedford Park, a mile north of downtown, you can visit the Gold Bug Mine (page 105).

Sutter Creek. About 30 miles south of Placerville on State 49, this picturesque village has a main street lined with attractive old buildings, some sporting overhanging balconies. To learn their history, pick up a free city guide at the Bubble Gum Book Store.

The Sutter Creek Inn up the street (one of two side-by-side inns) was the 1859 home of one of the state's first senators. The Downs House, a block west on Spanish Street, was built in 1873 for a mine foreman.

Tiny Amador City, 2 miles north, is another sightseers' mecca. The brick Imperial Hotel has reopened as an inn and restaurant. The Mine House inn was once headquarters for the Keystone Mine.

Jackson. Though modern facades have transformed many of the old buildings along Main Street, this city has preserved some of its rich heritage. Lively National Hotel at the foot of the street claims to be the state's oldest continually operating hotel. A visitor center (junction of State 49 and State 88) has free guides to area cities.

Visit the county museum on Church Street (open 10 A.M. to 4 P.M. Wednesday through Sunday; donations requested) to learn about Jackson's mining role. Don't let the size of wee St. Sava's Serbian Orthodox Church on North Main fool you; it's the mother church for the western hemisphere.

The Kennedy and Argonaut mines at the north edge of town have been closed for decades, but headframes, some buildings, and huge tailing wheels built to carry waste to a settling pond over the hills still stand. To get a close look at the wheels, follow Jackson Gate Road northeast of downtown to Tailing Wheels Park. Along the road lie several of the city's best Italian restaurants, an antique store housed in the county's oldest building, and two bed-and-breakfasts.

State 88 (open all year) heads east over Carson Pass past several good summer trout lakes (Bear Reservoir, Silver Lake, and Caples Lake) and a couple of winter ski areas (the largest is Kirkwood).

About 12 miles east of Jackson off State 88, a side road leads north to the mining camp of Volcano, Indian Grinding Rock State Historic Park (huge outcropping used by Miwok Indians as a mortar, reconstructed village, and museum), and Daffodil Hill, where you'll see an explosion of spring color in a free hillside garden.

San Andreas to Angels Camp. Follow a sign marked "Historic" to get behind San Andreas' modern mask. The Calaveras County Museum (a three-building complex that includes the I.O.O.F. Hall, courthouse, and jail) a block east of Main Street is worth a stop. Black Bart was tried in the courthouse and awaited trial in the jail. The museum is open 10 A.M. to 4 P.M. daily (small fee). West of town, the intriguing Pioneer Cemetery dates back at least to 1851.

Thanks to Mark Twain, Angels Camp, 12 miles south, is probably best noted for its frog-jumping contest in May. You'll find a few remembrances of gold-mining days—the Angels Hotel, the ubiquitous I.O.O.F. Hall, and the indoor-outdoor mining museum at the north end of town.

Murphys detour. You'll feel as if the clock had stopped when you take State 4 east to Murphys (9 miles from State 49). Gingerbread Victorians peek from behind white picket fences, and tall locust trees border the main street.

The Murphys Hotel, opened in 1856, displays an illustrious register of temporary residents—U.S. Grant, Thomas Lipton, Horatio Alger, Charles Bolton (Black Bart), and more. Across the street, the Old Timers Museum displays gold rush memorabilia (open Friday through Sunday, small admission).

Southern mines

The placer and quartz veins in the southern gold country never rivaled those to the north. Tourists on their way to Yosemite arrived almost as soon as the prospectors.

Sonora. Sonora, at the junction of State highways 49 and 108, is as bustling today as a century ago, but considerably less rowdy. Layers of modernity cover the aged buildings lining Washington Street, the main thoroughfare, but a drive along narrow, hilly streets reveals many relics of the past.

Pick up a walking tour guide of Victorian homes at the century-old jail and museum at 158 W. Bradford Road or at the Tuolumne County Visitors Bureau offices, 55 W. Stockton Road. Graceful St. James Episcopal Church on Washington Street, built in 1860, is one of the gold country's most beautiful frame structures.

Columbia State Historic Park. Four miles north of Sonora via State 49 and Parrotts Ferry Road is Columbia, once called the "Gem of the Southern Mines" for its gold output. This living museum is an ideal place to learn about mining and miners.

Though it attracts thousands of visitors on summer days and appears quite commercial, the town is historically authentic. Stop by the park headquarters for a brochure outlining a 1½-hour stroll through the traffic-free streets. Children enjoy panning for treasure, riding the jouncing horse-drawn stagecoach, sipping sarsaparilla at a saloon, or even getting a haircut at the state's oldest barbershop.

From June through September, a free bus carries visitors to an operating gold mine. Theatrical performances take place in summer at the Fallon House Theater, and both the City Hotel and Fallon House are back in business as hostelries and restaurants.

Jamestown. Fire has been the enemy of this little town 3 miles south of Sonora, but a few proud structures remain, including some of the region's oldest operating inns. A profusion of antique stores, several places to pan for gold, and a couple of good restaurants add to its appeal.

At Railtown 1897 State Historic Park, you'll find the steam locomotives, vintage rolling stock, and 26-acre roundhouse and shop complex of the Sierra Railway. Nearly 200 feature movies, television shows, and commercials have been filmed along the narrow gauge line, which once connected mines with Central Valley shipping centers.

The park is open daily May through September, weekends and holidays the rest of the year, from 10 A.M. to 5:30 P.M. (small admission charge). Rail excursions over some of the original line run spring and through September (see page 126).

Coulterville. About halfway between Sonora and Mariposa, this photogenic little community is enriched by the presence of the Jeffrey Hotel (once a stagecoach stop, now an inn), built in 1851 of rock and adobe with walls 3 feet thick. The adjoining Magnolia Saloon displays firearms, minerals, coins, and other memorabilia.

Across the street are the remains of the Coulter Hotel and the Wells Fargo building (a museum), once operated by Buffalo Bill's brothers. In the small plaza are the local "hangin' tree" and the Whistling Billy, a small steam engine once used to haul ore from the Mary Harrison Mine north of town. The Sun Sun Wo adobe at the east end of Main Street is all that remains of a once-sizable Chinese population.

Mariposa. Halfway between Merced and Yosemite National Park, Mariposa has one of the choicest bit of architecture of the gold rush era. The two-story courthouse at the north end of town has been in use continuously since it was erected in 1854.

Don't miss the California State Mining and Mineral Museum in the fairgrounds on State 49 about 1½ miles south of its junction with State 140. One wing contains 20,000 gems and minerals. Artifacts and photographs in another wing tell the story of mining. A scale model of a stamp mill whirls into action with the push of a button. Dioramas in a tunnel cut into a hill behind the museum depict miners drilling and blasting. Hours are 10 A.M. to 6 P.M. daily (to 4 P.M. on Sunday). A moderate admission is charged.

Oakhurst. At the southern terminus of State 49, Oakhurst (called Fresno Flats in its heyday) shows little evidence of its hectic mining past, but the historical park at 427 High School Road displays remnants of it. The French-style chateau on the hill at 48688 Victoria Lane is Erna's Elderberry House, a mecca for diners.

Inside the Mines

Piles of tailings, jutting headframes, rusty monitors, and an occasional stamp mill—these reminders of the industry that changed California's destiny crop up throughout the gold country. But it's also possible to get a peek inside the mines that once burrowed into these hills.

At the Empire Mine State Historic Park in Grass Valley (1 mile east of State 49 on Empire Street), tours of one of the state's deepest and most productive sites include a brief entry into the mine itself. Visitors also see offices, shops, and the owner's residence. The 784-acre park (small admission) is open 10 A.M. to 5 P.M. daily except in winter. For details, call (916) 273-8522.

At Placerville's Gold Bug Mine, you can walk into a tunnel and examine an old stamp mill. The mine is open 10 A.M. to 4 P.M. daily in summer, weekends only in spring and autumn (small fee). Take Bedford Avenue to Gold Bug Park 1 mile north of U.S. 50. For information, call (916) 622-0832.

A summer visit to Columbia State Historic Park can include a tour to a nearby working gold mine. Free buses transport visitors from Main Street. For information, call (209) 532-4301.

At the California State Mining and Mineral Museum in Mariposa, you can walk through a 150-foot-long mine tunnel.

In Yosemite National Park's high country, LeConte Falls on the Tuolumne River tumbles over glaciated cliffs on its rush down the canyon.

Yosemite National Park

By any standards one of the nation's most spectacular parks, Yosemite is loved to death. More than 3 million people visit the century-old park annually, 70 percent of them arriving during the summer and most never venturing outside the 7 square miles of Yosemite Valley.

Though its monumental granite walls and high-diving waterfalls make the valley a logical place to begin a visit, there remain almost 1,200 square miles of less crowded splendor to explore: glaciers, giant sequoias, alpine meadows, trout-filled streams and lakes, and 13,000-foot Sierra Nevada peaks.

The Awhaneechee Indians were the park's first residents, camping, fishing, hunting, and collecting acorns here in summer. Trappers and prospectors glimpsed the valley, but no one else entered it until the U.S. Cavalry came on the scene in 1851. Word of its beauty spread quickly, and four years later the first party of tourists arrived to see the great U-shaped valley created by glaciers some two million years ago.

Park preservation

Yosemite is more than just another pretty place—it's the nation's first federally mandated park and the model upon which our national park system was based. In 1864, when President Lincoln signed legislation deeding Yosemite to California as a public trust (not a national park), the grant contained two separate wonders: Yosemite Valley and the Mariposa Grove of giant sequoias (now part of the park).

Hetch Hetchy Valley (later flooded by a dam on the Tuolumne River to give San Francisco drinking water) and the high country along the Sierra crest were added in 1890, when Yosemite National Park was created. Much of the credit for the establishment of the national park goes to pioneer environmentalist John Muir, who lobbied for its creation.

Yosemite is also a case study of what happens to an area that becomes too popular. Weekend traffic clogs valley roads and overflows parking lots, fragile areas are trampled by careless hikers and campers, and more than 1,000 structures clutter the valley floor.

Though a master plan to return the valley to a more natural state was never fully implemented, in part because of a lack of funds, some progress has been made. Computerized reservations for valley lodging and campsites simplify the search for a place to sleep, and free shuttle buses and paved bicycle paths link all of the valley's camping, lodging, and visitor centers, making it possible to get along just fine without a car. But the question of whether or not visitor areas should be limited in order to protect the environment remains a controversial one.

Park highlights

Yosemite is the Sierra Nevada's crown jewel. Within its limits lie ecosystems as diverse as foothill woodlands and alpine tundra, a grand backdrop for a bonanza of recreational possibilities.

Yosemite Valley. Barely 7 miles long and only a mile at its widest point, the valley is actually more like a canyon. Granite ramparts draped with thundering falls in the spring and etched in sharp relief by snow in winter soar more than 3,000 feet above the meadow, and great domes and pinnacles fringe canyon rims. The Merced River threads its way along the valley floor through groves of pines and oaks, thickets of shrubbery, and patches of flowers and ferns.

Visitor facilities are all in the valley's eastern end: lodging and convenience stores at Curry Village, Yosemite Lodge, and the historic Ahwahnee Hotel; a grocery and other services at Yosemite Village, where you'll also find the park headquarters and visitor center. A quarter-mile trail from the village leads to the base of 2,425-foot Yosemite Falls, the continent's highest waterfall.

You'll find a variety of activities available, from free nature walks and art classes to bicycle and raft rentals, horseback rides, and rock-climbing lessons. Details are printed in the free "Yosemite Guide," available at entry stations, most service facilities, and the Valley Visitor Center at busy Yosemite Village.

The visitor center also provides a basic overview of the park's natural history (as does the small nature center at Happy Isles to the east). The Indian Cultural Museum next door contains an exquisite collection of basketry. In the reconstructed village behind, you'll see tool making, basket weaving, beadwork, and Indian games demonstrated daily in summer.

Glacier Point. To appreciate its glacier-scoured geology fully, you have to leave the valley. At Glacier Point Overlook on the south rim you can see the entire valley, from Yosemite Falls to the sheared granite wall of Half Dome. Beyond rise the snow-clad peaks of the high country.

Glacier Point is a circuitous 30-mile drive from the valley. Take Wawona Road south to Chinquapin, and turn left onto Glacier Point Road (closed in winter about a mile beyond Badger Pass Ski Area). Stop at the Wawona Tunnel pullout for a classic view from Bridalveil Fall to Half Dome and beyond.

Bus service from the valley offers an option for those who'd like a one-way hike from the rim to the valley. Early morning is the best time to start out on the 9-mile Panorama Trail, longest and grandest of the routes to the valley. Take a picnic and water: spectacular overlooks can stretch this into a leisurely day-long outing.

Wawona & the Big Trees. The magnificent Mariposa Grove of giant sequoias lies near the park's south entrance (State 41), 36 miles from the valley. In this grand forest, more than 200 trees measure at least 10 feet in diameter. Largest—30 feet around and 210 feet tall—and probably the oldest is Grizzly Giant. A walk among the trees offers grand vertical views.

...*Yosemite*

Guided tours (fee) run from the valley to the grove in summer, with a stop at Wawona's lovely 1800s hotel and the Pioneer Yosemite History Center. If you drive on your own, park in the lot at the edge of the grove. One-hour tram tours carry visitors through the grove every 15 minutes from May to October (moderate fee). Or you can follow a 2½-mile trail to the upper grove.

Along the Tioga Road. If you leave Yosemite without a visit to the wild and uncrowded backcountry, you'll miss some of the park's finest scenery and best experiences. This land of majestic peaks, rocky chasms, wildflower-trimmed meadows, brilliant blue lakes, and innumerable rivers is accessible mainly by Tioga Road (State 120), usually open late May through October.

Just driving through, you learn a good deal about the natural history of these mountains from roadside exhibits. You'll discover even more if you do some exploring on foot.

Rustic cabins and lodges, tent camps, and more secluded campsites provide a choice of overnight accommodations. To prevent overcrowding, wilderness permits are now required for any overnight stay in the backcountry. They are available free at the Valley Visitor Center, Wawona, Big Oak Flat Information Station, or Tuolumne Meadows. It's a good idea to get your permit a day ahead, as trailheads fill up most summer weekends. Or you can reserve by mail from February through May; send a brief itinerary to Wilderness Permits, Box 577, Yosemite National Park, CA 95389.

Pick up backcountry maps and trail guides at park visitor centers and stores.

High Sierra loop. Five walk-in camps lie within a short day's hike of one another around Tuolumne Meadows. The woodstove-heated tent villages and cabins have comfortable beds and linens, showers and toilet facilities, hearty breakfasts and dinners, and, if you request them, box lunches for the trail. All you need to carry is a day pack with extra clothes, toiletries, and personal gear. The camp cost is $66 per night including meals; trail lunches are an extra charge.

If you prefer to sleep under the stars, you can reserve dinner or breakfast at the camps, which will also store food overnight for you so it won't attract bears (otherwise, be sure to use the cables or hooked poles provided for hanging your food).

Reservations, in great demand, are taken in early December for the next summer, but cancellations have been known to occur; call (209) 454-2002. Or you can try to reserve space on guided hikes or saddle trips.

You need to be in reasonably good shape to make these hikes. With trail elevations as high as 10,300 feet, hiking can be strenuous, requiring steady walks of as long as seven hours between camps.

Visitor strategy

Planning your Yosemite visit is essential, particularly if you're staying in the valley. Though it never hurts to call for last-minute cancellations, campsites and lodging are usually booked months in advance in summer. The quality of your experience will be better if you can avoid this peak period, especially around Memorial Day, Fourth of July, and Labor Day holidays.

Pick a season. For visitors who want to escape the crowds by visiting the high country, summer is still the time to go. While the valley is open year-round, most of Yosemite's 1,189 square miles are accessible only spring through autumn.

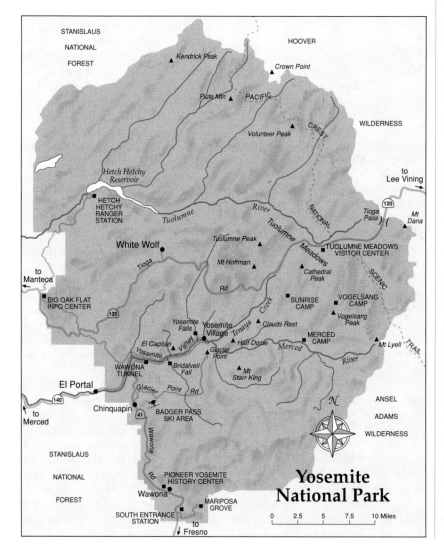

Yosemite
National Park

Off-season visits (before Memorial Day and after September) can be spectacular. In autumn, the valley quiets down somewhat, campgrounds empty, nights get nippy, and leaves turn from green to crimson and gold. One reward of a Yosemite spring vacation is a chance to view the waterfalls at their best, roaring over cliffs to splash through misty rainbows on the valley floor.

For many people, winter's solitude restores the grandeur of the valley, returning its sense of wildness. Frosty weather makes hiking difficult but signals the beginning of snow fun. You can skate, sled, and ski tour against a backdrop of snow-etched canyon walls.

The park's ski season at Badger Pass (see page 124) usually lasts from Thanksgiving to mid April. A free bus shuttles visitors from the valley, about 20 minutes away. More than 350 miles of cross-country trails are also open.

Getting there. Yosemite Valley is a 4-hour drive from the San Francisco area. The park can also be reached by Amtrak and Greyhound to Merced. Two companies offer daily bus service between Merced and Yosemite year-round; for details call Yosemite Gray Line, (209) 383-1563, or Via Yosemite, (209) 722-0366. Yosemite Gray Line also offers service to the park from Fresno (location of the closest major airport). Rental cars are also available at the Fresno airport.

Three highways penetrate the park; you can pick up any of them from State 99, which runs north-south through the Central Valley. Curvy State 120, the Tioga Road (closed in winter), runs from Manteca on the west all the way to Lee Vining on the east side of the park. It's 81 miles from Merced to Yosemite Valley on State 140, the lowest and least winding of the main roads. From Fresno to the southern entrance via State 41 is an 89-mile drive.

Major roads from the west are kept open year-round; State 140 has first priority for snow removal. Always carry chains in winter. For current road conditions, call (209) 372-4605.

Getting around. Whenever and wherever possible, leave your car and use public transportation. Frequent free shuttle buses will whisk you through the valley from campgrounds and lodgings to major facilities and many trailheads.

Cycling is another easy way to get around. A good 9 miles of paved paths loop through the eastern end of the valley. You can rent single-speed bikes at Yosemite Lodge or Curry Village.

In summer, 2-hour narrated tram tours (fee) leave Yosemite Lodge every half-hour daily; there's an evening run on full moon nights. Buses are also available to Glacier Point, Mariposa Grove, and Tuolumne Meadows. Though they are seldom full, it's wise to reserve space by calling (209) 372-1240.

Lodging. Valley accommodations range widely in choice and price. Curry Village has rustic tent cabins (about $30 for two people), modern Yosemite Lodge and nearby cabins are mid-priced, and majestic stone-and-timber Ahwahnee offers luxury (around $185). All locations have restaurants; try the Ahwahnee's Sunday brunch even if you're staying elsewhere.

Lodging is also available at Wawona (pool, tennis court, 9-hole golf course, stables) and, in the high country off Tioga Road, at Tuolumne Meadows (tent cabins, central dining hall) and White Wolf (tent cabins, dining room). The Wawona Hotel, a national historic landmark near the Mariposa Grove, is open from mid-spring to early autumn. Tuolumne Meadows and White Wolf open when the weather permits.

Yosemite reservations may be made up to a year in advance; call (209) 252-4848. A deposit of one night's stay is required. To try for a cancellation, check the front desk of the hotel of your choice.

Another alternative is to establish a base outside the park. You can often find last-minute motel space in El Portal, Mariposa, Oakhurst, and other towns within an hour of the valley. Marriott's new Tenaya Lodge is an upscale choice in Fish Camp south of the park on State 41 (shuttle service provided).

Camping. Valley campgrounds are open from Memorial Day through the end of September. At least two in the valley and one at Wawona stay open year-round. Campgrounds in the high country remain open as long as weather permits.

During the camping season, campgrounds in Yosemite Valley, Hodgdon Meadow, Crane Flat, and Tuolumne Meadows are on a reservation basis through Ticketron. Sites can be reserved up to eight weeks ahead. To get applications for reservations at High Sierra camps for the following summer, call (209) 252-4848 in early November. They must be returned by the first Monday in December. For additional information, see page 120.

East of the Sierra

An ancient lake and a mining ghost town are two reasons to head east of Yosemite National Park.

Spectacular tufa formations surround Mono Lake (off U.S. 395 at Lee Vining), a 60-square-mile body of salty alkaline water that is a resting spot for millions of migratory birds. There's a visitor center on the south shore.

To the north is one of the West's best preserved mining ghost towns.

Bodie State Historic Park includes 170 weathered buildings from the town's gold-mining heyday of the 1870s. Rangers give free history talks at 3 P.M. daily except Monday and Thursday. To get to Bodie, take State 270 east from U.S. 395; the last 3 miles are unpaved.

In summer, you can reach U.S. 395 from Yosemite via the Tioga Road. Snow closes this and other roads from the west in winter.

Central Valley

The flat Central Valley provides strong contrast to its east-west boundaries: the towering peaks of the Sierra Nevada and the hills of the Coast Range. At its southern edge rise the Tehachapi Mountains, while the foothills of the southern Cascades and the northern Coast Range rim it on the north.

It's a big valley, extending 465 miles from north to south and varying from 30 to 60 miles in width. Actually, it's two valleys, the Sacramento and the San Joaquin. Both have namesake rivers meandering through much of their lengths.

Though the San Joaquin Valley extends south beyond Bakersfield, our coverage in this book ends at Fresno.

For a description of the southern part of the valley, see our companion book, the *Southern California Travel Guide*.

A traveler's view

Thanks to irrigation, the 18,000-square-mile Central Valley is the richest agricultural region in the world. Orchards, vineyards, and such staple crops as onions, sweet potatoes, grain, and cotton form the area's economic base.

Recreation is plentiful throughout the valley, whose lakes and rivers afford many opportunities for rafting, waterskiing, fishing, and picnicking. The Delta, a vast inland sea, provides more than 1,000 miles of interconnecting waterways ideal for houseboating.

Sacramento, the valley's largest city and the state capital, brims with pioneer history and gold rush allure. It's also home to the West's first art museum and the state's first theater. The railroad museum in Old Sacramento is the largest of its kind in the world.

Nearby Stockton, on a wide stretch of the Delta, is the area's major port, hosting oceangoing freighters. Farther south lie Modesto, Merced, and Fresno, agricultural communities that also act as gateways to the gold country and high Sierra regions.

Planning a trip

The Central Valley sizzles in midsummer, but residents and visitors cool off in the many lakes, rivers, and mountain retreats nearby. The rest of the year is pleasant except for occasional dense, low-lying fogs in winter.

Where to stay. Sacramento makes a good base for exploring the valley. Most of the major highways through central California pass through or around the city. And it's served by a number of major carriers and commuter airlines, as well as Amtrak and Greyhound.

The rapidly growing city (current population hovers around 370,000) offers a variety of accommodations, including the restored *Delta King* riverboat, the upscale Sterling Hotel (a refurbished 19th-century mansion), and several downtown bed-and-breakfast inns.

All large valley cities have some air, rail, and bus service (Fresno's regional airport is particularly busy). Rental cars are available in major cities.

Getting around. You'll need a car to explore this far-flung area. Interstate 5, on the valley's western side, is the most heavily traveled route between Southern and Northern California. A swift but somewhat monotonous freeway, it bypasses the towns that grew up along State 99, the slower highway to its east.

A number of east-west feeder roads connect the two routes, passing through small farming communities, and the two highways join at Red Bluff, just north of the valley.

Sacramento lies about halfway between San Francisco and Lake Tahoe on Interstate 80, the region's major east-west artery. From Sacramento, U.S. 50 also reaches east into the Sierra toward Lake Tahoe and Nevada beyond. Interstate 580 from the Bay Area slices through the valley, connecting with Interstate 5 near Stockton.

An impressive landmark in downtown Sacramento since 1874, the golden-domed State Capitol contains art and history displays. Free tours take place daily.

Contacts

These agencies offer information on attractions and accommodations. See additional contacts throughout this chapter.

Sacramento Convention & Visitors Bureau
1421 K St.
Sacramento, CA 95814
(916) 449-6711

Sacramento Visitor Information Center
1104 Front St.
Sacramento, CA 95814
(916) 442-7644

Fresno Convention & Visitors Bureau
808 M St.
Fresno, CA 93721
(800) 543-8488

Sacramento

Sacramento's history began with the splash of Captain John A. Sutter's anchor in the American River in 1839. Sutter, a Swiss immigrant, had navigated up the Sacramento River from San Francisco en route to a 50,000-acre parcel of land granted him by the Mexican government. On a knoll not far from the anchorage, he built a fort to protect his 76-square-mile holding, established an embarcadero, and called the area New Helvetia.

When gold was discovered at Sutter's sawmill in Coloma, Sacramento quickly became a lusty boomtown, connected to other communities like Marysville and Red Bluff by river steamer and sailing schooner. When the gold ceased to pan out, agriculture developed, and the city emerged as a supply center.

Outdoor family fun

Although it's adorned with wide, tree-lined boulevards and elegant Victorian houses and boasts a variety of recreational activities and attractions, Sacramento is often overlooked by visitors. Yet it's a rewarding stop.

Cruises. Riverboats ply the Sacramento on 1½-hour narrated cruises from spring through autumn. Short cruises depart from the L Street Landing in Old Sacramento, the redeveloped historic district. Longer trips through the Delta between Sacramento and San Francisco leave from the port (west side of the river, south of Interstate 80) on weekends from May to October (see page 124).

American River Parkway. A 23-mile-long strip of green connects several parks (picnic sites, hiking and riding trails, boat-launching facilities, and an 18-hole golf course) along the banks of the American River between Nimbus Dam to the northeast and the stream's junction with the Sacramento River. A paved bicycle trail runs 30-plus miles from Discovery Park to Folsom Lake.

William Land Park. Bounded by Freeport and Riverside boulevards, 13th Avenue, and Sutterville Road, this large park in south Sacramento offers several child-pleasers: the Sacramento Zoo (open daily; small fee) and Fairytale Village (open daily February through November, variable winter schedule; small fee). The park also has pools, gardens, a public golf course, baseball diamonds, picnic grounds, and a grove of flowering cherries. In summer, Shakespeare finds evening audiences in the park's outdoor amphitheater.

Gibson Ranch County Park. Northeast of the downtown area, a 326-acre 1870s ranch delights youngsters, who can feed farm animals, watch milking demonstrations, see early-day farm equipment, and fish in a lake alive with ducks, mudhens, geese, and muskrats. To get there, take Watt Avenue north to Elverta Road, turn left and follow it to the entrance. The free park is open daily from 7 A.M. to dusk.

Sacramento Science Center. The dry title belies the interesting displays at this combination natural history and physical science complex, located northeast of downtown at 3615 Auburn Boulevard. A live animal hall of more than 45 species of mammals, birds, and reptiles hosts weekend shows at 2 and 4 P.M. Planetarium shows take place weekends at 11 A.M. and 3 P.M. A trail roams through the nature area outside (picnic tables available). A modest admission is charged; shows are extra.

Capital beginnings

It's not surprising that Sacramento became the state capital in 1854. Its prime location has always made it a vital link in the state's river, rail, and highway network. California's first railroad began here in 1856, and a few years later the city became the western terminus of the Pony Express line.

Capitol Park. An oasis on hot summer days, the 40 well-landscaped acres surrounding the capitol building include plantings from around the world. A 10-day Camellia Festival in March showcases the park's more than 800 varieties. You'll also notice several monuments and a wealth of squirrels.

Capitol tour. Office buildings line the Capitol Mall corridor as you near the domed capitol at 11th Street between L and N. A $68-million restoration has returned 19th-century grandeur to the massive structure.

Two different guided tours take place every hour between 9 A.M. and 4 P.M. weekdays, from 10 A.M. on weekends. A third tour is added in summer. Free tickets are issued a half-hour before each tour from the office in the basement. Or you can wander through seven historic rooms on your own after picking up a free brochure. A short film describes the building.

Old Governor's Mansion. This elegant 19th-century Victorian at 16th and H streets was home to 13 California governors. Now vacant, it's open only for guided tours, which take place daily on the hour from 10 A.M. to 4 P.M. Expect a small admission fee.

Old Sacramento

This four-block-long historic district along the east bank of the Sacramento River (between Capitol Mall and I Street) preserves the largest collection of gold rush–era buildings on the Pacific Coast. Visitors stroll plank sidewalks past 100 fully restored brick-and-frame structures, many housing turn-of-the-century museums. No ghost town, this 28-acre area teems with restaurants, gift shops, and offices.

Start your walking tour at the visitor center (1104 Front Street), open daily from 9 A.M. to 5 P.M. Maps there show landmarks and attractions.

You'll pass the 1849 Old Eagle Theater (Front and J streets), the period schoolhouse (Front and L), and the B. F. Hastings Building (2nd and J), where museums commemorate the Pony Express, Wells Fargo, and the California Supreme Court.

California State Railroad Museum. This impressive interpretive railroad museum (2nd and I streets), the largest in the world, is the area's premier attraction. More than 20 restored locomotives and cars and a wealth of historical railroad exhibits are on display. A film describes 19th-century railroads. The authentic reconstruction of the nearby 1876 Central Pacific Passenger Station recalls the sights and sounds of the era. On summer weekends, a steam train takes passengers on a 45-minute ride (see page 126).

Tickets good for a same-day visit to both locations (open 10 A.M. to 5 P.M. daily) are $5 for adults, $2 for children 6 to 17. Train rides are extra.

Sacramento History Museum. The facade of the red brick building at Front and I streets housing memories of the city's colorful past is a true replica of the public building (city hall, jail, and waterworks) constructed on this site in 1854. Inside, it looks more like an ultramodern mall, with a sunken theater, an extensive gold collection, a canning line, and a re-created 1920s farm kitchen. The museum is open 10 A.M. to 4:30 P.M. Tuesday through Sunday; a modest admission fee is charged.

Delta King. You can overnight aboard the 285-foot stern-wheeler moored along the riverfront or visit its museum, theater, shops, restaurant, and lounges. A sister ship of the *Delta Queen* (now on the Mississippi River), it carried passengers between Sacramento and San Francisco in the 1920s and 1930s.

Other city attractions

Sutter's reconstructed fort, the West's oldest art museum, and showcases for almonds, Indian artifacts, and vintage cars make other interesting stops around town.

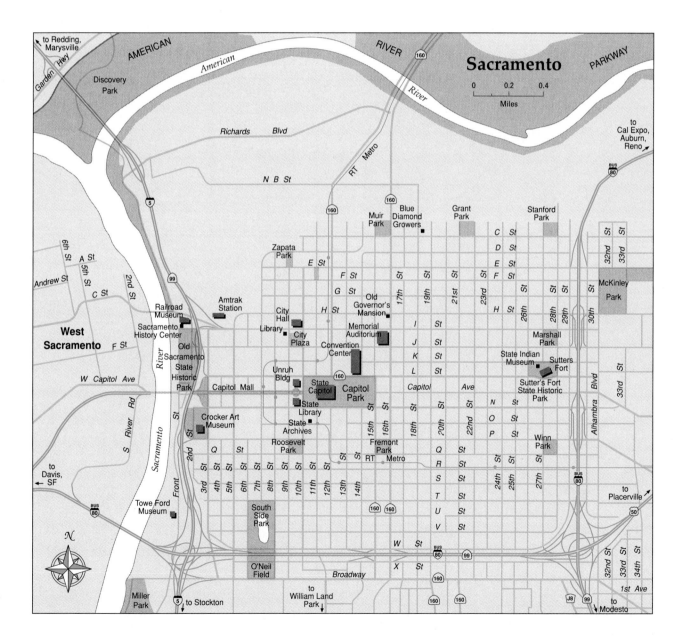

Evening strollers and cyclists pass Old Sacramento's riverfront park; the restored stern-wheeler Delta King, now a hotel, floats in front of the Tower Bridge. Tracks carry steam-powered excursion trains.

...Sacramento

Sutter's Fort State Historic Park. Headset narration allows visitors to tour Captain Sutter's first settlement at their own pace. The fort looks much as it did in 1846, with blacksmith shops, a prison, and living quarters. Located at 2701 L Street, it's open daily (except major holidays) from 10 A.M. to 5 P.M. The modest admission includes headsets.

State Indian Museum. At 2618 K Street (adjacent to Sutter's Fort), this recently revitalized museum interprets the tribal life of California's Native Americans, with displays of artifacts, jewelry, and clothing. The basket collection is particularly good. Hours and admission fees are the same as at the fort.

Crocker Art Museum. The elegant craftsmanship of this stately Victorian mansion built by Judge E. B. Crocker in 1873 to house his private art collection made a perfect setting for its grand displays. But a glass pavilion connecting it to the Crockers' actual home has added space. Of particular interest are its Asian art and contemporary California paintings. On the first floor, a Discovery Gallery caters to children's interests.

The museum, at 216 O Street, is open Tuesday through Sunday, 10 A.M. to 5 P.M. (to 9 P.M. on Thursday). Admission is modest.

Towe Ford Museum. Car buffs shouldn't miss this unique collection of antique Fords at 2200 Front Street. It's the world's most complete, with every year and model from 1903 to 1953 including Phaetons, roadsters, woodies, and other fondly remembered styles. On weekends, shuttle buses run between it and the Sacramento Visitor Information Center (see page 110). Open 10 A.M. to 6 P.M. daily, the museum charges admission of $5 for adults, $2.50 for teenagers, and $1 for children.

Blue Diamond Growers. Nuts are the theme at this almond factory (18th and C streets). Free guided tours (9 and 10 A.M., 1 and 2 P.M. weekdays) include a film (also shown Saturday).

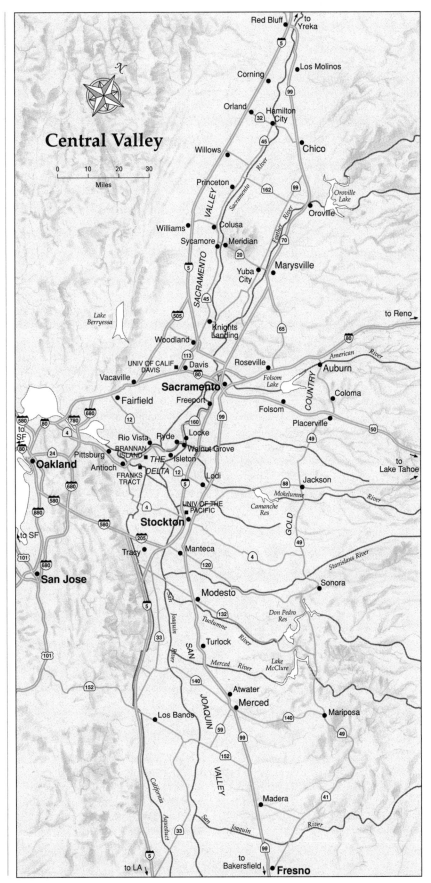

Along the Sacramento

The quiet towns and countryside along the banks of the Sacramento River north of the capital city seem little changed since their beginnings in the early 1900s. To explore by car, you'll have to stray slightly off busy interstates onto two-lane, lightly traveled back roads that follow the river's meanderings. If possible, plan your drive for spring or early summer: cottonwoods have leafed out, fruit orchards are in bloom, crops are planted, and summer's heat hasn't yet descended on the valley.

Boating. If you pick your time and place, there's plenty of elbow room on the river for fishing, boating, and waterskiing. Most towns and fishing resorts along the route have boat-launching facilities. Your best bet for gas to the north of Colusa is Los Molinos, about a mile east of the river.

How to get there. If you're heading east on Interstate 80, turn north on State 113 at Davis (home of a University of California campus). To reach State 113 from Sacramento, exit Interstate 5 at Wood-land (full of turn-of-the century architectural gems) and follow the signs.

Along the route

At Knights Landing, a small community somewhat reminiscent of towns along Mark Twain's Mississippi, turn left onto 4th Street, a narrow levee road along the river's south bank, to reach State 45. As the road angles northwest across open farmland, note the rice "checks"—flooded paddies surrounded by low levees.

Past the town of Sycamore, detour east across the river on State 20 to visit the quiet streets of Meridian. A small grocery store near the river can provide the makings for a picnic lunch.

Colusa, 5 miles farther north on State 45, is a popular swimming and waterskiing center. A 67-acre recreation area on the west bank of the river has a launching ramp, picnic sites, a sandy beach, and unimproved campsites.

Three miles southwest of town lies one of the Sacramento Valley's four wildlife refuges, winter home for millions of migratory wildfowl. For a walking tour, pick up a map at the headquarters.

At Princeton (about 15 miles north of Colusa), you can board the last operating ferry on the Sacramento River for a 2-minute ride across the river. State 45 continues north 23 miles to Hamilton City. From here, you can turn west to reach Interstate 5 at Orland or head east to Chico, off State 99.

Chico

At the north end of the Central Valley lies the college town of Chico, founded in 1849 on a ranch purchased by John Bidwell, a Civil War–era general and former gold miner. If his antebellum-style house and its surrounding parkland (now a 2,400-acre state park) look familiar, you might have seen them in such movies as *Gone with the Wind*.

Guided tours of the mansion, located at 525 The Esplanade, take place from 10 A.M. to 5 P.M. daily (small admission). The large park (picnic sites, playing fields, wilderness areas) winds along Chico Creek 10 miles into the foothills.

Detours from Interstate 5

Two favorite outings lie near Sacramento within easy striking distance of Interstate 5: Vacaville, 30 miles west on Interstate 80, and Folsom, 15 miles east off U.S. 50.

Vacaville. Much of this city's visitor appeal centers an the Nut Tree, a dining spot–cum–amusement park and shopping center. Now a large complex of restaurants and stores complete with private airport, it all started with a single black walnut tree planted in 1860 to shade passersby on the Emigrant Trail.

An addition to the property is the large factory outlet center (open daily to 9 P.M.) on the south side of Interstate 80. And a block away (junction of Interstate 80 and 505), you can work your way through the giant mazes of the WOOZ ($6.50 adults, $5 ages 5 through 12); call (707) 446-3977 for seasonal hours.

Folsom. The gaslight and restored buildings along Sutter Street whisper of this town's gold-mining past. The chamber of commerce is in the old Southern Pacific depot at Sutter and Wool streets; old cars are on display outside. A blacksmith shop and miner's cabin stand nearby.

Johnny Cash helped familiarize people with Folsom State Prison, 2 miles north of town. A gift shop at the main gate sells items crafted by the prisoners, and a fascinating museum documents the history of incarceration in California.

The 75-mile shoreline of Folsom Lake is all part of a state recreation area popular with boaters, waterskiers, anglers, campers, and picnickers. Hikers and horseback riders have 65 miles of trails to roam.

The Delta

The Sacramento–San Joaquin Delta, an irregularly bounded area of almost 740,000 acres (50,000 of which are water), extends from Sacramento south to Tracy and from Stockton east as far as Pittsburg. With almost 1,000 miles of navigable sloughs bearing such astonishing names as Hog, Little Potato, Lost Whiskey, Little Conception, and Lookout, it's a boater's haven.

Once a densely forested everglade, the area was denuded to feed the furnaces of old riverboats. The muddy expanses that remained were later transformed into hundreds of levee-rimmed islands (many still called "tracts"), where enterprising farmers prosper with asparagus and fruit crops.

Fed by two of the West's largest rivers, the Sacramento and the San Joaquin, the Delta also accepts tribute from the Mokelumne, Stanislaus, Tuolumne, Merced, and Kings rivers before tumbling on into the San Francisco Bay.

Exploring the Delta

One of the most startling experiences for new visitors to the Delta is to look across a flat field of swaying grain and see the profile of a freighter moving silently along a levee top. Yet it's as characteristic of the region as the sudsy wake of a water-skier's craft or the bobbing of a fishing boat.

Interstates 5, 80, 580, and 680 encircle this vast waterway, yet you hardly know it's there. To gain access by car, you have to travel State highways 4, 12, or 160 and some of the county roads. A detailed map of the region can be obtained from area tackle shops; or send $2.75 to Delta Map, P.O. Box 9140, Stockton, CA 95208.

Boating. The best and most popular way to explore this watery world is by boat. Bring your own or rent anything from a houseboat to a fishing skiff. One- and two-day boat tours are also available from Sacramento, Stockton, and San Francisco (see page 124). Shorter summer cruises also depart from Brentwood and Isleton.

Houseboats can be rented all through the Delta. For a listing of agencies, contact the chambers of commerce for Antioch—(415) 757-1800—and Stockton—(209) 466-7066.

The basic navigational guide in the Delta region is Chart 5527SC (San Joaquin River). Chart 5528SC is a guide to the Sacramento River from Andrus Island to Sacramento, including the northern reaches of the Delta. For information and the price of the charts, write to the Distribution Division (C44), National Ocean Survey, Riverdale, MD 20840.

For free pamphlets on state boating regulations and water safety, write to Commanding Officer (B), 12th Coast Guard District Office, 630 Sansome Street, San Francisco, CA 94126.

Fishing. Autumn is the peak run of one of the Delta's most sought-after game fish, the striped bass. Salmon and steelhead also pass through here on their autumnal migration up the Sacramento River, but the area seldom presents ideal water conditions for trout fishing. Year-round residents include catfish, black bass, bluegill, and giant sturgeon. Bait and tackle shops can update you on fishing conditions and provide the names of good guides.

Cycling. Biking the Delta means two-wheeling along level, lightly traveled roads atop levees separating low-lying fields from higher waters. A spring ride lets you survey acres of blooming pear tree tops while avoiding summer's heat and high winds (though winds can be a problem year-round). Three convenient spots to park your car and begin your ride are at Brannan Island State Recreation Area (day-use fee), Sacramento County's Hogback Island Access ($3, weekends only), and the River Road in Walnut Grove. To see freighter traffic, cycle on Sherman and Andrus islands; Grand, Sutter, and Ryer islands have pear orchards.

Camping. Brannan Island State Recreation Area has about 150 campsites for tents and motor homes and a public boat launch; phone (916) 777-6464 for fees and reservations. Private campgrounds are scattered throughout the Delta; detail maps show locations.

Dining. To serve the recreational flotilla on the Delta, a number of restaurants are anchored along the water. Architecture ranges from steamboat revival to neoclassical, and cuisine runs from crayfish to chateaubriand. Most restaurants have their own dock space; some are open only in summer.

Brannan Island and west Stockton offer the greatest variety. Other landmark eateries include Grand Island Mansion (an opulent estate open for Sunday brunch only), Ryde Hotel (a Prohibition-era hotel and restaurant), and Giusti's (a rustic Italian restaurant at Snodgrass Slough).

Delta towns

Sightseeing along the Delta reaps rewards. You can buy fresh produce at roadside stands, pack a picnic to enjoy at Brannan Island park, or poke around riverfront communities like Walnut Grove, Freeport, Locke, and Ryde.

State 160 (the Delta Highway) winds 45 miles along the Sacramento River. It's a slow but scenic route between the Central Valley and the Bay Area.

Isleton. Many of the shops in this once-important riverboat port and canning center now stand vacant, though there are a few exceptions. Quong Wo Sing Company store has been owned by the same family for four generations. If you're visiting in early spring, turn onto Isleton Road from State 160 to see the sandhill cranes that winter here.

Locke. Built around 1915 by members of a Chinese association who worked on Delta levees, railroads, and farms, Locke today has fewer than 100 residents. A stroll along its wooden walkways past false-front buildings gives you an inkling of its much livelier past. The Dai Loy Gambling House Museum is a big draw, as is Al's Place, a saloon noted for its hamburgers and steaks.

San Joaquin Valley

South of Sacramento, the Central Valley follows the course of the San Joaquin River, which flows northward to meet the Sacramento. State 99 and Interstate 5 are its north-south corridors, Interstate 580 (south of Stockton) and State 152 the major routes westward toward the coast. Of all of the cities straddling State 99, Stockton and Fresno offer the most visitor attractions.

A longtime agricultural center, the valley is noted for its acres of orchards and vineyards and, farther south, cotton fields. The grapes grown around Lodi and Stockton are pressed into premium wines. Free tasting rooms in the Stockton area welcome visitors.

Stockton area

A boomtown in the 1850s, Stockton today is an important port city connected to the San Francisco Bay Area by a 76-mile deep-water channel. Docks along the western edge of town serve some 700 freighters a year. Several excursion boats offer regular river cruises. For information, contact the Stockton–San Joaquin Convention and Visitors Bureau, 46 W. Fremont Street, Stockton, CA 95202; phone (800) 888-8016.

City attractions. Down at the harbor, Stockton Waterfront Warehouse (445 W. Weber Avenue) offers waterside dining choices. At Pacific Avenue and Stadium Drive, the ivy-covered, Gothic-style buildings and green lawns of the venerable University of the Pacific give it the ideal campus look.

The free Haggin Museum in Victory Park (Pershing Avenue at Rose Street) documents county history. It's particularly noted for its fine collections of Hudson River School paintings and California Indian baskets.

An oasis for families with small children is Pixie Woods Wonderland in Louis Park (Monte Diablo and Occidental streets). Amidst a fantasyland setting are amusement rides and a petting zoo (admission). It's open 11 A.M. to 6 P.M. Wednesday through Friday and noon to 5 P.M. weekends from mid-June to early September. Hours are shorter in spring and autumn; it closes in winter.

Fresno

A 19th-century farming town, fast-growing Fresno is now the state's eighth-largest city and the valley's financial and agricultural center. Its downtown is parklike. To get your bearings, stop by the Fresno Convention and Visitors Bureau (808 M Street), open 8 A.M. to 5 P.M. weekdays.

Dining options. In the early 1900s Basque shepherds came from France and Spain to work on ranches around the valley. In the winter they lived in Fresno boarding hotels, two of which still stand. For a typical Basque family-style lunch, visit the Santa Fe (935 Santa Fe Street) or Yturri (2546 Kern Street) hotels near the railroad station. The Yturri also serves dinner.

Because Fresno has been a favorite of Armenian immigrants since the 1880s, you're as likely to find lavash as French bread in its markets. For fresh picnic fixings, stop by these two downtown bakeries: Hye Quality (2222 Santa Clara Street) and Valley (502 M Street). Or have lunch at George's Shish Kebab (Galleria, 2405 Capitol Street).

Restored homes. Two of the city's restored 19th-century houses are open for tours (small fee). Guided walks through the Meux Home (1007 R Street) take place noon to 3:30 P.M. Friday through Sunday. A bonus to visiting the Edwardian mansion of raisin baron Theodore Kearney (7160 West Kearney Boulevard, 7 miles west of downtown) is the chance to wander around its spacious grounds. Tours are offered from 1 to 4 P.M. Friday through Sunday.

Museums. The Fresno Metropolitan Museum of Arts, History, and Science (1555 Van Ness Avenue) houses a sizable collection of paintings, ranging from old masters to trompe l'oeil; there is also an array of Ansel Adams' photographs and historical exhibits. The museum (small fee) is open Wednesday through Sunday, 11 A.M. to 5 P.M.

The Fresno Art Museum (2233 N. 1st Street) offers rotating exhibits, foreign film programs, concerts, and a gift shop. There's a small charge to visit.

Roeding Park. A pioneer nurseryman planted verdant Roeding Park (Olive or Belmont exits off State 99) with hundreds of trees, making this 157-acre oasis a great spot to picnic. Here, too, are camellia and rose gardens, tennis courts, lakes, a children's Story Land (fee), and Fort Miller Block House, where free historical exhibits are open afternoons from May to October.

Chaffee Zoological Gardens, at the southeastern corner of the park, contains more than 700 animals, Asian birds, and reptiles. Of particular interest are the elephant compound, reptile house, and denizens of the tropical rain forest and Australian Outback. The zoo (fee) is open 10 A.M. to 5 P.M. daily.

Other valley stops

Micke Grove Park and Zoo (Lodi, 9 miles north of Stockton). The San Joaquin County Historical Museum, a zoo, a Japanese garden, and shady picnic sites are only some of the reasons to stop at this 120-acre county park (open daily, per-car admission).

McHenry Mansion and Museum (15th and I streets, Modesto). Though movie mogul George Lucas is the favorite son these days, the McHenrys were one of Modesto's pioneer families. Their 1863 restored home is open for free tours Tuesday through Thursday and Sunday afternoons.

Castle Air Museum (Castle Air Force Base, 6 miles north of Merced). Some three dozen lovingly restored military planes are displayed, from World War II to the present. They range in size from a drone too small to carry a pilot to the gigantic B-52. The free museum is open daily, 10 A.M. to 4 P.M. A restaurant and gift shop add to its appeal.

A young "conductor" poses proudly at the Western Railway Museum, a 25-acre, open-air collection of vintage rolling stock in the Delta region (see page 126).

Northern California
An Activity Guide

Camping at National Parks

Advance planning will help you get the most out of a camping trip to one of California's national parks or monuments. For information and campsite fees (currently $3 to $12 per night), contact the individual parks listed below or the National Park Service, Western Regional Information Office, Fort Mason, Bldg. 201, Bay and Franklin Streets, San Francisco, CA 94123; phone (415) 556-0560.

Maximum RV length accepted varies from campground to campground—be sure to check ahead of time.

Lassen Volcanic National Park (see page 90). Information: (916) 595-4444. The park's seven campgrounds are open only from June to fall; heavy snows limit park access in winter. State 44 and State 89 lead to the park, located 47 miles east of Redding. Most campgrounds close in September, but two—Butte Lake and Manzanita Lake—remain open into October.

Three campgrounds are reached by the Lassen Park Road, a 30-mile paved scenic route winding through the western part of the park. Largest of the park campgrounds is *Manzanita Lake* (179 tent/RV sites, sanitary disposal station, disabled facilities, elevation 5,890 feet), at Manzanita Lake near the park's northwest entrance. About 4½ miles northeast is *Crags* (45 tent/RV sites, pit toilets, elevation 5,700 feet). Another large camping area is *Summit Lake, North and South* (48 tent and 46 tent/RV sites, disabled facilities, elevation 6,695 feet), about 12 miles southeast of Manzanita Lake on Lassen Park Road.

In the park's northeast corner is *Butte Lake Campground* (98 tent/RV sites, disabled facilities, elevation 6,100 feet), located 18 miles southeast of Old Station off State 44 (last 6½ miles unpaved). At the southwest entrance is *Southwest Campground* (21 tent sites, flush toilets, adjacent food service, elevation 6,700 feet). Two re-

mote campgrounds near the southeast corner of the park are *Juniper Lake* (18 tent/RV sites, no piped water, pit toilets, elevation 6,790 feet), 13 miles northwest of Chester on the Chester–Juniper Lake Road; and *Warner Valley* (18 tent/RV sites, pit toilets, elevation 5,650 feet), 17 miles northwest of Chester on the Chester–Warner Valley Road.

Lava Beds National Monument (see page 93). Information: (916) 667-2282. Open year-round is *Indian Well Campground* (40 tent/RV sites, elevation 4,770 feet).

Pinnacles National Monument (see page 57). Information: (408) 389-4526. There are 23 year-round tent sites at *Chapparal Campground*, 11 miles northeast of Soledad on State 146.

Point Reyes National Seashore (see page 69). Information: (415) 663-1092. No vehicle campgrounds. Four hike-in campgrounds (charcoal braziers, pit toilets, no drinking water; reservations necessary) are open year-round by permit, available at the Bear Valley Visitor Center.

Redwood National Park (see page 81). Camping facilities within this federally administered area are located in three state parks. Campsite reservations can be made between 48 hours and 8 weeks prior to date of arrival through the MISTIX reservation system (see page 121).

Del Norte Coast Redwoods State Park. Information: (707) 464-9533. Located 9 miles south of Crescent City, this park is open April to October (8 tent and 107 tent/RV sites, disposal station, elevation 400 feet).

Jedediah Smith Redwoods State Park. Information: (707) 464-9533. Located 9 miles northeast of Crescent City off U.S. 199, the park is open all year (108 tent/RV sites, disposal station, disabled facilities, elevation 250 feet).

Prairie Creek Redwoods State Park. Information: (707) 488-2171. Located north of Orick off U.S. 101, the park has two campgrounds, both open year-round: *Elk Prairie* (74 tent/RV sites, disposal station, disabled facilities, elevation 150 feet), 6 miles north of Orick; and *Gold Bluffs Beach* (25 tent/RV sites, no piped

water, elevation 0 feet), 8 miles north of Orick off U.S. 101 via Davidson Road.

Whiskeytown Unit of the Whiskeytown-Shasta-Trinity National Recreation Area (see pages 84–85). Information: (916) 241-6584. Open year-round are *Oak Bottom* (100 tent and 50 RV sites, reservations available, disposal station, elevation 1,250 feet), located 13 miles west of Redding off State 299; and undeveloped *Brandy Creek* (37 RV sites, elevation 1,250 feet), located 14 miles west of Redding off State 299 on Kennedy Memorial Drive.

For camping in Shasta-Trinity National Forest, phone (415) 705-2874.

Yosemite National Park (see page 107). Information: (209) 372-0264. Three all-year campgrounds and 11 seasonal areas offer more than 1,800 campsites. Five campgrounds are in Yosemite Valley; others are along Tioga Road and Big Oak Flat Road, off Glacier Point Road, and near Wawona. Reservations (recommended May through September) may be made for some campgrounds up to 8 weeks in advance at local Ticketron outlets or by calling (800) 452-1111 (small fee).

Maximum length of stay is 30 days, except from June 1 to September 15, when stays are limited to 7 days in Yosemite Valley and 14 days outside the valley.

In Yosemite Valley (elevation 4,000 feet), campgrounds border the Merced River near the east end of the valley, generally between Yosemite Village and Curry Village. One valley automobile campground is kept open all year (specific site varies); others open in April or May and close in October or November. Campgrounds include *Lower River* (138 tent/RV sites, disposal station), *Upper River* (124 tent sites), *Lower Pines* (172 tent/RV sites, disabled facilities), *North Pines* (85 tent/RV sites), and *Upper Pines* (238 tent/RV sites, disposal station). *Sunnyside* is an all-year walk-in campground (35 tent sites).

Two additional all-year campgrounds are *Wawona* (100 tent/RV sites, elevation 4,000 feet), located 1 mile northwest of Wawona on State 41, and *Hodgdon Meadow* (105 tent/RV sites, elevation

4,872 feet), 9 miles west of Crane Flat just off Big Oak Flat Road.

Open June to September is *Bridalveil Creek Campground* (110 tent/RV sites, elevation 7,200 feet), off the Glacier Point Road about 8 miles east of Chinquapin.

The Tioga Pass Road cuts through Yosemite's high country. Opening in May is *Crane Flat Campground* (166 tent/RV sites, elevation 6,190 feet); opening in June are *White Wolf* (87 tent/RV sites, elevation 8,000 feet) and *Tuolumne Meadows* (314 tent/RV sites, disposal station, elevation 8,600 feet). Three other Tioga Road campgrounds also open in June, but with simpler facilities (no piped water, pit toilets): *Tamarack Flat* (52 tent/RV sites, elevation 6,315 feet), *Yosemite Creek* (75 tent/RV sites, elevation 7,659 feet), and *Porcupine Flat* (52 sites, elevation 8,100 feet). All campgrounds along the Tioga Road close by mid-October.

Walk-in campgrounds for backpackers are located in Yosemite Valley at *Backpackers Campground* (25 sites), and along the Tioga Road at *Tenaya Lake* (50 sites) and *Tuolumne Meadows* (25 sites). Hikers who wish to stay at Yosemite's famed High Sierra camps should make reservations months in advance; for information, phone (209) 454-2002.

Camping at State Parks

Camping at state parks and beaches gives you easy access to swimming, fishing, nature hikes, and other fun. We list some of the most popular beach and inland sites. A detailed guide to state park facilities is available for $2—contact the Publications Section, California Department of Parks & Recreation, P.O. Box 942896, Sacramento 94296-0001; phone (916) 322-7000.

Campsite reservations can be made for most parks between 48 hours and 8 weeks prior to date of arrival through the MISTIX reservation system. To charge reservations to a Visa or MasterCard number, or to obtain an informational brochure, phone (800) 444-7275 (California only) or (619) 452-1950 (out of state) on weekdays from 8 A.M. to 5 P.M., or weekends from 8 A.M. to 3 P.M.

Camping fees generally range from $7 to $20 per campsite per night, plus a $3.95 nonrefundable reservation fee. RV hookups or premium beachfront campsites may be slightly higher.

Self-contained recreational vehicles can overnight at several state parks and beaches on a first-come, first-served basis. Regular fees apply for en route sites.

BAY AREA

Big Basin Redwoods State Park, 9 miles northwest of Boulder Creek off State 9 on State 236 (Santa Cruz County); 146 campsites, disposal station. Hiking and equestrian trails, museum. Contact: (408) 338-6132.

Half Moon Bay State Beach, ½ mile west of Half Moon Bay (San Mateo County); 50 campsites, disposal station, en route camping. Fishing, nature program. Contact: (415) 726-6238.

Henry Cowell Redwoods State Park, 5 miles north of Santa Cruz on Graham Hill Road (Santa Cruz County); 113 campsites. Hiking and equestrian trails. Contact: (408) 335-4598.

Mount Tamalpais State Park, 11 miles west of Mill Valley on Panoramic Highway (Marin County); 16 tent campsites, en route camping. Hiking trails, visitor center. Contact: (415) 388-2070.

Samuel P. Taylor State Park, 15 miles west of San Rafael on Sir Francis Drake Boulevard (Marin County); 60 campsites, disposal station, en route camping. Swimming, hiking and equestrian trails. Contact: (415) 488-9897.

CENTRAL COAST

Manresa State Beach, 10 miles south of Santa Cruz off State 1 (Santa Cruz County); 64 campsites. Swimming, fishing, hiking. Contact: (408) 761-1795.

New Brighton State Beach, east end of Capitola off State 1 (Santa Cruz County); 108 campsites, disposal station, en route camping. Swimming, fishing. Contact: (408) 475-4850.

Pfeiffer Big Sur State Park, 2 miles southeast of Big Sur off State 1 (Monterey County); 217 campsites, disposal station. Swimming, fishing, hiking trails. Contact: (408) 667-2315.

Seacliff State Beach, in Aptos off State 1 (Santa Cruz County); 26 sites with hookups. Swimming, fishing, visitor center, museum. Contact: (408) 688-3241.

Sunset State Beach, 16 miles south of Santa Cruz off State 1 (Santa Cruz

County); 90 campsites. Swimming, fishing, hiking trails. Contact: (408) 724-1266.

GOLD COUNTRY & SIERRA

Calaveras Big Trees State Park, 4 miles northeast of Arnold on State 4 (Calaveras County); 129 sites, disposal station. Swimming, fishing, hiking and ski trails. Contact: (209) 795-2334.

Indian Grinding Rock State Historic Park, 11 miles northeast of Jackson off State 88 (Amador County); 21 campsites. Reconstructed Miwok village, visitor center, museum. Contact: (209) 296-7488.

Malakoff Diggins State Historic Park, 21 miles northeast of Nevada City on State 49 and Tyler Foote Crossing (Nevada County); 28 campsites. Swimming, fishing, hiking and equestrian trails, visitor center, museum. Contact: (916) 265-2740.

Plumas-Eureka State Park, 5 miles west of State 89 at Blairsden on County Road A14 (Plumas County); 67 campsites (summer), disposal station. Swimming, fishing, hiking and equestrian trails, museum. Contact: (916) 836-2380.

LAKES & RIVERS

Brannan Island State Recreation Area, 3½ miles south of Rio Vista off State 160 (Sacramento County); 100 campsites with water hookups, disposal station, dock. Swimming, fishing, visitor center. Contact: (916) 777-6671.

Clear Lake State Park, 3½ miles northeast of Kelseyville on Soda Bay Road (Lake County); 147 campsites, disposal station. Swimming, fishing, boating, hiking trails. Contact: (707) 279-4293.

Colusa–Sacramento River State Recreation Area, 9 miles east of Interstate 5 at the north end of Colusa (Colusa County); 22 campsites, disposal station, en route camping. Swimming, fishing, boating. Contact: (916) 458-4927.

Folsom Lake State Recreation Area, 5 miles northeast of Folsom (Placer, El Dorado, and Sacramento counties); 160 campsites, disposal station, rental boats, dock. Swimming, fishing, boating, waterskiing, hiking and equestrian trails. Contact: (916) 988-0205.

Lake Oroville State Recreation Area, 7 miles east of Oroville on State 162 (Butte County); 212 campsites, 75 sites with hookups, disposal station, rental boats, marina, en route camping. Swimming, fishing, waterskiing, hiking trails, visitor center. Contact: (916) 538-2200.

Woodson Bridge State Recreation Area, 6 miles east of Corning on South Avenue (Tehama County); 46 campsites, disposal station. Swimming, fishing, hiking trails. Contact: (916) 839-2112.

LAKE TAHOE

D. L. Bliss State Park, 6 miles south of Meeks Bay on State 89 (El DoradoCounty); 167 campsites (summer), disposal station. Swimming, fishing, hiking trails. Contact: (916) 525-7277.

Donner Memorial State Park, 3 miles west of Truckee on Donner Pass Road (Nevada County); 154 campsites (summer). Swimming, fishing, hiking trails, museum. Contact: (916) 587-3841.

Emerald Bay State Park, 8 miles north of South Lake Tahoe (El Dorado County); 100 campsites (summer), dock. Swimming, fishing, boating. Contact: (916) 541-3030 (summer) or 525-7232 (park district headquarters).

Grover Hot Springs, 4 miles west of Markleeville off State 89 on County Road E1 (Alpine County); 76 sites (May–October), hot spring pool. Swimming, fishing, hiking trails. Contact: (916) 694-2248.

Sugar Pine Point State Park, 1 mile south of Tahoma on State 89 (El Dorado County); 175 campsites, disposal station, dock. Swimming, fishing, hiking and ski trails, museum. Contact: (916) 525-7982.

Tahoe State Recreation Area, ½ mile northeast of Tahoe City on State 28 (Placer County); 39 sites (summer), dock. Swimming, fishing, boating. Contact: (916) 583-3074 (summer) or 525-7232 (park district headquarters).

NORTH COAST

Fort Ross State Historic Park, 11 miles north of Jenner on State 1 (Sonoma County); 25 campsites (April–November). Reconstructed Russian trading post and fort. Fishing, museum, visitor center. Contact: (707) 847-3286.

MacKerricher State Park, 3 miles north of Fort Bragg on State 1 (Mendocino County); 143 campsites, disposal station.

Fishing, hiking and equestrian trails. Contact: (707) 937-5804.

Manchester State Beach, 7 miles north of Point Arena off State 1 (Mendocino County); 45 campsites, disposal station. Fishing. Contact: (707) 937-5804.

Patrick's Point State Park, 5 miles north of Trinidad off U.S. 101 (Humboldt County); 123 campsites. Fishing, hiking trails, museum. Contact: (707) 677-3570.

Russian Gulch State Park, 2 miles northeast of Mendocino off State 1 (Mendocino County); 30 campsites. Fishing, hiking trails. Contact: (707) 937-5804.

Salt Point State Park, 20 miles north of Jenner on State 1 (Sonoma County); 130 campsites, disposal station. Fishing, riding. Contact: (707) 847-3221.

Sonoma Coast State Beach, north of Bodega Bay on State 1 (Sonoma County); 128 campsites, disposal station. Primitive 11-site environmental camp (April–November only). Fishing, hiking and equestrian trails. Contact: (707) 875-3483.

Van Damme State Park, at Little River on State 1 (Mendocino County); 72 campsites, disposal station, en route camping. Fishing, hiking. Contact: (707) 937-5804.

Westport–Union Landing State Beach, 16 miles north of Fort Bragg on State 1 (Mendocino County); 130 campsites, en route camping. Fishing. Contact: (707) 937-5804.

REDWOOD COUNTRY

Grizzly Creek Redwoods State Park, 18 miles east of U.S. 101 on State 36 (Humboldt County); 30 campsites. Swimming, fishing, nature trails, visitor center. Contact: (707) 777-3683.

Humboldt Redwoods State Park, 45 miles south of Eureka off U.S. 101 near Weott (Humboldt County); 214 campsites, disposal stations, en route camping. Swimming, fishing, hiking and equestrian trails, visitor center. Contact: (707) 946-2311.

Richardson Grove State Park, 8 miles south of Garberville on U.S. 101 (Humboldt County); 169 campsites, disposal station. Swimming, fishing, hiking trails. Contact: (707) 247-3318.

Standish-Hickey State Recreation Area, 1 mile north of Leggett on U.S. 101 (Men-

docino County); 162 campsites. Swimming, fishing. Contact: (707) 925-6482.

SHASTA-CASCADE

Castle Crags State Park, 6 miles south of Dunsmuir off Interstate 5 (Shasta County); 64 campsites, en route camping. Fishing, hiking. Contact: (916) 235-2684.

McArthur–Burney Falls Memorial State Park, 11 miles northeast of Burney on State 89 (Shasta County); 128 campsites, disposal station, en route camping. Swimming, fishing, boating, waterskiing, hiking trails. Contact: (916) 335-2777.

Golf Courses

If you take your golf game on the road, you'll find an ever-increasing choice of courses to play in Northern California. Because of their popularity, you need to reserve tee times well in advance. Our sample of public, resort, and semiprivate courses allowing public play gives some idea of what's available. For a complete roundup, contact local visitor bureaus. Yardage listed is from the regular tees.

BAY AREA

Half Moon Bay Golf Links, 2000 Fairway Dr., Half Moon Bay; (415) 726-4438. Very scenic Palmer/Duane public course; 18 holes, par 72; 6,447 yards; rating 71.0, slope 130.

Pebble Beach golfers

Harding Park Golf Course, Harding Rd. and Skyline Blvd., San Francisco; (415) 664-4690. Municipal course with narrow, tree-lined fairways; 27 holes, par 72; 6,586 yards; rating 71.3, slope 119.

Lincoln Park Golf Course, 34th and Clement Sts., San Francisco; (415) 221-9911. Scenic, hilly public course; 18 holes, par 68; 5,149 yards; rating 64.5, slope 106.

Pasatiempo Golf Course, 18 Clubhouse Rd., Santa Cruz; (408) 459-9155. Semiprivate Alister MacKenzie course overlooking Monterey Bay; 18 holes, par 71; 6,154 yards; rating 71.4, slope 134.

Tilden Park Golf Course, Grizzly Peak Blvd. and Shasta Rd., Berkeley; (415) 848-7373. Hilly public course with lots of trees; 18 holes, par 70; 5,823 yards; rating 67.8, slope 114.

MONTEREY PENINSULA

Del Monte Golf Course, 1300 Sylvan Rd., Monterey; (408) 373-2436. The Monterey Peninsula's oldest public course; 18 holes, par 72; 6,007 yards; rating 69.5, slope 119.

Laguna Seca Golf Club, 10520 York Rd., Monterey; (408) 373-3701. Robert Trent Jones public course with many bunkers and two lakes; 18 holes, par 71; 5,711 yards; rating 68.5, slope 119.

The Links at Spanish Bay, 2700 17-Mile Dr., Pebble Beach; (408) 624-6611, ext. 66. Authentic Scottish links public course bordering Pacific Ocean; 18 holes, par 72; 6,078 yards; rating 72.1, slope 133.

Pacific Grove Municipal Golf Links, 77 Asilomar Blvd., Pacific Grove; (408) 648-3177. Scenic coastal public course; 18 holes, par 70; 5,553 yards; rating 66.3, slope 114.

Pebble Beach Golf Links, 17-Mile Dr., Pebble Beach; (408) 624-3811, ext. 228. Popular resort course famed for magnificent ocean views; 18 holes, par 72; 6,357 yards; rating 72.7, slope 139.

Poppy Hills Golf Course, 3200 Lopez Rd., Pebble Beach; (408) 625-2035. Robert Trent Jones, Jr. public course with tree-lined fairways and rolling greens; 18 holes, par 72; 6,288 yards; rating 71.7, slope 134.

Rancho Cañada Golf Course, 1 mile east of State 1, Carmel Valley Rd., Carmel; (408) 624-0111. Public course set against Santa Lucia Mountains. *East:* 18 holes, par 71; 5,822 yards; rating 67.3, slope 111. *West:* 18 holes, par 72; 6,071 yards; rating, 69.6, slope 120.

Spyglass Hill Golf Course, Stevenson Dr. and Spyglass Hill Rd., Pebble Beach; (408) 625-8563. Outstanding, challenging Robert Trent Jones resort course; 18 holes, par 72; 6,277 yards; rating 73.1, slope 135.

SIERRA

Edgewood Tahoe Golf Course, Loop Pkwy. at Stateline, NV; (702) 588-3566. Scenic resort course on south shore of Lake Tahoe; 18 holes, par 72; 6,960 yards; rating 72.8, slope 133.

Graeagle Meadows Golf Course, State 89, Graeagle; (916) 836-2323. Public course in towering pines of Plumas National Forest; 18 holes, par 72; 6,655 yards; rating 70.7, slope 118.

Incline Village Championship Course, 955 Fairway Blvd., Incline Village, NV; (702) 832-1144. Resort course on Nevada side of Lake Tahoe; 18 holes, par 72; 6,446 yards; rating 70.5, slope 124.

La Contenta Lakes Golf & Country Club, 1653 State 26, Valley Springs; (209) 772-1081. Gold-country public course nestled in foothills; 18 holes, par 72; 6,409 yards; rating 71.3, slope 127.

Lake Tahoe Golf Course, State 50 West, South Lake Tahoe; (916) 577-0788. Public course with mountain and lake views; 18 holes, par 71; 6,169 yards; rating 67.9, slope 110.

Northstar-at-Tahoe Golf Course, Basque Dr., off State 267, Truckee; (916) 587-0290. Robert Muir Graves resort course; 18 holes, par 72; 6,294 yards; rating 69.3, slope 130.

Tahoe Donner Golf Course, Northwoods Blvd., Truckee; (916) 587-9440. Resort course, tight fairways lined with huge pines; 18 holes, par 72; 6,595 yards; rating 71.5, slope 127.

Tahoe Paradise Golf Course, State 50, Tahoe Paradise; (916) 577-2121. Hilly public course with lots of trees; 18 holes, par 66; 4,070 yards; rating 60.0, slope 95.

WINE COUNTRY

Napa Municipal Golf Course, 2295 Streblow Dr., Napa; (707) 255-4333. Championship public course with lots of water; 18 holes, par 72; 6,506 yards; rating 70.7, slope 115.

Silverado Country Club & Resort, 1600 Atlas Peak Rd., Napa; (707) 257-0200. Challenging championship resort courses. *North:* 18 holes, par 72; 6,351 yards; rating 70.9, slope 126. *South:* 18 holes, par 72; 6,213 yards; rating 70.4, slope 123.

Sonoma Golf Club, 17700 Arnold Dr., Sonoma; (707) 996-0300. Top-rated public course; 18 holes, par 72; 6,583 yards; rating 72.3.

OTHER AREAS

Bodega Harbour Golf Links, 21301 Heron Dr., Bodega Bay; (707) 875-3538. Seaside resort course designed by Robert Trent Jones, Jr.; 18 holes, par 70; 5,630 yards; rating 69.2, slope 125.

Haggin Oaks Golf Course, 3645 Fulton Ave., Sacramento; (916) 481-4506. Municipal golf course close to downtown. *South:* 18 holes, par 72; 6,344 yards; rating 69.3, slope 110. *North:* 18 holes, par 72; 6,660 yards; rating 69.9, slope 112.

Lake Shastina Golf Resort, 5925 Country Club Dr., Weed; (916) 938-3201 or (800) 358-4653 in California. Partly open, partly wooded Robert Trent Jones, Jr. resort course; 27 holes, par 72; 6,594 yards; rating 70.9, slope 109.

Skiing

Many Northern California skiers head for Lake Tahoe, with its concentration of top resorts. Other ski areas are in the central Sierra, south of Lake Tahoe, and in the Shasta/Lassen area.

LAKE TAHOE AREA

Alpine Meadows, Alpine Meadows Road off State 89 between Truckee and Tahoe City; (916) 583-4232. Lifts: 1 quad, 2 triple, 8 double chairs; 2 pomas. Summit: 8,637 feet.

Boreal Ridge, Castle Peak exit off Interstate 80 at Soda Springs near Donner Summit; (916) 426-3666. Lifts: 1 quad, 1 triple, 8 double chairs. Summit: 7,800 feet.

Diamond Peak at Ski Incline, 2 miles off State 28 at Incline Village, NV; (702) 832-1177. Lifts: 1 quad, 6 double chairs. Summit: 8,540 feet. Cross-country: 35 km of groomed trails.

Donner Ski Ranch, on old U.S. 40, 3 miles east of Interstate 80 (Norden/Soda Springs exit); (916) 426-3635. Lifts: 1 triple, 3 double chairs. Summit: 7,835 feet.

Granlibakken, on Granlibakken Road off State 89, 1 mile south of Tahoe City; (916) 583-4242. Lifts: 1 poma, 1 rope tow. Summit: 6,500 feet.

Heavenly Valley, on Ski Run Boulevard off U.S. 50, South Lake Tahoe; (916) 541-1330. Lifts: 1 quad, 7 triple, 9 double chairs; 1 aerial tram, 6 surface. Summit: 10,100 feet.

Homewood, on State 89, 6 miles south of Tahoe City; (916) 525-7256. Lifts: 1 quad, 2 triple, 2 double chairs; 5 surface. Summit: 7,880 feet.

Mount Rose, 11 miles northeast of Incline Village, NV on State 431; (702) 849-0704. Lifts: 1 quad, 3 triple, 2 double chairs. Summit: 9,700 feet.

Northstar-at-Tahoe, on State 267 between Truckee and Kings Beach; (916) 562-1010. Lifts: 2 quad, 3 triple, 3 double chairs; 1 gondola, 2 surface. Summit: 8,600 feet. Cross-country: 40 km of groomed trails.

Soda Springs Ski Area, on old U.S. 40, 1 mile east of Interstate 80 (Norden/Soda Springs exit); (916) 426-3666. Lifts: 1 double, 2 triple chairs. Summit: 7,352 feet.

Squaw Valley U.S.A., on Squaw Valley Road off State 89, 5 miles north of Tahoe City; (916) 583-6985. Lifts: 3 quad, 7 triple, 16 double chairs; 1 aerial tram, 1 gondola, 4 surface. Summit: 9,050 feet.

Sugar Bowl Ski Resort, on old U.S. 40, 2 miles east of Interstate 80 (Norden/Soda Springs exit); (916) 426-3651. Lifts: 1 quad, 7 double chairs; 1 gondola. Summit: 8,383 feet.

Tahoe Donner, on Donner Pass Road ½ mile off Interstate 80 (Truckee–Donner Lake exit); (916) 587-9444. Lifts: 2 double chairs, 1 tow. Summit: 7,350 feet. Cross-country: 68 km of groomed trails.

CENTRAL SIERRA

Badger Pass, on Glacier Point Road in Yosemite National Park off State 41; (209) 372-1330. Lifts: 1 triple, 3 double chairs; 2 surface. Summit: 8,100 feet. Cross-country: 57 km of groomed trails.

Cottage Springs, on State 4, 27 miles east of Angels Camp; (209) 795-1209. Lifts: 1 double chair, 1 surface. Summit: 6,500 feet.

Dodge Ridge, off State 108, 32 miles east of Sonora; (209) 965-3474. Lifts: 2 triple, 5 double chairs; 4 surface. Summit: 8,200 feet.

Iron Mountain, 42 miles northeast of Jackson at State 88 and Mormon Emigrant Trail; (209) 258-4672. Lifts: 2 triple, 3 double chairs. Summit: 7,800 feet.

Kirkwood, on State 88 at Carson Pass, 35 miles south of South Lake Tahoe; (209) 258-6000. Lifts: 4 triple, 6 double chairs; 1 surface. Summit: 9,800 feet. Cross country: 80 km of groomed trails.

Mount Reba/Bear Valley, on State 4, 52 miles east of Angels Camp; (209) 753-2301. Lifts: 2 triple, 7 double chairs. Summit: 8,500 feet.

Sierra Ski Ranch, off U.S. 50, 12 miles west of South Lake Tahoe; (916) 659-7453. Lifts: 1 quad, 2 triple, 6 double chairs. Summit: 8,852 feet.

Sierra Summit, on State 168, 64 miles northeast of Fresno at Huntington Lake; (209) 893-3316. Lifts: 2 triple, 3 double chairs; 4 surface. Summit: 8,709 feet.

SHASTA/LASSEN

Lassen Park Ski Area, on State 89 in Lassen National Park, 49 miles east of Red Bluff; (916) 595-3376. Lifts: 1 triple chair, 2 surface. Summit: 7,200 feet.

Mount Shasta Ski Park, between Mt. Shasta City and McCloud off State 89 on Ski Park Hwy.; (916) 926-8610. Lifts: 2 triple chairs, 1 poma. Summit: 6,600 feet.

Plumas-Eureka Ski Bowl, 5 miles off State 70 at Johnsville; (916) 836-2317. Lifts: 3 pomas. Summit: 6,150 feet.

Boat Cruises

Viewing Northern California's waterways from the deck of a boat is usually the best, and certainly the most scenic, way to get to know them. We've rounded up a sampling of what's available; for a complete list of area cruise operators, check with the visitor bureau for that region (addresses at the front of each chapter).

FERRIES

Bay Area. *Golden Gate Ferries,* Ferry Building at foot of Market Street, (415) 332-6600; runs between the city and Sausalito/Larkspur in Marin County. *Tiburon–Angel Island Ferry,* Tiburon, (415) 435-2131; shuttles to Angel Island State Park daily in summer, weekends and holidays the rest of the year.

Sacramento River. *Princeton Ferry,* State 45, Princeton; river's last-operating car ferry, free 2-minute trip.

SIGHTSEEING CRUISES

Bay Area. *Blue & Gold Fleet,* Pier 39, (415) 781-7877; 1¼-hour bay cruises beginning at 10 A.M., 3-hour dinner-dance cruise departing at 8 P.M. weekends. *Hornblower Dining Yachts,* Pier 33, (415) 394-8900; lunch and dinner cruises aboard a re-created 1900s motor yacht. *Red & White Fleet,* Pier 41, (415) 546-BOAT; 45-minute narrated bay cruises departing daily from 10:45 A.M. from Piers 41 and 43½, round-trip ride to Marine World/Africa USA in Vallejo, Alcatraz, and Angel Island State Park. *Questuary,* foot of Broadway, Oakland, (415) 452-2214; 1-hour cruises of the Oakland-Alameda Estuary Wednesday through Sunday.

The Delta. *Delta Riverboat Cruises,* Sacramento, (916) 372-3690; 1- and 2-day cruises between Sacramento and San Francisco. *Matthew McKinley,* (916) 441-6481, and *River City Queen,* (916) 448-7447; paddle-wheeler cruises on Sacramento River, Old Sacramento Waterfront. *Island Queen,* Stockton, (209) 941-4835; paddle-wheeler cruises on the San Joaquin River.

Humboldt Bay. *M.V. Madaket,* foot of C Street, Eureka, (707) 445-1910; 75-minute narrated cruises daily at 5 P.M. May through September.

Lake Tahoe. *M.S. Dixie,* Zephyr Cove, (702) 588-3508, Emerald Bay cruises daily spring to autumn, south shore cruises Tuesday through Saturday afternoon in summer. *North Tahoe Cruises,* Round House Mall and Marina, Tahoe City, (916) 583-0141; 2-hour historical trips on northwest shore daily late spring to autumn.

Tahoe Queen, foot of Ski Run Boulevard, South Lake Tahoe, (916) 541-3364; Emerald Bay sightseeing and dinner cruises year-round, winter ski shuttle to north shore.

Monterey Bay. *Spellbinder Sailing Tours*, Fisherman's Wharf, Monterey, (408) 655-2281, harbor cruises aboard a 50-foot wooden yacht.

Napa River. *Napa Riverboat Co.*, Napa Valley Marina, 1200 Milton Road 8 miles southwest of Napa, (707) 226-2628; 3-hour cruises on Napa River.

Whale Watching

After feeding all summer in the Bering Sea and Arctic Ocean, California gray whales head south each winter to birthing and breeding grounds 4,000 miles away in Baja California. This migration (mostly during December and January) brings the large mammals so near the shore that they can be seen from land at several points.

Males and noncalving females begin trickling north again in March. Cows with calves appear beyond the surf line from April into May.

One of the best places from which to watch the parade is at Point Reyes National Seashore (see page 69). Arrive early on weekends; you might wait up to 2 hours for a shuttle from the visitor center to the lighthouse. Call (415) 669-1534 for information.

Other good sites (from north to south) include these coastal headlands: Redwood National Park's Crescent Beach, at the end of Endert's Beach Road 4 miles south of Crescent City; Mendocino Headlands (whale festival in March); Salt Point State Park, 20 miles north of Jenner; Bodega Head, at the end of Bay Flat Road, 4 miles west of Bodega Bay; and busy Point Lobos State Reserve, south of Carmel on State 1.

Several companies offer whale-watching excursions by boat. Contact the following operators directly for schedules and prices.

Bay Area. *Blue & Gold Fleet*, P.O. Box Z-2, Pier 39, San Francisco, CA 94133, (415) 781-7890; *Dolphin Charters*, 1007 Leneve Pl., El Cerrito, CA 94530, (415) 527-9622; *Oceanic Society Expeditions*, Fort Mason Center, Building E, San Francisco, CA 94123, (415) 474-3385; *Whale Center*, 3929 E. Piedmont Ave., Oakland, CA 94611, (415) 654-6621.

Monterey Bay. *Monterey Sport Fishing*, 96 Fisherman's Wharf #1, Monterey, CA 93940, (408) 372-2203; *Princess Monterey Cruises*, 90 Old Fisherman's Wharf #1, Monterey, CA 93940, (408) 372-2628; *Randy's Whale Watching Trips*, 66 Fisherman's Wharf, Monterey, CA 93940, (408) 372-7440; *Shearwater Journeys*, P.O. Box 1445, Soquel, CA 95073, (408) 688-1990; *Tom's Fisherman's Supply*, 2210 E. Cliff Dr., Santa Cruz, CA 95062, (408) 476-2648; *Wharf Charters*, P.O. Box 396, Capitola, CA 95010, (408) 462-3553.

North Coast. *King Salmon Charters*, 1110 King Salmon Ave., Eureka, CA 95501, (707) 442-3474; *New Sea Angler & Jaws*, P.O. Box 1148, Bodega Bay, CA 94923, (707) 875-3495; *Pacific Adventures*, P.O. Box 268, Cotati, CA 94928, (707) 795-8492; *Lady Irma II Cruises*, Noyo Harbor, P.O. Box 103, Fort Bragg, CA 95437, (707) 964-3854.

River Runs

Take a raft full of people, mix together with a wild and scenic river, and you've got the adventure known as white-water rafting. Commercial outfitters design trips to combine thrilling plunges down untamed rapids with relaxing floats on tranquil pools.

Trips can last from a few hours to a few days. Longer excursions include camping and planned activities such as hiking and gold panning. Plan on spending $50 to $120 (includes lunch) for a one-day excursion, depending on location.

Outfitters operate on these major Northern California rivers: Klamath (near the Oregon border), upper Sacramento (north of Redding), Trinity (northwest of Redding), Salmon (west of Yreka), Middle Fork of the Eel (northern coast), East Carson (south of Lake Tahoe), American (east of Sacramento), Stanislaus (east of Modesto), Merced (east of Merced), and Tuolumne (southeast of Modesto).

For a free directory of river-rafting companies operating in Northern California, call (800) 552-3625. The list, published by the California Western River Guides Association, briefly describes trips.

The California Office of Tourism (address on page 4) can also furnish a list of operators.

Spelunking

Strictly speaking, spelunking is exploring caves left in their natural state, wiggling along on hands and knees through narrow passages and tight spaces. But most of the caverns open to the public in Northern California can be visited on a walk-through basis, via guided tours. Others, such as Lava Beds National Monument (see page 93) and Pinnacles National Monument (see page 57) can be explored on your own.

California Caverns at Cave City, P. O. Box 78, Vallecito, CA 95251; (209) 736-2708. John Muir wrote eloquently about his visit to the West's first commercially developed cave; other early tourists carved their names in its walls. A 1½-hour guided tour ($5.50 adults, $2.75 children 6 to 10) leaves every hour daily from 10 A.M. to 5 P.M. in summer, 10 A.M. to 4 P.M. in autumn; true spelunking is offered by reservation. From State 49 in San Andreas, take Mountain Ranch Road east about 8 miles to the turnoff.

Lake Shasta Caverns, P.O. Box 801, O'Brien, CA 96070; (916) 238-2341. Visits here have a novel flair. First a catamaran ferries you across an arm of Lake Shasta; then a bus drives you up to the cave, 800 feet above the lake. Dazzling formations include rocky draperies as grand as those in any opera house. Daily tours ($12 adults, $6 children 4 to 12) are offered hourly from 9 A.M. to 4 P.M. April to October and 10 A.M., noon, and 2 P.M. November through March. Total tour takes 2 hours. From Interstate 5, exit on Shasta Caverns Road, 15 miles north of Redding.

Mercer Caverns, P.O. Box 509, Murphys, CA 95222; (209) 728-2101. This earthquake-born, mostly vertical cave (visitors descend and then climb 440 stairs) is bounded on one side by a sheer rock wall. The 1-hour tour ($4.50 adults, $2.25 children 5 to 11) visits 10 "rooms"; it's offered 9 A.M. to 5 P.M. in summer, weekends the rest of the year. From Murphys, take Sheep Ranch Road north 1 mile.

Moaning Cavern, P.O. Box 78, Vallecito, CA 95251; (209) 736-2708. There are two ways to get the bottom of this cave: on a spiral staircase or by rappelling down (no experience needed) on secure ropes. Guided tours of the cavern ($5.50 adults, $5 seniors, $2.75 children 6 to 12) take place daily from 9 A.M. to 6 P.M. in summer, 10 A.M. to 5 P.M. in winter. The adventurous can continue deeper on a 3-hour spelunking expedition (reservations required). From Vallecito on State 4 take Parrotts Ferry Road south 1½ miles to the turnoff.

Subway Cave, Lassen National Forest, 55 S. Sacramento St., Susanville, CA 96130; (916) 257-2151. On a self-guided ⅓-mile tour of this lava tube, interpretive plaques explain the sights in colorfully named chambers. Bring a flashlight. To reach the cavern (always open), take State 44 east from Redding to Old Station; the cave is just north of town on State 89.

Train Rides

If riding the rails is your passion, Northern California offers some nostalgic excursions and interesting museums. Several trains operate year-round; others are geared for summer vacationers. Reserve space on the Napa Valley train 6 to 8 weeks in advance; it's also wise to have reservations for the Skunk on summer weekends.

Blue Goose–Short Line Railroad, Yreka, CA 96097; (916) 842-4146. A 3-hour run from Yreka to the old railroad town of Montague offers views of the countryside around Mount Shasta. The line operates from Memorial Day to Labor Day. Diesel trains ($7 adults, $3.50 children) leave at 9:30 A.M. Wednesday through Friday; steam trains ($9 adults, $4.50 children) depart at 10 A.M. weekends.

Central Pacific Freight Depot, Front and K Sts., Old Sacramento, CA 95814; (916) 448-4466. On a visit to the renowned California State Railroad Museum (see page 113), you can enjoy steam train rides May through Labor Day weekends (no trains on July 4th weekend). Trains depart on the hour from 10 A.M. to 5 P.M. from a circa-1867 reconstructed station. Fares for the 45-minute, 7-mile run are $3 adults, $1 children 6 to 17. Tickets are good for a same-day museum visit.

Napa Valley Wine Train, 1275 McKinstry St., Napa, CA 94559; (707) 253-2111 or (800) 522-4142. The train's elegant decor and fine food and wine make it a favorite with tourists, though many residents resent its intrusion. The 36-mile, 3-hour tour (no stops) operates daily Tuesday through Sunday plus holiday Mondays. Excursion fare is $25 weekdays, $29 weekends. Add $22 for champagne brunch (weekends) or lunch, $45 for dinner.

Niles Canyon Railway, (415) 862-9063 (for recorded information). Diesel- and steam-powered engines pull open-air passenger cars through a deep, wooded gorge between the East Bay towns of Sunol and Fremont. The 45-minute round-trip excursions follow the route of the old Western Pacific *California Zephyr*. Volunteers offer rides from 10 A.M. to 4 P.M. on the first and third Sunday of the month. Donations help maintain the line. The Sunol train station is at the junction of Main Street and Kilkare Road.

Railtown 1897, P.O. Box 1250, Jamestown, CA 95327; (209) 984-3953. This state historic park can make a number of claims to American railroading fame: it boasts the oldest steam locomotive still riding the rails, uses the only standard-gauge steam roundhouse, and has been a filming site for more than 200 television shows and movies. In summer, guided roundhouse tours (including a film on the line's history) take place from 10 A.M. to 4:30 P.M. daily ($2 adults, $1.25 children). On summer weekends and holidays, 1-hour runs carry passengers over 8 miles of Sierra countryside. Fares are $7.95 adults, $3.95 children 3 to 12.

Roaring Camp & Big Trees Railroad, P.O. Box G-1, Felton, CA 95018; (408) 335-4400. You'll travel a sinuous, narrow-gauge track up a summit and through the redwoods of the Santa Cruz Mountains aboard this 1880 steam train. Narrated 75-minute trips take place daily. Hours vary depending on the season. Admission is $10.50 adults, $7.50 children 5 to 17. The simulated logging camp of Roaring Camp (Graham Hill and Mount Herman roads near State 17) offers weekend barbecues and picnic grounds.

Santa Cruz, Big Trees & Pacific Railway, P.O. Box G-1, Felton, CA 95018; (408) 335-4400. The Suntan Special, another excursion from Roaring Camp (see above), leaves the redwood-covered mountains for a several-hour stop at Santa Cruz's beach and boardwalk. Trains run week-

ends in spring and autumn and daily in summer, with an extra train on moonlit Saturday nights. Southbound trains depart at 10:30 A.M. and return at 4 P.M.; the northbound express leaves Santa Cruz at noon, returning at 6:30 P.M. Round-trip fares are $16 adults, $8.50 ages 5 to 17.

Skunk Train (California Western Railroad), P.O. Box 907, Fort Bragg, CA 95437; (707) 964-6371. This old logging train through the redwoods between Fort Bragg on the coast and Willits on U.S. 101 dates back to 1885. It's affectionately dubbed the Skunk because old-timers said you could smell the yellow, self-powered railcars before you could see them. The 80-mile, all-day round-trip ride includes a midpoint stop at Northspur (refreshments and souvenirs); half-day trips to Northspur from either Fort Bragg or Willits are also available. In summer a Super Skunk steam train puffs out from Fort Bragg every morning. Round-trip fares are $20 adults, $10 children 5 through 11; half-day fares are $16 adults, $8 children. Reservations are suggested for summer and holiday weekends. Call for schedules.

Western Railway Museum, 5848 State 12, Suisun City, CA 94585; (707) 374-2978. Located at Rio Vista in the Delta, the 25-acre museum and park complex (open weekends only) showcases a grand collection of vintage rolling stock. Your entrance fee ($4 adults, $2 ages 12 to 17 and seniors, $1 ages 3 to 11) includes unlimited rides on electric trolleys and, on some weekends, 12-mile round-trips behind a diesel engine. Grounds include an attractive picnic area and a large bookstore.

Yosemite Mountain–Sugar Pine Railroad, 56001 State 41, Fish Camp, CA 93623; (209) 683-7273. Near the southern entrance to Yosemite National Park, an old logger steam train and Jenny rail cars loop through the Sierra National Forest on 4-mile tours. The steam train operates daily from mid-June through August, weekends only in May, September, and October, departing at 11 A.M. and 12:30 P.M., with extra trains at 2 and 3:30 P.M. from June through August. Jenny rail cars operate daily from late March through October.

Steam train fares are $8.50 adults, $4 children 3 to 12. Jenny fares are $5.75 adults, $3 children 3 to 12. An evening ride (barbecue and entertainment) is held on Saturday nights June through September. A museum on the grounds is free.

Index

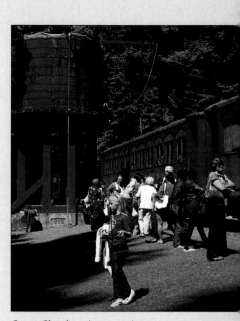

Super Skunk train excursion

Sunset
Proof-of-Purchase
ISBN 0-376-06559-1

128 ■ *Northern California Index*

Southern California
——TRAVEL GUIDE——

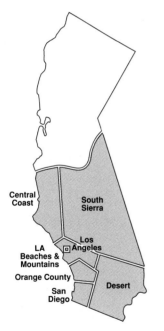

By the Editors of Sunset Books
and Sunset Magazine

Sunset Publishing Corporation
Menlo Park, California

Research and Text
Barbara J. Braasch

Book Editor
Phyllis Elving

Coordinating Editor
Suzanne Normand Mathison

Design
Cynthia Hanson
Kathy Avanzino Barone

Maps
Eureka Cartography

Cover: Colorful toyon boughs frame Avalon Harbor, largest anchorage on Santa Catalina Island. Cover design by Susan Bryant. Photography by Jeff Gnass Photography.

Our thanks...

to the many people and organizations who assisted in the preparation of this travel guide. Special appreciation goes to city and county visitor bureaus, chambers of commerce, and other visitor service agencies throughout Southern California.

We would also like to thank Joan Beth Erickson for her editorial contributions to this manuscript and Lois Lovejoy for her illustration of the California poppy.

Photographers

Carr Clifton: 91; **Betty Crowell:** 15, 114; **Jeff Gnass Photography:** 98; **Cliff Hollenbeck Photography:** 2, 75, 122; **Dave G. Houser:** 23, 51, 83, 119; **Dennis Junor:** 54; **Marie Mainz:** 35, 46; **David Muench:** 59, 78, 86; **Marc Muench:** 62, 127; **Chuck Place Photography:** 31, 67, 111; **David Ryan/Photo 20-20:** 94; **Jonathan Selig/Photo 20-20:** 18, 26; **Larry Ulrich Photography:** 10, 38, 43, 70, 103, 106.

Editor, Sunset Books
Elizabeth L. Hogan

First Printing May 1991

Copyright © 1991, 1979, 1974, 1970, 1964, 1959, Sunset Publishing Corporation, Menlo Park, CA 94025. Sixth Edition. World rights reserved. No part of this publication may be reproduced by any mechanical, photographic, or electronic process, or in the form of a phonographic recording, nor may it be stored in a retrieval system, transmitted, or otherwise copied for public or private use without prior written permission from the publisher. Library of Congress Catalog Card Number: 90-71700. ISBN 0-376-06760-8. Lithographed in the United States.

Disney-inspired paraphernalia, like these suspenders, make the ultimate Southern California souvenir.

Contents

Exploring the Southland

Wacky, wild, and mostly wonderful, Southern California has long been a land of dreams and a magnet for visitors. Millions of people vacation here each year, and thousands settle in permanently.

What is it that draws them? Certainly weather, lifestyle, and a healthy economy are prime factors. Mellowed by the fine subtropical climate, Southern Californians have adopted a more casual—and often innovative—way of life, in the process becoming trendsetters in food, fashion, architecture, and entertainment. And no other single geographical area offers such a combination of natural and man-made attractions, from lofty Sierra peaks and miles of dramatic coastline to the make-believe worlds of Hollywood and Disneyland.

The Southland's popularity has created many of its problems—sprawling cities, crowded highways, and that coined-for-L.A. word, smog. But to visitor and resident alike, the Southland's allure more than compensates for its disadvantages.

Contacts

Agencies listed on the first page of each chapter in this book can provide information about accommodations and attractions in their locales. Contact the following office for general information about traveling in California.

California Office of Tourism
801 K St., Suite 1600
Sacramento, CA 95814
(800) 862-2543 *(for maps and brochures)*
(916) 322-1397 *(for specific travel questions)*

Southern California's image as a carefree, sun-splashed haven was propelled into the national consciousness more than a century ago. A massive advertising campaign by the Southern Pacific and Santa Fe railroads attracted thousands of newcomers in the 1880s with visions of swimming in the blue Pacific, picking oranges from acres of fruit-filled groves, and enjoying shirt-sleeve fun in the snow. Such variety still exists, though it's harder these days to locate a beachside parking lot, find a nearby orange grove, or negotiate bumper-to-bumper mountain roads.

In fact, it's difficult to imagine anyplace with more to offer the visitor. Large cities, with all their cultural and commercial possibilities, add overlays to the landscape between ocean and mountains. Yet the wilderness is close at hand; high bluffs shelter secluded Pacific coves, waterfalls cascade down mountain reaches, and desert badlands stretch for miles in sand and silence.

The lowest point in the western hemisphere (Death Valley's Badwater) is here, not all that far away from the nation's highest point outside of Alaska (Mount Whitney in the Sierra Nevada). Desert resorts offer a wealth of recreational activities, and a fringe of beaches is dotted with bronzed beauties and wave-borne surfers.

Land of entertainment

Southern California sets the pace for the rest of the country in entertainment. Hollywood, Sunset Boulevard, Disneyland, and the Rose Bowl—these are bywords nationwide. You'll find more man-made amusements and attractions here, in fact, than anywhere else in the world.

Since the first moving picture was filmed in Hollywood in 1913, the world has been smitten with the processes as well as the products of this land of illusion. Movie and television studios let you peek behind the scenes, and some of them double as full-scale amusement parks. Celebrity-hunting is a big game, too, and many people come to the area hoping to rub elbows with the stars (we offer some tips on pages 20 and 21).

When Walt Disney created Disneyland in the 1950s in Anaheim, his first and foremost theme park set the standard for family fun. Then another Walter, Knott, expanded his nearby Berry Farm into 150 acres of amusements, and Orange County's reign as an entertainment capital began. To the south, one of the world's best zoos and renowned Sea World marine park are among San Diego's family-oriented attractions.

Southern California is also proud of its cultural complexes. Some of the world's finest museums, theaters, and music centers are here. "Under the stars" performances are popular, too, thanks to the balmy weather. In summer, the famed Los Angeles Philharmonic performs in the Hollywood Bowl, while across the Hollywood Hills top-name entertainers draw crowds for evening concerts at Griffith Park's Greek Theatre. San Diego's Balboa Park is the outdoor setting for summer musicals, and Santa Barbara offers song and dance spectacles in its Mission Bowl.

Land of diversity

The Indians were here first: the Diegueño and the Chumash along the southern coast and the Agua Caliente inland around the Coachella Valley's mineral springs. Traces of their cultures are still evident around San Diego, Palm Springs, and Lompoc.

The first Europeans arrived in 1542, when Portuguese navigator Juan

Continued on page 8

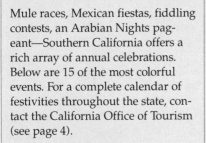

Fairs & Festivals

Mule races, Mexican fiestas, fiddling contests, an Arabian Nights pageant—Southern California offers a rich array of annual celebrations. Below are 15 of the most colorful events. For a complete calendar of festivities throughout the state, contact the California Office of Tourism (see page 4).

Tournament of Roses, January 1 in Pasadena. Elaborate floral floats, marching bands, and equestrian teams parade through the city before the Rose Bowl football game (free curbside or limited grandstand seating). Contact: (818) 449-4100 or (213) 681-3724.

National Date Festival, mid-February (beginning Presidents' Day weekend) in Indio. An elaborate outdoor Arabian Nights pageant (free) and daily camel and ostrich races highlight this 10-day festival marking the end of the date harvest. Contact: (619) 347-0676.

Hullabaloo Days, March or April (Palm Sunday weekend) in Calico. Mojave Desert ghost town celebrates its mining heritage with flapjack races, horseshoe pitching, pole climbing, and the world tobacco spitting championships. Contact: (619) 254-2122 or (714) 780-8810.

Cinco de Mayo, May 5 in Los Angeles and other cities with sizable Hispanic populations. Celebrate colorful Mexican holiday—commemorating an 1862 victory in the fight for independence from France—on Olvera Street in the Old Town section of Los Angeles. Contact: (213) 628-7833 or (213) 625-5045. San Diego celebrates on the weekend closest to May 5 at Old Town. Contact: (619) 237-6766.

Mule Days, May (Memorial Day weekend) in Bishop. Marking the start of the annual summer mule-

packing season in the Sierra, this 4-day event demonstrates the versatility of mules in competitions ranging from steer roping to chariot racing. The wild packers' scramble is a highlight. Other events include a parade, country and western dances, barbecues, pancake breakfasts, and an arts and crafts show. Contact: (619) 873-8405.

Lompoc Valley Flower Festival, mid-June in Lompoc. With its flower fields at peak bloom, the "flower seed capital" celebrates with field tours, flower shows, a parade, an arts and crafts fair, food booths, and other events. Contact: (805) 735-8511.

Festival of Arts & Pageant of the Masters, July–August in Laguna Beach. Works by more than 150 top artisans go on display, a children's art workshop is held, and great works of art are created in pageant tableaux. Contact: (714) 494-1145. The simultaneous Sawdust Festival features local arts and crafts and continuous entertainment. Contact: (714) 494-3030.

Old Spanish Days, first week of August in Santa Barbara. The city's oldest and largest annual festival celebrates Santa Barbara's Spanish and Mexican heritage with 5 days of colorful activities—parades, two Mexican marketplaces, food and crafts booths, a rodeo, a carnival, and nightly shows. Contact: (805) 962-8101.

Nisei Week Japanese Festival, mid-August in Los Angeles. The city's "little Tokyo" offers a week of traditional sports competitions (aikido, karate, and kendo), arts displays (bonsai, calligraphy, and ceramics), and other special events (including a parade). Contact: (213) 687-7193.

Los Angeles County Fair, September (beginning after Labor Day) in Pomona. The world's largest county fair features acres of home arts, floral, and

agricultural displays, plus livestock judging, wine competition, a circus, horse racing, carnival rides, and headliner entertainment. Contact: (714) 623-3111.

Danish Days, second or third weekend of September in Solvang. Along Copenhagen Street and in the city park, you can eat traditional Scandinavian fare, watch village dancers, listen to folk music, and see a parade on Saturday. Contact: (805) 688-0701.

Clam Festival, third weekend of October in Pismo Beach. Along with a parade, a fishing derby, a clam dig, sports and games, live entertainment, and crafts booths, there's plenty of clam chowder at this lively celebration. Contact: (805) 773-4382.

Annual 49ers Encampment, November (Veterans Day weekend) in Death Valley. This commemoration of the 1849 crossing of Death Valley features a liar's contest, a fiddling competition, a horseshoe tournament, art and lapidary shows, country and western music, and a barbecue. Contact: (619) 852-4524.

Trek to the Nation's Christmas Tree, second Sunday in December in Kings Canyon National Park. Participants leave Sanger (west of the park on State 180) at noon for the 50-mile bus caravan to the park's huge General Grant sequoia, site of a moving ceremony. Reserve bus seats by November 1. Contact: (209) 875-4575.

Christmas Boat Parades, December 17–23 in Newport Beach and mid-December in San Diego. Local yachts strung with lights parade on Newport Harbor for 7 successive nights. Contact: (714) 644-8211. In San Diego, fishing boats join with other vessels for a parade of lights from Harbor Island to Seaport Village. Contact: (619) 236-1212.

Stepping into a Spanish mission is like walking back in time. Beginning in 1769, Spain established a chain of 21 missions in California—institutions mandated not only to spread Christianity to the native Indian population but also to settle the frontier. These were California's first European communities, and today they constitute the oldest historic relics along the Pacific coast.

The mission chain is strung out along or near U.S. 101, which closely follows the original "royal road"—El Camino Real—started as a footpath linking the settlements. Eleven of the missions, plus two sub-missions, are in the area covered by this book. Five of these were begun by Father Junipero Serra, the Franciscan priest designated by Spain as the original father-president of the missions—and thus often considered the founder of California.

What you see today is a far cry from when the missions were miniature cities, teeming with activity. Thanks to restoration efforts, though, you can get some idea of what life must have been like in those early days. Missions welcome visitors daily on self-guided tours (some close on major holidays); most charge a small fee. Many still function as churches.

San Diego de Alcala. Father Serra founded California's first mission on July 16, 1769 atop Presidio Hill. It was moved to its present Mission Valley site in 1774. Taped tours include a small museum with Serra's records and relics.

Santa Ysabel. Inland Indians found it difficult to get to San Diego, so a branch mission was established 60 miles to the east in 1818. The present stucco chapel dates from 1924. Located on State 79 near Julian, the mission still serves area Indians.

San Luis Rey de Francia. Started in 1798 by Father Fermin Lasuen, Father Serra's successor, this impressive mission once included nearly 6 acres of buildings and had 3,000 Indian neophytes. Now well restored, the present 1815 church is framed with fine gardens. San Luis Rey is 5 miles east of Oceanside off State 76.

San Antonio de Pala. Established in 1815 as a sub-mission to San Luis Rey de Francia, this active church and school serves a Pauma Indian congregation. The chapel frescoes were painted by Indian artists. The gift shop and museum close Monday. Pala is on State 76 east of Interstate 15.

San Juan Capistrano. The picturesque ninth mission was founded in 1775, abandoned, and reestablished a year later by Father Serra. Its chapel is the only place standing where he is known to have said Mass. An 1812 earthquake destroyed much of the original mission and took many lives. Today, the mission is known for the swallows that still arrive from Argentina each year around St. Joseph's Day (March 19). Take Ortega Highway exit west from Interstate 5.

San Gabriel Arcangel. Founded in 1771 and moved to San Gabriel in 1774, the cathedral-style mission is presently closed because of earthquake damage. You can still tour the lovely grounds (534 Mission Drive), site of the state's oldest winery.

San Fernando Rey de España. Founded in 1797, this mission has been damaged several times by quakes, the last in 1971. A careful replica of the 1806 church now stands among manicured gardens 5 blocks east of Interstate 405 on San Fernando Boulevard.

San Buenaventura. Ventura's mission was the last one founded by Father Serra, in 1782. The expansive grounds are gone, but the red-trimmed church at 224 E. Main Street, reconstructed after the quake of 1812, looks much like its first incarnation. Among the museum relics are the original wooden bells.

Santa Barbara. The Queen of the Missions graces a hillsite above the city at Laguna and Los Olivos streets. Founded in 1786 and completed in 1820, the mission was enlarged by a second tower in 1831 (rebuilt in 1833).

Santa Ines. This well-restored mission in the heart of Solvang was founded in 1804 and served as temporary quarters for the state's first educational institution; the present building dates from 1817.

La Purisima Concepcion. Perhaps the most worthwhile stop along the route, this 1787 mission is now a completely restored 967-acre state historic park. Rooms are furnished as they would have been in the early 1800s; mission-era crafts are demonstrated in summer. Head west about 15 miles from U.S. 101 on State 246 toward Lompoc.

San Luis Obispo de Tolosa. Father Serra's fifth mission (in the heart of the city at Monterey and Chorro streets) was founded in 1772. The present building was finished in 1794. Once modernized with wooden siding, it has been restored to its original simple appearance.

San Miguel Arcangel. Nine miles north of Paso Robles off U.S. 101, Mission San Miguel was founded in 1797 by Father Lasuen. The present church was completed in 1818. Simple and severe on the outside, it glows inside with colorful murals.

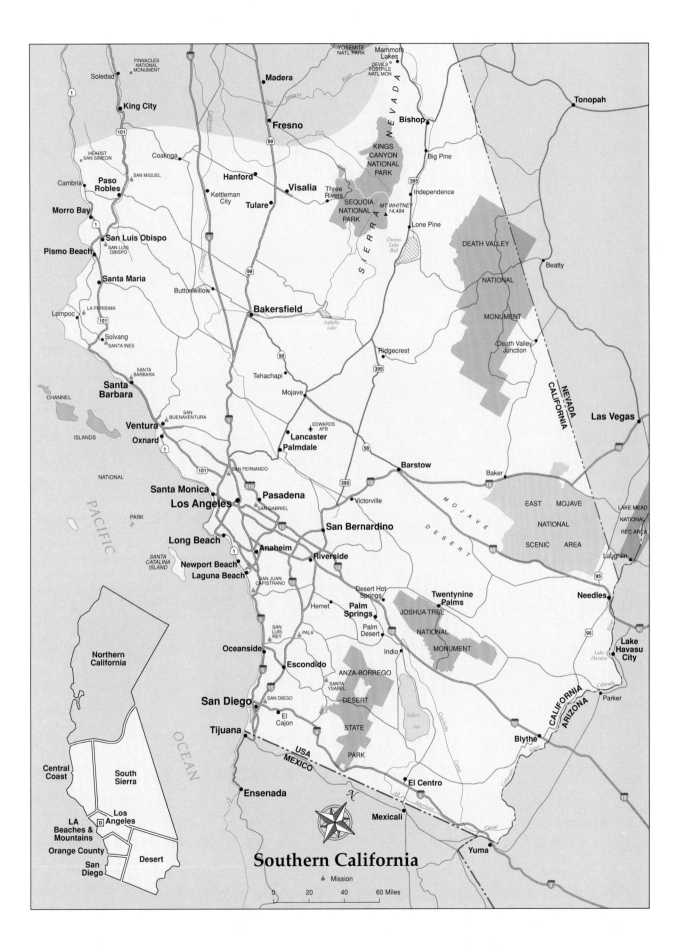

Southern California

Mission ⛪

0   20   40   60 Miles

...from page 4

Rodriguez Cabrillo landed at what is now San Diego. Colonization nonetheless didn't begin until the first Spanish mission was established in 1769. As a chain of missions extended northward (see page 6), Southern California's cities grew up around them. A walk through San Diego's Old Town, the Pueblo de Los Angeles, or the streets of Santa Barbara provides insight into the Spanish era.

The Hispanic influence remains strong, but more recently still more cultures have added to the area's rich diversity: Chinese, Japanese, Filipino, Korean, Vietnamese, and others. L.A.'s Chinatown, Japantown, and Koreatown showcase the lifestyles of these ethnic groups. But Southland diversity extends even beyond its great ethnic mix. From frontier days, this land has attracted and absorbed all sorts of lifestyles and life views, the mixture seeming to create an energy of its own.

About this book

Southern California is defined as much by personality as by geography. For the purposes of this book, we've chosen a generous interpretation, stretching north into the San Joaquin Valley and the Sierra Nevada and taking in both Inyo and Mono counties, major recreation targets for Southland residents though arguably "northern" in terms of geography. The book covers the Central Valley as far north as Visalia and the coast as far as Morro Bay and San Simeon, site of Hearst Castle.

The area north of this imaginary boundary is described in Sunset's companion *Northern California Travel Guide.*

This book begins with the sprawling West Coast anchor city of Los Angeles, starting point for the majority of Southland visits. Subsequent chapters cover L.A.'s coastal and mountain attractions, Orange County, San Diego, desert areas, the southern Sierra and surrounding region, and the central coast.

The map on page 7 shows how we've divided the state, chapter by chapter. Regional maps within each chapter, and detailed downtown maps of Los Angeles, San Diego, and Santa Barbara, are offered as further aids in planning driving or walking tours.

A special guide at the back of the book breaks down the state by activity. Look here for specifics on camping in national parks and at state beaches plus directories of golf courses, theme parks, zoos, boat tours, whale-watching excursions, winery tours, health spas, bicycling routes, and ski resorts.

Some destinations may be covered in special features or in the activity guide as well as in the chapter describing that region; use the index at the back of the book to make sure you locate each entry.

A note on prices and hours: We've made every effort to be up to date. Admission fees and hours are constantly changing, however, so check locally to be sure.

When to visit

Southern California's biggest asset is its dry, subtropical climate. Very little rain, low humidity, little variation in temperature, and a lot of sun make it possible to enjoy outdoor activities the year around. Any time of the year is good somewhere in the sunny Southland.

Since this is a year-round destination, accommodations are usually not priced for a three-month "tourist season." The one exception is the desert, where room rates are on an inverse ratio with the temperature: the cooler the season, the higher the rates.

Southern California tourism does peak in the summer in terms of visitor numbers. Though the desert is *hot* (into the 100s) and you're likely to find smog around Los Angeles and its inland valleys, action picks up in the summertime along the coast and in the mountains.

What little rain there is falls mostly in winter, when resorts and wilderness parks in the desert are the goal of devoted sunseekers. Avid skiers can head north to Mammoth Mountain, one of the country's top ski areas.

Spring and autumn provide the Southland's mildest weather and the choice seasons for many of the largest fairs and festivals (see page 5). Wildflowers carpet desert floors and spread up into higher elevations beginning in mid-February and extending through June. For some of the best flowering displays, turn to page 88.

How to get around

Southern California offers a choice of entry points—sprawling international airports, teeming freeways, busy ports, or rejuvenated railway terminals. No matter how you arrive, though, you'll need some form of transportation to explore the many attractions in and around the major cities.

If you're not driving your own car, rental cars are available in all large cities. If this is your first visit or you haven't been here recently, get a detailed map and plot your course before you take to the road.

Forget hair-raising tales you may have heard about freeway driving. This inter-connecting highway system is usually the fastest, most direct, and often only way to get around. If you avoid the freeways when people are going to and coming from work, learn where to get on and off easily, watch the traffic flow, and keep to your own lane, you should have few problems.

Southern California's Rapid Transit District operates a good bus and light rail system in and around L.A., including minibuses linking points of interest downtown, trolleys to Long Beach, and service to Disneyland. In Orange County, Palm Springs, and San Diego, shuttles are available to whisk passengers to major attractions. A trolley connects the latter city with Tijuana, just across the border in Mexico.

Don't overlook sightseeing tours as a means of getting around. They give good background information and spotlight the high points of an area. For details, check with your hotel desk or an area visitor center.

Where to stay

Accommodations are as varied as the region's topography, ranging from elegant self-contained resorts and high-rise city hotels to more modest hotels, motels, bed-and-breakfast inns, and RV parks. Advance reservations are almost always advisable, especially in summer and on weekends year-round.

This guide takes a look at landmark hotels in the Los Angeles area, historic hostelries in San Diego County, selected desert oases in and around Palm Springs, coastal B & Bs, and health spas. For more comprehensive suggestions in any area, write or call the contacts listed on the first page of each chapter.

Many of Southern California's national parks and state beaches offer campgrounds—see pages 120 and 121. For a listing of national forest campgrounds, contact the U.S. Forest Service, 830 Sansome St., Room 527, San Francisco, CA 94111; (415) 556-0122.

Information sources

Advance planning will help you make the most of your Southern California trip. For up-to-the-minute information on transportation, accommodations, dining options, and special events, contact visitor and convention bureaus and chambers of commerce listed in each chapter. For general information about the state, contact the California Office of Tourism (address on page 4). In addition, several agencies provide help for travelers with special needs.

Handicapped travelers. In the last few years California has made great strides in assisting disabled travelers. Special license plates and permits, available from the state's Department of Motor Vehicles, allow the physically impaired to park in convenient slots close to entryways. California also honors permits and plates issued by other states.

For additional information, contact the Department of Motor Vehicles, P.O. Box 942869, Sacramento, CA 94269-0001; (916) 732-7243. Many attractions provide free or rental wheelchairs. And most new and recently refurbished hotels have a few rooms equipped especially for the handicapped. For referrals, contact the California Travel Industry Association at 2500 Wilshire Blvd., Suite 603, Los Angeles, CA 90057; (213) 384-3178.

Senior citizens. Older travelers will receive hotel and transportation discounts, special dining rates, and reduced entrance fees at many places in Southern California. The age of eligibility varies widely, so ask about these special fares in advance.

Dining Delights

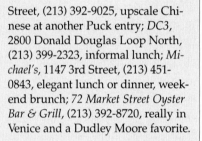

A wealth of fresh produce and seafood, a delicious diversity of ethnic cuisines, and an influx of innovative chefs make the Southland's dining scene as eclectic as its attractions. Prices are equally varied. Lunch might be $4 for tacos for two on L.A.'s Olvera Street or $24 for a tuna melt at upscale Trumps in West Hollywood.

Free dining guides preview restaurants in major cities around the area. The monthly *Los Angeles* magazine (available at newsstands) lists hundreds more throughout the region. We mention other notable dining spots throughout this book and take a look at some San Diego waterfront choices on page 63.

Trendy eateries in Beverly Hills, Los Angeles, and Santa Monica are frequent haunts of celebrities. Getaways around Santa Barbara and Palm Springs also attract the famous. If you're hoping to glimpse a well-known face, you'll usually need advance reservations (often difficult to get) and plenty of money. But even if you don't see a soul you recognize, you'll have

eaten in some of the area's hottest spots.

Note: Telephone area codes in certain western and southern portions of Los Angeles County will change from (213) to (310) on February 1, 1992.

Los Angeles. *Champagne,* 10506 Little Santa Monica Boulevard, (213) 470-8446, dress-up dining; *Eureka,* 1845 S. Bundy Drive, (213) 447-8000, Wolfgang Puck's latest boutique brewery and diner; *Morton's,* 8800 Melrose Avenue, (213) 276-5205, forget about finding a table on weekends; *Spago,* 8905 Sunset Boulevard, (213) 652-4025, pizza supreme by Puck.

Beverly Hills. *Bistro,* 246 N. Cañon Drive, (213) 273-5633, venerable dining spot with French cuisine; *Jimmy's,* 201 Moreno Drive, (213) 879-2394, French with a flourish; *La Scala,* 9455 Little Santa Monica Boulevard, (213) 275-0579, Italian favorite.

Santa Monica. *Border Grill,* 1445 4th Street, (213) 451-1655, inexpensive and innovative Mexican and South American fare; *Chinois on Main,* 2709 Main

Street, (213) 392-9025, upscale Chinese at another Puck entry; *DC3,* 2800 Donald Douglas Loop North, (213) 399-2323, informal lunch; *Michael's,* 1147 3rd Street, (213) 451-0843, elegant lunch or dinner, weekend brunch; *72 Market Street Oyster Bar & Grill,* (213) 392-8720, really in Venice and a Dudley Moore favorite.

Santa Barbara. *Cold Spring Tavern,* 5995 Stagecoach Road, (805) 967-0066, out-of-the-way retreat; *El Encanto,* 1900 Lasuen Road, (805) 687-5000, secluded dining with a view; *Michael's Waterside,* 50 Los Patos Way, (805) 969-0307, classic cuisine and attention; *Ranch House,* S. Lomita Avenue, Ojai, (805) 646-2360, garden setting for garden-fresh food.

Palm Springs. *Bono,* 1700 N. Indian Avenue, (619) 322-6200, Sonny sans Cher; *Cunard's,* 78045 Calle Cadiz, La Quinta, (619) 564-4443, open for winter season; *Las Casuelas Nuevas,* 70-050 State 111, Rancho Mirage, (619) 328-8844, branch of popular Mexican eatery.

Los Angeles

California's largest city, in terms of both area and population, sprawls over 464 square miles, roughly the size of the entire state of Rhode Island. Almost 3½ million people call Los Angeles home (only New York City is bigger nationwide), and L.A. County is approaching 9 million residents. Some 50 million more people visit annually.

Why do they come? Despite L.A.'s very real problems of traffic and smog (generally at its worst in summer), its charms are many. A fine setting between mountains and sea is enhanced by year-round sunshine, and an innovative lifestyle has made the area a trendsetter in the fields of fitness, fashion, food, and film.

Entertaining is big business in Los Angeles, and the city boasts some of the country's premier hotels, shops, and restaurants, plus a wealth of elaborate—and unique—amusements. If you think museums, concerts, and theaters are the measure of a city, you'll find some fine ones here. But where else would you also discover cemeteries listed as tourist attractions, pizza elevated to an edible art form, and replicas of Ice Age creatures emerging from a tar pit?

Huge and constantly changing, L.A. is best approached by breaking it into small components. This chapter focuses on the attractions that draw most visitors, from the glamour of Hollywood and the movie studios to the upscale glitter of Beverly Hills or the cultural melange of the downtown area. Roundups of city museums, favorite diversions for children, and a host of free attractions are evidence of the depth of the city's capacity to please visitors.

For a look beyond the city core to the beach and mountain playgrounds that frame Los Angeles, turn to the chapter beginning on page 30.

A pattern of growth

Los Angeles started as a Spanish village in 1781, when 44 settlers recruited by the California provincial governor, Felipe de Neve, reached the banks of the Los Angeles River after a seven-month colonizing expedition from Sonora, Mexico. They marked off the lots that gave birth to El Pueblo de Nuestra Señora la Reina de los Angeles—the town of Our City the Queen of Angels.

Eventually the city with the tongue-tangling name became Mexican (after independence from Spain in 1822), and then finally Yankee (after its surrender in 1847). Today, L.A. is a collection of communities where you can savor sights, sounds, foods, and goods from around the world. It has the nation's largest Hispanic population (more than 3½ million in the greater L.A. area), and only Honolulu boasts a greater Asian population.

The cattle ranches and citrus groves that gave Los Angeles its first claim to fame have long since given way to freeways, industrial growth, and dense residential sprawl. Instead, L.A. is now a world trade center and a leader in the financial, aerospace, and oil industries. One early enterprise does remain, however. Sunny weather allowing year-round filming of movies made the L.A. area an entertainment capital early in the century, and the city has yet to relinquish the title, thanks to the number of movies, television shows, and radio broadcasts produced here.

Planning a trip

Year-round sunshine helped make Los Angeles famous in the first place. The sun may be filtered through smog much of the time these days, but the benign climate still makes for a nearly seamless 12-month tourist season.

First-timers and even those who haven't been to L.A. for awhile may need help in finding their way around. Stop by one of the two offices of the Los Angeles Convention and Visitors Bureau (addresses below) for maps, visitor guides, discount coupons to at-

Sleek skyscrapers define downtown L.A.'s business district. To the right rise the futuristic glass silos of the Westin Bonaventure Hotel.

Contacts

These agencies offer information on attractions and accommodations. See additional contacts throughout this chapter.

NOTE: Telephone area codes in western and southern portions of Los Angeles County will be changed from (213) to (310) as of February 1992.

Los Angeles Convention and Visitors Bureau
Downtown Visitor Information Center
695 S. Figueroa St.
Los Angeles, CA 90017
(213) 689-8822
Hollywood Visitor Information Center
The Janes House
6541 Hollywood Blvd.
Hollywood, CA 90028
(213) 461-4213

Beverly Hills Visitors Bureau
239 S. Beverly Dr.
Beverly Hills, CA 90212
(213) 271-8174

tractions, and free tickets to television shows. The downtown center is open 8 A.M. to 5 P.M. daily except Sunday; the Hollywood center opens at 9 A.M.

Getting there. Los Angeles International Airport (Century and Sepulveda boulevards) is the world's third largest in terms of passenger traffic. The free LAX "A" shuttle makes a circuit of the international and seven domestic terminals at the lower level. An information board in each terminal baggage claim area lists most ground transportation. Get information and tickets for many scheduled and on-call shuttles at sidewalk booths in front of the terminals. SuperShuttle, (213) 338-1111, is one of the least expensive (around $12 to downtown, less to the Westside). Hotel and rental car courtesy trams, taxis, and limos depart from marked islands on the lower level.

Four other major metropolitan airports—Burbank (14 miles northwest of the city center), Long Beach (22 miles south), Orange County (30 miles southeast), and Ontario (40 miles east)—provide supplemental service.

If you're arriving by train, Amtrak uses the handsome Union Station depot at 800 N. Alameda Street, close to El Pueblo and the Civic Center. Greyhound and Trailways share a bus terminal at 6th and Los Angeles streets.

Getting around. Driving L.A.'s maze of freeways can be a daunting experience for newcomers, but a car is almost a necessity for any ambitious sightseeing. Two suggestions: Avoid peak times—6:30 to 9:30 A.M. and 3:30 to 6:30 P.M.—and plan routes in advance. Good map sources are the Automobile Club of Southern California, 2601 S. Figueroa Street (AAA members only) and Thomas Brothers Maps and Travel Bookstore, 603 W. 7th Street.

Interstate 5, California's major north-south artery, slices through the heart of L.A., entering from the north as the Golden State Freeway and exiting as the Santa Ana Freeway. Interstate 405 (San Diego Freeway) offers access to the city's western and southern reaches. The direct route from the east is Interstate 10 (San Bernardino Freeway), which becomes the Santa Monica Freeway downtown at the Civic Center. Interstate 110 (Harbor Freeway) connects L.A. and the port at San Pedro.

The city's public transportation system (RTD) has route maps to local attractions at its downtown customer center, Level B Arco Plaza, 515 S. Flower Street (closed weekends); (213) 626-4455. Frequent daytime DASH (Downtown Area Short Hop) shuttles cover the heart of the city. An extensive light-rail system should be completed in 1992. The first section—the Blue Line to Long Beach—opened in 1990.

Taxi service is available from the airports, train and bus terminals, and major hotels. Cabs do not cruise the streets looking for passengers.

Tours. Half-day and longer city sightseeing tours give a good orientation. Gray Line and several other companies offer scheduled tours year-round; check your hotel desk for schedules. Customized shopping, dining, and celebrity-seeking tours are also available. The Los Angeles Convention and Visitors Bureau has details (see page 11).

Free bus tours of downtown Los Angeles depart from the firehouse at Old Town Plaza (see page 16) on the first and third Wednesday of each month. Reservations are required for the 2-hour tours; call (213) 628-1274.

Los Angeles Conservancy conducts guided walking tours of historic downtown L.A. at 10 A.M. Saturday from the Olive Street entrance of the Biltmore Hotel (506 S. Grand Avenue). Tours last 2 hours and cost $5; call (213) 623-2489 for reservations.

Accommodations. For a detailed accommodation guide, contact the Los Angeles Convention and Visitors Bureau (page 11). Some top-of-the-line lodgings are listed on the facing page.

Rooms can also be booked through the Southern California Hotel Reservation Center; for rates and confirmations, call (800) 527-9997 in California, (800) 537-7666 outside the state.

Entertainment. Star-studded theatrical and musical performances are year-round attractions. Visitors' guides and the Sunday "Calendar" section of the *Los Angeles Times* list current events.

The theaters and concert halls of the downtown Music Center (135 N. Grand Avenue) play host to city ballet, opera, symphony, and theatrical companies. The Los Angeles Theatre Center, an intimate four-theater complex at 514 N. Spring Street, offers works from the Los Angeles Actors Theatre.

Plays and musical performances are also held at other large entertainment centers, like Century City's Shubert Theatre, Universal City's Amphitheatre, and Hollywood's Pantages Theatre. In summer, the Greek Theatre and the Hollywood Bowl are popular for outdoor plays and concerts.

Spectator sports. The L.A. area teems with sports activities. Suburban Inglewood (near LAX) is home to beautifully landscaped Hollywood Park race track and to the Great Western Forum, setting for Lakers pro basketball and Kings ice hockey games.

In Exposition Park southwest of downtown off Interstate 110, the Los Angeles Memorial Sports Arena hosts Clippers basketball games, the L.A. Memorial Coliseum features college and pro football (Raiders), and the Swimming Stadium is a venue for water sports competitions.

The Dodgers play pro baseball just north of the L.A. Civic Center at Dodger Stadium, and free polo practices are held Tuesday and Thursday evenings in Griffith Park's Equidome.

Shopping. From the chic and pricey boutiques of Rodeo Drive in Beverly Hills to Olvera Street's souvenir stands, L.A. is a browser's paradise. Of special interest are the downtown wholesale garment and jewelry districts (see page 14). Old Town, Little Tokyo, and Chinatown offer a wealth of gift shops.

For a riot of scents and colors, pay an early-morning visit to the Flower Mart around 6th and San Julian streets, or wander through the food stalls of Grand Central Public Market at 3rd and Hill streets or the Farmers Market at 3rd and Fairfax (see page 17).

Museum shops and art galleries offer other gift possibilities; the largest Westside gallery concentrations are along Melrose, La Brea, La Cienega, and Robertson avenues.

Landmark L.A. Lodgings

Noted for ambience, architecture, and location, some of L.A.'s classic hotels have become visitor attractions in themselves, worth a look even if you're not planning a stay. Most are old-timers that have undergone recent face-lifts; a couple are newer beauties.

Double rooms at the "budget" lodgings among the group start at $100 or so; rates are considerably steeper for most of these hotels. For detailed information on rates and amenities, call hotels directly or obtain a copy of the lodging guide published by the Los Angeles Convention and Visitors Bureau (address on page 11).

For more help, check with the Automobile Club of Southern California (AAA members only), a travel agent, or the Southern California Hotel Reservation Center, (800) 527-9997 in California, (800) 537-7666 nationwide.

Bel-Air Hotel, 701 Stone Canyon Rd., Los Angeles, CA 90077; (213) 472-1211. Constantly rated as one of the world's most romantic retreats, the tranquil Bel-Air Hotel is tucked into a wooded canyon above Sunset Boulevard. Private bungalows sprinkled throughout 12 acres of lush gardens look out to a waterfall and a swan-filled lake.

Beverly Hills Hotel, 9641 Sunset Blvd., Beverly Hills, CA 90210; (800) 792-7637. A restaurant in this sprawling Mission-revival hotel (1912) features favorite dishes of celebrities who have used the property as a hideout. Movie moguls still make deals over breakfast or lunch in the Polo Lounge.

Beverly Wilshire Hotel, 9500 Wilshire Blvd., Beverly Hills, CA; (800) 421-4354. The impressive hotel across from Rodeo Drive has long been a haven for the rich and the royal. The Regent Group, its current owners, recently completed a handsome renovation of rooms, lobby, and restaurants.

Biltmore Hotel, 506 S. Grand Ave., Los Angeles, CA 90071; (800) 421-8000. A $40 million face-lift returned the glow of 1920s youth to one of the city's grande dames. New entry court, relocated lobby, additional dining rooms, impressive health club, and new and refurbished rooms are highlights.

Century Plaza Hotel, 2025 Avenue of the Stars, Los Angeles, CA 90067; (800) 228-3000. Designed by architect Minoru Yamasaki and built in the 1960s on land once owned by Twentieth Century Fox Studio, the soaring Century Plaza resembles a modernistic Rockefeller Center; the tower is a 1980s addition. The first astronauts to reach the moon were honored here at a Presidential State Dinner.

Checkers Hotel, 535 S. Grand Ave., Los Angeles, CA 90071; (800) 628-4900. Guests of the old Mayflower Hotel that once occupied the site would never recognize this renovated version. The chic boutique hostelry has 190 antique-furnished rooms and a top-rated restaurant.

Hollywood Roosevelt Hotel, 7000 Hollywood Blvd., Hollywood, CA 90028; (800) 950-7667. First home of the Academy Awards, this lovingly restored hotel in the heart of Hollywood has a jazz bar, a restaurant, a health club, and a mezzanine lined with "tinsel town" history.

Queen Mary Hotel, Pier J, Long Beach, CA 90801; (800) 421-3732. Once the largest and fastest luxury liner afloat, the venerable ship has 12 decks open for tours (see page 40). Staterooms and restaurants have been refurbished and several prestigious shops added to the ship hotel, now part of the Disney family.

Ritz-Carlton Huntington Hotel, 1401 S. Oak Knoll, Pasadena, CA 91109; (800) 241-333. The Huntington Hotel was Pasadena's social hub from the time of its opening in 1914 until the main building was razed in the late 1980s because it didn't meet earthquake standards. A new and larger replica now stands on the site, surrounded by nicely refurbished cottages and some of the hotel's acclaimed original gardens.

St. James's Club, 8358 Sunset Blvd., Los Angeles, CA 90069; (800) 225-2637. Clark Gable and Marilyn Monroe were among the movie stars who had apartments in this art deco building with the grand view. Still a favorite with celebrities, it's now a private club with an elegant restaurant and spa. Membership privileges are extended to overnight guests.

Westin Bonaventure, 404 S. Figueroa St., Los Angeles, CA 90071; (800) 228-3000. Five mirror-glass silos make this futuristic hotel a latter-day landmark. Marble, brass, and glass gleam around its Flower Street entry and lobby area, part of a renovation to make the hotel and its shopping complex more "pedestrian-friendly."

Westwood Marquis Hotel, 930 Hilgard Ave., Los Angeles, CA 90024; (800) 421-2317. Once a girls' dormitory, later an apartment building, this is now an all-suites hotel with impressive pools, gardens, and restaurants (Garden Room's Sunday brunch is notable). The Westwood setting makes it a base for strolls to the village, U.C.L.A., and the Armand Hammer Museum.

Downtown L.A.

Fear of earthquakes forced Los Angeles to grow out, not up. But when height restrictions were removed in 1957, the city began to soar. High-rise office buildings, hotels, and "in-city" residences rose on the site of now-flattened Bunker Hill (once home to elegant Victorian mansions) and south along the Harbor Freeway. Newest and as-yet tallest of the skyscrapers is the 73-story world headquarters of the First Interstate Bank at Library Square, 5th and Hope streets.

Just east of the Harbor Freeway between 11th Street and Pico Boulevard sprawls the Los Angeles Convention Center, site of large business gatherings and trade shows. Across the freeway and a bit farther south, the University of Southern California (page 17) stands adjacent to Exposition Park, site of several notable museums (page 27) and the Los Angeles Memorial Coliseum (page 17). Just across from U.S.C., Jewish culture is highlighted at the Skirball Museum (3077 University Avenue, scheduled to move to 2701 N. Sepulveda Boulevard in 1992).

An overview

Finding your way around downtown is relatively easy. Traffic isn't bad except during weekday rush hours, and parking garages are plentiful if not cheap. In the evening and on weekends, the area is virtually deserted.

Transportation. DASH shuttles loop through the downtown area every few minutes from 6:30 A.M. to 6:30 P.M. weekdays and 10 A.M. to 5 P.M. Saturday. You'll need exact change (25 cents).

Hotel and dining scene. Downtown hotels make good choices for convention-goers or anyone planning to take in shows at the Music Center, Theatre Center, or Japanese American Cultural and Community Center; see page 13 for a listing of some of the choices.

Outside of a handful of such noted restaurants as Engine Co. No. 28, Original Sonora Cafe, Pacific Dining Car, Rex II Ristorante, and Steppes on the Court, most fine dining downtown takes place in hotels. The Biltmore serves tea in its street-level Rendez-vous Court from 2 to 5 P.M. daily.

Shopping. The central city's major shopping malls are Levels B and C of the subterranean Arco Plaza (5th and Flower streets), the Broadway Plaza (7th and Flower), the Seventh Market Place (7th and Figueroa), and the shops at the Westin Bonaventure Hotel.

Bargain hunters head east to the Jewelry District (Hill Street from 5th to 8th) and the Garment District (between Los Angeles and San Pedro streets from 7th to Pico). Though geared to the wholesale market, many shops are open to the public; the Cooper Building (860 S. Los Angeles Street) is a vertical discount center with 76 stores and several fast-food restaurants.

A city walk

Contrary to popular opinion, people do walk in L.A. It's the best way to get a close look at major attractions in the surprisingly compact downtown area. Our route takes a leisurely half-day.

The walk follows the general routes of DASH shuttles. You can board the B Line at the end of your walk to return to your starting point, or even make the entire tour by bus. (Transfer to the A Line to see Little Tokyo and the Temporary Contemporary Museum.)

Financial District. A cluster of high-rise bank buildings and corporate offices flanking the Harbor Freeway makes up the downtown business and financial heart. Above-street promenades connect many structures.

To get an overall view, start from the 35th-floor rooftop lounge of the futuristic Westin Bonaventure Hotel (5th and Flower). Then cross the footbridge over 5th Street to reach the landscaped garden atop the 52-story Arco Plaza Complex. Underneath its twin towers is one of the country's largest subterranean shopping centers.

Along both sides of Flower to the north of 4th Street hulk the World Trade Center and the Security Pacific headquarters building; note the latter's water-filled garden plaza. At 4th and Hope, walk through the glass-enclosed garden pavilion between the Wells Fargo Bank headquarters and the IBM towers to Grand Avenue. (A free history museum on the ground level of the bank is open from 9 A.M. to 4 P.M. weekdays—see page 29.)

Across Grand is the massive California Plaza shopping, office, and housing development. The dazzling red sandstone building at 250 S. Grand houses the Museum of Contemporary Art (see page 27).

Music Center. Two blocks north, at 1st and Grand, L.A.'s Music Center is the city's cultural heart and home to such respected companies as the Los Angeles Philharmonic and the Joffrey Ballet. A landscaped mall links the elegant Dorothy Chandler Pavilion, largest of the center's three halls, to the intimate Mark Taper Forum and the Ahmanson Theatre. The Frank Gehry–designed Walt Disney Concert Hall joins the trio in 1994.

For information on touring the center, see page 17. You might round out your visit with a stop at one of the three restaurants in the complex or at the performing arts–oriented gift shop.

Civic Center. L.A.'s Civic Center is one of the largest government complexes in the country. The building with the reflecting pool west of the Music Center houses the Department of Water and Power; the other municipal buildings lie to the east.

The 32-story, pyramid-shaped City Hall at 200 N. Spring Street—Southern California's tallest building when it was built in 1928—offers views as far as Mount Wilson, 15 miles away, on rare clear days. The observation deck on the 27th floor is open 10 A.M. to 4 P.M. weekdays. Near City Hall at 202 W. 1st Street is the Los Angeles Times Building (see page 17).

Many of the Civic Center's major buildings stand at the perimeter of

Beyond a pennant-adorned courtyard in the heart of the city stands the Dorothy Chandler Pavilion, largest of the Music Center halls and home to the Los Angeles Philharmonic and Joffrey Ballet companies as well as the annual Oscar ceremonies.

...Downtown L.A.

landscaped Los Angeles Mall, a sunken shopping center between Main and Los Angeles streets that includes the Los Angeles Children's Museum (see page 29).

Little Tokyo. This redeveloped Japanese neighborhood southeast of the Civic Center, roughly bounded by 1st, Alameda, 3rd, and Los Angeles streets, combines peaceful gardens with colorful collections of shops and restaurants. The garden atop the south wing of the New Otani Hotel (120 S. Los Angeles Street) and another at the Noguchi Plaza's Japanese American Cultural and Community Center south of San Pedro and 2nd streets (also

the setting of the handsome Japan America Theatre) are particularly noteworthy.

From Noguchi Plaza, cross 2nd Street to reach the stores and eateries of Japanese Village Plaza. Across the plaza, at 1st and Central, stands the original Museum of Contemporary Art, now an annex known as the Temporary Contemporary (see page 27). The Japanese American National Museum is in a rehabilitated Buddhist temple at 815 E. 1st.

El Pueblo de Los Angeles. To reach L.A.'s Old Town, where the city began, head north on Main Street across the freeway. The 44-acre state historic monument is bounded by Alameda, Arcadia, Spring, and Macy streets.

To get the most out of a visit, join a free guided tour (Tuesday through Saturday at 10 and 11 A.M., noon, and 1 P.M.) from the Docent Center fronting on the plaza. Or pick up a self-guided walking tour map at the visitor center in the Sepulveda House (622 N. Main Street). A 20-minute film on the history of the park is shown daily except Sunday at 11 A.M. and 2 P.M. The center is open Monday through Friday from 10 A.M. to 3 P.M., Saturday until 4:30 P.M.

Park highlights include a display of antique firefighting equipment in the two-story Old Plaza Firehouse (134 Paseo de la Plaza), the Old Plaza Church on North Main (the city's oldest), and the restored Avila Adobe at 10 E. Olvera Street, which dates back to about 1818 (closed Monday). All are open to visitors at no charge.

Lively Olvera Street, a block-long Mexican marketplace, is the Pueblo's greatest magnet. Streetside shops and stalls sell handicrafts and such treats as sugary *churros* (Mexican-style donuts). Restaurants serve typical Mexican cuisine (El Paseo Inn is a local favorite). Shops are open daily from 10 A.M. to 8 P.M., later in summer. A museum dedicated to the history of Chinese Americans in the U.S. Southwest introduces the district north of the Pueblo.

Chinatown. Walk 3½ blocks north on Broadway to the main entrance to Chinatown, several blocks of shop-lined lanes with names like Gin Ling (a pedestrian mall), Sun Mun, and Lei Ling. Like Olvera Street, the area is touristy, although it's also a cultural center for Chinese Americans. Food markets stock intriguing wares, shops offer everything from Hong Kong reproductions to antiques, and restaurants specialize in moderately priced tank-fresh seafood.

The district's most authentic Chinese section is on North Spring Street, southeast of the tourist zone. You can buy a walking tour map of the area from the Chinese Historical Society of Southern California at 970 N. Broadway or 982 Gin Ling Way.

To return to the starting point of your downtown walk, catch the southbound B Line bus on Broadway.

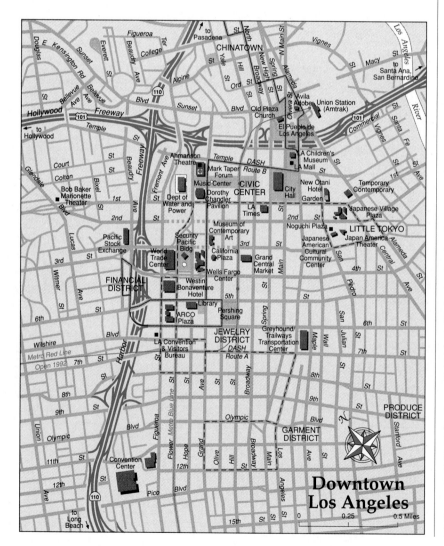

Downtown Los Angeles

Fun & Free in L.A.

The 12 tours listed below are examples of things you can do in Los Angeles without spending a cent. Other ideas for cash-free entertainment sprinkled throughout the chapter include television tapings, museum visits, strolls through the city's rich ethnic neighborhoods, and a trek to Mann's Chinese Theatre to view hand, foot, paw, and hoof prints of Hollywood stars.

For more suggestions, pick up a visitor guide listing events, tours, exhibits, sports, and musical happenings. It's available at visitor information centers (addresses on page 11).

Farmers Market, 3rd Street and Fairfax Avenue; (213) 933-9211. Pick up a map of this 20-acre market-restaurant-shopping complex at the office on the second floor above Gate 1. The market got its start in 1934, when 18 hard-pressed farmers decided to sell their produce directly to the people. Now boasting more than 160 stalls, shops, cafes, and dining plazas, it is expanding to include a theater and a hotel.

Hours are 9 A.M. to 6 P.M. Monday through Saturday, 10 A.M. to 5 P.M. Sunday (an hour later in summer). Du-Par's Restaurant, noted for pancakes and pies, is open from 6 A.M. until midnight.

Forest Lawn, 1712 S. Glendale Avenue, Glendale; (213) 254-3131. Only in L.A. are cemeteries renowned for their art collections, museums, and theaters. The Forest Lawn visitor center displays gems and biblical coins and offers guides to artwork (10 A.M. to 4 P.M. daily). At another Forest Lawn cemetery (6300 Forest Lawn Drive, Hollywood Hills), you can see a film on the birth of liberty.

Lawry's California Center, 520 W. Avenue 26 off the Pasadena Free-

way just northeast of Interstate 5; (213) 224-6840. A 45-minute tour of this handsome complex showcases test kitchens and seasoning plant facilities, ending in the gift, wine, and food shops. Tours are given at 11:45 A.M. and 12:30, 1:30, and 2:30 P.M. weekdays; two restaurants are open for lunch daily (except major holidays), dinner May through November.

Los Angeles Memorial Coliseum, 3911 S. Figueroa Street; (213) 747-7111. Tours of the site of the 1932 and 1984 Olympic Games are offered when no events are scheduled; call for information. While in Exposition Park, stop to smell the blossoms at the world's largest rose garden; peak periods are April and May, September and October.

Los Angeles Music Center, 1st Street and Grand Avenue; (213) 972-7483 for tour reservations. Hour-long tours of the center's three theaters let you view sets and props of current productions and an eclectic and impressive art collection. Tours begin every half-hour from 10 A.M. to noon Saturday.

Los Angeles Times, 202 W. 1st Street; (213) 237-5757. The nation's largest standard-size daily newspaper offers hour-long tours weekdays, except holidays, at 11:15 A.M. and 3 P.M. (no children under 10).

Lummis Home, 200 E. Avenue 43 off the Pasadena Freeway; (213) 222-0546. Wander on your own through the stone "castle" that was home to Charles Fletcher Lummis, founder of the Southwest Museum (see page 27). Now headquarters of Southern California's Historical Society, the house is open 1 to 4 P.M. Wednesday through Sunday.

Mormon Temple, 10777 Santa Monica Boulevard; (213) 474-1549. Unless you're a Latter-Day Saint, your tour of

this huge temple is on film in the visitor center, but anyone can walk through the beautiful gardens. The center is open daily from 9 A.M. to 9:30 P.M.

Pacific Coast Stock Exchange, 233 S. Beaudry (between 2nd and 3rd streets west of the Harbor Freeway); (213) 977-4500. A visitors' gallery on the 12th floor gives you a view of the trading floor. Exchange hours, 6:30 A.M. to 1:30 P.M. weekdays, coincide with those of the New York Stock Exchange.

Rancho La Brea Tar Pits, Wilshire Boulevard and Curson Avenue; (213) 936-2230. Ice Age fossils trapped in bubbly black pits some 40 centuries ago have been recreated in asphalt at the scene of their demise. You can see them from a viewing station west of the George C. Page Museum (see page 27). Guided tours depart the observation pit (open weekends 10 A.M. to 5 P.M.) Thursday through Sunday at 1 P.M., except on major holidays.

University of Southern California, Exposition Boulevard and S. Figueroa Street next to Exposition Park; (213) 743-2983. Make an appointment to take an hour-long walking tour of one of the West's oldest private universities (weekdays from 10 A.M. to 2 P.M.). For a tour through the 1890s museum (weekdays by appointment), phone (213) 743-5213. A free art gallery is open Tuesday through Saturday afternoons.

Watts Towers, 1765 E. 107th Street; (213) 569-8181. Simon Rodia, an immigrant Italian tilesetter, spent 33 years creating these three 99-foot towers from cement, steel rods, broken tile, bottles, and seashells. He completed the task in 1954. For a good view, stop at the adjacent art center.

"Where Music Meets the Stars" is the theme of the Hollywood Bowl's popular summer concert series. Sellout crowds jam the outdoor amphitheater to enjoy performances ranging from classical favorites to pops and jazz.

Hollywood

Hollywood Boulevard is a comparatively short street, but it may be the best known of all L.A.'s thoroughfares—and it's a major magnet for Southland visitors. At first glance this may look like any Main Street of any town, but its wealth of art deco architecture has elevated it to the status of a national historic district.

In its heyday, from the 1920s to the 1950s, Hollywood boasted some of L.A.'s largest movie palaces and most exclusive department stores. Studios such as Paramount and Metro Goldwyn Mayer ate up acres of real estate. And uphill, such cinema royalty as Gloria Swanson and Tyrone Power built hideaways.

When retail business moved to the suburbs and the movie industry expanded into other areas of the city, Hollywood lost its luster. But the faded star is staging a comeback. The Hollywood Roosevelt Hotel (7000 Hollywood Boulevard), where the first Academy Awards were presented, has been renovated, and an ambitious 2½-block redevelopment project around Sid Grauman's 1927 Chinese Theatre at 6925 Hollywood Boulevard—now called Mann's—offers state-of-the-art cinemas, specialty shops, and the Hollywood Exposition Museum, dedicated to the entertainment industry.

Exploring Tinsel Town

Hollywood is still a lot of fun. On a day's excursion, you might take a bus tour, visit a museum, and lunch at an old restaurant near a studio. Or take a look at the boulevard's architecture, search out the hillside Hollywood sign and Rudolph Valentino's crypt, and then catch a film in a resplendent movie house.

Guided tours. An excellent introduction to the boulevard is a walking tour led by actor-members of Hollywood Heritage, a preservation organization. The 2-hour Saturday and Sunday morning tours stop in movie palaces and turn down side streets. Cost is $6; to reserve a place, call (213) 465-5993.

For a wider overview, take a double-decker bus trip with Hollywood Fantasy Tours. The guides' patter includes the omnipresent movie trivia, but there's substantial history, too. You'll see landmarks like Capitol Records (1750 Vine Street), built in 1954 to resemble a record stack. The 2-hour excursions leave 1744 N. Highland Avenue at 10:30 A.M. and 1 P.M. daily; cost is $12 adults, $10 children. For reservations, call (213) 469-8184.

Grave Line Tours, Hollywood Boulevard and Orchard Avenue, takes you on a hearse-drawn tour of the city's more macabre side. Call (213) 876-0920 for information.

On your own. If you prefer to choose your own route, park in any of the lots or parking structures on or near Hollywood Boulevard.

You can't explore the boulevard without stepping on one of Hollywood's earliest attempts to spruce up. The Walk of Fame, begun in 1958, features some 2,500 celebrity-named stars inset along both sides of the street for the half-mile from Gower Street to Sycamore Avenue and along Vine Street from Sunset Boulevard to Yucca Street. To view them in order, start outside the Hollywood Roosevelt Hotel.

Eating spots. Golden-age restaurants still exist. The most famous is Musso & Frank Grill, 6667 Hollywood Boulevard, known since 1919 for no-nonsense American food. Dating from the same year, C.C. Brown's Ice Cream Parlour, 7007 Hollywood Boulevard, lays claim to having served the country's first hot fudge sundaes. (Both are closed Sunday.)

Nickodell Melrose Restaurant (5507 Melrose Avenue, east of Vine) has served steaks to Paramount Pictures personnel for more than 40 years. And tiny Formosa Cafe (7156 Santa Monica Boulevard) is a favorite with people from Warner Hollywood Studios. Crammed with Elvis memorabilia, the cafe serves old-fashioned American-Chinese dishes (closed Sunday).

Movie magic

Three studios in the Hollywood area offer peeks into the world of filming. Paramount and KCET Television are still operating studios that you can tour (see page 20). The third pays homage to the industry's early days.

You can only drive by Charlie Chaplin's picturesque studio at 1416 N. La Brea Avenue. The storybook hamlet of tiny buildings from the early 1900s now houses A & M Records offices.

Hollywood Studio Museum. When Cecil B. DeMille came to Hollywood in 1913, he rented part of a barn to use as a studio. It sat on the Paramount lot for decades, playing bit parts in the TV series *Bonanza*, and then was moved to its present location at 2100 N. Highland Avenue (across from the Hollywood Bowl) and opened to show off movie memorabilia. The studio is open from 10 A.M. to 4 P.M. Tuesday through Sunday; admission is modest.

Around town

Two ways to put Hollywood into perspective are from the hills above the boulevard or at the quiet cemetery on its boundary.

Hillside views. For a brief foray into the hills in back of town, drive or climb up to Yamashiro (1999 N. Sycamore Avenue). Built in 1913 in the style of a 16th-century palace, the former mansion is now a Japanese restaurant.

To see how close you can come to the fabled Hollywood sign that overlooks the town, head up Beachwood Drive (off Franklin Avenue). The 50-foot-high letters were erected for this 1920s housing development, Hollywoodland; the "land" disappeared years ago.

Hollywood Memorial Cemetery. You can pick up a free map at this memorial park to find monuments to De Mille, Fairbanks, Valentino, and other Hollywood legends. The cemetery is just north of the Paramount studio at 6000 Santa Monica Boulevard.

The star-gazing game—hunting for celebrities—is avidly practiced around L.A. If your curiosity is piqued but your observation time limited, the best way to sight famous faces may be to drop by places where they work.

The following is a rundown of movie studios with back-lot tours and TV shows looking for audiences, along with "homes of the stars" tour possibilities. Even if you don't see your favorite celebrities in person, you can visit their stars on Hollywood's Walk of Fame (see page 19), measure your feet against their footprints in the forecourt of Mann's Chinese Theatre (6925 Hollywood Boulevard), or buy star-related memorabilia at movie and television studio shops.

Studio tours

Movie studios created L.A.'s aura of glamour in the heyday of the 1920s and 1930s, and film and TV studios still play a big role in attracting visitors to the area.

Universal Studios Hollywood, Lankershim Boulevard east of the Hollywood Freeway in Universal City; (818) 508-9600. The best-known studio in Southern California, Universal has evolved into a sprawling theme park as well as a major producer of films and television. A simulated 8.3-magnitude earthquake and a visit with King Kong currently make the biggest impression on children, but the studio constantly adds attractions.

Plan to spend a full day for your behind-the-scenes look at film-making. A narrated tram ride takes you through famous sets on the 420-acre back lot and lets you see yourself on live action shows. Trams leave frequently, but you might be assigned a boarding time; while you wait, you learn about

special effects. You tour the studio's entertainment center on your own.

The Universal box office is open from 8 A.M. to 5 P.M. daily in summer, 9:30 A.M. to 4 P.M. the rest of the year (closed Thanksgiving and Christmas). Admission is $22 adults, $16.50 ages 3 to 11 and over 55; parking costs $3.

Burbank Studios, 4000 Warner Boulevard, Burbank; (818) 954-1744. Less glitzy than Universal, bustling Burbank Studios houses both Warner Brothers (here since 1928) and Columbia Pictures. Guides lead 10 to 12 persons at a time through sound stages, a $20 million wardrobe inventory, and back lots such as Midwest Street, where Ronald Reagan starred in *King's Row*. Expect a lot of walking.

A prop room stores a chandelier from Errol Flynn's *Captain Blood* and lamps from *Casablanca*, two of the classics shot here.

The 2-hour tours leave at 10 A.M. and 2 P.M. weekdays, with additional tours at 9:30, 10:30, and 2:30 in summer (closed holidays). Call for reservations and directions at least a week in advance. Admission is $20; children under 10 are not admitted. Reservations are also required for lunch in the Blue Room (extra).

Paramount Pictures, 5555 Melrose Avenue, Hollywood; (213) 468-5575. Limited first-come tours at this studio right in the heart of Hollywood provide glimpses of movie and TV production. You may visit the room where technicians create and dub sounds not recorded with the actors' dialogue—everything from gunshots to footsteps.

Two-hour tours ($10) start at 11 A.M. and 2 P.M. weekdays; no children under 10 are admitted. Arrive early at the visitor center on the Gower Street side. After the tour, you may want to stop at the studio store.

NBC Television Studio, 3000 W. Alameda Avenue, Burbank; (818) 840-3537. A 1¼-hour walking tour offers highlights of a television production studio: set construction, special effects, make-up, and wardrobe. You'll also get a look at yourself on camera. Don't expect to watch a show being taped—for that you need studio audience tickets (see facing page).

Continuous tours ($6.50 adults, $4.50 children 5 to 14) are offered from 8:30 A.M. to 4 P.M. weekdays, 10 A.M. to 4 P.M. Saturday, 10 A.M. to 2 P.M. Sunday (closed major holidays). A garden cafe offers lunch or snacks while you wait.

KCET Television. The oldest continually operating studio—since 1912—lets you tour its complex at 4401 Sunset Boulevard most Tuesday and Thursday mornings with advance notice. Call (213) 667-9242 at least a week ahead for reservations for the free 90-minute behind-the-scenes look. Children under 6th-grade level are not allowed on the tour.

Now a major public television studio, this studio once housed silent film companies and then B-movie giant Monogram Studios, which made the Bowery Boys and Charlie Chan series.

Live filming

For a chance to watch live film and TV shootings, you can purchase daily schedules of locations where movie and television crews are filming. Some sites are more active than others, so luck and timing play a role in what you may see.

Hollywood on Location. This company's filming lists and maps ($29) even mention what stars are expected to be on hand. The lists are published weekdays only, at 9:30 A.M. Pick them up from offices at 8644

Wilshire Boulevard (west of La Cienega), Beverly Hills. To reserve a copy, call (213) 659-9165.

Motion Picture Coordination Office. For a minimal charge, this industry office gives you a copy of the daily location list for shooting around L.A. (Don't expect the details available from Hollywood on Location.) Call (213) 485-5324 for information, or stop by the office at 6922 Hollywood Boulevard.

TV shows

Most television sitcoms, game shows, and talk shows are taped live in the L.A. area, and you can be part of the studio audience. You'll learn what goes into producing your favorite show, how the sets look, and how sequences are pieced together.

Most studios restrict audiences to 16 years and up, though some drop the age to 12. No cameras or food are allowed.

Winter is the peak production period for most shows. Crowds shrink as summer tourists return home, increasing your chances of getting a ticket. Most shows tape in early afternoon and early evening, sitcoms generally on Tuesday, Wednesday, and Friday and game shows all week long. Some shoot for only 45 minutes, others for up to 3 hours at a time.

Tickets are free (on a first-come basis) but don't guarantee admittance. Lining up early is the key. To play it safe, arrive a good 2 hours in advance, considerably earlier for the most popular shows. (In summer some audience hopefuls wait as long as 7 hours.)

ABC, NBC, CBS, and Paramount offer tickets at on-site offices and by mail. Some independent studios offer seats through agencies. A few tickets (usually to new or less popular shows) are available daily outside Mann's Chinese Theatre in Holly-wood. For additional information, check with visitor information centers (addresses on page 11).

Most tickets are available a week ahead; for popular shows, they may be gone in 2 hours. To find which ones are available, and how many you can get (most programs have limits), call the studio or the audience service directly.

The best way to have a ticket in hand is to order it by mail at least 3 weeks in advance of your visit. Send a stamped, self-addressed envelope; include the name of the show and preferred date.

Ticket agencies. Audiences Unlimited is good for game shows. Offices are in Hollywood at Fox Television Center (5746 Sunset Boulevard; open 8:30 A.M. to 6 P.M. weekdays) and in Panorama City at Panorama Mall (corner of Van Nuys and Roscoe boulevards; open 10 A.M. to 9 P.M. weekdays, 10 A.M. to 7 P.M. Saturday, 11 A.M. to 6 P.M. Sunday). Tickets are available starting Wednesday the week before shooting. Call (818) 506-0067, or write to Audiences Unlimited, 100 Universal City Plaza, Building 153, Universal City, CA 91608.

Audience Associates, (213) 467-4697, offers guaranteed reserved seating a day or two ahead and bus rides to the studios. Audiences Inc., (714) 527-0246, has some success with same-day requests, including *Arsenio Hall Show* tickets.

ABC. The office at 1776 Talmadge Street in Los Angeles is open 9 A.M. to 5 P.M. weekdays; for details, call (213) 557-4396. To order by mail, write to ABC Show Tickets, 4151 Prospect Ave., Los Angeles, CA 90027.

CBS. Ticket office and mail-order address is 7800 Beverly Blvd., Los Angeles, CA 90036. Hours are 9 A.M. to 5 P.M. daily. For information, call (213) 852-2458.

NBC. Most tickets are available on the day of the program only. Office and mail-order address is 3000 W. Alameda Ave. (corner of Olive Avenue), Burbank, CA 91523. Hours are 8:30 A.M. to 5 P.M. weekdays, 9:30 A.M. to 4 P.M. weekends. From 9 A.M. to 5 P.M., you can call (818) 840-3537 for information.

Paramount Television. The ticket office is at 780 N. Gower Street, Hollywood (no mail orders). Hours are 8 A.M. to 4 P.M. weekdays. For details, call (213) 468-5575.

Homes of the stars

Most of L.A.'s celebrities hide out in the hills above Hollywood, in the canyons of Bel Air, around the crest of the Santa Monica Mountains in Beverly Hills, or farther west near Pacific Palisades and Malibu. You can drive around on your own or join a bus or van tour. Several leave from Mann's Chinese Theatre.

Bus tours. Gray Line offers daily narrated tours of the Hollywood and Beverly Hills area; call (213) 481-2121 for details. Hollywood Fantasy Tours, (213) 469-8184, often uses double-decker buses with open-air seating topside. Starline Sightseeing Tours offers general area tours as well as a rib-tickling tour past stars' homes; call (213) 463-3131.

Tour lengths and prices vary according to destination; most operators provide pickup at area hotels. You may need reservations.

Touring on your own. To drive past some stars' former abodes, buy a map from one of the hawkers along Sunset Boulevard. Maps may not be accurate, but they provide a pleasant way to spend a couple of hours.

Westside

Many of L.A.'s most exclusive shops, restaurants, art galleries, and entertainment centers are west of downtown in the fashionable communities of Beverly Hills, Century City, Westwood, and Bel Air.

To visit this area, get off the freeways and drive some of the city's famed boulevards: Wilshire, Sunset, and Santa Monica. Almost every attraction in the western sector of L.A. is on or near these thoroughfares.

Wilshire Boulevard. Stretching 16 miles from the center of L.A. to the Pacific Ocean, Wilshire is one of the city's prestige streets, often compared to New York's Fifth Avenue. Launched in the 1920s with the opening of the Miracle Mile (the area between La Brea and La Cienega avenues, now known as Mid-Wilshire), the thoroughfare was soon lined with upscale stores, prominent business firms, smart apartment houses, plush restaurants, and well-known hotels.

From the Harbor Freeway northwest to Lafayette Park, Wilshire cuts through a melting pot of Hispanic and Asiatic cultures. A few blocks to the west, Koreatown's colorful shops, markets, and restaurants turn the section south of Wilshire between Vermont and Western avenues into a tourist attraction. An interesting stop is the Korean Shopping Center (3300 W. 8th Street), a small arcade with several boutiques.

• Mid-Wilshire draws visitors to the Hancock Park area, site of the La Brea Tar Pits, the George C. Page Museum, and Los Angeles County Museum of Art (page 27).

Sunset Boulevard. Gloria Swanson immortalized this street on film; she even lived on the famous thoroughfare, across from the Beverly Hills Hotel. Her home is gone, but other celebrities live nearby.

Even if you're not a star-gazer, Sunset is a worthwhile drive. Beginning at El Pueblo downtown (see page 16), it proceeds through Hollywood, wanders past estates (and the exclusive Beverly

Hills Hotel) at the base of the Santa Monica Mountains, and finally intersects with the Pacific Coast Highway 25 miles away in Malibu.

There's still plenty of activity in West Hollywood's 20-block swath of neon and nightclubs known as the Sunset Strip, though its character has changed. Where fans once gathered to watch the movie colony of the 1930s and 40s enter Trocadero, Mocambo, and Ciro's nightclubs, the young and trendy now stroll in and out of loud, gaudy lounges and glorified hamburger stands. The street costumes and billboard art seem to catch people's eyes these days more than the view, but the garden of Butterfield's Restaurant (8426 Sunset Boulevard), once Lionel Barrymore's home, offers a good vantage for looking out over the city.

Santa Monica Boulevard. Originating in the Silver Lake district east of Hollywood, Santa Monica parallels Sunset for a stretch, then turns south, cutting through Beverly Hills and across Wilshire on its way to the ocean. Though not as glamorous a thoroughfare as Wilshire and Sunset, it offers an entrée to Century City. And if you take Wilshire to Beverly Hills, Santa Monica is a good alternate route back to Los Angeles and Hollywood.

Other notable streets. The trendy section of Melrose Avenue stretches from artsy West Hollywood (center of L.A.'s gay community) west to Beverly Hills. Weekends are lively, with crowds thronging to avant-garde shops and restaurants between La Brea and San Vicente. The Pacific Design Center at Melrose and San Vicente (known familiarly as the Blue Whale) is the center for interior design (not open to the general public). Nearby at Beverly and La Cienega, the dramatic Beverly Center (L.A.'s largest retail building) contains an eclectic collection of stores, restaurants, and theaters.

Fairfax Avenue (between Beverly Boulevard and Melrose) is the heart of L.A.'s largest Jewish neighborhood; this is the place to look for Jewish delicates-

sens, bakeries, bookstores, and newsstands. Farmers Market at 3rd and Fairfax bustles with food stands, produce stalls, and shops (see page 17). Cafe Largo (432 N. Fairfax) hosts evening poetry readings and offbeat entertainers that attract the younger celebrity set.

Beverly Hills

One of Southern California's most eagerly sought addresses, Beverly Hills is home to many well-known personalities of stage and screen and, consequently, a mecca for visitors who come to mix and mingle in the affluent city where stars live, dine, and shop.

Flags mark the Academy of Motion Picture Arts & Sciences (8949 Wilshire Boulevard), home of the Oscars. Exhibits related to motion pictures are open to the public weekdays from 9 A.M. to 5 P.M. The academy's library collection, at 333 S. La Cienega Boulevard, is also open to the public.

Though completely surrounded by Los Angeles, Beverly Hills is a fiercely independent municipality. At the busy intersection of Olympic Boulevard and Beverly Drive, a monument honors celebrities who helped preserve the community when annexation seemed likely.

Beverly Hills' boundaries extend roughly from San Vicente Boulevard on the east to Century City and Benedict Canyon Boulevard on the west, and from Olympic Boulevard on the south to the hills above Sunset Boulevard on the north. But most visitors are mainly interested in the shopping area, a triangle of streets bounded by Wilshire Boulevard, Cañon Drive, and Little Santa Monica Boulevard (separated from Santa Monica Boulevard by railroad tracks).

Getting around. Two-hour-free parking structures in the heart of town are well marked. A motorized trolley ($1) shuttles passengers around the main shopping area Tuesday through Saturday. For details, call the Beverly Hills Trolley at (213) 271-8174.

*You don't need a Rolls Royce to shop on Rodeo Drive in Beverly Hills, but you do
need an appointment to look at the exclusive fashions in bijan.*

...*Westside*

For maps, shopping and restaurant guides, and touring information, stop by the Beverly Hills Visitors Bureau, 239 S. Beverly (south of Wilshire in the center of the city's latest dining row).

Rodeo Drive. Several major department stores have luxurious branches along Wilshire Boulevard, but *the* shopping street is Rodeo Drive, north of the Beverly Wilshire Hotel. Strolling the 3-block stretch past Giorgio, Hermes, Gucci, Tiffany, and other sites of conspicuous consumption has become a spectator sport. When browsing palls, patio and sidewalk cafes guarantee good views of the passing scene.

Gardens. Two Beverly Hills estates open their gates for garden touring. Greystone Park, 905 Loma Vista Drive (in the hills above Sunset Boulevard at Doheny Drive), offers superb views from 18½ acres of formal gardens, woods, and lakes. The free gardens are open daily from 10 A.M. to 5 P.M.; the mansion is closed to the public.

You'll need advance reservations to visit the lush patio gardens of the city's oldest residence, the Virginia Robinson estate at 1008 Elden Way. Built in 1911, the home is open from 10 A.M. to 1 P.M. Tuesday through Friday; call (213) 276-5367. A small admission is charged to tour the grounds.

Century City

The somewhat sterile-looking contemporary enclave southwest of Beverly Hills was once the back lot of Twentieth Century Fox. Though filming continues, the studio (10201 Pico Boulevard) is not open for public tours. But you can glimpse the facades of the *Hello, Dolly!* set through the gates.

The entrance to the Avenue of the Stars, Century City's main thoroughfare, is from Santa Monica Boulevard just south of Wilshire. No cars park along the broad street; all lots are underground. The Century City Marketplace at 10250 Santa Monica has a variety of eating spots and specialty stores.

The ABC Entertainment Center, across from the fan-shaped Century Plaza Hotel at 2025 Avenue of the Stars (see page 13), features the large Shubert Theatre (setting for Broadway productions), two first-run cinemascopic theaters, shops, restaurants, and clubs.

Westwood Village

Known primarily as home to the University of California at Los Angeles (U.C.L.A.), Westwood is also L.A.'s movie theater capital (most of the new films preview here) and the location of the prestigious Armand Hammer Museum of Art and Cultural Center (see page 27). Marilyn Monroe and Natalie Wood are among celebrities buried in the cemetery at Lindbrook and Glendon avenues.

The intersection of Wilshire and Westwood boulevards is one of the area's busiest, and all of the main shopping streets are clogged with daytime browsers and nighttime diners, strollers, and theater-goers.

To avoid the weekend gridlock, take the DASH bus that operates Friday evening (7 P.M. to 2 A.M.) and Saturday (from 11 A.M.) from the Federal Building at Wilshire and Veteran boulevards. The bus stops at all theaters; a ride costs 25 cents.

Village streets. Dining outlets of all types, trendy clothiers, bookstores, video shops—Westwood appeals to the upscale collegiate. Movie-goers make the pedestrian crossing in the 900 block of Broxton Avenue, between the landmark Village and Bruin movie palaces, the city's liveliest.

Contempo-Westwood Center (10886 LeConte Avenue), once a Masonic temple, is now entrenched as a shopping, dining, and art center. The 500-seat Westwood Playhouse here presents plays, musicals, and revues.

U.C.L.A. This mammoth educational center enrolls more than 34,000 students and has more than 85 buildings on its 411-acre campus south of Sunset Boulevard. Free tours familiarize visitors with the university's facilities, architecture, and history, or you can wander around on your own.

On 1½-hour walks, guides point out landmarks like Royce Hall (one of the original buildings, a concert center), Wight Art Gallery, an outstanding 20th-century sculpture garden, botanic gardens, and sports complexes. Tours depart the visitor center in the Ueberroth Building, 10945 Le Conte Avenue, at 10:30 A.M. and 1:30 P.M. weekdays. Call (213) 206-8147 for information on weekend walks and other special tours.

The visitor center is open weekdays from 8 A.M. to 6 P.M. On-campus parking next to the center costs $3. A shuttle between Westwood Village and the campus stops at the visitor center; the bus operates every 5 to 10 minutes weekdays from 7:15 A.M. to 6 P.M.

City Mountains

L.A. has a mountain range right in its midst, an east-west chain that extends 47 miles west from the Los Angeles River into Ventura County. The Santa Monicas embrace 150,000 acres of rugged heights and steep canyons; almost half is parkland. At their eastern end lies Griffith Park; their western peaks wade right into the ocean.

Roads from Malibu and Agoura (in the San Fernando Valley) reach interior parks like former Paramount and Twentieth Century Fox filming sites. You get good views from Mulholland Drive, which stretches from the Pacific Coast Highway to the Hollywood Freeway (unpaved for 10 miles between Topanga Canyon and San Diego Freeway).

For information on outdoor activities, contact the Santa Monica Mountains National Recreation Area, 22900 Ventura Blvd., Woodland Hills, CA 91364; (818) 888-3770.

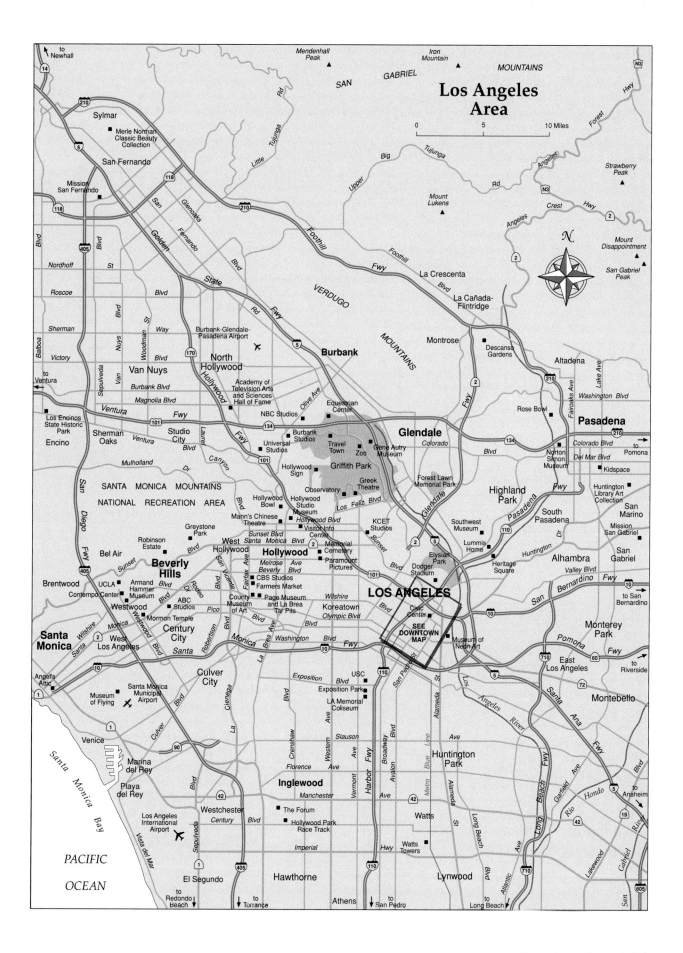

Los Angeles Area

One of the city's most striking architectural works, the Museum of Contemporary Art building in downtown Los Angeles hints by virtue of its bold exterior at the dramatic collection displayed inside.

L.A.'s Grand Museums

It's been said cities wear museums the way admirals proudly display a chest of gleaming medals. If so, L.A.'s acclaimed awards range from Ice Age fossils to contemporary art. The museums profiled below—along with Malibu's J. Paul Getty Museum, San Marino's Huntington Museum, and Pasadena's Norton Simon, all discussed in the following chapter—contain the area's major collections of art, history, and science.

Armand Hammer Museum of Art and Cultural Center. Located at 10889 Wilshire Boulevard in Westwood, this innovative new museum houses Hammer's personal collection of Western European art. Exhibits include 10,000 Daumier works and the only Leonardo Codex in the western hemisphere. The museum has a below-level garage. Admission is $4.50 adults, $2.50 children; hours of operation are 11 A.M. to 7 P.M. (closed Tuesday). Contact: (213) 443-6471.

California Afro-American Museum. This free museum in Exposition Park (600 State Drive) offers an excellent introduction to Afro-American life and culture. Exhibits range from books clandestinely published by blacks in the antebellum South to contemporary sculpture. Hours are 10 A.M. to 5 P.M. daily. Contact: (213) 744-7432.

California Museum of Science and Industry. There's always something new at the West's most popular science center, crammed with hands-on exhibits. Open daily from 10 A.M. to 5 P.M., the museum is in Exposition Park at 700 State Drive. Admission is free; IMAX Theater programs are $5 for adults, $3.50 for children and seniors. Recorded show information: (213) 744-2014 or 2015.

George C. Page Museum. Skeletons and re-creations of mastodons, dire wolves, imperial mammoths, and other prehistoric animals trapped in the Rancho La Brea Tar Pits during the Ice Age are displayed in this museum at 5801 Wilshire Boulevard, almost directly above their engulfing ooze. More than a million plant and animal fossils have been recovered from the site over the years. A 15-minute film depicts life in the Pleistocene era and shows how the remains were uncovered.

At an observation building in the northwest corner of the park, you can see the bubbling asphalt-laden water. The free observatory is open weekends from 10 A.M. to 5 P.M. The museum is open Tuesday through Sunday from 10 A.M. to 5 P.M.

Museum admission is $3 for adults, $1.50 for students and seniors, and 75 cents for children 6 to 12 (free for everyone the second Tuesday of each month). Contact: (213) 936-2230.

Los Angeles County Museum of Art. From pre-Columbian art to 20th-century sculpture, this encyclopedic collection at 5905 Wilshire Boulevard takes several hours to view. The museum's size was doubled when the Anderson building (a wedge of limestone and glass with a heroic entry portal), a central courtyard, and the Pavilion for Japanese Art (home for the internationally renowned Shin'enkan paintings) were added to the original Ahmanson, Hammer, and Bing pavilions in the late 1980s.

Admission is $5 adults, $3.50 students and seniors, $1 children ages 6 to 12 (free for everyone the second Tuesday of each month). The museum is open 10 A.M. to 5 P.M. weekdays, 10 A.M. to 6 P.M. weekends (closed Monday and major holidays).There's a parking lot southeast of the museum at Wilshire Boulevard and Spaulding Avenue (fee). A plaza cafe is open for lunch. Contact: (213) 857-6111.

Museum of Contemporary Art. The bold architecture of the museum building makes a fitting showcase for the important collection it houses. Art from the 1940s through abstract expressionism is displayed, including works by Pollock, Rauschenberg, Nevelson, and Diebenkorn.

The downtown museum is at 250 S. Grand Avenue. An auxiliary facility at 152 N. Central Avenue, dubbed the Temporary Contemporary, was the museum's original home.

Both museums are open Tuesday through Sunday from 11 A.M. to 6 P.M. (Thursday until 8 P.M.). Admission is $4 for adults, $2 for seniors and students, free for children under 12 and for all visitors after 5 P.M. Thursday. Contact: (213) 621-2766.

Natural History Museum. Egyptian mummies, reconstructed dinosaurs, glittering gems, dioramas of animals in natural settings, antique automobiles, Hollywood memorabilia—this museum is almost overwhelming in its diversity. The Discovery Center is packed with hands-on exhibits for children.

The museum (900 Exposition Boulevard in Exposition Park) is open Tuesday through Sunday from 10 A.M. to 5 P.M. (closed on major holidays); the Discovery Center is open from 11 A.M. to 3 P.M. Admission is $3 for adults, $1.50 for juniors and seniors, and 75 cents for children 5 to 12 (free the first Tuesday of the month). Contact: (213) 744-3466.

Southwest Museum. This hillside museum west of the Pasadena Freeway at 234 Museum Drive contains one of the country's best displays of Native American art and artifacts, from prehistoric times to the present.

There's hillside parking above the building, but it's more interesting to park below and enter through a diorama-lined tunnel. An elevator whisks you up to the gallery. Admission to the museum (open Tuesday through Sunday, 11 A.M. to 5 P.M.; closed holidays) is $3 for adults, $1.50 for seniors and students, $1 for children 7 to 18. Contact: (213) 221-2163.

Most of the Hispanic collection is housed in nearby Casa de Adobe (4605 N. Figueroa Street), once part of a Mexican/Californian rancho. This free museum operates on the same schedule as the Southwest Museum.

San Fernando Valley

Bounded by the Santa Monica, Santa Susana, Verdugo, and San Gabriel mountains, the 250-square-mile San Fernando Valley has been growing in leaps and bounds since the 1940s. If it were a single city, its nearly 1½ million population would rank it among the country's top ten. But, except for a few holdouts like Burbank and San Fernando, it's all part of Los Angeles.

Often smog-filled, this basin gets little respect from residents in other parts of L.A. Its middle-class lifestyle, though, has spawned more swimming pools per square mile than anyplace outside of Palm Springs, and the "valley girl talk" at Sherman Oaks Galleria mall added words to our vocabulary.

Most of the visitor interest centers on Universal, Burbank, and NBC studios (see pages 20–21) and on North Hollywood's new Academy of Television Arts and Sciences Hall of Fame (Lankershim and Magnolia boulevards). But a few historic remnants, including the San Fernando Mission (see page 6) also draw visitors "over the hill."

Getting around. The Hollywood Freeway (U.S. 101) and the San Diego Freeway (Interstate 405) enter the valley from Los Angeles. Most visitors from the north arrive on the Golden State Freeway (Interstate 5) or the Ventura Freeway (U.S. 101 as it cuts inland from the coast).

The valley is laid out in a grid pattern, with major thoroughfares running in a straight line for 20 miles. Ventura Boulevard, the main artery, extends east-west through the valley for 21 miles.

Los Encinos State Historic Park. The valley's recorded history began more than 200 years ago when the Portola party camped here. Old olive trees, the 1849 Osa adobe, and some turn-of-the-century sheep ranch buildings stand on the site at 16756 Moorpark Street in Encino. There's a small charge to visit the park, open Wednesday through Sunday from 10 A.M. to 5 P.M.

William S. Hart Park. Once the home of a Western star of the silent screen, the ranch house at the bottom of the hill contains mementos of his career; the Spanish-style mansion atop the hill houses vintage weapons, Native American artifacts, and fine Western art. A herd of bison roams the range.

The ranch (Newhall Avenue and San Fernando Road, Newhall) is open from 10 A.M. to dusk daily; free mansion tours operate every hour from 10 A.M. to 5 P.M. weekends, 10 A.M. to 3 P.M. Wednesday through Friday. There's free shuttle service from the park entrance.

Placerita Canyon State and County Park. Gold was discovered here in 1842, six years before the strike at Sutter's Mill began Northern California's gold rush. As the story goes, a shepherd named Don Francisco Lopez dreamed about gold while taking a nap. Being hungry when he awoke, he pulled up a clump of wild onions and found nuggets clinging to the roots, the first glimpse of a deposit that netted $80,000.

The oak tree under which he rested still stands in this small park about 5 miles east of Newhall off U.S. 14. It's a pleasant place to picnic or hike.

L.A.'s Playground

Sprawling Griffith Park is the site of the city's zoo, an observatory and planetarium, an outdoor theater, a bird sanctuary, an equestrian center, and an antique vehicular museum. And that's not all: its 4,107 acres contain golf courses, tennis courts, cycling paths, polo grounds, a swimming pool, and a cricket field.

Griffith Park straddles the eastern end of the Santa Monica Mountains in the northern part of the city. More than half of its rugged terrain is a sort of domesticated wilderness laced with miles of horseback and hiking trails. But its flat perimeter is easily accessible from the Ventura, Golden State, and Hollywood freeways. Both Western and Vermont avenues lead into the park from the south.

For free maps and information on Griffith Park's attractions and activities, stop by the visitor center (open daily, 10 A.M. to 5 P.M.) at 4730 Crystal Springs Drive, off Riverside Drive south of the zoo. A 1926 carousel operates opposite the center. See page 29 for information about the zoo and Travel Town transportation museum.

Greek Theatre. Nestled among the foothills near the park's southern edge, this 6,000-seat natural amphitheater is a popular setting for summer concerts; call (213) 410-1062.

Griffith Observatory. From its perch on the slopes of Mount Hollywood in the southern part of the park, the observatory commands a spectacular view of the city at night. A 600-seat planetarium theater replicates eclipses, northern lights, and other celestial phenomena. Another show pulses with laser light and sound.

Admission to the observatory and its science exhibits is free. The observatory is open Tuesday through Sunday from 7 to 10 P.M. The science hall is open Sunday through Friday from 12:30 to 10 P.M. (from 2 P.M. weekdays in winter), Saturday from 11:30 A.M. to 10 P.M.

L.A. for Children

Where do you take the younger set after they've toured Universal Studios, seen the footprints in Mann's Chinese Theatre, and (with luck) watched a filming somewhere in the city? The answer might be to a puppet show, on a train or stagecoach ride, to the zoo, or to a children's museum. Even without kids in tow, adults are likely to enjoy many of the following diversions.

This is only a sampling of what's available in the greater L.A. area. Among other good choices are Santa Monica's Angel's Attic and Pasadena's Kidspace (page 41) and the Long Beach Children's Museum (page 40). The whole family will enjoy fossils at Rancho La Brea Tar Pits (page 17), "please touch" displays at both the Museum of Science and Industry and the Discovery Center in the Natural History Museum (page 27), and planetarium and laserium shows at Griffith Park (page 28).

The only place young children are *not* encouraged is in the audience of a television filming. Because of the fear of disruption, kids usually must be 16 to get a ticket.

Los Angeles Children's Museum. The museum in the mall at Civic Center (310 N. Main Street) is just for kids, although adults may tag along to watch youngsters make a recording, take part in a videotape filming, paint their faces, or build with giant foam blocks. Exhibits show ages 2 to 12 how to learn by doing.

In summer, the museum is open weekends 10 A.M. to 5 P.M., weekdays from 11:30 A.M. to 5 P.M. Hours the rest of the year are 2 to 4 P.M. Wednesday and Thursday, 10 A.M. to 5 P.M. weekends. Admission is $4 (adults free weekday afternoons during the school year).

Wells Fargo History Museum. The Old West lives downtown at 333 S. Grand Avenue, where the whole family learns about the rigors and adventures of early-day travel by climbing aboard a stagecoach for a simulated ride. Among the historic highlights: an 1880s ore cart, a fist-size gold nugget, and photos of notorious bandit Black Bart. The free museum is open 9 A.M. to 4 P.M. weekdays.

Bob Baker Marionette Theater. Dancing skeletons, toy soldiers, and skate-boarding clowns are among the whimsical characters that make this puppet theater the most endearing—and enduring—in the country. Performances take place daily at 10:30 A.M. weekdays and 2:30 P.M. weekends. The $7 admission fee includes the show, a backstage tour, and refreshments.

The theater is located west of the Harbor Freeway at 1345 W. 1st Street. Reservations are a must; phone (213) 250-9995.

Gene Autry Western Heritage Museum. Walt Disney Imagineering created the exhibits and sound tracks in seven galleries tracing America's Western heritage. You're introduced to soldiers and Indians, trappers and sodbusters, outlaws and good guys in white hats—and some of the actors who played them. Of special appeal to kids of all ages is The Spirit of Imagination gallery (film clips and other Hollywood cowboy artifacts).

To reach the museum (4700 Zoo Drive at the edge of Griffith Park), take the Golden State Freeway (Interstate 5) north from downtown to the Zoo Drive exit. Museum hours are 10 A.M. to 5 P.M. Tuesday through Sunday. Admission is $4.75 for adults, $3.50 for students and seniors, $2 for children 2 through 12. A museum shop and restaurant round out the amenities.

Los Angeles Zoo. More than 2,000 mammals, birds, and reptiles live on this fine zoo's 113 hillside acres. Key exhibits include a large Koala House and a walk-in aviary. Adventure Island, a special children's section of the zoo, has five major Southwest environments: sea lions cavort along the Shoreline, bats inhabit the Cave, mountain lions roam around the Mountain, prairie dogs poke their heads above the Meadow, and roadrunners dash about the Desert. Other zoo child-pleasers are the nursery orphans and the domestic array at the Spanish Hacienda.

The Los Angeles Zoo is on Zoo Drive in the northern part of Griffith Park, at the intersection of the Ventura and Golden State freeways (State 134 and Interstate 5). Hours are 10 A.M. to 5 P.M. daily (to 6 P.M. in summer), except Christmas. Admission is $6 for adults, $5 seniors, and $2.75 for children 2 to 12, including various animal shows presented throughout the day (check the schedule when you arrive). Camel and elephant rides cost extra.

Travel Town. More than 30 steam locomotives and railroad cars, fire trucks, a horse-drawn milk wagon, and an 1849 circus wagon are part of the allure of this indoor/outdoor transportation museum in Griffith Park. Children of all ages love riding the miniature train that circles the park.

The museum opens daily at 10 A.M. and closes sometime between 4 P.M. and 6 P.M., depending on the day of the week and the season. There's no fee to visit, though donations are encouraged. Train rides cost $1.50 for adults, $1.25 for children under 14, and $1 for seniors. Travel Town is on Zoo Drive in the northern part of Griffith Park.

L.A.'s Beaches
& Mountains

L.A.'s sandy front door and back-yard mountains add impressive dimensions to any Southern California visit. Residents and tourists alike flock to the string of beaches around the city; more than 50 million hit the sands annually. And the nearby mountains swarm with local hikers and campers, or sledders and skiers, depending on the season. But the attractions don't stop with splendid scenery and outdoor recreation; along the shore and in mountain valleys are fine museums, historic sites, and gardens to tour.

Beach playgrounds

Stretching some 75 miles from Malibu on the west to Long Beach on the south, L.A.'s western and southern shores are used as a summer coolant by the city's huge population. It's usually about 10° cooler at beach communities than it is inland, and water temperatures are around 67° from July on into autumn.

But the beaches are more than just hot-weather destinations. They're a key part of the L.A. lifestyle, inviting every aquatic pleasure from boating and fishing to surfing, snorkeling, and scuba diving.

Mountain retreats

The San Gabriel and San Bernardino mountain ranges rise abruptly to peaks over 10,000 feet, separating Los Angeles from desert lands to the north and forming an imposing backdrop for the teeming city.

Lower elevations of the frontal slopes are closed in summer because of fire danger, but alpine lakes and pine-clad slopes higher up offer quick relief from the inland area's heat and smog. In winter, locals head for the hills to belly-thump down slopes on improvised sleds or ski at such resorts as Lake Gregory–Crestline and Big Bear.

The Santa Monicas, the state's only east-west mountain range, march right into the Pacific Ocean west of the city, their rocky tops forming the offshore Channel Islands. Mountains and beaches meet at Point Mugu, where this chapter begins.

Planning a visit

Many visitors to L.A. establish cool summer bases in beach towns like Santa Monica (a short distance from Westside attractions), Marina del Rey (close to the L.A. airport), or Long Beach (near Orange County).

Cabins, bed-and-breakfasts, motels, and a few large hotels welcome mountain-goers. Lake Arrowhead and Big Bear have the best accommodations.

Getting there. Long Beach Municipal Airport is a convenient alternative to LAX or Orange County traffic. More than 40 daily flights offer service from 27 cities across the country. For mountain destinations, the closest large airport is at Ontario; a few air charters also serve larger resorts.

Though there is shuttle service from Los Angeles and Long Beach airports to a few beach hotels, light-rail service between L.A. and Long Beach (see page 40), and spotty city bus transportation, a car makes it easier to explore both coastline and mountains.

State 1, the Pacific Coast Highway, ties the beach communities together. Inland, Interstate 405 provides coastal access from the north and south, and Interstate 10 reaches the beach from the east at Santa Monica. Access roads to the San Gabriels and the San Bernardinos are easily reached from Interstate 210 and Interstate 215.

At Marina del Rey's harbor, Fisherman's Village imparts a turn-of-the-century, Cape Cod ambience for shopping and dining. Tour boats offer cruises of the man-made marina, the West Coast's largest.

Contacts

These agencies offer information on attractions and accommodations. See additional contacts throughout this chapter.

NOTE: Telephone area codes in coastal and southern portions of Los Angeles County will be changed from (213) to (310) as of February 1992.

Santa Monica Convention & Visitors Bureau
P.O. Box 5278
Santa Monica, CA 90405
(213) 393-7593

Long Beach Area Convention and Visitors Council
One World Trade Center, Suite 300
Long Beach, CA 90831-0300
(800) 234-3645

Pasadena Convention & Visitors Bureau
171 S. Los Robles Ave.
Pasadena, CA 91101
(818) 795-9311

Inland Empire Tourism Council
800 N. Haven, Suite 100
Ontario, CA 91764
(714) 941-7877
For mountains, inland valleys

The Beaches

The county's long stretches of sand and water, from Santa Monica Bay southwest to Long Beach Harbor, are dotted with fishing piers, marinas, museums, and shopping complexes. Carefully tony and innocently shabby, purveying cracked crab and caramel corn, these beach communities are where Southern California's sandcastle vision of health and happiness is made real.

Days start early at the shore, especially the crescents along Santa Monica Bay. By 7 A.M. anglers are in position on piers and fleets of beach-cleaning machines are raking the sand. They're soon joined by joggers and—if radio prognostications are favorable—by surfers.

State beaches provide a variety of facilities; the map on the facing page shows their locations. For state beach camping, see page 121.

Beach parking can be a problem. Bring plenty of quarters to feed meters at city and county parks.

Point Mugu to Point Dume

The south slope of the Santa Monica Mountains drops abruptly into the sea in the westernmost section of a Los Angeles area beach tour, forming rocky headlands and intimate pocket beaches. Farther to the east you'll find good swimming beaches.

Point Mugu to Malibu has the cleanest ocean along the metropolitan coast, with clear water, healthy kelp beds, the best shore and offshore fishing and diving, and some very good surfing.

Zuma Beach. Just west of Point Dume off State 1, L.A.'s largest county-owned beach offers excellent swimming, except for occasional summer riptides. Big parking lots, tots' playgrounds, volleyball courts, and food stalls make it a popular place.

Point Dume Whale Watch. A stairway from Westward Beach Road at Point Dume leads up to a good spot from which to watch the annual winter whale migration (see page 124).

Malibu & east

Surfing movies in the 1950s and 60s helped popularize L.A.'s beaches. *Gidget* and *Beach Blanket Bingo* were just two of a whole genre of beach films set in Malibu. But this community has long been home for celebrities who brave winter surf and mud slides for summer fun. David Letterman, Larry Hagman, Rob Lowe, and Goldie Hawn are but a few of the prominent citizens who might be glimpsed around town.

Maybe that's why there's such a high concentration of oceanview restaurants along State 1, including Geoffrey's, Alice's, Don the Beachcomber, Malibu Sea Lion, Moonshadows, Charthouse, and Gladstones 4 Fish. Some are expensive; others have surprisingly down-to-earth tabs. Zonker Davis Accessway (named after a "Doonesbury" comic strip character) is one of several public-access footpaths that thread between the beachhouses to the sand.

At Malibu's pier, you'll find sportfishing boats and a restaurant. You can fish from the pier with a license, and buy bait and tackle.

History and birds. A showcase of Spanish-Moorish architecture, the Adamson House at 23200 Pacific Coast Highway was built in 1929 on what was then the last undivided Spanish land grant in California. Now it is part of the Malibu Lagoon Museum. After touring the house and 13 acres of gardens, visit the former garage to see exhibits on Malibu from Chumash Indian days to the present. The museum is open from 10 A.M. to 2 P.M. Wednesday through Saturday; for details, call (213) 456-8432. Admission is free for seniors.

East of the house, at Malibu Lagoon State Beach, restoration gave new life to a 5-acre coastal wetlands visited by more than 250 species of birds. Kiosks explain bird and plant life. The beach fronting the lagoon is a surfer's haven.

J. Paul Getty Museum. One of America's richest art museums stands on a bluff at 17985 W. Pacific Coast Highway, between Sunset and Topanga Canyon boulevards.

A wealthy American industrialist who began collecting art in the 1930s, Getty left the bulk of his estate to the museum when he died in 1976. His interests centered on Greek and Roman antiquities, Renaissance and Baroque paintings, and European decorative arts. Though greatly expanded now (recent acquisitions include Van Gogh's *Irises*), the museum's collections still reflect Getty's imprint. Hands-on displays in a second-floor gallery help explain exhibits.

The building itself is a replica of the Villa dei Papiri, an ancient Roman country house at Herculaneum destroyed by the eruption of Vesuvius in 79 A.D. Its gardens include trees, flowers, shrubs, and herbs similar to those that might have been growing two thousand years ago at the villa.

The museum is open Tuesday through Sunday from 10 A.M. to 5 P.M. year-round except on major holidays. Admission is free, but you'll need a parking reservation. No walk-in traffic is permitted. Call (213) 458-2003 at least a week in advance of your visit; the office is open daily from 9 A.M. to 5 P.M.

Plan on spending about 3 hours to thoroughly explore the museum, perhaps taking lunch in the Garden Tea Room and visiting the bookstore.

By the mid-1990s, a new J. Paul Getty Center off Interstate 405 and Mulholland Drive will showcase the paintings, drawings, manuscripts, and decorative arts now on display in the Malibu museum, plus others previously in storage. The Greek and Roman collections will remain at the present Malibu site.

Inland forays

From Malibu, Sunset Boulevard winds along the base of the Santa Monicas en route to downtown L.A. Just a mile or so inland from the coast highway lie two peaceful parks worth a detour.

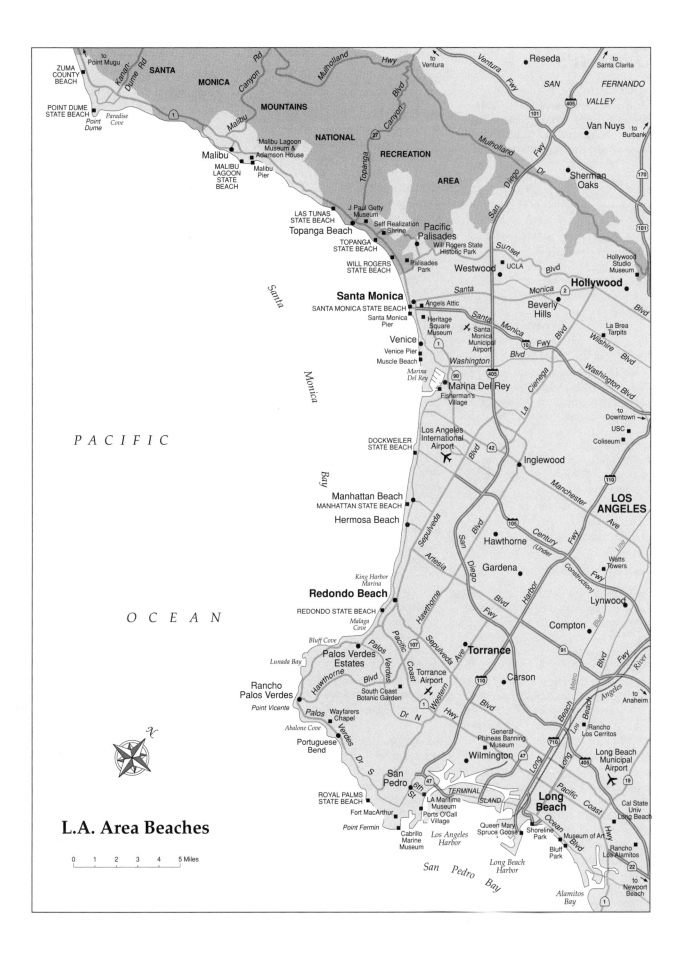

L.A. Area Beaches

PACIFIC

OCEAN

ZUMA
COUNTY
BEACH

to Point Mugu

to
Ventura

to
Santa Clarita

Reseda

SANTA

MONICA

Kanan-Dume Rd

Malibu Canyon Rd

Mulholland Hwy

Ventura Fwy

405

SAN

FERNANDO

VALLEY

POINT DUME
STATE BEACH

Point
Dume

Paradise
Cove

1

MOUNTAINS

Van Nuys

to
Burbank

170

Topanga Canyon

NATIONAL

27

RECREATION

Mulholland

San Diego Fwy

101

Sherman
Oaks

101

Malibu

MALIBU
LAGOON
STATE
BEACH

Malibu Lagoon
Museum &
Adamson House

Malibu Pier

AREA

Santa

Monica

LAS TUNAS
STATE BEACH

J Paul Getty
Museum

Self Realization
Shrine

Pacific
Palisades

Hollywood
Studio
Museum

Topanga Beach

TOPANGA
STATE BEACH

Will Rogers State
Historic Park

Sunset

Blvd

Westwood

UCLA

2

Monica

Beverly
Hills

Hollywood

Blvd

Santa

WILL ROGERS
STATE BEACH

Palisades
Park

Santa

La Brea
Tarpits

Wilshire

Blvd

Santa Monica

SANTA MONICA STATE BEACH

Angels Attic

Santa
Monica

10 Fwy

Blvd

Bay

Santa Monica
Pier

Heritage
Square
Museum

Santa
Monica
Municipal
Airport

Washington Blvd

Venice

1

Washington

to
Downtown

USC

Venice Pier

90

La Cienega

Coliseum

Muscle Beach

Marina
Del Rey

405

Marina Del Rey

42

Fisherman's
Village

Los Angeles
International
Airport

Inglewood

LOS
ANGELES

DOCKWEILER
STATE BEACH

Blvd

110

Manchester

Ave

Manhattan Beach

MANHATTAN STATE BEACH

Sepulveda

San Diego

105

Century

(Under

Hawthorne

Watts
Towers

Hermosa Beach

Blvd

Construction)

Artesia

Gardena

Blvd

Harbor

Fwy

Lynwood

King Harbor
Marina

Redondo Beach

Hawthorne

Compton

Blue

Line

REDONDO STATE BEACH

Malaga
Cove

91

Blvd

Fwy

Los Angeles River

Bluff Cove

Pacific Coast

107

Sepulveda

Torrance

110

Carson

to
Anaheim

Palos Verdes
Estates

Lunada Bay

Palos

Verdes

Blvd

Torrance
Airport

Western

Ave

Rancho
Los Cerritos

Rancho
Palos Verdes

Hawthorne

South Coast
Botanic Garden

Beach

Long Beach

Point Vicente

Palos

Wayfarers
Chapel

1

Hwy

General
Phineas Banning
Museum

710

405

Long Beach
Municipal
Airport

Abalone Cove

Verdes

Dr N

Wilmington

47

19

Portuguese
Bend

Dr S

San
Pedro

6th
St

47

TERMINAL
ISLAND

Long
Beach

Cal State
Univ
Long Beach

ROYAL PALMS
STATE BEACH

LA Maritime
Museum

Ocean

Blvd

Fort MacArthur

Ports O'Call
Village

Queen Mary
Spruce Goose

Shoreline
Park

Museum of Art

Point Fermin

Cabrillo
Marine
Museum

Los Angeles
Harbor

Bluff
Park

Rancho
Los Alamitos

22

San

Pedro

Bay

Long Beach
Harbor

to
Newport
Beach

Alamitos
Bay

1

0 1 2 3 4 5 Miles

...Beaches

Self-Realization Fellowship Lake Shrine. A quiet retreat at 17190 Sunset Boulevard, this 10-acre hillside meditation garden contains a spring-fed lake, shrines, gazebos, a waterfall, and a windmill chapel. You can visit between 9 A.M. and 4:45 P.M. except on Mondays, holidays, and occasional Saturdays (no admission charge).

Will Rogers State Historic Park. Cowboy philosopher Will Rogers lived in the large (31 rooms) but unassuming house on this 186-acre Pacific Palisades ranch from 1928 until his death in 1935. On tours you'll see the Western paintings, rugs, lariats, and saddles that played such an important part in his life.

Stables, polo fields (matches are held most weekends), and riding and hiking trails make up the rest of the spread. The entrance road to the hillside park overlooking the Pacific is at 14253 Sunset Boulevard. The park is open daily from 8 A.M. to 7 P.M. (per-car admission charge); house tours take place from 10 A.M. to 5 P.M.

A state beach named for the humorist lies beneath Pacific Palisades, south of Sunset Boulevard on State 1.

Santa Monica

At Santa Monica the shore turns south for a splendid sweep of 20 miles of almost wholly accessible, broad, sandy beach encompassing eight public beaches, five fishing piers, and two small craft harbors. Then it rounds the Palos Verdes Peninsula for 15 rocky miles before losing itself among the channels of two big harbors, Los Angeles and Long Beach. A bike path stretches 19 miles south from Santa Monica to the bluffs at Palos Verdes.

Exploring the city. Over the last few years, Santa Monica has been transformed from a slightly stodgy seaside community that did little to encourage visitors into a dynamic city noted for its upscale art galleries, restaurants, and shops as well as its famed beach.

Make your first stop the Santa Monica Visitor Center at the south end of beautiful Palisades Park (1400 Ocean Avenue, between Santa Monica Boulevard and Broadway).

New hotels like Loews, Park Hyatt, and Guest Quarters Suites have joined such longtime favorites as the Miramar-Sheraton, Pacific Shore, Shangri-la, and two Holiday Inns. More than 400 restaurants, cafes, and pubs are crowded into the city's 8 square miles, including the elegant Michael's, Wolfgang Puck's Chinois on Main, and Ivy at the Shore. Patrick's Roadhouse (106 Entrada Drive at Pacific Coast Highway) is so popular that you need reservations for breakfast on weekends; call (213) 459-4544.

Boutiques, chic stores, and art galleries line Montana Avenue from 7th to 17th streets and fill Santa Monica Place mall (between 2nd and 4th streets, Broadway and Colorado Avenue). Renovated Main Street and the Third Street Promenade hold other one-of-a-kind shops. A remodeled, turn-of-the-century egg warehouse (2437 Main Street) is now the city's downtown art museum.

For a look at local history, visit the free Heritage Square Museum at 2612 Main Street. Period furnishings and old photographs decorate the rooms of this 1894 house (open Thursday through Saturday from 11 A.M. to 4 P.M. and Sunday from noon). Children love the antique toys and dolls displayed at Angel's Attic, 516 Colorado Avenue (see page 41).

Airplane buffs will enjoy the exhibition of antique aircraft—from World War I biplanes to Spitfires and P51s—at the Museum of Flying (Santa Monica Airport, 2772 Donald Douglas Loop North near Ocean Park Boulevard). Next door is the trendy DC3 Restaurant, a huge hangar-style eatery.

Santa Monica Pier. Hard-hit and truncated by a 1983 storm, the West Coast's oldest pleasure pier has been restored once more. A gathering place for generations of residents, the pier at the foot of Colorado Avenue in the midst of Santa Monica State Beach is the perfect place from which to view the action on the esplanade below and the cliffside park above.

Arcades, amusement rides, restaurants, shops, and a Victorian-era merry-go-round vie for attention. A roller coaster and 11-story ferris wheel are being added. Some activities are free—fishing from the pier (no license required) or watching nearby surfers, volleyball players, and acrobats.

Venice

Venice of America was the formal name for the watery resort of isthmuses and canals built by Abbot Kinney in 1904 as a mecca of art and enlightenment. Grand hotels lined Windward Avenue, symphony orchestras performed at the Summer Assembly, and gondoliers plied their fleet along the waterways. Later Kinney added plunges, bathhouses, amusement piers, and a midway where thrill rides whirled within screaming distance of the ocean's breakers.

Venice thrived as a West Coast Coney Island well into the 1920s. Then misfortunes—flood, fire, the imposition of L.A.'s blue laws—spun the town into decline. By 1929, even the famous canals had been largely filled in and paved.

Today's version, though, remarkably resembles Kinney's original dream. Part souk, part circus, it harbors artists, writers, restaurateurs, remnant hippies, and retirees. Other beach towns are relaxing. Venice is not.

Ocean Front Walk. Any stroll, bike ride, or roller skate along Ocean Front Walk, with its array of outdoor cafes, shops, vendors, and street artists, is entertaining. Walkers take the sidewalk nearest the buildings; cyclists and roller skaters ride a few yards nearer to the ocean. (You can rent bikes or skates anywhere along the walk.)

You might start your tour near the Venice Pavilion at the foot of Windward Avenue about a mile seaward of Lincoln Boulevard (State 1). Muscle Beach lies south of Windward; to the north are several good cafes (among them Sidewalk and Figtree's) with ringside views of fire-eaters and fortune-tellers.

Venice Pier. The fishing pier at the foot of Washington Street is organized for round-the-clock angling (no license needed). Bays at short intervals expand its perimeter to about 400 yards.

Bright umbrellas line the beach along one of Santa Monica's broad stretches of sand. Excellent swimming, diving, surfing, and fishing make the area a favorite destination for both vacationers and L.A. area residents.

...Beaches

Canals. To take a look at the few remaining canals, turn inland on South Venice Boulevard and then south onto Dell Avenue. You can stroll the bridges and the canal banks, even though sidewalks are sometimes missing. At Sherman Canal and Dell Avenue, a restoration project uses concrete blocks and native pickleweed to stablize the canal banks.

Marina del Rey

When you see the forest of masts at Marina del Rey, it's easy to believe that this man-made recreational boat harbor is the world's largest. To reach the visitor center from State 1, head seaward on Mindanao Way to 4701 Admiralty. Here, you can pick up maps and information on parking, restaurants, entertainment, and hotels, including the glamorous new Ritz-Carlton entry.

Touring the harbor. Narrated harbor tours depart Fisherman's Village docks on Fiji Way on the hour from 11 A.M. to 4 P.M. daily (see page 124). Buy tickets ($5) at the blue boathouse near the lighthouse in Fisherman's Village (13755 Fiji Way).

Rent-a-Sail, at Fisherman's Village, rents sailboats, motorboats, catamarans, and canoes.

Fisherman's Village. Though touristy and usually crowded on weekends, this New England–style shopping and dining complex is worth a look. Some 40 shops feature everything from seashell statues to fine jewelry. You'll hear live jazz from 2 to 5 P.M. many Sundays. After shopping, take a stroll along the esplanade to view incoming boats.

Manhattan, Hermosa & Redondo Beach

There's little visible glamour in this trio of older seaside cities, but you'll find more youthful beach aficionados per square yard than almost anywhere else along the coast.

Both Manhattan and Hermosa Beach have public fishing piers, each with bait and tackle shops, rest rooms, and snack shops. Redondo State Beach adjoins a marina complex (King Harbor) of restaurants, motels, yacht clubs, and boat facilities. Next door, shops and restaurants line two piers that give a good view of the 1½-mile beach.

Two oceanside boulevards, the Esplanade in Redondo Beach and the Strand in Hermosa Beach and Manhattan Beach, offer plenty of people-watching action.

Palos Verdes Peninsula

Following scenic Palos Verdes Drive south around the peninsula is a pleasant alternative to State 1. Beginning in plush Palos Verdes Estates and ending at San Pedro's Point Fermin Park, it follows the rugged clifftop for a 15-mile stretch, passing several noteworthy attractions and a number of ocean overlooks en route to the busy ports of Los Angeles and Long Beach.

Three coves below the cliffs are accessible to the public. Malaga Cove lies next to Torrance County Beach on Paseo de la Playa; Bluff Cove and Lunada Bay are reached by following Paseo del Mar west to trailheads.

South Coast Botanic Garden. This 87-acre oasis, once a mine and later a landfill project, makes a pleasant detour off Palos Verdes Drive at 26300 Crenshaw Boulevard. The garden (open 9 A.M. to 5 P.M. daily) has native plants, ground covers, and flowering trees. There's a small fee to tour.

Point Vicente Interpretive Center. Adjacent to the lighthouse at 31501 Palos Verdes Drive W., the center has exhibits on area history and geology and on the California gray whale. An observation area on the second floor provides panoramic views. The center is open daily, 10 A.M. to dusk; there's a token admission charge.

Wayfarers Chapel. On a hill at Portuguese Bend sits a striking glass chapel designed by Lloyd Wright, son of the famed architect, for the Swedenborgian church. A 50-foot white stone campanile surmounts the chapel. The grounds are landscaped with plants mentioned in the Bible. The chapel (5755 Palos Verdes Drive S.) is open daily from 9 A.M. to 5 P.M. for free self-guided tours.

Point Fermin Park. Near the Old Point Fermin Lighthouse, this 37-acre blufftop facility is a good place from which to explore tidepools, watch for whales, and observe the windsurfing activities at Cabrillo Beach. The restored lighthouse, built in 1874 of lumber brought around Cape Horn, is not open to the public.

Los Angeles Harbor

The ports of Los Angeles and Long Beach share the world's second largest man-made harbor (Rotterdam is first). Shielded by a 9-mile breakwater, its maze of channels, inlets, and islands covers 50 miles of developed waterfront.

The port (which includes San Pedro, Terminal Island, and Wilmington) is a leader in total tonnage processed and in modern handling techniques. It's also the center of the country's seafood canning industry and home to more than 100 commercial fishing vessels.

Soaring 185 feet above the harbor's main channel, Vincent Thomas Bridge (50-cent toll) connects San Pedro with Terminal Island and Long Beach. Under the bridge's western end lies the Catalina Terminal, departure site for ferries and seaplanes to Santa Catalina Island (see facing page).

Concrete bunkers and a small museum in Fort MacArthur, above Angel's Gate Park near the harbor entrance, testify to the protection planned for the harbor during World War II.

Now noted as the West Coast's premier cruise center, San Pedro has been busily changing its image from industrial to recreational. It's added a marina, the World Cruise Center, several upscale hotels, trendy restaurants, and new shopping complexes along 6th Street in the revitalized downtown.

Cabrillo Marine Museum. Southern California's largest collection of marine life is found in the free museum at 3720 Stephen White Drive, down the hill from Fort MacArthur and adjacent to Cabrillo Beach. Aquariums contain an assortment of creatures from anchovies

Santa Catalina Island

California's only offshore resort has lured local pleasure-seekers since the 1890s, but it took chewing gum magnate William Wrigley, Jr. to thrust the 76-square-mile isle into the national limelight.

First he built a mountaintop summer mansion (now the elegant Inn at Mount Ada). Then he brought his Chicago Cubs baseball team over for spring training, and then, in 1929, he built the huge, circular Casino Building. It's not actually a casino, but it *is* a signature landmark in the little town of Avalon at the island's south end. Broadcasts from its ballroom brought the nation the big-band sounds of the 1930s and 40s.

No longer do you arrive by steamer. But you can still cross the 22 miles from the mainland by sea, bands still perform occasionally in the Avalon Ballroom, and your hotel—though somewhat modern-ized—may date back to the early 1900s.

Transportation. Getting to Catalina is part of the fun—by boat, plane, or helicopter. Flights from Los Angeles and Orange counties take about 15 minutes, from San Diego 30 minutes.

Ferries from Long Beach and San Pedro shuttle passengers to and from Avalon on almost an hourly basis (more limited service is available from Newport Beach and San Diego). Crossings take from 1½ to 2 hours. For details, phone Catalina Cruises, (213) 410-1062, or Catalina Express, (213) 519-1212.

Touring. Since Avalon is only 1 square mile, it's best explored on foot. You can board a shuttle or rent a bicycle or golf cart to view its attractive shops and restaurants, but cars are off-limits to visitors. To get the lay of the land, walk along Crescent Avenue to the Chamber of Commerce office at the 1909 Green Pleasure Pier (center for boat tours and rentals, fishing trips and gear, diving rentals) or the Island Company's Visitor's Information Center at 423 Crescent.

Daily guided tours of the Casino show off its well-preserved art deco movie palace and ballroom. A free museum (open daily from 10:30 A.M. to 4 P.M.) contains historical mementos.

Half-day bus tours transport visitors to the island's rugged interior for a look at scenery and wildlife, including a free-roaming herd of 400 bison descended from a few left after Zane Grey's 1925 filming of *The Vanishing American.* One tour stops at an Arabian horse ranch.

Glass-bottom boat trips explore the colorful undersea marine life and vegetation of the island's legendary clear waters. From May through September, several coastal and sunset dinner cruises are added. A nighttime Flying Fish Boat Tour lets you watch winged fish perform acrobatics 25 feet above the water.

Some 50 miles of trails and a handful of campgrounds welcome hikers. Contact the Los Angeles County Department of Parks and Recreation in Avalon, (213) 510-0688, for free hiking permits and campsite information.

Lodging. Avalon offers more than 40 hotels, motels, and inns, ranging from moderate to luxurious. A 2-night stay is usually required on summer weekends.

For information, write to the Catalina Island Chamber of Commerce & Visitor's Bureau (Box 217, Avalon, CA 90740) or call the Island Company's Visitor's Information Center, (800) 428-2566.

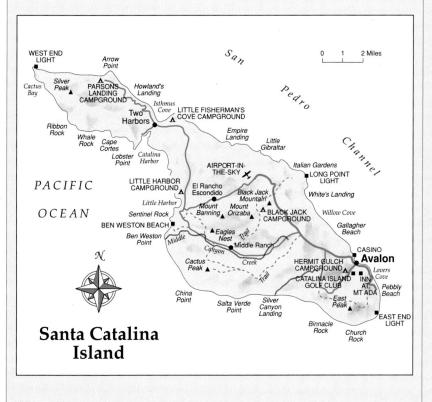

Santa Catalina Island

Once the pride of the British fleet, the elegant Queen Mary now rides serenely at anchor in the Long Beach Harbor. The regal liner, both a hotel and a floating museum, and the adjacent Spruce Goose wooden flying boat are part of Disney's entertainment empire.

...Beaches

to sharks. The museum is open from noon to 5 P.M. Tuesday through Friday and from 10 A.M. to 5 P.M. weekends. There's a $5.50 charge to park in the beach lot.

Ports O' Call Village. An extensive shopping and dining complex faces the harbor's main channel at Berth 77 on Harbor Boulevard. Ever-changing and constantly expanding, the colorful center (open 11 A.M. to 9 P.M. daily) currently contains 75 shops and 15 restaurants on 15 acres.

Several companies offer hour-long narrated harbor cruises from the village. Most operate on weekends and summer weekdays. Whale-watching cruises take place from December through March. For details on cruises, see page 124 or contact the San Pedro Chamber of Commerce, (213) 832-7272.

Los Angeles Maritime Museum. On San Pedro's waterfront at Berth 84 (foot of 6th Street), this museum houses a wealth of nautical displays, from 19th-century steam sloops to World War II battleships. Included are an 18-foot model of the *Titanic* and a 21-foot scale model of the *Queen Mary*. The mu-

seum is open 10 A.M. to 5 P.M. Tuesday through Sunday except on major holidays; donations are encouraged.

General Phineas Banning Museum. The man who founded the town of Wilmington north of L.A.'s harbor built a 30-room colonial showcase in 1864 and landscaped it with acres of beautiful gardens. Now completely restored, the mansion at 401 E. M Street (2 blocks east of Avalon Boulevard off the Pacific Coast Highway) is a museum filled with 19th-century antiques. Hourly tours take place Tuesday through Thursday and weekends from 12:30 to 3:30 P.M. A donation is suggested.

Top Spots Underwater

A mask, fins, a snorkel, and a bathing suit are all you need to get an intimate look at colorful undersea life in summer. Add a wet suit for the rest of the year.

For greatest visibility and safety, you'll have the best luck in coves and other protected waters on calm days. Avoid heavy surf; it kicks up sand and clouds the water. Conditions change rapidly, so check with lifeguards on arrival.

The following are some of Southern California's best snorkeling spots, listed from north to south.

Malibu. Paradise Cove to the south of Point Dume has some good rocky spots close to shore just west of the pier. Unless it's calm, visibility is less than 10 feet. Nearby kelp beds are great for scuba, but inexperienced snorkelers should avoid them.

Palos Verdes Peninsula. Abalone Cove, a county beach below Wayfarers Chapel (page 36), has some of the finest snorkeling within easy reach of Los Angeles. Swim close to rocky outcroppings in the warm, shallow underwater reserve.

Santa Catalina Island. You'll find clear, sparkling water at Avalon's Lover's Cove, just southeast of the passenger boat dock. Children can swim close to shore in shallow water. You can rent equipment at island dive shops.

Newport Beach area. "Big" and "Little" Corona, just east of Newport Harbor's entrance jetty, shelter good snorkeling beneath their cliffs. Flat, sandy bottoms and rocky reefs grace both areas, and swim lines and kelp beds protect snorkelers from boat traffic. To get there from Pacific Coast Highway in Corona del Mar, turn southwest onto Marguerite Avenue. Drive right on Ocean Boulevard to Big Corona, then left to Little Corona.

Farther south at Reef Point, part of Crystal Cove State Park, you can expect to see perch, brilliant orange garibaldi, lobster, and octopus among the reefs. Access is from the parking lot just down from Crystal Cove.

Laguna Beach. Northwest of Laguna's main beach, three fine snorkeling areas are tucked under cliffs in a protected ecological reserve. Best parking for Rock Pile (also popular with surf-

ers), Picnic Beach, and Divers Cove is on Cliff Drive beside Heisler Park.

About a mile southeast of the main beach, Woods Cove offers a large rock and reef a short swim offshore. Enter from Diamond Street. Moss Point (good diving) can be reached from Moss Street, two blocks from Diamond. Laguna's surf conditions differ daily, so check first at the main guard tower.

La Jolla. La Jolla Cove, best-known part of an underwater park, has a great variety of undersea activity. On a calm day, strong swimmers can explore beyond the cove; check with the lifeguard first.

Casa Cove (also known as "The Children's Pool") lies just to the southwest. Though protected by a breakwater, it can still be rough, and only outside the breakwater does it have the underwater range of La Jolla Cove.

Patchy reefs and a sandy bottom (6 to 10 feet deep) make Marine Street Beach (foot of Marine Street) and Windansea Beach (foot of Bonair Street) good choices.

...Beaches

Long Beach

An important naval base, port, and manufacturing center, Long Beach has resurfaced as a resort and recreational center as well. Thanks to thoughtful planning, the state's fifth-largest city (second in L.A. County) is no longer the "Coney Island of the West." Indeed, the former Pike amusement area is to become a high-rise complex with hotels, shops, offices, and residences.

Today, downtown Long Beach features sleek high-rises, a sophisticated city transit system, and an attractive pedestrian promenade stretching from the shore to Long Beach Plaza mall between Pine Avenue and Long Beach Boulevard, 3rd and 6th streets. (Long Beach Children's Museum at the mall has imaginative play paraphernalia for tots to preteens; moderate admission fee.) Even the oil drilling rigs that dot the harbor have been cleverly concealed on palm-studded, man-made islands.

Getting around. The city is linked to Los Angeles, 22 miles to the north, by the Long Beach Freeway (Interstate 710) and connected to other coastal towns by Pacific Coast Highway (State 1) and the San Diego Freeway (Interstate 405).

The Metro Blue Line light-rail system, operated on the same route used by the famed Big Red Cars from 1902 to 1964, makes its 22-mile run to downtown L.A. in 50 minutes. Trains depart from the Willow Street Station (at Long Beach Boulevard) every 10 to 15 minutes during the day, every 20 minutes in the evening until midnight.

Make your first stop the Long Beach Visitor Center (3387 Long Beach Boulevard, at the corner of Wardlow). The center provides maps and information on events, lodging, and dining.

Ocean Boulevard. Several attractions lie along Ocean Boulevard, which parallels the bayshore. The Long Beach Convention & Entertainment Center at Pine and Ocean is the site of the Terrace Theater (home to symphony, civic light opera, ballet, and opera companies), the more intimate Center Theater, and the Arena (for sporting events).

About 1½ miles east, the Long Beach Museum of Art (2300 E. Ocean Boulevard) is an avant-garde museum of modern culture housed in a charming early-1900s house. The museum and adjoining bookstore and gift shop are open Wednesday through Sunday from noon to 5 P.M. (a small donation is suggested).

Farther southeast on Ocean, the Bluff Park Historic District encompasses several blocks of carefully preserved residences built early this century.

At the south end of Ocean in Alamitos Bay is Naples, a tiny group of islands threaded by canals and linked by walkways. Best way to get a look at the delightful maze of homes is from the water. Gondola Getaway at 5437 E. Ocean Boulevard, (213) 433-9595, offers hour-long cruises departing Alamitos Bay from sunrise to midnight. You can also rent kayaks and small boats at Alamitos Bay.

Waterfront. Parks, marinas, tourist-oriented shopping complexes, and hotels line the harborside. Harbor cruises and Catalina trips (see page 37) are offered from several locations.

Shoreline Park, at the foot of Pine Avenue, is a 100-acre aquatic playground with fishing platforms, picnic sites, and an RV park. Next door, Shoreline Village is fashioned after an early 1900s seaside hamlet. Specialty shops and restaurants cover 7 acres along the water. A ride on one of the hand-carved Looff carousel animals (vintage 1906) is sufficient reason to make the trip.

Every April, Shoreline Drive becomes a raceway during the Toyota Grand Prix. This nerve-jingling, ear-popping event attracts some 200,000 visitors from all over the world.

Queen Mary and Spruce Goose. Across Queensway Bay at Pier J looms the regal *Queen Mary*, a retired Cunard liner that sailed under the British flag from 1939 to 1967. Almost as famous is Howard Hughes' *Spruce Goose*, the huge wooden airplane housed nearby under the world's largest clear-span aluminum dome. London Towne, a replica of an English village, now sits beside them, but the whole area may

see dramatic changes. Disney, which recently took over the properties, has announced plans to build a 350-acre nautical theme park and resort alongside the pier.

The 1,000-foot-long *Queen Mary*, also run as a hotel, is open daily for tours, dining, and shopping (London-based Harrods and Pringles operate branches aboard the ship). A self-guided tour covers the bridge, engine room, officers' quarters, and upper decks.

The *Spruce Goose*, flown only once, predated the jumbo jet by more than two decades yet has nearly the same wing span. You can enter the enormous plane and peer into the cockpit, see a cutaway engine display, and view films from the aviation career of eccentric billionaire Hughes.

One ticket ($17.50 for adults, $9.50 for children 5 to 11) covers both attractions; a guided Captain's Tour of the ship costs an additional $5. The ticket center is open daily from 10 A.M. to 6 P.M.

To reach the site, exit Interstate 710 at Harbor Scenic Drive and follow the signs; or cross the channel on Queensway Bridge from Shoreline Drive.

Spanish ranchos. There's no charge to visit two charming remnants of former cattle-ranching days, both owned by the city.

Rancho Los Cerritos (4600 Virginia Road) once served as headquarters for a 27,000-acre cattle ranch. Built in 1844 and remodeled in 1930, the two-story house is open Wednesday through Sunday from 1 to 5 P.M. (weekend guided tours on the hour from 1 to 4 P.M.). From Interstate 405, exit north on Long Beach Boulevard; turn left at San Antonio Drive, then right onto Virginia.

Rancho Los Alamitos (6400 Bixby Hill Road) is one of the area's finest restored adobes. The 1806 adobe and 4-acre garden were part of a working cattle ranch until 1953. Once owned by Jose Figueroa, an early California governor, the adobe is filled with original furnishings.

One-hour guided tours of the house and barns are offered Wednesday through Sunday from 1 to 5 P.M.; you walk through the gardens on your own. From Interstate 405, take Palo Verde Avenue south to the rancho gate.

"Only in L.A." might be an appropriate comment after visiting some of the intriguing and lesser-known museums around the area. From the world's oldest rock to neon art, here's a small sampling of lively collections.

American Heritage Park, 1918 N. Rosemead Boulevard, El Monte; (818) 442-1776. Tanks, trucks, jeeps, and an assortment of large artillery make this private military museum look like the staging ground for an invasion. Open noon to 4:30 P.M. weekends, weekdays by appointment. Admission: $2 adults, $1 ages 10 to 16, and 50 cents ages 5 to 10.

Angel's Attic, 516 Colorado Avenue, Santa Monica; (213) 394-8331. Antique dolls and dollhouses, vintage toy soldiers, model trains, and other century-old toys crowd the rooms of a lovingly restored Victorian. Open 12:30 to 4:30 P.M. Thursday through Sunday. Admission: $4 adults, $3 seniors, $2 children 12 and under.

Barnsdall Art Park, 4800 Hollywood Boulevard, Hollywood; (213) 485-4581. A Frank Lloyd Wright–designed house, L.A.'s Municipal Art Gallery, and a junior art center crown Olive Hill at the eastern end of the boulevard. The gallery is open to visitors from 12:30 to 5 P.M. daily except Monday. Admission: $1 ages 14 and above. For recorded information on Hollyhock House guided tours, call (213) 662-7272. Admission: $1.50 ages 12 and up.

Cabrillo Marine Museum, 3720 Stephen White Drive, San Pedro; (213) 548-7562. Southern California's largest display of marine life includes aquariums, a tidepool, and a collection of whale bones you can touch. Open noon to 5 P.M. Tuesday through Friday, 10 A.M. to 5 P.M. weekends. Free admission.

California Museum of Photography, 3824 Main Street, Riverside; (714) 787-4787. Here you'll see the state's grandest display of photographic masterpieces. A history of photo technology includes three-dimensional stereographs. Open 10 A.M. to 5 P.M Tuesday through Saturday (to 9 P.M. Wednesday), noon to 5 P.M. Sunday. Admission: $2 adults, $1 seniors, free for children under 12.

Frederick's of Hollywood Museum, 6608 Hollywood Boulevard, Hollywood; (213)466-8506. This homage to intimate apparel includes garments worn by celebrities for films and videos, such as Lana Turner's black slip from *The Merry Widow* and some of Madonna's concert attire. Open 10 A.M. to 8 P.M. Monday through Thursday, 10 A.M. to 9 P.M. Friday, 10 A.M. to 6 P.M. Saturday, and noon to 5 P.M. Sunday. Free admission.

Heritage Square, 3800 Homer Street, Los Angeles (Avenue 43 exit off Interstate 110); (818) 449-0193. A village of eight eclectic structures built between 1865 and 1914 showcases the area's early architecture. Among the vintage buildings are Victorian houses, a small church, and a railroad station. Open noon to 4 P.M. weekends. Admission: $4.50 adults, $3 seniors and ages 12 to 17, free for children under 12.

Kidspace, 390 S. El Molino Avenue, Pasadena; (818) 449-9143. A mechanical robot greets children at the door to this hands-on museum. Two- to 12-year-olds enjoy a variety of learning equipment, from face paints to fire engines. Open 2 to 5 P.M. Wednesday, 12:30 to 5 P.M. weekends. Admission: $3.25, $2.75 seniors.

Max Factor Museum, 1666 N. Highland Avenue, Hollywood; (213) 463-6668. Cosmetics are the focus of the museum dedicated to the man who made up the faces of many screen idols, but you'll also find actors' hairpieces, celebrity autographs, and other paraphernalia. Open 10 A.M. to 4 P.M. Monday through Saturday. Free admission.

Merle Norman Classic Beauty Collection, 15180 Bledsoe Street, Sylmar; (818) 367-2251. Not makeup, but more than 200 classic and antique cars compose this award-winning collection; thirty are on display. A fourth-floor gallery displays musical instruments, including a Wurlitzer theater organ. Open Tuesday through Saturday; call for reservations. Free admission.

Museum of the Holocaust, 6505 Wilshire Boulevard, Beverly Hills; (213) 651-3175. The haunting story of the Nazi persecution of the Jews is presented in film, documents, and personal memorabilia. Docents may be concentration camp survivors. Open 9 A.M. to 4:30 P.M. weekdays (to 3 P.M. Friday), 1 to 5 P.M. Sunday. Free admission.

Museum of Neon Art, 704 Traction Avenue, Los Angeles; (213) 617-0274. This futuristic museum offers a colorful—and electrifying—look at artworks of bubbling gas and glass. You'll see the latest neon artistry as well as some vintage pieces. Open 11 A.M. to 5 P.M. Tuesday through Saturday. Admission: $2.50 adults, free for children under 15.

Raymond M. Alf Museum, Webb School, 1175 W. Baseline Road, Claremont; (714) 624-2798. Tracing life from the beginning of time, this paleontological museum displays fossilized plants, insects, and mammals. Oldest of the exhibits is a rock that dates back 3.8 billion years; among the most interesting is a footprint of a prehistoric man. Open 1 to 4 P.M. Monday through Thursday during the school year. Donations encouraged.

Mountains & Valleys

Southern Californians really can ski and surf the same day—given favorable traffic. Ski season in the San Gabriel and San Bernardino mountains, a couple of hours north and east of L.A., often extends well into spring. While the runs may not appeal to experts, beginning and intermediate skiers flock to the slopes shortly after the first good snowfall (see page 126).

These recreationally rich mountain ranges also offer a wealth of summer activities: boating, camping, cycling, hiking, picnicking, parasailing, and waterskiing. Sightseers attend weekend arts festivals and explore village craft shops.

Mountain communities have accommodations for all tastes, from rustic to resort, and a variety of restaurants from fast food to continental cuisine. En route to the mountains, valley towns hold their own discoveries: gardens, historic landmarks, and some outstanding museums.

Pasadena

The San Gabriel Valley's grande dame, this attractive residential community at the base of the San Gabriel Mountains is best known for the colorful New Year's Day Tournament of Roses Parade and annual Rose Bowl football game. A revitalized Old Town shopping and dining area (roughly bounded by Arroyo Parkway, Pasadena Avenue, Union Street, and Green Street), fine museums, noted gardens, and a full calendar of performing arts are other reasons to visit.

You can pick up visitor guides and self-guided auto tour maps from the Pasadena Convention & Visitors Bureau (see page 30).

Gamble House. One-hour guided tours through one of the best works of renowned architects Charles and Henry Greene are offered Thursday through Sunday from noon to 3 P.M. Admission to the house, located at 4 Westmoreland Place, is $4 for adults, $3 for college students (children free).

Tournament House & Wrigley Gardens. A 4½-acre site at 391 S. Orange Grove Boulevard contains the ornate mansion once owned by chewing gum magnate William Wrigley, Jr. Free guided tours of the mansion, now headquarters for the Tournament of Roses Association, take place from 2 to 4 P.M. Wednesday, February through August. The formal rose gardens are open year-round except December 31 and January 1.

Pasadena Historical Society. Guided tours of the 18-room mansion at 470 W. Walnut offer glimpses of an earlier, more elegant lifestyle. Open from 1 to 4 P.M. on Tuesday, Thursday, and Sunday (closed in August), the museum includes historical displays and the Finnish Folk Art Museum. Admission is $4.

Norton Simon Museum of Art. The cornerless, tile-clad museum at 411 W. Colorado Boulevard baffles design critics, but most admire its classic setting. Its well-regarded collection of artwork spans the globe, from Indian and Southeast Asian sculpture to European old masters, American impressionist and modern paintings, and medieval tapestries. Galleries and gardens display sculpture. The museum is open Thursday through Sunday from noon to 6 P.M. Admission is $4 for adults, $1.50 for seniors and students.

Pacific Asia Museum. Appropriately housed in an old building that looks like the Chinese Imperial Palace, Southern California's only Asian arts museum is built around a peaceful courtyard with a koi-filled brook. Located at 46 N. Los Robles Avenue, the center is open Wednesday through Sunday from noon to 5 P.M., with guided tours on Sunday (modest admission charge).

Brookside Park. With the Rose Bowl in its center, this park in Arroyo Seco Canyon covers more than 500 acres. Here, too, are a four-pool aquatic center, municipal golf course, playgrounds, picnic areas, and hiking trails. On the second Sunday each month, the Rose Bowl hosts a gigantic swap meet and flea market; take Rosemont Avenue to the stadium entrance.

Around the San Gabriel Valley

Of the three large valleys around Los Angeles, the San Gabriel is certainly the most lush, in terms of greenery, and the most plush, in terms of wealth and architecture. It contains one of Southern California's finest museums, and a trio of impressive parks (one a race track) are worthy detours off Interstate 210 (Foothill Boulevard). The fourth in the chain of California missions is here as well—Mission San Gabriel Arcangel (see page 6).

Huntington Library, Art Collections, and Botanical Gardens. Don't miss a visit to this magnificent museum in San Marino. Pacific Electric tycoon H.E. Huntington willed his entire estate to the public, so there's no charge to visit, though $2 donations are encouraged.

The mansion contains one of the best collections of British and French 18th-century art in America, including Thomas Gainsborough's well-loved *Blue Boy* and Thomas Lawrence's *Pinkie*. An American art gallery displays paintings and furnishings from the 1730s to the 1930s.

The separate library boasts a rich assortment of British and American history and literature as well as many rare books and manuscripts, among them a Gutenberg Bible, Chaucer's *Canterbury Tales*, and Benjamin Franklin's hand-written autobiography.

Highlights of the 150 acres of gardens include desert plantings, a palm garden, Japanese-style oases, the region's first commercial avocado grove, and a Shakespearean-inspired retreat. A garden restaurant serves lunch from 1 to 4 P.M.

The museum is at 1151 Oxford Road north of Huntington Drive. Gates are open Tuesday through Sunday from 1

Cabins dot the wooded shores of Big Bear Lake in the San Bernardino Mountains, about two hours by car from Los Angeles. This all-year resort is among a number of cool, high-country retreats to the north and east of the L.A. basin.

...Mountains & Valleys

to 4:30 P.M.; tours are offered weekdays at 1 P.M. L.A. County residents need reservations to visit on Sunday; call (818) 405-2141.

Descanso Gardens. Once a private estate, this 165-acre garden in La Cañada Flintridge becomes a riot of color from October through March, when more than 100,000 camellias blossom. Peak blooming season for the multitude of old roses is May to early June, while the 4-acre All-American Rose Selection specimens blossom from May until December. Lilacs and orchids peak in April.

Descanso (1418 Descanso Boulevard) is open 9 A.M. to 4:30 P.M. daily except Christmas. There's a modest admission charge, and the gardens are free the third Tuesday of each month. You can take a guided tram tour ($1.50) from 1 to 3 P.M. Tuesday through Friday, 11 A.M. to 4 P.M. weekends. A teahouse in a serene Japanese garden operates Tuesday through Sunday from 11 A.M. to 4 P.M.

Los Angeles State and County Arboretum. Plantings from around the world are featured in this 127-acre arboretum (301 N. Baldwin Avenue, Arcadia).

Peacocks roam the grounds amid historic buildings that date from the time the property was Rancho Santa Anita. On a self-guided tour, you see a tropical jungle, demonstration home gardens, gardens using unthirsty plantings, and several greenhouses.

The arboretum is open daily from 9 A.M. to 5 P.M. except on Christmas. Guided walking tours are offered at 11 A.M. Wednesday. The modest admission charge is waived on the third Tuesday of each month. Guided tram tours ($1.50) take place weekdays from 12:15 to 3 P.M., weekends from 10:30 A.M. to 4 P.M.

Santa Anita Park. One of the country's most famous thoroughbred tracks lies near the arboretum (285 W. Huntington Drive, Arcadia). During racing season (October to November and late December to late April) fans throng to the 500-acre park. If you don't want to see a race, you can watch morning workouts (7:30 to 9:30 A.M.) and admire the well-landscaped grounds for free. There's a charge to park.

San Gabriel Mountains

The San Gabriels have been called L.A.'s mountain playground because they're easily accessible to hikers, riders, campers, picnickers, and skiers. In spring, scenic waterfalls are only a short stroll from canyon roads. The high-country wilderness areas can only be reached by trail.

The Angeles Crest Highway (State 2), access road to Mount Wilson Observatory, ascends the mid-range from La Cañada Flintridge (19 miles to the observatory). Open daily from 10 A.M. to 4 P.M. except on major holidays and in bad weather, the observatory offers views of the whole L.A. basin on the occasional clear day. There's a visitors' gallery for the 100-inch telescope (you can't actually look through the lens). To check on weather conditions, call (818) 449-4163.

State 39 from Azusa stretches up past San Gabriel Reservoir to Crystal Lake, and San Antonio Canyon Road curls up to Mount Baldy's ski slopes.

For area information and maps, write to Angeles National Forest Supervisor, 701 N. Santa Anita Avenue, Arcadia, CA 91006, or phone (818) 574-5200.

Pomona-Walnut Valley

The valley midway along the base of the San Gabriels and San Bernardinos is usually designated as Pomona-Walnut. Though smoggy and hot in summer, it's an area rich in culture, history, and entertainment.

Ontario's international airport is the region's gateway. You can pick up a guide to area attractions, including winery tastings, from the Greater Ontario Visitors & Convention Bureau at 421 N. Euclid, (714) 984-2450 (open weekdays). Ontario also offers samples of another agricultural product, olives. Stop in at the century-old Graber Olive House (315 E. 4th Street) for a walking tour of the processing plant; it's in full operation from October to December during the fall harvest, but you can visit anytime (open daily).

Pomona. Best known as the site of the huge Los Angeles County Fair every September, Pomona is also noted for horses and antiques. Some 400 antique dealers line a two-block mall downtown on E. Second Street between Garey Avenue and Gibbs Street.

At 2 P.M. on the first Sunday of the month (except in summer), the W. K. Kellogg Arabian Horse Center presents a 1-hour show with a flashy cast of 15 to 20 specially trained mounts. After the show, visitors can wander around the stables until 5 P.M. The modest ticket price includes a film on the ranch.

To reach the center (now part of California State Polytechnic University),

Ramona Pageant

Often called California's greatest outdoor spectacle, the dramatization of *Ramona* has been performed in a natural outdoor amphitheater outside Hemet every spring since 1923. More than 350 residents of this small town (southeast of Riverside) take part in the elaborate production of Helen Hunt Jackson's 1884 novel of early California Indian history.

Reservations are a must for the popular play, which is held on three successive weekends starting in late April. To get a ticket application form, send a stamped self-addressed envelope with your request to Ramona Pageant Association, 27400 Ramona Bowl Road, Hemet, California 92344. For information on dates, prices, and transportation, phone (714) 658-3111.

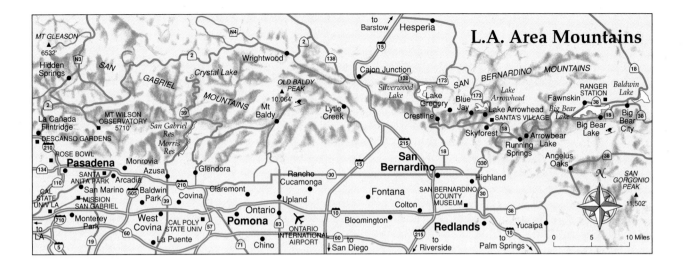

exit Kellogg Drive from Interstate 10, go about half a mile southwest and turn left on Citrus Lane, then turn right on Eucalyptus Lane. For more information, call (714) 869-2224.

Claremont. Home to such prestigious colleges as Claremont McKenna, Pomona, Scripps, Harvey Mudd, and Pitzer, the city of Claremont is also the setting for Rancho Santa Ana Botanic Gardens, an 85-acre collection of native plantings. The free garden (open daily except major holidays) is at its most colorful from February to June, when the poppies bloom. Enter from College Avenue north of Foothill Boulevard.

Chino. This city is devoted to flight. Head for the airport (7000 Merrill Avenue) to see the Planes of Fame Air Museum, a respected collection of vessels from 1896 through World War II. The museum (about $5 for adults, $2 for children 5 to 10) is open daily except Christmas. An annual air show is held the third weekend in May.

Riverside. It's ironic that the city that gave birth to California's navel orange industry is now often smothered by crop-damaging smog. To glimpse its more romantic past, stop by the Riverside Municipal Museum at 3720 Orange Street or tour the nicely restored Heritage House, a few blocks away at 8193 Magnolia Avenue.

The free museum is open 9 A.M. to 5 P.M. Tuesday through Friday and 1 to 5 P.M. on weekends. Free mansion tours

take place from noon to 2:30 P.M. Tuesday and Thursday, noon to 3:30 P.M. Sunday.

Nearby, the landmark Mission Inn (bounded by 6th, 7th, Main, and Orange streets) is being renovated.

Redlands. A wealth of beautifully restored Victorians can be seen on a drive-by tour. Purchase a guidebook from the Chamber of Commerce, 1 E. Redlands Boulevard.

Edwards Mansion, a Victorian at 2064 Orange Tree Lane (California Street exit off Interstate 10), is now a restaurant. Next door, the free San Bernardino County Museum (open 9 A.M. to 5 P.M. Tuesday through Saturday and Sunday afternoon) has a not-to-be-believed collection encompassing anthropology, archaeology, ornithology, history, and fine arts.

San Bernardino Mountains

Pine forests, hidden lakes, fabulous vistas, and crisp, cool air lure vacationers year-round to the San Bernardino range. Peaks here commonly top 10,000 feet, and Mount San Gorgonio reaches 11,502 feet. Yet this alpine land is only an hour's drive from San Bernardino via State 18 (also known as the Rim of the World Drive) or snaky State 330 (shortest route to Big Bear Lake). Many campgrounds lie along State 38, a longer back-door approach to Big Bear.

To get maps of the 660,000-acre San Bernardino National Forest's suggested

walking and driving tours, contact the U.S. Forest Service at 1824 Commercenter Circle, San Bernardino, CA 92408-3430; (714) 383-5588. Maps cost $2 each.

Lake Arrowhead. This man-made lake in its picturesque resort setting offers a variety of water sports and beautiful scenery. Stop at the marina to find out about waterskiing instruction, lake cruises, boat rentals, and swimming and fishing areas. In the village, some 60 shops and restaurants attract browsers. Upscale resorts, motels, cabins, and campgrounds dot the shoreline.

On your way up to the lake, short side roads lead past lookouts and to smaller resorts such as Strawberry Peak, Crestline, Lake Gregory (an old Mormon settlement), and Blue Jay (outdoor ice rink). Children love the shops, rides, and petting zoo at Santa's Village in Skyforest, open daily from 10 A.M. to 5 P.M. in summer and from mid-November through December. Admission is $8.50.

Big Bear Lake. One of the Southland's largest all-year recreation spots, Big Bear is popular with summer boaters, jetskiers, parasailers, anglers, horseback riders, hikers, and campers. A Bavarian-style festival in October draws large crowds, and slippers and sliders crowd the three ski resorts in winter. Small souvenir stores jostle up against craft shops, restaurants, inns, and motels along the lake's southern shore.

Orange County

*O*nce little more than a sleepy ag- ricultural region scented by orange blossoms, Orange County was trans- formed by the magic wand of Walt Disney in the 1950s into the state's larg- est tourist mecca. Today it resembles a spread-out, continuous world's fair with enough diversions to earn the nickname Vacationland USA.

The link along the Pacific between Los Angeles and San Diego counties, Orange County reaches inland into the wilderness of the Santa Ana Moun- tains. Its towns, one after another, are part of the urban continuum of the Los Angeles metropolitan area, with here and there only a hint of the county's rural past.

Lure of the land

In addition to renowned Disneyland, a sampling of Orange County's man- made attractions includes ever-ex- panding Knott's Berry Farm, celebrity- studded Movieland Wax Museum, the jousting hall of Medieval Times, and Wild Rivers' refreshing plunges.

Thanks to the prestigious homes and marinas along its 42 miles of shoreline, the county's Pacific rim is dubbed Gold Coast. It extends from north of Hunt- ington Beach (self-proclaimed surfing capital of the world) through the sea- side communities of Newport Beach, Balboa, Corona del Mar, Laguna Beach, and Dana Point south to San Clemente.

Inland towns lie on land that once nourished bean fields and orchards.

For an upside-down and backward view of the world, take a heart-stopping ride on Montezooma's Revenge at Knott's Berry Farm in Buena Park. This family- oriented theme park started as a roadside fruit stand.

The University of California at Irvine and Saddleback Valley's foothill parks and recreational retreats sprawl over part of what was once a vast Spanish rancho. Remnants of mission days re- main at San Juan Capistrano.

Planning a trip

More than 35 million people a year vacation in Orange County. The climate helps: with an annual rainfall of only 15 inches and an average temperature of 70°, this is a year-round playground. When summer days are hot and smog- gy in the interior, residents head for the beach.

Getting there. Alaska, America West, American, Continental, Delta, Mid- way, Northwest, TWA, United, and a number of commuter airlines fly di- rectly into John Wayne/Orange County Airport in Santa Ana. Rental cars, taxis, and limousines are avail- able at the airport.

Two scheduled ground shuttles, Airport Coach and Airport Cruiser, and a number of on-call airport vans make nearby Los Angeles, Long Beach, and Ontario airports satisfactory alternates. One-way fares from Los Angeles (35 miles from Anaheim) run around $12.

Interstates 5 (Santa Ana Freeway) and 405 (San Diego Freeway) are the major ties to Los Angeles. Easiest route from the east is Interstate 10 (San Ber- nardino Freeway) to State 91 (Riverside Freeway). State 1 (Pacific Coast High- way) skirts the ocean.

Amtrak trains between Los Angeles and San Diego stop at Fullerton, Ana- heim Stadium, Santa Ana, San Juan Capistrano, and San Clemente. Trains make 8 daily trips in each direction.

Greyhound buses connect Orange County with other parts of the coun-

try. The Southern California Rapid Transit District also offers bus service from its main Los Angeles terminal (6th and Los Angeles streets) to Disneyland, Knott's, and Movieland Wax Museum.

Getting around. The area has one of the best county-wide transit systems in Southern California. Bus maps and schedules are widely distributed; check with your hotel, or pick one up at the visitors bureau in the Convention Cen- ter (on Katella Avenue across from Disneyland).

Contacts

These agencies offer information on attractions and accommoda- tions. See additional contacts throughout this chapter.

Anaheim Area Visitor & Convention Bureau
P.O. Box 470
Anaheim, CA 92803
(714) 999-8999

Buena Park Convention & Visitors Office
6280 Manchester Blvd., Suite 103
Buena Park, CA 90621
(714) 994-1511

Newport Beach Conference & Visitors Bureau
366 San Miguel, Suite 200
Newport Beach, CA 92660
(800) 942-6278

Laguna Beach Chamber of Commerce
357 Glenneyre (P.O. Box 396)
Laguna Beach, CA 92652
(714) 494-1018

Many hotels and motels offer free shuttle service to Disneyland, Knott's, and other major attractions and shopping areas. For a moderate fee, you can ride Pacific Coast Sightseeing buses to major destinations around Orange County and Los Angeles. Buses stop at most large hotels and motels; check at the front desk or phone (714) 978-8855.

Lodging. The largest clusters of motels and hotels are around Disneyland in Anaheim and in Buena Park, home to Knott's. Business travelers find chain hotels around the airport and at Newport Center in Newport Beach.

For lodging suggestions around Disneyland or elsewhere in the county, contact the Anaheim Area Visitor & Convention Bureau (see address on page 47) or the Southern California Hotel Reservation Center, (800) 527-9997 in California, (800) 537-7666 outside the state.

Campers and RV owners have a choice of several private parks in Anaheim and the surrounding area. State and county beaches offer limited camping (see page 121).

Entertainment. The three-theater complex at the striking Orange County Performing Arts Center (600 Town Center Drive, Costa Mesa) presents musical theater, symphony, opera, and dance. Across the way, the intimate South Coast Repertory Theatre hosts classic and contemporary productions. For information on these and other events, contact the Anaheim Area Visitor & Convention Bureau (page 47).

Activities. No matter the sport, it's available in Orange County, from tennis, jogging, and cycling to wind surfing, sailing, and snorkeling. Golfers will need reservations for busy public courses (see page 123). Hikers and horseback riders head for mountain canyons or coastal trails. Surfers find the best wave action at Huntington Beach and Newport Beach.

Spectator sports abound. The California Angels baseball team and Los Angeles Rams football team share the 70,000-seat Anaheim Stadium (2 miles east of Disneyland at Katella Avenue and State College Boulevard). Los Alamitos Race Course (4961 Katella Av-

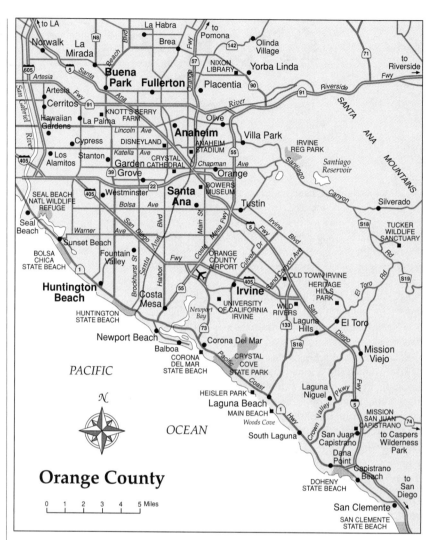

Orange County

0 1 2 3 4 5 Miles

enue) hosts year-round horse racing Tuesday through Saturday at 7:30 P.M.

Shopping. The range and variety of chic shopping in Orange County makes it an attraction in itself. Upscale malls and trendy boutiques, galleries, and specialty stores are scattered all around the region.

Laguna Beach may be better known for its art galleries, but it boasts more goldsmiths and jewelers per square foot than anywhere else in the country. In the market for antiques? San Juan Capistrano has numerous antique shops; they look right at home in the historic setting. Newport Beach's most posh outlets are tucked away in converted cannery buildings on the Balboa Peninsula.

For the Southland's busiest and largest shopping showplace, head for ele-

gant South Coast Plaza in Costa Mesa (Bristol Street exit off Interstate 405). When you arrive, pick up a map of the acres of department stores, specialty shops, and restaurants in the mall's Carousel, Jewel, and Crystal Court sections. (The Crystal Court is in a separate complex across Bear Street.)

Across Sunflower Street to the north, South Coast Plaza Village adds even more shopping and dining choices, including Antonello Ristorante, one of Orange County's finest.

Glamorous Fashion Island (Newport Center Drive off Pacific Coast Highway) contains all of the large upscale emporiums like Neiman-Marcus, Bullock's Wilshire, and Robinson's. Unique boutiques are found at the center's Atrium Court area. Lunch from food stalls around the lower-level Farmers Market is a treat.

World of Fun

The possibilities for entertainment in Orange County are endless. You might raft along a waterfall, cheer for a jousting knight, eat a slice of boysenberry pie while strolling the streets of a ghost town, watch a lagoonside water and light show, climb aboard a stomach-jerking roller coaster, or join Dorothy and her friends on the "yellow brick road."

And that doesn't even include Disneyland, the best-known park of all; to help plan a trip to the Magic Kingdom, see page 50.

Where to look. Three major attractions are clustered around Buena Park, 20 miles southeast of downtown Los Angeles and just a tempting 5 miles from Disneyland in Anaheim. Wild Rivers Waterpark is in Laguna Hills, about 15 minutes southeast by freeway. Other parks, amusement centers, special-interest museums, and theaters are sprinkled around Orange County.

You'll never see them all in one day, or even several. Tour companies offer limited-time visits to major attractions. If you prefer a less hurried pace, go on your own, with a good street map to help you get around.

Disneyland Hotel. Right across the street from Disneyland, this hotel is almost a destination in itself. It's connected to the park by fast monorail from Tomorrowland.

The 60-acre resort complex has 11 theme restaurants and lounges and 35 specialty shops. Activity revolves around the large marina, with its lush tropical gardens and waterfalls, koi ponds, and palm-studded beach.

Twice nightly, a pulsating Dancing Waters and Lights Fantastic Show is presented (no charge). In summer, a free Polynesian show is added. The hotel is also a good spot from which to get a free look at Disneyland's nightly fireworks.

You have to be a guest to swim in one of three pools or to get a preferred court at nearby Tennisland, but the other attractions are open to the public.

Knott's Berry Farm

Walter and Cordelia Knott came to Orange County to start a berry farm in 1920. When the Depression hit, Mrs. Knott began selling her homemade berry preserves at a fruit stand along the highway. Later she added chicken dinners. From those humble beginnings came the 150 acres of rides and attractions that make Knott's the country's third most popular theme park (after Disneyland and Florida's Disney World).

To reach Knott's (8039 Beach Boulevard, Buena Park), exit Interstate 5 at Beach and drive south about 2 miles. Pacific Coast Sightseeing Knott's Express bus connects the park with Disneyland and major hotels.

One entrance fee includes unlimited use of all rides and attractions ($21 for adults, $17 children 3 to 11, $15 seniors over 60 and handicapped). Winter hours are 10 A.M. to 6 P.M. weekdays, later on weekends; in summer, the park stays open to midnight Sunday through Friday, to 1 A.M. Saturday. Strollers and wheelchairs are available for your use at the park.

What you see. Five major theme areas offer adventure from Wild West to white water. More than 160 rides, shows, and attractions are concentrated on the west side of Buena Park's Beach Boulevard. Some spill across the street, like the full-scale reproduction of Independence Hall.

Everything is designed for family enjoyment, from the vaudeville show in the Calico Saloon (where the strongest drinks are sarsaparilla and boysenberry punch) to the Good Time Theatre, a 2,150-seat showcase for daytime ice shows and evening musical entertainment (some headliner concerts cost extra).

Dinner lines can be long at the popular chicken and steak restaurants, located near the gift shops and boutiques in the park's California Marketplace section along Beach Boulevard. It's a good idea to put your name in early.

Theme areas. When Walter Knott decided to provide guests with amusement while they waited for dinner, a Western-style Ghost Town was born. Start here for a sense of what Knott's was like in the early days. Visitors can ride shotgun on the stagecoach, pan for gold, tour a mine, or drop down a water flume. Passengers aboard the smoke-belching Denver & Rio Grande narrow gauge will be suitably affrighted by bandits.

Camp Snoopy, a more recent addition, is designed especially for children 3 to 7. Snoopy and other members of the "Peanuts" gang greet young guests. Thirty tot-sized attractions include a petting zoo, balloon ride, roller coaster, and pony-driven carousel; adults aren't even allowed on most of the rides. There's even a restaurant with scaled-down burgers.

Mexican food stalls and artisans and an authentic Denzel carousel enliven Fiesta Village, also home to a few stomach-gripping rides, like Montezooma's Revenge (360° loop coming and going), Tampico Tumbler, and Slingshot. But most of the park's thrill rides (20-story Parachute Sky Jump, XK-1 aircraft, Boomerang roller coaster, and others) lie in the Roaring 20s section. Here, too, are bumper cars, soap box derbies, game arcades, a dolphin and sea lion show, and the Kingdom of Dinosaurs ride through a landscape inhabited by huge animated creatures.

The Wild Water Wilderness area features Bigfoot Rapids, a white-water rafting experience (be prepared to get wet). Find out about Bigfoot from the on-duty naturalist or watch a show in the Wilderness Dance Hall.

Movieland Wax Museum

Just north of Knott's, at 7711 Beach Boulevard, is the biggest gathering of celebrities in the world. Featured at Movieland are more than 240 wax likenesses of film and television stars. You'll find more glitter and glamour here than in Hollywood and encounter more stars than on the busiest day at

Continued on page 52

More than 12 million visitors a year pour through the gates of Disneyland, making it the nation's most popular amusement park. To keep visitors coming back, the 76-acre Anaheim park is constantly adding more attractions, and future plans call for creation of another entire theme park nearby.

Children and adults alike find themselves enchanted by the Magic Kingdom's illusion and entertainment. The clean and well-landscaped park offers thrill and fantasy rides, musical performances, animated peeks at the past and the future, colorful parades, theme restaurants, shops, a sky full of fireworks at night—and, of course, Mickey Mouse.

Planning a visit. Disneyland is about an hour's drive east of downtown Los Angeles via Interstate 5. Freeway signs indicate the exit to the park (1313 Harbor Boulevard, Anaheim). Trams take visitors from parking lot to entrance. Shuttle services operate from many hotels.

Don't expect to whiz through all of Disneyland in a day. Seven themed areas offer hundreds of rides, arcades, and other adventures. First-timers might consider a 2½-hour tour of major attractions, about $10 over the regular admission. Circle rides on the Disneyland Railroad (at the entrance) or Tomorrowland's monorail also give good overviews.

The park is open 10 A.M. to 6 P.M. weekdays and 9 A.M. to midnight on weekends, with extended hours for summer and some holidays.

Lines for rides are shortest when the park first opens, a half-hour before it closes, and during parades. Many families get there early, leave around lunchtime, and return in the early evening. (Have your hand and parking pass stamped for re-entry.)

Know what your "must-see" attractions are before you arrive, then get right in line for the most popular ones—like Splash Mountain, Captain EO, Star Tours, Space Mountain, and Pirates of the Caribbean. Also note show and parade times.

Wheelchairs and strollers are available, and a "baby station" off Main Street offers a place—and supplies—to feed, change, and rock the youngest visitors. Kennels at the main gate accommodate pets for a small fee.

For additional information, contact the Anaheim Area Visitor & Convention Bureau (address on page 47).

Cost. An Unlimited Passport admission covers all rides and attractions, excluding arcades, shops, and restaurants. One-day passports are $27.50 for adults, $22.50 for children 3 to 11. Two- and three-day passports reduce per-day rates slightly. Parking is $3.

Attractions. Walkways lead into the themed areas from a central plaza at the end of Main Street 1890, your point of entry.

Adventureland offers a jungle boat ride, the treehouse of the Swiss Family Robinson, and the "enchanted" Tiki Room. New Orleans Square has a Mississippi steamwheeler, the Pirates of the Caribbean ride, and the Haunted Mansion.

In Frontierland, you can careen down Thunder Mountain on a runaway train or raft to Tom Sawyer's island. Critter Country is home to Splash Mountain flume ride and Country Bear Playhouse.

Fantasyland begins when you cross the moat of Sleeping Beauty's Castle. Tomorrowland keeps pace with science with Space Mountain, Star Tours, and Captain EO.

New as of 1991 is an area themed to characters from Disney television shows. Future plans call for a a Young Indiana Jones Adventure show and two more theme areas—Mickey's Starland and Hollywoodland.

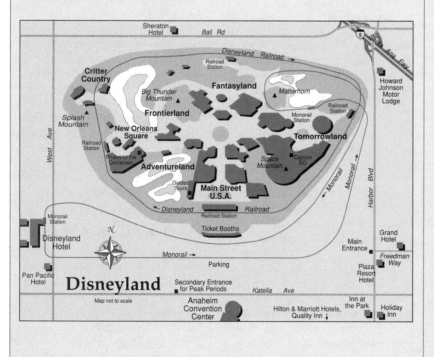

Going nose to nose with Pinocchio, one of Disneyland's popular resident characters, requires a boost from mom. Orange County's Magic Kingdom is the nation's most popular theme park.

...World of Fun

any studio lot. One caution: The sets seem so realistic that you may be tempted to touch the figures; if you do, you trigger an alarm.

Movieland is open daily 9 A.M. to 10 P.M. from Easter week through Labor Day, 10 A.M. to 9 P.M. the rest of the year. Tickets are $9.95 for adults, $5.95 for children 4 to 11.

Across the street, Movieland also operates the Ripley's Believe It or Not collection of oddities (separate admission fee).

Medieval Times

Across the street from Movieland, at 7662 Beach Boulevard in Buena Park, Medieval Times offers 11th-century entertainment in a castlelike setting. Guests watch tournament games, jousting matches, and sword fights while they feast in Middle Age fashion—with their fingers.

Performances take place nightly, with matinees on weekends. Free tours are offered weekdays from 9 A.M. to 4 P.M. Prices for the dinner (includes beverages and show) are $26 to $30 for adults, $18 to $19 for children. For reservations, call (800) 438-9911 in California, (800) 826-5358 outside the state.

Wild Rivers Waterpark

Forty wet rides, slides, and attractions make Wild Rivers a refreshing summer stop. Float around on an inner tube, go white-water rafting, peer through a waterfall, or just work on your tan. Facilities include changing rooms, showers, and lockers; gift shops can provide suntan lotion, towels, and even swimsuits.

Wild Rivers is just west of the junction of Interstates 5 and 405 in Laguna Hills (8800 Irvine Center Drive); head south from Interstate 405 at the Irvine Center Drive exit, or take Lake Forest Drive west from Interstate 5 and then turn right onto Irvine Center. The park is open mid-May through September; call (714) 768-WILD for times. Entrance is $15.95 ages 10 and over, $11.95 children 3 to 9, $7.95 over 55 or after 4 P.M. in summer.

Specialty sightseeing

Small and specialized museums and an "only in California" glass cathedral offer new dimensions when you need a break from thrill rides.

Children's Museum. Kids are welcome to touch the exhibits at this learning center a few miles north of Disneyland (301 S. Euclid Street, La Habra). Set in and around an old railroad depot, the museum has model trains, a theater, a science gallery, and a nature walk (small admission). The museum is open 10 A.M. to 4 P.M. Tuesday through Saturday (closed major holidays).

Richard Nixon Library & Birthplace. Opened in 1990, this 9-acre site northeast of Anaheim in Yorba Linda includes the house where the former president was born, a 52,000-square-foot library highlighting historical events of his life, and a garden. Attractions are open from 8:30 A.M. to 5 P.M. daily ($3.95 adults, $2 seniors, free 11 and under).

The library is at 18001 Yorba Linda Boulevard; from State 57, exit east at Yorba Linda Boulevard.

Museum of World Wars and Military History. Close to Knott's (7884 E. La Palma Avenue, Buena Park), this intriguing collection belies its rather dull name. Military and historical relics from 1776 to 1945 create realistic battle settings; more than 200 uniformed figures stand among them.

The museum (modest admission) is open Monday through Saturday from 10 A.M. to 6 P.M., Sunday from noon to 6 P.M. (closed major holidays).

Hobby City Doll and Toy Museum. Antique dolls, teddy bears, and toy soldiers reside at this museum (1238 S. Beach Boulevard, Anaheim). More than 3,000 dolls and toys are housed in a half-scale model of the White House. The museum is open from 10 A.M. to 6 P.M. except on major holidays.

Crystal Cathedral. The enormous glass and steel edifice at Chapman and Lewis streets in Garden Grove is the Crystal Cathedral, home of television evangelist Robert Schuller's Reformed Church in America. Hour-long tours include a look at one of the world's largest pipe organs (Monday through Saturday from 9 A.M. to 3:30 P.M., Sunday from 1:30 to 3:30 P.M.). Donations are encouraged.

Charles W. Bowers Museum. Newly expanded, Santa Ana's fine cultural arts museum at 2002 N. Main Street specializes in art from the Americas and Pacific Rim countries. A fascinating potpourri of African artifacts is also on display. Galleries are devoted to Southwest and Northwest Indian art.

The renovated museum will be open by the end of 1991 (Tuesday through Saturday, 10 A.M. to 5 P.M., and Sunday afternoon; donations accepted). Take the Main Street exit off Interstate 5.

Countryside retreats

In the countryside, several locations provide a pleasant contrast to the acres of homes found elsewhere.

Caspers Wilderness Park. A bit of old California, this 5,500-acre county park lies 7 miles inland from San Juan Capistrano via State 74 (Ortega Highway). You can picnic free beside the highway; there's a fee for picnicking in meadows within the park and for overnight camping. A hiker's and horseback rider's domain, the park has almost no facilities; bring your own water.

Tucker Wildlife Sanctuary. In the Santa Ana Mountains just past the charming old town of Modjeska, this beautiful oasis of trees, flowers, foliage, and wildlife is operated by California State University at Fullerton. The sanctuary is open from 9 A.M. to 4 P.M. daily, except Monday (small donation). To reach it from Interstate 5, take El Toro Road inland.

Irvine Regional Park. Created in 1897, this oasis of native sycamore trees and 500-year-old oaks is a good place to picnic, hike, and ride ponies or paddleboats. A small zoo is a good introduction to native Southwest creatures. To get to the park, take Chapman Avenue east from Interstate 55 in Orange.

Orange Coast

Orange County's coast presents two faces—wide, flat stretches of sand from the town of Seal Beach south to the Balboa Peninsula and more picturesque bluff-backed coves southward from Corona del Mar to San Clemente. Watch your driving all along this coast. Cars park wherever there's an inch of space, and it's not uncommon to see a horizontal surfboard with legs attached dashing across the highway.

Seal Beach & south

Seal Beach residents work hard to keep a low profile for their pleasant little town, not boasting about the fishing pier at the end of Main Street and the nice stretch of swimming and surfing beach that fronts the quiet community. Most visitors pass it by, only noticing the oil pumps, refineries, and storage tanks that line the inland side of State 1 as far south as Huntington Beach.

Sunset Beach. Boaters head for neighboring Sunset Beach's marina, aquatic park, and launching and trailer-parking facilities. The broad sandy stretches at Sunset and adjoining Surfside beaches are popular with residents.

Bolsa Chica State Beach. This day-use beach (fire rings, rest rooms, and lifeguards) to the south is 6 miles long, but only its northern end, a 3-mile strip of sand between the ocean and highway, is lined with sun-lovers. Steep cliffs between the road and beach make access difficult at the southern end. Some trails and a stairway near 16th Street penetrate the bluffs, and a cycling path and walkway extends its length. Clamming, diving, and fishing are popular here; grunion runs occur between March and August.

On the landward side of the highway across from the beach, Bolsa Chica Ecological Reserve's salt marshes provide a landing site for birds on the Pacific Flyway. A mile-long loop trail winds through part of the reserve's 530 acres.

Huntington Beach

Named Pacific City when it was first settled in 1902, this community was meant to rival Atlantic City. But unlike its East Coast counterpart, Huntington Beach rose to fame on the strength of wave action. The annual OP Surfing Championships take place Labor Day weekend, but you can watch surfers "hang ten" any day.

Most of the early-morning and late-day action takes place around the main pier at the foot of Main Street, being rebuilt because of storm damage. The state beach that stretches 2 miles south of the pier is spectacular on summer nights, when its 500 fire rings are ablaze with bonfires.

The new pier area (to be completed by the end of 1992) and the Waterfront Hilton Hotel (Huntington Street and Pacific Coast Highway) are the beginning of an ambitious redevelopment program. New and refurbished shopping centers, hotels, and condominium complexes will keep the city under construction for several years.

Huntington Harbor, west of downtown, consists of eight man-made islands top-heavy with luxury homes, waterside shops, and restaurants among a maze of marinas. A tour boat from Peter's Landing complex gives a look at the project.

Newport Beach–Balboa

In 1902, an ad for Newport Beach–Balboa claimed: "The best fishing on the Pacific coast, surf that's foamy and playful, a bay studded with islands around which you may row, fish, yacht, picnic, and stroll." It's still true if you know where to look.

Peeks at the Past

The bean fields, orange groves, and cattle ranches that once covered so much of Orange County's inland area have almost vanished. A few faint traces of the past have been preserved in two historic parks.

Old Town Irvine. Little is left of the famous Irvine Ranch that once sprawled over one-fifth of Orange County. The planned community of Irvine already occupies more than half its 108,000 acres. But you can get a look at some of the original ranch buildings when you pay a visit to Old Town Irvine, a renovation of the vintage town that once was the ranch's shipping center.

Onetime warehouses, granaries, and other outbuildings now house shops, galleries, offices, a restaurant, and a hotel. (Half of La Quinta Inn's guest rooms were converted from lima bean silos.) Other businesses occupy a former blacksmith shop, foreman's house, and general store.

Free walking tours take place from 10 A.M. to noon on the first Saturday of the month, but you can visit anytime. From Interstate 5, take Sand Canyon Avenue west, turn left at Burt Road, then turn right into the parking lot.

Heritage Hills Park. This peaceful preserve in the Laguna Hills area is the county's first historic park. To see an original adobe and three restored turn-of-the-century structures, exit Interstate 5 on Lake Forest Drive; head east for 2 miles, and turn north on Serrano Road.

The park is open daily from 8 A.M. to 5 P.M.; house tours take place at 11 A.M., 2 and 3 P.M. Just down the road is Serrano Creek Park, a pleasant place for a picnic or a jog.

To Southland surfers, the day is measured out in waves to ride into shore. These shimboarders catch the crest of a frothy breaker at Laguna.

...Orange Coast

The Balboa Peninsula, with its two piers, and Balboa Island offer the most visitor attractions, set against a backdrop of yacht clubs and ultra-expensive homes. Upper Newport Bay lures campers, bird-watchers, and water-lovers.

Newport Center, to the south, is the area's vast professional and financial complex, site of sleek hotels and Fashion Island (see page 48). Close by lies Newport Harbor Art Museum (850 San Clemente Drive), open Tuesday through Sunday; patio lunch is offered on weekdays.

To reach the Newport Beach–Balboa area, take State 1 (Pacific Coast Highway), State 55, or Jamboree Road from Interstate 405. Newport Beach Conference and Visitors Bureau, at the north end of Balboa Peninsula (address on page 47), has maps and brochures.

Balboa Peninsula. Access to this long, skinny sandspit is via Newport Boulevard. A good first stop is the free Newport Harbor Nautical Museum, 1714 W. Balboa Boulevard, where exhibits highlight the area's boating background and fishing history; hours are 10 A.M. to 3 P.M. Wednesday through Sunday.

If you turn southeast on Via Lido at the north end of the peninsula, crossing over a humpbacked bridge leads to Lido Isle, a posh residential area dredged up from the harbor's bottom. Boats tie up right at the back doors of these waterfront homes. Investigate the charming little labyrinth of shops and restaurants along the street before you reach the bridge.

Farther south along Newport Boulevard, browse around Cannery Village, an intriguing conglomeration of boutiques, galleries, restaurants, boat yards, and antique shops housed in former fish canneries. One converted warehouse, The Factory, has more than 30 tiny shops under one roof.

Newport Pier (west of the intersection of Newport and Balboa boulevards) sits over the deep marine canyon where the McFaddens built the county's first commercial wharf in 1888. Look for the dory fishing fleet, last on the Pacific Coast; its catch has been sold at market here since 1891. Baldy's Tackle at the pier's head, in business since 1922, rents bikes and beach gear. There's a seafood restaurant at the end of the pier.

To entice folks beyond the bustling Newport Pier area, developers built Balboa Pier and Pavilion in 1905. Drive southeast on Balboa Boulevard to pier parking at Palm Avenue. It's a 4-minute walk to the end of the pier where Ruby's 1940s-style diner serves hamburgers, floats, and shakes.

The ground-floor restaurant in Balboa Pavilion (now a center for deep-sea fishing, parasailing, and whale-watching trips) has photos from Victorian through big-band eras. To the left of the pavilion, the Fun Zone offers rides, ticket booths, and docks for harbor tours, boat rentals, and waterside restaurants. The little ferry to Balboa Island leaves from here.

Expert body surfers challenge the waves at the Wedge, the area between the jetty and the beach at the tip of the peninsula.

Balboa Island. Built from a sandbar in 1906 as a subdivision of tiny lots, the island's homes sit cheek by jowl. Shops are crunched into about 3 short blocks along Marine Avenue. While you browse, try a local favorite: a Balboa Bar (vanilla ice cream hand-dipped in chocolate) or a chocolate-dipped frozen banana. A bayfront boardwalk circles the island, offering fine harbor views.

Upper Newport Bay. Newport Dunes Aquatic Park offers access to a 15-acre lagoon on the upper arm of Newport Bay. This private park (fees for day use and overnight camping) has picnic tables, dressing rooms, showers, wading pool, fire rings, and launching ramp. Paddleboards, kayaks, sea cycles, and sailboats can be rented for use on the quiet, warm waters.

A vast estuary on the east shore of the upper bay is a wildlife preserve. In fall, it swarms with ducks, geese, and other birds on the Pacific Flyway. Tours take place Saturdays in winter.

To reach the park and the preserve, turn west on Backbay Drive from Jamboree Boulevard just north of its intersection with State 1.

Around Corona del Mar

Most tourists only see the attractive shops and restaurants lining the Coast Highway in Corona del Mar. To get beyond them to the popular palm-lined state beach, turn west on any of the flower-named streets between Orchid and Iris.

Sherman Gardens. Photographers and horticulturists will enjoy a stop at Sherman Library and Gardens, 2647 E. Coast Highway. Early California architecture serves as a backdrop for annual plantings and tropical greenery. The gardens are open daily from 10:30 A.M. to 4 P.M.; there's a small charge.

Crystal Cove State Park. One of the Southland's newest state beach parks stretches 3¼ miles along the coast between Corona del Mar and Laguna and inland toward Irvine. Three coves offer swimming, surfing, snorkeling, and tidepooling; the offshore area is designated an underwater park for divers. Access to Crystal Cove is through a small colony of beach cottages, happily ramshackle remnants of an earlier era.

Laguna Beach

In a county that has changed dramatically over the last decades, Laguna Beach fights hard to keep its tone of tasteful Bohemianism. Hillside cottage studios, erected by artists who settled the town around the turn of the century, still stand next to more pretentious residences. Art galleries are prominent throughout town, and two annual art events—the summer Festival of Arts and Pageant of the Masters and the Winter Festival in February—draw large crowds.

To get to Laguna from Newport Beach, follow State 1 southeast 10 miles; from Interstate 405, take Laguna Canyon Road (State 133) 8 miles south. Traffic on the Coast Highway through town is a problem, particularly on summer weekends, and parking is a nuisance; 2-hour meters are the stroller's bane.

Art heritage. An art lover's first stop should be the Laguna Art Museum, Cliff Drive and North Coast Highway. The permanent collection in this hot

...Orange Coast

pink gallery (open 11 A.M. to 5 P.M. Tuesday through Sunday; small admission) stars California painters.

Many of the galleries on Forest Avenue, Laguna's eucalyptus-shaded artist's row, specialize in traditional works; you'll find more contemporary pieces along the Coast Highway. Several times a month the Chamber of Commerce hosts gallery tours; call (714) 494-1018 for information.

Town sights. Ocean views from Heisler Park (near the art museum) found their way onto many an early-century canvas; painters still daub here. Paths wind among bird of paradise plants; steps descend to the tidepools of the Glenn E. Vedder Marine Ecological Reserve. Stroll northwest past the lawn bowling grounds, in use most days.

You can picnic in the park or try a restaurant near the museum. Las Brisas, 361 Cliff Drive, offers Mexican brunches and dinners and the postcard-perfect setting you expect at Laguna. The Cottage Restaurant, 308 N. Coast Highway, is another local favorite (breakfast, brunch, and dinner).

From Las Brisas restaurant, take the path down to Main Beach and the country's most scenic basketball court. Pick-up games are hotly competitive—as is the beach volleyball. Shoppers will want to cross over at the Forest Avenue intersection to reach Lumber Yard Village shopping center; others might walk along the highway to white-towered Hotel Laguna, a landmark from 1930. Its handsomely restored lobby holds historic photos of Laguna; the restaurant has a gull's-eye ocean view. Rooms are tidily old-fashioned.

Dana Point & south

This resort area was named for Richard Henry Dana, Jr., author of *Two Years Before the Mast*, who was aboard the brig *Pilgrim* when it pulled into the cove to pick up cowhides in the 1830s. His statue stands not far from a full-size replica of the ship at the harbor (open Sundays March to Thanksgiving from 11 A.M. to 2:30 P.M.; admission fee).

Laguna Niguel. Atop a bluff in this newly annexed northern section of town sits the Ritz-Carlton at Laguna Niguel, one of the state's few oceanfront resorts built in recent times. The chic 393-room hostelry, opened in 1984, offers all amenities—golf, tennis, swimming, and glamorous restaurants.

You can sip a drink at the hotel and watch the surfers on the beach below catch the day's last ride. Or enjoy Salt Creek Beach, a bluff-backed county facility, with plenty of comfortable terrain for sunbathing and reading. The entrance is about half a mile south of Crown Valley Parkway.

Harbor. Dana Point Harbor Drive leads down from the Coast Highway to the 2,500-slip marina, numerous casual restaurants, three nautically inclined shopping centers, and a motel. Spread out on the bluff above, Dana Point Resort overlooks the entire area.

Visitors can rent boats, go parasailing and deep-sea fishing, or reserve a spot on December-to-March whale-watching trips. On Dana Island, inside the breakwater, grassy strip parks offer places to rest or look for crabs and starfish along the rocky shore.

The Orange County Marine Institute (open daily except Sunday, free admission), at the northwest end of the harbor, contains aquariums, marine exhibits, information on the area's tidepools, and a gift shop. The tall ship *Californian*, primarily a training vessel for young people, is moored nearby several months a year.

The lighthouse on Del Prado Avenue, north of Dana Point Resort, houses a free Nautical Heritage Museum, full of ship models, antiques, and memorabilia (open 10 A.M. to 4 P.M. Monday through Friday).

Doheny State Beach. Though the harbor is short of sand, there's plenty of it at this wide state beach to the east. Doheny offers camping combined with good surfing and safe waters. The lagoon at the northwest end is a wild bird habitat.

South to San Clemente. The pretty little town of San Clemente is best known as a retreat of former President Richard Nixon. Take Avenida del Mar from Interstate 5 to get to the beach and pier. There's no scenic coast drive, but marked accesses lead down from the bluffs to small coves.

Just south of San Clemente and over the county line, San Onofre Nuclear Power Plant is a startling contrast to the beach scene. There's an information center off the highway.

San Juan Capistrano

Once a sleepy little town that sprang up around the mission founded by Father Junipero Serra in 1776, San Juan is now a photogenic suburban community with Spanish-style homes and shops. From State 1, drive inland a couple of miles on Camino Capistrano. The turn-off from Interstate 5 also leads right to the center of town (Camino Capistrano and Ortega Highway), site of the mission and the Amtrak depot.

Mission. The mission and its grounds (small admission fee) are well worth visiting on your own or with a guide. To arrange for a guided tour, call the visitor center, (714) 493-1424, in advance of your stay. If you arrive between March and October, you may see some of the famous swallows that summer here, although they're far outnumbered by pigeons these days.

The mission chapel is the only remaining church where Father Serra is known to have said Mass. Next to it is a replica of the mission church destroyed in an 1812 earthquake (ruins remain).

Around town. Good restaurants, art galleries, craft shops, and antique stores crowd the downtown area. The city's historical society conducts guided tours ($1) at 1 P.M. most Sundays. Meet the guide at El Peon, across from the mission entrance, or call (714) 493-8444 for further information. To look at historic adobes on your own, pick up a walking-tour map at the O'Neill Museum (31831 Los Rios Street).

Capistrano's recently renovated depot has been operating as a train station since 1895. Refurbished vintage cars line its tracks. The indoor-outdoor Rio Grande Bar & Grill restaurant is a favorite setting for Sunday brunch and an afternoon of Dixieland jazz.

B&Bs along the Coast

Breakfasts in flower-filled courtyards, wine on oceanfront terraces, take-along picnic lunches for cycling tours—these are only some of the touches offered by coastside inns. A few bed and breakfasts lie just a stone's throw from a beach, some are tucked into neighborhoods noted for historic architecture, and others survey hills and valleys a few miles inland.

Part of the charm of B & Bs is the chance they offer visitors to learn about the area from their host and other guests. It's a good way to exchange ideas on activities, restaurants, and "must sees." Inns seem to attract a compatible crowd.

The following is but a sampling of the small hostelries available in the Southland. Those described here are all situated in coastal towns, listed from south (San Diego) to north (Cambria). For a free guide to the hundreds of bed and breakfast inns throughout the state, write to the California Office of Tourism, Box 9278, Van Nuys, CA 91409, or phone (800) TO-CALIF.

Make reservations well in advance; inns book months ahead for summer weekends. All of the inns listed below serve breakfast. Most prohibit children, pets, and smoking. Facilities for handicapped are indicated, where available. Rates include breakfast for two: I= below $80, M=$80–$125, E=above $125.

Britt House, 406 Maple St., San Diego, CA 92103; (619) 234-2926. Beautifully restored Victorian, 9 rooms and cottage, each with distinctive decor; most share baths; 1 wheelchair access. Delicious afternoon tea; breakfast in parlor or rooms. M

Heritage Park, 2470 Heritage Park Row, San Diego, CA 92110; (619) 295-7088. An 1889 charmer moved to Old Town; 9 rooms; 1 handicapped room; antiques; breakfast in bed or garden; dinner by arrangement; vintage movies. M

Bed & Breakfast Inn at La Jolla, 7753 Draper Ave., La Jolla, CA 92037; (619) 456-2066. Fifteen rooms with private baths; 1 wheelchair access; some ocean views; walk to village shops and restaurants. M–very E

Rock Haus, 410 15th St., Del Mar, CA 92104; (619) 481-3764. California bungalow overlooking the ocean; 10 rooms, some with private baths; wine and canapes. I–E

Carriage House, 1322 Catalina St., Laguna Beach, CA 92651; (714) 494-8945. Imaginatively furnished New Orleans–style colonial; 6 spacious suites with kitchens; breakfast in dining room off courtyard. M–E

Eiler's Inn, 741 S. Coast Highway, Laguna Beach, CA 92651; (714) 494-3004. Turning its back to busy highway, inn offers 12 simple rooms around lush courtyard; buffet breakfast; afternoon tea; sun deck. M–E

Doryman's Inn, 2102 W. Ocean Front, Newport Beach, CA 92663; (714) 675-7300. Overlooking beach and dory fleet, 10 luxurious rooms with fireplaces and sunken tubs; restaurant below; breakfast on balcony or in room. M–very E

Seal Beach Inn, 212 5th St., Seal Beach, CA 90740; (213) 430-3915. Garden entrance sets tone for French Mediterranean ambience; 22 rooms; breakfast room; swimming pool; 1 block from ocean. M–E

Lord Mayor's Inn, 435 Cedar Ave., Long Beach, CA 90802; (213) 436-0324. Restored home of first mayor; 5 rooms with antiques; gardens; full breakfast. I–M

Venice Beach House, 15 30th Ave., Venice, CA 90291; (213) 823-1966. Bungalow in eclectic beach town; 9 rooms, 4 with private bath; bicycles; picnic lunches. I–E

La Mer, P.O. Box 23318, Ventura, CA 93001; (805) 643-3600. An 1890 Cape Cod with European flavor; 5 rooms; fireplaces; antiques; gardens; picnic baskets. M–E

Bayberry Inn, 111 W. Valerio St., Santa Barbara, CA 93101; (805) 682-3199. Lovely Colonial-Federal building; 8 rooms; croquet; bicycles; large breakfast. M–E

Old Yacht Club Inn, 431 Corona del Mar Dr., Santa Barbara, CA 93103; (805) 962-1277. City's first inn in two buildings near beach; 9 rooms; beach chairs and towels; bicycles; picnic baskets; Saturday dinner. I–E

Ballard Inn, 2436 Baseline, Ballard, CA 93463; (805) 688-7770. Santa Ynez Valley retreat for wine touring, Solvang shopping; 15 rooms, some with fireplaces; 1 handicapped. E

Rose Victorian Inn, 789 Valley Rd., Arroyo Grande, CA 93420; (805) 481-5566. Lawn with arbor and gazebo surrounds former pioneer rancher's home; 11 rooms on 3 stories; restaurant; antiques; hearty breakfast and dinner. E

Beach House, 6360 Moonstone Beach Dr., Cambria, CA 93428; (805) 927-3136. Three-story beach house; 7 rooms with baths; gardens; bicycles. M–E

J. Patrick House, 2990 Burton Dr., Cambria, CA 93428; (805) 927-3812. Contemporary American-style log house; 8 rooms; handicapped access; gardens; picnic baskets. M

San Diego

San Diego has been charming visitors since the 1500s. At first glance, the city's modern facade belies its age. But California's oldest European settlement is ever mindful of its rich Spanish-Mexican heritage. Monuments report it and buildings preserve it. A legacy of Spanish place names and graceful architecture reflect the city's pride in its past.

California's history began here when Juan Rodriguez Cabrillo landed at Point Loma in 1542. Sixty years later Sebastian Vizcaino also reached the grand bay he named San Diego. But the West Coast's first settlement was not established until 1769, when Father Junipero Serra, a member of Gaspar de Portola's expedition, founded Mission San Diego de Alcala.

The village that grew up around the mission became the anchor for Spanish domain in California. Today the once-sleepy seaside community is the West Coast's second largest city.

Lay of the land

Seventeen-mile-long San Diego Bay is in many ways the heart of this water-oriented city. Vast, natural, and almost landlocked, the great harbor is one of the world's best deep-water anchorages. Host to ships from all ports, it's also home for most of the Navy's Pacific fleet as well as the world's largest sportfishing fleet.

Inland lie the modern city, Old Town (where the city began), and a world-famous park and zoo. East of the downtown, along Interstate 8, is Mission Valley, site of major shopping centers, hotel row, San Diego's mission, and Jack Murphy Stadium (venue for pro football and baseball).

Up the coast lie seaside towns, noted spas, colorful flower fields, and wide beaches. The interior holds a wealth of surprises, from impressive Wild Animal Park to the old mountain mining village of Julian. To the south, Mexico's colorful bargains are an easy 16-mile drive—or trolley ride—from downtown San Diego.

Planning a visit

A splendid natural setting, an equable climate (average temperature of 70° with low humidity), and a wealth of attractions and events make San Diego a favorite year-round vacation site.

Getting there. San Diego's international airport, Lindbergh Field, is only 3 miles northwest of downtown along the bay. Rental cars, taxis, and limos are available from the airport.

Greyhound provides bus service to San Diego. Amtrak passenger trains offer several daily round-trips between Los Angeles and San Diego, with stops at San Juan Capistrano, Oceanside, and Del Mar.

Interstate 5, en route south from Los Angeles to the border, skirts Mission Bay and Old Town before entering the heart of the city. Interstate 15 connects San Diego with the San Bernardino Mountains to the north, and Interstate 8 is the major east-west route.

Getting around. A network of freeways can get you anywhere within minutes. Except during rush hours, it takes only about 20 minutes to cross into Mexico or to drive up the coast to Del Mar.

Motorists can follow a 59-mile scenic drive all around town and into the surrounding area. Start at the Broadway Pier (foot of Broadway) or anywhere you see road signs bearing a white sea gull symbol.

The refurbished Santa Fe Depot downtown (Broadway and Kettner Boulevard), the Amtrak station, is also

Contacts

These agencies offer information on attractions and accommodations. See additional contacts throughout this chapter.

San Diego Convention & Visitors Bureau
1200 Third Ave., Suite 824
Department 700
San Diego, CA 92101-4190
(619) 236-1212

Escondido Convention & Visitors Bureau
720 N. Broadway
Escondido, CA 92025
(800) 848-3336; (619) 745-4741

Julian Chamber of Commerce
P.O. Box 413
Julian, CA 92036
(619) 765-1857

A graceful belltower and a simple adobe facade characterize Mission San Diego de Alcala, founded in 1769 as the first link in California's 21-mission chain.

the departure point for the San Diego Trolley, the city's light-rail transit system. Bright red cars run through the city to the border in about 40 minutes, including frequent stops for loading passengers; a $1.50 ticket takes you the whole distance. An extension connects bayside hotels and attractions. Trolley cars operate daily between 5 A.M. and 1 A.M. For schedules, call (619) 233-3004.

For an overview of city attractions, ride the trackless Old Town Trolley. You can get on or off along the way or stay aboard for a 2-hour tour. Start at Old Town to keep history in perspective.

Ferries and water taxis can be a scenic way to reach some destinations—see page 61.

Where to stay. San Diego and its northern coastal reaches offer a wide selection of hotels, motels, and bed-and-breakfast inns. You'll find clusters of accommodations near all the city's main attractions. Make early reservations for summer and holiday weekend stays. Campers also need to reserve beachside parks well in advance (see page 121). Mission Bay's Campland on the Bay, (619) 274-6260, also fills up early.

Activities. San Diego County claims more good public beaches (70 miles) than anywhere else in the state. If you tire of swimming and sunning, you can opt for soaring, parasailing, skin diving, and deep-sea fishing—all year-round activities.

The city known as "Sports Town, U.S.A." hosts professional baseball (Padres), football (Chargers), and soccer (Sockers), as well as world-class sailing, golf, and tennis tournaments. Almost 80 courses suit golfers to a tee. Cycling and jogging routes trail along the ocean and through Balboa Park.

Clusters of stores at Seaport Village, Horton Plaza, and Old Town lure the less athletic. And Tijuana's craft-filled shops lie tantalizingly nearby.

You can see performances by local theater companies, symphony, opera, and ballet on several downtown stages. For ticket information for these and other San Diego events, call ARTS TIX, (619) 238-3810. Its office (closed Monday) is in Horton Plaza. You can save money by ordering half-price tickets on the day of performance.

For recorded information on what's happening around town, you can call (619) 239-9696.

Hotels with a Past

Good looks and longevity distinguish seven of San Diego County's hotels. Three are downtown beauties, three overlook the ocean, and one sits amid apple orchards and gold mines.

The architecture of these renovated grande dames alone makes them worthy of admiration. If you plan a stay, check current rates; several are definite splurges.

Horton Grand Hotel, 311 Island Avenue, San Diego, CA 92101; (619) 544-1886. Two Victorian hotels, once slated for demolition, were dismantled and later reassembled as this Gaslamp Quarter hostelry. Staff wear 19th-century costumes; rooms have fireplaces, four-posters, and curtain swags. Afternoon tea is served in the glass-enclosed lobby. A small museum displays mementos of the past.

Horton Plaza Hotel, 901 Fifth Avenue, San Diego, CA 92101; (619) 232-9500. A 1913 office building was converted in 1987 to this all-suites hotel. The facade still has its original Corinthian and Alaskan marble and Australian gum wood trim.

U.S. Grant Hotel, 326 Broadway, San Diego, CA 92101; (619) 232-3121. When first opened in 1910, the marble-paved U.S. Grant was downtown's most posh. After falling into disrepair over the years, it was refurbished and reopened in 1985. Take afternoon tea under the lobby's wedding cake chandeliers or dine in the elegant, wood-paneled Grant Grill.

Hotel del Coronado, 1500 Orange Avenue, Coronado, CA 92118; (619) 435-6611. This red-roofed beauty, still Coronado's focal point, celebrated her centennial in 1988. Distinguished guests over the years have included U.S. presidents, Thomas Edison, Henry Ford, Robert Todd Lincoln, the Duke of Windsor, and Wallis Simpson.

Take a self-guiding tour of the intricate corridors and cavernous rooms of this Victorian-style wooden wonder (rental cassettes available) or roam the grounds.

Colonial Inn, 910 Prospect Street, La Jolla, CA 92037; (619) 454-2181. When it opened in 1913, this clifftop hotel was La Jolla's first. Recently restored and expanded, the hotel's older section is charming.

La Valencia Hotel, 1132 Prospect Street, La Jolla, CA 92037; (619) 454-0771. Presiding over La Jolla village, this pink, Mediterranean-style hostelry was famous in the 1920s as a Hollywood hideaway. Join the locals for lunch on the Tropical Patio.

Julian Hotel, 2032 Main Street (P.O. Box 1856), Julian, CA 92036; (619) 765-0201. Set in the middle of a former ghost town, this Victorian charmer owes its past to mining and its present to tourism. The region is noted for gold-rush relics and apple pie.

The Waterfront

San Diego should be viewed from the water. The city's beautiful harbor offers parks for strolling and playing, piers and embankments for fishing, boat-launching facilities, beaches, and lots of places to watch the ships go by. And it boasts a striking convention center, marinas, bayside resort hotels, shops, and restaurants oriented to the water. Two wildlife reserves at the south end of the bay offer views of life on the marsh.

Only 1½ to 2 miles wide, San Diego Bay provides a close look at a complex assortment of military and sportfishing ships, from state-of-the-art fishing vessels to yachts of world-ranked sailors.

Getting around

Car-free options for seeing the bay include ferries, water taxis, light-rail and trackless trolleys, and bicycles.

Ferries. Ferry service was discontinued for some time after the swooping San Diego-Coronado Bridge was built in 1969, but it was resumed a few years ago. Boats carry pedestrians and cyclists between the Broadway Pier (on Harbor Drive at the foot of Broadway) and Coronado's Old Ferry Landing, a complex of shops and restaurants by Landing Park. Ferries operate daily from 10 A.M. to 10 P.M., longer on Friday and Saturday ($1.50 one way).

Water taxis. Water taxis shuttle pedestrians around the bay, making regularly scheduled stops at major waterfront hotels. For on-call service to shopping areas and restaurants, call BAY-TAXI; the tariff is a fairly steep $5.

Light-rail trolleys. An extension of the San Diego Trolley runs from downtown along Harbor Drive to the convention center. The Chula Vista Nature Interpretive Center, west of the E Street stop, can also be reached by trolley.

Trackless trolleys. The Old Town Trolley makes waterfront stops on routes around the city. The Coronado Trolley Lines links Old Ferry Landing with the Hotel del Coronado and Le Meridien.

Bicycles. Miles of bicycle paths open the bay to cyclists. One route rounds the top of the bay; another streaks from Glorietta Bay to South Bay wetlands. A favorite route starts at the parking lot of Spanish Landing Park, near the airport, heads east paralleling the waterfront, then crosses by ferry to Coronado.

Many hotels rent bikes, as does a shop at Old Ferry Landing on Coronado. To get a free San Diego cycling map, call (619) 231-2453.

Harbor tours

The best way to get your bearings is from the water. A variety of vessels depart from the well-marked dock on Harbor Drive at the foot of Broadway. Cruises loop close along the shoreline, exposing a full range of air, surface, and undersea craft and harbor activity otherwise hidden from sight.

Harbor Excursion's 2-hour cruises—past Ballast Point sub base, North Island carrier docks, the repair docks south of Coronado bridge, and Silver Strand's amphibious base—give the best look at the bay's military presence. For best viewing, stand topside, on the right facing forward. For schedule and ticket information, call (619) 234-4111.

Along the Embarcadero

To sample the waterfront scene, join the parade of walkers, joggers, and cyclists along the Embarcadero, a landscaped boardwalk that extends along the bayshore from the Coast Guard Station next to the airport all the way south to Seaport Village, about 4 miles. Special stops along the route include a floating museum and the shops and museums of a re-created seaport. Small landscaped parks offer plenty of people-watching opportunities.

Although Naval yards are off-limits, vessels moored at the Broadway Pier hold open house on weekend afternoons. Cruise ships may also be spotted at the adjacent B Street Pier. Home port for the shrinking tuna fleet is the G Street Pier, where a bay-view plaza and a restaurant at the pier's end permit good views of the sleek seiners and tubby trawlers.

Maritime Museum. The three ships of the Maritime Museum, now berthed together around a floating pier north of the excursion boat dock, are worth a half-day visit. The square-rigger *Star of India*, in service since 1863, is the world's oldest iron-hulled merchantman still under sail. Go aboard the painstakingly restored ship for a hint of sea life as it was more than a century ago. Volunteers work on rigging and sails some Sundays.

The *Berkeley*, an 1898 former San Francisco ferry, is full of exhibits and models. Visit on weekdays to see the model-building shop at its most active. Next door you can board the 1904 steam yacht *Medea*.

The museum is open daily; a moderate admission is charged.

Seaport Village. Shops and restaurants designed to evoke the past make tidy Seaport Village, at Pacific Highway and Harbor Drive, popular with bayside browsers. The shopping center's 45-foot-high tower is a re-creation of a lighthouse in the state of Washington; the refurbished turn-of-the-century carousel, operating daily, once twirled on Coney Island.

Shelter & Harbor islands

Two man-made isles in San Diego Bay accommodate boaters, sailors, anglers, and atmosphere-seekers. Once mud and sandpiles built up by dredging in the bay, Shelter and Harbor islands are now attractive resort areas studded with forests of boat masts.

Shelter Island. Really a peninsula, Shelter Island is connected to Point Loma by a salty causeway. Among the island's attractions are a fishing pier, a boat-launching ramp, marinas, restaurants, and hotels. Tropical blooms, torches, and "Polynesian" architecture lend a South Seas flavor. Winding paths provide good strolling, cycling, and bay-

Downtown San Diego buildings soar skyward to take full advantage of bayside views.
Alive with boats of all sizes, the grand natural harbor is one of the country's best
deep-water anchorages.

...Waterfront

watching spots. The Friendship Bell is a gift of Yokohama, San Diego's sister city in Japan.

Harbor Island. Opposite the airport, Harbor Island features high-rise hotels, restaurants, parks, and marinas. You can view it from a peaceful vantage point in Spanish Landing Park on Harbor Drive. On this island's western tip, a Spanish-style building houses a lighthouse and restaurant.

Coronado

Coronado's relative isolation gives it the flavor of an island. Actually it's connected to the mainland by a long, scenic sand spit and a graceful bay bridge. Low guard rails on the span open up a view stretching all the way south to Mexico.

The regal Hotel del Coronado is the focal point of the area (see page 60). Across from the hotel, a picturesque boathouse (now a restaurant) sits at the edge of Glorietta Bay, a small boat harbor with a public launching ramp. Adjoining it are a municipal golf course and a long public beach with fine sand —and occasional sound effects from planes landing at nearby North Island Naval Air Station. (Caution: Watch for stingrays on the beach early in the season.)

Although overshadowed by its more glamorous neighbor, the Glorietta Bay Inn (formerly John D. Spreckels' home) still hosts visitors. Between the complex of shops and restaurants that make up the Old Ferry Landing and Coronado's new Tidelands Park (just north of the bridge) sits Coronado's newest hotel, Le Meridien.

At the north end of the peninsula, the Naval Air Station is one of the oldest in existence. The flat island was the departure point for Charles Lindbergh's historic 1927 flight across the Atlantic. (A replica of his plane is a highlight in San Diego's Aerospace Museum in Balboa Park—see page 69.)

Southward along the narrow spit separating ocean from bay is Silver Strand State Beach, another fine stretch of shoreline.

Point Loma

The high promontory that shelters San Diego Bay from the Pacific Ocean offers grand harbor views. On a clear day you can see from the mountains of Mexico to beyond the La Jolla mesa and from the sprawling city of San Diego to the Coronado Islands and out to sea.

Cabrillo National Monument. At the tip of Point Loma stands Cabrillo National Monument, one of the smallest, most historic, and most visited monuments in the country (outdoing even the Statue of Liberty). Cabrillo's statue, a gift from Portugal (homeland of the great navigator), faces his actual 1542 landing spot at Ballast Point. The nearby visitor center explains Cabrillo's discovery of San Diego Bay and the events following it.

A glassed-in observatory at the monument permits fine views of the California gray whale migration that occurs each year from mid-December through mid-February (see page 124). The well-preserved lighthouse on the high bluff was used from 1855 until 1891, when the waterside lighthouse (still in use) was built.

Follow the nature trail to see a surprisingly unique plant community and some of the best tidepools in Southern California (you're invited to look but not touch).

The monument is open daily from 9 A.M. to sunset; there's a per-car admission charge. To reach Point Loma from downtown, take Rosecrans Street south from Harbor Drive and follow the signs. From Mission Bay, take Sunset Cliffs Boulevard and follow the signs to Catalina Boulevard. En route to the monument you'll pass through Fort Rosecrans National Cemetery, part of a U.S. Navy installation.

View Dining

Ask a dozen San Diegans about the best waterside dining places and you'll get 12 different answers. But everyone's likely to agree that any of the following restaurants will give you a fine view of the water.

The codes (I, M, E) offer some idea of the dinner tab for two (not including wine or tip): I=under $25, M=$25-$50, E=$50+. Most also serve lunch; some offer weekend brunch.

Anthony's Star of the Sea Room (E), 1360 Harbor Drive, (619) 232-7408; elegant ambience; dinner only; coat and tie.

Chart House (M), 1270 Prospect Street, La Jolla, (619) 459-8201; good chain choice; cove setting.

Fish Market and Top of the Market (I-M), 750 Harbor Drive, (619) 232-3474; mostly seafood downstairs; add tablecloths, other entrées at "Top."

George's at the Cove (E), 1250 Prospect Street, (619) 454-4244; alfresco dining; popular with locals.

Grand Island Cafe (I), Seaport Village, (619) 239-5216; patio right on the water.

Mister A's Restaurant (E), 2550 Fifth Avenue, (619) 239-1377; power lunch or dinner atop downtown high rise; continental cuisine.

Peohe's (E), 1201 First Street, Old Ferry Landing, Coronado, (619) 437-4474; views of distant city skyline; fresh seafood menu.

Reuben E. Lee (M), 880 E. Harbor Island Drive, (619) 291-1870; replicated riverboat; popular Sunday brunch.

Tom Ham's Lighthouse (I-M), 2150 Harbor Island Drive, (619) 291-9110; waterside setting; Sunday brunch; evening entertainment.

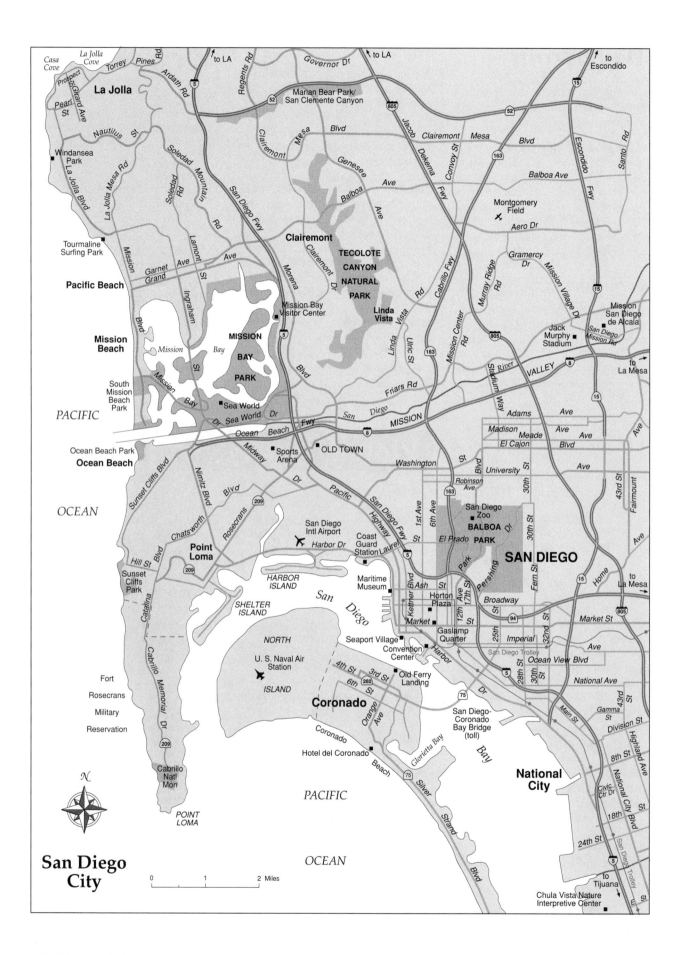

Downtown

San Diego's first downtown was a scrabble of adobe buildings in what is now Old Town. Then Alonzo Horton, an entrepreneur from Wisconsin, decided to move the town closer to the harbor. He bought 960 acres of land in 1867 and laid out streets around a small park, Horton Plaza, which has been the city's center ever since.

After years of neglect, San Diego's downtown has undergone a face-lift. Restored historical buildings and an eye-catching shopping mall make the area attractive to both residents and visitors. Completed in 1989, the convention center (at the foot of Fifth Avenue), with its striking sail-like rooftop, helps define the urban center.

New, refurbished, and rebuilt hotels welcome guests. Restaurants top skyscrapers to take advantage of views, while atriums, breezeways, and vest-pocket parks enliven the downtown area at street level. Theater, dance, and symphony performances add life, as do sidewalk cafes, jazz bistros, and street performers.

You can get your bearings at two visitor information centers downtown, at Horton Plaza (First Avenue and F Street) and on G Street between Second and Third avenues.

Horton Plaza

With its eclectic blend of department stores, boutiques, restaurants, theaters, and markets, the gaily painted, four-block-square Horton Plaza coaxes visitors away from suburban malls. There is much to engage the senses: tantalizing smells, eye-catching banners and displays, and strolling musicians.

Bounded by Broadway, G, First, and Fourth streets, the 11½-acre complex includes more than 150 shops. At one entrance, a stairway and plaza lead down to the Lyceum, two stages that are home to the San Diego Repertory Theatre.

A multilevel parking garage makes it convenient to shop or explore the adjacent historic area.

Gaslamp Quarter

A restored area south of Horton Plaza is worth a look. Bounded by Fourth, Sixth, Broadway, and the waterfront, it's one of the country's largest national historic districts.

The onetime heart of the city was a favorite haunt of Wyatt Earp and other 19th-century notables, but it fell on hard times in the late 1890s when businesses moved north of Broadway. In later years, it became a haven for gamblers, prostitutes, and opium dealers.

Though parts of the quarter are still redolent of its past, massive redevelopment has gentrified the region with brick sidewalks, period street lamps, benches, and trees. More than 100 splendid representations of Victorian architecture now house art galleries, antique shops, hotels, restaurants, and office buildings.

The Gaslamp Quarter Theatre Company puts on contemporary plays in the intimate Elizabeth North Theatre and the larger, elegant Hahn Cosmopolitan Theatre.

Touring the area. The William Heath Davis House (410 Island Avenue) is headquarters for the Gaslamp Quarter Foundation. Built in 1850 and moved here in 1984, it's the oldest house downtown. Join a 2-hour narrated stroll every Saturday (small donation requested), or pick up a map and strike out on your own. For information, call (619) 233-5227.

The Centre City Development Corporation also sponsors free weekend bus and walking tours. For information and reservations, call (619) 696-3215.

If you're touring on your own, take special note of the historic buildings on the east side of Fifth Avenue, between E and F streets. Their detailing is typical of commercial construction in the Victorian era.

The Royal Pie Bakery (554 Fourth Avenue) makes a tempting stop and a fine historical footnote: a bakery has operated at this address since 1875, even when the second floor was a notorious brothel. Or drop into the Horton Grand Hotel (see page 60) for tea, cocktails, or a meal. The hotel restaurant, Ida Bailey's, is named for one of the city's former madams.

Around town

Walking is also a good way to take a look at downtown San Diego's large entertainment complexes, small museums, and intriguing shopping opportunities.

Arts. Downtown renaissance turned a former movie theater at Seventh and B streets into a performing hall for the San Diego Symphony. Opera, ballet, musicals, and concerts are offered at the Civic Theatre and at Golden Hall, part of the Convention and Performing Arts Center on First Avenue.

Library. San Diego's public library, at the corner of Eighth and E streets, is one of the most modern and well-stocked facilities in the country. Its collection contains 4,000-year-old Sumerian cuneiform tablets.

Shopping. Antique buffs will enjoy the Olde Cracker Factory at Kettner Boulevard and Harbor Drive. More than 40 dealers display a wide range of antiques and collectibles. For another kind of shopping experience, the Farmers Market at Horton Plaza showcases fresh produce and specialty foods.

Museums. The Firehouse Museum, located at 1572 Columbia Street, reveals a glittering array of firefighting equipment and a host of amusing oddities. The museum is open Thursday through Sunday; donations are requested.

The grand mansion at 1925 K Street, now called Villa Montezuma, is a fine museum of Victorian architecture and decorative arts, including an outstanding stained glass collection. A small admission fee is charged to visit the museum, open Wednesday through Sunday afternoon. No high-heeled shoes are permitted.

Old San Diego

In 1769, Father Junipero Serra chose a commanding site overlooking the bay for the mission that would begin the settlement of California. A fort built to protect the mission gave the place its name, Presidio Hill. Soon a town began to sprout at the foot of the hill.

Some buildings and relics of the Spanish, Mexican, and American settlements that thrived here survive; others have been reconstructed. The most interesting lie within Old Town San Diego State Historic Park, an area bounded by Wallace, Congress, Twiggs, and Juan streets.

Old Town

Old Town is no sterile museum display; many colorful shops and restaurants are tucked around patios in its historic buildings. Locals rub elbows with tourists in garden restaurants at Bazaar del Mundo, a popular shopping complex in the historic Casa de Pico hacienda between Juan and Calhoun streets at Wallace.

Old Town is near the junction of Interstate 5 and Interstate 8 north of the airport; follow signs from Interstate 5.

Getting around. Park streets are reserved for strollers. Free ranger-led walking tours take off daily at 2 P.M. Get information from park headquarters at Wallace Street and San Diego Avenue, or call (619) 237-6770. Historical society tours are offered Saturday at 1:30 P.M. from the Whaley House at San Diego and Harney.

Highlights. Most of the old houses center on the plaza, once the scene of bullfights. The flagpole has flown Spanish and Mexican flags for two centuries; the American flag was added in 1846.

Casa de Estudillo (Mason Street end of the plaza), the first Spanish casa on the plaza, was the home of the commandante of Monterey and San Diego. Nearby Seeley Stables houses horse-drawn vehicles and western artifacts. Admission to the house and stables is free, but donations are welcome.

Casa de Bandini (Mason and Calhoun streets), built by wealthy Don Juan Bandini (known for lavish fandangos and dinners), is now a Mexican restaurant. The house was Commodore Stockton's headquarters during the American occupation of California in 1846, played host to Kit Carson, and was a stagecoach station in the 1860s.

The Whaley House (corner of San Diego Avenue and Harney Street), Southern California's oldest brick structure, has served as a dairy, funeral parlor, theater, saloon, courthouse, and Sunday school (the city's first).

The restored house is open Wednesday through Sunday. Admission includes entrance to the adjacent Derby-Pendleton House, shipped around Cape Horn and put together with wooden pegs in the 1850s.

Heritage Park. Stroll through the park at Juan and Harney streets to take a look at some of the city's oldest Victorians. Seven restored 1880-era houses (one housing a charming bed-and-breakfast inn) and a venerable Jewish temple line hillside Juan Street.

Presidio Park

Five years after Father Serra dedicated Alta California's first mission, its hillside location was already too small. So the building was moved 6 miles east in 1774 into Mission Valley (see page 6).

On its former site adjacent to Old Town rises the handsome Serra Museum (open Tuesday through Saturday and Sunday afternoon; admission fee). The site of the original mission chapel is marked by a towering cross.

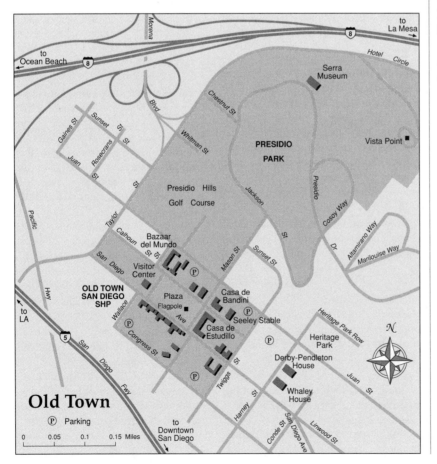

Old Town

P Parking

0   0.05   0.1   0.15 Miles

Sea World trainer introduces a young guest to one of the marine park's smiling performers, a killer whale who dazzles audiences with aquatic acrobatics.

Two City Parks

Two of San Diego's most outstanding attractions are examples of careful planning and foresight. Balboa Park, conceived in the 1860s, and Mission Bay Aquatic Park, developed a century later, attract millions of tourists yearly. They come to see one of the world's largest wild animal collections, a huge aquarium, and a raft of museums.

Balboa Park

It took more than a century for the 1,400 acres of rattlesnake-infested, hilly chaparral set aside in 1868 as a city park to become the verdant public garden you see today. And most of its impressive architecture is the result of two world fairs.

The 1915 Panama-California International Exposition contributed the Moorish and Spanish Renaissance buildings along El Prado, the central promenade, including the ornate California Tower with its 100-bell carillon, and also the world's largest outdoor organ (free concerts Sunday at 2 P.M.). The 1935 California-Pacific International Exposition added the Old Globe Theatre and the Spanish Village Arts & Crafts Center (a collection of craft shops near the zoo).

The park provides an idyllic setting for a concentration of top attractions: the world-famous San Diego Zoo, science and natural history museums, art galleries, performing arts centers, and a renowned space theater. Here, too, lie botanical gardens, playgrounds, picnic groves, a municipal golf course, a miniature railroad, and a 1910 carousel.

Getting around. The park's main entrance is from Laurel Street on the west side; it can also be reached from Park Boulevard, to the east. Parking is plentiful around El Prado's cluster of museums, the Palisades region to the south, and near the zoo.

Pick up maps and other park information at the visitor center in the House of Hospitality in the central El Prado area. Horse-drawn carriages carry visitors up and down the car-free mall.

A museum passport, available at the visitor center or participating museums, offers admission discounts. Many museums are closed Monday.

Museums of note. The rebuilt Casa de Balboa at the center of the park houses several small museums—Photographic Arts, San Diego History, Model Railroad, and Hall of Champions (sports). Next door, the Science Center's hands-on exhibits are popular with youngsters. Across the plaza, the Natural History Museum concentrates on southwestern desert and marine life.

The Museum of Man, in the California Tower at the other end of the plaza, appeals to anthropology buffs of all ages. It's noted for its American Indian research. Mummies and craft demonstrations please children.

The San Diego Museum of Art collection spans the ages, from early Asian to 20th century. The Sculpture Garden Cafe is a popular lunch spot. In the adjacent Timken Art Gallery, American and European art on display includes a number of Russian icons. The Centro Cultural de la Raza (south in the park's Pepper Grove area) focuses on contem-

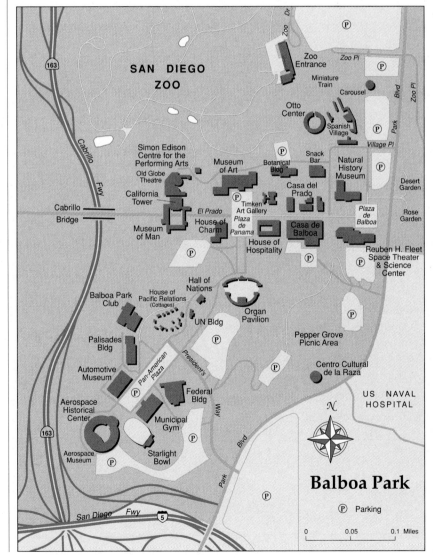

porary Indian, Mexican, and Chicano art and culture.

The Aerospace Museum, a few blocks south of El Prado, greets visitors with a replica of *The Spirit of St. Louis*, Lindbergh's famous plane. Other exhibits cover the whole history of flight, from gliders to space capsules. Nearby, the Automotive Museum is another memorial to transportation.

Theaters. The 580-seat Old Globe Theatre, in a grove behind the California Tower, is part of the Simon Edison Centre for the Performing Arts. The three-theater complex includes an outdoor stage.

The Starlight Bowl, near the open-air Aerospace Museum, presents summer musicals. It's in the flight path for Lindbergh Field, so performers learn to "freeze" when planes pass overhead and resume when they can be heard.

In the Science Center building on El Prado, the Reuben H. Fleet Space Theater's huge, dome-shaped Omnimax screen was the prototype for similar theaters around the world. The screen is a tilted hemisphere; when films shot through a special fish-eye lens are projected onto it, you feel as if you're in the movie.

San Diego Zoo. Simply put, this zoo is extraordinary. More than 3,400 animals, representing some 800 species, roam its lush, 100-acre grounds. But what make this zoo unique are its cleverly designed moated enclosures simulating natural habitats, its rare and exotic inhabitants, and its endangered species breeding programs.

Cuddly koalas cling to eucalyptus branches, Malayan sun bears play in a rain forest, and majestic Sumatran tigers stride through a tropical mist. Colorful flamingos collect on the lagoons, eagles perch high overhead in a giant walk-through aviary, and peacocks strut independently through the grounds of this cageless environment.

In a separate enclosure, the Children's Zoo brings tots nose to nose with the animal kingdom's younger set. Even drinking fountains and restroom facilities are scaled down. Adults, too, crowd around the nursery and the hatchery.

Seeing the entire zoo takes time, careful planning, and plenty of walking. There's no better way to get the lay of the land than to join a guided bus tour. The 3-mile safari saves steps, travels to regions not easily reached by walkers, and introduces visitors to stage-struck animals cued by the driver.

Another way to get around is aboard the Skyfari, an aerial tramway which rises 170 feet over the zoo's grottos and mesas. When you're not spying on the animal activity below, you'll enjoy a fine overview of Balboa Park.

The zoo is open all year from 9 A.M. to dusk (later in summer). A one-price admission package is offered combining entrance fee, bus tour, and aerial tram fees (see page 122).

The zoo has food service, strollers, wheelchairs, and shops.

Mission Bay Aquatic Park

The beautiful bay right on the edge of downtown San Diego has lived through several incarnations since Cabrillo gave it the name "False Bay" after mistaking it for San Diego's harbor. It has gone from a productive estuary to a silt and trash collector to the world's largest municipal aquatic park.

But it took 20 years of community action to create the 4,600-acre playground you see today. Dredging and development transformed Mission Bay into a maze of islands and lagoons, with 27 miles of beaches, free public boat-launching ramps, picnic areas, campgrounds, playgrounds, golf courses, and miles of landscaped coves.

Along the waterfront, the sandy stretches of Mission Bay are protected from the ocean by a narrow jetty of sand. One of the lively beach communities, Pacific Beach, is often compared to the beach town of Venice near Los Angeles.

Attractions. Sea World, a huge water wonderland of aquariums, exhibits, and shows, is Mission Bay's main tourist destination, but water sports of every type are its reason for being. Marinas rent everything from paddle boats to ocean-going sloops.

Several beaches on the 1½-mile waterskiing course are set aside as pickup and landing sites. Anglers try their luck from the shore or aboard sportfishing boats. Catches within the bay include halibut, flounder, bass, croaker, and perch.

For a map of the area and information on its resort hotels, restaurants, camping choices, and recreational facilities, stop by the Mission Bay visitor center just off Interstate 5 at East Mission Bay Drive.

Sea World. This lushly landscaped, 135-acre marine life park on Mission Bay is one of the world's largest oceanariums. Outstanding aquarium exhibits and a variety of water shows make Sea World a good destination for the entire family.

One of the park's finest exhibits is the Penguin Encounter, a climate- and light-controlled environment for some 400 birds. You'll see penguins belly-flopping in the water, waddling along snowbanks, and building rock nests to raise their chicks. Your view is from a moving sidewalk on the warm side of the glass. The catchy exhibit includes a 6-minute film.

Other park "stars" include Baby Shamu—pride of the killer whale clan. At the Forbidden Reef exhibit, you can feed bat rays and get close to moray eels and other intriguing denizens of the deep.

A tram carries visitors up 70 feet over the bay. The 320-foot Sky Tower offers unobstructed views of Mission Bay and San Diego.

The park is open daily from 9 A.M. to dusk (to 11 P.M. in summer). It will take you 8 hours or more if you aim to catch all the shows and view every single exhibit. On summer nights, special shows and a laser light and fireworks display are added, and musicians, mimes, and jugglers stroll the grounds.

A one-price park admission, $22.95 for adults and $16.95 for children 3 to 11 years old, includes all shows and exhibits; parking is free. Rides and a guided 90-minute peek behind the scenes are extra.

Sea World is on the southern edge of Mission Bay Aquatic Park. To get there from Interstate 5, follow Sea World Drive west.

Early morning light warms the wind-carved bluffs at Torrey Pines State Reserve, a coastal preserve north of San Diego set aside to protect some of the world's rarest trees.

La Jolla & the North Coast

Acres of flowers, quaint seaside communities, beaches, luxurious spas and golf courses, missions, and parks are a few of the reasons to explore San Diego's north coast.

La Jolla

A 15-minute drive north on Interstate 5 from the heart of San Diego, La Jolla is really a part of that city. But this region has always had its own personality. Although La Jolla offers a wealth of sporting, shopping, and museum-touring activities, the town does little to invite visitors—and that's part of its appeal.

Most people come to enjoy the Mediterranean-like setting of the scenic site, nestled atop cave-pocked cliffs along 7 miles of curvaceous coastline. According to Indian legend, "jolla" (pronounced hoya) means "hole" or "cave," but the Spanish translation of "jewel" or "gem" is more common.

Exploring the village. Newer high-rise developments to the north and east contrast sharply with the small-town feeling of La Jolla's heart. In the center of the village, art galleries, boutiques, and restaurants line the streets, and architecturally pleasing small hotels welcome guests.

La Jolla is best seen by walking rather than driving—parking places are hard to find, pedestrian traffic is erratic, and the layout of the village is confusing. Although Girard Avenue is the main street, it's more fun to walk along the mile or so of cliffside Prospect Street from the cottage shops and plazas at the north end to the art museum on to the south.

Restaurants along the route often occupy old houses; some offer a sea view. Locals often join visitors in the courtyard cafe of the venerable La Valencia Hotel or nearby in the refurbished Colonial Inn.

The La Jolla Museum of Contemporary Arts (700 Prospect Street) is well worth a stop to view some of California's best contemporary painting,
sculpture, photography, and design. A bookstore and cafe invite loitering. The museum is open Tuesday through Sunday from 10 A.M. to 5 P.M. and Wednesday until 9 P.M. (admission free after 5).

La Jolla's curving streets are somewhat confusing. If you come north from the main part of San Diego, the quickest route to the center of town is west from the Ardath Road exit off Interstate 5.

Recreation. The area's beaches are a magnet; they vary considerably. La Jolla Shores, to the north, is long, flat, and relatively shallow out some distance, ideal for families and surfers. The private La Jolla Beach and Tennis Club marks its southern end.

Sunbathers and swimmers dot scenic La Jolla Cove (below the cliffs in the village center). Snorkelers and beachcombers explore tidepools and coral reefs. An annual Rough Water Swim in September is an exciting international competition. A cliffside walk along the cove offers grand ocean views.

South of Coast Boulevard Park (ideal for expert body surfers) lies Children's Pool, a small beach with a curving breakwater that keeps the surf gentle. At the foot of Bonair Street, Windansea Beach is a favorite with snorkelers (see page 39).

To visit one of the caves in the pockmarked cliffs, go into the curio shop at the end of Coast Boulevard. You'll pay a small admission charge to descend 133 wooden stairs into the cave (not recommended for the infirm).

Cycling is a good way to investigate the town and oceanfront. La Jolla hosts an annual Grand Prix Bicycle Race.

The Golden Triangle. A newer section of La Jolla lies off La Jolla Village Drive east of Interstate 5. Called the Golden Triangle (it's bounded on the east by Interstate 805), this is a high-rise region of offices, condominiums, hotels, restaurants, and shopping malls.

Of particular interest is the extensive collection of folk art from around the world at the Mingei International Museum in Building 1-7 of the University
Towne Centre shopping complex on the south side of La Jolla Village Drive.

Torrey Pines Mesa

The northern edge of La Jolla, a former wilderness thick with groves of eucalyptus and stands of rare pine trees, is the setting for an aquarium, noted golf courses, a hang glider port, and the impressive campus of the University of California at San Diego. From the village, take Torrey Pines Road north to reach the mesa.

Scripps Institution. On the pier north of La Jolla Shores Beach sprawls Scripps Institution of Oceanography, noted for its ocean study and now part of UCSD. An aquarium, open daily from 9 A.M. to 5 P.M., gives visitors a diver's view of aquatic flora and fauna. There's a parking fee, and donations are requested in the museum. The pier itself is not open to the public.

Offshore, San Diego-La Jolla Underwater Park preserves shoreline and underwater life.

Salk Institute. Named for the man who helped vanquish polio, this biological research center near UCSD is conspicuous for its surrealistic architecture. Tours are offered weekdays; phone (619) 453-4100 for times.

Torrey Pines State Reserve. A 1,750-acre preserve protects a gnarled and twisted grove of trees that were growing here when Cabrillo's ships first sighted California. These pines grow only here and on Santa Rosa Island, off the coast of Santa Barbara.

Well-marked trails threading the park lead to cliffs, canyons, and 6 miles of beach. To hike along the ocean, use the park's north entrance off Interstate 5 and consult a tide table to avoid being caught by rising waters.

Torrey Pines Reserve opens at 8 A.M. and closes at 10 P.M. from April to October, 5 P.M. in winter. Admission is free, but there's a charge to park. No picnicking is permitted in the reserve.

...La Jolla & the North Coast

North Coast

Along the coast between Torrey Pines and Oceanside, small towns are interspersed with state and county beaches. To poke around, leave the freeway at Del Mar and follow city streets instead. An inland side trip east of Oceanside takes you to one of California's finest missions and to the town of Fallbrook, heart of the country's avocado-growing region.

Del Mar. Visitors flock to this coastal town for the racing season (late July to mid-September) at Del Mar Thor-oughbred Club, founded by Bing Crosby in the 1930s. Its famed fairgrounds are also the site of the annual county fair in June. For a bird's-eye view of some of its luxurious beachfront homes, take a balloon tour; a number of companies offer flights. Boutiques, galleries, and restaurants overflow the downtown Del Mar Plaza, Camino del Mar at 15th Street.

Rancho Santa Fe. Take Via de la Valle exit inland from Interstate 5 for a pleasant drive around Rancho Santa Fe, originally a Spanish land grant and now graced with estates and horse ranches. Douglas Fairbanks and other movie stars of the 1920s and 30s had homes in the area. Those eucalyptus trees you see everywhere were planted by the Santa Fe Railway in an unsuccessful experiment in using the wood for railroad ties.

Encinitas and Leucadia. Although suburban growth has cut into the flower fields, this region radiates color from May through September. The area is the world's leading grower of poinsettias. The Quail Botanical Gardens, east of Encinitas Boulevard, offers self-guided tours Saturday at 10 A.M.

Carlsbad. In the 19th century, this town built its reputation on its mineral waters. The spring is long gone, but Carlsbad is still noted for spas. Several small hotels have spa facilities; inland, famed La Costa is an elite retreat (see page 125).

Oceanside. Surfers, boaters, and anglers flock to this beach city, San Diego County's third largest. It's the scene of many popular regattas and races. The long wooden pier juts into the sea for 1,900 feet, attracting throngs of fisherfolk; visitors enjoy the view from a restaurant at the end of the pier. At one end of the 4-mile beach lie a large marina and Cape Cod Village, a shopping and dining complex.

Oceanside is the gateway to Camp Pendleton Marine Corps base. Visitors are welcome to drive through part of its grounds. The former ranch of Pio Pico, the last of Mexico's governors, lies within its gates.

Mission San Luis Rey. One of the most impressive restorations in the chain of California missions (see page 6) is just 5 miles east of Oceanside via State 76 (Mission Avenue). Founded in 1789, Mission San Luis Rey was the largest and most populous in the Americas. The mission, still a seminary, is open to the public Monday through Saturday and Sunday afternoon.

Fallbrook. Antique shops and avocado orchards are but two of Fallbrook's delights. Here, too, are cactus and macadamia nurseries, a koi farm, golf courses, and a handful of good restaurants. Pick up a map from the Chamber of Commerce at 300 N. Main Street weekdays, or call (619) 728-5845. From Oceanside, take State 76 east about 15 miles, then South Mission Road 6 miles north.

Border Bargains

Visitors to San Diego have long made the trek south to Tijuana in search of bargains. But now you can find them north of the border as well.

The San Diego Factory Outlet Center lies just half a mile north of the San Ysidro border crossing (14 miles south of downtown San Diego). Among its factory stores are outlets for Bass shoes, Black & Decker, Corning, Gitano, Koala Blue, Mikasa, Nike, Revere, and Van Heusen.

What is a factory outlet? Fairly new to the West, factory outlets are long-time favorites in New England and the South. They're places where name-brand manufacturers sell directly to consumers at cost or just above wholesale prices, allowing discounts of 40% to 70% off retail.

Goods are usually first-quality, surplus items identical to what you'd find in major department stores. To avoid competing with local retailers, outlets usually don't advertise, and several use names different from the familiar products they sell. Izod, Monet, and Ship 'N Shore brands, for instance, are sold at Fashion Flair; Banister Shoe is actually the U.S. Shoe Company, which makes Bandolino, Capezio, Evan Picone, Joyce, Pappagallo, and other well-known brands.

Planning your visit. Most shoppers spend at least half a day at the center, so plan to wear comfortable shoes. Pick up a center map at any store or at the mall's U.S.-Mexico visitor center.

Stores accept personal checks and credit cards. Hours are generally 10 A.M. to 7 P.M. Monday through Saturday, 11 A.M. to 6 P.M. Sunday. Tuesday is typically the lightest shopping day.

Plenty of parking is available at the center and nearby. Several food outlets offer quick dining.

To get to the center, take the last U.S. exit southwest off Interstate 5; then turn right on Camino de la Plaza. The center will be on your right. For additional details, call (619) 690-2999.

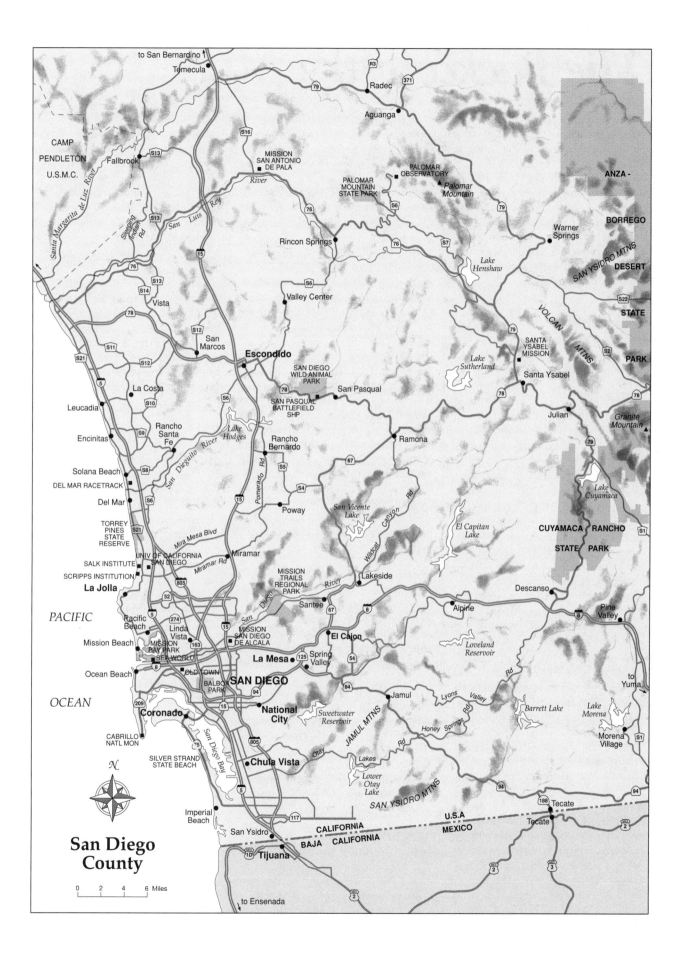

CAMP
PENDLETON
U.S.M.C.

to San Bernardino

Temecula

R3

79

Radec

371

Aguanga

S16

Fallbrook

S13

MISSION
SAN ANTONIO
DE PALA

PALOMAR
OBSERVATORY

PALOMAR
MOUNTAIN
STATE PARK

Palomar
Mountain

ANZA -

BORREGO

S13

River

76

S6

79

Warner
Springs

Santa Margarita de Luz River

Sleeping Indian Rd

San Luis Rey

Rincon Springs

76

S7

Lake
Henshaw

SAN YSIDRO MTNS

DESERT

15

76

S13

S14

Vista

78

S6

Valley Center

79

VOLCAN
MTNS

S22

STATE

S12

San
Marcos

SANTA
YSABEL
MISSION

S2

S11

S21

Escondido

Lake
Sutherland

Santa Ysabel

PARK

5

La Costa

S10

SAN DIEGO
WILD ANIMAL
PARK

S6

78

San Pasqual

78

Leucadia

S9

Rancho
Santa
Fe

Lake
Hodges

SAN PASQUAL
BATTLEFIELD
SHP

Rancho
Bernardo

Julian

79

Granite
Mountain

Encinitas

San Dieguito River

Ramona

Solana Beach

S8

S5

Pomerado Rd

Lake
Cuyamaca

DEL MAR RACETRACK

S6

S4

67

CUYAMACA RANCHO

S1

Del Mar

15

Poway

San Vicente
Lake

Wildcat Canyon Rd

El Capitan
Lake

STATE   PARK

TORREY
PINES
STATE
RESERVE

S21

Mira Mesa Blvd

UNIV OF CALIFORNIA
SAN DIEGO

Miramar

SALK INSTITUTE

Miramar Rd

MISSION
TRAILS
REGIONAL
PARK

River

Lakeside

Descanso

SCRIPPS INSTITUTION

805

Pine
Valley

La Jolla

52

Santee

67

8

Alpine

8

PACIFIC

5

San Diego River

274

Pacific
Beach

Linda
Vista

15

MISSION SAN DIEGO
DE ALCALA

El Cajon

Loveland
Reservoir

Mission Beach

163

MISSION
BAY PARK

La Mesa

125

Spring
Valley

54

to
Yuma

Ocean Beach

8

SEA WORLD

OLD TOWN

SAN DIEGO

94

94

Jamul

Lyons   Valley

Barrett Lake

Lake
Morena

OCEAN

209

BALBOA
PARK

National
City

Sweetwater
Reservoir

JAMUL MTNS

Honey Springs Rd

Rd

94

S1

Coronado

15

805

Rd

Morena
Village

CABRILLO
NATL MON

75

San Diego Bay

Otay

Lakes

SILVER STRAND
STATE BEACH

Chula Vista

Lower
Otay
Lake

SAN YSIDRO MTNS

188

Tecate

94

N

Imperial
Beach

117

U.S.A

Tecate

2

San Ysidro

CALIFORNIA

MEXICO

BAJA   CALIFORNIA

San Diego
County

1D

Tijuana

0   2   4   6 Miles

2

3

to Ensenada

2

The Backcountry

A land of rural charm and historical interest, San Diego's backcountry is full of surprises: wineries, ranches, mining towns, Indian museums, a mountain observatory, and the not-to-be-missed San Diego Wild Animal Park. Camp overnight in a forested state park, unwind around Escondido, or check into a time-mellowed gold-country hotel. Some of the region's highlights might be sampled in a day, but two or three days could go by rapidly.

Escondido

It's about a 40-minute drive north from San Diego on Interstate 15 to the charming city of Escondido. En route, red tile roofs are all you can see of the resort community of Rancho Bernardo from the freeway. But it's worth turning off just to visit the Mercado, an enclave of some 40 art and craft shops, studios, and restaurants. Weekends are lively.

In and around Escondido. Popularity came late to Escondido, but in the last few years the city's population has almost doubled (currently 100,000). Lawrence Welk liked Escondido so much that he built a resort here around his mobile home and added a theater, motel, restaurant, and three public golf courses. The complex is off Interstate 15 a few miles northeast of town; exit north on Mountain Meadow Road.

Near Escondido's new Civic and Cultural Center, Grape Day Park holds some of the city's relocated historic buildings: its first library (now a museum), a turn-of-the-century barn and windmill, a Victorian-era ranch house, and the 1888 Santa Fe railroad depot. The buildings, located at 321 N. Broadway, are open Thursday through Saturday afternoons.

Wine country. Escondido is in the center of a wine-growing region, and more than a dozen wineries nearby welcome visitors with tours and tastings. Three are south of the city along Interstate 15; the others cluster about 30 miles north around Rancho California Road, east of Temecula.

Ferrara Winery, the county's oldest, is a state historical site. The tasting room (1120 W. 15th Avenue) is open 9 A.M. to 5 P.M. weekdays and 10 A.M. to 5:30 P.M. on weekends. You can pick up a sandwich at the deli and enjoy the vineyard view from the patio pavilion.

You can picnic under a grape arbor after touring and tasting at Thomas Jaeger Winery (13455 San Pasqual Road); bring your own lunch, or pick up the makings here. The winery is open daily from 10 A.M. to 5 P.M. Culbertson Vineyard & Winery (32575 Rancho California Road) also boasts a charming cafe and a visitor center.

San Pasqual Battlefield State Historic Park. On State 78 about 8 miles east of Escondido (next to San Diego Wild Animal Park) is the site of one of the least-known battles in U.S. history, and almost the only one fought in the conquest of California. A 10-minute video at the visitor center depicts the December 6, 1846 struggle between General Pico's native California troops and General Kearney's U.S. Army. The U.S. troops lost in what historians call the bloodiest battle of the Mexican War.

San Diego Ostrich Ranch. Also on San Pasqual Valley Road (State 78) you can commune with an ostrich, the world's largest bird. There's no charge to view these ungainly creatures. One warning: They love to peck at objects like glasses and earrings, so don't stand too close.

Bates Bros. Nut Farm. Pack a lunch and follow County Road S6 about 8 miles north from Escondido to reach this Valley Center site (15954 Woods Valley Road). The farm's huge retail store displays nuts from all over the world, along with jams, jellies, and candies. Visitors can tour a processing plant, pet farm animals, and picnic.

Deer Park Vineyard. You won't find deer at this attraction north of Escondido off Interstate 15 (29013 Champagne Boulevard). But you can see some vintage automobiles, do a little wine tasting, or have a picnic lunch.

West of town. State 78 heads west of Escondido to reach the coast near Carlsbad. If you get hungry along the way, stop in the town of San Marcos (about 5 miles west of Interstate 15). Old California Restaurant Row here offers plenty of dining options at 12 ethnic restaurants (1020 San Marcos Boulevard), and an open-air market takes place on Saturday afternoon.

Turn north on Santa Fe Avenue in nearby Vista to reach the Southwestern Antique Gas & Steam Engine Museum in hilly Guajome Park (also the site of a historic adobe). The threshers, binders, and other early farm equipment you see on display rev up in June and October for a Threshing Bee and Antique Engine Show. For further details, call (619) 565-3600.

San Diego Wild Animal Park

This innovative wild animal preserve was developed as a breeding ground for the San Diego Zoo and a sanctuary for rare and endangered species. On 1,800 acres resembling African veldt and Asian plain, more than 2,500 animals representing 240 species roam almost as freely as they would in their native habitats. This compares with 3,400 animals on the parent zoo's 100 acres.

Visitors are kept mostly at a distance so they won't disturb the animals. A narrated monorail tour quietly skirts the park perimeter, offering glimpses of elephants, water buffaloes, lions, leopards, wildebeests, rhinos, zebras, and other creatures. The 5-mile tour takes about 50 minutes.

A couple of tips: The right side of the tram affords best viewing. Bring a pair of binoculars, and try to schedule your ride in early morning or late afternoon when the animals are most active and visible.

Another viewing opportunity is to join a photo safari and be driven right into the herds on a flat-bed truck. These caravans are expensive—about $50 per passenger.

*Yesteryear's furnishings overflow an antique store's yard in bucolic downtown Julian,
a turn-of-the-century mining town noted today for its wildflowers and apple orchards.*

...Backcountry

A 1½-mile walking trail offers spectacular vistas for animal observation and photography as well as picnicking sites. Exhibits near the park entrance include a lowland gorilla grotto, a free-flight aviary, and an animal nursery. Animal shows are scheduled throughout the day.

Gardeners will enjoy the park's landscaping. An interesting 1-acre water-wise garden displays a variety of "unthirsty" plants.

The park is open from 9 A.M. to dusk daily; summer hours include some night tours. The ticket price, which includes entrance, monorail tours, animal shows, and exhibits, is $14.50 for adults and $7.50 for children 3 to 15. For detailed information, call (619) 234-6541.

To reach the park from Escondido, head east on State 78 (San Pasqual Valley Road); from San Diego, take Interstate 15 north and Via Rancho Parkway exit east onto San Pasqual Valley Road and follow the signs.

Pala Mission

In a tranquil river valley on State 76 about 5 miles east of Interstate 15 stands Mission San Antonio de Pala, a branch of Mission San Luis Rey (see page 72). This is the only original chapel building in the entire mission chain still used by American Indians as a church and chapel.

Built in 1815, the mission is adorned with frescoes and has an attractive campanile. Behind the mission rears Tourmaline Queen Mountain, once teeming with miners.

Palomar Observatory

Southeast of Pala, State 76 winds through Pauma Valley to the turnoff for Palomar Observatory, some 5 miles beyond Rincon Springs. It's a twisting but scenic 11½-mile drive up Palomar Mountain through chaparral- and rock-covered countryside.

High atop the mountain lie the great white dome of the 13-story observatory, operated by the California Institute of Technology, and a museum and exhibit hall. A self-guided tour briefs you on the workings of one of the country's largest telescopes.

The observatory is open daily from 9 A.M. to 4 P.M. You may want to wear a sweater; the interior of the dome must be kept at nighttime temperatures, since even a few degrees of variation can cause distortion.

From the road to the observatory, turn west to reach Palomar Mountain State Park (hiking, picnicking, camping). Vehicles with heavy loads should approach the observatory and park from the Lake Henshaw turnoff to the southeast, a more gradual incline.

Santa Ysabel

The white stucco chapel of Mission Santa Ysabel was rebuilt in 1924 in the style of the original 1818 mission (see page 6). Five Indian reservations still use it. A donation is suggested to tour.

Santa Ysabel's old general store, at the crossroads of State 78 and State 79, supposedly dates back to 1870. State 78 leads west into Anza-Borrego Desert State Park (see page 88).

Julian

High in the pine- and oak-covered hills, the tiny gold-rush town of Julian was once the county's second largest. A strike in 1870 briefly created a boom; at its end, the town settled comfortably into an agricultural and ranching existence. Julian is 7 miles southeast of Santa Ysabel where State 78 and State 79 again separate.

Main Street retains its original false-front buildings and wooden sidewalks. The refurbished Julian Hotel, circa 1887, and a host of bed-and-breakfast inns, many in old houses clinging to hillside sites, welcome guests. Other historic buildings house the stage stop and post office, a onetime jail, and an old-fashioned soda fountain.

Julian is famous for its apples; several bakeries and almost every restaurant in town make apple pies. Apple Day, the first weekend in October, naturally attracts crowds of visitors. But so do the Wildflower Show in spring and the autumn Weed Show. For information, contact the Julian Chamber of Commerce (see page 58).

Pioneer Museum. You can rediscover some of Julian's legendary artifacts—for starters, its first bathtub and oldest pool table—at the town's restored Pioneer Museum. The eclectic exhibits also include one of the state's finest lace collections, practical wedding gowns from the 1800s, a bookcase belonging to President Ulysses Grant, and a 1920s permanent wave machine that closely resembles an electric chair. Gold-mining equipment and a cider press are more recent additions.

The museum, located at 2811 Washington Street (off State 78/79 two blocks south of the town center) is open 10 A.M. to 4 P.M. daily (weekends only in winter). A $1 donation is suggested.

Gold mines. The George Washington Mine, the first in the area, can still be reached by a footpath from the end of Washington Street. The mine is closed, but you can look into a reconstructed assay office and blacksmith shop.

Guided 1½-hour tours of another mine, the Eagle, are offered daily from 9 A.M. to 4 P.M. ($6 adults, $4 children). To reach the mine, take C Street east from town and follow the signs.

Cuyamaca Rancho State Park

A wilderness of rugged mountain terrain and intermittent streams, Cuyamaca Rancho State Park is blessed with a wealth of seasonal wildflowers and bird and animal life. The big park (24,677 acres) about 40 miles east of urban San Diego is popular with hikers, horseback riders, and campers.

Peaks jutting 4,000 to 6,500 feet are cloaked in dense forests of ponderosa and Jeffrey pine, fir, incense cedar, and live and black oak. Views from here extend as far as the ocean to the west and the desert to the east.

Formerly an Indian gathering place and then a Spanish rancho, the park gets its name from a Spanish translation of an old Indian word for "the place where it rains." Exhibits at the park headquarters depict activities of early-day settlers.

To reach the park from San Diego, head east on Interstate 8 and turn north on State 79.

Mexico, just a few minutes away from San Diego, lures many of the city's tourists. For shopping and sports, Tijuana is a favorite day trip. Plan a longer stay to explore the border towns of Tecate and Mexicali and the charming seaport of Ensenada, south of Tijuana.

No passports are required to visit Mexico. You won't even need a tourist card unless you plan to stay longer than 72 hours or go more than 75 miles south of the border (the destinations described here are all within the limit).

Tijuana. Mexico's most-visited city has made an effort to clean up its tawdry, raffish image. Crown jewel of the new look is the Tijuana Cultural Center at Paseo de los Heroes and Avenida Independencia north of downtown.

The complex has a fine museum, shops displaying handicrafts from all over the country, and a performing arts center. A small fee admits you to the spherical Omnitheater's film on Mexican history and culture, shown in English daily at 2 P.M.

Most of Tijuana's tourist shops and restaurants are around a 7-block stretch of spruced-up Avenida Revolucion downtown. Here, too, is Fronton Palacio, home for fast-paced jai alai.

Horse and dog racing takes place at Agua Caliente Racetrack evenings and weekends; bull rings offer corridas from mid-May to mid-September. And golfers and tennis enthusiasts are welcome at Tijuana's country club. Call Tijuana Visitors Bureau, (619) 298-4105, for details on sports, or stop by an information booth at the border or on Avenida Revolucion.

Ensenada. Todos Santos Bay 66 miles south of Tijuana is the setting for Ensenada, a casually charming resort town, sportfishing center, and port for several cruise ships. Shops, small hotels, restaurants, and boat rental offices line Lopez Mateos, the main street.

For details on daily tours of Bodegas de Santo Tomas, the country's largest winery, check with the tourist office at Avenida Lopez Mateos 13-B. The government-sponsored Centro Artesanal de Ensenada next door has a good craft display.

South of town, Estero Beach attracts swimmers and surfers; La Bufadora blowhole is another 14 miles. A rustic hot springs lies 10 miles inland.

Tecate. This small, simple, clean town's primary attractions are a brewery and nearby Rancho La Puerta spa. Stop by the tourist office on the south side of the plaza on Callejon Libertad for a visitor's guide.

Mexicali. A cultural tour of Baja California's state capital might include stops at the university's regional museum (Avenida Reforma and Calle L) and the former state governor's residence (Avenida Alvaro Obregon 1209), where a gallery displays works of Mexican artists.

Most visitors come for a day to wander around shops and dine at restaurants near the border. Zona Rosa, next to the Civic Commercial Center on Calzada Independencia at the southern edge of the city, is an attractive shopping and dining area.

Mexicali hosts colorful charreadas (Mexican rodeos) once a month in the winter and twice-monthly bullfights during the winter and on holidays.

Shopping tips. From piñatas and bright paper flowers to furniture and fine silver jewelry—Mexico's handicrafts are attractive and comparatively inexpensive. Duty-free stores display European perfumes, clothing, and crystal.

U.S. currency is accepted happily anywhere along the border. Most stores offer discounts for cash. Bring small bills; getting change can be a problem. Bargaining is the name of the game in markets. Elsewhere, stores have set prices.

U.S. Customs allows each person to bring back $400 in goods without duty (including 1 liter of alcohol, if you're over 21) each 30 days. Handicrafts are usually duty free.

Driving in Mexico. Most motorists enter Mexico at the Tijuana-San Ysidro crossing. To avoid the usual long lines, returning travelers often use the less busy crossing at Otay Mesa just east of Tijuana's airport. To reach that crossing from the U.S. side, take State 17 east from Interstate 5 or 805.

Tecate's port of entry (closed midnight to 6 A.M.) is 32 miles southeast of San Diego off State 94. The Mexicali crossing is through Calexico, about 2 hours east of San Diego via Interstate 8.

Exercise caution when driving in Mexico; an automobile accident is a criminal offense for which you can be detained until claims are adjusted. Your U.S. automobile insurance is not valid in Mexico; it's a good idea to buy a short-term policy from a Mexican insurance firm on your way to the border.

If you're only going to Tijuana, you can easily park your car in San Ysidro, walk across the border, and catch a cab downtown.

Public transportation. Taking the trolley to the border is fun and inexpensive (currently $1.50). Trolleys between downtown San Diego and San Ysidro run daily from 5 A.M. to 1 A.M.

Frequent Greyhound and Mexicoach service also connect San Diego with Mexico's border towns.

Desert Destinations

*S*outhern California's deserts are a surprise. Seemingly barren stretches of sand and cactus, they hide a wealth of plants and animals and a whole range of visitor activities. You can wind-surf on man-made lakes, rock-hunt in hidden valleys, and explore scenic old mining towns and deep underground caverns. Or you can opt for poolside sunning and rounds of golf at world-class resorts and spas, glamorous counterpoints to the sparse desert surroundings.

Throughout most of the year the desert possesses a desolate grandeur, but in spring it comes alive in an unforgettable explosion of color. The natural beauty of this blooming landscape is preserved in several state and national parks, from Antelope Valley's California Poppy Reserve to the East Mojave National Scenic Area.

Lay of the land

A collection of glittering resort communities—often called the Sunshine Strip—lines the Coachella Valley from Palm Springs southeast to Indio. The area's popularity is nothing new: the Cahuilla Indians were lured here centuries ago by its warm springs and the sheltering palm oases in the San Jacinto Mountains that rise to the west.

North and south of the valley sprawl two grand desert preserves, Joshua Tree and Anza-Borrego. Their time-carved

Resembling giant desert candles, blossoming yuccas stretch skyward against a backdrop of granite boulders at Joshua Tree National Monument. This unique high and low desert park lies northeast of Palm Springs.

canyons and wind-blown mesas reveal the subtle differences between high and low deserts.

To the southeast lies Salton Sea, a getaway for swimmers, boaters, anglers, campers, and bird-watchers. Eastward, where the Colorado River forms the California-Arizona border, the dams that tamed the river created lakes that beckon boaters and waterskiers.

The immense Mojave Desert encompasses much of southeastern California. Within this great high desert you'll find everything from ghost towns to Edwards Air Force Base, landing site for NASA space flights.

Planning a visit

Among the great virtues of this vast land is that it seems far removed from more populous regions, yet it's easy to reach from anywhere in Southern California. And it offers get-away-from-it-all experiences to suit a variety of tastes, from camping under the stars to relaxing at some of the state's finest accommodations.

When to go. The desert's magnet is its climate, especially from mid-October to mid-May. Days are generally sunny, warm, and cloudless, the air dry. Winter temperatures are comfortable, 70° to 90° during the day; nights can dip to 25°, although 40° is more usual. In summer, daytime temperatures hover around 100° or more, but low humidity makes it bearable. Rainfall is scant, falling mostly in brief storms from November through April. Spring and autumn usually have good weather, fewer people, and reduced room rates.

Getting around. Interstate 10 is L.A.'s main escape route to Palm Springs (120 miles) and other Coachella Valley oases. Interstate 15 stretches along the

northern edge of the East Mojave National Scenic Area en route to Las Vegas, and Interstate 40 skirts the southern edge on its way from Barstow to Needles. State 14 gives access to the Mojave's western edge.

Even though the desert's largest cities have commercial plane and bus service, you need a vehicle to do much exploring. Palm Springs, gateway to Coachella Valley resorts, is served by national and commuter airlines.

Lodging. Coachella Valley offers the desert's widest choice of lodging, from well-landscaped RV parks to deluxe megaresorts (see page 84). Elsewhere, you'll find the most motels and services at Lancaster/Palmdale, Victorville, Barstow, Needles, and Blythe.

Contacts

These agencies offer information on attractions and accommodations. See additional contacts throughout this chapter.

Palm Springs Desert Resorts Convention & Visitors Bureau
69-930 Highway 111, Suite 201
Rancho Mirage, CA 92270
(619) 770-9000

Desert Information Center
408 E. Fredericks St.
Barstow, CA 92311
(619) 256-8617

California Deserts Tourism Association
P.O. Box 364
Rancho Mirage, CA 92270
(619) 328-9256

The Sunshine Strip

Green golf courses and turquoise swimming pools, palm trees and tennis courts, Bob Hope and Frank Sinatra—to many, these symbolize the air-conditioned, irrigated continuum of resort communities from Palm Springs to Indio. But traces of the Coachella Valley's early days can still be found in mountain canyons and pioneer adobes, commercial date groves, and elegant old resorts.

Palm Springs may be the best known of the desert resort communities, but the 20-mile stretch of State 111 between "The Springs" and Indio boasts the valley's newest shopping and entertainment complexes as well as many of its most popular retreats. Desert Hot Springs, a few miles north of Palm Springs, has long been a spa setting.

How it all began

An ancient lake that filled the Coachella Valley for centuries began receding around 1500. The Cahuilla Indians, who had depended on the lake for fish, found other sources of food and adapted to the new environment. Some Cahuillas still live around the valley, many at nearby Morongo and Agua Caliente reservations. They also own prime valley real estate, such as the bubbling hot springs under the Spa Hotel & Mineral Springs in Palm Springs (corner of Tahquitz–McCallum Way and Indian Avenue).

The region first gained its reputation as a health spa about a century ago. Those first valley resorts were short on luxury; dry air was the elixir they promoted.

In the 1920s and 30s, the area became a refuge for the rich and famous. Hollywood celebrities like Greta Garbo, Clark Gable, and Errol Flynn patronized La Quinta Hotel when it opened in 1926. Now this hostelry 15 miles southeast of Palm Springs—the valley's oldest still in operation—has been transformed into a chic resort famous for its golf courses.

The presence of celebrities is still very much felt in these desert resort towns.

Streets, public buildings, and sports events bear their names, and tour buses patrol their neighborhoods to give visitors a glimpse of how they live.

Activities

A surprising diversity of activity welcomes valley visitors: golf, tennis, horseback riding, cycling, swimming, picnicking, hiking, ice skating, and hot-air ballooning. Spas offer extensively equipped health clubs. For a complete listing of facilities, contact the Palm Springs Desert Resorts Convention & Visitors Bureau (see page 79).

Spectators can watch California Angels spring training baseball games, polo matches, tennis tournaments, and almost 200 golf tournaments a year, including the prestigious Bob Hope Classic (January), Dinah Shore LPGA Championship (April), and Skins Game (November).

Musical and theatrical performances are presented in Palm Desert at the Bob Hope Cultural Center and the College of the Desert, and in Palm Springs at the convention center and the Walter Annenberg Theatre.

A world of shopping awaits along Palm Canyon Drive in Palm Springs and on El Paseo, 2 miles of trendy boutiques and galleries in Palm Desert.

Exploring the valley

For an all-encompassing valley view, soar aloft in a hot-air balloon or go sightseeing by helicopter or plane. Several companies offer rides; check the Yellow Pages for phone numbers.

Desert Off-Road Adventures offers a 3-hour jeep safari of the Coachella Valley backcountry, wandering some 20 miles through Indian canyons and past a bighorn sheep reserve. For information and prices, call (619) 773-3187.

Two companies offer tours past stars' homes and other attractions along the Sunshine Strip. The longer tours are a good introduction to historic landmarks, museums, parks, and shopping areas. One-hour tours focus on the most

popular sights: the huge hedged estates of Walter Annenberg and Frank Sinatra, the discreet homes of Goldie Hawn and Lena Horne, and Bob Hope's spaceship-shaped abode.

Gray Line Tours, (619) 325-0974, has daily 2½-hour bus tours at 9:30 A.M. and 1:30 P.M. from October through May 15. Celebrity Tours, (619) 325-2682, has 1- and 2-hour bus tours daily. Call for times. Both pick up at major hotels and other locations.

Palm Springs

It's easy to find your way around Palm Springs. State 111, the exit off Interstate 10 to Palm Springs, becomes Palm Canyon Drive, the city's main street (one-way heading south). Indian Avenue, a block east, runs one-way north through the central part of the "village." Tahquitz–McCallum Way is the dividing line for north and south street numbering.

Balmy winter weather often means bumper-to-bumper traffic and scarce parking in the busy downtown area. To avoid these headaches, hop aboard the Sun Trolley shuttle that loops through the village between 9 A.M. and 7 P.M. from November through May. Fare is 50 cents.

Palm Springs is also the departure point for an aerial tramway into the San Jacinto Mountains—see page 85.

Village Green Heritage Center. For a peek at Palm Springs' past, visit this collection of pioneer buildings at 221 S. Palm Canyon Drive. The center includes Cornelia White's pioneer railroad-tie house (originally part of the valley's first hotel), McCallum Adobe (home of the city founder), and Ruddy's General Store Museum (a re-creation of a typical general store of the 1930s).

Hours are noon to 3 P.M. Wednesday and Sunday, 10 A.M. to 4 P.M. Thursday, Friday, and Saturday from mid-October through May. The rest of the year, the buildings are open weekends only, noon to 6 P.M. There's a small fee to enter each building.

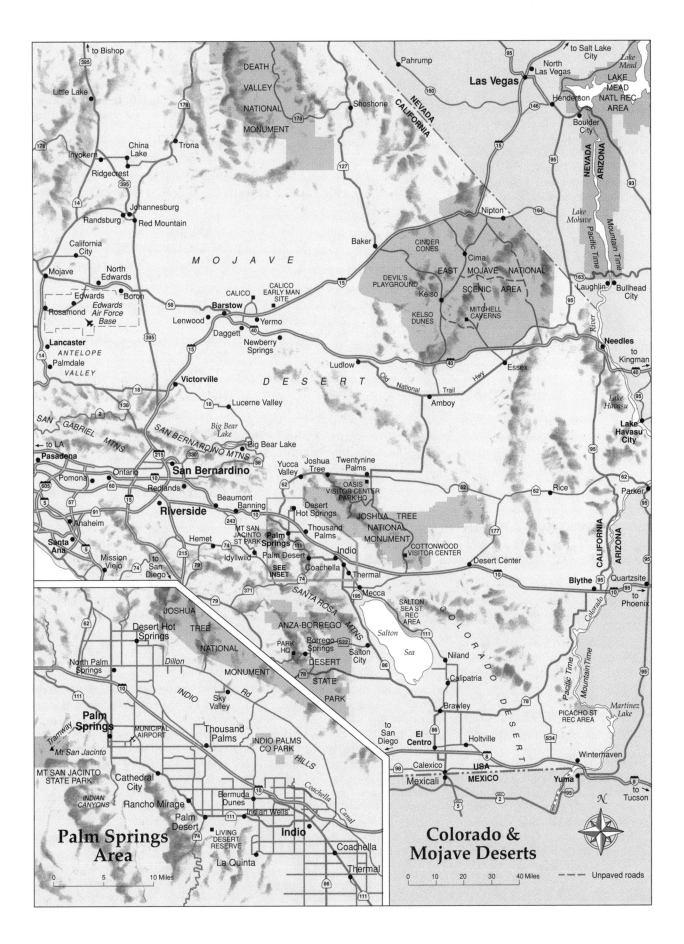

...Sunshine Strip

Desert Museum. Don't miss seeing the handsome museum and cultural center at 101 Museum Drive, behind the Desert Fashion Plaza. One wing displays Western art, the other contemporary. A natural sciences section concentrates on the desert environment and Indian culture. The landscaped sculpture gardens are worth a look.

The museum is open 10 A.M. to 4 P.M. Tuesday through Friday, to 5 on weekends (closed Monday and in summer). Admission is free on the first Tuesday of each month.

Moorten Botanical Garden. A stroll through this private preserve gives you a good look at desert plantings and wildlife. The 4-acre garden displays more than 2,000 unusual specimens from arid regions around the world, and some of them create surprisingly verdant spots. Benches provide a place to sit and watch the birds.

Located at 1701 S. Palm Canyon Drive, the garden is open daily from 9 A.M. to 5 P.M. (small admission fee).

Oasis Water Resort. Children of all ages combat desert heat with a visit to the 21-acre Oasis Water Resort, 1500 Gene Autry Trail. One of the biggest of the Southland's water parks, it operates daily from March through early September and on weekends through October, opening at 11 A.M. and closing at 6 P.M. in spring and autumn, 8 P.M. in summer.

Admission is $14.95 for anyone taller than 60 inches, $9.95 for those 40 to 60 inches, less after 5 P.M. There's an additional charge for parking.

Desert Hot Springs

As the name denotes, activity in this popular resort revolves around its mineral spas. The gushing springs, which can reach temperatures of 207°, are cooled to under 110° for therapeutic and recreational uses.

Spas. The most famous of the area's spas is Two Bunch Palms (see page 84), once a hideaway for Al Capone. Its waters are open only to guests at the resort, but many others are open to the public. For information, contact the Chamber of Commerce, 13560 Palm Drive, Desert Hot Springs, CA 92240; (800) 346-3347 in California, (619) 329-6403 outside the state.

Cabot's Old Indian Pueblo Museum. The desert has long attracted its share of eccentrics, and Cabot Yerxa was one of them. His unconventional home and unusual memorabilia are now a museum.

In 1913, Yerxa walked into the valley with a quart of water and a paper bag of food. His pueblo, inspired by Indian architecture, is largely the work of his own imagination. The cement and adobe maze has 35 tiny rooms with 150 windows pieced together from odd-shaped glass.

Scattered throughout the house are such exotic mementos as an 8-foot stuffed brown bear, pictures of prospector Yerxa in Alaska with his friend Theodore Roosevelt, and an Indian medicine man's vestments made from elk skin and human hair.

The museum, 67-616 E. Desert View Avenue, is open 9:30 A.M. to 4:30 P.M. daily except Tuesday. You pay a small fee and get an informal tour.

Palm Desert

This resort town midway along the Sunshine Strip is beginning to rival Palm Springs for shopping, sports, culture, and attractions. The Palm Desert Town Center (State 111 at Monterey Avenue) boasts large department stores, more than 100 shops, and an all-year indoor ice-skating rink. The College of the Desert and the Bob Hope Cultural Center host many special events.

Aerie Sculpture Garden and Gallery. Part nature preserve, part artists' showplace, this 2½-acre Palm Desert garden combines native plants with some 40 sculptures created from metal, acrylic, and stained glass. A free pamphlet maps the route along a ⅓-mile trail. The reflecting pool and plant misters attract bighorn sheep, raccoons, eagles, and ravens.

Aerie is open 1 to 4 P.M. Friday through Monday and by appointment; call (619) 568-6366. Admission is $2.50. To reach the garden, drive south 2½ miles on State 74; turn on Cahuilla Way,

Desert Driving

Desert travel should be an adventure, but don't let a breakdown or extreme weather conditions turn it into a disaster. If you aren't familiar with backcountry desert driving, here are some precautions you should take:

■ Give friends a copy of your itinerary and date of return.

■ Carry at least a gallon of drinking water per day per person; bring extra for vehicles.

■ Wear layered clothing. It slows dehydration and minimizes exposure in hot weather, insulates you in cold weather.

■ Don't count on being able to pick up supplies beyond the last town, or find help fast in case of trouble. Carry extra food and gas. Take first-aid gear and a sleeping bag.

■ Always travel with a good map. Desert map sources include the American Automobile Association (free to members), U.S. Geological Survey (Box 25286, Federal Center, Denver, CO 80225), and Bureau of Land Management (1695 Spruce Street, Riverside, CA 92507).

■ Road conditions can change rapidly in bad weather. Before setting out, always check with a local source such as a park ranger.

*Acres of golf courses carpet the Coachella Valley between Palm Springs and Indio,
like this one at Marriott's Desert Springs Resort in Palm Desert. East of the desert playground, the abruptly rising San Jacinto Mountains are often snowcapped in winter.*

83

...Sunshine Strip

north on Cat Canyon Road, and west on Cholla Way to Aerie Road.

Living Desert. A 1,200-acre wild animal park and botanical garden re-creates the flora and fauna of eight different desert habitats. You'll see big-horn sheep, Arabian oryx, coyotes, and reptiles. Bats and other creatures active at night inhabit a special display.

An ethnobotanical garden contains plants used by Native Americans for food, fiber, soap, and other purposes. Another section of the reserve features Joshua trees and other high-desert succulents. All areas are described in a trail guide.

The Living Desert sanctuary, at 47900 S. Portola Avenue, is about 1½ miles south of State 111. It's open 9 A.M. to 5 P.M. daily from September through mid-June. Admission is $5 for adults, $2 for children 3 to 15.

Indio

Early Coachella Valley date farmers envisioned a scene straight from Morocco—endless rows of date palms swaying in desert breezes. Towns were dubbed Arabia, Mecca, and Oasis. The communities that remain don't exactly present the Byzantine image their founders intended. But the date industry has thrived, and dates are such a major crop southeast of Indio that the town is often dubbed the date capital of the nation.

State 111 in western Indio is the "Date Strip." Groves alternate with date stores adorned with brightly painted plywood pavilions and Moorish cupolas. Here's your chance to buy a fancy gift pack or try a date milkshake. At Shields Date Gardens, you can watch a film on the love life of a date or wander through a fine rose garden.

National Date Festival. This popular week-long event in mid-February began in 1921 as an effort to bring tourism to the valley. Held in connection with the Riverside County Fair, festivities include a national horse show, an Arabian Nights pageant, and some hilarious ostrich and camel races.

Coachella Valley Museum. The city's tidy museum and cultural center at 82-616 Miles Avenue is housed in a small, cool adobe that was a doctor's home and office in the 1920s. Exhibits include Cahuilla Indian artifacts and old farm and household equipment.

From autumn through spring, the museum is open 10 A.M. to 4 P.M. Tuesday through Saturday, noon to 4 Sunday; in summer, it's open weekends only. Visitors pay a small fee to tour.

Desert Oases

Each new desert resort built along the Sunshine Strip (Highway 111 between Palm Springs and Indio) seems more plush than the last. Surrounded by green fairways and boasting glamorous spa, tennis, and dining facilities, these self-contained retreats might be worth an occasional splurge.

As examples of what you'll find in top-of-the-line lodging, we list one deluxe resort from each community. For a listing of all area accommodations, contact Palm Springs Desert Resorts Convention & Visitors Bureau (see page 79).

Listings below include published rates for double rooms during the peak winter season; check for latest information. Rates are usually reduced in spring and autumn; they often drop as much as 50 percent in summer.

DoubleTree Resort (formerly Desert Princess Resort), Vista Chino at Landau (P.O. Box 1644), Palm Springs, CA 92263; (619) 322-7000. Facilities: 289 units, 2 restaurants, pool and spa, 10 tennis courts, 2 racquetball courts, 18 holes golf, rental bikes. Rates: $195–$220.

Hyatt Grand Champions Resort, 44-600 Indian Wells Lane, Indian Wells, CA 92210; (619) 341-1000. Facilities: 336 units, 3 restaurants, 4 pools, health club, 12 tennis courts, tennis stadium, 36 holes golf. Rates: $220–$325.

Indian Palms Resort & Country Club, 48-630 Monroe Street, Indio, CA 92201; (619) 347-0688. Facilities: 59 units, 2 restaurants, small pool and spa, 9 tennis courts, 27 holes golf. Rates: $64–$74.

La Quinta Hotel Golf & Tennis Resort, 49-499 Eisenhower Drive (P.O. Box 69), La Quinta, CA 92253; (619) 564-4111. Facilities: 640 casitas, 5 restaurants, 25 pools and 35 spas, 30 tennis courts, 36 holes golf. Rates: $195–$285.

Marriott's Desert Springs Resort & Spa, 74-855 Country Club Drive, Palm Desert, CA 92260; (619) 341-2211. Facilities: 891 units, 5 restaurants, 3 lagoon-sized pools, health spa, 18 tennis courts, 36 holes golf. Rates: $235–$330.

Ritz-Carlton, Rancho Mirage, 68-900 Frank Sinatra Drive, Rancho Mirage, CA 92270; (619) 321-8282. Facilities: 238 units, 3 restaurants, pool, health club, 10 tennis courts. Rates: $275–$395.

Two Bunch Palms, 67-425 Two Bunch Palms Trail, Desert Hot Springs, CA 92240; (619) 329-8791. Facilities: 44 villas, restaurant, mineral springs, tanning bins, mud baths, pool, 2 tennis courts, mountain bikes. Rates: $100–$365.

Into the Mountains

When days warm up in the Coachella Valley, residents and visitors alike head for the nearby mountains to picnic in the lush canyons behind Palm Springs or ride a tram up to the cool wilderness area around Mount San Jacinto.

The craggy ramparts of the San Jacintos rise abruptly from near sea level to 10,084 feet. Although the tram is the most dramatic way to reach their upper reaches, you can also get there by way of Banning (Interstate 10 to State 243) or via Riverside and Hemet (Interstate 215 to State 74 to State 243).

Jumping-off spot for exploring the upper Jacintos by car or foot is the forested community of Idyllwild southwest of Palm Springs, where you'll find hotels, motels, restaurants, camping supplies, pack and saddle stock.

Indian canyons

The scenic canyons tucked into the folds of the mountains behind Palm Springs have been the traditional summer retreat of the Cahuilla Indians for centuries. Today the canyons attract hikers, horseback riders, bird-watchers, and photographers as well.

A toll road through the Agua Caliente Indian Reservation gives access to the canyons. Follow Palm Canyon Drive south to the reservation, about 5 miles from the heart of Palm Springs. The toll gate is open daily from 9 A.M. to 4 P.M. except in summer (usually mid-May to mid-October), when the hazard of fire is too extreme.

The road into the canyons is narrow and winding; the last half-mile requires cautious driving. For further information, call the local Bureau of Indian Affairs office, (619) 325-2086.

Palm Canyon. This 14-mile-long canyon 7 miles beyond the toll gate is noted for its fine stands of Washingtonia palms, many of them more than 1,500 years old. You can view the canyon from above at Hermit's Bench parking area (souvenirs, soft drinks, rest rooms) or from a steep trail that drops down into the canyon.

For a pleasant day's outing, bring a picnic lunch; there are tables but no drinking water. A trail, popular with horseback riders, winds through the palm groves.

Andreas Canyon. Beyond Palm Canyon, the parking area for Andreas Canyon lies half a mile off the main road in a grove of shady sycamores and cottonwoods (picnic tables, rest rooms). A particularly impressive grove of native California fan palms stands nearby. A trail follows an all-year stream about 4 miles to the head of the canyon.

Murray Canyon. Hidden between Andreas and Palm, Murray Canyon is accessible by hiking trail from Andreas Canyon. It's also popular with horseback riders. Most of the year a clear stream flows through the canyon.

Aerial tramway

To beat the heat on the valley floor, catch a tram to the top of Mount San Jacinto, where the air is pine scented and the temperatures are some 40° cooler. The trip up the mountain begins in rugged Chino Canyon at the north edge of Palm Springs. Valley views are spectacular on the 14-minute climb, but try to plan your trip for a clear day; a desert haze will obscure the view.

At the top. The two 80-passenger trams move up and down one of the sheerest mountains in North America, over granite recesses deeper than the Grand Canyon. The mountain station, 8,516 feet above the valley floor, has a restaurant (open for lunch and dinner), a gift shop, and an observation deck. A free movie shows you how the tram was built in the early 1960s.

From the mountain station, it's a 6-mile hike to the summit of Mount San Jacinto. A paved trail also leads down to Long Valley, a popular picnic site. Mules can be rented to make the trek in summer. During winter, the valley welcomes cross-country skiers.

At the base. To get to the tram, take State 111 north from Palm Springs and follow the signs. Gray Line offers bus service.

Tram rides begin at 10 A.M. Monday through Friday, 8 A.M. weekends and holidays. In summer, the last trip leaves the valley at 9 P.M. and returns at 10:45 P.M. The rest of the year, the last trip is 7:30 P.M., the return at 9:15 P.M. The tram closes for two weeks of maintenance on the first Monday in August.

Round-trip admission for the 2½-mile ride is $13.95, $8.95 for children 3 to 12. You can carry hiking or backpacking gear at no extra charge.

Mount San Jacinto State Park

This mountainous state park and wilderness area offers more than 50 miles of hiking trails. Only two state campgrounds are accessible by car, but primitive camping is available in state and federal wilderness areas.

Hikers and horseback riders alike need day-use permits to enter the wilderness section of the park. Apply in person at Long Valley Ranger Station at the top of the aerial tramway or at the state park or forest service office in Idyllwild. Backpackers need overnight permits in advance. For maps and further information, call (714) 659-2607.

San Gorgonio Pass

West of Palm Springs, Interstate 10 slices through the divide between the San Jacinto and San Bernardino mountains. The Cahuilla Indians operate the small Malki Museum on their Morongo Reservation (north side of San Gorgonio Pass). The free museum is open Tuesday through Sunday; exit north from the freeway just east of Banning on Fields Road and follow the signs.

Detour off the freeway at Beaumont and Banning for springtime views of cherry and peach orchards in bloom. From the freeway between Banning and Palm Springs, you'll see rows of power-generating wind machines sprouting up like huge, surrealistic cactus.

A showcase for spectacular wildflower productions, the vast Anza-Borrego Desert State Park sprawls grandly over a half million acres of mostly untamed desert.

Two Desert Parks

Contrast the high and low deserts on visits to two vast nature preserves: Joshua Tree National Monument and Anza-Borrego Desert State Park. Both are within easy striking distance of the Palm Springs area on either side of Interstate 10, Joshua Tree to the north and Anza-Borrego to the south.

Joshua Tree National Monument

This beautiful sanctuary, a transition area between the low Colorado Desert and the high Mojave Desert, is a rare preserve showcasing dramatic desert plants and wildlife. In spring, it's carpeted with wildflowers.

Although you can drive, hike, climb, picnic, and camp in its more than 850 square miles, Joshua Tree is less a playground than a showcase for a living desert so unique that legislation is under consideration to expand it and elevate it to national park status.

The giant desert plants that give the monument its name are concentrated in the higher western half. If you travel all the way across the monument, you'll see a clear delineation between the scrub vegetation and delicate wildflowers of the low desert in the eastern and southern regions and the more grandiose plants of the high desert.

You could do a day's trip from the Palm Springs area to take in scenic highlights. Plan to stay in or near the monument if you want to do much hiking or scrambling over the huge granite boulders scattered about in improbable jumbles.

For more information, contact Joshua Tree National Monument, 74485 National Monument Drive, Twentynine Palms, CA 92277; (619) 367-7511.

How to get there. The main entrance is from the north off state 62 at Twentynine Palms, about 50 miles north and east of Palm Springs (less than an hour's drive). At monument headquarters south of the highway, rangers provide brochures and information on touring.

Just outside the monument, Twentynine Palms (which has far more than 29 palms) was once a watering spot for prospectors. A small museum (6136 Adobe Road) displays mementos of early days. The free museum is open Tuesday through Sunday afternoons year-round.

You can also enter the monument from the town of Joshua Tree (17 miles west of the main entrance on State 62) or, from the south, via Cottonwood Springs Road off Intersatate 10 some 25 miles east of Indio. Paved roads connect the three entrances, making loop trips possible. It's about 45 miles from the southern entrance to the main entrance, but don't expect a quick drive through the monument; speed limits are low and vista turnouts frequent.

When to go. Because much of Joshua Tree is high desert, the weather is pleasant most of the year. Altitude ranges from 1,000 to 6,000 feet in the mountainous regions. Most roads are at the 3,000- to 4,000-foot level, so it seldom gets too hot for comfort even in summer. And desert nights can be cold. Occasional strong winds can whip up dust storms.

Where to stay. Black Rock Canyon campground can be reserved through Ticketron; others are first come, first served. Facilities include tables, firepits, and toilets. Bring your own water and fuel; you can fill water containers at the visitor center.

There are no motels or restaurants within the park. Limited accommodations are available in towns around the park, including Twentynine Palms and Yucca Valley to the north.

Plants and animals. Trademark plant of the high Mojave Desert, the Joshua tree (*Yucca brevifolia*) is actually a giant member of the lily family. Supposedly named by Mormon pioneers, who also called it the "praying plant" because of its upstretched arms, it grows at 3,000- to 5,000-foot elevations in the central and western parts of the park.

Joshua trees can attain heights of 40 feet. From about February to April, foot-long clusters of greenish white blossoms adorn their branches; each plant flowers only every second or third year.

The eastern half of the national monument is dominated by creosote bush, spidery-branched ocotillo, and cholla cactus. Several oases within the park are shaded by stately fan palms.

The spring wildflower show depends upon winter rains, which average about 5 inches. In a normal year, a colorful display begins in lower elevations as early as March. Lost Palms Oasis Trail is one good place to spot blooms (see page 88).

Desert wildlife is abundant because of the monument's variety of altitude and climate. About 250 kinds of birds and 38 species of reptiles and amphibians have been sighted.

Signs of the past. To step back a century, visit the Desert Queen Ranch. Also called Keys Ranch, this little-known landmark is better preserved than many ghost towns. Rangers lead hour-long tours to the ranch from mid-February through Memorial Day and from mid-October to mid-December. Schedules are posted at the visitor center.

You'll see traces of Indian, cattle rustling, and mining days. But the dominant presence is that of William Keys, a colorful character who homesteaded here after World War I. The tour includes the now-derelict ranch house, tiny schoolhouse, dam, and orchard. Scattered around is old-time farm gear.

Desert views. A self-guided nature trail leads to a palm oasis from monument headquarters. Among numerous other trails, a walk through Cholla Cactus Garden (midway between northern and southern entrances) is interesting.

A few miles into the park from the north, Hidden Valley supposedly once sheltered cattle rustlers among its massive boulders. Keys View, at the end of the paved road south from Hidden Valley, offers vistas stretching from the

...Two Desert Parks

Salton Sea (235 feet below sea level) to the San Jacinto and San Gabriel mountains (over 10,000 feet above sea level).

The 18-mile Geology Tour Road southwest of park headquarters affords sweeping views and takes you past old mines and a fine stand of barrel cactus.

Anza-Borrego Desert State Park

Largest state park in the contiguous United States, Anza-Borrego's nearly 600,000 acres (1,000 square miles) contain fabled badlands, seasonal waterfalls, cool piney heights, natural springs, and waves of wildflowers in spring. You can't see it all in one visit.

Anza-Borrego offers an easily accessible introduction to the harsh beauty of the Colorado Desert, an extension of Mexico's vast Sonoran Desert. Its gullied badlands are its most extraordinary phenomenon, but there's far more to the park than that: subtle fragrances of sage and cottonwood, about 600 species of animals—and terrain nearly as untouched as that found by early Spanish explorers.

Juan Bautista de Anza pioneered a route through this desert in 1774, and the park name honors him. The second part of the name is a Spanish word for sheep; some desert bighorns still live in the more remote northern reaches of Anza-Borrego.

The park's visitor center (open daily from October through May, weekends only the rest of the year) is at Borrego Palm Canyon, 3 miles west of the small community of Borrego Springs on State 22. The building looks as if it was burrowed out of the desert; it's topped with cement and six feet of sand.

For additional information, contact Anza-Borrego Desert State Park, P.O. Box 299, Borrego Springs, CA 92004; (619) 767-4205.

How to get there. By car, Anza-Borrego is 1½ hours south of Palm Springs and 2 hours east of San Diego. Take State 111 east from Palm Springs, turn south on State 86, and head west on State 22 to Borrego Springs. From San Diego, take State 78 east.

When to go. The most comfortable time to visit the park is from late autumn to mid-May. Summer gets torrid, but the dry air keeps it from being unbearable. In this part of the desert, temperatures can vary as much as 50° within a 24-hour period; evenings are always cool.

Accommodations. Borrego Springs, a private enclave in the center of the park, has restaurants, trailer parks, modest motels, and two surprisingly luxurious resorts, Rams Hill Country Club (18-hole golf course) and La Casa del Zorro. For a list of lodgings, contact the Chamber of Commerce, Borrego Springs, CA 92004; (619) 767-5555.

Desert camping here varies from highly developed (Borrego Palm Canyon) to primitive (wherever you wish, with a few restrictions). Reservations for developed sites are recommended on weekends and holidays; call MISTIX, (800) 444-7275.

Around the park. More than 600 miles of roads offer a choice of scenery and terrain. Probably the most famous viewpoint in the park is Font's Point north of Borrego Palm Canyon, overlooking the spectacularly undulating Borrego Badlands. Other roads and trails lead to groves of California fan palms and stands of smoke trees (among the finest anywhere) and to clusters of the park's signature plant, the fat-boled, low-to-the-ground elephant tree (*Bursera microphylla*).

Ranger-led nature walks, auto caravans, and campfire programs are offered from the visitor center on weekends and holidays in season.

Blossom Trails

When the desert flowers, its brilliance is dazzling. Bright colors contrast vividly with the landscape's usually more subdued hues.

Several areas offer particularly extravagant spring displays. From early March through May, you can call the Wildflower Hotline, (818) 768-3533, to find out which regions have the best blossoms.

Antelope Valley. About 50 miles north of Los Angeles, a 1,745-acre California Poppy Reserve was established in 1976 on some of the state's most consistent poppy-bearing land.

The reserve (15101 West Lancaster Road, 10 miles west of Lancaster off State 138) is open daily from 10 A.M. to 4 P.M. during the blooming period (usually mid-March through May). There's a small per-car entry fee. Four loop trails let you get close to the flowers. Shelters have picnic tables.

Joshua Tree National Monument. From February to April, you should find flower-filled canyons along the 4-mile Lost Palms Oasis Trail from Cottonwood Springs, a mile east of the visitor center on Interstate 10. Call (619) 367-7511 for prime viewing times.

Anza-Borrego Desert State Park. The 1½-mile trail to Palm Canyon from Borrego Palm Canyon Campground is overpopular from February to early March, but it's an excellent introduction to classic desert flora. Or you can pick up a wildflower map, updated weekly, at the visitor center.

To plan a visit around the peak period, send a stamped, self-addressed postcard (with words such as "The flowers are blooming!" written on the back) to Wildflower Notification, Visitor Center, Anza-Borrego Desert State Park, Borrego Springs, CA 92004. It will be returned when the show starts.

Salton Sea

Sandwiched between the rich farmlands of the Imperial Valley and the resorts of the Coachella Valley, the 35-mile-long Salton Sea is one of the world's largest inland bodies of salt water and a mecca for water-sports enthusiasts.

Once dry wasteland, the sea was formed in 1905 when the Colorado River overstepped its bound. Billions of gallons of floodwaters were trapped below sea level.

With no natural outlet to dilute the minerals in its waters, the shallow sea has become increasingly salty over the years. A desalinization project is now underway in an attempt to stabilize the salinity level—and prevent the Salton Sea from becoming a dead sea.

It isn't only fish who depend on the Salton Sea. This is an important link on the Pacific Flyway, host to 373 species of birds at one time or another. Spectacular skeins of Canada and snow geese shadow the skies above the sea in autumn, and a third of North America's white pelicans winter here.

When to visit. Salton Sea is a hot place in summer—temperatures can be well above 100°. Winter temperatures are in the comfortably low 50s to high 80s. Water temperatures drop as low as 50° in midwinter and climb as high as 90° in summer. Best months to visit are November and December and February through April; strong winds hamper water activity in January.

How to get there. Located 20 miles southeast of Indio, Salton Sea is ringed by good highways. State 86 runs to the west, State 111 to the east. State 78 from Anza-Borrego Desert State Park joins State 86 along the lake's southwest shore.

Recreational choices

Fishing, boating, swimming, water-skiing, bird-watching, and duck hunting are among the area's attractions. Racers consider Salton Sea one of the fastest bodies of water in the world; because it's 235 feet below sea level, internal combustion engines run more efficiently here. A storm alert system warns boaters of occasional strong winds that can create high waves.

Although the continuing concentration of minerals in the sea has made it far saltier than the Pacific Ocean, fish introduced in the 1950s by the Department of Fish and Game have adapted and survived. And a freshwater fish, tilapia, has managed to proliferate here since it entered via the Coachella Valley canal system.

Because of the concentration of minerals, fish caught in the Salton Sea have elevated levels of selenium. Pregnant women and small children are advised not to eat them, and others should limit their consumption.

Salton Sea State Recreation Area. Headquarters of the 17,913-acre recreation area lies at the northern end of the lake about 22 miles southeast of Indio on State 111. The visitor center here is open from Labor Day to Memorial Day.

Varner Harbor is the hub for boating and fishing activities. A marina offers boat-launching facilities. The breakwater is popular with croaker fishers; corvina and sargo fishing is best from a boat.

The recreation area has both primitive and improved campsites and picnic areas. Campsites are available on a first-come, first-served basis, except for a 40-site area (25 with full hookups) that you can reserve by calling MISTIX, (800) 444-7275.

For information on facilities, contact Park Ranger, Salton Sea State Recreation Area, P.O. Box 3166, North Shore, CA 92254; (619) 393-3052.

Salton Sea National Wildlife Refuge. State 111 takes you along the sea's eastern edge for several miles before swinging away from the water. The sea then drops from sight, and you could easily miss one of its most fascinating sights: a great gathering of birds along the south shore.

A short detour gives you a close look. Turn west on Sinclair Road about 4 miles after State 111 turns south at Niland. Then it's about 4½ miles to the wildlife refuge headquarters.

Look for snowy egrets, great blue herons, and snow and Ross geese on the 2-mile nature trail along the lake. The setting is serene, but hardly quiet. In winter, when geese are present in force, their bickering makes an impressive din. A lookout tower gives a good vantage point.

Nearby desert sights

Dusty side roads and rocky trails around Salton Sea lead to hot mineral springs, Indian relics, rock-hunting grounds, ancient shell deposits, colorful canyons, and sand dunes.

From State 86 west of the sea, watch for the "bathtub ring" that marks the onetime shore of Lake Cahuilla, which covered the Salton Sink from about 900 to 1400 A.D. You'll see it along the base of the foothills west of the highway near the Imperial-Riverside county line.

Mecca Hills. Three canyons—Painted, Box, and Hidden Spring—in choice desert country just north of Salton Sea are favorites of hikers. All are off State 195, a few miles west of Mecca. Smoke trees and desert ironwood present a spring show of purple blossoms.

Travertine Rock. A mound of enormous boulders can be seen about 100 yards off State 86 some 6 miles south of its intersection with State 195. Once partially submerged by Lake Cahuilla, the mound—not a true travertine, but a calcareous tufa rock—is covered with a scaly, knobby limestone. A climb to the top (about 200 feet) affords a good view.

South of Travertine Rock, along State 86, amateur geologists and rock collectors find a happy hunting ground. Look for brightly colored quartzites, flints, granites, schists, and sandstone around the south end of the sea, the farther from the highway the better.

Along the Colorado

Once described as "too thick to drink and too thin to plow," the Colorado River forms a natural boundary between California and Arizona. It served as a canoe thoroughfare for early American Indians and, later, as a watercourse for paddle-wheel steamers.

The river today is an important water supplier for the Los Angeles Basin. But the dams that tamed it also turned it into a watery playground. Most of its 265-mile length from Hoover Dam in Nevada to the Mexican border invites recreational use. You can float an innertube down a calm stretch east of Blythe or head for the marinas that dot the shoreline at Lake Havasu.

Summers are hot in this low desert region, temperatures climbing above 100°. But July and August, with quiet and warm waters, offer outstanding boating, fishing, and waterskiing.

Around Needles

Needles sits near the junction of Interstate 40 and U.S. 95, just south of Nevada's southern tip. Established in 1869 as a steamboat landing and supply station on the Old Emigrant Trail, Needles grew with the coming of the railroad. The train depot and adjacent "Harvey House" hotel have been carefully preserved.

Good beaches line the river here; a marina and golf course add to the city's appeal. Anglers congregate downstream in the Havasu National Wildlife Refuge; a valid fishing license and a special use stamp lets you fish from the river or from the Arizona side.

Twenty-six miles upstream from Needles, the Nevada town of Laughlin is popular with Southlanders as the nearest major casino destination.

Park Moabi. This park, 11 miles southeast of Needles on Interstate 40, surrounds a lagoon that opens onto the river directly across from the wildlife refuge. Launching facilities, boat docking, and boat rentals (including houseboats) are available. Secluded inlets invite camping.

Topock Gorge. A scenic stretch of the Colorado accessible only by boat lies just below the Interstate 40 crossing. Mohave Canyon, 15 miles in length, leads south to Lake Havasu.

Neither roads nor trails approach the canyon, but boaters can explore bays, sloughs, caves, and side canyons that cut into its steep, colorful walls. While onshore camping is prohibited in many areas, houseboats may anchor overnight in sheltered bays. You can rent boats and motors at Park Moabi or across the river in Topock, Arizona.

Deep trolling may yield striped bass or trout; catfish are plentiful for bait fishers plumbing holes in warmer bays.

Lake Havasu

The intensely blue waters of sinuous Lake Havasu (3 miles across at its widest point, 45 miles long) make a refreshing break in the stark desert. This picturesque Colorado River reservoir, created by the construction of Parker Dam in 1938, fluctuates so little it has been spared the shoreline band that disfigures most reservoirs.

Lake Havasu State Park, a 13,000-acre preserve on the Arizona side of the river, has its headquarters at Pittsburgh Point on the island linked by London Bridge to Lake Havasu City.

Getting around. Lodging and facilities are centered at Lake Havasu City, Arizona. For information on the area, contact the Visitor and Convention Bureau, 1930 Mesquite Ave., Suite 3, Lake Havasu City, AZ 86403; phone (602) 453-3444.

To get to Lake Havasu City, turn south off Interstate 40 onto Arizona State 95, about 10 miles east of Topock. It's about a 20-mile drive.

From the California side, a road off U.S. 95 reaches the west side of the lake at the Chemenuevi Valley Indian Reservation (no facilities).

Boats can only be launched at a few points around the lake. More than 1,500 campsites (some accessible only by boat) are scattered along its shore.

Activities. Boaters can spend a full day exploring, often combining boating and waterskiing. You can ski for an hour in one direction, if you have the endurance. Powerful winter winds, which can turn the lake into a choppy sea, usually taper off by March. If one occurs while you're on the lake, take shelter at one of the refuges along the shore.

Anglers like Havasu for many reasons, one being that spring and autumn, most pleasant weatherwise, are also the best fishing seasons. There is no closed season, and you may fish all day and all night.

London Bridge. In 1825, the first stone of the New London Bridge was laid on the banks of England's Thames River; in 1971, the entire bridge stood on the shore of Lake Havasu. The 928-foot span manages to maintain a massive dignity despite its incongruous setting.

At one foot sits the London Bridge Resort and the English Village, with Tudor-style shops and restaurants. (Britain's union jack flies here, and the Lord Mayor of London visits on October 10 during an annual celebration.) Across the bridge lie the marina and Nautical Inn Resort. Also on the island is a busy commuter airport.

Lower Colorado

Now thoroughly tamed by a succession of dams, the lower reaches of the Colorado River attract lovers of warm-water angling, waterskiing, jetskiing, scenic cruising, and camping. Fishing is good for black bass, bluegills, crappies, and catfish.

Boats and other equipment can be rented at several places along the river at the town of Blythe. For information, contact the Blythe Chamber of Commerce, 201 S. Broadway, Blythe, CA 92225; (619) 922-8166.

Also of interest are the Blythe Intaglios about 15 miles north of town off U.S. 95. The giant figures created in the earth's surface by Indians centuries ago are the best known examples of this primitive art form in North America.

In the western reaches of the Mojave Desert, stunning spring displays of California poppies beckon visitors to the Antelope Valley.

The High Desert

The Mojave Desert stretches across southeastern California from the Nevada border to the town of Lancaster, northeast of Los Angeles. This is the high desert, ranging in elevation from 3,000 to 5,000 feet.

In spring, following winters of gentle rainfall, some 250 species of wildflowers paint an impressionistic canvas of color across the Mojave.

East Mojave National Scenic Area

Proposed federal legislation would preserve 1½ million acres of scenic area near the California-Nevada border as Mojave National Park. Currently managed by the Bureau of Land Management as a national scenic area, this vast piece of desert encompasses 16 mountain ranges, four dry lakes, a year-round stream, and countless washes, mesas, buttes, and badlands.

Among its inventory of scenic attractions, East Mojave has unique caverns (see facing page), lava beds, and sand dunes. All lie between Barstow and Needles (page 90); access is from Interstate 15 or Interstate 40.

Camping. Frontier freedom is the keynote of the present camping policy; you can pitch a tent and unroll a sleeping bag anywhere within 300 feet of a road, although you must stay more than 600 feet away from a waterhole.

Hole-in-the-Wall and Mid-Hills, two BLM camping areas with limited facilities (water, privies, fire rings, and tables), sit among piñons and junipers between 4,000 and 5,600 feet.

To get there, take Interstate 40 to Essex Road (about 100 miles east of Barstow, 40 miles west of Needles). Take Essex about 10 miles north to Black Canyon Road (good signed dirt strip). Drive north about 8 miles to Hole-in-the-Wall; Mid-Hills is 6½ miles farther.

Cinder Cones. Apollo astronauts trained for the 1969 moon landing in the blackened landscape of these 25,600 acres of lava beds and upthrust cinder cones, now a national natural landmark. Old mining roads give access; stick to them, as the cinder crumbles easily. The extinct volcanic cones are noteworthy for their petroglyphs.

From Baker (60 miles northeast of Barstow on Interstate 15), drive east on Kelbaker Road for about 10 miles. Park on the shoulder or follow a dirt road into the cones.

Kelso Dunes. The 70-square-mile Kelso Dunes are the most extensive in the West. Easily reached on a half-mile walk from the road, they're best if viewed at sunrise and sunset, when the slanting light clearly defines their shifting humps and ridges.

To reach the dunes, continue on Kelbaker Road about 22 miles beyond the cinder cones (see above). You'll pass the historic old Kelso train depot, slated to become a visitor center. A signed dirt road leads west about 3 miles to the main dunes. The dunes can also be reached by a dirt road off Interstate 40 (31 miles east of Ludlow).

Barstow area

A good base for exploring the high desert, the town of Barstow at the junction of Interstates 15 and 40 was founded in 1886 as a railroad depot for the Atchison, Topeka & Santa Fe. The train station (1611 E. Main Street) is now a shopping and dining complex.

Mojave River Valley Museum (270 E. Virginia Way) chronicles the area's history; the free museum is open daily 11 A.M. to 4 P.M.

The California Desert Information Center (831 Barstow Road) makes a good place to start backcountry exploration. Maps, exhibits, and displays on history, wildflowers, and wildlife enhance any visit. Jointly managed by the BLM and the city's Chamber of Commerce, the center is open from 9 A.M. to 5 P.M. daily; or call (619) 256-8617.

Calico Ghost Town. Founded in 1881 on the heels of one of the West's richest silver strikes, Calico once boasted more than 3,500 residents, two hotels, a church, a one-room schoolhouse, 13 saloons, and a small Chinatown. The town burned and was rebuilt twice, finally closing down when the price of silver dropped in 1896.

In 1951, Calico awoke to experience a new boom—tourists, not prospectors. The town was restored and opened to the public by Walter Knott of Knott's Berry Farm fame, whose uncle had grubstaked the original prospectors.

Today, this is a regional park where you can explore miles of tunnels at the high-producing Maggie Mine, ride the Calico-Odessa Railway, take a cable tram, and poke through buildings that are probably a bit tidier than before.

A campground (hookups) lets you spend a night in the "Old West." Motels are found nearby in Yermo and Barstow. Calico is north of Interstate 15 about 9 miles east of Barstow, 3½ miles west of Yermo.

Annual celebrations attract crowds: Calico Hullabaloo in April, Calico Spring Festival in May, Calico Days in October, and Western Fine Arts Festival in November. For information, contact Calico Ghost Town, P.O. Box 638, Yermo, CA 92398; (619) 254-2122.

Calico Early Man Site. An archeological dig 15 miles northeast of Barstow dates man's presence in North America back more than 50,000 years. The site was discovered in 1942 by an amateur archeologist. Twenty years later the National Geographic Society and the San Bernardino County Museum began excavation. To date, more than 6,000 artifacts have been discovered.

Free tours at the site off Interstate 15 are offered Wednesday through Sunday at 1:30 and 3:30 P.M., plus 9:30 and 11:30 A.M. Thursday through Sunday.

Roy Rogers/Dale Evans Museum. Southwest of Barstow at Victorville, this museum salutes the careers of the two Western stars—and equine costars Trigger, Buttermilk, and Trigger, Jr., who are stuffed and mounted for viewing along with canine pal Bullet. A video theater lets you see the whole crew in action. The museum, at 15650 Seneca Road, is open 9 A.M. to 5 P.M. daily except Thanksgiving and Christmas (moderate admission).

Northern Mojave

In the vast reaches of the northwestern Mojave Desert, the terrain ranges from high, imposing peaks to low, crystalline sinks of primeval lakes. Human history is recorded in ancient Indian petroglyphs and in 19th-century mines and mining towns.

Modern man's mark includes secluded military bases and missile sites. At Boron (on State 58 just west of U.S. 395) lies the world's largest open-pit borax mine. Its neighbor to the south is Edwards Air Force Base, offering free weekday tours; call (805) 258-3446.

Randsburg. A pleasant stop off U.S. 395 about 27 miles north of State 58, photogenic Randsburg was once a gold and silver mining center. Though the Yellow Aster Mine recently reopened and some 150 diehard prospectors work old claims nearby, it's almost a ghost town today.

Butte Street's weather-beaten buildings house antique stores, a general store and soda fountain, and a small hotel and tea room. The Floozy House, a former bordello behind the White House Saloon, is now an inn.

The Desert Museum (161 Butte Street) exhibits an impressive display of mining memorabilia. Open weekends, it's worth the small fee to tour.

China Lake. An extraordinary concentration of prehistoric petroglyphs can be seen in Renegade Canyon within the China Lake Naval Weapon Center firing range. Day-long tours are offered from the Maturango Museum in Ridgecrest. To join one, write to the museum, P.O. Box 1776, Ridgecrest, CA 93556, or call (619) 375-6900.

You can visit the museum (local history, natural history, geology) from 10 A.M. to 5 P.M. Tuesday through Sunday. To get there, leave U.S. 395 or State 14 at the Ridgecrest-China Lake exit and continue to 100 E. Las Flores. A small admission fee is charged.

Little Lake. About 20 miles north of China Lake, other notable Indian petroglyphs are found at Little Lake off U.S. 395. Some of the rock drawings are visible from the shore; you can rent a rowboat to see others. The greatest concentration is on the west shore and at the southeast end of the lake.

Camping fees at a private facility (tables, fireplaces, water) include bank-fishing privileges.

Western Mojave

The Antelope Valley corner of the Mojave Desert slopes gradually upward to the west as it narrows between the rolling foothills of the converging Tehachapi and San Gabriel mountains. Without its Joshua trees, the pastoral valley would not look like a desert at all. It's particularly attractive when wildflowers bloom (see page 88).

The Western Mojave has undergone a population explosion in recent years, as aerospace industries and spillover from the San Fernando Valley have brought an influx of desert dwellers. Lancaster, the largest city, is a good base for exploring, and the sprawling city park off State 14 (take the L exit) is a pleasant spot to stretch your legs.

You get more than just a scenic look at the valley if you pull off State 14 (heading north) at the lookout point a few miles south of Palmdale. A plaque shows the location of the San Andreas Fault, California's dominant rift zone. The fault line extends west across the valley to its highest elevation at Big Pines Summit (6,862 feet).

Burton's Tropico Gold Mine. The Tropico was one of the Southland's most successful gold mines, remaining in operation until 1956. On tours of the mine, visitors get a chance to see the 900-foot-deep shaft, a stamp mill, and mining equipment. Buildings on the property house collections of rocks, gems, period clothing, and old newspapers.

To reach the mine from Lancaster, take State 14 north 11 miles to Rosamond Boulevard, go west about 5 miles to Tropico Mojave Road, and follow the signs. The mine and museum are open from 10 A.M. to 4:30 P.M. Thursday through Sunday. Admission is modest. For information, call (805) 256-2644.

Exotic Feline Breeding Compound. Practically next door to the Tropico Mine, this breeding compound for exotic cats offers free tours of leopard and tiger enclosures daily except Wednesday from 10 A.M. to 4 P.M. Donations help fund research and build natural habitats for the animals. For further information, call (805) 256-3332.

A Cavern Tour

Visitors have been admiring Mitchell Caverns since prospector Jack Mitchell opened them to the public in 1932. Caverns such as these that combine all three types of cave formations—dripstone (stalagmites, stalactites), flowstone (ribbons, draperies), and erratics (helictites, shields)—occur only once in 40,000 caves.

Now a natural preserve in the Providence Mountains State Recreation Area, the caverns are open from mid-September through mid-June. Ranger-led 1½-hour tours (small fee) depart the visitor center at 1:30 P.M. weekdays and 10 A.M., 1:30 P.M., and 3 P.M. weekends and holidays. Bring a sweater; year-round temperature inside the caverns is 65°.

The caverns are reached from a 17-mile paved road off Interstate 40, about 100 miles east of Barstow and 40 miles west of Needles. Views from the visitor center, some 4,300 feet above the desert floor, are stunning. A few short trails and six primitive campsites (limited water) complete the facilities.

South Sierra Country

Superlatives come easy when you're talking about the region in and around the southern part of the Sierra Nevada. This area encompasses a legendary desert, the tallest peak in the lower continental United States, the Southlanders' favorite ski destination, some of the country's oldest and most massive trees, and much more.

To the west of the towering mountain range lies the southern half of the vast Central Valley, acre for acre the world's richest agricultural region.

A few of the places described in this chapter hardly seem part of Southern California when you locate them on a map. But such northerly attractions as Mammoth Mountain are much more aligned to the Southland by virtue of access and economy than they are to the northern part of the state.

Highs & lows

Two adjacent national parks—Sequoia and Kings Canyon—contain several thousand acres of giant sequoias (*Sequoiadendron giganteum*) within their combined area of 1,300 square miles. On the eastern edge of Sequoia National Park, majestic Mount Whitney's 14,495-foot peak looms above other magnificent granite mountains.

The rugged backcountry of both parks is a hiker's domain of peaks and canyons, threaded with an intricate trail system that includes the southern end of the famed John Muir Trail. Camp-

Like massive sentinels from the past, Sequoia National Park's groves of ancient giants dwarf—and awe— visitors. Some of the trees are more than 2,500 years old.

grounds in the heart of the parks are cool summertime retreats.

To the east of the Sierra, Death Valley National Monument is an ideal winter destination. Nowhere else in California is nature's palette more vividly displayed than on this wind-carved landscape. Badwater, on the valley floor 282 feet below sea level, is the lowest point in the Western Hemisphere.

Between Death Valley and the Sierra is the Owens Valley, where wanderers will discover ghostly remains of mining communities and a 4,000-year-old bristlecone pine forest.

Planning a visit

There's air service to the region's larger cities (American and America West to Bakersfield, commuter lines elsewhere). But you'll need a car to thoroughly explore the area. Interstate 5 and U.S. 99 are the major north-south arteries west of the mountains. U.S. 395 through the Owens Valley offers access to the mountains from the east.

When to go. Sequoia and Kings Canyon are year-round playgrounds, though the more remote areas are not accessible in winter. The road connecting the two parks may be closed by snow at times. For recorded weather information, call (209) 565-3351.

Mammoth Mountain, north of Kings Canyon, is one of the state's longest-operating ski areas, sometimes open as late as the Fourth of July weekend. From spring through summer, the region plays host to hikers, backpackers, anglers, and mountain climbers.

The best time to visit the desert is February to May, after winter rains but before the intense heat of summer. In spring, the desert blushes with thousands of square miles of wildflowers.

The Central Valley, too, sizzles in summer. Residents escape then to nearby lakes and mountain parks.

Where to stay. Accommodations range from campgrounds, cabins, and lodges to resorts, roadside motels, and city hotels. Visalia and Bakersfield offer the greatest choice of lodging in the southern part of the Central Valley. Death Valley and Mammoth have both modern resort facilities and campgrounds. Some accommodations and camping areas in Sequoia and Kings Canyon are open all year.

Contacts

These agencies offer information on attractions and accommodations. See additional contacts throughout this chapter.

National Park Service
Sequoia and Kings Canyon
National Parks
Three Rivers, CA 93271
(209) 565-3456

**Mammoth Lakes Visitor
Information Center**
P.O. Box 48
Mammoth Lakes, CA 93546
(800) 367-6572

Death Valley National Monument
Death Valley, CA 92328
(619) 786-2331

**Greater Bakersfield Convention
& Visitors Bureau**
P.O. Box 1947
Bakersfield, CA 93303
(805) 325-5051

Sequoia & Kings Canyon

Giant trees, awesome canyons, cascading streams, and sparkling lakes greet visitors to two spectacular national parks in the southern Sierra. Much of their natural beauty can be explored by road or trail. Bus tours, self-guided nature trails, naturalist-conducted walks, and pack trips allow everyone to sample this unspoiled mountain country.

Developed visitor amenities are concentrated in the western reaches of the parks, primarily along the 46-mile Generals Highway connecting Sequoia and Kings Canyon national parks. You can pick up maps and other material at visitor centers in the Ash Mountain, Giant Forest, Lodgepole, and Grant Grove areas—all reached via the winding Generals Highway.

Vast expanses of the two parks are road-free high country. Inhabited only by wildlife for nine months out of the year, this backcountry invites hikers and backpackers in summer. The main traffic arterial is the John Muir Trail, which begins to the north in Yosemite National Park and runs south for 225 miles. From the east side of Sequoia, the Whitney Portal Trail joins the John Muir Trail near Mount Whitney's summit (see Lone Pine, page 99).

Activities. Summer is the time for hikers and backpackers. For backcountry travel, wilderness permits and reservations (with a trail-entry date) must be obtained in advance. For information, call (209) 565-3307.

Horseback riders can hire mounts at Grant Grove in Kings Canyon for day-long trail rides. Guided day and overnight rides into the backcountry depart from Lodgepole, Cedar Grove, and Mineral King areas of the parks.

Fishing is good for brook, brown, rainbow, and golden trout. Most anglers head for the South Fork of the Kings River in Kings Canyon park. In Sequoia, the best fishing accessible by road is along the Kaweah River's Middle Fork. A California fishing license, available in both parks, is required for anyone 16 or older.

In winter, cross-country skiers head for the small Wolverton Ski Area (near Giant Forest) and Grant Grove.

How to get there. Sequoia and Kings Canyon, joined end to end along the Sierra ridge and administered jointly, can be reached easily from the west. State 198 runs 70 miles from Visalia to Sequoia, entering at Ash Mountain—headquarters for both parks. The KOA Campground in Visalia offers guided day-long bus tours of the parks; call (800) 322-2336.

From Fresno, it's 55 miles on State 180 to the Big Stump entrance of Kings Canyon.

Generals Highway, the connector between the two parks, offers dramatic views. It's a difficult drive for motor homes and large trailers, especially the 16 miles between Ash Mountain (southern entry) and Giant Forest.

The scenic highway was completed in 1934. A hint of the care taken to preserve the natural beauty along its route is Tunnel Rock, a great boulder left in the path of the road.

Where to stay. At altitudes ranging from 2,100 to 7,500 feet, more than 1,300 campsites in the two parks offer a choice of scenery and geology. Some campgrounds allow trailers (no hookups available). All except Sequoia's Lodgepole are on a first-come, first-served basis. You can reserve Lodgepole sites through Ticketron; this campground and a few others at lower elevations are open all year.

Giant Forest Lodge in Sequoia offers motel-type rooms, tent cabins, and two-room cabins, as well as a cafeteria and a summer-only restaurant and lounge; by the mid-90s, overnight facilities will be moved out of Giant Forest to the new Clover Creek area 5 miles beyond Lodgepole. The smaller Stony Creek Lodge, midway between Grant Grove Village and Giant Forest Village, has a restaurant.

Grant Grove Lodge in Kings Canyon (open all year) has modest roofed or canvas-topped cabins without baths in a pine forest; there's also a coffee shop. Cedar Grove, along the banks of the Kings River, offers limited lodging from mid-May to mid-September. Bearpaw Meadow Camp offers tent camping, dining facilities, and hot showers from the end of June until Labor Day.

To make reservations for lodges and cabins, write to Reservations Manager, Sequoia & Kings Canyon Guest Services, Sequoia National Park, CA 93262. You can also call (209) 561-3314 all year for information and reservations.

Sequoia spectacles

The first national park in California and the second in the entire national park system, Sequoia was established in 1890 to protect groves of giant sequoias. More of the huge trees grow here than anywhere else in California—their only native habitat. In 1978, the park was enlarged with the addition of the Mineral King area.

Giant Forest. Crowning the park's sequoia groves is the largest living thing in the world—the General Sherman Tree. The massive sequoia is 102 feet in base circumference, 36½ feet thick, and 275 feet tall; some 140 feet above ground, a limb almost 7 feet in diameter extends from the trunk.

The General Sherman Tree stands in the Giant Forest, the most developed area of the park. The 2-mile Congress Trail, which begins near the General Sherman Tree, takes you to yet other spectacular specimens: Senate, House, and Founder's groves, as well as President McKinley and Chief Sequoyah trees. Booklets at the trailhead explain what you'll see along the way.

Moro Rock. Walk or drive 2 miles from Giant Forest to ascend this massive boulder more than 6,000 feet above the valley floor. Steps lead 300 feet to its summit—and a 360° view.

Crystal Cave. This stalactite-hung cavern 9 miles west of Giant Forest is open daily in summer for guided tours ($3 for adults, $1.50 for children 6 to 12).

Heather Lake. Sequoia's most accessible alpine lake lies 4 miles by trail from Wolverton Ski Area. Pear Lake, 2 miles beyond, is cradled in a barren granite basin.

Mineral King. Once a silver-mining area, this rugged region in the park's southern reaches is now a peaceful retreat for summer campers and hikers. A high valley set amid a rugged mass of spectacular peaks and canyons, Mineral King lies at the end of a narrow road that winds 29 miles east from Three Rivers (southwest of the park on State 198). Inaccessible in winter, the road is not recommended for trailers or RVs anytime.

Kings Canyon highlights

To the north of Sequoia, Kings Canyon has the distinction of being both one of the oldest and one of the newest national parks. When established in 1940, it absorbed tiny General Grant National Park, a sanctuary set up shortly after Sequoia was created in 1890.

Now the old section of the park is known as the General Grant Grove.

Kings Canyon is actually two entirely separate areas. The smaller west side contains the most developed section—General Grant Grove. Much of the rest is a bewildering maze of jagged peaks and rugged canyons. Densely forested, with an elevation that varies from 4,600 to 6,600 feet, the park is usually comfortably cool.

General Grant Grove. Most visitors head for General Grant Grove, which contains almost all the park's facilities and also the world's second largest tree. The General Grant sequoia has a base circumference of 108 feet—actually 6 feet larger than the General Sherman Tree in Sequoia National Park, though the General Grant has a smaller total volume. Both trees were standing in the Bronze Age more than 3,000 years ago. General Grant has been designated as the nation's official Christmas tree, and an impressive yuletide ceremony is held here every year on the Sunday before Christmas.

Informative campfire programs are given every summer night in the nearby amphitheater. For park lore, join one of the trips led daily by rangers; schedules are posted in the village.

Kings Canyon region. The park's other developed area is reached by a 30-mile stretch of State 180 from Grant Grove. The road, closed in winter, drops 2,000 feet before attaining its destination. Parking overlooks on sweeping curves allow far-reaching views of the deep canyons of the Middle and South forks of the Kings River and the peaks that rise beyond.

About 20 miles beyond Grant Grove is marble-walled Boyden Cavern; guided tours are conducted daily in summer and early autumn.

Cedar Grove, in a canyon along the South Fork of the river, is the popular base point for trail rides into the high country. The level valley floor is good for cycling. Rangers lead a variety of walks during the day and present nightly campfire programs in summer.

Big, Bad Bodie

"Goodbye, God, I'm going to Bodie," wrote a little girl in her diary in 1881 when her family moved to what was then one of the wildest mining camps in the West. Her dismay was not unfounded; there was allegedly at least one murder a day in "big, bad Bodie." A busy red light district and 65 saloons kept the town jumping day and night.

Bodie's boom was short-lived, but since 1964, the 486 acres that make up the town have been a state historic park—one of the best preserved Western mining ghost towns in existence.

Recently, controversy has again surrounded Bodie as drilling rigs once more bore into the bluffs around town. Efforts by a large mining corporation to search for

gold on the ridge above town, using modern equipment and methods, have park people worried about damage to structures and to the visitor experience. As one ranger put it, "It's ironic. Gold made Bodie, and gold could unmake Bodie."

Booms and busts. The town was named for a prospector who discovered gold here in 1859 and died in a blizzard soon after. Its heyday really began in the late 1870s with the discovery of several rich veins of gold. By 1879, 10,000 people called Bodie home, making it the largest settlement between Sacramento and Salt Lake City.

The boom was over by 1882, though some sporadic activity occurred in the 1890s and again in the 1920s and 30s.

Today, the 170 weathered buildings that remain are maintained in a condition of "arrested decay." A detailed park map with a self-guided walking tour to some 69 sites costs $1. Rangers offer free history talks at 3 P.M. daily except Monday and Thursday. On weekends and holidays from Memorial Day to Labor Day, free tours of the old Standard Mine take place at 11 A.M. and 2 P.M.

How to get there. To reach Bodie (open all year), take U.S. 395 to State 270 (north of Mono Lake and east of Yosemite National Park); the last 3 miles are unpaved and often inaccessible in winter. A modest day-use fee is charged per vehicle. Bring your own lunch; there are no stores or overnight facilities.

Just beyond the jumbled rocks of the Alabama Hills in Owens Valley, a trail ascends mighty Mount Whitney, tallest peak in the contiguous United States.

East of the Sierra

The full impact of the Sierra Nevada is rarely appreciated until you see its abrupt east face, the one it turns toward the desert. This side of the range, to the east of Sequoia and Kings Canyon and west of Death Valley, has much to offer vacationers: high desert country, spectacular mountain scenery, uncrowded trails, good fishing, ghost towns, spring wildflowers, and excellent skiing in winter.

U.S. 395 leads north and south through the whole section, linking a chain of little towns. From this arterial highway, you can go east into Death Valley or west a short distance into the towering mountains.

Travelers to the Owens Valley will find motels and restaurants in Lone Pine, Independence, and Big Pine. Bishop, at the top of the valley, provides the widest selection. The Mammoth region has a variety of lodgings.

Owens Valley

The bending and cracking of the earth's surface that created the Sierra Nevada and the parallel White, Panamint, and Inyo ranges also sank a long, deep trough between them—Owens Valley, a place of hot springs, craters, lava flows, and earthquake faults.

Lone Pine. Gateway to the Owens Valley, the small town of Lone Pine has long been a favorite site for filming movies and commercials. Many early Westerns were shot west and northwest of town on Movie Flat Road.

Thirteen miles west of Lone Pine is the start of the Whitney Portal Trail, a steep, 10¾-mile path to the summit of Mount Whitney. Hikers need permits; write to the U.S. Forest Service, P.O. Box 8, Lone Pine, CA 93545.

The Eastern Sierra Interagency Visitor Center, south of town at the junction of U.S. 395 and State 136, has maps and information on the whole area.

Independence. Turnoff for the Kearsarge Pass entrance to the Sierra high country, tiny Independence is the home of the excellent Eastern California Museum (155 N. Grant Street). The historical museum is open Wednesday through Monday from 10 A.M. to 4 P.M.; donations are requested.

One block north of Center Street on U.S. 395 stands the restored mansion known as Commander's House. Open weekends during summer (donations requested), this 11-room structure is the only survivor of Camp Independence, established in 1862 to protect early Owens Valley residents.

Seven miles south of Independence are the remains of the World War II Japanese-American internment camp of Manzanar.

Ancient Bristlecone Pine Forest. The world's largest bristlecone forest grows in a 28,000-acre area of the White Mountains. Stunted and twisted by the harsh forces of nature, the ancient trees —some more than 4,000 years old— resemble pieces of driftwood decorated with green needles.

The pines are about 20 miles from U.S. 395. Turn east onto State 168 (Westgard Pass Road) just north of Big Pine; a winding but well-marked side road (usually open late June through October) climbs up to the Schulman Memorial Grove. Take warm clothing, food, and water, and make sure your gas tank is full; there are no services after Big Pine.

Bishop. The valley's most bustling metropolis, Bishop (population 3,500) is at its most vibrant in autumn, when groves of cottonwood and aspen are ablaze. The town stages a colorful Mule Days celebration on Memorial Day weekend and a rodeo on Labor Day. The Chamber of Commerce (690 N. Main Street) has information on area attractions.

Laws. The once-active railroad town of Laws makes a worthwhile break from the long drive through Owens Valley. It's just off U.S. 6 about 5 miles northeast of Bishop.

The 11-acre Laws Railroad Museum and Historical Exhibit displays period buildings daily, weather permitting, from March through mid-November, and on weekends the rest of the year; donations are encouraged.

Mammoth & more

One of the country's largest ski areas, Mammoth Mountain has some 30 lifts, 150 trails, and 30,000 vertical feet of ski runs. Summer visitors hike and backpack into the John Muir Wilderness and fish and boat in area lakes.

Mammoth draws most of its winter crowd from Southern California— it's easily reached from the south over U.S. 395 (about 300 miles from Los Angeles) but cut off from the west when passes are closed by snow.

The resort town of Mammoth Lakes, about 42 miles northwest of Bishop, makes a good base for exploring the 200,000-acre region promoted as Mammoth Lakes Recreational Area. A visitor center, an aerial tram, and cozy mountain lodges welcome visitors. Trails lead to such unusual geologic formations as Devils Postpile National Monument, a sheer wall of basaltic columns more than 60 feet high. Forest Service campgrounds, usually crowded in summer, are virtually deserted after September.

Hot Creek. Soaking in Hot Creek's mineral springs is a popular pastime. The water in the 4-foot-deep pool is unusually buoyant—and very hot. Ask for directions at the U.S. Forest Service Visitor Center on State 203, about 3 miles off U.S. 395.

Mono Lake. Ancient Mono Lake, 60 square miles of salty, alkaline water in a lunarlike setting, is a breeding ground for gulls and a resting spot for millions of migratory waterfowl. To learn about the birds and the lake's spectacular tufa formations, stop by the state reserve on the south shore. Mono Lake lies off U.S. 395 at Lee Vining, 26 miles north of Mammoth.

Death Valley

The forbidding name given to this desert valley doesn't ring true after you have spent a spring day here. It's actually a valley of light, color, and life. You can drive, hike, and camp for weeks among its 14 square miles of dunes, 200 square miles of salt flats, and 11,000-foot mountains.

The valley probably got its name in January 1850 when one 49er is known to have died here—but not from heat or thirst. A party of nine others may also have perished, and pioneers crossing the area certainly suffered extreme hardships. But measured against the rest of the western desert, Death Valley's record of human lives lost is reassuringly low.

Administered as a national monument since 1933, Death Valley is distinguished from other desert valleys by its great size, diverse scenery, and colorful history. It's also unique among deserts for its great extremes of temperature and topography. A record high of 134° was set in 1913. Elevations range from 282 feet below sea level near Badwater to 11,049 feet above sea level at nearby Telescope Peak.

Desert geology. Fossils of prehistoric mammals discovered here show that the arid salt flats and gravel desert of Death Valley were once a fertile plain. As the climate became drier, ancient lakes evaporated into salt deposits and mud playas. Wind reduced granite to sand and blew it into dunes. Since the wind blows from all directions, the dunes remained intact.

Plants and animals. The popular belief that nothing lives or grows in Death Valley is discounted by the diverse animal and plant life that has tenaciously adapted to the burning heat and dryness. Only the central salt flats are barren.

Nearly 1,000 species of plants and trees, including ferns, lilies, and orchids, flourish in the monument. Twenty or more flowering plants—including the yellow Panamint daisy, the blue-flowered Death Valley sage, and the small-blossomed goldcarpet—grow nowhere else in the world. Ancient bristlecone pines live high on Telescope Peak.

You're not likely to see many animals—most emerge only at night. But many creatures, including bighorn sheep and wild burros, do live in a 2-mile area between Telescope Peak and Badwater.

Even fish exist in this desert. Descended from Ice Age ancestors, the rare pupfish or "desert sardine" thrives in Salt Creek, Saratoga Springs, and Devil's Hole—an astonishing example of rapid evolutionary adaptation.

Planning a visit

From November through mid-April, Death Valley's tourist facilities are in full operation and the climate is mild. It's only in summer that visitors experience the blazing sun and intense heat usually associated with desert climes. If you must cross the valley in summer, make sure your car is in good condition, carry extra water, and travel at night when temperatures drop.

How to get there. The national monument hugs the California-Nevada border and spills over into Nevada at its northeast corner. The closest major air terminal is at Las Vegas, Nevada, 160 miles southeast of the monument. Light planes can land at Furnace Creek and Stove Pipe Wells.

From U.S. 395, it's 60 miles from Lone Pine to Towne's Pass on State 136/State 190, the most spectacular and best route from the west into Death Valley. From the southwest, State 178 runs 75 miles from U.S. 395 into the park, entering just west of Wildrose campground; there's a high-clearance gravel section for about 6 miles before Wildrose.

Another approach is from the southeast on State 127, which meets State 190 to the east of the monument at Death Valley Junction.

Where to stay. Accommodations are rarely a problem in Death Valley, but reservations are suggested, particularly around President's Day, Easter, Thanksgiving, Christmas, and the annual Death Valley 49ers Encampment in early November.

Lodging within the monument runs from rustic to resort. Rates at the luxurious Furnace Creek Inn (swimming pool, tennis courts, stables, and 18-hole golf course) include meals. The Furnace Creek Ranch, a mile down the road, has more modest motel-style rooms or cabins. The inn is open from October through mid-May; the ranch remains open year-round. For information and reservations, contact Furnace Creek Inn and Ranch Resort, P.O. Box 1, Death Valley, CA 92328; phone (619) 786-2345.

Stovepipe Wells Village, on State 190 about 25 miles northwest of Furnace Creek, has motel-style rooms, swimming pool, restaurant (closed in summer), grocery store, and service station. The mailing address for information and reservations is Death Valley, CA 92328; you can call (619) 786-2387.

Camping. Most of the monument campgrounds have scenic backdrops ranging from whispering sand dunes to sweeping mountain views. The most improved campgrounds are in the valley. Texas Spring and Furnace Creek (the latter open all year but very hot in summer) are both close to the visitor center; Ticketron reservations are accepted for Furnace Creek.

Campgrounds at higher elevations are open in summer. Campers must furnish their own firewood, and backcountry campers should come prepared to boil the water they use. At some campgrounds, you must provide your own water.

In the frequented parts of the valley, camping is strictly confined to established campgrounds. Backcountry camping is permitted if you don't litter or have ground fires.

The Wildrose campsites, open year-round, provide a nice change of pace from other campgrounds. Located at 3,500 feet on the west side of the Pan-

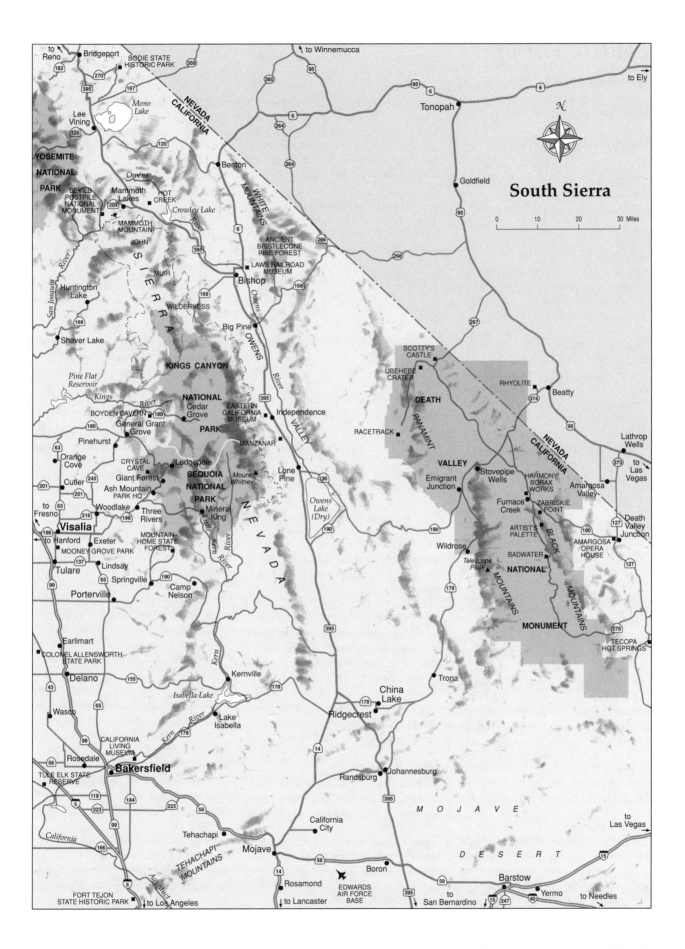

...Death Valley

amint Range just inside the southwest entrance, this facility has tables, fireplaces, pit toilets (no water).

Valley highlights

At first glance, Death Valley seems little different from the surrounding desert. But upon closer scrutiny, you'll begin to perceive its unique dimensions.

The mountain face, seemingly unbreached when seen from afar, is really slotted with fascinating labyrinths that lead on and on. The featureless salt flat is actually a vast maze of miniature crystalline alps. The distant sand ridges are mountains in their own right—but mountains that yield underfoot and restore themselves to an unmarked pristine state with every fresh breeze. The unnatural splotch on the far hillside is a waste pile marking an abandoned mine, its tunnels, shafts, headframes, and railroad beds still more or less intact.

Death Valley can be explored on more than 500 miles of well-maintained roadways. Most of the area's unique attractions lie no more than an easy stroll from one of them. This area is also well suited for cycling, as major attractions are concentrated in a few areas near relatively flat paved roads. A four-wheel-drive vehicle opens up still more backcountry.

Furnace Creek. Because of an excellent and dependable water supply from nearby springs, this region near the center of the monument on State 190 has always been the hub of activity. You can buy maps and other useful publications at the year-round visitor center and tour a museum of local geology, plants, and wildlife. Naturalist-led walks and programs are conducted from November 1 through Easter.

Borax Museum. An outdoor exhibit of equipment once used to extract and refine borax and other minerals is on display in Furnace Creek. The Borax Museum is a parking lot of the past, with stagecoach and buggy, buckboard and wagon, railroad handcar and locomotive.

Also on the grounds are a crude mining machine, a hand-operated stamp mill, and the 1883 mining office-bunkhouse that once stood in Twenty Mule Team Canyon. The great 20-mule-team wagons, nearly as sound as when they were hauling tons of borax from the 1880s until 1907, mark the site of the restored Harmony Borax Works 2 miles north of the museum.

Scotty's Castle. At the northern end of the monument, you can tour an incredible desert mansion built in the 1920s by a locally legendary character known as Death Valley Scotty. Walter Scott and his wealthy friend Alfred M. Johnson spent $2 million and 10 years to complete the Spanish-Moorish house.

Scotty's flamboyant escapades are part of Death Valley folklore, and the castle is testimony to his natural showmanship and eccentric personality. Tours are conducted daily; a moderate admission fee is charged. You can use the picnic area without charge.

Rhyolite. A booming city of 12,000 at the start of the 20th century, Rhyolite is now a ghost town. Among the surviving structures of the old mining town are an elaborate railroad depot (now a museum and store) and the Rhyolite Bottle House, its walls built from 51,000 beer bottles set in adobe. The owner sells desert glass and curios. Rhyolite is just northeast of the national monument on State 374 in Nevada, 2½ miles west of Beatty.

Unusual formations. To sample the desert's color, view a sunrise from Zabriskie Point (southeast of Furnace Creek on State 190) or follow the 9-mile scenic Artist's Drive south of Furnace Creek among the foothills of the Black Mountains. Halfway through the canyon, Artist's Palette hillside burns with intense hues when viewed early or late in the day.

Dante's View, on the crest of the Black Mountains, is one of the most spectacular scenic overlooks in the United States. It rises 5,775 feet above Badwater. The lowest point in the Western Hemisphere, Badwater lies 282 feet below sea level. At close range, the region's crusted pools reveal weird rock salt formations.

Charcoal kilns that look like giant stone beehives almost blend into the hillside of the Panamint Mountains. Once used to reduce pines and junipers to charcoal for the Modoc Mine smelter 25 miles to the west, the century-old kilns appear as good as new. To reach them, take the Upper Wildrose Canyon road from Wildrose Ranger Station.

In the northern part of the monument 16 miles west of Scotty's Castle, you can view a crater created 3,000 years ago by a volcanic explosion. Ubehebe Crater is half a mile wide and 500 feet deep.

The Racetrack, 27 miles south of the crater, is a mud flat that's the setting for the "mystery of the moving rocks." When wet, the Racetrack is so slippery that high-velocity winds skid great boulders across its surface as easily as if they were pebbles.

West of the monument

The Amargosa Opera House in Death Valley Junction is the setting for Marta Becket's one-woman dance performances. The ballerina even painted her own "audience," a realistic, wall-size mural depicting 260 members of a Spanish court, ranging from bawdy commoners to sedate nobles.

Performances are held Monday, Friday, and Saturday nights at 8:15 P.M. from November through April (except in December) and on Saturday only in May, October, and December. For performance details and admission prices, write Amargosa Opera House, Death Valley Junction, CA 92328, or call (619) 852-4316.

South of Death Valley Junction, State 127 passes through Tecopa Hot Springs, where visitors can splash in free mineral baths. The springs once belonged to Indians who believed they had healing powers and brought their lame and sick to bathe. When they turned over the site to white settlers, it was agreed that the water would remain free to all comers—and so it has.

Clusters of trailers around the bathhouses make the settlement visible for miles. For information, write to the Death Valley Chamber of Commerce, 2 Post Office Row, Tecopa, CA 92389.

Amid the picturesque ruins of Death Valley's Harmony Borax Works stands an original 20-mule-team rig. Above the other-era scene, snow dusts the national monument's 11,049-foot Telescope Peak.

San Joaquin Valley

Encompassing the southern half of California's great Central Valley, the San Joaquin Valley to the west of the Sierra ranks high among the nation's producers of food, fuel, and fiber. Sunshine, fertile soil, a long growing season, and water from surrounding mountains create ideal conditions for cotton, citrus fruits, grapes, nuts, and many other fruits and vegetables. The valley is also the state's top oil-producing region; you're likely to see an oil well pumping in the midst of a vineyard or potato field.

For the traveler, sunshine and the vast reservoir system that irrigates the valley make for good boating, swimming, and rafting. Valley towns can also be pleasant places to break a trip. Unexpected treats such as Wasco, the world's top rose-growing area, lie a short distance off main highways. In summer, millions of blooms line State 43 west of Bakersfield.

How to get there. Airlines, Amtrak, and bus lines serve larger valley cities. Interstate 5 skirts the sparsely populated western edge of the valley, and State 99 cuts through the valley's center; both offer easy north-south access. State 58 and State 178 are major east-west routes across the bottom of the Sierra range.

From Los Angeles, motorists enter the valley on the "Grapevine" route over the Tehachapis. Today's smooth freeway gives no indication of the troubles experienced by earlier travelers over this pass. Winter storms do sometimes cause temporary road closures due to icing. Throughout the valley, low-lying dense winter fog can be a problem for motorists at times.

Where to stay. Valley cities such as Bakersfield and Visalia, and Fresno farther north, are gateways to national parks and the high country of the Sierra Nevada. Nearby lakes and rivers offer added recreational opportunities. Motor inns and motels are only an offramp away from State 99, more infrequent along Interstate 5.

Bakersfield

Situated on the south bank of the Kern River at the southern end of the San Joaquin Valley, Bakersfield is county seat for Kern County and a major highway junction. Not only is Bakersfield a center for agriculture, petroleum, and tourism; it's also recognized as the state's country music capital.

The city has a host of playgrounds, parks, golf courses, and tennis courts. Lake Ming and Hart Park lie due east of town. Southern California's largest man-made lake, Isabella, lies about 45 miles east in the Sierra foothills. The nearby Kern River provides a natural setting for fishing, white-water rafting, hiking, camping, picnicking, and horseback riding.

The Basque influence is still felt in Bakersfield, legacy of sheepherders who came here a century ago. Several restaurants, including Matia's, Wool Growers Cafe, and the Noriega Hotel (established in 1897), offer traditional meals. Most are located in the east side of the city near the railroad station. You can buy a sourdough sheepherder loaf at Bakersfield's century-old Pyrenees Bakery (717 E. 21st Street).

Kern County Museum's Pioneer Village. Frontier history comes alive at a 14-acre museum at 3801 Chester Avenue. Some 56 buildings (originals and restorations) are laid out as a vintage model town of the 1860-1930 era. Indoors, the main museum building houses fossils from nearby McKittrick oil field, a diorama of birds and mammals, Indian relics, and a most unusual curiosity—a dog-powered butter churn.

The museum and village are open weekdays from 8 A.M. to 5 P.M., weekends and holidays from 10 A.M. to 5 P.M. (closed New Year's, Thanksgiving, and Christmas). Museum admission is free; there's a small fee to explore the village.

California Living Museum. Thirteen miles northeast of Bakersfield off State 178, this combination natural history museum and zoo displays hundreds of California desert animals in their native habitats. Included are a reptile house, one of the state's largest walk-in aviaries, a desert tortoise enclosure, and a children's petting zoo. Located at 14000 Old Alfred Harrell Highway, the museum is open Tuesday through Sunday from 10 A.M. to sunset. A small admission fee is charged.

Tule Elk State Reserve. At Buttonwillow, 22 miles west of Bakersfield via State 58, you can view a small band of tule elk at a 965-acre sanctuary. Now an endangered species, these animals once roamed the Central Valley's vast marshland. The reserve is 3 miles west of Interstate 5.

Fort Tejon State Historic Park. An old military post south of Bakersfield once quartered the Army's most unusual unit, the First Dragoons and Camel Corps. Established by the U.S. Army in 1854, the park is handily situated off Interstate 5 near Lebec (30 miles south of Bakersfield).

The post is open daily year-round. After touring its museum, reconstructed barracks, and officers' quarters, you can picnic on the grounds in the shade of some lovely old trees. A living history program is presented the first Sunday of each month. On the third Sunday of each month from April through October, a mock Civil War skirmish is staged for visitors at 10 A.M., noon, and 2 P.M.

Visalia vicinity

Founded in 1852, Visalia is the oldest city in the southern San Joaquin Valley. Self-guiding walking tour maps of its historic district can be picked up weekdays from the Chamber of Commerce, 720 W. Mineral King Avenue.

State 198 heads east from Visalia to Sequoia National Park. During the peak summer season, many travelers use the city as a base for exploring the nearby mountain area.

Mooney Grove Park. Acres of oaks and date palms shade this pleasant park 5 miles south of Visalia, open daily in summer, Thursday through Monday the rest of the year. Detour from the highway to picnic and enjoy lake scenery; a small per-car fee is charged.

Tulare Historical Museum. A museum in the onetime railroad town of Tulare, about 8 miles south of Visalia, traces county history from a century or so ago, when much of the area lay beneath one of the largest bodies of water west of the Mississippi. Tulare Lake today is a ghost that reappears only in the wettest years.

To visit the museum, located at 444 W. Tulare Avenue, take State 137 west 1¼ miles from State 99. It's open Thursday through Saturday and Sunday afternoons (small admission charge).

Colonel Allensworth State Park. A fascinating detour off State 99 about 30 miles south of Visalia, this historic park was once a town settled and governed entirely by blacks. Seven buildings, including a library and private homes, have been restored.

The town was founded in 1908 by Allen Allensworth, a former slave from Kentucky who was once sold because he tried to learn to read. The park is open daily, but you can only go inside the buildings on weekends. The small campground (water, rest rooms) is seldom filled. Turn off State 99 at Earlimart; drive west 7 miles on County J22, then south a mile on State 43.

Mountain Home State Demonstration Forest. John Muir's favorite grove of sequoias is enshrined about 8 crow-flying miles from the southern border of Sequoia National Park. This 4,500-acre forest and Balch Park, the 160-acre park that it surrounds, receive less attention than their famous neighbor; summer weekdays can be downright quiet.

The giant sequoias in the 53-acre Adams Memorial Redwood Grove are the main draw, but the whole area is interesting. The Yaudanchi Yokuts made their summer home here near the Tule River, leaving numerous bedrock mortars. Hedrick Pond, once the site of a lumber mill, is stocked with rainbow trout. Campgrounds offer some 200 spaces (no hookups, no reservations); you pay only in Balch Park.

Gateway to Mountain Home is Porterville, about 15 miles east of State 99 via State 190. From there, drive 17 miles east on State 190 past Springville, then north on County J37 for 3½ miles and east 18 miles on Bear Creek Road.

Detour to Hanford

The little town of Hanford, 18 miles west of Visalia on State 198, makes a refreshing detour on any drive through the San Joaquin Valley. Its rich history, classic architecture, charming shops, and nationally noted restaurant make it a perfect place for a short stay or an overnight stop.

Founded by the Southern Pacific Railroad in 1877, Hanford was named for its popular paymaster, James Hanford, who paid workers millions of dollars in gold and was alleged to have signed more checks than any other person in American history.

Pick up a self-guiding tour map at the Chamber of Commerce office (213 W. Seventh Street; open 8 A.M. to 5 P.M. weekdays) or at the Amtrak station 2 blocks down the street.

Cozy Irwin Street Inn near Courthouse Square heads the short list of accommodations. For lodging information, call the Chamber of Commerce at (209) 582-0483.

Courthouse Square. Built in the late 1800s, the courthouse fronting on the picture-perfect town square has been restored in recent times. Today it houses gift shops, boutiques, and a bar and restaurant. In good weather, flower and fruit stands and an antique carousel attract residents and tourists outside the building.

Behind the courthouse, the dark red building called La Bastille served as the city jail before its transformation into a restaurant. Nearby stand other architectural gems. The Superior Dairy, an old-fashioned ice cream parlor, has been in business for more than 60 years.

China Alley. Hanford's more exotic historical buildings are found in China Alley, a few blocks east of downtown. At the end of the last century, when jobs on railroads and farms brought as many as 800 Chinese families to Hanford (including future Chinese statesman Sun Yat-sen), China Alley was home to boardinghouses, gambling dens, and herbalist shops.

In those early days, the Taoist Temple, built in 1893, served as the Chinese community center. The temple can be toured by request; call (209) 584-3236. The wooden structure nearby that houses King's Hand Laundry started life as a hotel for immigrants.

Hanford's name turns up in more than a few out-of-town address books thanks to the Imperial Dynasty Restaurant, owned and operated by the Wing family for more than a century. Chef Richard Wing pioneered the Chinese-accented French fare that has become so trendy elsewhere.

For a splendid nine-course splurge, make reservations three or four days in advance by calling (209) 582-0196.

Central Coast

Stretching between Ventura County and the Monterey Peninsula, California's Central Coast embraces some of the state's loveliest beaches and a series of intriguing seaside communities. Tucked into inland valleys are resorts and inns, celebrity retreats, wineries, apple farms, and Arabian horse ranches. Six old Spanish missions—at Ventura, Santa Barbara, Solvang, Lompoc, San Luis Obispo, and San Miguel—welcome visitors.

Offshore, the Channel Islands offer glimpses of unique wildlife at one of the country's newest national parks. Cruises from Oxnard, Ventura, and Santa Barbara allow you to explore this beautiful marine sanctuary (see page 117). Other ocean-going opportunities include coastal deep-sea fishing and whale watching.

Coastal highlights

Santa Barbara, 90 miles north of Los Angeles, is one of the oldest and prettiest cities along the coast. Spreading along a wide and gently curving beach, it lies on a sunny sheltered plain backed by the rugged mountains of the Santa Ynez range. The city's stunning setting, lush landscaping, and distinctive Spanish architecture have lured generations of vacationers.

The wide beaches of Ventura and Oxnard to the south offer choice surfing and fishing sites. Inland around the resort town of Ojai, hikers, cyclists, and horseback riders find miles of trails.

Up the coast lie the Danish village of Solvang, the flower fields around

The state's own "Rock of Gibraltar," a 576-foot volcanic remnant, rises above the fishing port of Morro Bay and provides nesting for peregrine falcons.

Lompoc, gracious Santa Maria, and the clam beds of Pismo Beach. Beyond San Luis Obispo, State 1 hugs the coast from Morro Bay to San Simeon, site of the incredible Hearst Castle.

Planning a visit

With its ideal climate, easy accessibility, varied attractions, and wealth of activities, the Central Coast is popular year-round. Summer attracts the most visitors, though fog can be a factor then. If you visit in summer, make reservations well ahead for Hearst Castle tours. Hotels, seaside motels and inns, guest ranches, and beach campsites are also booked well in advance during the summer.

Some of the area's warmest and sunniest days occur in spring and autumn. It's easier to find accommodations then, and rates are significantly lower than during the summer. Fishing holds up well into autumn, and ocean temperatures, though cool in early spring, remain warm enough for swimming into November.

Winter days can be sparkling along this section of coast. All attractions are open, the crowds are gone, and surf-viewing is at its best.

How to get there. American, United, and smaller commuter airlines serve Santa Barbara. Commuter airlines also fly to Santa Maria and San Luis Obispo. Amtrak has service to Santa Barbara and San Luis Obispo. Greyhound offers daily bus service.

Driving is the best way to see the area. Look for rental car agencies in larger towns. A combination of U.S. 101 and the narrower and somewhat more meandering State 1 skirts much of the coast. Other highways give access to the region's inland destinations.

Where to stay. You'll find a wealth of lodging choices all along the Central Coast, including deluxe resorts, guest ranches, city hotels, bed and breakfasts, and budget-priced motels.

In the 1930s and 40s, movie stars made famous such deluxe retreats as the Ojai Valley Inn, the Alisal guest ranch near Solvang, and Santa Barbara's Biltmore Hotel, El Encanto Hotel, Montecito Inn, and San Ysidro Ranch—all of which still welcome guests.

Camping is permitted at some state beaches and state parks. Private campgrounds are sprinkled throughout the area. Reserve far in advance for weekends throughout the year and anytime in summer.

Contacts

These agencies offer information on attractions and accommodations. See additional contacts throughout this chapter.

Santa Barbara Visitor Information Center
One Santa Barbara St.
(P.O. Box 299)
Santa Barbara, CA 93102
(805) 965-3021

Solvang Visitors Bureau
1571 Mission Dr.
(P.O. Box 70)
Solvang, CA 93463
(800) 468-6765

San Luis Obispo Chamber of Commerce
1039 Chorro St.
San Luis Obispo, CA 93401
(805) 543-1323

Santa Barbara

Santa Barbara's colorful history dates back to the Chumash Indians, who settled the region in large numbers thousands of years ago. When the Spanish arrived in the 1700s, they called this place *La Tierra Adorada*—the beloved land. Today's visitors, beguiled by the city's climate and setting, find it hard not to share the enchantment.

When a 1925 earthquake destroyed many post-Victorian structures and forced the early demolition of others, it opened the way for Santa Barbara to express its heritage in the course of rebuilding. Today, the city reflects that history in its Spanish and mission-style architecture—adobe construction, tile roofs, bell towers, and the Mediterranean love of colorful accents. To ensure the perpetuation of this style, an architectural review board approves the design of every commercial and public building.

Not all of Santa Barbara's urban charm is man-made, however; nature contributes a gentle lushness that enhances the traditional-looking buildings. Stately palms ring many buildings, bougainvillea tumbles down whitewashed walls, and fir trees (decorated at Christmastime) mark pedestrian crossings downtown.

Santa Barbara's cultural calendar is testimony to the city's love for plants—the International Orchid Show is held here every spring, and the Santa Barbara Fair & Expo in April includes a flower show. The city pays homage to its past during the colorful Old Spanish Days Fiesta in August.

Visitors are often puzzled by Santa Barbara's layout. Streets have the unsettling habit of bending abruptly and taking off in another direction, or of ending at U.S. 101, which divides downtown's historic section from the beach. To decipher the street system, pick up a map at the Visitor Information Center along the waterfront near Stearns Wharf (corner of Santa Barbara Street and Cabrillo Boulevard). Other useful brochures on attractions around the city are also available.

Heart of the city

Downtown Santa Barbara is designed for strolling. With few exceptions, buildings are no taller than four stories, the result of a strictly enforced height ordinance that can't be varied without voter approval. New construction is designed to blend with existing buildings. Convenient city lots and garages make it easy to park; and the first 90 minutes are free.

State Street, the city's landscaped main artery, provides an entrée to the historic area bounded by Victoria, Chapala, Ortega, and Santa Barbara streets—the original core of the city that surrounded the Spanish Presidio. Plaques and markers identify the early buildings; a few of them are open to visitors. Pick up a free map of the self-guided walking tour at the visitor center or county courthouse. Or join Heritage Tours of Santa Barbara for a narrated walk through history; tours leave Plaza de la Guerra Monday through Saturday at 10 A.M. and Sunday at 1 P.M.; there is a fee. For information, call (805) 962-8578.

Santa Barbara Museum of Art. One of the country's finest small museums is located at the corner of State and Anapamu streets.

The museum building is bright, airy, and—unlike other city landmarks—modern. Soft, natural light falls on Greek, Roman, and Egyptian sculptures and priceless glassware. An encircling gallery and adjacent halls contain impressive collections of Asian, European, and American art.

The museum is open Tuesday through Sunday, except major holidays; admission is charged. Guided tours are offered daily at 2 P.M.

Santa Barbara County Courthouse. Built in 1929, the courthouse resembles a Spanish-Moorish castle. Its buildings and grounds cover a square block bounded by Santa Barbara, Anacapa, Anapamu, and Figueroa streets. An English translation of the motto above the entrance arch on Anacapa Street reads, "God gave us the country. The skill of man hath built this town."

Two-story murals in the Assembly Room colorfully depict Santa Barbara history, including the arrival of Juan Rodriguez Cabrillo in 1542, the founding of Mission Santa Barbara in 1786, and Colonel John C. Fremont's 1846 heralding of American rule in California. For an unequalled view of the city, take the elevator to the top.

The courthouse is open daily; free guided tours are offered Tuesday through Saturday at 2 P.M., with additional tours Wednesday and Friday at 10:30 A.M.

Historical Society Museum. Many of the city's historic treasures are housed in this museum, situated at the corner of De la Guerra and Santa Barbara streets. One wing is a library; the other is devoted to exhibits of the Mexican, Spanish, and Early American periods. On display are a carved statue of Saint Barbara, intriguing letters, early costumes, and relics of writer Richard Henry Dana's visits to the city.

The museum is open afternoons Tuesday through Sunday, except major holidays. Donations are requested.

Casa de Covarrubias. Built in 1817, the L-shaped adobe at 715 Santa Barbara was the site of the last meeting of the Mexican Assembly. Adjoining it is the adobe that served as Colonel John C. Fremont's headquarters after the American takeover in 1846. Both are open to visitors.

Lobero Theatre. On the site of the city's first theater (at the corner of Anacapa and Cañon Perdido streets), this showpiece was built in 1873 by Italian musician Jose Lobero. It's now the setting for contemporary productions.

Arlington Center for Performing Arts. Another palatial movie theater from a different era is worth a look. The Arlington, at 1317 State Street, is home to the city's symphony orchestra.

El Presidio de Santa Barbara State Historic Park. Ongoing restoration is bringing back some of the city's oldest structures at this park at 122 and 123 E. Cañon Perdido. El Cuartel (Guards House) and La Cañeda Adobe are part of the original Spanish fort on the site blessed by Father Serra in 1782. The padre's quarters and the chapel are reconstructions on original foundations. The park, including a museum shop in El Cuartel, is open 10 A.M. to 5 P.M. Monday through Saturday, noon to 4 P.M. Sunday.

El Paseo. A delightful shopping arcade reminiscent of Old Spain has been built in and around the adobe home of the De la Guerra family, begun in 1819 by mission Indians. A brick in the passageway bears the date of completion, 1826. Casa de la Guerra was the setting for a Spanish wedding fiesta in Dana's *Two Years Before the Mast*.

Import and specialty shops are now located here at 814 State Street. Across the street is the plaza where the first City Council met in 1850 and where the first City Hall was located.

The Waterfront

Santa Barbara boasts one of the most inviting stretches of coastline anywhere. Miles of wide, gently curving beaches, fringed with palms, offer space for swimmers, surfers, picnickers, scuba divers, anglers, and grunion-hunters. A picturesque 92-acre yacht harbor, protected by a long breakwater, shelters the local fishing fleet as well as hundreds of pleasure craft.

Attractive hotels and motels face the beach along Cabrillo Boulevard, an oceanfront drive popular with strollers, cyclists, and roller skaters. A Sunday arts and crafts show at Palm Park along the waterfront overflows for a mile along the boulevard.

Stearns Wharf. Constructed in 1872 and restored in 1981, Stearns Wharf is California's oldest working pier. Fishing is still popular, but the 3-block-long wharf at the foot of State Street is also the site of restaurants, shops, and a seafood market. The Santa Barbara Winery tasting room at the wharf is open daily from 10 A.M. to sunset for the sampling of area wines.

From the pier, harbor cruises depart several times a day. Or you can board the Santa Barbara Trolley here for a 90-minute tour of the town.

Sea Center. A small marine museum and aquarium at Stearns Wharf offers winter whale-watching cruises and field trips to the Channel Islands (see page 117). The museum is open daily; there is a small admission charge. A relief map of Santa Cruz Island highlights the displays at the Nature Conservancy Center next door.

Water sports. Motorboats and sailboats in several classes can be rented at the yacht harbor. A boat-launching ramp and a large parking area for boat trailers lie at the foot of Bath Street. Most waterskiing takes place between the wharf and East Beach. If the water is choppy, stay inside the breakwater.

Some of the area's best surfing and snorkeling can be found a few blocks north or south of the wharf. Arroyo Burro and Leadbetter beaches, both west of the breakwater, offer rough but inviting surf.

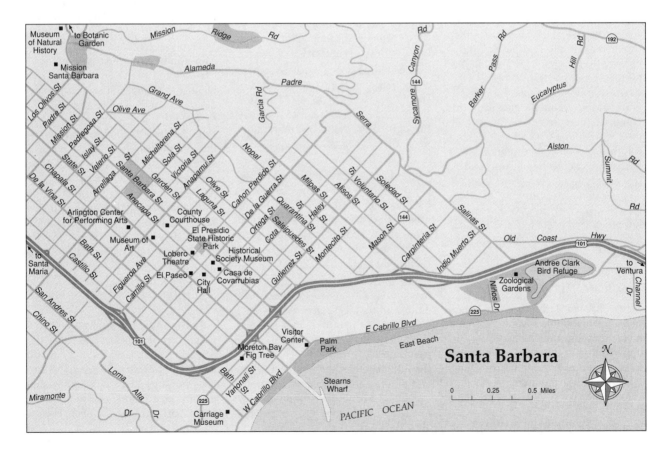

...Santa Barbara

No license is necessary for pier fishing; still-fishing with shrimp for bait may produce a nice haul of tasty perch. Offshore fishing is about as productive here as anywhere along the California coast. Charter boats from Sea Landing west of the wharf take anglers out for half-day and full-day fishing excursions in pursuit of albacore, marlin, and sailfish.

Zoological Gardens. In a charming garden setting just north of the ocean and E. Cabrillo Boulevard are some 200 elephants, lions, monkeys, sea lions, exotic birds, and other animals. A miniature train takes visitors on a tour of the zoo ($4 adults, $2 children). In the farmyard area, children can pet and feed domestic animals. Athletic seals show off in a sealarium with viewing portholes to accommodate visitors of any height. The zoo, at 500 Niños Drive, is open daily; an admission fee is charged.

Andree Clark Bird Refuge. On E. Cabrillo Boulevard next door to the zoo, a beautifully landscaped preserve gives shelter to geese, swans, and other freshwater fowl. Footpaths and a bikeway skirt a lagoon. Feeding the birds is discouraged.

Four Seasons Santa Barbara Biltmore Hotel. Channel Drive, to the east of the bird refuge, leads past the lush and colorful gardens surrounding Santa Barbara's most prestigious resort hotel. It also provides an entrée to the exclusive residential community of Montecito. Two more of the city's best known hostelries are in Montecito—the Montecito Inn (built by Charlie Chaplin) and the San Ysidro Ranch.

A scenic drive

Many of Santa Barbara's major attractions are highlighted along a 24-mile scenic drive around the city. You can obtain a map of the route at the Visitor Information Center near Stearns Wharf (One Santa Barbara Street).

One of the prettiest parts of the drive leads into the hills behind town. Mission Canyon Road begins at Mission Santa Barbara and heads north to the Museum of Natural History and the Santa Barbara Botanic Garden. Alameda Padre Serra winds southeast from the mission through the 500-foot-high foothills known as The Riviera. This pleasant residential area (the location of El Encanto Hotel) offers beautiful views of the city and the ocean beyond. To return to the downtown area, take Gutierrez Street.

Mission Santa Barbara. Overlooking the city from a knoll at the end of Laguna Street sits the tenth of the 21 missions founded by the Spanish in California. Established in 1786 by Father Fermin Lasuén, Santa Barbara is the only mission to remain continuously in the hands of the Franciscans.

Its unique stone facade makes the "Queen of the Missions" a popular subject for photographers. The two-towered design was copied from a Roman book on architecture written by Vitruvius in 27 B.C. (The book is still in the mission archives.)

Three of the mission's original rooms remain, one a primitive kitchen. The chapel, curio room, and library contain relics of mission life. Entrance to the cemetery is through a Roman arch hung with skulls and crossbones.

The mission is still in use as a parish church; its altar light has burned constantly since the chapel was built. You can take a self-guided tour Monday through Saturday and Sunday afternoon; there is a small fee.

Museum of Natural History. Located 2 blocks north of Mission Santa Barbara, at 2559 Puesta del Sol Road, the museum is set amid 2 acres of wooded grounds. Well-conceived exhibits focus on regional plants and animals and prehistoric Indians.

The museum is open daily except major holidays (admission fee). Free guided tours take place Sunday at 2 P.M. Within the museum complex, Gladwin Planetarium's closed-circuit television lets groups of people view the skies together. Shows are Saturday and Sunday afternoons and Saturday evening; a Wednesday afternoon show is added in summer. Call (805) 682-4334 for information.

Santa Barbara Botanic Garden. Indigenous California plants, from wildflowers to redwoods, grow in natural settings on 65 acres in Mission Canyon, just 1½ miles above the mission. More than 5 miles of trails wind through sections representing canyon, desert, Channel Island, arroyo, and redwood forest plant life, following historic Mission Creek to the dam and aqueduct built in 1806 to supply water to the mission.

The garden bursts with color in spring and summer. Flowering shrubs and brilliant wildflowers blaze in the meadow section, ceanothus (wild lilac) contributes white and blue shades to the landscape, and cacti and yucca bloom in the desert. The garden, at 1212 Mission Canyon Road, is open daily all year from 8 A.M. to dusk. Guided tours are offered Thursday at 10:30 A.M. and Sunday at 11 A.M. Admission is charged.

Earl Warren Showgrounds. Horse shows are popular events in Santa Barbara. The Earl Warren Showgrounds on the west side of town (Las Positas Road at U.S. 101) hosts most of them, including the Santa Barbara National Horse Show in August.

Moreton Bay fig tree. At the corner of Chapala and Montecito streets just west of Stearns Wharf stands the largest tree of its kind in the United States. Native to Australia, the fig was planted by a little girl in 1877. Today, it's reckoned that 10,000 people could stand in its shade; its branch spread is estimated at 160 feet.

Carriage Museum. Vintage surreys, hansoms, and buggies are on display in this free museum (hours vary) at 129 Castillo Street, a few blocks west of the wharf. Look sharp for the building; it sits back from the street next to an open field.

Polo Grounds. The public is invited to watch polo matches at the Santa Barbara Polo & Raquet Club, just east of the city at Carpinteria. From U.S. 101, take the Santa Claus Lane exit. Games usually take place Sunday afternoon from April through October. There is an admission fee.

For many vacationers, Santa Barbara is the pot of gold at the end of a rainbow. Its stunning setting, handsome Spanish architecture, and wealth of cultural and recreational offerings make it a good base for exploring California's Central Coast.

Into the Valleys

For a change of pace from the ocean scene, poke about in the valleys around Santa Barbara and Ventura. Just a few minutes away from vacation-packed beaches, you can enjoy peaceful back-country driving, pleasant wine tasting, and uncrowded lakeside camping. Rolling hills and soft meadows dominate the inland landscape, and quiet little communities fit right in with the leisurely atmosphere.

Santa Clara Valley

From the coastal cities of Ventura and Oxnard, southbound travelers have several alternatives to U.S. 101. State 126 heads east through the fertile Santa Clara Valley, eventually meeting Interstate 5 just north of Six Flags Magic Mountain amusement park. State 1 follows the coast south.

Ventura. A stop in Ventura can be rewarding. Miles of broad beaches, a great fishing pier, and a well-developed harbor appeal to swimmers, surfers, anglers, and boaters. From October to March, monarch butterflies winter in and around the city. Ventura's harbor is the year-round embarkation point for cruises to the Channel Islands.

Pick up a touring map of the area from the Ventura Visitors and Convention Bureau (89-C S. California Street). The county's handsome Museum of History and Art, 100 E. Main Street, houses Chumash Indian, Spanish, and early pioneer artifacts. Hours are from 10 A.M. to 5 P.M. Tuesday through Sunday; admission is free.

Across the street is modest Mission San Buenaventura, the last mission founded by Father Serra. Fascinating relics turned up by archeologists digging next to the mission are on display at the free Albinger Archaeological Museum (closed Monday).

Picnickers can head for Plaza Park at Santa Clara and Chestnut streets or the beach promenade at the southern end of California Street. The promenade and the western end of Surfer's Point Park are good places to watch beach activity.

Follow signs from U.S. 101 to reach the harbor. En route, you pass the historic Olivas Adobe. The grounds are open daily; house tours are given on weekends from 10 A.M. to 3 P.M.

Hotels, restaurants, and shops are part of the harbor scene. The tidy building at the end of Spinnaker Drive is the visitor center for Channel Islands National Park. Exhibits and a film describe the islands, visible from the center on a clear day. The office of Island Packers, tour operator for the islands, is next door. For more information on trips to the park, see page 117.

Oxnard area. South of Ventura on State 1, Oxnard started life as a farming community, became a Navy town, and is now developing into a tourist destination. From the city's Channel Islands Harbor, charter companies run fishing and whale-watching cruises; in summer, boats take visitors to Channel Islands National Park. A public boat-launching ramp lies just south of Channel Islands Boulevard. Fisherman's Wharf, a New England–style village at the harbor, welcomes browsers, shoppers, and diners.

South at Port Hueneme, a free museum pays tribute to the Civil Engineer Corps and the Seabees. Displayed in Building 99 of the Naval Construction Battalion Center are cultural artifacts from around the world. Located at Ventura Road and Sunkist Avenue, the museum is open Monday through Saturday from 9 A.M. to 4:30 P.M. and Sunday from 12:30 to 4:30 P.M., except on national holidays. Visitors obtain a pass at the gate; children under 16 must be accompanied by an adult.

Santa Paula. The little town at the junction of State 150 and State 126 is a shipping center for lemon-rich Santa Clara Valley. One of California's earliest oil booms took place here, a fact memorialized in the free museum at Tenth and Main streets.

Six Flags Magic Mountain. At the eastern end of the Santa Clara Valley,

State 126 intersects Interstate 5. Just south lies Six Flags Magic Mountain, a 260-acre theme park where rides let the adventuresome try white-water rafting, take a splashing dash through a water flume, race through a mine in a runaway car, ride a jet boat, and go skydiving. Six roller coasters, including the world's fastest and tallest looper, guarantee thrills.

Other attractions include an amphitheater with live entertainment, restaurants, and craft shows. Small fry love Bugs Bunny World and the petting zoo. You can visit the park daily in summer, on weekends and holidays (except Christmas) the rest of the year. Gates open at 10 A.M. A ticket for all rides and entertainment is about $23; seniors and children under 4 feet tall pay $12 (free under 3 years).

Ojai Valley

For a pleasant lake and mountain side trip between Ventura and Santa Barbara, use State 33 and State 150 to reach Ojai. Tucked among hillsides covered with citrus and avocado groves, this little resort town has long been a retreat for well-to-do Los Angelenos.

Some say that Ojai (pronounced o-high) comes from an Indian word meaning "nest." Certainly the moon-shaped valley is well insulated against fog, wind, and smog by both its altitude and the Topa and Sulphur mountain ranges.

Lake Casitas. The lake west of town hosted the rowing competition of the 1984 Olympics. It's a favorite spot for campers, boaters, and anglers (swimming and waterskiing are prohibited). Activities are concentrated at the upper end of the reservoir; boat rentals are available at the landing. Campsites are numerous and spacious, though few are tree shaded; trailers are permitted. Day-use and overnight camping fees are moderate. An observation point at the dam on the southeastern end of the lake is reached from State 33 or Santa Ana Road.

Ojai and beyond. A tennis and golf resort, a haven for horseback riders, and a refuge for artists, the community of Ojai maintains a leisurely pace reminiscent of early Spanish days. Even its architecture is vaguely Spanish in feel. The handsome Ojai Valley Inn and Country Club, the area's premier resort, is open to the public.

Cultural activities share the spotlight with sports. A music festival in June and a Mexican Fiesta in September are but two of the yearly highlights. The country's oldest tennis tournament is held here in April.

Beyond the serene little valley stretch miles of wild and rugged mountain terrain with creeks, campsites, and pleasant picnic sites. North on State 33, Wheeler Gorge is the largest and most popular of the public camping parks. En route, note scenic Matilija Dam. Farther north, a side road leads to Piedra Blanca, a spectacular outcrop of white sandstone rocks.

Goleta Valley

Bordered by the luxurious residential development of Hope Ranch to the east and squeezed between the Santa Ynez Mountains and the Pacific, Goleta Valley just northwest of Santa Barbara boasts some of the coast's best beach parks—Goleta, El Capitan, Refugio, and Gaviota—and several notable attractions. One quick trip off U.S. 101 is to the seaside campus of the University of California at Santa Barbara—actually at Goleta, not Santa Barbara.

Cycling is popular with area residents and visitors alike; rentals are available, and bikeways are well marked. An easy ride leads past historic landmarks, along the beach, and into the university campus.

Goleta Depot Railroad Museum. In Lake Los Carneros Park, a restored Victorian railroad station has become a museum. Tours of the grounds (Wednesday through Sunday afternoons) give visitors a nostalgic look at the era of steam locomotives. You can ride miniature trains in summer and at the annual Depot Day celebration on the third Sunday of October. To reach the depot, take Los Carneros Road exit north from U.S. 101.

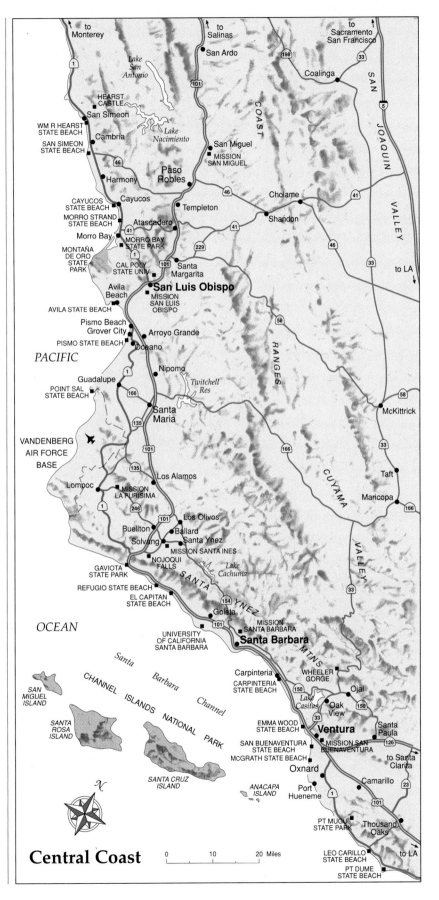

Central Coast

Quaint Santa Ynez Valley town of Solvang celebrates its Scandinavian roots during an annual Danish Days festival held in September. Traditionally attired women prepare aebleskiver, a puffy pancake.

114

...Into the Valleys

Stow House. This gracious country home, built in 1872, was once the heart of a vast ranch. Wide verandas and gingerbread detailing adorn the exterior; inside, rooms are furnished with period antiques. Next door, the Howard Sexton Memorial Museum features a blacksmith shop and farm implements.

Both structures, located near the Goleta Depot north of U.S. 101, are open Sunday afternoon from 2 to 4 P.M. (closed in January); admission is free.

Santa Ynez Valley

Snuggled between mountain ranges behind Santa Barbara is the Santa Ynez Valley, where stagecoach-era towns provide a scenic contrast to Vandenberg Air Force Base at the western end of the lush basin. The valley's equine residents graze along whitewashed fences that demarcate the many horse ranches; some ranches welcome visitors.

A happy blend of climate and geology has turned the valley into one of the state's best wine regions. Tours and tasting are offered at a couple dozen wineries. Pick up a wine-touring map at the visitor center in Santa Barbara, or contact the Santa Barbara County Vintners' Association, P.O. Box 1558, Santa Ynez, CA 93460; (805) 688-0881.

State 246 enters the valley through the Danish community of Solvang. State 154, a former stagecoach route from Santa Barbara, traverses the length of the valley, rejoining U.S. 101 just beyond Los Olivos.

Lake Cachuma. Along State 154 about 11 miles west of the San Marcos summit sprawls Lake Cachuma Recreation Area, a 9,000-acre county park. Along the shoreline, oaks shade camping and trailer spaces, fire pits, and picnic tables; shower and laundry facilities are available.

In winter, the lake is stocked with fingerling rainbow trout and Kamloops trout from British Columbia. Cool spring and autumn months provide the best fishing; angling slows in summer. Tackle and boat rentals are available. No swimming or waterskiing is allowed, but three swimming pools are open from April through October.

The year-round recreation area charges for admission, parking, and overnight camping. It's crowded in summer, so plan to arrive early.

Valley towns. Scattered around the valley are picturesque small towns that seem little affected by the state's growth.

Santa Ynez deliberately maintains its Old West atmosphere with high-front buildings and a "Western Town" complex. The white-steepled church at the corner of Tivola and Lincoln streets, built in 1897, is one of the valley's oldest. At 3596 Sagunto Street, a museum and carriage house offer insights into 19th-century life. Both are open Friday through Sunday from 1 to 4 P.M.; the carriage house is also open Tuesday through Thursday from 10 A.M. to 4 P.M.

Los Olivos, once a stop for the Butterfield Stage Lines, still serves food to travelers at Mattei's Tavern, the old inn. Also of interest around town are galleries, tasting rooms, and the elegant little Los Olivos Grand Hotel.

Nearby Ballard, established in 1880, was the valley's first settlement. The little red schoolhouse (2425 School Street) is now a historic landmark.

Buellton, at the crossroads of U.S. 101 and State 246, offers access to Santa Ynez Valley and Solvang 3 miles to the west. Buellton got on the map as the "home of split pea soup," a specialty of Andersen's Restaurant.

Solvang. Solvang's windmill structures, copper and thatched roofs crowned with artificial nesting storks, gas lights, cobblestone walkways, and horse-drawn trolley suggest a quaint environment manufactured solely for the tourists who throng its streets. But this town is solidly Scandinavian in heritage, food, and customs.

About two-thirds of the 3,500 or so residents are of Danish descent. Danish educators from Minnesota selected the area as the site for a folk school in 1911, when the only building in town was the Mission Santa Ines.

Patterned after a typical rural Danish meetinghouse, the Bethania Lutheran Church on Atterdag Road contains a scale model of a fully rigged ship hanging from its ceiling, a common Scandinavian tradition. The pulpit is hand carved. Danish-language services are held the first Sunday of each month.

Solvang's fine bakeries have made the town famous. Look for Danish pancakes, too—thin ones, or the puffy balls called *aebleskiver*. Eat them with *medisterpølse*—pale, thick sausages. Several restaurants serve the traditional *smørrebrød*.

Shopping leans toward Scandinavian imports, with an emphasis on gourmet and delicatessen foods, housewares, toys, apparel, and gifts.

Tourists flock to the colorful Danish Days celebration in mid-September and to the summer Theaterfest. For information, stop at the Visitors Bureau, 1571 Mission Drive (open daily).

Mission Santa Ines, the old Spanish mission still in use today, is just east of Solvang's main business district. Founded in 1804, it's one of the best restored of all the missions. The chapel, museum, and cemetery are open daily.

Nojoqui Falls. One of the state's most graceful waterfalls highlights a drive between Solvang and the coast. From Solvang, drive south on Alisal Road for about 6½ miles. If you're coming from U.S. 101, turn off about 5 miles north of Gaviota Pass on a road marked "To Nojoqui Falls County Park." A short walk along a woodsy path brings you to the waterfall, best in spring.

Mission La Purisima. If you visit just one mission—especially if you're traveling with children—it should be Mission La Purisima Concepcion, 15 miles west of Buellton and 5 miles east of Lompoc in a quiet rural setting off State 246. Carefully restored and operated as a state historic park, the mission presents a row of simple facades: church, craft workshops, and padres' living quarters. A colorful fiesta is held here the third Sunday in May.

Lompoc. Lompoc Valley produces more than half the world's flower seeds. From May to September, thousands of acres of fields are in bloom; you can catch glimpses from the roads. A festival in late June includes a floral parade.

Up the Coast

The Spanish and Indian influence in this part of the Central Coast is revealed in such musical place names as Guadalupe, Santa Maria, Oceano, Nipomo, Arroyo Grande, San Luis Obispo, Morro Bay, Cayucos, and Cambria.

Take your choice of routes: U.S. 101 is faster but bypasses most of the historic and recreational spots; State 1 takes a more rural direction along the ocean. At San Luis Obispo, the highways diverge, State 1 heading north to the shore at Morro Bay and U.S. 101 veering inland toward Paso Robles and nearby Mission San Miguel (see page 6).

Explorations from U.S. 101 lead to ranching and wine-growing valleys around the Santa Lucia Mountains. Most of the wineries are clustered around Paso Robles, though a few in the Edna Valley region south of San Luis Obispo on State 227 offer tasting rooms. Stop at Templeton Corner, a tasting outlet for dozens of boutique wineries, on the main street of the tiny town of Templeton.

Nipomo (off U.S. 101 just north of State 166) was a private ranch before becoming an important stopover on the old El Camino Real between the Santa Barbara and San Luis Obispo missions. Although most of its historic structures are gone, the adobe ranch house still stands. Jocko's restaurant draws crowds for spicy beans and big steaks.

A few miles north in Arroyo Grande you'll find Western storefronts, an old jail, and other historic remnants. Attractive Lopez Lake, 10 miles inland, has camping sites (full hookups), boat rentals, a sandy shore, and a water slide.

If you drive State 1, Guadalupe offers the first look at the coast's most extensive sand dunes. Follow Main Street west to Rancho Guadalupe County Park; occasional high winds shift sands and force some road closures. On the town's lone street, Basque House is but one of the restaurants serving good food, not atmosphere.

Around Pismo Beach. The town of Pismo Beach was named for its resident mollusk, the Pismo clam. The bay's broad, surf-swept arc provides an ideal environment for clams; but because the shore is too accessible to clam-loving humans, the greater part of the clam beds has been made into a preserve.

Monarch butterflies brighten the town from November through March. Fishing is good from the end of the long pier, where you can charter deep-sea boats.

Pismo State Beach. Some 6 miles of shoreline from the town of Pismo Beach south to the Santa Maria River make up one of the state's finest beach parks; you'll find campgrounds, picnic areas, rest rooms, and showers here. The park's southern reaches include the vast expanse of Pismo Dunes Preserve, where visitors picnic, hike, and slither up and down the sandy slopes. Vehicles are prohibited in the preserve.

The southern entrance to the park is through Oceano, once an aspiring seaside resort. A few Victorian-era gingerbread houses still stand.

Avila State Beach. Popular with locals, Avila State Beach nestles within the northern arc of San Luis Obispo Bay. Warm water makes the ocean ideal for swimming. Facilities include a pier, charter boats, a launching ramp, and rental concessions for gear.

Above the quiet bay, luxurious San Luis Bay Inn offers great views and a golf course. A detour off San Luis Bay Drive leads through oak-lined See Canyon, a major apple-producing area. You can buy apple varieties here that you won't find in supermarkets.

San Luis Obispo

Cupped in a small valley, San Luis Obispo, the region's focal point, makes a good base for exploring the countryside. The town grew up around Mission San Luis Obispo de Tolosa, established in 1772. Among local lodgings are the colorful and curlicued Madonna Inn, the modern Victorian-style Apple Farm Inn, and the country's first motel (Motel Inn). Good restaurants and shops abound.

Detouring off the freeway that slices through San Luis Obispo, you'll discover a surprising showcase of California architectual history. A brochure available from the Chamber of Commerce (1039 Chorro Street) describes some 20 attractions along a 2-mile walking or driving tour. Highlighted are the mission, the County Historical Museum, and the 1874 Ah Louis store, which once served as a bank and post office for Chinese railroad workers.

San Luis is livelier than you might expect a museum town to be, hosting a Spanish Fiesta in May, a Jazzfest over the Fourth of July weekend, and a Mozart Festival in August.

Every Thursday the town throws a party. Higuera Street is blocked off near the mission, and local farmers truck in their produce. By 6 P.M. the downtown spills over with people buying, selling, eating, browsing, or swapping gossip.

Mission Plaza. Located in the heart of town at Chorro and Monterey streets, the mission was the first to be built with a tile roof. Today the restored building is a parish church and museum. The mission is open daily; a minimum donation is requested.

Across the street from the mission, the county's historical museum, housed in a 1905 Carnegie library, keeps an eclectic collection of regional memorabilia dating back to the Chumash and Salinian Indian periods. It's open 10 A.M. to 4 P.M. Wednesday through Sunday; admission is free.

The well-landscaped plaza fronting the mission was designed by Cal Poly students. Footbridges span the creek that meanders through town, leading to shops and restaurants.

Cal Poly. California Polytechnic State University, famous for its schools of architecture and agriculture, sits on rolling hills overlooking the city from the northeast. Students at Cal Poly, no ordinary campus, learn by doing—at the campus nursery, chicken farm, or printing press. Campus-produced jams, milk, and a very popular salsa are sold

Channel Islands National Park

Scattered off the coast between Santa Barbara and San Diego lie the eight volcanic islets that make up the Channel Islands, among the first parts of California to be explored by Europeans. Cabrillo anchored near Anacapa Island in 1542; in 1769, Portola made reference to it in his log.

Once home to thousands of Chumash Indians and later a destination for hunters, the islands are mainly nature preserves now where boaters, hikers, and campers can view a kind of American Galapagos. Windswept canyons and meadows support plants and wildlife found nowhere else.

On clear days, the islands are visible from the mainland. The closest, Anacapa (actually three tiny islands), lies 11 miles from shore. The popular tourist destination of Santa Catalina Island is also part of the Channel Islands (see page 37).

Natural wonders. To ensure the preservation of rare and endangered plants and wildlife, five of the islands—Anacapa, San Miguel, Santa Rosa, Santa Barbara, and privately owned Santa Cruz—were designated as the Channel Islands National Park in 1980. The rich waters surrounding the park are a national marine sanctuary.

Beaches and rocky inlets are refuges for seals, sea lions, and sea elephants. Other local residents include island foxes, cormorants, and California brown pelicans.

Tidepools teem with activity, and giant kelp forests in the offshore waters shelter more than 1,000 species of marine life, visible to scuba divers and snorkelers. Migrating gray whales are sighted from December through April.

Plant enthusiasts won't be disappointed with the unique trees, shrubs, and wildflowers. The vivid blooms of the giant coreopsis steal the show in late winter, painting the islands with splashes of brilliant yellow.

An island visit. Island Packers, the park concessioner, offers trips to Santa Barbara, Santa Cruz, Santa Rosa, and San Miguel islands in summer. Service to Anacapa is available year-round. Boats leave the harbor at Ventura at 9 A.M. daily in summer and during the winter whale migration, returning at 5 P.M. Island Packers also makes daily summer runs for campers and, in April and May, half-day non-landing excursions.

For reservations, write to Island Packers, 1867 Spinnaker Drive, Ventura, CA 93001; phone (805) 642-1393. For information and prices, call (805) 642-7688.

Channel Islands Adventures provides air tours to Santa Cruz and Santa Rosa islands all year from Camarillo. Day trips include a picnic lunch. From April through October, a four-day weekend or five-day midweek package includes airfare, meals, and island accommodations in a two-story adobe ranchhouse dating back to 1864.

For information and reservations, contact Channel Islands Adventures, 305 Durley Avenue, Camarillo, CA 93010; phone (805) 987-1678.

Primitive camping (no food or water is provided) is permitted on Anacapa, San Miguel, Santa Rosa, and Santa Barbara. Reserve ahead for camping sites and for ranger-guided walks on San Miguel and Santa Rosa.

For information, write to the Superintendent, Channel Islands National Park, 1901 Spinnaker Drive, Ventura, CA 93001, or stop at the visitor center at the tip of Ventura's harbor. Photographs, displays, an indoor tidepool, and a 25-minute film make this a worthwhile stop.

The Nature Conservancy operates 90 percent of Santa Cruz Island as a preserve; the other 10 percent has been owned by the Gherini family since the 1800s. Permission to visit the island is strictly limited. Landing permits for private boats can be obtained from the Santa Cruz Island Company, Box 23259, Santa Barbara, CA 93121; phone (805) 964-7839.

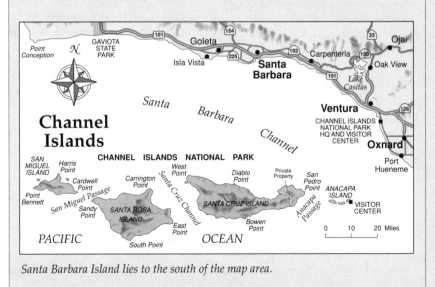

Santa Barbara Island lies to the south of the map area.

...Up the Coast

at the student store (closed Sunday) near the visitors parking area.

North on State 1

From San Luis Obispo, State 1 cuts through photogenic hills and rolling farmlands, wending its way northwest to Morro Bay. In summer, the valley's blue skies are usually blanketed by fog, and temperatures drop abruptly.

Montaña de Oro State Park. Los Osos, 12 miles west of San Luis Obispo, is the gateway to one of the state's most beautiful parks. Unlimited ocean vistas are a part of its lure. Hikers explore Valencia Peak and other hills that overlook the nearly 100 miles of coastline from Point Sal in the south to Piedras Blancas in the north.

Made up largely of rugged cliffs and headlands, the 5,600-acre park contains little coves with relatively secluded sandy beaches. Spring wildflowers abound; the predominantly yellow color inspired the park's name, which means "mountain of gold" in Spanish. About 50 campsites are located near the old Rancho Montaña de Oro headquarters beside Islay Creek.

Morro Bay. The fishing town of Morro Bay 12 miles northwest of San Luis Obispo spreads along the eastern shore of the estuary that gives it its name. Motels, shops, and seafood restaurants ring the waterfront. Sightseeing boats cruise around the harbor; a clam taxi shuttles hikers, picnickers, and birdwatchers to the 4-mile-long spit separating bay and ocean.

Chess players congregate around the giant board at the foot of the centennial stairway that leads from Harbor Street to the waterfront. Boats dock right behind the fish markets; a battalion of pelicans awaits one false move.

Morro Rock, which separates Estero Bay (to the north) from the harbor, was a landmark for Spanish explorers. The 576-foot-high rock, westernmost in a chain of long-extinct volcanoes that form the picturesque backbone of San Luis Obispo County, is a protected nesting site for peregrine falcons.

Morro Bay State Park. Spacious and verdant, the inviting park a mile south of town spills over the hillside and down to the bay. It's a good place to camp, picnic, rent a boat, or play golf.

On the way to the park, stop by the Museum of Natural History for a view of the bay and Morro Rock. Fascinating displays and movies feature local wildlife and area history. Open daily, the museum charges a modest fee.

Cayucos. Take the Ocean Avenue exit off State 1 to visit Cayucos, a funky beach town with a pier long enough to get anglers out beyond the surf line. The town was once known for abalone, but overfishing killed the industry; only some shell decorations around town serve as a reminder. Several antique shops, some modest restaurants, and a few other stores line the main street.

Harmony. Don't blink or you might miss this former dairy town, population 18, several miles south of Cambria. About a block long, it has a pottery shop, a couple of design studios, a glassblower, a restaurant, and a wedding chapel made from a wine cask.

Cambria. Fine galleries, restaurants, and shops line artsy Cambria's Main Street, the link between the two villages that make up the town. Although a number of intimate inns are sprinkled around town, reservations are at a premium on weekends and in the summer. Coastal parks are good vantage points from which to watch the winter migration of California's gray whales.

Hearst Castle

Media tycoon William Randolph Hearst called his San Simeon estate "the ranch," an understatement if ever there was one. The opulent grandeur of his hilltop hideaway might have drawn the envy of Kublai Khan.

Some 40 miles up the coast from San Luis Obispo, the gilded towers of Hearst Castle glitter like gems among a strangely eclectic but glamorous collection of mansions, terraced gardens, pools, art objects, bunkhouses, and garages. The estate that crowns La Cuesta Encantada—Hearst's Enchanted Hill—cost nearly three million Depression-era dollars and took Hearst and architect Julia Morgan from 1919 to 1947 to build.

In 1957, the Hearst family turned the palatial residence over to the state. It's now a state historic monument toured by more than 1 million visitors annually—second only to Disneyland as California's most popular attraction.

Tours. Guided tours give glimpses of a way of life that rivaled the most extravagant fantasies enacted by Hearst's movie-star guests. Because of the vastness of the estate—123 acres of grounds, three guest houses, and a main house with 38 bedrooms, 14 sitting rooms, 2 libraries, a kitchen, and a theater—four tours are offered.

Tour 1 takes in the gardens, a guest house, the pools, and the main floor of the mansion. Tour 2 covers the upper floors of the main building, including Hearst's private quarters and personal libraries, guest rooms, and kitchen. Tour 3 includes the guest wing of the main building, a guest house, gardens, pools, and a home movie theater. Tour 4, available only from April through October, visits the wine cellar, pools, underground vaults, and bowling alley.

Each tour lasts about 2 hours and requires considerable walking and climbing. Comfortable shoes and a sweater or jacket are advised, as part of each tour is outdoors. Tour 1 is the best introduction to the property.

Although a limited number of tickets are sold at the visitor center each day on a first-come, first-served basis, advance reservations for the tours, which cost $10 each, are recommended. Reserve by phone or in person at any MISTIX outlet. In California, the toll-free number is (800) 444-7275; out of the state, phone (619) 452-1950. Hearst Castle is open daily, except New Year's Day, Thanksgiving, and Christmas.

Lodging. For information on accommodations, contact San Simeon Chamber of Commerce at (805) 927-3500 or Cambria Chamber of Commerce at (805) 927-3624. You can reserve San Simeon State Beach campsites through MISTIX two months ahead.

On a tour of Hearst Castle in San Simeon, visitors pause at the Neptune Pool fronting the mansion. William Randolph Hearst's former estate took three million Depression-era dollars and almost three decades to build.

An Activity Guide

Camping at National Parks

Advance planning will help you get the most out of a camping trip to one of California's national parks or monuments. For information and fees (currently $6 to $10 per night), contact the individual areas listed below or the National Park Service Information Office, 30401 Agoura Rd., Agoura Hills, CA 91301, phone (818) 597-9192.

Three campgrounds (in Sequoia National Park and in Death Valley and Joshua Tree national monuments) accept reservations up to 8 weeks in advance through Ticketron. To charge reservations (small fee), call (900) 370-5566.

Maximum RV length varies from campground to campground—be sure to check ahead of time.

Channel Islands National Park (see page 117). Information: (805) 644-8157. Primitive camping is permitted on Anacapa, San Miguel, Santa Barbara, and Santa Rosa islands; reservations are required. You must bring your own food and water.

Island Packers provides transportation to the islands (see page 117); make boat reservations at least 2 weeks in advance. Various ecological organizations also lead trips; contact park headquarters.

Death Valley National Monument (see page 100). Information: (619) 786-2331. All-year campgrounds include *Furnace Creek*, near monument headquarters (34 tent and 136 tent/RV sites, disposal station, disabled facilities, elevation -196 feet; reservations accepted) and unimproved *Wildrose*, near the State 178 entrance (30 tent/RV sites, no water, pit toilets, elevation 4,100 feet).

Open from November to April are *Sunset*, near Furnace Creek (1000 tent/RV sites, disposal station, disabled facilities, elevation -190 feet); nearby *Texas Spring* (40 tent and 53 tent/RV sites, disposal station, elevation 0 feet); and *Stovepipe Wells* (24 tent and 175 tent/RV sites, disposal station, elevation 0 feet).

Emigrant, 9 miles southwest of Stovepipe Wells (10 tent/RV sites, elevation 2,100 feet), is open April to October. Two unimproved, high-altitude camping areas farther south are open March through November.

Devils Postpile National Monument (see page 99). Information: (619) 934-2289. Located 13 miles west of Mammoth Lakes off State 203, Devils Postpile has one campground (24 tent/RV sites, elevation 7,600 feet), open June to October.

East Mojave National Scenic Area (see page 92). Information: (619) 326-3896. Developed Bureau of Land Management campgrounds are open all year at *Mid-Hills* (26 tent/RV sites, elevation 5,600 feet), 15½ miles southeast of Cima off Cedar Canyon Road, and *Hole-in-the-Wall* (9 tent/RV sites, elevation 4,200 feet), 25½ miles northwest of Essex off Interstate 40. *Providence Mountains State Recreation Area*, 21 miles northwest of Interstate 40 on Essex Road, is also open year-round (6 tent/RV sites, elevation 4,300 feet).

Joshua Tree National Monument (see page 87). Information: (619) 367-7511. Open October to April is *Black Rock Canyon*, 5 miles southeast of Yucca Valley off State 62 (100 tent/RV sites, disposal station, elevation 4,000 feet; reservations recommended). Open all year is *Cottonwood*, 32 miles northeast of Indio off Interstate 10 (62 tent/RV sites, disposal station, elevation 3,000 feet).

Other undeveloped campgrounds (pit toilets but no water), all free, are on side roads south of State 62. Open year-round are *Hidden Valley* (62 tent/RV sites, elevation 4,200 feet); *Indian Cove* (114 tent/RV sites, elevation 3,200 feet); *Belle* (20 tent/RV sites, elevation 3,800 feet); and *Jumbo Rocks* (130 tent/RV sites, elevation 4,400 feet). Open October to May are *White Tank* (20 tent/RV sites, elevation 3,800 feet) and *Ryan* (27 tent/RV sites, elevation 4,300 feet).

Kings Canyon National Park (see page 96). Information: (209) 565-3456. Six campgrounds are clustered in two areas along State 180: north of Wilsonia near Grant Grove Village (6,600-foot elevation) and along the South Fork of the Kings

River near Cedar Grove (4,600-foot elevation). All have tables, fire rings, water, flush toilets, and showers; camping limit is 14 days from mid-June to mid-September, 30 days the rest of the year.

Near Grant Grove Village, *Azalea* is open year-round (30 tent and 87 RV sites, disposal station, disabled facilities). Open May to September are *Sunset* (30 tent and 154 tent/RV sites) and *Crystal Springs* (25 tent and 42 tent/RV sites).

Near Cedar Grove, *Sentinel* is open May to October (83 tent/RV sites, disabled facilities). Open June to October are *Sheep Creek* (111 tent/RV sites, disposal station) and *Moraine* (120 tent/RV sites).

Santa Monica Mountains National Recreation Area (see page 24). Information: (818) 888-3770. Encompassing some 150,000 acres of federal, state, county, and city lands, the NRA includes state-operated coastal campgrounds at *Leo Carillo State Beach* and *Point Mugu State Park* (page 121). North of State 1 off Las Virgenes Road is *Malibu Creek State Park* (64 tent/RV sites, elevation 500 feet).

Sequoia National Park (see page 96). Information: (209) 565-3456. Campgrounds have tables, fire rings, toilets, and water; most have a 14-day camping limit from mid-June to mid-September, 30 days otherwise.

Along the General's Highway (State 198) are three all-year campgrounds: *Dorst* (190 tent/RV sites, elevation 6,720 feet); *Lodgepole* (163 tent and 98 RV sites, disposal station, showers, disabled facilities, elevation 6,700 feet; reservations accepted); and *Potwisha* (44 tent/RV sites, disposal station, disabled facilities, elevation 2,100 feet). Open April to October is *Buckeye Flat* (28 tent sites, elevation 2,800 feet). Some campgrounds are to be relocated in the mid-90s.

In the Mineral King area, open May to September, are *Atwell Mill* (23 tent sites, elevation 6,645 feet) and *Cold Springs* (37 tent sites, elevation 7,500 feet). Open all year (limited winter access) is *South Fork* (13 tent/RV sites, elevation 3,650 feet).

Camping at State Beaches

Camping at state beaches and coastal parks gives you easy access to surfing, swimming, surf fishing, clamming, skin diving, and other fun along the Pacific. The following listings capsulize camping facilities south to north. A detailed guide of state park facilities is available for a fee—contact the Publications Section, California Department of Parks & Recreation, P.O. Box 942896, Sacramento, CA 94296-0838; phone 916/322-7000.

Campsite reservations can be made between 48 hours and eight weeks before date of arrival through the MISTIX reservation system. To charge reservations to a Visa or MasterCard number, phone (800) 444-7275 (California only) or (619) 452-1950 (out of state) on weekdays from 8 A.M. to 5 P.M., on Saturday and Sunday from 8 A.M. to 3 P.M.

Camping fees generally range from $7 to $20 per campsite per night, plus a $3.95 non-refundable reservation fee. RV hookups may be slightly higher. Reduced fees apply for anyone 62 years or older.

Self-contained recreational vehicles can overnight at several state beaches on a first-come, first-served basis. Regular fees apply for "en route" sites.

SAN DIEGO COUNTY

Silver Strand State Beach, 4½ miles south of Coronado; en route camping, food service. Surfing, swimming, sailboarding, fishing. Contact: (619) 435-5184.

San Elijo State Beach, ½ mile northwest of Cardiff-by-the-Sea (Birmingham Drive off Interstate 5); 171 campsites, disposal station, store. Surfing, swimming, skin diving, fishing. Contact: (619) 753-5091 or (619) 729-8947.

South Carlsbad State Beach, 3 miles south of Carlsbad; 222 campsites, disposal station, store. Surfing, swimming, skin diving, fishing. Contact: (619) 438-3143 or (619) 729-8947.

San Onofre State Beach South, 3 miles south of San Clemente off Interstate 5 (Basilone Road); 221 campsites, disposal station, store, hike-in 20-site primitive campground (summer), en route camping (summer). Swimming, fishing, hiking trails. Information: (714) 492-4872 or (714) 492-0802.

ORANGE COUNTY

San Clemente State Beach, 2 miles south of San Clemente off Interstate 5; 160 campsites, 72 with hookups for vehicles to 30 feet. Surfing, swimming, fishing, hiking. Check conditions—ocean has rip currents. Contact: (714) 492-3156.

Doheny State Beach, 2 miles south of San Juan Capistrano on State 1; 121 campsites, disposal station, food service. Surfing, swimming, fishing, marine life refuge and diving area offshore, interpretive center. Contact: (714) 496-6171.

Bolsa Chica State Beach, 3 miles north of Huntington Beach; en route camping only, cold showers, fire rings, dressing rooms, food service. Swimming, fishing, nature trail. Contact: (714) 846-3460.

LOS ANGELES COUNTY

Dockweiler State Beach, west of L.A. Airport at the west end of the Imperial Highway; 158-site RV campground (hookups), disposal station, store. Swimming, fishing, volleyball. Contact: (213) 305-9503.

Leo Carillo State Beach, 28 miles west of Santa Monica on State 1; 138 campsites (50 near beach accessible only to vehicles less than 8 feet in height), disposal station, store (weekends only in winter). Surfing, swimming, skin diving, fishing, tidepools, nature trail. Migrating whales visible November–May. Contact: (818) 706-1310.

VENTURA COUNTY

Point Mugu State Park, 15 miles south of Oxnard; 50 developed and 100 primitive campsites, disposal station. Swimming, fishing, hiking, exhibits. Contact: (818) 706-1310.

McGrath State Beach, 3½ miles south of Ventura; 174 campsites, disposal station. Swimming, fishing, nature trail, wildlife area. Contact: (805) 654-4744 or (805) 654-4611.

Emma Wood State Beach, 3 miles north of Ventura; 61 campsites operated by Ventura County, (805) 643-3951; en route camping. Group camp, campsites for hikers and bicyclists operated by state. Swimming, fishing, bike path. Contact: (805) 643-7532 or (805) 654-4611.

SANTA BARBARA COUNTY

Carpinteria State Beach, 12 miles south of Santa Barbara; 174 campsites (119 with hookups), disposal station. Surfing, swimming, fishing, interpretive display. Contact: (805) 684-2811 or (805) 654-4611.

El Capitan State Beach, 20 miles northwest of Santa Barbara; 140 campsites, disposal station, store; en route camping. Surfing, swimming, fishing, nature trail, bike path. Rocky shore with tidepools. Contact: (805) 968-3294.

Refugio State Beach, 23 miles northwest of Santa Barbara; 85 campsites, store. Swimming, fishing, bike path. Contact: (805) 968-3294.

Gaviota State Park, 33 miles west of Santa Barbara; 59 campsites, store (weekends only in winter). Bring drinking water. Swimming, fishing, boating, hiking and equestrian trails. Contact: (805) 567-5013.

SAN LUIS OBISPO COUNTY

Pismo State Beach, 2 miles south of Pismo Beach; Oceano Campground has 82 sites (42 with hookups), North Beach Campground 106 sites, disposal station. Fishing, hiking trails, monarch butterfly preserve (winter season). Contact: (805) 489-2684.

Montaña de Oro State Park, 12 miles west of San Luis Obispo; 50 undeveloped sites; en route camping. Fishing, hiking and equestrian trails, nature trail. Contact: (805) 528-0513 (summer only) or (805) 772-2560.

Morro Bay State Park, Morro Bay; 115 campsites, 20 sites with hookups, disposal station, food service; en route camping. Fishing, boating, nature walks and programs, 18-hole golf course. Outstanding marine area, shore bird habitat. Exhibits on natural history, wildlife, ecology, Native American life. Contact: (805) 772-2560.

Morro Strand State Beach, Morro Bay; 104 campsites. Swimming, fishing. Contact: (805) 772-2560.

San Simeon State Beach, 5 miles south of San Simeon; 132 developed, 115 primitive campsites, disposal station. Fishing, hiking trails. Contact: (805) 927-2010.

Theme Parks & Zoos

From San Diego in the south to Bakersfield in the north, Southern California is dotted with elaborate amusement parks and vast zoological gardens.

THEME PARKS

Disneyland, Harbor Boulevard exit off Interstate 5, Anaheim; (714) 999-4565. See page 50 for description. *Hours:* 10 A.M. to 6 P.M. weekdays, 9 A.M. to midnight weekends (9 A.M. to midnight weekdays in summer, 8 A.M. to 1 A.M. summer weekends). *Admission:* $27.50 adults, $22.50 children 3 to 11. *Other costs:* Parking, food, souvenirs, wheelchair/stroller rental, kennels.

Knott's Berry Farm, Beach Boulevard exit off Interstate 5, Buena Park; (714) 220-5200. See page 49 for description. *Hours:* Daily except Christmas, 10 A.M. to 6 P.M. weekdays, to 10 P.M. Saturday and 7 P.M. Sunday (10 A.M. to midnight daily in summer). *Admission:* $21 adults, $17 children 3 to 11. *Other costs:* Parking, food, souvenirs, some headliner performances, wheelchair/stroller rental.

Baby giraffe enjoys a handout at San Diego Wild Animal Park.

Oasis Water Resort, 1500 Gene Autry Trail, Palm Springs; (619) 325-SURF. Inner-tube river ride, free-fall and speed slides, splash pools, wave pool. *Hours:* 11 A.M. to 6 or 8 P.M. daily March through Labor Day, weekends through October. *Admission:* $14.95 anyone over 60 inches, $9.95 for those 40 to 60 inches. *Other costs:* Parking, food, foam surfboards, lockers.

Raging Waters, Raging Waters Drive off Interstate 210, San Dimas (near Pomona); (714) 592-6453. Forty-four acres of get-wet attractions, including 10 slides, wave pool. *Hours:* Open mid-May to mid-October, 10 A.M. to 7 P.M. weekends only in spring and fall, daily in summer (varying extended hours). *Admission:* $15.95 anyone 48 inches or taller, $8.95 for children 42 to 48 inches, $6.95 seniors. *Other costs:* Parking, lockers, rafts, snacks.

Santa's Village, State 18, Sky Forest, San Bernardino Mountains; (714) 337-2481. Santa's workplace with shops, rides, and petting zoo. *Hours:* Daily, 10 A.M. to 5 P.M. mid-June through mid-September and mid-November through December; call for other times. *Admission:* $8.50 ages 3 through adult. *Other costs:* Food, gifts.

Sea World, Sea World Drive off Interstate 5, Mission Bay, San Diego; (619) 226-3901. See page 69 for description. *Hours:* 9 A.M. to 5 P.M. in winter, to 6 P.M. spring and fall, to 11 P.M. summer. *Admission:* $22.95 adults, $16.95 children 3 to 11. *Other costs:* Food, gifts, wheelchair/stroller rental.

Six Flags Magic Mountain, Magic Mountain Parkway off Interstate 5, Valencia; (805) 255-4111. See page 112 for description. *Hours:* Daily, 10 A.M. to 10 P.M. or later, in summer; weekends and school vacations rest of year, 10 A.M. to 6 P.M. *Admission:* $23 adults and children over 4 feet, $16 seniors, $14 children under 4 feet (free under 2 years). *Other costs:* Parking, food, souvenirs, some concerts, wheelchair/stroller rental.

Universal Studios, Lankershim Boulevard off U.S. 101, Universal City; (818) 508-9600. See page 20 for description. *Hours:* Daily except Thanksgiving and Christmas; call for seasonal hours. *Admission:* $22 adults, $16.50 seniors and children 3 to 11. *Other costs:* Parking, food, souvenirs, wheelchair/stroller rental.

Wild Rivers Waterpark, Irvine Center Drive off Interstate 405, Laguna Hills; (714) 768-WILD. See page 52 for description. *Hours:* Open mid-May through September; call for seasonal hours. *Admission:* $15.95 ages 10 and older, $11.95 children 3

to 9, $7.95 seniors over 55. *Other costs:* Parking, bodyboards, lockers, snacks.

ZOOS

California Living Museum, 14000 Old Alfred Harrell Highway, 13 miles east of Bakersfield off State 178; (805) 872-CALM. Botanical gardens and native wildlife zoo, with reptile house, walk-in aviary, desert tortoise enclosure, petting park. *Hours:* Tuesday through Sunday, 10 A.M. to sunset. *Admission:* $3.50 adults, $2.50 seniors, $2 children 4 through 17.

Los Angeles Zoo, Zoo Drive, Griffith Park, near the junction of Interstate 5 and State 134; (213) 666-4090. See page 29 for description. *Hours:* Daily except Christmas, 10 A.M. to 5 P.M. (6 P.M. in summer). *Admission:* $6 adults, $5 seniors, $2.75 children 2 to 12. *Other costs:* Food, souvenirs, elephant or camel rides, wheelchair/stroller rental.

Moonridge Animal Park, Moonridge Road, Big Bear Lake, San Bernardino Mountains; (714) 866-3652. Small mountain wildlife complex. *Hours:* 8 A.M. to 4 P.M. daily in summer. *Admission:* Free.

San Diego Zoo, Balboa Park; (619) 234-3153. See page 69 for description. *Hours:* Daily, 9 A.M. to 4 P.M. (to 5 P.M. July through Labor Day). *Admission:* $10.75 adults, $4 children 3 to 15, including aerial tram; $3 extra for guided bus tour. *Other costs:* Food, souvenirs, wheelchair/stroller rental.

San Diego Wild Animal Park, Rancho Parkway exit off Interstate 15 to San Pasqual Valley Road, Escondido; (619) 747-8702. See page 74 for description. *Hours:* Daily, 9 A.M. to 5 or 6 P.M, to 11 P.M. in summer. *Admission:* $14.50 adults, $7.50 children 3 to 15. *Other costs:* Parking, wheelchair/stroller rental.

Santa Ana Zoo at Prentice Park, 1801 E. Chestnut Ave., Santa Ana; (714) 835-7484. Primate collection, petting zoo, playground. *Hours:* Daily except Christmas and New Year's, 10 A.M. to 5 P.M. *Admission:* $2 adults, 75 cents seniors and children 3 to 12. *Other costs:* Wagon rental.

Santa Barbara Zoological Gardens, 500 Niños Drive, west of U.S. 101; (805) 962-6310. See page 110 for description. *Hours:* Daily, 10 A.M. to 5 P.M. in winter, 9 A.M. to 6 P.M. in summer. *Admission:* $4 adults, $2 seniors and children 2 to 12. *Other costs:* Snacks, souvenirs, carousel and train rides, wagon/stroller rental.

Golf Courses

If you take your golf game on the road, you'll find an ever-increasing choice of places to play in Southern California. Because of their popularity you need to reserve tee times well in advance. Our sample of public and resort courses gives some idea of what's available. For a more complete roundup, contact local visitor bureaus and chambers of commerce. Yardage listed is from the regular tees.

GREATER LOS ANGELES AREA

Brookside Golf Course, 1133 N. Rosemont Ave., Pasadena; (818) 796-0177. Flat public courses with lots of trees; near Rose Bowl. *Koiner:* 18 holes, par 72; 6,661 yards; rating 71.6, slope 117. *Eonay:* 18 holes, par 70; 5,689 yards; rating 66.3, slope 104.

Griffith Golf Courses, 4730 Crystal Springs Dr., Los Angeles; (213) 663-2555. Two championship public courses in Griffith Park next to the zoo. *Harding:* 18 holes, par 72; 6,488 yards; rating 69.1, slope 108. *Wilson:* 18 holes, par 72; 6,802 yards; rating 70.9, slope 109.

Industry Hills Golf Club, 1 Industry Hills Pkwy., City of Industry; (818) 965-0861. Two championship public courses. *Dwight D. Eisenhower:* 18 holes, par 72; 7,192 yards; rating 70.9, slope 130. *Babe Zaharias:* 18 holes, par 72; 6,735 yards; rating 70.3, slope 130.

Rancho Park Golf Course, 10460 W. Pico Blvd., Beverly Hills; (213) 838-7373. Popular flat public course; usually lush fairways; 18 holes, par 71; 6,585 yards; rating 71.2, slope 108.

ORANGE COUNTY

Anaheim Hills Public Country Club, 6501 E. Nohl Ranch Rd., Anaheim; (714) 637-7311. Hilly, challenging Richard Bigler public course near Disneyland; 18 holes, par 71; 6,180 yards; rating 68.4, slope 116.

Costa Mesa Golf Course, 1701 Golf Course Dr., Costa Mesa; (714) 754-5267. Lush public club and facilities with vast practice area. *Los Lagos:* 18 holes, par 72; 6,542 yards; rating 69.0, slope 110. *Mesa Linda:* 18 holes, par 70; 5,486 yards; rating 63.3, slope 96.

Newport Beach Golf Course, 3100 Irvine Ave., Newport Beach; (714) 852-8681. Premier executive public course; 18 holes, par 59; 3,490 yards; rating 51.7, slope 83.

The Links at Monarch Beach, 33080 Niguel Rd., Laguna Niguel; (714) 240-8247. Challenging Scottish link–style resort/public course designed by Robert Trent Jones, Jr.; 18 holes, par 70; 5,900 yards; rating 67.2, slope 117.

SAN DIEGO AREA

Balboa Park Municipal Golf Course, Golf Course Dr., San Diego; (619) 232-2470. Two-tier public courses in parklike setting. *18-hole course:* par 72; 6,300 yards; rating 68.3, slope 110. *9-hole course:* par 32; 2,197 yards.

La Costa Country Club, Costa del Mar Rd., Carlsbad; (619) 438-9111, (800) 854-5000. Renowned resort hotel and spa. Dick Wilson/Joe Lee–designed resort courses. *North:* 18 holes, par 72; 6,983 yards; rating 69.8, slope 117. *South:* 18 holes, par 72; 6,896 yards; rating 69.3, slope 117.

Mission Bay Golf Center, 2702 N. Mission Bay Dr., San Diego; (619) 273-1221. Popular flat public course; 18 holes, par 58; 3,175 yards.

Pala Mesa Resort, 2001 State 395, Fallbrook; (619) 728-5881. Championship resort course has distinctly different 9s—one is hilly, the other wooded; 18 holes, par 72; 6,472 yards; rating 69.4, slope 117.

Rancho Bernardo Inn & Country Club, 17550 Bernardo Oaks Dr., Rancho Bernardo; (619) 277-2146. Resort course located in long, winding valley; 18 holes, par 72; 6,388 yards; rating 69.5, slope 118.

Torrey Pines Inn & Golf Club, 11480 N. Torrey Pines Rd., La Jolla; (619) 452-3226. Outstanding public facility; choice of two challenging Billy Bell courses. *North*: 18 holes, par 72; 6,659 yards; rating 69.6, slope 116. *South:* 18 holes, par 72; 7,021 yards; rating 72.2, slope 124.

PALM SPRINGS AREA

Indian Wells Golf Resort, Grand Champions Hotel, Indian Wells; (619) 346-GOLF. Two excellent resort courses. *East:* 18 holes, par 72; 6,686 yards; rating 69.4, slope 110. *West:* 18 holes, par 72; 6,478 yards; rating 68.7, slope 109.

La Quinta Hotel Golf & Tennis Resort, La Quinta; (619) 345-2549. Stark rocks of Santa Rosa Mountains frame distinctive Pete Dye resort courses; 54 holes, each 18-hole course par 72. *Dunes:* 6,874 yards; rating 70.6, slope 129. *Mountain:* 6,834 yards; rating 71.4, slope 136. *Citrus:* 7,135 yards; rating 70.9, slope 123. Dunes and Citrus courses open only to resort guests.

Mission Hills Resort Hotel & Golf Club, Rancho Mirage; (619) 328-3198. Pete Dye championship resort course open to hotel guests and public; 18 holes, par 70; 6,743 yards; rating 70.3, slope 126.

Palm Springs Municipal Golf Course, 1885 Golf Club Dr., Palm Springs; (619) 328-1956. Outstanding city public course; 18 holes, par 72; 6,701 yards; rating 69.6, slope 102.

PGA West, 56150 PGA Blvd., La Quinta; (619) 564-7170. Call a day ahead for tee times. Pete Dye–designed resort course. *TPC Stadium:* 18 holes, par 72; 7,261 yards; rating 71.2, slope 130. *Nicklaus:* 18 holes, par 72; 7,264 yards; rating 69.2, slope 122.

SANTA BARBARA AREA

Alisal Golf Course, 1054 Alisal Rd., Solvang; (805) 688-4215. Excellent ranch-hotel facility. Designed by Billy Bell, resort course meanders along a seasonal creek; 18 holes, par 72; 6,286 yards; rating 68.5, slope 114.

La Purisima Golf Course, 3455 State 246, Lompoc; (805) 735-8395. Designed by Robert Muir Graves and Damian Pascuzzo, public course incorporates ideas derived from golf design seminars; 18 holes, par 72; 7,105 yards; rating 72.5, slope 132.

Ojai Valley Inn & Country Club, 1203 Country Club Rd., Ojai; (805) 646-5511. World-class resort course designed by George Thomas and Billy Bell has contrasting 9s—one flat, the other rolling hills; 18 holes, par 70; 5,909 yards; rating 68.9, slope 117.

Sandpiper Golf Course, 7925 Hollister Ave., Santa Barbara (near Goleta); (805) 968-1541. Reminiscent of Scotland, outstanding Billy Bell seaside public course has sweeping fairways and spacious greens; 18 holes, par 72; 7,053 yards; rating 71.3, slope 126.

Boat Cruises

Viewing Southern California's coast from the deck of a boat is usually the best way, and certainly the most scenic, to get your bearings. From south to north, the following operators all offer boat tours.

SAN DIEGO

Bahia Belle, 998 W. Mission Bay Dr.; (619) 488-0551. Mission Bay cruises aboard sternwheeler.

Classic Yacht Charters, 555 W. Beech St. #518; (619) 234-0306. Bay cruises.

Harbor Excursions, 1050 N. Harbor Dr.; (619) 234-4111. Two-hour look at military presence on the bay.

Invader Cruises, 1066 N. Harbor Dr.; (619) 234-8687. Bay cruises on schooner, sternwheeler, or motor yacht.

San Diego-Coronado Ferry, Broadway and Harbor Drive; (619) 233-6872. Fifteen-minute shuttles.

San Diego Harbor Excursion, 570 N. Harbor Dr.; (619) 234-4111. Daily bay cruises.

NEWPORT/BALBOA

Cannery Cruises, Cannery Restaurant, Balboa Peninsula; (714) 675-5777. Weekend brunch and dinner cruises.

Catalina Passenger Service, Balboa Pavilion; (714) 673-5245. Year-round 45- and 90-minute harbor tours.

Hornblower Yacht Cruises, Newport Harbor; (714) 631-2469. Sunday brunch and dinner cruises.

Pavilion Queen, Balboa Pavilion; (714) 673-5245. Sunday buffet cruises.

LONG BEACH/SAN PEDRO

Buccaneer/MardiGras Cruises, San Pedro; (213) 548-1085. Harbor and dinner cruises on schooner or paddlewheeler.

Catalina Channel Express, P.O. Box 1391, San Pedro, CA 90733; (213) 519-1212. Channel crossings to Catalina Island.

Catalina Cruises, Shoreline Village & Queen Mary, Long Beach; (213) 410-1062. Narrated harbor cruises, shoreline cocktail cruises.

Los Angeles Harbor Cruises, Village Boat House, Ports O'Call; (213) 831-0996. Daily one-hour harbor tours.

Spirit Cruises, Ports O'Call, Berth 76, San Pedro; (213) 831-1073. Harbor cruises, summer weekend cocktail cruises.

Spirit of Los Angeles, Ports O'Call, San Pedro; (213) 514-2999. Lunch and dinner daily, weekend moonlight cruises.

MARINA DEL REY

Hornblower Dining Yacht, Dock 52, Fisherman's Village; (213) 301-9900. Harbor tours, Sunday champagne brunch cruises on Mississippi-style riverboat.

SANTA BARBARA

Capt. Don's Harbour Cruises, Stearns Wharf; (805) 969-5217. One-hour cruises May–October.

MORRO BAY

Clam Taxi, 699 Embarcadero; (805) 772-8085. Sandspit shuttle and tour boat.

Tiger's Folly, 1205 Embarcadero; (805) 772-2257. Paddlewheeler.

Whale Watching

After summers spent feeding in the Bering Sea and Arctic Ocean, California gray whales head south each winter to birthing and breeding grounds 4,000 miles away in Baja California.

This December-through-January migration brings the large mammals so near to shore that they can be seen from land at several points. Males and noncalving females begin trickling north again in March. Cows with calves appear outside the surf line from April on into May.

One of the best places from which to watch the passing parade is the whale-watching station at San Diego's Cabrillo National Monument on Point Loma. Sightseeing boats offer even closer looks. The following cruise operators are grouped from south to north.

OCEANSIDE/SAN DIEGO

Baja Expeditions Inc., P.O. Box 3725, San Diego, CA 92103; (619) 581-3311. January–March trips to Baja California.

Biological Adventures, Fisherman's Landing, 2838 Garrison, San Diego, CA 92106; (619) 222-0391. December–March.

H&M Landing, 2803 Emerson St., San Diego, CA 92106; (619) 222-1144. December–February.

Helgren's Oceanside Sportfishing Trips, 315 Harbor Dr., Oceanside, CA 92054; (619) 722-2123. December–April.

Islandia Sportfishing, 1511 W. Mission Bay Dr., San Diego, CA 92109; (619) 222-1164. December–January.

San Diego Natural History Museum, P.O. Box 1390, San Diego, CA 92112; (619) 232-3821. December–February.

DANA POINT/ NEWPORT BEACH

Burns Charters, 2602 Newport Blvd., Newport Beach, CA 92663; (714) 675-2867. December to season's end.

Catalina Passenger Service, Davey's Locker, 400 Main St., Balboa, CA 92661; (714) 673-5245. December–March.

Dana Wharf Sport Fishing, 34675 Golden Lantern, Dana Point, CA 92629; (714) 496-5794. October–February.

Orange County Marine Institute, 24200 Dana Point Harbor Dr., Dana Point, CA 92629; (714) 831-3850. November–March.

LONG BEACH/SAN PEDRO

Catalina Cruises, P.O. Box 1948, Catalina Terminal, San Pedro, CA 90733; (213) 410-1062. December–March.

Queen's Wharf, 555 Pico Ave., Long Beach, CA 90802; (213) 432-8993. December–April.

Spirit Cruises, Berth 76, Ports O'Call, San Pedro, CA 90731; (213) 831-1073. January–March.

VENTURA/ SANTA BARBARA

Capt. Don's Harbour Cruises, P.O. Box 1134, Summerland, CA 93067; (805) 969-5217. February–March.

Island Packers, 1867 Spinnaker Dr., Ventura, CA 93001; (805) 642-1393. December–March.

Santa Barbara Museum of Natural History, 2559 Puesta del Sol Rd., Santa Barbara, CA 93105; (805) 962-0885. November–March.

Sea Landing Sportfishing, Breakwater, Santa Barbara, CA 93109; (805) 963-3564. February–April.

MORRO BAY

Virg's Fish'n Inc., 1215 Embarcadero, Morro Bay, CA 93442; (805) 772-1223. December–March.

Wine Touring

You'll see vineyards throughout the Southland, but the majority of wineries and tasting rooms are in three widely separated districts: Temecula, the Santa Ynez Valley, and Paso Robles.

The elaborate Robert Mondavi Wine & Food Center in Orange County (1570 Scenic Avenue, Costa Mesa) stages a variety of wine tastings, concerts, art shows, and cooking demonstrations that are open to the public. For details on upcoming events, call (714) 979-4510.

Not far from Old Town in Los Angeles is that city's oldest winery, San Antonio (737 Lamar Street), open daily from 8 A.M. to 6 P.M. for touring and tasting. From Interstate 5, take the Main Street exit west, continue 5 blocks to Lamar, and drive south 2 blocks.

TEMECULA

Tucked into the southwest corner of Riverside County about 60 miles north of San Diego, the hilly Temecula area is known for fruity white wines. Reds such as Petite Sirah have also gained attention.

Almost a dozen wineries provide tours and tastings. Most can be reached from the Rancho California Road exit off Interstate 15. Cafe Champagne (open 11 A.M. to 9 P.M. daily), at the John Culbertson Winery, offers a delicious alternative to picnicking.

For a complete list of wineries, contact the Temecula Valley Chamber of Commerce, 40945 County Center Dr., Suite C, Temecula, CA 92390; (714) 676-5090.

SANTA YNEZ VALLEY

The wineries in the scenic valley near Santa Barbara are easy to reach from main highways—U.S. 101, State 246, and State

154. For a list of 22 wineries welcoming guests, write to the Santa Barbara County Vintners' Association, P.O. Box 1558, Santa Ynez, CA 93460, or call (805) 688-0881. Maps can also be picked up at wineries.

"One-stop" tasting rooms offer a chance to compare wines from a number of sources. Los Olivos Tasting Room, 2905 Grand Avenue, Los Olivos, is open 11 A.M. to 8 P.M. daily (small charge for tasting). Stearns Wharf Vintners, on the pier in Santa Barbara, offers free tasting from 10 A.M. to 5 P.M. daily.

PASO ROBLES

Two dozen Paso Robles wineries are open for tasting, most from 10 A.M. to 5 P.M. daily. Almost all lie along U.S. 101 (the north-south route) or State 46 (the east-west corridor). Many wineries have pleasant picnic sites.

Start your tour on the main street of the tiny town of Templeton a few miles south of Paso Robles. Templeton Corner serves as a central tasting room for boutique wineries. Pick up a winery map here, or contact the Paso Robles Chamber of Commerce, 548 Spring St., Paso Robles, CA 93446; (805) 238-0506.

A popular wine festival is held the third Saturday in May in Paso Robles' downtown City Park.

Health Spas

If you're worried about staying fit on vacation, take heart. Southern California—particularly San Diego County—is noted for its fine spas. They come in as many sizes and shapes as their patrons.

A dictionary definition of a spa is "any locality frequented for its mineral springs." So our directory samples modest, therapeutic settings where people still "take the waters" as well as exclusive, beauty-oriented retreats. Advance reservations are required almost everywhere; some spas offer day-use facilities.

SAN DIEGO AREA

Cal-A-Vie, P.O. Box 1567, Vista, CA 92084; (619) 945-2055. Week-long health and beauty programs include fitness training, massage, and exercise.

The Golden Door, P.O. Box 1567, Escondido, CA 92033; (619) 744-5777. Expensive week-long health and beauty programs, luxurious lodging.

La Costa Hotel & Spa, 2100 Costa del Mar Rd., Carlsbad, CA 92009; (619) 438-9111. Large resort with variety of fitness and basic spa programs for men and women, pools, jogging trail, 23 tennis courts, 2 golf courses, 8 noted restaurants (open to public).

Murrieta Hot Springs Resort, 28779 Via las Flores, Murrieta, CA 92362; (800) 458-4393. Hot springs with mud and mineral baths, 3 pools, 14 tennis courts, and fitness facilities; 2-day packages with accommodations in lodge and cottages.

Rancho La Puerta, P.O. Box 2548, Escondido, San Diego, CA 92033; (800) 443-7565. Just over the border in Tecate, this was the modest first version of Golden Door (see preceding); week-long packages include meals and exercise classes (massage and beauty services extra).

DESERT AREA

Bermuda Resort, 43019 Sierra Highway, Lancaster, CA 93534; (805) 942-1493. Fitness and weight-loss plans, extra-cost massage and beauty treatments.

Desert Hot Springs Hotel & Spa, 10805 Palm Dr., Desert Hot Springs, CA 92240; (619) 329-6495. Motor inn with cluster of hot mineral pools, dining room, massage.

The Palms at Palm Springs, 572 N. Indian Ave., Palm Springs, CA 92262; (619) 325-1111. Individually tailored fitness programs; packages include low-calorie meals (2-day minimum).

Spa Hotel & Mineral Springs, 100 N. Indian Ave., Palm Springs, CA 92262; (619) 325-1461. Palm Springs grew up around these Indian-owned mineral springs; hotel offers 2-night and 7-night spa packages, day-use rates.

CENTRAL COAST

The Ashram, P.O. Box 8009, Calabasas, CA 91372; (818) 888-0232. Exclusive star retreat for shape-up breaks, focusing on fitness, vegetarian cuisine.

The Oaks at Ojai, 122 E. Ojai Ave., Ojai, CA 93023; (805) 646-5573. Fun-and-fitness spa with overnight packages that include low-calorie meals, exercise classes, evening programs.

Sycamore Mineral Springs Resort, 1215 Avila Beach Dr., San Luis Obispo, CA 93401; (805) 595-7302. Small motor inn 1 mile from beach, in-room spas, outdoor hot springs.

Cycling

Unlike Southern California's freeways, its bicycle routes are uncrowded. Many offer a different view of the region than you'll see from a car, and in some cases two wheels simply provide the best way to tour an area. We highlight a few particularly inviting routes. Rental bikes are available in most areas.

GREATER L.A.

Stretching from the Santa Monica Pier to the bluffs at Palos Verdes, the 19-mile paved South Bay Bike Trail passes Venice's bizarre bazaar of street vendors and entertainers, Marina del Rey (leave the path at Fiji Way to reach Fisherman's Village), and the rest of beach-town row.

ORANGE COUNTY

Bikeways parallel the shore at Bolsa Chica State Beach in Huntington Beach and stretch the length of Balboa Peninsula in Newport Beach. The ferry to Balboa Island lets you take your bike along.

SAN DIEGO

Bicycle paths open up miles of waterside cycling along the harbor. Other routes show off inland terrain. For a map of all bike trails, call (619) 231-2453. Many hotels rent bikes, as does a shop at Coronado's Old Ferry Landing.

Waterfront. A 4½-mile pathway shared by cyclists, pedestrians, and joggers runs along the waterfront from the west end of Spanish Landing Park (west of the airport along Harbor Drive) to the south arm of Embarcadero Marina Park. From here, you can cross by ferry to explore Coronado and Silver Strand State Beach (8 level miles of unimpeded views).

DESERT

In winter, the sun-washed desert is an excellent place for cycling. A number of bikeways in the Palm Springs area offer routes especially suited to families with young children, and Death Valley's level terrain and stunning scenery are best seen at a bike's pace.

Palm Springs Area. Tahquitz Bikeway, a 10-mile route between Palm Springs and Rancho Mirage, skirts two golf courses before leaving landscaped neighborhoods for a desert wash. You can pick it up at the corner of Sunny Dunes Drive and Sunrise Way. If you don't want to go the whole way, a 1½-mile ride takes you to DeMuth Park, a good place for a picnic.

Free maps and rentals are available at bike shops such as Mac's Bike Rentals (700 E. Palm Canyon Drive).

Death Valley. Cycling in the national monument requires special considerations. Check weather conditions with a ranger, be prepared for flats, carry liquids and snacks, and dress in layers for changing temperature conditions. You'll need to provide your own wheels—the monument has no bike rentals.

The following are round-trip mileages, difficulty ratings, and best times to visit six attractions around Furnace Creek by bike.

Badwater: 36 miles; some long, gradual climbs; moderately strenuous; go in the morning.

Artists Palette: 13 miles, 2½-mile climb, then rolling; moderately strenuous; best in late afternoon.

Golden Canyon: 6¼ miles plus 2- to 3-mile hike up to Zabriskie Point or Red Cathedral; level, easy; afternoon ride.

Zabriskie Point: 9 miles; 888-foot climb; moderate; go at first light to watch the illumination of Golden Canyon and Manly Beacon peak.

Twenty Mule Team Canyon: 16 miles southeast (2¾ unpaved); steady climb; moderate; late afternoon.

Mustard Canyon (turn left from State 190 at Harmony Borax Works): 4½ miles (1½ unpaved); flat, easy; morning or afternoon.

CENTRAL COAST

Though cycling in the cities during rush hours should be avoided, several coastal routes are rewarding. Check with the Ventura Visitors and Convention Bureau (address on page 112) for designated bike tours. One takes you to the Channel Islands National Monument headquarters, another through the historical downtown.

Santa Barbara is full of beautiful cycling paths. You can bike from the city to Goleta via Cathedral Oaks Road; paths explore the University of California campus at Santa Barbara.

At Morro Bay, you can cycle north from downtown on Embarcadero to Morro Rock; another recommended route takes you along Main Street and out State Park Road to the Museum of Natural History and Morro Bay State Park.

Skiing

L.A.-area skiers head up to the nearby San Bernardino and San Gabriel mountains for non-taxing fun. Serious sport means an all-day drive north to Mammoth Mountain.

GREATER L.A. AREA

Bear Mountain, Big Bear Lake off Big Bear Blvd.; (714) 585-2519. Lifts: 1 quad chair, 5 double chairs, 3 triple chairs, 2 pomas. Summit: 8,805 feet.

Mount Baldy, Mount Baldy Rd., San Gabriels; (714) 981-3344. Lifts: 4 double chairs. Summit: 8,600 feet.

Mountain High East and West, State 2, Wrightwood; (619) 249-5471. Lifts: 2 quad, 9 double, 3 surface chairs. Summit: 8,200 feet.

Mount Waterman, State 2, La Cañada Flintridge; (818) 440-1041. Lifts: 3 double chairs. Summit: 8,023 feet.

Ski Sunrise, State 2, Wrightwood; (619) 249-6150. Lifts: 1 quad, 3 surface chairs. Summit: 7,600 feet.

Snow Forest, south of Big Bear Village; (714) 866-8891. Lifts: 1 triple, 3 surface chairs. Summit: 8,000 feet.

Snow Summit, State 18 east of Big Bear, Big Bear Lake, CA 92315; (714) 866-5766. Lifts: 2 quad, 2 triple, 6 double chairs. Summit: 8,200 feet.

Snow Valley, State 18, Running Springs; (714) 867-2751. Lifts: 8 double, 5 triple chairs. Summit: 7,440 feet.

MAMMOTH

June Mountain, State 158, June Lake; (619) 648-7733. Lifts: 5 doubles, 2 quad, 1 minipoma, 1 tram. Summit: 10,200 feet.

Mammoth Mountain, north of Bishop off State 395, Mammoth Lakes; (619) 934-2571. Lifts: 5 quad, 7 triple, 14 double chairs; 2 gondola, 2 surface. Summit: 11,053 feet.

SOUTHERN SIERRA

Montecito-Sequoia Nordic Resort, contact 472 Deodara, Los Altos, CA 94024; (800) 227-9900. Groomed and backcountry touring trails, ski school, and rentals in Sequoia National Forest between Sequoia and Kings Canyon national parks.

Index

ABC, 21
ABC Entertainment Center, 24
Academy of Motion Picture Arts &
    Sciences, 22
Accommodations, 8–9, 57, 60
    Central Coast, 107
    Desert, 79, 84
    Los Angeles, 12, 13
    Orange County, 48
    San Diego, 60
    Sierra, 95
Aerie Sculpture Garden, 82
Amargosa Opera House, 102
American Heritage Park, 41
Anaheim, 47, 48, 50–51, 52, 122,
    123
Ancient Bristlecone Pine Forest, 99
Andreas Canyon, 85
Andree Clark Bird Refuge, 110
Angeles National Forest, 44
Angel's Attic, 29, 34, 41
Antelope Valley, 88, 91, 93
Anza-Borrego Desert State Park,
    86, 88
Arcadia, 44
Arlington Center for Performing
    Arts, 108
Armand Hammer Museum of Art
    and Cultural Center, 24, 27
Arroyo Grande, 57, 116
Avalon, 37
Avila State Beach, 116

Badwater, 4, 95, 102, 126
Baker, 92
Bakersfield, 95, 104
Balboa, 48, 53, 55, 124
Balboa Park, 68–69
Ballard, 57, 115
Banning, 85
Barnsdall Art Park, 41
Barstow, 79, 92
Basques, 104
Bates Bros. Nut Farm, 74
Beaches, 121. See also individual
    beaches
    Long Beach, 40
    Los Angeles, 30–39
    Orange County, 39, 53, 56
    San Diego area, 39, 63, 69, 71
    Santa Barbara, 109
Beaumont, 85
Bed-and-breakfast inns, 57
Beverly Hills, 9, 11, 13, 21, 22–24,
    41, 123
Bicycle trips, 126
Big Bear Lake, 43, 45, 126
Big Pine, 99
Bishop, 5, 99
Blythe, 90
Boat trips, 124
Bob Baker Marionette Theater, 29
Bodie, 97
Bolsa Chica State Beach, 53, 121
Borax Museum, 102
Boron, 93
Borrego Springs, 88
Brookside Park, 42, 123
Buellton, 115
Buena Park, 46, 47, 48, 49, 52, 122
Burbank, 20, 21
Burbank Studios, 20
Burton's Tropico Gold Mine, 93

Cabot's Old Indian Pueblo Museum,
    82
Cabrillo Marine Museum, 36, 39, 41
Cabrillo National Monument, 63
Calabasas, 125
Calico, 5, 92
California Afro-American Museum,
    27
California Living Museum, 104, 122
California Museum of Photography,
    41
California Museum of Science and
    Industry, 27

California Polytechnic State Univer-
    sity, 116, 118
California State Polytechnic Univer-
    sity, 44–45
Cambria, 57, 118
Camping, 9, 120, 121
Camp Pendleton, 72
Carlsbad, 72, 123, 125
Carpinteria State Beach, 121
Carriage Museum, 110
Casa de Adobe, 27
Caspers Wilderness Park, 52
Catalina Island, 37, 39
Caverns, 93, 96
Cayucos, 118
CBS, 21
Century City, 24
Channel Islands National Park, 112,
    117, 120, 126
Charles W. Bowers Museum, 52
Children's activities, 29
Children's Museum, 52
China Lake, 93
Chinatown, 16
Chino, 45
Cinder Cones, 92
Claremont, 41, 45
Climate, 8
Coachella Valley, 79, 80–84
Coachella Valley Museum, 84
Colonel Allensworth State Park, 105
Colorado Desert, 87, 88
Colorado River, 90
Corona del Mar, 55
Coronado, 60, 61, 63, 121
Costa Mesa, 48, 123, 125
Crystal Cathedral, 52
Crystal Cave, 96
Crystal Cove State Park, 55
Cuyamaca Rancho State Park, 76

Dana Point, 56, 124
Death Valley, 4, 5, 95, 100, 102,
    120, 126
Del Mar, 57, 72
Descanso Gardens, 44
Desert Hot Springs, 80, 82, 84, 125
Desert Museum, 82
Devils Postpile National Monument,
    99, 120
Disneyland, 4, 49, 50–51, 122
Dockweiler State Beach, 121
Doheny State Beach, 56, 121
Dorothy Chandler Pavilon, 14, 15
Driving tips, 12, 77, 82

Earl Warren Showgrounds, 110
Eastern California Museum, 99
East Mojave National Scenic Area,
    92, 120
Edwards Air Force Base, 79, 93
El Capitan State Beach, 121
El Monte, 41
El Paseo, 109
El Presidio de Santa Barbara State
    Historic Park, 109
El Pueblo de Los Angeles, 16
Emma Wood State Beach, 121
Encinitas, 72
Ensenada, Mexico, 77
Escondido, 58, 74, 125
Exotic Feline Breeding Compound,
    93
Exposition Park, 14, 17, 27

Fairfax Avenue, 22
Fallbrook, 72, 123
Farmers Market, 17, 22
Festivals, 5, 44,
Filming locations, 20–21
Fisherman's Village, 36
Forest Lawn, 17
Fort MacArthur, 36
Fort Tejon State Historic Park, 104
Frederick's of Hollywood Museum,
    41
Fresno, 96, 104
Furnace Creek, 102

Gamble House, 42
Garden Grove, 52
Gaslamp Quarter, 65

Gaviota State Park, 121
Gene Autry Western Heritage
    Museum, 29
General Grant Grove, 5, 97
General Phineas Banning Museum,
    39
George C. Page Museum, 24
Getty Museum, 32
Giant Forest, 96
Glendale, 17
Goleta Depot Railroad Museum,
    113
Goleta Valley, 113, 115
Golf courses, 83, 84, 123
Greek Theatre, 12, 28
Greystone Park, 24
Griffith Observatory, 28
Griffith Park, 28, 29

Hancock Park, 22
Handicapped travel, 9
Hanford, 105
Harbor Island, 61, 63
Harmony, 117
Harmony Borax Works, 103
Health spas, 125
Hearst Castle, 118, 119
Heather Lake, 97
Hemet, 44
Heritage Hills Park, 53
Heritage Park, 66
Heritage Square, 41
Heritage Square Museum, 34
Hermosa Beach, 36
History, 4, 8
Hobby City Doll and Toy Museum,
    52
Hollyhock House, 41
Hollywood, 4, 13, 18, 19, 20, 21, 41
Hollywood Bowl, 12, 18
Hollywood Memorial Cemetery, 19
Hollywood on Location, 20–21
Hollywood Park race track, 12
Hollywood Studio Museum, 19
Horton Plaza, 60, 65
Hot Creek, 99
Huntington Beach, 48, 53
Huntington Library, Art Collections,
    and Botanical Gardens, 42, 44

Idyllwild, 85
Independence, 99
Indian Canyons, 85
Indian Wells, 84, 123
Indio, 5, 84
Irvine, 53
Irvine Regional Park, 52

John Muir Wilderness, 99
Joshua Tree National Monument,
    78, 79, 87–88, 120
J. Paul Getty Museum, 32
Julian, 58, 60, 75, 76

KCET Television, 19, 20
Kelso Dunes, 92
Kern County Museum's Pioneer Vil-
    lage, 104
Kidspace, 29, 41
Kings Canyon National Park, 5, 95,
    96, 97, 120
Knott's Berry Farm, 4, 46, 47, 49,
    122
Koreatown, 22

La Brea Tar Pits, 17, 27, 29
La Cañada Flintridge, 44, 126
Laguna Beach, 5, 39, 47, 54,
    55–56, 57
Laguna Hills, 52, 53, 122
Laguna Niguel, 56, 123
La Habra, 52
La Jolla, 39, 57, 60, 63, 71, 123
Lake Arrowhead, 45
Lake Cachuma, 115
Lake Casitas, 112
Lake Havasu, 90
Lake Isabella, 104
Lancaster, 88, 93, 125
La Quinta, 84, 123
Lawry's California Center, 17
Laws, 99
Lee Vining, 99

Mammoth Mountain skier

Leo Carillo State Beach, 121
Leucadia, 72
Little Lake, 93
Little Tokyo, 5, 14, 16
Living Desert, 84
Lobero Theatre, 108
Lompoc, 5, 115, 123
London Bridge, 90
Lone Pine, 99
Long Beach, 13, 30, 36, 37, 38, 40,
    57, 124
Lopez Lake, 116
Los Angeles, 5, 9, 10–39, 41,
    42–45, 57, 121, 122, 123, 126
    accommodations, 12, 13, 57
    airports, 12, 30
    beaches, 30–39, 121
    bicycle trips, 126
    dining, 9, 14, 19
    downtown, 14–16
    driving tips, 12
    entertainment, 11, 12, 20–21
    festivals, 5
    freeways, 12
    galleries, 14, 16, 24, 26, 27, 41
    golf courses, 123
    history, 11
    markets, 12, 17, 22
    mountains, 30, 42–45
    movie studios, 19, 20–21
    museums, 14, 16, 17, 19, 24, 26,
        27, 29, 34, 36, 39, 41
    shopping, 12, 14, 22
    skiing, 126
    sports, 12
    tours, 12, 19, 20, 21
    transportation, 12, 14, 30
    valleys, 42–45
Los Angeles Children's Museum, 29
Los Angeles Convention Center, 14
Los Angeles County Museum of Art,
    27
Los Angeles Harbor, 36, 39
Los Angeles Maritime Museum, 14,
    39
Los Angeles Memorial Coliseum,
    14, 17
Los Angeles Music Center, 14, 15,
    17
Los Angeles State and County
    Arboretum, 44
Los Angeles Times, 14, 17
Los Angeles Zoo, 28, 29, 122
Los Encinos State Historic Park, 28
Los Olivos, 115, 125
Lummis Home, 17

Magic Mountain, Six Flags, 112,
    122
Malibu, 32, 39

Sunset
Proof-of-Purchase
ISBN 0-376-06760-8